Our beloved *Polites*

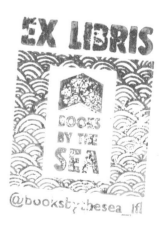

Our beloved *Polites*

Studies presented to P.J. Rhodes

Edited by
Delfim Leão, Daniela Ferreira,
Nuno Simões Rodrigues, Rui Morais

ARCHAEOPRESS ARCHAEOLOGY

ARCHAEOPRESS PUBLISHING LTD
Summertown Pavilion
18-24 Middle Way
Summertown
Oxford OX2 7LG
www.archaeopress.com

ISBN 978-1-80327-170-5
ISBN 978-1-80327-171-2 (e-Pdf)

Cover: EM 13537: Epigraphic Museum, Athens, Photo by K. Takeuchi
© Hellenic Ministry of Culture and Sports / Hellenic Organization of Cultural Resources Development.

This book is available direct from Archaeopress or from our website www.archaeopress.com

In Memoriam Professor P.J. Rhodes

(1940–2021)

Contents

A Tribute to P. J. Rhodes: An Overview

This volume was initially conceived as a natural outcome of the academic debate planned for the congress to be held on the occasion of the celebration of P.J. Rhodes' 80th birthday, in September 2020, at the University of Coimbra, an institution with whose researchers the honorand has been collaborating for almost two decades, particularly in the area of ancient Greek law. Unfortunately, the development of the pandemic situation made it impossible to hold this celebration according to the originally intended parameters. Notwithstanding, this did not detract from the main objective of all those scholars and friends (to whom we are so profoundly grateful) who were involved in the organisation and promotion of the event: to celebrate the person and the career of one of the most remarkable historians of ancient Greece, whose contribution to this area of knowledge is so splendidly demonstrated in John Davies' opening text. On 17 June 2021, there was a brief preliminary presentation of the contributions of the tribute in an online meeting, which was attended by the honoree. Sadly, his unexpected death a few months later (on 27 October) prevented P.J. Rhodes from appreciating the volume in its final form, but the tribute to one of the most brilliant scholars of ancient Greek history has been realised entirely in the terms in which it was presented to him.

The volume has been organised in four parts that map closely onto four prominent areas of P.J. Rhodes' research into ancient Greece: History and Biography, Law, Politics, and Epigraphy.

In the First Part, are included essays on political history, cultural memory and transmission and on some of the events that marked the historical process of the Greeks and several historical personalities. Denis Correa deals with agonistic intertextuality between Herodotus and Hecataeus in *Histories* 2.143. Following P. J. Rhodes method, the author asks questions Herodotus *qua* historian in relation to his goals and limitations and proposes an explanation for the perception of competition and emulation that may be recognised in his writings, focusing particularly on the controversy between Herodotus and Hecataeus. Then, following previous studies on the subject, Robert W. Wallace presents a new reading of Thucydides' suggestion that Athens' two expeditions to Sicily were intended as conquest manoeuvres. Wallace argues that the historian's suggestions frame Thucydides' accounts of Athenian expeditions to Sicily and that they seem inconsistent with various internal remarks, raising the question whether the historian later inserted what may be a misrepresentation of Athens' intentions in order to reinforce larger moral lessons from Athens' defeat. The author's main thesis is that the central sections in both Sicilian expeditions suggest that, at the time of his writing, Thucydides had not yet grasped his overarching theme, which he envisaged as Athens' overweening ambition, probably until Athens' defeat in 413/2. Once he hit upon his central thesis, Thucydides went back through his accounts of these expeditions inserting lines, especially at their beginning and end, just as he did with Athens and its allies. Thucydides is also the main topic of Amanda Ledesma Pascal's chapter, which analyses the inclusion of the mythological story of Alcmaeon in Thucydides' historiographical narrative. Although considered a secondary digression, this story has a Herodotean flavour and often causes admiration among Thucydides' critics, since one of the main features of the historian is the exclusion of myth from his narrative. But as Ledesma Pascal also reminds us, both narrator and audience shared mythical tradition, with the purpose of the excursus seeming to have been to invite readers to reflect on all its implicit consequences. After Ledesma Pascal's contribution, Antonis Tsakmakis deals with the reference to the battle of Ephesus (409 BC) in the Cairo papyrus of the *Hellenica Oxyrhynchia*. Comparing this information to other sources such as Xenophon's *Hellenica* and Diodorus Siculus, the conclusion is that the three agree in most of the details concerning the battle. But there is a divergence on the allies of the Ephesians. Who were they? While Xenophon says that the Persians, Syracusans and Selinuntines were those allies, the papyrus refers to Spartans, reflecting a pro-Spartan attitude. The author explores this divergence, stressing that Xenophon's account, in alignment with a historiographic tradition which is dominated by prejudices against Ionians, tacitly denies any decisive role to the Ephesians in the defense of their own city, while the Oxyrhynchus historian draws a distinctly positive picture of these Ionian Greeks. Martina Gatto focuses on Lycurgus and how his life and political achievements, such as the constitution of Sparta, are present in Ephorus' fragments. The author considers that, in Ephorus' mind, the Lycurgan *politeia* was the key to the political and military ascent of Sparta and its hegemony in Greece until its defeat by Thebes. So, Ephorus' portrayal of Lycurgus was particularly important within his work. Therefore, Gatto outlines the main elements of the Spartan legislator's elaborated representation in Ephorus, which is significantly different from the representations that Herodotus and Xenophon made of the same personality. Nuno Simões Rodrigues makes an intertextual reading of two passages of Plutarch: one considering the Sacred Band of Thebes and the other dealing with a story about Alcibiades' and Socrates' comradeship on the battlefield. Taking account of the context of pederasty and same-sex relations in Ancient Greece, the author suggests that the passage on Alcibiades and Socrates should be read within the context of the topic of the Theban Sacred Band, considering it a possible way for Plutarch to pass on a message concerning Greek sexual customs and practices. Then, Chiara Maria Mauro proposes to identify traces of information once included in ancient *periploi*, or coastal pilot books, and determine its origin. Since the quantity and quality of this information increased during the Hellenistic Age, the focus is placed here on the previous period, running from the 6th to the end of the 4th century BC. Mauro considers this time frame to be crucial for understanding the development and transmission of nautical issues, as it was the time when geographicalliterary documents called *periploi* appeared. Gertjan Verhasselt studies Heraclides' epitomes of Aristotle's constitutions, discussing their validity as a source for our knowledge of the lost ones, which are the majority. In fact, the *Athenaion Politeia* is the only surviving Aristotelian constitution. All that remains of the other constitutions are fragments. Verhasselt discusses Heraclides' method and reliability as an epitomist of Aristotle by comparing the section on Athens with the original Aristotelian text. This method sheds light onto the filter through which the other constitutions are now known to us. Since Heraclides' epitome of the Athenian case gives a heavily distorted picture of the original, the author argues that we should be cautious about the excerpts on other constitutions. The last chapter in this section belongs to Antony Keen, who discusses who the mother of Ptolemy XII Auletes was or, better said, could not have been. The topic was motivated to the author after rewatching the 1983 series *The Cleopatras*. Keen starts by underlining how brief and fragmented the sources are on this topic and period, being not concerned with demonstrating that Auletes' mother was, or was not, Egyptian, or Greek, or Syrian, but rather merely that she did not belong to the Ptolemaic royal house. The author concludes that Ptolemy XII Auletes was the illegitimate son of Ptolemy IX Lathyros, by an unknown mother.

The Second Part of the book brings together essays on Greek law. Delfim Leão focuses on Aristophanes' references to the laws of Solon. Leão stresses that they are comparatively scarce, but, despite their relative paucity, those occurrences prove that Aristophanes was familiar with Solon's laws, which he uses mainly for parodic purposes. The article presents analysis of those passages in their proper context and compares them with passages from other authors in order to discuss their validity as sources for the study of Solon's laws. The second paper included in this part belongs to Davide Napoli and is centered on the method and purpose of Antiphon's *Tetralogies*, and their connection to the sophistic reflection on ancient Greek language and law. Napoli argues that the *Tetralogies* use a legal form to problematise legal principles, hence leading Athenian legal practice to demonstrate its own limitations. Thus, the *Tetralogies* might help us to redraw the boundaries of theory and practice in sophistic thought. Lorenzo Sardone proposes to re-examine Demosthenes' authorship of the *Against Aristogeiton*. The author takes account of new elements of assessment about the orator and the historical, political, and cultural background of the 4th century BC Athens. Sardone stresses the importance of the usage of such words as *physis* and *nomos*, considering they are not casual, but acquire a deep evocative meaning for the learned Athenian audience. In fact, the presence of the opposition between law and nature in the *Against Aristogeiton* suggests that its author had a good knowledge of this philosophical topic, and this is one of the reasons why the author argues that Demosthenes perfectly seems to fit as the author of the speech. Ália Rodrigues' essay analyses the ways in which the figure of the *nomothetes* is represented and characterised in 4th century BC legal narratives. Rodrigues argues that in all kinds of legal narratives (historical, philosophical, legal) there is a welldefined representation of the Lawgiver within the topic of the creation of Constitutions. Furthermore, the author shows that the uniformity of the Lawgiver's representation is maintained through the language used to describe the *nomothetes* and his activity. Therefore, the image of the Lawgiver as well as the idea of legal procedure were built not only in courts but also outside them. Next, Brenda Griffith-Williams focuses on the importance of adoption within the Athenian inheritance system for both family (*oikos*) and state (*polis*), stressing the significance and implications of an empty house (*oikos eremos*). Sources show that posthumous adoptions were a relevant issue in Classical Athens, since estates left vacant after the last owner had died leaving no direct heir became a problem to be solved in court. The author concludes that we cannot rule out the possibility that one of the Athenian archons at some time had an active role in the arrangement of posthumous adoptions. If the archon's legal duty was not concerned with the continuity of Athenian families, but with the supervision of estates left vacant after the last owner had died leaving no direct heir, that would be entirely consistent with the administrative functions over which the archon had charge. Aikaterini-Iliana Rassia reminds the reader of how often the notions of *adikia* ('injustice') and *asebeia* ('impiety') were used seemingly interchangeably, both being notions that qualify kinds of human transgression. Part of the confusion of the semantic overlap between *adikia* and *asebeia* is that both notions can be indistinguishably applied in both secular and religious matters. However, argues the author, the way we choose to interpret this semantic overlap often affects our broader understanding of the value terms of injustice and impiety in relation to social and religious matters. The focus of Rassia's chapter is placed on the analysis of the semantic overlap of *adikia* and *asebeia* attested in the sacred regulation of the Amphiareion at Oropos, one of the most important healing sanctuaries of ancient Greece. Michael Gagarin discusses what Greeks like the Cretans of the Hellenistic period meant when they referred to *hieroi nomoi* or 'Sacred Laws'. Although we have doubts about such category of laws in ancient times, the expression appears in the sources, and it meant something for those who used it. As the author argues, the conclusions reached in the chapter will not provide any further guidance on ways to organise a modern collection, but may help reassure us that in forming such collections we are not radically departing from the Greek notion of sacred laws. Closing this part of the volume, Gerhard Thür demonstrates the variety of meanings that the expression καθάπερ ἐκ δίκης ('from a court procedure') could assume in papyrus contracts of the Ptolemaic and Imperial Era (the expression is a formula often found in these documents). Comparing these texts with other sources beyond Graeco-Egyptian papyri, Thür concludes that, depending on the context, the formula can pass the idea of full executive force but also mean legal irrelevance. It also acts as an instrument to dishonour, that would be particularly effective in a society marked by the ancient values of honour and shame.

The Third Part presents essays on Greek Politics and Political Thought. John Davies shows how written sources, such as literary texts, can be used to construct the history of individuals of ancient Athens, considering the methods, limitations, and achievements that these sources can offer to the historian of Ancient Greece. Davies stresses the caution that the historian must have when dealing with these sources. They often offer the historian the names of individuals, which Davies organises in three categories: names embedded in narrative or discursive text (e.g. lyric and dramatic poetry, historical narratives), names decontextualised as an item in a list or as an example selected for inclusion in a discourse, and names recontextualised in a later construct, typically a biography. The essay concerns mainly the second category. Still, the author makes several methodological and practical remarks on the three types of names/sources, showing how important the topic is to build a prosopography. Roger Brock's essay concerns the elements or social code that mark out the elite as a select minority, characterised by a control of membership through the use of unstated, subtle and elusive coded language and the monitoring of standards of correct behaviour. This is coherent and consistent with the aristocratic ideal, the ideal of an established elite, which could only be learned through socialisation: the oligarchic ideal was a well-constructed exclusionary code, argues Brock. Subsequently, Aitor Luz Villafranca proposes to study archaic tyranny within the consolidation of civic consciousness and citizenship in Greek *poleis*. The author analyses the role of tyranny in the changes of archaic aristocratic polis systems, as well as the emergence of the portrayal of the tyrant as a monster, which came to be used as a political tool by oligarchy. Lynette Mitchell, for her part, focuses on the concept of the border in Ancient Greece. She sets out to explore some of the themes of border politics in the Greek world by focussing on two sets of battles: the battles of Tanagra and of Oenophyta in 458/7, and the Athenian attack on Tanagra in 426 and the battle of Delium in 424 BCE. This series of events allows the author to explore their impact not only on themes in Greek international relations in the fifth century, but also on the importance of liminality – borders, borderlands, and border zones – in the Greek political and diplomatic landscape. Carlo Santaniello's essay focuses on an ancient tradition that suggests that Empedocles had "popular" or antioligarchic feelings. In fact, asks the author, why should Empedocles dissolve the Thousand, of which he was certainly a member, as he belonged to one of the noblest and richest families? Santaniello criticises this tradition, arguing that Empedocles might simply have challenged an attempt of the Thousand to support a new would-be tyrant, in the same way as he had formerly rejected the humiliations inflicted upon the participants in a symposium by a host with tyrannical aspirations. The author also considers doubtful some recent attempts at finding comparisons or confirmations of the philosopher's alleged democratic feelings in the *Peri physeos*. He then concludes that none of the surviving texts endorse any hypothesis regarding a democratic Empedocles. This part of the volume is closed by Ian Worthington's paper, which deals with

Athens' history after the Classical Period. Pertinently, the author focuses on a less "golden" age of the polis, stressing the resilience of its people who never stopped fighting against new foreign rulers, although circumstances persistently contradicted the goal of having freedom back. In this context, a man like Demosthenes, who fought for Athens' independence and freedom, gained special meaning for the Athenians of the Hellenistic and Roman periods. The existence of a statue then dedicated to him proves it and, as Worthington argues, must have been used as symbol against Macedonian rule, first, and Roman power, after.

The fourth and last part of the book is dedicated to Epigraphy. It starts with Robin Osborne's contribution, which presents a reflection on how the material form of inscriptions affects the historical use of inscribed texts. Osborne focuses on two specific aspects of epigraphic texts: their being written for display in a particular place and their freezing of a particular moment in time. The author argues that, by taking these aspects into account, epigraphic texts acquire additional dimensions that enable a rather richer history to be written. In his paper, András Patay-Horváth considers the remaining parts in the Serpent Column of Delphi (a list of 31 *poleis* that participated in the Battle of Plataea and a damaged preamble), but he deals mainly with the lost ones. Patay-Horváth argues that the traditional reading of the preamble is likely to be correct, since it gives all the necessary information about the dedicators. The author also argues that the dedicatory inscription was most probably incised on the lost base of the monument. It was likely to have been a very simple inscription, naming only the Hellenic symmachy led by Sparta, and most probably the fact that it was erected as a military victory monument. As far as Andrea Giannotti is concerned, his main goal is to investigate to what extent the language of Athenian tragic plays is related to the language of epigraphy, in particular that of honorific decrees praising the deeds and virtues of foreign benefactors. Greek drama provides many examples of reciprocal relationships between people which mirror the logic of honorific practice. A comparative analysis of specific tragic episodes, such as Aegeus' in Euripides' *Medea*, and epigraphic testimonies can thus help us estimate to what extent the logic of honorific practice permeated Athenian society, as well as understand the significance of the logic of benefactions and exchanges in the world of Attic tragedy. Kazuhiro Takeuchi's essay deals with the sacrificial calendar of Thorikos, which was first published in 1983. Although the issues of its chronology and sacrificial ritual are still under debate, as the author remarks, it is pertinent to present a fresh look on this topic, based on autopsy. This method allows the author to offer epigraphical commentaries and propose new restorations concerning the oath of the *euthynos* ('auditor') and the *euthynai* ('audits') of officials appended to the end of the inscription. Takeuchi raises the issue about the date and the lettering of the document. Finally, the last contribution is Adele C. Scafuro's, whose chapter deals with a famous passage in 'Philip's Letter to the Athenians', in which the Macedonian king mentions repeated attempts to put an end, by arbitration, to his dispute with the Athenians over the island of Halonessos. Scafuro considers that Philip offered a formal *proklesis* to the Athenians for the arbitration of their dispute and explains why a *proklesis* may be appropriate in some contexts but inappropriate in others, such as diplomatic situations. The author also takes the authenticity issue of the letter into account, as well as a comprehensive overview of its reception and hermeneutics. In the end, Scafuro argues that 'Philip' properly resorts to a technical term of arbitration proceedings, used by cities that are bound together by agreements, considering this an indication of the genuineness of the document (e.g. as representing the author's intimate knowledge of international affairs).

The preparation of a coherent manuscript is a laborious and highly demanding task, to whose copy-editing Carlos Martins de Jesus devoted many hours of his time. The same can be said of David Wallace-Hare, who so generously and attentively reviewed the texts of non-native English-speaking authors. Special thanks must be given, as well, to the internal and external referees who read the papers, strongly contributing to improve them. The final quality of the volume owes much to their diligent commitment. Finally, a word of sincere appreciation to David Davison and to Archaeopress, for having accepted to publish the book and make it available to readers.

We have left to the end the greatest of thanks, which is due to P.J. Rhodes, for having enlightened and inspired generations of Classicists. May the work of the editors of this volume not detract from the exceptional quality of the scholar they endeavour to honour.

Delfim Leão,
Daniela Ferreira,
Nuno Simões Rodrigues,
Rui Morais

PJR: An Appreciation

John Davies

What was written and delivered via the electronic gathering at Coimbra as an Appreciation has had at the last moment to become an Elegy. The Editors' invitation to revise the text presents a dilemma. To leave the text unchanged risks incongruity and insensitivity: to change it significantly risks needless overlap with other tributes to Peter as scholar and human being, both those in this volume and those to come elsewhere. I have therefore changed virtually nothing of my text except the tense of some verbs.

It was both a privilege and a pleasure to have been able to offer this affectionate salutation to so long-standing a friend and colleague as Peter Rhodes, for our paths through life ran in parallel in ways that reflect aspects of the sociology of scholarship. Typically for our generation, we were both products of high-status and fiercely selective English grammar schools in a period when meritocracy was in vogue in Britain and when a few of the financially poorer and less distinguished colleges in Oxford and Cambridge saw competitive advantage in recruiting such applicants as ourselves, rather than applicants from independent fee-paying schools (the so-called 'public schools'). Wadham in Oxford was one such college, and in consequence first I, then Peter a few years later, had the good fortune to find ourselves there and to be taught ancient history by George Forrest (later Wykeham Professor of Greek History): I have described elsewhere how Forrest's personality and teaching style made the subject come alive and inspired a long succession of his students to follow him into the specialism.

A second shared experience followed, as first I, then Peter, came under the influence of David Lewis as the supervisor of the post-graduate projects that eventually gave us our doctorates and the entrée to university careers. Peter in his turn commented on that influence elsewhere, for I think he found it easier than I did to relate to Lewis's high expectations and hyper-laconic postcard-sized guidance. In retrospect, though, it is clear that we both responded constructively to his vision of studies that bypassed the traditional parade-ground of ancient Greek history, politico-military narratives, and instead explored how Greek societies and their institutions worked in practice. Both in the thesis that became his first big book, *The Athenian Boulé*, and in many other publications, Peter largely stayed true to the institutional side of that vision, while I have inclined more to its social and economic side. But our careers continued in parallel, his too with spells at Merton College Oxford and at the Washington Center for Hellenic Studies, a lectureship outside Oxford which became a personal Chair at Durham, and election as Fellow of the British Academy, not to mention many shorter-term honorific awards. Throughout the decades, his energy and industry were exceptional, enviable, and very efficiently employed: I can do no more here than touch very briefly on some of the most prominent themes of his activity.

I begin, not with his innumerable reviews or with his equally innumerable edited-volume chapters and journal papers, but with his books, because they displayed those 'prominent themes' in their most concentrated form. Above all, they showed him as 'editor', in no fewer than three of the four possible roles that that term encompasses. (He wisely avoided the fourth role, the thankless task of actually editing a journal, but as a member of editorial committees of no fewer than eight journals over the decades he played a generous supportive role in that sector of scholarship too.) In the first of those three editorial roles, his activity as editor, translator, and commentator of literary texts was incessant for forty years. It began with his second *mega biblion*, the full-dress *Commentary on the Aristotelian Athenaion Politeia*. It then moved to single books of Thucydides and Herodotos by way of the *Old Oligarch* and a translation of Thucydides, and more recently embraced *the Laws of Solon*.

The second role, that of editing, translating, and commenting on inscriptions, was an equally intense activity. He was never a hard hands-on epigraphist, but rather one who used, assembled, and explained them for general utility. A volume of mid-fourth century inscriptions in translation in 1972 began the sequence, but it abruptly changed course when David Lewis's final illness, combined with David's competing priorities, compelled Peter to take by far the major responsibility for compiling and editing what became *The decrees of the Greek states* in 1997. This is a characteristically painstaking compilation of evidence from across the Greek-inscribing world, so designed as to document how the range of distributions of power within Greek states was reflected in the formulae of the preambles of inscribed public decrees. It became his third *mega biblion*: one surmises that the intimate acquaintance with the whole Greek epigraphic corpus that it gave him helped to engender the step-change that was visible six years later in his fourth, the book of fourth-century inscriptions that is now known to us all as RO. Compiled jointly with Robin Osborne, it replaced Marcus Tod's 1948 volume of the same title, which in turn had replaced Hicks' pioneering effort of 1882, and it was a real step-change. All such compilations have been in essence a teaching tool for university courses, but the additions to each entry in RO of full-dress lemmata, full translations, some apparatus criticus, and detailed explanatory commentaries have raised its format and content much closer to the gold standard for full epigraphic publication. Nor did the editors stop there, for the editors then changed places on the title page and gave us OR for the fifth century: what we shall call the pre-478 volume when it appears remains to be seen. Together the volumes will form a magnificent trilogy.

There remains the third and last form of editorship, represented by eight examples of what has become our profession's signature art-form: edited book-form assemblages of papers, whether of conference proceedings, of a scholar's collected works, or of selected or solicited contributions to a theme. Three are singletons: a source-book in translation on *The Greek city-states*, the editorial responsibility for David Lewis's posthumous *Selected Papers*, and a collection of essays by 14 scholars on *Athenian democracy*. Others have been collaborations – with Lynette Mitchell for *The development of the polis in Archaic Greece*, with E.E. Bridges and Edith Hall for *Cultural responses to the Persian wars*, with Edward Harris and Delfim Leão for *Law and drama in ancient Greece*, with Polly Low and Graham Oliver for *Cultures of commemoration*, and with Valerij Gouschin for *Deformations and crises of ancient civil communities*. I cite them all in detail because collaborators' names tell one story (of wide and amicable collegiality) and the book titles tell another (of a wide range of thematic interest), but both sets reflect the central place which PJR occupied for decades in the communal mission to reconstruct the complex but patchily documented culture of Classical Greece and to present it lucidly and precisely.

I now turn from PJR as editor to PJR as reviewer. I do so not just because of the lucidity and sane judgment of his reviews but also, and primarily, because the intensity of his activity since 1970 that their numbers reflect was a polysemic marker: of his willingness to perform an essential but unglamorous and sometimes distracting task, of the choices that he made and of the profile that review editors have discerned, but especially of his acquisition of intellectual capital. To write a review is also to invest in one's own store of knowledge. To focus such activity over the decades, as he did, is to give oneself an unshakeable command not just of the 'bibliography' of a subject but also of its flows and tensions and inter-relationships. But the strategy is effective only if it is concentrated, achieving near-total coverage of an author, say, or of a region or a period or a specific culture-form. In this respect Peter's list is eloquent. Apart from a few outliers and from his surveys of publications in Greek history in *Greece & Rome* in 1988-91, the titles reviewed were almost wholly concerned with one or other of three interlaced subjects: Athens, Thucydides, and ancient Greek institutions and political theory. So have the four book-length monographs of his that I have yet to cite: first, *Ancient democracy and modern ideology*, with a meaningful title to which I return in a moment, secondly *A history of the Classical Greek world 478-323 BC*, thirdly *Alcibiades, Athenian playboy, general and traitor*, and fourthly *A short history of ancient Greece*.

If, keeping in mind that consistency of focus within reviews and monographs, one turns to his list of journal papers and chapters in edited volumes, one finds that -- hardly surprisingly -- they show exactly the same profile. There were a few ventures into foreign parts – to a sentence in Suetonius, to Sparta twice, to Boiotia, Macedonia, Miletos, and Sicily once each – and a near-dozen that reflected his affectionate loyalty to Durham and to his colleagues, but otherwise one is looking at the yield across those three interlaced subjects from that concentrated investment.

Does that concentration constitute a limitation? There is a case for the answer 'Yes', insofar as it gave him fewer opportunities to show how polities and institutions can be safely compared across time or space, and it has deprived the reader of what would have been equally carefully thought out and documented studies of other more neglected times and regions of Antiquity. But the far stronger case is for 'No'. How do I best put it? With some trepidation, I ask you to imagine in your mind's eye an old wooden box that is stored up in the dusty attic of an old house and is simply labelled 'Athens'. It is stuffed-full of preserved and rescued fabrics and clothing of every kind and pattern that have been dumped there by generations of families – standard undamaged basic items (a waistcoat, an evening dress), unfinished garments, curtains, complete and fragmentary display pieces, roll-ends, torn and broken remnants, discards, heirlooms --- and of a quality that varies from the choice to the mundane, from shoddy to classic. The inexpert will open the box and despair. Yet a skilled tailor or seamstress who knows the range and potential of such materials can select, refurbish, combine, and reshape them so cleverly as to be able to present a new, elegant, robust and well-made product time and again. Peter was that tailor. Seemingly effortlessly (but the relentless hard work in study and library has to be imagined and factored in) and in response to endless requests for lectures and invitations to contribute to a volume, the list of creations grew so steadily, and latterly so fast (at least 4 or 5 a year since he retired), as to provide a complete conspectus of how Athenian and Greek public life and institutions worked in practice. When his forthcoming *Studies on fourth-century Athens* finally appears, it will surely be seen as a *Summa historica* and as yet another indispensable *mega biblion*.

Three words suffice to characterise this corpus: authority, lucidity, and caution. The first is obvious: for decades he knew the texts and documents and bibliography about Athens and Classical Greece as well as, and very probably better than, anyone else in the world, and he used that knowledge crisply, appositely, and constructively in the interests of fostering his readers' understanding of past realities. Secondly, whether describing or narrating or arguing, he always wrote simply: he wished to be understood. Thirdly, he stayed close to the evidence, showed his working, used his knowledge to demolish the extravagant or ill-founded ideas of others, and yet remained deeply cautious and critically aloof. One of his six *mikra biblia* provides a perfect illustration. This is his Presidential Address to the Classical Association at Bristol in 2015, entitled *Ktema es aei (A possession for all time)*. Its 22 pages[1] bring text and author sympathetically alive, steer the reader through the interpretative debates, and yet keep their distance. This is very firmly not Thucydid-olatry, but in many ways Thucydides emerges vastly the better for being treated as a human being, with his foibles and obsessions, as well as a composer, making and using the historical record in order to reflect on the human condition.

But texts and institutional realities were not his only preoccupation, for an earlier *mikron biblion, Ancient democracy and modern ideology*, entered a much larger and even more contested arena. It and a later essay explored the relationship between two currently live questions: first, Where was power actually located during the two centuries of the Athenian democracy?, and secondly How far, when we ask that and other questions about Athens, should we be preoccupied with the possible utility of the answers for the political societies of the present day? The first question needs a descriptive answer, but one framed in terms both of evidence and of analytical concepts, whether modern (such as legitimacy, sovereignty, clientage, charisma, and networks) or those of the culture in question (*kharis, timé, eudaimonia*, etc.). The second needs a normative answer, and therefore one that locates the descriptive evidence not only within a lattice of human rights and values which may or may not be deemed to be universal and timeless, but also within a fiercely reductive debate about the sociology of knowledge. That debate is inclined to delegitimate much of the necessary working vocabulary as 'constructs' (and to some degree rightly so, for the shade of Foucault cannot be excised – or exorcised – from any debate on these matters). It is not melodramatic to assert that behind his responses to these two questions, and behind the detailed summaries of much modern scholarship, Peter was exercising a mission. It was one of measured resistance to the (nowadays largely American-led) tendency to look to ancient Greece, and especially to 'democratic Athens', for lessons for today's world, and instead to assert the absolute need to 'aspire to objectivity and disengagement' while still desiring 'to make the Greek and Roman world intelligible and interesting to inhabitants of our own world'.

Here, and everywhere else in his work, one detects a strong didactic streak. It goes back to his first source-book of 1972 in a series that was designed to serve the upper-school and undergraduate market, and it ran through his entire oeuvre. It cannot be chance, either, that the concentration identified above was reflected precisely in the two principal focuses of his teaching in Durham, Greek history and Greek political theory and practice. If I may (though I suspect Peter did not greatly approve) resort momentarily to economist-speak, his 'investment' generated 'production' of 'goods' with great 'efficiency' for an entire set of

---

[1] He published a longer and differently organised study (Rhodes 2015c) in the same year.

concurrent and complementary 'markets', from the school-room and the lecture-hall to the international journal and 'the standard work on the subject'. We all try to do it, but few of us do it so effectively at all levels of scholarship and sophistication.

Even with all that said, one final group of readers has yet to be mentioned. Not all of Peter's 'ventures into foreign parts' were desk- and library-based affairs. Annually and for many years, fortunate friends and colleagues found their email Inboxes suddenly filled with another instalment of 'Peter's travels', a detailed and lively description in 3-7 pages of where he had been for work or pleasure. I lack early instalments, though I know of those for Russia in 1997 and Iran in 2000. My set starts with Poland and the Baltics in 2001, then jumps to Corfu, Barcelona, and Egypt in 2007, Mitteleuropa in 2009, Syria in 2010 (now a pitiful piece to re-read), and Poland again and southern France in 2011. Thereafter Perm in Russia appears year after year, and outside Europe Azerbaijan, Georgia, and Armenia come in 2015, Cuba and New England in 2016, India and Japan in 2018, Minsk, Morocco, and Utrecht in 2019 – and understandably nothing at all in 2020. Together they comprise a remarkable catalogue of adventure, observation, and reportage. In part, as he made very clear, they reflected his activity and popularity as a lecturer: in part they reflected the sort of informal international network of colleagues and former students which many of us academics tend to assemble: but above all they reflected his own sense of curiosity about places and peoples, his confidence in travelling alone or as a member of a tourist group across the accessible world, and his very firm view of a 'holiday' not as sunburnt sloth on a beach but as a carefully planned programme of active exploration in a deliberately chosen area. It all amounts to a revealing and honest self-portrait, all the more valuable for being unselfconscious.

My final sentence had been: 'We congratulate him on his enterprise and vitality, we thank him most warmly for informing and entertaining us, we hope that the stream of scholarship will continue for many years to come, and we wish him well for the resumption of "Peter's travels" when circumstances and governments allow.' I retain it perforce as it was, painful though it now is to re-read.

References

Davies, J.K. 1999. Professor William George Grieve Forrest. *Annual of the British School at Athens* 94 (1999), pp. 475-83.

Rhodes, P.J. 2003. *Ancient democracy and modern ideology*. London: Duckworth.

Rhodes, P.J. 2015a. *Ktema es aei (A possession for all time)*. London: The Classical Association.

Rhodes, P.J. 2015b. Directions in the study of Athenian democracy. *Scripta Classica Israelica* 34 (2015), 49-68.

Rhodes, P.J. 2015c. *Thucydides*. London: Bloomsbury.

P.J. 2019. *John Davies, Greek historian*, in Z.H. Archibald and J. Haywood (eds), *The power of individual and community in Ancient Athens and beyond. Essays in honour of J.K. Davies*: 311-315. Swansea: Classical Press of Wales.

Part I - History and Biography

The Controversy Between Herodotus and Hecataeus: History and Competition in the *Histories* 2.143.

Denis Correa

Federal University of Recôncavo da Bahia
Centre for Classical and Humanistic Studies (CECH)
tecnocaos@gmail.com

Abstract

The report from Herodotus 2.143 about both his own and Hecataeus' conversations with Egyptian priests is a major controversy of Classical historiography. Scholars have approached it as some sort of misrepresentation that intended to undermine Hecataeus' reputation, or as a point made by Herodotus about the methodological flaws of his predecessor, although it is hard to believe that it happened exactly as Herodotus represented it. Some scholars already acknowledged the role of agonistic intertextuality in this passage as a structuring element of tradition and it changes the perspective about why and how Herodotus criticizes Hecataeus. Fifth-Century prose writing did not have yet an established context of communication, like the one that Greek poetry has in the ceremonial recitation in Pan-Hellenic festivals, or later in the systematic reading and criticism of texts in the schools of rhetoric and philosophy from the Fourth-Century onwards. In the lack of such kind of established setting for textual communication, I propose that Herodotus incorporated within the narrative a dramatization of Hecataeus' visit to the Egyptian temple as a way of competing against him. My focus is on the rhetorical and agonistic aspects of the passage to understand how Herodotus intended to drain Hecataeus' reputation and project himself in the same textual tradition.

Keywords

Herodotus, Hecataeus, historiographical controversies, agonistic intertextuality

> What we need to do with the ancient historians, and with all ancient texts, is what sensitive scholars had been trying to do even before the days of modern literary theory. We must use all the means at our disposal to establish what the writers were trying to do, how they set about doing it, what material was available to them, what limitations they were subject to, what limitations we are subject to in studying them - and then, if we are historians, we must make the best use of them that we can in investigating the questions which we want to investigate. The results will not be as clear-cut for us as they are for total believers or total unbelievers, but life is like that.

(Rhodes 1994: 157).

With these lucid words, P.J. Rhodes stated his defense of ancient Greek historians against modern skeptical views about their methods and styles of writing. Regarding Herodotus, these views were embodied at that time especially by D. Fehling (1971, 1989) and O.K. Armayor (1978), and before that by W.A. Heidel (1935), among others. I will not revisit these arguments, nor the criticism against them, but focus instead on recent contributions about agonistic intertextuality between Herodotus and Hecataeus, considering critically the following passage in the *Histories* 2.143:[1]

> Some time ago the writer[2] Hecataeus was in Thebes. He traced a genealogy of his own lineage back to a divine ancestor in the sixteenth generation. So the priests of Zeus there did to him what they did to me too (except that I have not traced my genealogy): they took me into the temple, showed me the wooden figures there, and counted them for me, up to the number I have mentioned (see 2.142), since every high priest sets up his own statue in the temple while he is still alive. The priest started with the statue of the one who had died most recently and went through the whole lot, until they had shown them all, and while showing me the statues and counting them out, they demonstrated how in each generation the son succeeded his own father. In response to the fact that Hecataeus traced a genealogy back to a divine ancestor in the sixteenth generation, they traced an alternative genealogy on the basis of their counting of the statues, and they refused to accept this idea that a human being could be descended from a god. In tracing their alternative genealogy, they claimed that every one of the figures represented a *piromis* descended from a *piromis* (in Greek this would be a 'man of rank').

Whenever I read about this passage or talk about it with Herodotean scholars, there is always the shadow of the question: can we trust Herodotus? Admittedly, this is an inadequate way of approaching the subject[3], so I would rather stick with Rhodes and ask similar questions he did: what did Herodotus try to do ? What limitations he had in doing it? How he did it? Which limitations we have in trying to understand it? I will discuss the first two questions as a review of some modern scholarship and then, when turning to the other two, I will focus on my interpretation of 2.143, with a wider concern about the role of textual controversy within Greek historiography. Herodotus, I suggest, connected himself with Hecataeus in a competitive way to drain authorial reputation from his rival. That kind of agonistic intertextuality had a fundamental role in establishing a shared framework of textual communication where authors can connect with rivals and compete against their authorities and claims of truth.

What did Herodotus try to do and what limitations did he have?

Both 'believers' and 'unbelievers', expressions used by Rhodes above, agreed that Herodotus wants to reveal the failure of his predecessor in establishing a critical review of his genealogical claims when confronted with Egyptian records of the past. The 'unbelievers' stressed that Herodotus was dishonest for inventing sources and/or concealing that he relied on Hecataeus to produce his account on Egypt (Heidel 1935: 93–117; Fehling 1989: 77–85; Armayor 1978: 63–67). The 'believers' focused on Herodotus' improvement of the historical method through criticism against Hecataeus' failure to see how the Egyptian historical records subvert the time structure of Greek genealogy (Lateiner 1989: 93–95; Lloyd 1988: 105–114; 2007: 231–232,

---

[1] English version by Waterfield (1998: 210), but I made minor changes to give focus to the use of the verb γενεαλογέω, which Waterfield translates with variant expressions.

[2] For λογοποιός to describe Hecataeus, see Alganza Roldán (2012: 31–43; 2015: 6–19). It is hard to be sure if it has a negative connotation, because at chapter 5.36 the same word is used and Hecataeus has a positive role as wise advisor for the Milesians, while in the controversy about the Pelasgians 6.137 Hecataeus is identified also by the patronymic.

[3] See Lloyd (2002: 426), Marincola (2007: 51–52), and Moyer (2002: 73).

344–347). This second view may encompass the dismissal of Herodotus' intertextuality with Hecataeus, and the description of the Milesian contribution to Greek historical thought as 'arbitrary empiricism' (Lateiner 1989: 93) and 'dull listing of facts' (Thomas 2000: 212). Most of the fragments from Hecataeus were transmitted by Stephanus of Byzantium (6th century AD), a lexicographer whose scope and selection could be the source of such perception of his work. These and other aspects are summarized by F. Pownall's commentary on the relevant fragments (2016a: T4 and F300).

S. West (1991: 147–149) argued that we probably could not find this story on Hecataeus' work and neither on Egyptian sources, and the improvement of the historical method by Herodotus ignored skepticism against wood statues immune to woodworms and the continuous transmission of the priesthood by father to son through millennia without any interruption. For West (1991: 149–154), the story is a narrative device to deliver abstract ideas, similar to many other similar instances in the work. The episode 'may be somewhat astringent' about the genealogical work of Hecataeus (West 1991: 154–159), but his portrayal is not so bad if we consider his role as an equal inquirer on Egypt and advisor to the Milesians at the Ionian Revolt (5.36 and 5.125). However, if this is the case, what is the role of Hecataeus in 2.143? Why did Herodotus choose to place him there, instead of focusing on his reasoning in 2.142 and 2.144–146?

I. Moyer (2002: 70–75), on the other hand, endorsed the remarks from A. B. Lloyd (1988: 105–114; 2007: 236–237, 344–347) that Herodotus got something right from actual Egyptian evidence. Considering the Egyptian king-lists records, the figures he offered at 2.142 are not absurd (although he made some wrong calculations), so his reasoning could have some ground on the Egyptians' own perception of their long history and their reorientation to the ancient and glorious past in the context of Persian domination (Moyer 2002: 75–82). Herodotus' travels and inquiries compelled him to question the Greek nobility's desire to link themselves with divine ancestors in a few generations, so he used the Egyptian framework of time to historicize some aspects of Greek collective memory. Moyer (2002: 83–85) emphasizes how Herodotus represents Hecataeus as 'the ignorant Greek', as an inquirer he is 'disavowed' and his critical approach to Greek traditions seems to be 'minimal'.[4]

This kind of bad judgment about Hecataeus' work cannot ignore the contribution from L. Bertelli (2001: 76–89) about how some of his fragments satisfy fundamental features of historical discourse, which included a hypothesis about the development of historical chronology based on the conversion of generations in years that may have some influence from Egyptian knowledge of the past (2001: 89–94). More importantly, Bertelli (2001: 67–76) introduced his views with a discussion about the origin of Greek historiography in which the old 'technological determinism' of the advent of writing is replaced by the decisive role of the 'agonistic intertextuality',[5] that is, a triangular relationship between author, predecessor and a common topic which competitively connects authorities and claims of truth, a feature that Hecataeus satisfies in his criticism against tradition. Bertelli also remarked how Herodotus

---

[4] See also how Thomas (2000: 212–221, 259–260, 272–273) minimizes Hecataeus' contribution.
[5] That set of ideas was first introduced by Assmann (1992: 286; 2011: 260–261), but with a slightly different terminology which I will discuss below.

at the same time criticizes Hecataeus but follows his footsteps in being critical of Greek traditions.

Recently, C. Condilo (2017: 242–262) considered the fragments of genealogical works from Pherecydes and Hellanicus, and concluded that Hecataeus' critical attitude to tradition appealed to Herodotus because it was based on similar grounds of inquiry and autopsy. Condilo's (2017: 263–264) main concern is about Herodotus' critical standing on Greek genealogy, and therefore Hecataeus' presence in 2.143 constitutes a meta-narrative or meta-*historie* in which Herodotus is judging his ability to perform a critical revision of tradition, especially his failure in evaluating the impact of Egyptian historical tradition in his genealogical work. So, for Condilo, Herodotus judged the superiority of Hecataeus in comparison with other genealogists, and at the same time, presented himself as a better representative of this kind of critical attitude. Of course, the passage is integrated into a wider debate about the conciliation of Egyptian and Greek chronologies from 2.142 to 2.146, which includes the digression about Herakles (2.43–2.45) and other genealogical occurrences, as Condilo showed (2017: 265–272).

In sum, the 'believers' and 'unbelievers' saw the controversy as a question of historical method, and often this interpretation was connected to the bad judgment of one of the two antagonists, either Herodotus or Hecataeus. Probably this was due to our modern inability to acknowledge that there was no set of conventions[6] in which Herodotus could refute Hecataeus on the grounds of a shared and institutional structure to evaluating claims of truth[7]. Even when scholars acknowledge that categories like 'science' and 'fiction' are inappropriate to understand Herodotus' statements, there is still the problem that he is claiming a truthful representation of reality by inventing a narrative to make his points against Hecataeus. Bertelli and Condilo showed how Herodotus regarded Hecataeus as his best predecessor and precisely because of that he was competing against him. Greek culture is very competitive, so there is no need to presume mendacity from Herodotus or dull ignorance from Hecataeus to understand this instance of agonistic intertextuality. So, the improvement of the historical method should be seen as a posterior result of Herodotus' authorial competition, which is his main motivation, not mendacity, and neither a search for scientific standards. He is creating these standards by using rhetorical strategies and literary conventions from different areas of knowledge[8] to prevail over his rival, and his awareness of the limitations of what he can do with these methods is everywhere in the *Histories*.[9]

An aspect noted by J. Marincola (1987: 121–132, 137) is that Book 2 has an unusual presence of autobiographical statements claiming inquiry and autopsy: 30 from a total of 44 in the whole text, while in the last books about the Persian Wars they almost disappear. That is why the long-lasting debate about the reliability of Herodotus often focused on the evidence of the Egyptian book, but if we reject the simplistic dichotomy between the *father of history* or the *father of lies*, we can understand better what drove Herodotus. Those statements could be

---

[6] See Parke (1946: 80–92) about this subject.

[7] For the role of institutions, like schools of rhetoric and philosophy, in the development of tradition, see Assmann (2011: 257–260), Marincola (1997: 221), and Nicolai (2007: 13–23; 2014: 33–41).

[8] I refer to the notion of 'intellectual milieu' developed by Thomas (2000: 161–200); see also Fowler (1996; 2006), Hornblower (2002: 385–386), and Raaflaub (2002: 156–164).

[9] The more explicit passages are 1.123 and 7.152, but often Herodotus' authorial voice states that he did not believe in what he heard of, for example, in 1.182 and 2.73.

related to his affirmation that Egypt is the place with the most wonders in the world (2.35), but Marincola (2007: 13–15, 35–36) also remarked how they represent Herodotus as an Odyssean persona in travels through marvelous places. So, they are not ubiquitous along with the narrative, neither are they a systematic way of ensuring accuracy: they are part of the mise-en-scène for a report of travel to a marvelous place, and they help to build a sense of wonder and suspense (Marincola 2007: 51–57). As an emulation of traveler's report – like the *Odyssey*, the *Arimaspes*[10], and the *Periodos Ges* from Hecataeus – they are also a sign of Herodotus' rivalry with these predecessors. Reports of denials of autopsy concerning the phoenix, of which he saw only a picture (2.73), and the floating Island of Chemmis (2.156), could be seen either as refutations of the marvel or deliberate moves leaving the possibility open (Marincola 2007: 58–59); or also the anticipation of what the audience may know about these marvels, and since antiquity some readers saw the passages above as implicit references to Hecataeus.[11]

Of course, autobiographical claims of inquiry and autopsy are also related to the truthfulness that the author wants to build within the report, but to Marincola (2007: 60–65) this truthfulness is not concerned with accuracy in the Thucydidean sense, but with a set of contrasts, similitudes, and a sharing features that help the Greeks understand not only Egypt but also themselves and their place within this vast world.[12] Herodotus and Hecataeus were far from being part of a few Greeks who visited Egypt: besides the Greek settlement of Naucratis on the Delta, Herodotus mentions Ionian mercenaries (2.154), and King Amasis permitting eleven Greek cities to set altars where they could honor the gods and make commerce[13] (2.178). The wise Solon visited Egypt (1.30 and 2.177), the courtesan Rhodopis[14] got rich in Naucratis (2.134–135), and Syloson of Samos met a warrior named Darius in the streets of Memphis, an encounter which later will lead to ill-fated deeds to Samos when the Persians tried to establish Syloson as a tyrant (3.139–149). The Greek presence in Egypt should be considered as a factor in the claims of inquiring and sightseeing: it could be a way of providing useful and attractive information to travelers, and a sign of competition against Hecataeus or even Hellanicus, who also wrote about Egypt (Pownall 2016b).

Accordingly, more than the Persian Wars, Egypt was a polemical topic where writers competitively tested their claims and their reputations. However, how could they compete without the conventions and the traditions which set the standards where one could judge the reliability of a historical claim?[15] How could they argue against a writer without a shared framework of textual communication? That leads to my next question.

---

[10] Herodotus makes frequent claims of inquiry and autopsy also in the Scythian *logos*, another travel report through a land where Greek presence was thriving at the time. It is also the place for a controversy against the poet Aristeas of Proconesus, which parallels his agonistic intertextuality with Hecataeus, see Fowler (1996: 85), Gagné (2020: 237), Luraghi (2001: 155), and Marincola (2007: 64–66).

[11] See *BNJ* 1 F305, F324a and 324b, and the commentary by Pownall (2016a).

[12] See also Condilo (2017: 271–272) and Vanniccelli (2001: 211–212).

[13] It is hard to miss the polemical and geopolitical meaning of this passage, especially when Herodotus (2.178.13-14) condemns other Greek cities that claim to participate in this sacred precinct.

[14] Herodotus refuted the absurd story of Rhodopis being responsible for the construction of Mycerinus' Pyramid by claiming autopsy of the dedication of a tenth of her fortune at Delphi: she was rich, but not enough. This is an example of how claims of autopsy relate to travel report conventions and worked as rhetorical weapons against views that needed to be refuted.

[15] Methodological reasoning in ancient historiography is often tied to the refutation of specific claims, see Bakker (2002: 20–24), Correa (2019: 133–136), Lateiner (1989: 92), and Thomas (2000: 213–215).

How did Herodotus do it and what limitations do we have in understanding it?

Competition was the usual setting a Greek would apply to solve many kinds of disputes and achieve a reputation in many kinds of craft.[16] However, prose-writing has no institution to host contests between writers, like the religious festivals hosted poetical contests or the formal occasions where polemical speeches were made. Authorial competition was a way of assuring authority to textual discourse in Greek writing culture, especially in the context where writing was not monopolized by professionals, as was in Bronze Age scribal culture, which allowed the penetration of oral culture in the development of Greek writing culture.[17] I reprise here Assmann's and Bertelli's 'agonistic intertextuality' as triangular relationships between authors, predecessors, and common topics that competitively connect authorities and claims of truth. By critical attitude against authorities, like Homer and Hesiod, Hecataeus could be seen as the first instance of agonistic intertextuality in Greek prose (Bertelli 2001: 77–78).[18] Herodotus similarly addresses the claims of rivals in Book 2, by refuting Ionian theories about the Nile river (2.15–29) and the critical review of Greek genealogical chronology due to his knowledge of Egyptian records (2.142–146). These agonistic statements of Herodotus about thriving common topics at the time also encompass a story in which Hecataeus makes foolish statements in front of Egyptian priests.

However, Assmann mentions 'agonistic intertextuality' only *en passant*,[19] his focus is on the concept of 'hypoleptic discourse'. The meaning of the Greek term ὑπόληψις is 'reply' or 'the act of taking up a matter where another leaves off' (Liddell et al. 1996: 1887), but Assmann uses it unconventionally[20]. He wants to draw attention to how a writer makes references to other texts within the same framework of discourse in the form of a controlled variation. The main achievement of hypoleptic discourse is the gradual development of logical rules in the search for truth, from which derived the modern ideas of philosophy and science (Assmann 2011: 255–267). Here I do not intend to discuss entirely these theories, but rather explore how this notion of competitive textual discourse could be related to the *Histories* 2.143.

Plato mentions ὑπόληψις when describing how the tyrant Hipparchus settled the competition between rhapsodes at the Panathenaic festival, where one rhapsode would take up the Homeric poem exactly where the previous one had left.[21] Diogenes Laertius prefers ὑποβολή (Liddell

---

[16] About the role of competition in the development of textual traditions and rational thought, see Corcella (2006: 53–55), Lloyd (1983: 69–81, 118, 166, 208–213; 1987: 56–70; 2014: 12–28, 32–41, 54–55, 86–88, 114–115), Marincola (1997: 158–174, 218–236) and Most (1990: 47).

[17] This discussion is obviously beyond my scope, but besides Assmann (1992; 2011: 241–275) and Bertelli (2001: 67–72), it is important to consider the criticism of earlier theories about orality and literacy in Greek culture from Thomas (1989: 21–35; 1992: 16–28, 53–65).

[18] Although with no focus on competition, see Boedeker (2000: 113–114) and Luraghi (2006: 84–86) about how intertextuality is a fundamental aspect of the genre of prose-writing created by Herodotus.

[19] Assmann uses the expression only in the German edition (1992: 286) of his book and in a footnote he ascribes it to a non-published communication of Heinrich von Staden. In the English version (2011: 260–261), the expression and the footnote were suppressed to focus on his concept of hypoleptic discourse. Anyway, 'agonistic intertextuality' started to be used for Greek historiography since Bertelli (2001) as a synonym expression to Assmann's notion of hypoleptic discourse. See also Scanlon (2015: 19–20).

[20] Assmann (2011: 255–257) relates it to the notion of εἰς αὐτὸ ἡ ἐπίδοσις ('adding to itself', *De Anima* 417b6–7) and to the distinction between nature (repetition) and history (in which extension and supplementation are allowed). However, I am more interested in the rhapsodic roots of the expression.

[21] Plato *Hipparch.* 228b: καὶ τὰ Ὁμήρου ἔπη πρῶτος ἐκόμισεν εἰς τὴν γῆν ταυτηνί, καὶ ἠνάγκασε τοὺς ῥαψῳδοὺς Παναθηναίοις **ἐξ ὑπολήψεως** ἐφεξῆς αὐτὰ διιέναι.

et al. 1996: 1876) when crediting Solon with the institution of sequential and competitive performances.[22] We know through Lycurgus (*Against Leocrates* 102) that a specific law guided these competitions, and Herodotus (5.67) attests its political relevance: the tyrant of Sicyon Cleisthenes, the grandfather of the Athenian Cleisthenes, expelled the rhapsodes because in Homeric singing contests they celebrated their enemies from Argos. Poetic competition in religious festivities is a well-known aspect of Greek culture, and Hesiod himself claimed to have won a trophy by singing at the games of Amphidamas in Chalcis (*OD*, 654–662). These competitions also relate to dramatic performances at the festivals in honor of Dionysus, as well as elegiac poetry that could have some of its original performance 'in some sort of festive, perhaps agonistic, context' (Bowie 2001: 50–61).

Assmann (2011: 257–260) integrates this notion into other instances of hypoleptic discourse in which there is the habit of competitively linking up different discourses, like oratory and philosophy[23]. About historiography, C. Darbo-Peschanski (2007: 124–126, 196–198, 355–362) showed how ὑπόληψις and ὑποβολή rearranged the time structure from poetical discourse into historical time. Although unrelated to Assmann, this discussion has the common ground of how ὑπόληψις is about the tension between continuity and interruption of different discourses. In sum, hypoleptic discourse is a shared frame of textual communication where an author could 'respond' to a 'predecessor', even if it is a text from centuries ago, to achieve a better performance about the subject. It encompasses poetical competitions, philosophical antilogies, and medical and historical controversy. Herodotus himself offers an example of hypoleptic framing of discourse when Artabanus responds to king Xerxes (7.10.6–11):[24]

> My lord, unless opposing views are heard, it is impossible to pick and choose between various plans and decide which one is best. All one can do is go along with the opinion that has been voiced. However, if opposing views are heard, it is possible to decide. Think of a piece of pure gold: taken by itself it is impossible to tell that it is pure; only by rubbing it on the touchstone and comparing gold with gold can we tell which one is best.

Modern scholars have often noted the polemical and adversarial bent in ancient historiography. The prominence of autobiographical statements of inquiry and autopsy in Book 2 of the *Histories* was frequently conceived as participating in scientific discourse. Here I want to explore how the innovations derived from these instances of agonistic discourse, and especially 2.143, serve to connect the text with others in adversarial way. This is not to say that oral and written competition is the same, simply because, for example, a writer can always choose against whom he wishes to argue. But we cannot assume that historical controversies are products of the disinterested search for truth from some individuals. Development in historical thinking were incorporated into a very competitive culture, and it may have borrowed conventions from competitive poetry, such as amoebean bucolic, and oratory and have given a more relevant role to the claims of truth and the methods of achieving it. On the whole, when engaging critically against an opponent, the writer can absorb his authority for himself – this is what I call to drain a reputation.

---

[22] Diog. Laert. 1.57: Τά τε Ὁμήρου **ἐξ ὑποβολῆς** γέγραφε ῥαψῳδεῖσθαι, οἷον ὅπου ὁ πρῶτος ἔληξεν, ἐκεῖθεν ἄρχεσθαι τὸν ἐχόμενον.

[23] About ὑπόληψις in philosophy, see Bien (1974: 1252–1254) and Gutschker (2002: 272–273).

[24] English version by Waterfield (1998: 477).

In sum, the role of this chapter has been to understand *Histories* 2.143 as an expression of authorial rivalry, in which Herodotus connects himself with Hecataeus to drain his authority and reputation. In doing so, Herodotus made a decisive contribution to the development of public and logical rules in the search for truth. In my view, he employed three persuasive strategies to connect himself to Hecataeus and compete against him. I am not concerned with stating theoretical schemes for these strategies, as they are narrative and rhetorical devices very common within the *Histories*, rather I highlight more macro-level strategies serving this purpose.

The first strategy is a well-known Herodotean feature: dramatization.[25] By this term, I mean the presentation of historical reasoning through a narration of actions. As West pointed out, we can see the conversation between Hecataeus and Egyptian priests in the same manner we see the encounter between Solon and Croesus: it is a narrative device to express abstract ideas about complex events.[26] Even if these actions have never taken place, they help us to understand the narrative in different ways: they anticipate events that have not happened yet, or expose how they could have happened differently, or yet discloses how Herodotus judged events and characters. If we exclude chapter 2.143 and just jump from 2.142 to 2.144–146, we have the complete argumentation about the redefinition of Greek chronology by the standards of Egyptian records, so there was no need to include 2.143 to state the case. However, the story dramatizes the divergence through actions. With the Nile river polemics (2.15–28) we have a direct refutation of three theories in the first-person voice and with complex logical argumentation, in section 2.143, on the other side, we have a series of dramatized actions: Hecataeus tells his genealogy (Herodotus does not), the Egyptian priests took both to the temple, showed and counted the statues, and refuted Hecataeus. Theoretically, the Egyptians could be concerned with defending their priesthood and their claims of stability and continuity (Moyer 2002: 78–80), but their vocabulary and argumentation reveal Herodotus' methods and concerns. So, Herodotus himself does not contest his opponent, he dramatizes the priests doing it for him: the evidence and the historical reasoning are presented by them, not by the writer.

That leads us to the second strategy: displacement.[27] Herodotus is the narrator of what occurred between Hecataeus and the priests, and a non-action character that had the same encounter and did not trace his own genealogy. Again, if we read 2.142 and jump directly to 2.144–146 the argumentation is complete, so why does he disrupt the timeline to put himself there? I see no other reason than competing against Hecataeus while presenting two opposite attitudes in front of the priests. He steps aside[28] and dramatizes the Egyptian priests offering the same argument that he would employ himself. In that way, Herodotus presents himself as a moderate, humble, and wise inquirer, while Hecataeus is portrayed as nothing like that (Pownall 2016a: F300). If Hecataeus indeed told in his work something that later Herodotus

---

[25] See West (1991: 147–154) and Marincola (1987: 133–135; 2007: 35–36).

[26] The same Hecataeus is dramatized as a wise advisor for the Milesians in 5.36 and 5.124–126. About the famous encounter between Solon and Croesus, see Leão (2020: 271–295).

[27] See Irwin (2005: 261) about the Odyssean strategy of "playing both sides". Displacement as rhetorical strategy could also relate to what Bakker (2006: 94) describes as the "syntactic" style of Herodotus: "moving from one *logos* to the next may involve a shift in time or space, and so a 'putting together' ('syntaxis') of two different places or two different times: different times are linked to one place, or different places to one time, as the historian moves backwards and forwards".

[28] Cf. a similar attitude to the other mention of Hecataeus in the controversy about the Pelasgians (6.137).

reshaped in the form of this story in 2.143 we may never know for sure, but there is a clear framing of the story by which Herodotus creates a displacement (in both narrative and chronological senses) to connect himself with Hecataeus, as the paralleled vocabulary makes clear (2.143.1: Ἑκαταίῳ [...] γενεηλογήσαντί [...] ἐμοὶ οὐ γενεηλογήσαντι ἐμεωυτόν). In this way, the audience could compare 'gold with gold' as Artabanus suggested to king Xerxes (see above).

The last persuasive strategy is another device in which Herodotus achieved mastery: irony.[29] First of all, it is ironic because nothing in this story is about the literal verbal utterance about what is told: Herodotus wants to reveal himself in a light that he would never do something like his opponent did. The more evident irony is the verbal utterance of a story in which a notorious wise man is refuted about his own genealogy, but there is also dramatic irony implicated in the audience's awareness of what Hecataeus ignores. In chapter 2.142, Herodotus had already stated for the audience that the Egyptians have records of 11,340 years with no appearance of a god in human form, so Hecataeus executed his useless performance of his genealogy not only for the priests but also for the Herodotean audience, which is invited to watch his theatrical and historiographical peripeteia.

Conclusions

While I endeavoured to deal with these long-lasting questions, Rhodes (1994: 161) offered me wise advice about how to approach the work of someone who was, at the same time, so distant and so close to our modern standards:

> Herodotus' world was different from ours; his assumptions and his priorities were different from ours; but he was (among other things) what we can recognize as a historian, and he can be used by historians today.

By emulating conventions from competitive discourses like poetry and oratory Herodotus is not distant from other competitive and scientific textual traditions of the same period, like medicine. Lloyd (1983: 69–81, 118, 166, 208–13) analogously contextualized adversarial discourse within ancient medical literature in competition for clients among physicians and other healers. When approaching the wider subject of inquisitive thought, Lloyd (1987: 56–70; 2014: 32–41, 64–55, 86–88, 114–115) asked how competition could relate to a certain Greek 'egotism', and whether it could be a major incentive to innovation in science, but also an inhibitor of it. The 'abiding Greek obsession with all forms of contests and competitions' (Most 1990: 47) could reveal a lot about what ancient historians tried to do with their argumentations, and how they developed the canons of historiography, both aesthetically and methodologically. We often fail to notice competitiveness as a relevant aspect when they engaged against rivals due to our assumption that they already have a similar shared framework of textual communication, with its defined rules and institutions, as we have today in modern scholarship.

---

[29] The study of Herodotean ironies from Rutherford (2018) is different from the one formulated in the current chapter, which sees the ironical aspects of 2.143 as more evident than many passages approached by Rutherford. See also Condilo (2017: 264–269) and her brief commentary about the ironic tone of the passage.

Herodotus was aware of the limitation of his inquiries, but, when engaged against a belief that he wanted to dismantle, he would use any rhetorical tool available to him. In 2.143, he connected himself with a previous authority and overcame a rival by using many rhetorical strategies which included rational reasoning, but also ironic and agonistic dramatization where one could compete and achieve a reputation as a better inquirer and writer. In this way, he helped establish a shared framework of textual communication through which authors could connect with rivals and compete against their authorities and claims of truth. So, even if this story was created to dramatize a competition against a predecessor, it can be seen as and important development in historiography on par with any other methodological contributions from Herodotus.

Bibliography

Alganza Roldán, M. 2012. Hecateo de Mileto, «historiador» y «mitógrafo». *Florentia Iliberritana* 23: 23–44.

Alganza Roldán, M. 2015. ¿Historiadores, logógrafos o mitógrafos? (Sobre la recepción de Hecateo, Ferécides y Helánico). *Polymnia* 1: 3–24.

Waterfield, R. 1998. *The Histories*. Oxford and New York: Oxford University Press.

Armayor, O.K. 1978. Did Herodotus Ever Go to Egypt. *Journal of the American Research Center in Egypt* 15: 59–73.

Assmann, J. 1992. *Das kulterelle Gedächtnis: Schrift, Erinnnerung und politische Identität in frühen Hochkulturen*. München: Beck.

Assmann, J. 2011. *Cultural Memory and Early Civilization: Writing, Remembrance, and Political Imagination*. Cambridge: Cambridge University Press.

Bakker, E.J. 2002. The Making of History: Herodotus' *Histories apodexis*, in E.J. Bakker, J. F. Jong, and H. Wees (eds) *Brill's Companion to Herodotus*: 3–32. Leiden: Brill.

Bakker, E.J. 2006. The syntax of *historie*: How Herodotus writes, in C. Dewald and J. Marincola (eds) *The Cambridge Companion to Herodotus*: 92–102. Cambridge: Cambridge University Press.

Bertelli, L. 2001. Hecataeus: from Genealogy to historiography, in N. Luraghi (ed.) *The Historian's Craft in the Age of Herodotus*: 57–94. Oxford: Oxford University Press.

Bien, G. 1974. Hypolepsis. *Historisches Wörterbuch der Philosophie* 3: 1252–1254.

Boedeker, D. 2000. Herodotus' Genre(s), in M. Depew and D. Obbink (eds) *Matrices of Genre: Authors, Canons, and Society*: 97–114. Cambridge; London: Harvard University Press.

Bowie, E.L. 2001. Ancestors of Historiography in Early Greek Elegiac and Iambic Poetry?, in N. Luraghi (ed) *The Historian's Craft in the Age of Herodotus*: 45–66. Oxford: Oxford University Press.

Condilo, C. 2017. Agonistic intertextuality: Herodotus' engagement with Hecataeus on genealogies. *Journal of Ancient History* 5.2: 228–279.

Corcella, A. 2006. The New Genre and Its Boundaries: Poets and Logographers, in A. Rengakos and A. Tsakamakis (eds) *Brill's Companion to Thucydides*: 33–56. Leiden: Brill.

Correa, D. 2019. The Aristotelian Athenaion Politeia as 'poor history'? Historiography, rhetoric, and the controversies about Solon in the Fourth Century. *Histos* 13: 129–145.

Darbo-Peschanski, C. 2007. *L'Historia. Commencements grecs*. Paris: Gallimard.

Fehling, D. 1989. *Herodotus and his 'Sources': Citation, Invention and Narrative Art*. Leeds: F. Cairns.

Fowler, R. 1996. Herodotos and his contemporaries. *Jounal of Hellenic Studies* 116: 62–87.

Fowler, R. 2006. Herodotus and his prose predecessors, in C. Dewald and J. Marincola (eds) *The Cambridge Companion to Herodotus*: 29–45. Cambridge: Cambridge University Press.

Gagné, R. 2020. Mirages of ethnicity and the distant north in Book IV of the Histories: Hyperboreans, Arimaspians, and Issedones, in T. Figueira and C. Soares (eds) *Ethnicity and Identity in Herodotus*: 237-257. London; New York: Routledge.

Gutschker, T. 2002. Aristoteles in der politischen Philosophie des 20. Jahrhunderts. In *Aristoteles in der politischen Philosophie des 20. Jahrhunderts.*, 272–273. Stuttgart: Metzler Verlag.

Heidel, W.A. 1935. Hecataeus and the Egyptian Priests in Herodotus, Book II. *Memoirs of the American Academy of Arts and Sciences* 18.2: 53–134.

Hornblower, S. 2002. Herodotus and his sources of information, in E.J. Bakker, J.F. Jong, and H. Wees (eds) *Brill's Companion to Herodotus*: 373–386. Leiden: Brill.

Irwin, E. 2005. *Solon and Early Greek Poetry: The Politics of Exhortation*. Cambridge: Cambridge University Press.

Lateiner, D. 1989. *The Historical Method of Herodotus*. Toronto: University of Toronto Press.

Leão, D. 2020. Barbarians, Greekness, and Wisdom: The Afterlife of Croesus' Debate with Solon, in T. Figueira and C. Soares (eds) *Ethnicity and Identity in Herodotus*: 271–295. London and New York: Routledge.

Liddell, H.G., and Scott, R. 1996. *A Greek-English Lexicon*. Oxford: Clarendon Press.

Lloyd, A.B. 1988. *Herodotus Book II Commetary 99-192*. Leiden: Brill.

Lloyd, A.B. 2002. Egypt, in E.J. Bakker, J.F. Jong, and H. Wees (eds) *Brill's Companion to Herodotus*: 415–436. Leiden: Brill.

Lloyd, A.B. 2007. Book II, in O. Murray and A. Moreno (eds) *A commentary on Herodotus Book I-IV*: 1–56. Oxford and New York: Oxford University Press.

Lloyd, G.E.R. 1983. *Science, Folklore, and Ideology: Studies in the Life Sciences in Ancient Greece*. Cambridge: Cambridge University Press.

Lloyd, G.E.R. 1987. *The Revolutions of Wisdom: Studies in the Claims and Practice of Ancient Greek Science*. Berkeley; Los Angeles; Oxford: University of California Press.

Lloyd, G.E.R. 2014. *The Ideals of Inquiry: An Ancient History*. Oxford: Oxford University Press.

Luraghi, N. 2001. Local Knowledge in Herodotus' Histories, in N. Luraghi (ed) *The Historian's Craft in the Age of Herodotus*: 138–160. Oxford: Oxford University Press.

Luraghi, N. 2006. Meta-historie: Method and genre, in C. Dewald and J. Marincola (eds) *The Cambridge Companion to Herodotus*: 76–91. Cambridge: Cambridge University Press.

Marincola, J. 1987. Herodotean Narrative and the Narrator's presence. *Arethusa* 20: 121–137.

Marincola, J. 1997. *Authority and Tradition in Ancient Historiography*. Cambridge: Cambridge University Press.

Marincola, J. 2007. Odysseus and the Historians. *Syllecta Classica* 18: 1–79.

Most, G.W. 1990. Canon Fathers: Literacy, Mortality, Power. *Arion* 1.1: 35–60.

Moyer, I.S. 2002. Herodotus and an Egyptian Mirage: The Genealogies of the Theban Priests. *The Journal of Hellenic Studies* 122: 70–90.

Nicolai, R. 2007. The Place of History in the Ancient World, in J. Marincola (ed) *A companion to Greek and Roman historiography*: 13–26. Malden: Blackwell.

Nicolai, R. 2014. The Canon and Its Boundaries, in G. Colesanti and M. Giordano (eds) *Submerged Literature in Ancient Greek Culture: an introduction*: 33-45. Berlin; Boston: de Gruyter.

Parke, H.W. 1946. Citation and recitation: a Convention in Early Greek Historians. *Hermathena* 67: 80–92.

Pownall, F. 2016a. Hekataios of Miletos (1) I. Worthington (ed). *Brill's New Jacoby*.

Pownall, F. 2016b. Hellanikos of Lesbos (4) I. Worthington (ed). *Brill's New Jacoby*.

Raaflaub, K.A. 2002. Philosophy, Science, Politics: Herodotus and the intellectual trends of his time, in E.J. Bakker, J.F. Jong, and H. Wees (eds) *Brill's Companion to Herodotus*, 149–186. Leiden: Brill.

Rhodes, P.J. 1994. In Defence of the Greek Historians. *Greece and Rome* 41.2: 156–171.

Rutherford, R. 2018. Herodotean Ironies. *Histos* 12: 1–48.

Scanlon, T.F. 2015. *Greek Historiography*. West Sussex: Wiley Blackwell.

Thomas, R. 1989. *Oral Tradition and Written Record in Classical Athens.* Cambridge: Cambridge University Press.

Thomas, R. 1992. *Literacy and Orality in Ancient Greece*. Cambridge: Cambridge University Press.

Thomas, R. 2000. *Herodotus in Context: Ethnography, Science and the Art of Persuasion*. Cambridge: Cambridge University Press.

Vannicelli, P. 2001. Herodotus' Egypt and the Foundations of Universal History, in N. Luraghi (ed) *The Historian's Craft in the Age of Herodotus*: 211-240. Oxford: Oxford University Press.

West, S. 1991. Herodotus' portrait of Hecataeus. *Journal of Hellenic Studies* 111: 144–160.

Thucydides on Athens' Goals in Sicily, 427-424 and 415-412 BC

Robert W. Wallace

Professor of Classics, Northwestern University
rwallace@northwestern.edu

Abstract

Thucydides' statements that Athens' two expeditions to Sicily aimed to conquer that island frame his accounts of both expeditions, placed at their beginning and end. These statements seem inconsistent with various internal remarks, raising the question whether he later inserted what I think misrepresent Athens' intentions in order to reinforce his larger moral lessons from Athens' defeat. The central sections in both expeditions, downplaying imperialism, suggest that when he wrote them Thucydides had not yet grasped his overarching theme, which he saw as Athens' overweening ambition, probably until Athens' defeat in 413/2. The central sections of both accounts indicate that Athens' purpose was to reduce the power of Syracuse, Sicily's major naval power and a Spartan ally.

Keywords

Thucydides, Peloponnesian War, Athens' Sicilian expedition, Nicias, Alcibiades.

In his review of my *Areopagos* book, Peter Rhodes (1990: 242) summarized my novel views of the pre-Ephialtic Areopagos and said, 'With much of this I disagree; but Wallace argues carefully and courteously, and readers may judge that his interpretation of the evidence is to be preferred to mine'. I and my adviser Mr. Badian were moved by Peter's kind words. Here I present another novel idea, on Thucydides' statements that Athens' two expeditions to Sicily aimed to conquer that island. These statements, which frame his accounts of these expeditions, seem inconsistent with various internal remarks, raising the question whether he later inserted what I think misrepresent Athens' intentions in order to reinforce his larger moral lessons from Athens' defeat.[1]

As many scholars have observed, Thucydides fragments his brief, almost speech-free presentation of Athens' first expedition to Sicily intermittently across books 3.86 to 4.65, by strictly following his method of dating by seasons, and not to distract from Athens' second expedition in Books 6 and 7, the climax of his history. In 427 Syracuse and its neighbor Leontini were at war (3.86.2). Syracuse, he writes, was allied with all of Sicily's Dorian cities except Camarina. These cities were Sparta's allies in the Peloponnesian War, but so far took no part in it. The Leontines were allies of Camarina, Naxos, Rhegion, and Athens. In late summer 427 Leontini's allies 'send to the Athenians to dispatch a fleet' in accordance with their 'ancient alliance' and Ionian origins (3.86.3). 'Closed in by the Syracusans by land and sea, they persuade the Athenians to send ships and the Athenians sent [twenty: 3.86.1] ships, on the pretext (*prophasis*) of kinship, but wishing to prevent the export of Sicilian grain to the Peloponnese, and making 'a previous attempt (*propeira*) if they could bring matters in Sicily

---

[1] Thucydides translations are mostly edited from standard versions. They aim only to be accurate.

under their control (*hupocheiria*)' (3.86.4). Many have suggested that *propeira*, a rare word, presupposes Athens' second expedition. If so, Thucydides wrote this sentence sometime after 415-413. Otherwise, neither Gomme (1956) nor Hornblower (1991) annotates these lines, evidently accepting them at face value. Westlake (1969: 105-10, followed by Kagan 1974: 182) defends both reasons for the first expedition given by Thucydides, attributing them to different opinions in the assembly.

An alternative purpose for Athens' first expedition is evident from Thucydides' narrative, although 3.86.4 ignores it: military action against Syracuse, Sicily's most powerful city and Sparta's ally. In Thucydides' fragmented account, in the winter of 427/6 (3.88) the Athenians sailed with the Rhegians against the Aeolian islands, allies of Syracuse, and laid waste their land, although the islands did not submit. In the summer of 426 (3.90), saying he will mention only Athens' most important military actions, Thucydides records that the Syracusans killed one Athenian general; he notes Athenian successes against Mylai and Messana, Syracusan allies; and in 3.99 he adds that the Athenians defeated Lokri, a Syracusan ally. The next winter (3.103), the Athenians fight some Sikels allied with Syracuse; the Lokrians; and (3.115) Himera and again the Aeolian islands. 'Athens' allies in Sicily [note: not the Athenians themselves] now sailed to Athens and persuaded the Athenians to send more ships', because 'Syracuse controlled their territory and was assembling a fleet'. Athens sent 40 more ships and three generals, one going on in advance, two others following with the main fleet which was diverted to Pylos and then delayed at Corcyra (4.1-3, 24.3). This fleet did not leave for Sicily until the end of the summer 425, too late for that year's campaigning season. The Lokrians defeat a new Athenian general. Incited by the Lokrians, Syracuse and its allies reinforce their fleet at Messana but are defeated in the straits by 16 Athenian and eight Rhegian ships, followed by more fighting also involving Naxians and Sikels who killed more than a thousand Messanians. The Athenians and Leontines counterattack. 'After this the Greeks in Sicily continued to make war on each other by land, without the Athenians' (4.24.4-25).

In 424 representatives of the Sicilian states met at Gela, to settle their differences instead of allowing the Athenians to exploit them by continued external interference (4.58). In a disproportionately lengthy speech, Thucydides has Hermokrates warn the Sicilians that the Athenians 'are here with a few ships watching for our mistakes, speciously (*euprepos*) using the respectable concept of alliance to take advantage of normal hostilities'. If we call them in while we are fighting each other, 'it is likely that, when they see us worn out, they will one day come in person with a larger armada and try to bring all these things under them' (4.60.1). Thucydides' Hermokrates does not say that the Athenians had just come with 60 ships in order to conquer Sicily. He fears this fate for the future (another sentence written after 415), reinforcing the conclusion that the current expedition did not have that purpose.

The Sicilians made peace, Athens' generals agreed and Athens was included in the treaty, and Athens' fleet sails for home (4.65.1-2). 'Upon their arrival at Athens, the Athenians banished [two of the generals] and fined [the third] for having taken bribes to depart when they might have conquered Sicily' (*ta en Sikeliai katastrepsasthai*: 4.65.3). Why did the Athenians punish these generals? In a fine article R. A. Knox (1985: 145-6) points out that at Gela they had little choice but to join the Sicilians. 'It is difficult to see what they could have done with their limited forces to disrupt a resolute Sicilian desire for peace', although Knox's main point is that the Athenians were typically hard on unsuccessful generals. However, if the Athenians intended to restraint the Syracusans militarily, the generals' concessions made that impossible. Did the Athenians intend 'to gain control' of Sicily (3.86.4) or 'to conquer' it (4.65.3)? In 427 the Athenians could hardly have thought twenty ships could do much against Sicily, and the military actions which Thucydides records over three years seem fairly desultory and only partly successful. As for Athens' sending 40 additional ships, at 3.115 Thucydides says they were 'thinking that the war in Sicily would thus be the sooner ended, and also wishing to exercise their navy'. When he wrote this sentence, he was evidently not thinking that Athens' purpose was to conquer Sicily (so also Kagan 1974: 182-85, with different reasons). In 3.86-4.65, Athens' military campaigns elsewhere get far more attention than in Sicily and Italy.

It seems most likely that the Athenians exiled their generals because they had been sent out to curtail the power of Sparta's ally Syracuse, but signing on to the Sicilians' general peace was contrary to that goal. Thucydides did not list Athenian military action against Syracuse as the purpose of the first expedition (3.86.4), and he says that the request for 40 ships came not from Athens' generals in Sicily but from Athens' allies, possibly because Syracusan military activities (some of which he mentions) could well have justified Athens' two expeditions. Instead, Thucydides wants to show that, especially after defeating Sparta at Pylos (4.37-41), Athens became excessively ambitious and prideful, 'so thoroughly had the present prosperity persuaded the Athenians that nothing could withstand them, and that they could achieve what was possible and what was impractical alike, with means ample or inadequate it mattered not. The reason for this was their general extraordinary success, which made them confuse their strength with their hopes' (4.65.4). Thucydides mentions Athens' desire to conquer Sicily only at the start and end of its first expedition. He gives no sign of it in his intervening narrative, but only statements that seem to contradict it.

Meanwhile (3.91), the Athenians had sent 60 ships and 2000 hoplites under Nikias 'to bring over' (*prosagagesthai*) the island of Melos, which had refused to join Athens' confederacy or be subject to (*hupakouein*) Athens. Nikias had no success. The Melos problem and Nikias' campaign get but half a sentence, followed by several pages of details adding little to the main story. Thucydides downplays this episode at Melos, as he does Athens' first Sicilian expedition.

In 424 Athens had unfinished business with Leontini, Melos, and Syracuse whose activities remained unchecked. In addition, Athens will soon be engaged by Egesta. In 422 the Athenians sent Phaiax and two other ambassadors on an exploratory diplomatic mission to persuade the Greek Sicilians to resist Syracuse and aid Leontini (5.4-5), the same goal they had in the first expedition. This mission accomplished little, beyond reconciling Athens with Lokri.

At the end of Book 5 the Athenians destroy Melos, the culmination in Thucydides (most scholars agree) of Athens' progressively savage and immoral behavior for which a crushing defeat in the second Sicilian expedition will be its punishment. Hornblower (1994: 217) notes that in Book 5 Thucydides suppresses any reference to Nikias' earlier unsuccessful expedition against that island.

Immediately following Melos' brutal destruction, Thucydides begins Book 6, 'The Athenians now wanted to sail to Sicily again with a larger force than [before], and overturn (*katastrepsai*) it if possible', repeating *katastrepsai* from 4.65.4, which Athens' three earlier generals had failed to do. Typically scornful of the demos (see e.g. Ste Croix 1954: 31-36), he adds, '*hoi polloi*

and Syracuse [he agrees with Nikias, these were Athens' opponents], and an attempt be made to have some of the Sikels revolt from the Syracusans, and to gain the friendship of others, in order to obtain grain and troops; and first of all to win over the Messanians, who lay right in the passage and entrance to Sicily and would afford an excellent harbor and base for the army. Thus, after bringing over the cities and knowing who would be their allies in the war, they might then indeed attack Syracuse and Selinos, unless the latter came to terms with Egesta and the former allowed the restoration of Leontini.

Lamachos on the other hand said they must sail straight to Syracuse, and fight their battle at once in front of the city while the people were still unprepared, and the panic was at its height...' If they attacked Syracuse suddenly, 'the rest of the Sicilians would be immediately less disposed to enter into alliance with the Syracusans, and would join the Athenians, without waiting to see which were the strongest' (6.47.1-49). On Lamachos' plan, evidently Athens' goal was to ally with the Sicilians against Syracuse.

'Having spoken to this effect, Lamachos nevertheless gave his support to the opinion of Alkibiades' (6.50.1). The Athenians sailed from Rhegion to Syracuse, and proclaimed from shipboard 'that the Athenians had come to restore the Leontines to their country, as being their allies and their kinsmen. They then sailed back to Catana' (6.50).

Patently, what Thucydides calls and several times repeats — 6.1, then 6.6 — the desire and 'urge' of the Athenians to conquer Sicily is nowhere evident, even before the allied fleet reached Sicily. The ambitions of even 'bold' Alkibiades extended no further than resolving the issues of Egesta and Selinos, if necessary by fighting Syracuse and Selinos. Nor did either Nikias or Alkibiades support Lamachos' idea, presumably because his plan involved an immediate attack on Syracuse. These speeches support what we have seen all along, both in 427-424 and now in 415. Athens' goal in Sicily was not conquering that island, but weakening or (if necessary) defeating Syracuse, Sicily's most powerful city and a Spartan ally.

As the culmination of what Thucydides saw as Athens' overweening imperialism immediately before disaster struck in Sicily, he has Alkibiades, now a traitor in exile, address the Spartans, claiming to possess superior knowledge about the Athenians. 'We sailed to Sicily first to conquer (*katastrephein*), if possible, the Sicilians, and after them the Italians also, and finally to assail the empire and city of Carthage.[3] In the event of all or most of these schemes succeeding, we were then to attack the Peloponnese... and with this fleet blockading the Peloponnese from the sea and assailing it with our armies by land, taking some of the cities by storm and besieging others, we hoped without difficulty to defeat them completely and after this to rule (*archein*) the whole of the Greek world... You have thus heard the history of the present expedition from the man who most exactly knows what our intentions were... If Syracuse is taken, all Sicily is held as well [just what Thucydides has the great Hermokrates say to the Syracusans in 6.33.2], and immediately Italy too, and the threat from there that I just mentioned would soon be at your door' (6.90.2-91.3). We might straightway conclude that Thucydides wrote this speech to demonstrate Alkibiades' puffery, in a sophistic tour de force. However, in 2.11.8 the Spartan king Archidamos (whom Thucydides greatly respected) states that the Athenians 'aspire to rule (*archein*) the rest of the world'. I believe Thucydides

---

[3] Alkibiades' speech was a ready source for Isokr. *On the Peace* 84-85.

hoped his readers would carry away Archidamos' and Alkibiades' darkest picture of Athenian imperialism. After all, he says, Alkibiades knew the truth.

Echoing his comment at the end of the first Sicilian expedition (4.65.4) and earlier of the Spartans (4.18-20), in Book 8 Thucydides writes, 'after the Spartans, the Chians are the only people I have known who knew how to be wise in prosperity, and who ordered their city the more securely the greater it grew... And if they were tripped up by one of the surprises which upset human calculations, they found out their mistake in company with many others who had believed, like them, in the speedy collapse of Athens' power' (8.24.4-5).

I conclude with two general remarks. First, in his fine book on Thucydides' structure, Hunter Rawlings (1981) traces various parallel accounts in the two halves of Thucydides' history, divided at 5.25. Although Rawlings doesn't comment on it, Thucydides evidently did the same with Athens' two Sicilian expeditions. His unified opus, crafted out of similar parts like Herodotus, culminates in claims of Athens' overweening ambition in Sicily, introduced in 3.86-4.65, then presented full blown in Books 6 and 7 when their ambitions are smashed.

Secondly, in a brilliant article which some conservative historians reject thinking him a demos-loving Marxist, Geoffrey de Ste Croix (1954: e.g. 16) observed that, while Thucydides states repeatedly in his 'editorial' voice that Athens' allies hated Athens, the narratives in his 'reporter' voice do not bear out that claim. Writing in a period when few criticized Thucydides, Ste Croix sought to smooth the waters by commending Thucydides' honesty in reporting facts which are inconsistent with his general thesis, which Ste Croix—I agree—thinks reflected anti-democratic and anti-Athenian prejudice. Our results here encourage a reconsideration of Ste Croix's explanation. The central sections in both Sicilian expeditions, downplaying imperialism, suggest that when he wrote them Thucydides had not yet grasped his overarching theme, which he saw as Athens' overweening ambition, probably until Athens' defeat in 413/2. Once he hit upon his central thesis, he went back through his accounts of these expeditions inserting lines especially at their start and finish, just as he did with Athens and its allies.

Bibliography

Balot, R., S. Forsdyke and E. Foster (ed.) 2017. *The Oxford Handbook of Thucydides*. Oxford: Oxford University Press.

Gomme, A.W. 1956. *A Historical Commentary on Thucydides*. Books II-III. Oxford: Oxford University Press.

Green, P. 1970. *Armada from Athens*. Garden City, New York: Doubleday.

Greenwood, E. 2017. Thucydides on the Sicilian expedition, in Balot et al. (eds) 2017: 161-77.

Hornblower, S. 1991, 1994, and 2008. *A Commentary on Thucydides*, vol. 1 (Books 1-3), vol. 2 (Books 4-5.24), and vol. 3 (Books 5.25-8.109). Oxford: Oxford University Press.

Kagan, D. 1974. *The Archidamian War*. Ithaca: Cornell University Press.

Kagan, D. 1981. *The Peace of Nicias and the Sicilian Expedition*. Ithaca: Cornell University Press.

Knox, R.A. 1985. So Mischievous a Beaste? The Athenian *Demos* and its Treatment of its Politicians. *Greece* and *Rome* 32: 132–61.

Liebeschuetz, W. 1968. Thucydides and the Sicilian expedition. *Historia* 17: 289-306.

Rawlings, H.R. III, 1981. *The Structure of Thucydides' History*. Princeton: Princeton University Press.

Rhodes, P.J. 1990. Review of R. W. Wallace, *The Areopagos Council, to 307 BC*. *Greece* and *Rome* 37: 242.

Ste Croix, G.E.M. de. 1954. The Character of the Athenian Empire. *Historia* 3: 1-41.

Schneider, Ch. 1974. *Information und Absicht bei Thukydides. Untersuchung zur Motivation des Handelns*. Göttingen: Vandenhoeck and Ruprecht.

Westlake, H.D. 1969. Athenian aims in Sicily, 427-424 B.C. *Essays on the Greek Historians and Greek History*: 101-22. Manchester: Manchester University Press. Reprinted from *Historia* 9, 1960: 385-402.

Reading Thucydides' Mythological Stories:
Alcmaeon in *The Peloponnesian War*

Amanda Ledesma Pascal †

IES Guadarrama
amanda_lepal@yahoo.es

Abstract

The critic of myth is an essential part of Thucydides' rationalism. As it is well known, he specifically bases the veracity of his account on the rejection of mythical stories. Therefore, some of his references to mythological figures seem very inconsistent with his logical thinking, and need to be explained. Focused on the figure of Alcmeon (2.102.6) and trying to shed light on Thucydides' critical assessment of this traditional tale, this paper seeks to contribute to a better understanding of such puzzling digressions.

Keywords

Thucydides; ancient historiography; myth; Alcmaeon

Thucydides' methodology is characterized by a rigorous selection of the narrative material, due to the historian's will of focusing on his main topic, the Peloponnesian War. In such an austere account, digressions, seldom as they are, have seemed therefore something anomalous and very inconvenient to the critic for a very long time.[1] When Thucydides' rationalism is critically addressed, digressions are not the only issue at stake, but they certainly are a very relevant one. In the last decades, however, many digressions have been thoroughly analysed, and their connection with the main narrative has been coming to light. As a result, it is now understood that, far from being superfluous or irrelevant, many excursuses play a significant role in Thucydides' work, and offer invaluable aid to its interpretation. When dealing with past history, Thucydides provides important clues on his very own perspective as an author, as convincingly argued by Tsakmakis.[2] Long digressions have attracted a certain amount of attention in recent years, benefiting our understanding of Thucydides' text greatly.[3] Notwithstanding, there remains a number of short excursuses whose integration in the work are not yet sufficiently understood. The description of the mouth of Achelous river with the related story of Alcmaeon's purification (Th. 2.102) is one of them. This paper is centered on this brief passage and it modestly aims to shed some light into its puzzling presence in the work.

The geographical description with its naturalistic explanation of the alluvial origin of the soil is generally considered the very core of the digression. From this point of view, the

---

[1] Cf. Tsakmakis 1995: 1-8. As observed by Pothou (2009: 20), a digression is a 'deviation in Thucydides' work (ἐκβολή), while it is an addition for Herodotus (προσθήκη)'.

[2] 'Thukydides' Umgang mit der historischen Überlieferung innerhalb seines eigenen Werkes soll seine auktoriale Perspektive bei der Abfassung der Geschichte des peloponnesichen Krieges in ihren wesentlichen Zügen fassbar machen' (Tsakmakis 1995: 3).

[3] Pothou (2009: 22; 155) also underlines their pertinence and Sancho Rocher (2017: 238ff.) underscores their sense regarding human nature as a tool for historical explanation (τὸ ἀνθρώπινον 1.22.4).

mythological content becomes secondary, a sort of digression within another digression,[4] with only a stylistic or entertaining function.[5] So, the excursus seems to have a Herodotean flavor,[6] and the reason of its inclusion in the work remains ultimately unexplained.[7] In an entirely unusual way, Thucydides displays geographical knowledge and erudition about Greek traditional lore as did early Ionian historians. In the absence of a satisfying interpretation, surprise[8] is the most frequent reaction to an episode which is inconsistent with Thucydides' method in many ways, and whose connection with the rest of his work is not obvious at all. Indeed, the description of the landscape is unexpected, for geographical details are very uncommon in Thucydides' *History*. Historical events usually unfold without lack of liveliness in places presented by the historian in a 'typological manner'.[9] Thus, when they appear, landscapes and geographical details are striking amid this abstract narrative, and they should draw the reader's attention. As for the mythological motif, internal contradiction is even more notorious. As it is well known, Thucydides' programmatically commits himself to banish τὸ μυθῶδες from his work.[10] Identifying τὸ μυθῶδες with our modern concept of myth would clearly be a naïve and simplistic interpretation.[11] However, it is also true that Thucydides' supposed inability to detach himself from myth in accounts such as Alcmaeons' story has contributed to this lack of identification[12]. Since these mythical stories are a rarity among critical fact presentations, it is surely worth trying to make sense out of this digression too, in spite of its extravagance.

It should firstly be borne in mind that such a division (geographical and mythological content) has been imposed on the text only for interpretative purposes. In fact, the whole excursus is a typical genealogical or foundational account. Time and space, fiction and reality, earth and water are typically intertwined in such stories.[13] That is the typical manner of Ionian school. In this particular case, comparison with Herodotus' *History* may be extremely fruitful, for a similar description of the mouth of Achelous river can be found there as well. In his own excursus, Herodotus makes an accurate analogy between the alluvial topography of Memphis and the mouth of Achelous river, without any mention of Alcmaeon myth.[14] Paradoxically, Thucydides' excursus proves to be more Herodotean than Herodotus' one. While writing this more traditional account, Thucydides plausibly had in mind the naturalistic data of his predecessor. It is not infrequent that Thucydides engages with Herodotus' text, and his dialogue is usually more sophisticated than is sometimes acknowledged. Instead of starting a controversy, he generally leads the reader to compare both visions of facts by imitating

---

[4] Pothou (2009: 27) names it 'digression intérieure', following Stahl ('Exkurs innerhalb des Exkurses').
[5] Cf. Pearson 1939; Hornblower 1991; Dewald 2005; Funke and Haake 2006; Pothou 2009.
[6] Cf. Pearson 1939: 53-54; Pothou 2009: 65; Sierra 2017: 71. Rood (2013: 119) accurately points to the risk of such a denomination: 'Easy recourse to the term "Herodotean" has the paradoxical effect of "buttressing the opposition" between Herodotus and Thucydides – as if labelling an apparently abnormal section "Herodotean" is enough to excuse the abnormality and stop further questioning'.
[7] For an interpretation of the story as proof of the recent development of the alluvial land, cf. Gray 2011: 84; for political reasons, cf. Sierra 2017.
[8] The mythological content is particularly surprising, cf. Hornblower 1991: 377-378; Sierra 2017: 69-71.
[9] Cf. Funke and Haake 2006: 383-384.
[10] Th. 1.21.1 and 1.22.2ff.
[11] Cf. Calame 1996 = 2003: ch.1. 'Illusions of Mythology'. For the contrast *mythos/logos* as already established in the fifth century and in Thucydides' work, cf. Fowler 2011: 66.
[12] 'Compare the theoretical affirmations of Thucydides in 1.21.1 and 1.22.2 ff. with his practical treatment of the "mythic" in 1.4, 1.8.4, 1.9.2, 2.15ff., 2.29.3f., 6.2.1, etc.' (Calame 1996 = 2003: 130 n. 51).
[13] Cf. Brulé 2005.
[14] Hdt. 2.10-11, as observed by Sierra (2017: 69ff.).

Herodotus' style.[15] Sometimes, as he does with the story of Alcmaeon, he even supplements Herodotus' account in a more digressive or anecdotal manner, as will be reviewed in more detail below.[16] Consequently, the mythical story of Alcmaeon is precisely the element which transforms a naturalistic and rationalistic commentary into a traditional foundational tale, and therefore carries the weight of the Thucydidean excursus. It is becoming clear that the account of Alcmaeon has usually been neglected for the sake of the geographical content, and consequently deserves more careful attention.

At this point, it is time to recall what exactly Thucydides tells us about Alcmaeon.[17]

λέγεται δὲ καὶ Ἀλκμέωνι τῷ Ἀμφιάρεω, ὅτε δὴ ἀλᾶσθαι αὐτὸν μετὰ τὸν φόνον τῆς μητρός, τὸν Ἀπόλλω ταύτην τὴν γῆν χρῆσαι οἰκεῖν, ὑπειπόντα οὐκ εἶναι λύσιν τῶν δειμάτων πρὶν ἂν εὑρὼν ἐν ταύτῃ τῇ χώρᾳ ἥτις ὅτε ἔκτεινε τὴν μητέρα μήπω ὑπὸ ἡλίου ἑωρᾶτο μηδὲ γῆ ἦν, ὡς τῆς γε ἄλλης αὐτῷ μεμιασμένης. ὁ δ'ἀπορῶν, ὥς φασι, μόλις κατενόησε τὴν πρόσχωσιν ταύτην τοῦ Ἀχελῴου, καὶ ἐδόκει αὐτῷ ἱκανὴ ἂν κεχῶσθαι δίαιτα τῷ ἀφ'οὗπερ κτείνας τὴν μητέρα οὐκ ὀλίγον χρόνον ἐπλανᾶτο. καὶ κατοικισθεὶς ἐς τοὺς περὶ Οἰνιάδας τόπους ἐδυνάστευσέ τε καὶ ἀπὸ Ἀκαρνᾶνος παιδὸς ἑαυτοῦ τῆς χώρας τὴν ἐπωνυμίαν ἐγκατέλιπεν. τὰ μὲν περὶ Ἀλκμέωνα τοιαῦτα λεγόμενα παρελάβομεν. (Th. 2.102.5-6)

The story goes that when Alcmaeon the son of Amphiaraus was a fugitive after the murder of his mother he received an oracle from Apollo indicating that he should settle in this land: the riddle was that he would not have release from the terrors until he found and set up home in a place which at the time when he killed his mother had not yet been seen by the sun nor yet existed as land, since all the rest of the earth was polluted by him. He was puzzled, but finally, so they say, thought of this sedimentation of the Achelous, and reckoned that over the long period of his wanderings after killing his mother there would have formed sufficient deposit to support a man's life. So he settled in the area around Oeniadae, became its ruler, and left the country its name from his son Acarnan. Such is the traditional story which has come down to us about Alcmaeon.

Thucydides tells the story of a murderer who, after having killed his mother and tried in vain to purify himself, solved Apollo's riddling oracle, reached purification in a new land, and became a founder. Everything in the story sounds odd in the context of the austere and rationalistic account of the war: the mention of Apollo,[18] the individual oracle and the Herodotean resonance of the riddle.[19] As we will see, the story itself is not odd at all. Although its connection with the main narrative is not clear, it is, in fact, a typical foundational tale. In order to try to interpret its significance in Thucydides' *History*, a detailed examination of the story's content is needed.

---

[15] 'Wenn er ihm gegenüber Stellung beziehen will, polemisiert er nicht offen, sondern erzwingt den Vergleich durch die Nachahmung herodoteischer Darstellungsmittel' (Tsakmakis 1995: 229). For the general interpretative value of this intertextuality, cf. Fragoulaki 2013: 28.

[16] For the Cylonian episode, cf. Rood 2013 and below.

[17] Greek edition is cited from E.H. Stuart Jones, Oxford (OCT) and translation from M. Hammond, Oxford University Press.

[18] Unusually for Thucydides, Apollo is named in this passage, cf. Hornblower 1997: 378.

[19] Cf. below.

As a foundational tale, Alcmaeon's story offers a twofold perspective about colonization, both historical and cultural. Delphi played a role in colonization and it was involved as well in crises like plague, famine, drought or war, which could start the foundation of a colony.[20] Such crises were supposed to be supernatural phenomena, generally caused by divine anger or divine punishment. The word μεμιασμένης points to the religious belief of pollution (μίασμα) on which the whole story relies. Its significance is stressed by this unique utterance.[21] Mingled with their fictional elements, mythical tales indeed carry a substantial amount of information about many religious practices and beliefs. The tale has been deemed, in fact, as 'the most obvious mythic example' of Delphic procedure in cases of murder pollution and purification: it is supposed that Delphic oracle generally revealed the cause and gave indications to the purification, while purification itself took place elsewhere, as in this particular instance.[22] Regarding purification, reference to the river has a historical background also, since, in ancient Greece, Achelous was worshipped in association precisely with Amphiaraus, Alcmaeon's father, among other purification deities.[23] Thucydides' account has been identified as the Delphic version of the story. This version tries to monopolize Delphic foresight and purification authority at the expense of figures like Amphiaraus.[24] As a warrior seer, Alcmaeon's father foresaw his own death at Thebes, requested revenge from his son upon his wife Eriphyle (who had forced him to go to war) and became a divine purification power at the very moment of his death. Keeping that in mind is certainly helpful in underlining the historical aspect of the presence of Delphi in Thucydides' account.

It is emerging through this analysis that Alcmaeon's tale is rich in historical and cultural references. Besides, since storytelling shapes religious beliefs, mythical tales bear precious information about them.[25] This is perhaps the most meaningful aspect of the tale: the system of pollution and purification beliefs fostered by its narrative. Reflected in mythical discourses of foundation, *miasma* beliefs are also a very significant element of culture in the phenomenon of colonization, as highlighted by Dougherty in the wake of Mary Douglas.[26] According to Dougherty's interpretation, purification turns the polluted into a sacred force, and so, violence is transformed into a metaphor in colonist-murderer discourses. Thucydides offers the opportunity to compare one of these mythical discourses, Alcmaeon's story, with a more historical description of colonization. The mythical discourse is not mentioned indeed in Thucydides' foundation account of Syracuse, where violence is not a mythical metaphor, but the real violence of colonization.[27] Still, the question is why Thucydides tells Alcmaeon's story, while remaining silent about many others. Given the lack of a plausible explanation, such internal inconsistency is detrimental to our understanding of Thucydides' rationalism, since *mythos* and *logos* seem to coexist in his work without any apparent reason.[28] As already seen, Thucydides' dialogue with Herodotus is a tool to critically assess traditional tales. It

---

[20] Cf. Malkin 1989.
[21] For *miasma*, cf. the landmark study of Parker 1983. For a summary of concepts, cf. Petrovic and Petrovic 2016: 4ff.
[22] Cf. Dyer 1969: 42-45; Parker 1983: 139.
[23] Cf. Sineux 2007: 143-144. The river represents 'la puissance des eaux jaillissantes'. For purification with water 'drawn from a flowing source', cf. Parker 1983: 226-227.
[24] Cf. Foster 2017: 136-183.
[25] For the hermeneutical value of Greek storytelling regarding Greek beliefs, cf. Kindt 2016.
[26] Dougherty (1993: 31-44) views the figure of the colonist-murderer 'as part of a religious system that channels the religious power inherent in the defiled into a positive, consecrating force'.
[27] Th. 6.3.2. Thucydides passes over the colonist murderer story, which has come to us thanks to Plutarch (*Moralia* 772e-773b); cf. Dougherty 1993.
[28] Fragoulaki (2013: 91) points to several registers in Thucydides, but incongruity remains.

is therefore likely that this critical assessment is present in the excursus we are analysing. In that case, everything points to the religious content as the core of the excursus and of Thucydides' critical interest.

As is frequent in colonial tales, Alcmaeon had to solve a riddling oracle in order to find 'an impossible landscape', for, unless he succeeded, 'he would not have release from the terrors' (λύσιν τῶν δειμάτων). In colonist discourses, colonist murderers manage to make the impossible possible, solve the riddle and find the new land. So, riddling oracles play a significant role in such tales.[29] Oracles are, thus, a vehicle of religious beliefs and, as it has been suggested, their enigmatic mode can bear a very special value.[30] Hence, it may be worth trying to understand what else the 'impossible landscape' riddle may mean from a wider perspective.

Apollodorus' account of this myth pinpoints 'barrenness of the land' as the consequence of *miasma*.[31] In contrast, pollution of the land is much more threatening in Thucydides' story due to its unspecified and universal effect. In fact, this is perhaps the deepest meaning of the riddle. The entire earth is jeopardized by the crime committed by Alcmaeon and by the blood of his mother: ὡς τῆς γε ἄλλης αὐτῷ μεμιασμένης.[32] *Miasma* can arise because of one single person, but its consequences can affect even entire cities and, in popular imagination, mankind at whole is put in danger. *Miasma* can indeed result in absolute annihilation.[33] With that in mind, the phrasing λύσιν τῶν δειμάτων sounds like a typical oracular formulation of the kind of troubles and fears which require purification, pointing to customary procedures and to common beliefs.[34]

As narratological analyses have brought to light, in Thucydides' *History* internal references are frequent and meaningful. Several interconnections can also be noticed between Alcmaeon's story and another excursus, the Cylon conspiracy. As stated by Rood, in his '"mythodic" depiction' of this episode, Thucydides has added an oracle not mentioned by Herodotus.[35] This similar style of both excursuses, supplementing Herodotean narrative, the recurrence of the word κατενόησε in both passages and the fact that these are two of only three occurrences of individual oracles in Thucydides' work[36] encourage comparison between Alcmaeon's story and the Cylon episode.

The relevance of the excursuses of Cylon, Pausanias and Themistocles has been illuminated by Tsakmakis. Together, the three episodes shape an answer to the Spartan request at the beginning of the war. The Spartans blamed Athens for the outbreak of the war because of an ancient guilt, the Cylonian sacrilege. The Spartan request targeted Pericles, heir of this ancestral curse as member of the Alcmaeonidae family. It is religious beliefs, and not historical data, which are relevant to this interpretation, and specifically, belief in the supernatural

---

[29] For riddle oracles and the 'impossible landscapes' in colonization discourses, cf. Dougherty 1993: 45-60.
[30] Kindt (2016: 160) suggests that 'we take seriously the enigmatic mode as a critically important aspect of how the human–divine relationship is set up in these stories'.
[31] Apollod. 3.7.5: γενομένης τῆς γῆς δι' αὐτὸν ἀφόρου. Cf. Pausanias 8.24.7-8.
[32] Harrison (1908: 221) notices that 'the story of Alcmaeon looks back to days even before the Erinys was formulated as a personality, to days when Earth herself was polluted, poisoned by shed blood'.
[33] Cf. Delcourt 1938=1986.
[34] Cf. Dyer 1969: 42; for a use of δεῖμα in the context of consulting the oracle, cf. Hdt. 8.36.1; for the poetic character of λύσιν τῶν δειμάτων and μεμιασμένην, cf. Hornblower 2004: 105-107.
[35] Hdt. 5.71. Cf. Rood 2013.
[36] Cf. Rood 2013: 134. Only individual oracles have riddling form in Thucydides.

causation of historical facts, the point of Cylon story.[37] The critical approach to such beliefs is a decisive moment in the process of rationalization attempted by Thucydides, whose *History* systematically tries to find rational and human causes, excluding all divine intervention from historical facts. Related to *miasma*, sacrilege (ἄγος) belongs to the same pollution and purification system and, in spite of all divergences, can also cause generalized destruction. The mythical account is, thus, integrated into this complex unit, designed critically to discard divine motivation from history. The connection between Alcmaeon's story and the curse of the Alcmaeonidae is evident. An Athenian audience could easily link both episodes due to the homonymy of both names.[38]

Although nearly forgotten in our time, the story of the matricide and epigonous warrior at Thebes was rather popular in classical Athens.[39] Thucydides' audiences were well acquainted with the legend, and the hero surely had a vivid presence in Athens thanks to the frequent theatrical treatment of his story. This is similar in many aspects to that of Orestes, another matricide and theatrical character whose fate is conversely well-known to this very day.[40] Thus, Alcmaeon's tragic personality may hold greater interpretative value than its supposed epic origin.[41] Athenian audiences were used to interpreting mythical paradigms and understanding myth in complex ways.[42] As in many Greek tragedies, conflict within the family is the core of the Alcmaeon myth on stage.[43] Family symbolism is relevant in Thucydides account of the hero as well. As pointed out by Fragoulaki, the human family provides a metaphor for intercommunal ties, and such ties were broken in the Peloponnesian War, according to Thucydides' interpretation of the facts.[44]

The significance and paradigmatic character of the excursus is stressed by its perfect detachment from the rest of the work.[45] Several occurrences of typical marks of quotation point to the traditional character of the story, and at the same time frame it and stress its importance: λέγεται, ὥς φασι, λεγόμενα, παρελάβομεν.[46] As the last word of the excursus, παρελάβομεν is complementary with τὰ λεγόμενα and closes the story at the end, in a similar

---

[37] Th. 1.126-138. Cf. Tsakmakis 1995: 154. For the Cylon account as a testimony of belief in ancestral fault, cf. Gagné 2013. For its oral tradition, cf. Thomas 1992.

[38] For the possible association of names and curses, cf. Hornblower 1991: 378.

[39] Cf. García Gual 2014.

[40] Cf. Delcourt 1959.

[41] The source of Thucydidean Alcmaeon account is allegedly the epic cycle, cf. Huxley, cited by Foster (2017: 166). As frequent in tragedy, *miasma* appears in one of Euripides' lost tragedies about Alcmaeon, cf. Kannicht (2004: 215), frag. 82.1-2: τὰ τῶν τεκόντων ὡς μετέρχεται Θεὸς / μιάσματα, with a possible reference to ancestral fault.

[42] In the words of Raaflaub (1987: 233, quoted by Vandiver 1991: 12), 'Athenian citizens were trained from early on (...) to grasp a wide variety of poetic allusions and moral and political "messages" in the annual theatrical performances. They had learned to understand the contemporary relevance of mythical paradigms presented to them on stage and to recognize the importance of new variations of traditional myths introduced with specific intentions by the poets. To them it was not difficult but normal to extrapolate beyond what was explicitly said, to connect what they saw and heard with what they knew and were concerned about otherwise, and to draw their own conclusions'.

[43] Cf. Arist. *Po.* 1453b 15-22. For 'harm to *philoi*' as 'a generic characteristic of ancient Greek tragedy', cf. Belfiore 2000. For lost plays about Alcmaeon, cf. García Gual 1991; Belfiore 2000; Gambón 2020. Aristotle (*Po.* 1453a 20) lists among the best tragedies those of Alcmaeon. For the possibility that the homonymy between the names contributed to the popularity of Alcmaeon myth in Athens, cf. Foster 2017: 180-181.

[44] Cf. Fragoulaki 2013: 6-9; Price 2001.

[45] As remarked by Munson (2017: 259-60), in contrast to Herodotus, there is no paradigmatic use of the heroic past in the Thucydidean speeches. For the heroes in Herodotus, cf. Vandiver 1991.

[46] Pothou (2009: 90-91) and Gray (2011: 84) mentions only three: λέγεται, ὥς φασι, λεγόμενα. Gray (2011) recognizes its function as marks of relevance; for his interpretation of the meaning, cf. above.

way as λέγεται opens it at the beginning. Within this frame, the 'self-contained unit'[47] of the mythical account and its meaning are visibly emphasized. The first person plural points to the shared character of Greek lore, reminding that both narrator and audience share this mythical tradition. With it Thucydides invites his audience to reflect on this tradition and its limitations, urging them to find a more rational interpretation of historical facts.

Bibliogaphy

Belfiore, E.S. 2000. *Murder among Friends: Violations of philia in Greek Tragedy*. New York: Oxford University Press.

Brulé, P. 2005. Dans le nom, tout n'est-il pas déjà dit? *Kernos* 18: 241-268.

Calame, C. 1996 (Engl. transl. 2003). *Myth and History in Ancient Greece: The symbolic creation of a colony*. Princeton, N.J: Princeton University Press.

Delcourt, M. 1938. (2nd ed. 1986) *Stérilités mystérieuses et naissances maléfiques dans l'antiquité classique*. Paris: Belles Lettres.

Delcourt, M. 1959. *Oreste et Alcméon: étude sur la projection légendaire du matricide en Grèce*. Paris: Belles Lettres.

Dewald, C. 2005. *Thucydides' War Narrative: A Structural Study*. University of Berkeley, Los Angeles, London: California Press.

Dougherty, C. 1993. *The poetics of colonization: From city to text in Archaic Greece*. New York: Oxford University Press.

Dyer, R. 1969. The Evidence for Apolline Purification Rituals at Delphi and Athens. *The Journal of Hellenic Studies* 89: 38-56.

Foster, M. 2017. *The seer and the city: Religion, politics, and colonial ideology in ancient Greece*. Oakland (California): University California Press.

Fowler, R. 2011. Mythos and Logos. *The Journal of Hellenic Studies* 131: 45-66.

Fragoulaki, M. 2013. *Kinship in Thucydides: Intercommunal ties and historical Narrative*. Oxford: Oxford University Press.

Funke, P. and Haake, M. 2006. Theatres of War: Thucydidean Topography, in A. Rengakos, and A. Tsakmakis (eds) *Brill's companion to Thucydides*: 369-384. Leiden: Brill.

Gagné, R. 2013. *Ancestral fault in ancient Greece*. Cambridge: Cambridge University Press.

Gambón, L. 2020. La tragedia fragmentaria griega y las versiones del mito de Alcmeón. *Argos* 1(40): 9-28.

García Gual, C. 1991. Tradición mítica y versiones trágicas: la venganza de Alcmeón. *Analecta Malacitana* 14.1: 5-18.

García Gual, C. 2014. *La venganza de Alcmeón: un mito olvidado*. Madrid: Fondo de Cultura Económica.

Gray, V. 2011. Thucydides' source citations: 'it is said'. *The Classical Quarterly* 61(1): 75-90.

Harrison, J. E. 1908. *Prolegomena to the study of Greek religion*. Cambridge: University Press.

Hornblower, S. 1991. *A Commentary on Thucydides*. Volume I. Oxford: Clarendon Press.

Hornblower, S. 2006. *Thucydides and Pindar: Historical Narrative and the World of Epinikian Poetry*. Oxford: Oxford University Press.

Kannicht, E. 2004. *Tragicorum Graecorum Fragmenta (TrGF)*. Vol. 5, *Euripides*. Göttingen: Vandenhoeck and Ruprecht.

---

[47] As noted by Foster (2017), 'the myth is a self-contained unit, marked off from the larger narrative with its own introduction and conclusion'.

Kindt, J. 2016. *Revisiting Delphi: religion and storytelling in ancient Greece*. Cambridge: Cambridge University Press.

Malkin, I. 1989. Delphoi and the founding of social order in archaic Greece. *Mètis. Anthropologie des mondes grecs anciens* 4.1: 129-153.

Munson, R.V. 2017. Thucydides and Myth: a complex Relation to Past and Present, in R.K. Balot, S. Forsdyke and E. Foster (eds) *The Oxford Handbook of Thucydides*: 257-266. New York: Oxford University Press.

Parker, R. 1983. *Miasma: Pollution and Purification in early Greek Religion*. Oxford: Clarendon Press.

Pearson, L. 1939. Thucydides and the Geographical Tradition. *The Classical Quarterly* 33.1: 48-54.

Petrovic, A. and Petrovic, I. 2016. *Inner Purity and Pollution in Greek religion. Volume I, Early Greek religion*. Oxford: Oxford University Press.

Pothou, V. 2009. *La place et le rôle de la digression dans l'oeuvre de Thucydide*. Stuttgart: F. Steiner.

Price, J.J. 2001. *Thucydides and Internal War*. Cambridge (UK), NY: Cambridge University Press.

Rood, T. 2013. The Cylon Conspiracy: Thucydides and the Uses of the Past, in A. Tsakmakis and M. Tamiolaki (eds) *Thucydides Between History and Literature*: 119-138. Berlin, Boston: De Gruyter.

Sancho Rocher, L. 2017. Los agentes de la historia en los excursos sobre el pasado de Tucídides. *Araucaria. Revista Iberoamericana de Filosofía, Política y Humanidades* 19.37: 235-256.

Sierra, M. C. 2017. *Tucídides 'archaiologikós': Grecia antes de la Guerra del Peloponeso*. Zaragoza: Libros Pórtico.

Sineux, P. 2007. *Amphiaraos. Guerrier, devin et guérisseur*. Paris: Les Belles Lettres.

Thomas, R. 1992. *Oral Tradition and Written Record in Classical Athens*. Cambridge: Cambridge University Press.

Tsakmakis, A. 1995. *Thukydides über die Vergangenheit*. Tübingen: Gunter Narr.

Vandiver, E. 1991. *Heroes in Herodotus: The interaction of myth and history*. Frankfurt am Main: Lang.

Ionians in the *Hellenica Oxyrhynchia:*
The Battle of Ephesus (*Hell. Oxy.* 1-3)

Antonis Tsakmakis

University of Cyprus
a.tsakmakis@ucy.ac.cy

Abstract

In classical Greek historiography the image of the Ionians is throughout negative. Herodotus and Thucydides question their military competence and, occasionally, treat them with irony. A notable exception to this tendency is the Oxyrhynchus historian, who presents the battle of Ephesus (409 BCE) as an achievement of the Ephesians (and not, like Xenophon, as a failure of the Athenians, and especially of their general Thrasyllus). The subtleties of the narrative, part of which is preserved on the Cairo papyrus of the *Hellenica Oxyrhynchia*, reveal a positive attitude towards Ionians. This attitude also contrasts with his usual writing style, which is particularly sensitive to leaders' shortcomings. These observations may add a further argument in favour of Theopompus of Chios, an Ionian, as the author of the work.

Keywords

Ionian War, Ionians, Battle of Ephesus, Thrasyllus, Tissaphernes, *Hellenica Oxyrhynchia,* Xenophon, Theopompus, Ethnic stereotypes, Praise in historical narrative

The Cairo papyrus of the *Hellenica Oxyrhynchia*, published in 1976,[1] contains parts from a narrative of the battle of Ephesus (409 BC), which is more detailed than the already known accounts of the same event in Xenophon's *Hellenica* (1.2.6-11) and Diodorus (13.64.1-2).[2] The battle was fought between the Athenians under the command of the general Thrasyllus and the Ephesians and their allies. Thrasyllus sailed towards the city commanding a force of 1000 hoplites, 100 horsemen and 50 triremes; he split the army in two divisions which disembarked a certain distance apart and failed to come together, with the result that they fought (and were defeated) in different places at different times.[3] The text on the papyrus begins with a damaged passage which refers, in all probability, to Thrasyllus' plans and landing. The best preserved section of the text deals with the attack of the Athenian hoplites, led by Thrasyllus, against the city.

The three literary sources agree on most of the details concerning the event, so that they complement and elucidate each other.[4] A striking divergence, however, concerns the Ephesians' allies: who were they and how important was their contribution to the repulsion

---

[1] First edition of the papyrus: Koenen (1976). It is included in the most recent edition of all available fragments of the work (Chambers 1993) and in the commentaries of Behrwald (2005), Billows (2016), Lérida Lafarga (2007), MacKechnie-Kern (1988).

[2] Diodorus follows Ephorus for this period, who depends on the *Hellenica Oxyrhynchia*. For a thorough discussion see Occhipinti 2016: 57-86.

[3] The commander of the second division is named in 1.1 as Pasion, probably to be identified with the general Pasiphon of Phrearrhioi who is mentioned on *IG* I³ 375.35 = Osborne and Rhodes (2017: no. 180); he was in Samos in 410/409 and probably joined Thrasyllus during his stopover of three days at the island on his way to Asia Minor; cf. X. *HG* 1.2.1-2).

[4] On topographical and historical questions see Bleckmann (1998: 149-162), and on chronological problems 272-293.

of the Athenians? Xenophon emphasizes the role of the Persian satrap Tissaphernes (pointing out that he had organized the sending of reinforcements for the defense of the city) and the help offered to the Ephesians by the Syracusans and Selinuntines, who happened to be in the city by the time of the attack. On the contrary, the Oxyrhynchus historian does not mention any of the above, but notes the presence of some Lacedaemonians in the Ephesian camp. Scholars who compared Xenophon's version with the new text, tried to explain the disagreement in terms of a choice between Sparta and Persia as the power with the most important impact on the Greek history of the period. Accordingly, each historian opted in favour of a different framing of the events: while Xenophon appears to be convinced about the role of Persia as a catalyst for the development of the Ionian war,[5] the anonymous historian, 'quite correctly saw that this was the war of Sparta.'[6] The details of his narrative reflect a pro-Spartan attitude and a tendency to downplay the significance of Persian help in the wars between the Greeks;[7] or, he might have realized the ethnic complexities in Asia Minor and wished to foreground the pan-hellenic mission of Sparta in this and the next decade.[8] Notwithstanding the fact that these explanations may be valid to a certain degree, they hardly account for all the peculiarities in the two narratives. In the following chapter, we argue that a more coherent interpretation of the two versions has to take a further factor into account, which has hitherto escaped the notice of interpreters: the characterization of the people who were first and foremost affected by the Athenian operation, namely the Ephesians themselves. While Xenophon's account, in alignment with a historiographic tradition which is dominated by prejudices against Ionians, tacitly denies any decisive role to the Ephesians in the defense of their city, the Oxyrhynchus historian draws a distinctly positive picture of these Ionian Greeks.[9]

'As a result of the Persian War, Ionia was excluded from Greek history', remarks a specialist on the history of this area.[10] Herodotus' and Thucydides' Athenocentric perceptions of Greek history in the 5th century left little room for the Greeks of Asia, who only appear in minor roles. The collective 'Ionians' (which mostly reflects a distant, external point of view), is regularly used with derogatory connotations. For Herodotus, they are the weakest among the Greeks and Ionians from areas other than Asia Minor were ashamed to be called by this name.[11] The destiny of Ionia was to be subjugated to the barbarians (Persians claimed control of all Asia: 1.4.4) and the only way for Ionians to avoid slavery would be to migrate (1.169-170; cf. also 9.106.1-3).[12] Thus, in the great combat between Greece and Persia, they were compelled to fight on the wrong side, and Themistocles only hoped that he could neutralize them with a trick (9.98.4).[13] The role of the Ionians as allies forced to follow a stronger power

---

[5] Xenophon's view of Persia and the Persians is not one-dimensional (cf. Vlassopoulos 2017); therefore, his analysis of the political and military relations between Greeks and Persians is not associated with stereotypes we encounter e.g., in Herodotus. On Persian policy in Asia Minor after the Sicilian expedition see Briant (2002: 591-596).

[6] Koenen (1976: 59).

[7] Lehmann (1977: 184-186).

[8] Bleckmann (1998: 159-161).

[9] Westelake (1979) is exclusively concerned with historical issues and does not address literary aspects of the sources.

[10] Greaves (2010: 12).

[11] Hdt. 1.143.2-3. Barbarian contempt for Ionians: 1.153.3, 5.107.

[12] Herodotus remarks that Ionia was the most beautiful country and had the best climate (1.142.1-2), but he does not relate the character of the Ionians to environmental factors. As Thomas (2000: 105) points out, 'Herodotus says nothing... about the effects of such a climate either on health or ethnic character'. On the other hand, Herodotus' low esteem for the Ionians is not related to their subjugation to a monarch or to miscegenation (cf. 1.146.2).

[13] The only Ionians who occupy a central role in Herodotus' narrative are the leaders who incite the Ionian revolt, an

is inherited to Thucydides: with their alliance with Athens, they only change masters (cf. Th. 6.76.4: ἐπὶ δεσπότου μεταβολῇ). In Thucydides, the opposition Ionians vs. Dorians is mostly exploited in speeches (1.124.1; 6.77.1; 6.82.2-3; cf. 3.92.5; 7.5.4), whereas the ethnic character of the war is occasionally undermined by the historian (7.57.4). However, the belief that Ionians are inferior to Dorians is taken for granted, so that Thucydides treats a double victory of Athenians over Peloponnesians and Milesians over the Argeians as a paradox (8.25.5).

Xenophon's account of the battle of Ephesus reveals a similar prejudice, since it suppresses the role of the Ephesians in the victory and underscores the contribution of all other parties involved. More specifically, Xenophon reports that, when Thrasyllus' intention to attack Ephesus was made manifest, 'Tissaphernes got to know of the plan and got together a large force to deal with it. He sent horsemen all round the country with instructions that everyone should move on Ephesus for the protection of Artemis' (1.2.6).[14] The satrap's claim to appear as the protector of the city is eloquently founded on his right to present himself as the patron of the sanctuary of Artemis, a fact which reminds Xenophon's reader that the appeal of the specific cult was broader than the Greek world and, consequently, places the event in a more complex historical context, in which the Ephesians appear as a negligible entity. The participation of the Ephesians' neighbours at the fight against the Athenians is confirmed a little later by the battle narrative, in a passage which includes even more details about the Ephesian camp: '... those in the city came out to meet him. There were the Ephesians themselves, the allied force brought up by Tissaphernes, the Syracusans (both the crews of the original twenty ships and also of five others under the command of Eucles, the son of Hippon, and Heraclides, the son of Aristogenes, which happened to have just arrived) and the crews of the two ships from Selinus.' The contribution of the Sicilian allies to the victory is emphasized not only by the expression οὗτοι δὲ πάντες, which introduces the subsequent peak of the battle narrative, but also with an explicit reference to the acknowledgement of their merits by the Ephesians themselves: 'The whole of this force moved first against the hoplites at Coressus and put them to flight, killing about a hundred and pursuing the rest to the shore. They then turned against the Athenians by the marsh, and these, too, were routed and about three hundred of them killed. The Ephesians put up a trophy at this spot and another one at Coressus. They awarded the prizes for valour to the Syracusans and to the men of Selinus, since both had fought with particular distinction. The prizes given were to individuals as well as to the troops as a whole. They also gave them the right, if any of them wished to avail themselves of it, to live in Ephesus tax free. And after Selinus had been destroyed they gave the Selinuntines the right of Ephesian citizenship as well.' It is obvious that amidst such an overwhelming amount of information on the allies and their brilliant performance, any achievement of the Ephesians is overshadowed. Their success is further belittled by Thrasyllus' shortcomings. In Xenophon's version, the Athenian general was responsible for a delay of seventeen days (1.2.7), which undoubtedly gave Tisssaphernes the time to organize the sending of the reinforcements. It is

event with devastating consequences on Greece. The military performance of the rebels was miserable, mainly due to their lack of training (6.12-14). Apart from a few, individual exceptions (e.g. 1.169.1), military excellence is denied to the Greeks of Asia Minor. Ionians excel in Cyprus (5.112.1), but this is a section where the opposition Greeks vs. barbarians is of key importance. Even in this case, it is the Samians who excelled: islanders are in some cases treated differently than the other Ionians (6.15.1: Chians in Lade; 1.27: distinction between continental Ionians and islanders).

[14] Translations of passages from Xenophon's *Hellenica* are by Warner (1979).

also to be noted that the Athenian historian is silent about the names of the Ephesian leaders, whereas he named the commanders of the Syracusan force.[15]

We can conclude that for Xenophon Ionians were not expected to successfully defend themselves against an aggressor.[16] Accordingly, the victory of the Ephesians was in need of an explanation. As a result, emphasis on the decisive contribution of Tissaphernes, the Syracusans and the Selinuntines to the repulsion of the Athenian attack, is supposed to increase the persuasiveness of the Xenophontic narrative.

In the parallel narrative of the *Hellenica Oxyrhynchia* a completely different attitude towards the Ephesians is manifest. The Ephesians and their commanders are the indisputable protagonists, the deeds of others are, at best, of secondary importance. The treatment of all ethnic groups involved in the narrative (or ignored by it) proves this.

a. The explicit mention of Lacedaemonians in 1.1 (for the text see Appendix) is a first, obvious departure from the Xenophontic version. Since these Lacedaemonians are not mentioned again, the most plausible interpretation of the passage is that they are military or political consultants. The situational context corroborates this suggestion: they appear in a passage which deals with enemy recognition and decision making concerning military action in response to an attack. This also explains why Xenophon ignores the Lacedaemonians: they played no role in the battle and did not influence the outcome. On the contrary, the Oxyrhynchus historian records their presence not only because his report is more detailed or because he is interested in the historical role of Sparta, but also because the present battle narrative pays special attention, as we will see, to military command. In addition, as the historian reveals, the Ephesians and Lacedaemonians perceive only Thrasyllus' men, while the second division was not visible to them yet. The fact that it was not only the Ephesians, but also the Lacedaemonians who failed to see the entire Athenian force frees the Ephesian commanders from any possible suspicion that this was their fault. Consequently, the passage ultimately serves the positive characterization of the Ionians.

b. In contrast to Xenophon, the historian does not seem to have made any mention of Tissaphernes, when he comes to mention the Ephesians' allies from the neighbouring areas (1.1; the allies are introduced in a way which suggests that this is their first mention in the present section, thus any reference to Tissaphernes in the same context is excluded). On the contrary, a likely reference to a past incident (obviously mentioned earlier in the work, but not known from elsewhere) points to existing ties between these people and the Ephesians and makes additional motivation for their assistance superfluous.

c. The allies are most likely to be identified with the ψιλοί mentioned during the battle (2.1: [παρ]ελ|θόντων δὲ τῶν Ἀθηναίων .[..........]ν|τες πάλιν οἱ ψιλοὶ τῶν ἀνόδ[ων .....] | εἰσβάλλουσι μετὰ τῶν .ο..τ.[......]η|[....]). The reconstruction of the text is uncertain, but, since the Athenians are the subject of a genitive absolute, the light-armed men in the

[15] Only one Ionian commander is named in the *Hellenica*, the Samian Hippeus (also an islander), whose name is introduced with an expression which betrays distance: Σάμιος ὀνόματι Ἱππεύς (1.6.29).

[16] Their political acumen is also exposed by Xenophon. The Ionian envoys sent to Sparta make a wrong estimation about the Persian reaction in case of a Greek invasion into Caria (3.2.12; in the fight that follows Ionians run away before the battle: 3.2.17).

main clause (ψιλοί, syntactic subject of the participle ...]ντες) cannot be Athenians.[17] Moreover, the emphatic statement that the Ephesian leaders ἀνεκαλοῦντο τοὺς ἑαυτῶν ὁπ[λ]ίτας in the previous sentence is likely to suggest a contrast to the other soldiers, who must have included non-Ephesian non-hoplites (this does not, of course, rule out the existence of Ephesian ψιλοί, as well). And this expression makes even more sense if these ψιλοί had been already mentioned in the text (the use of πάλιν and the lack of any further information about them accompanying their extant mention corroborate this estimation). As the previous section deals with the occupation of the heights by the Athenians and with Thrasyllus' intention to launch an attack on the city (ὡς κ[α]τὰ κράτος | ληψ[ό]μενοι τὴν πόλιν), the only expression in the extant text which can be related to the ψιλοί is the phrase καὶ πρὸς αὐτοὺς κατέφευ[γον (of course they might have been mentioned in a previous, missing part of text, as well, but in any case, this statement is hardly applicable to the Athenians, since these must be the antecedent of the pronoun). In this case, it is likely that some of the light armed allies (καί |τινες/ ἔνι|οι δέ[... ?) deserted, embarrassed as they were after the Athenians had occupied the καρτερὰ χωρ[ί]α. This behaviour contrasts nicely with the introductory remark about the devotion of these allies (1.1: πιστοτάτο[υ]ς τότε, which possibly, though not necessariliy, refers to a past incident), an example of the author's concealed sarcasm, which is a trademark of his writing style. More important, this development credits the Ephesians alone with the final victory against the Athenians.

d. The most striking feature in the presentation of the Ephesians is the way the author presents their leaders, who are named twice. The second mention (2.1: [Τ]ίμαρχος δ[ὲ] καὶ | Πο[σσ]ικράτης οἱ τῶν Ἐφεσίων ἡγε[μόν]ες)[18] is, strictly speaking, not necessary at all, since the reader had already been informed about the names of the two men. Its formal, solemn style, however, draws the reader's attention to their action at a very critical moment of the battle and credits them with the reversal of the situation. The first mention of the generals, however, is truly remarkable: τῶ[ν] δ' Ἐφεσίων ἡγοῦντο καὶ Τίμαρ|[χο]ς καὶ Ποσσικράτης οι... (the ensuing text, where more information on the two was possibly offered, is, unfortunately, damaged). The double καί emphasizes their joint leadership (both T. and P.). Apparently, it was not expected that both men were simultaneously serving as commanders. This unambiguously betrays the author's good knowledge of Ephesian affairs but also underlines the importance of this collaboration as a laudable act. We can only guess about the real circumstances: perhaps only one of the two men had a military function at this time; alternatively, they may have belonged to different political factions.[19]

e. If Xenophon is right about the fact that Syracusans and Selinuntians had fought on the side of the Ephesians, then the silence of the Oxyrhynchus historian about them is eloquent. It lets the Ephesians alone appear as those who defeated the Athenians.

To sum up, the narrative of the *Hellenica Oxyrhynchia* suggests an unreservedly positive evaluation of the Ephesians. More generally, the author treats Ionians in a completely

---

[17] Cf. Cuniberti (2009: 72).

[18] ἡγεμόνες is a generic term, not a military office. Its use serves to reinforce the impression of an *ad hoc* appointment (see below).

[19] Both men are now known to us from elsewhere, but a certain Timarchus appears on Ephesian coins dated between 415 and 394. His prominence in the period between Sicily and Cnidus is probably related to his pro-Spartan attitude; if Possicrates was active during the era of Athenian control, this might explain the stress on their common action here.

but did not offer any further information with which to compose his biography.[2] As we will see, Ephorus, on the other hand, writing in the fourth century, offered both a political and a biographical perspective.

The most relevant quotations that may help reconstruct Ephorus' view of the Spartan statesman derive from very different sources: Strabo, Polybius, Plutarch, Aelian, and Clement of Alexandria. Moreover, we shall include some minor fragments of Ephorus, such as a Pindaric scholium concerning Lycurgus' genealogy and a brief passage from Aelius Theon's *Progymnasmata*.[3] However, as a methodological principle, each fragment should not be evaluated in isolation from the others nor decontextualized from the text's original context.[4]

Furthermore, we should bear in mind that potential material from Ephorus on early Spartan political history might be found in other authors, such as Diodorus and Nicholas of Damascus, and might include passages in which Ephorus is not explicitly cited as a source.[5]

Let us now look more closely at the fragments. According to Strabo (F 118), Ephorus recognized the lawgiver as the sole creator of the *politeia*, and, thus, of all the main institutions of Sparta. Moreover, the historian offered a harsh criticism of Hellanicus of Lesbos, blaming him for an incorrect attribution of the Spartan *politeia* and for his silence on Lycurgus' political contribution.[6] In Ephorus' opinion, Hellanicus of Lesbos was wrong in attributing the constitution to the first rulers of the Spartan diarchy, the twins Eurysthenes and Prokles. With a polemical thrust, Ephorus compared the great honours for the lawgiver with the less noble treatment reserved for the two kings: while a temple was dedicated to and annual sacrifices celebrated for Lycurgus (μόνῳ γοῦν Λυκούργῳ ἱερὸν ἱδρῦσθαι καὶ θύεσθαι κατ' ἔτος), those whom Hellanicus identified as the supposed creators of the constitution did not receive similar veneration; on the contrary, Eurysthenes and Prokles had even not been allowed to assign their names to the ruling houses they founded.[7] The construction of the ἱερόν and the exceptional honours for Lycurgus were previously attested in Herodotus (without the annual offerings) and the contemporary Aristotle.[8]

In the last, corrupted part of the fragment, Ephorus also mentioned the pamphlet composed in exile by the king Pausanias II, who belonged to the Royal House of Agiads. Pausanias reported the oracles, including some eulogies, delivered by the Pythia to Lycurgus. Regardless of the pamphlet's controversial orientation (*in favour of* or *against* Lycurgus), which will not be

---

[2] Cf. Hdt. 1.65-66.1; Xen. *Lac. Pol.* (*passim*). On Xenophon' portrayal of Lycurgus, cf. David (2007b).

[3] Ephor. *FGrH* 70 F32 (= Theon *Progymn.* 96.1); F118 (= Strab. 8.5.5); F148 (= Pol. 6.45-46); F149 (= Strab. 10.4.16-22); F173 (= Schol. Pind. *Pyth.* 1.120b); F174 (= Clem. Alex. *Strom.* 1.170.3); F175 (=Aelian. *VH* 13.23); F205 (= Plut. *Lys.* 17.1-4). On the relevance of the Spartan constitution and Lycurgus in Ephorus' fragments, cf. Christesen (2010: 211-226); Parmeggiani: (2004: 96-112); Tigerstedt (1965: 210-215).

[4] Cf. Christesen (2010: 227); Schepens (2001: 206-207).

[5] Cf. Christesen (2010: 211). On the limits of using Diodorus as a source for reconstructing Ephorus, cf. Parmeggiani (2011: 349-394; 2014: 781-806).

[6] Hellan. *FGrH* 4 F116; Ephor. *FGrH* 70 F118 (= Strab. 8.5.5): Ἑλλάνικος μὲν οὖν Εὐρυσθέη καὶ Προκλέα φησὶ διατάξαι τὴν πολιτείαν, Ἔφορος δ' ἐπιτιμᾷ, φήσας Λυκούργου μὲν αὐτὸν μηδαμοῦ μεμνῆσθαι, τὰ δ' ἐκείνου ἔργα τοῖς μὴ προσήκουσιν ἀνατιθέναι.

[7] Ephor. *FGrH* 70 F118 (= Strab. 8.5.5). For Ephorus' presentation of Eurysthenes and Prokles; cf. Ephor. *FGrH* 70 F117 (= Strab. 8.5.4).

[8] Hdt. 1.66.1; Arist. F534 Rose[3] = F544 Gigon (= Plut. *Lyc.* 31.4). On the cultic honors for Lycurgus, cf. also: Nic. Dam. *FGrH* 90 F56; Paus. 3.16.6.

discussed here, it is essential to note that Ephorus had access to an authoritative local source on Spartan legislation, containing the Delphic oracles for Lycurgus.[9] From this brief mention, however, it is impossible to determine to what extent Ephorus could have relied on Pausanias for his description of Lycurgus.[10]

Another relevant fragment derives from Polybius (F148). In the sixth book of his *Histories*, the historian criticized Ephorus, Xenophon, Kallisthenes, and Plato, who strongly supported the tradition according to which Cretan and Spartan *politeiai* were similar.[11] Regardless of the dispute, Polybius' fragment highlights the importance of Lycurgus' role in the formation of the constitution: according to Ephorus (and the other authors mentioned), the Spartan lawgiver alone saw the essential points of governance, courage against enemies, and internal concord. Thus, Lycurgus eradicated the desire for money and all civic struggles in his homeland, guaranteeing Sparta's stability and harmony. Similar evaluations of Lycurgus' contribution in eliminating the *stasis* and the avariciousness from Sparta are made by Diodorus and by Strabo in another Ephorus' fragment.[12]

Furthermore, the latter passage of Strabo (F149) also includes the essential core of Lycurgus' biography. In his extensive account, the geographer summarizes the main points of Ephorus' thesis on the derivation of the laws of Sparta from the Cretan norms. The historian polemicized against those (generically named τινές) who believed that the Cretan costumes derived from the Laconic institutions, rather than *vice versa*.[13]

Ephorus described the Cretan *eunomia* as the original model of the Spartan constitution and as a unitary constitution for the whole island. In fourth century political thought, Crete and Sparta both had political systems often compared and universally admired by Greek conservatives.[14] It is no coincidence that Plato himself located his mythical city-state, Magnesia, on the island: as in Sparta, the Cretan legislative tradition constitution enjoyed great prestige amongst the political philosophers of the late classical period.[15] For instance, in Plato's *Laws*, Crete and Sparta shared many customs and institutions (*nomoi adelphoi*), even if the author did not claim that one borrowed from the other.[16] Similarly, Aristotle wrote extensively on many similarities amongst their institutions and suggested, like Ephorus, that the influence was from Crete to Sparta.[17] Nevertheless, the tradition linking these two constitutions is well attested even

---

[9] On the content and purpose of this debated *pamphlet*, cf. an updated bibliography in Nafissi (2017: 114 notes 26-27). The critical edition considered here for Strabo's corrupted text is Radt (2003: 477-478).

[10] According to Parmeggiani (2011: 637-638 n. 37), this *logos* might be more useful for Ephorus to reconstruct the political debate in Pausanias' times, rather than the archaic history of Sparta and Lycurgus' epoch; *contra* Barber (1935: 116), who considered Pausanias to be the main source for portraying Lycurgus. On Pausanias' pamphlet as a source for Ephorus' Sparta, cf. also Parker (2011 [*BNJ* 70]: F118).

[11] Ephor. *FGrH* 70 F148 (= Pol. 6.46.1-6).

[12] Ephor. *FGrH* 70 F148 (= Pol. 6.46.7-8); F149 (= Strab. 10.4.16-17); Diod. 7.12.2-8. For a broader discussion on the connection between the three passages, cf. Christesen (2010: 216-226); Parmeggiani (2011: 245-248).

[13] Cf. Ephor. *FGrH* 70 F149 (= Strab. 10.4.16-22).

[14] For the ancient debate on the resemblances and relationship between Spartan and Cretan regimes, cf. Cuniberti (2000); Hodkinson (2005: 227); Nafissi (1983-84); Perlman 2005: 300-308.

[15] On the Cretan *politeia* in the philosophical debate; cf. Huxley (1971); Perlman (1992; 2005).

[16] Cf. Plat. *Leg.* 3.683a.

[17] Cf. Arist. *Pol.* 2.1269a-1272b.

earlier, since Herodotus, in the fifth century, claimed that Lycurgus brought back his laws from Crete.[18]

According to Ephorus, several Spartan institutions, such as the γερουσία and the ἱππεῖς, kept the name and functions of the original ones from Crete; even the ephors (although with a different denomination) still had the same responsibilities as the corresponding κόσμοι.[19] Without going into too much detail of the discussion, in Ephorus' *Histories* the Spartans improved the original Cretan institutions through the indispensable contribution of Lycurgus: the latter visited the island and followed the ancient Cretan lawgivers' example in his political reforms.[20] However, despite the goodness of the Cretan laws and institutions, Lycurgus' *politeia* was superior to the initial model, ensuring long-lasting Spartan hegemony.[21]

More specifically, in his summary of Ephorus, Strabo discussed Lycurgus' chronology and travels in two paragraphs.[22] The chronology of the Spartan lawgiver was a further argument supporting opinion in favour of the temporal precedence of Cretan laws: Lycurgus was five generations younger than Althaemenes, who organized the colonial expedition to Crete; moreover, Althaemenes was the son of Cissus, founder of Argos and contemporary of Prokles of Sparta. Since Lycurgus was a direct descendant of the latter (the sixth successor to be exact: Λυκοῦργον δ᾽ ὁμολογεῖσθαι παρὰ πάντων ἕκτον ἀπὸ Προκλέους γεγονέναι), the argument of his opponents, according to which the constitution of Lycurgus was later than the Cretan *politeia*, is consequently rejected.[23]

Besides, Ephorus accepted the synchronism with Homer and, therefore, Ephorus' Lycurgus may reasonably be assigned a ninth century date.[24] A further indicator of this chronological framework is provided by the Pindaric scholium (F173), according to which Ephorus designated Lycurgus as the eleventh descendant of Heracles (οὗτος γὰρ ἐνδέκατός ἐστιν ἀπὸ Ἡρακλέους, ὡς Ἔφορος ἱστορεῖ).[25] Thus, combining the information from the two fragments, Lycurgus was the sixth descendant of Prokles, founder of the Eurypontid dynasty, and the eleventh from Heracles.[26]

However, although this genealogy (with few variants) is the most accepted and is coherent with Plutarch's account, there is no agreement on Lycurgus' chronology in the ancient tradition. The authors offered a wide range of proposals, from the return of the Heraclides (Xenophon), to the ninth century (c. 884 BC, Eratosthenes and Apollodorus), to the synchronism with Iphitus of Elis and the first Olympiad (Aristotle and Hermippus). Moreover, Cicero and Timaeus, trying to solve this chronological problem, postulated the existence of two different

---

[18] Cf. Hdt. 1.65.4.

[19] Cf. Ephor. *FGrH* 70 F149 (= Strab. 10.4.18).

[20] Cf. Ephor. *FGrH* 70 F149 (= Strab. 10.4.19).

[21] Cf. Parmeggiani (2011: 248).

[22] Ephor. *FGrH* 70 F149 = Strab. 10.4.18-19.

[23] Ephor. *FGrH* 70 F149 = Strab. 10.4.18.

[24] Ephor. *FGrH* 70 F149 = Strab. 10.4.19. For a generational framework and the date of Lycurgus in Ephorus, cf. Parker (2011 [*BNJ* 70]: F149).

[25] Ephor. *FGrH* 70 F173 (= Schol. Pind. *Pyth.* 1.120b).

[26] Cf. Plut. *Lyc.* 1.8. For Lycurgus Eurypontid, with some variants, cf. Simon. F123 Page = F628 *PMG*; Dieuch. *FGrH* 485 F5; Arist. *Pol.* 2.1271b 24-27; Ael. *VH* 13.23; Iust. 3.2.5. Only in Herodotus (1.65.4) and in Pausanias (3.2.3), Lycurgus belongs to the Agiad dynasty and he did not descend from Prokles but from Eurysthenes.

Lycurgi, who lived in two different epochs; Plutarch, for his part, accepted and registered this general disagreement.[27]

Returning to Strabo, the following section (19) is devoted to the events that led the lawgiver to leave Sparta and, later, return as a legislator, focusing on his journeys (Crete, Egypt, Chios, Delphi). This biographical account of Ephorus is not just a sort of 'appendix' to the central discourse, but rather a further argument in favour of the Spartan - Cretan relationship:

'(Ephorus says) the Cretans report that Lycurgus came to them for this reason: Lycurgus' elder brother was Polydectes; the latter died and left his wife pregnant. For a time, Lycurgus ruled in his brother's place; once a boy was born, to whom the throne was destined, he became the infant's guardian. Since a man, who was defaming him, declared that he knew full well that Lycurgus would reign, Lycurgus, suspecting, because of this rumour, that he would be accused of a plot against the child and fearing to be held responsible by his enemies if by any chance the infant should die, left for Crete. This, they say, was the reason for his journey: they claim that when Lycurgus arrived, he became acquainted with Thales, lyric poet and expert in legislation, and that he inquired from him how first Rhadamanthys and then Minos brought the laws to men as if their laws derived from Zeus. Next, he travelled to Egypt and learned the country's laws; and he met, as some say, Homer, who was living in Chios. Then he sailed again to Sparta and found Charilaos, his brother's son, reigning there. Then he started to implement the laws, visiting the god at Delphi, bringing the laws from there, just as Minos and his men had brought them from the cave of Zeus; most of his norms were similar to those of Minos'.[28]

Although Strabo summarizes only the essential points of Ephorus' discourse, he gives precise information on Lycurgus' story, which will be found in Plutarch's *Life* with the same narrative structure. The historian reported the circumstances that took place immediately after Polydectes' death: the king left his wife pregnant, and soon his brother Lycurgus became the newborn's tutor. However, allegations by his opponents of having organized plots against the heir forced the future legislator to leave and find refuge in Crete.[29] At this point, we find a description of Lycurgus' educational journeys outside Sparta, and such trips were not peculiar to him: 'didactic' itineraries to learn the customs, the *nomoi* or the wisdom of other peoples are among the essential elements of the biographical tradition of the nomothetes, and other Greek sages and philosophers.[30]

---

[27] Xen. *Lac. Pol.* 10.8; Arist. fr. 533 Rose[3] = fr. 541 Gigon; Eratosth. *FGrH* 241 F2; Apollod. *FGrH* 244 F64 (= Plut. *Lyc.* 1.2-3); Tim. *FGrH* 566 F127 (= *Lyc.* 1.4); Hermipp. *FGrH* 1026 F8a (*Lyc.* 23.3-4).

[28] Ephor. *FGrH* 70 F149 = Strab. 10.4.19: (...) Λέγεσθαι δ' ὑπὸ τῶν Κρητῶν ὡς καὶ παρ' αὐτοὺς ἀφίκοιτο Λυκοῦργος κατὰ τοιαύτην αἰτίαν· ἀδελφὸς ἦν πρεσβύτερος τοῦ Λυκούργου Πολυδέκτης· οὗτος τελευτῶν ἔγκυον κατέλιπε τὴν γυναῖκα· τέως μὲν οὖν ἐβασίλευεν ὁ Λυκοῦργος ἀντὶ τοῦ ἀδελφοῦ, γενομένου δὲ παιδὸς ἐπετρόπευεν ἐκεῖνον, εἰς ὃν ἡ ἀρχὴ καθήκουσα ἐτύγχανε· λοιδορούμενος δή τις αὐτῷ σαφῶς εἶπεν εἰδέναι διότι βασιλεύσοι· λαβὼν δ' ὑπόνοιαν ἐκεῖνος ὡς ἐκ τοῦ λόγου τούτου διαβάλλοιτο ἐπιβουλὴ ἐξ αὐτοῦ τοῦ παιδός, δείσας μὴ ἐκ τύχης ἀποθανόντος αἰτίαν αὐτὸς ἔχοι παρὰ τῶν ἐχθρῶν, ἀπῆρεν εἰς Κρήτην. ταύτην μὲν δὴ λέγεσθαι τῆς ἀποδημίας αἰτίαν· ἐλθόντα δὲ πλησιάσαι Θάλητι μελοποιῷ ἀνδρὶ καὶ νομοθετικῷ, ἱστορήσαντα δὲ παρ' αὐτοῦ τὸν τρόπον ὃν Ῥαδάμανθύς τε πρότερον καὶ ὕστερον Μίνως, ὡς παρὰ τοῦ Διός, τοὺς νόμους ἐκφέροι εἰς ἀνθρώπους, γενόμενον δὲ καὶ ἐν Αἰγύπτῳ καὶ καταμαθόντα καὶ τὰ ἐκεῖ νόμιμα, ἐντυχόντα δ', ὥς φασί τινες, καὶ Ὁμήρῳ διατρίβοντι ἐν Χίῳ, κατᾶραι πάλιν εἰς τὴν οἰκείαν, καταλαβεῖν δὲ τὸν τοῦ ἀδελφοῦ υἱὸν τὸν Πολυδέκτου Χαρίλαον βασιλεύοντα· εἶθ' ὁρμῆσαι διαθεῖναι τοὺς νόμους φοιτῶντα ὡς τὸν θεὸν τὸν ἐν Δελφοῖς, κἀκεῖθεν κομίζοντα τὰ προστάγματα, καθάπερ οἱ περὶ Μίνω ἐκ τοῦ ἄντρου τοῦ Διὸς παραπλήσια ἐκείνοις τὰ πλείω (...).

[29] Plut. *Lyc.* 3.1; 3.8-9; 4.1.

[30] Cf. Hölkeskamp (1999: 45-46); Szegedy-Maszak (1978: 202). Further expansion of Lycurgus' journeys is attributed by Plutarch to a local source, Aristokrates of Sparta (Aristocr. *FGrH* 591 F2 = Plut. *Lyc.* 4. 8).

As mentioned above, the first step of the journey is Crete: the Cretan *logoi* are the local sources of those events. The circumstances that followed the death of Polydectes are indicated because they justified Lycurgus' arrival on their island (λέγεσθαι δ' ὑπὸ τῶν Κρητῶν, ὡς καὶ παρ' αὐτοὺς ἀφίκοιτο Λυκοῦργος κατὰ τοιαύτην αἰτίαν). Clearly, Ephorus judged the local oral tradition to be reliable and assigned it considerable documentary value.[31]

According to Ephorus, the legislator met the melic poet Thales, who instructed him on Crete's laws and lawgivers. Regarding this expedition and the meeting with Thales, a comparison with Aristotle may be valuable. Aristotle, while admitting that Lycurgus went to Crete and supporting the mutual συγγένεια between Sparta and Crete, contested the master-disciple relationship between Thales and Lycurgus as being hardly reliable from a chronological viewpoint.[32]

As for the journey to Egypt, Herodotus and Isocrates, even before Ephorus, believed that the Lacedaemonians had customs comparable to the Egyptian ones. This association clearly influenced the legislator's biography since, in the account of Ephorus, the Spartans received Egyptian *nomima* thanks to Lycurgus' visit.[33] Diodorus later mentioned the Spartan lawgiver among the many Greek sages visiting the Nile country, and also Plutarch included the episode in his biography.[34]

To the best of our knowledge, Ephorus is also one of the first to attest a meeting between Homer and Lycurgus. However, we have another version, available in the Greek tradition, of the association between the lawgiver and the archaic poet. This alternative version, which probably goes back to Aristotle, considered Lycurgus to be responsible for collecting and divulgating in the Peloponnese the epic poems safeguarded in Ionia by the descendants of Creophylus of Samos. Plutarch clearly demonstrates that he knows both versions: in the opening of the *Life*, he declares himself to be aware that 'some' believed that Lycurgus and Homer had encountered each other in person; however, in the chapter dedicated to the legislator's travels, Plutarch excludes this episode in favour of the Aristotelian version.[35]

At this point, it is essential to focus on the origin of Lycurgus' legislation: how could the legislator imitate the *nomoi* of Crete and, at the same time, be inspired by Apollo through the Delphic oracle? The irreconcilability between the Delphic and the Cretan variants was previously highlighted by Herodotus, who considered them to be alternatives to each other. Xenophon, on the other hand, omitted the relationship with Crete, mentioning only the divine sanctioning of the legislation.[36] Thus, according to several scholars, the historian may have been the first to combine and integrate those versions together.[37] However, as Parmeggiani

---

[31] Cf. Nafissi (1983-84: 351); Parmeggiani (2011: 670).

[32] Arist. *Pol.* 2.1271b-72b; 2.1274a 25-31 (Thales-Lycurgus). On Aristotle and Ephorus, cf. Moggi (2014).

[33] Hdt. 2.167; Isocr. *Bus.* 17.

[34] Hecat. Abd. *FGrH* 264 F25 (Diodorus' source on Egypt); Diod. 1.96.1-2; 98.1; Plut. *Lyc.* 4.7-8.

[35] For the Aristotelian version on the Homeric poems and the descendants of Creophylus, cf. Heracl. Exc. 10.19-20 Dilts; *Lyc.* 4.5-6; Ael. *VH* 13.14. On the undetermined source in Plutarch about this meeting; cf. Plut. *Lyc.* 1.4; cf. also Manfredini and Piccirilli (1990: 219, 226-227). For the synchronism between Lycurgus and Homer, cf. Apollod. *FGrH* 244 F63b; Cic. *Brut.* 10. 40; *De Rep.* 2.18; *Tusc.* 5.3.7; Vell. Pat. 1.5-6; Dio. Chrys. *Or.* 2.44-45; Diog. Laert. 1.38.

[36] Hdt. 1.65.4; Xen. *Lac. Pol.* 8.5.

[37] Cf. Nafissi (1983-1984: 355); Tigerstedt 1965: 212.

rightly pointed out, a careful reading of the text reveals that the divine inspiration and the imitation from Crete were already incorporated in the Cretan local tradition that Ephorus reported.[38]

After concluding his journey, Lycurgus returned to Sparta, where he was able to put his theoretical knowledge into practice. First, he established the laws and then he visited the Oracle of Delphi, reporting the laws to the Spartans as *if* he had received them from Apollo (in the form of προστάγματα). Therefore, Lycurgus was an imitator of Minos, who, according to F147, behaved like his predecessor, Rhadamanthys. Each legislator personally claimed to have received the laws from the gods, giving legitimacy in the eyes of citizens to the law.[39] Thus, Ephorus focuses on the sacralization of the law as a political mechanism transmitted by imitation from one lawgiver to another.[40]

Moreover, Ephorus' critical and rationalizing attitude towards mythical accounts emerges in F32, where Aelius Theon explicitly attests that the Cretan *mythologoumena* concerning Minos, Rhadamanthys, and Lycurgus were subjected to critical scrutiny, presumably in the fourth book.[41] This reference is part of a more extensive section in which Theon analysed the Greek general tendency to rationalize the mythos, seeking plausible explanations for poetic and mythological tales.[42]

Additionally, we may find further evidence of the Minos-Lycurgus association in Clement of Alexandria. The fragment connects Ephorus' portrayal with Aristotle and Plato's statements, showing that all three authors believed that, just as Minos went to the cave of Zeus for nine years, Lycurgus was being instructed (παιδεύεσθαι) by visiting the Pythia periodically.[43]

Returning to Strabo, his account of the Spartan lawgiver does not present the last piece of the story: his death. In this case, however, we are fortunate to have a further passage of Aelian who explicitly refers to Ephorus completing his biography with Lycurgus' suicide by starvation in exile: λέγει δὲ Ἔφορος αὐτὸν λιμῷ διακαρτερήσαντα ἐν φυγῇ ἀποθανεῖν.[44]

As far as we know, Ephorus is the first source to attest to the suicide, accepted later also by Nicholas of Damascus and Plutarch.[45] According to the latter authors, the Spartans took an oath to observe the Lycurgan laws until he returned from his journey to Delphi; however, Lycurgus opted for everlasting exile, committing suicide to ensure they would never break

---

[38] Cf. Parmeggiani (2011: 669-670 and n. 143).

[39] On Minos and Rhadamanthys, cf. Ephor. *FGrH* 70 F147 (= Strab. 10.4.8).

[40] Cf. Camassa (2014: 77-79); Parmeggiani (2011: 247-248 and n. 471).

[41] Ephor. *FGrH* 70 F32 (= Theon *Progymn.* 96. 1). On the treatment of these topics in the fourth book, cf. Ephor. *FGrH* 70 F31a (=Theon *Progymn.* 95.8); F33 (= Strab. 10.4.9); F34 (=Theon. *Progymn.* 95.27).

[42] Theon *Progymn.* 95-96. On the *spatium mythicum* and *spatium historicum* in Ephorus, cf. Parmeggiani (1999).

[43] Ephor. *FGrH* 70 F174; Arist. fr. 535 Rose³ = fr. 540 Gigon (= Clem. Alex. *Strom.* 1.170. 3 Stählin): (...) τόν τε αὖ Λυκοῦργον τὰ νομοθετικὰ εἰς Δελφοὺς πρὸς τὸν Ἀπόλλωνα συνεχὲς ἀπιόντα παιδεύεσθαι γράφουσι Πλάτων τε καὶ Ἀριστοτέλης καὶ Ἔφορος.

[44] Ephor. *FGrH* 70 F175 (= Ael. *VH* 13.23).

[45] Lycurgus' death by starvation is found in all the following sources except in Nicholas, who may have summarized Ephorus' version, cf. Nic. Dam. *FGrH* 90 F56; Plut. *Lyc.* 29, 7-8; Tertull. *Apol.* 4. 6; *Suda* [λ 824] s.v. Λυκοῦργος. Since the historian is probably the primary source of Nicholas, it has been conjectured that Ephorus may have referred to the same location for Lycurgus' death, i.e., Krisa (Nic. Dam. *FGrH* 90 F56), cf. Parker (2011 [*BNJ* 70]: F175).

Tigerstedt, E. 1965. *The Legend of Sparta in Classical Antiquity*, I. Stockholm: Almqvist and Wiksell.

Verdegem, S. 2010. *Plutarch's Life of Alcibiades. Plutarch's Life of Alcibiades: Story, Text and Moralism.* Leuven: Leuven University Press.

Wickersham, J. 1994. *Hegemony and Greek historians.* Totowa: Rowman and Littlefield.

The Sacred Band of Thebes and Alcibiades' *Exemplum* (Plutarch, *Pel.* 18-19 and *Alc.* 7.3-6)[1]

Nuno Simões Rodrigues

University of Lisbon
CH and CEC-ULisboa/CECH-UC
nonnius@fl.ul.pt

Abstract

This essay aims to contextualize Alcibiades *exemplum* as Socrates lover, as referred by Plu. *Pel.* 18-19 and *Alc.* 7.3-6, within Greek sources references to the Sacred Band of Thebes. Alcibiades becomes then evidence of how in Athens not only the so-called 'pederastic model' was in practice, but also what we may call the 'military model'. Therefore, regarding homoeroticism and same-sex male sexuality, when compared with other regions in Ancient Greece, Athens seems not to have been an exception.

Keywords

Alcibiades, Sacred Band of Thebes, Homoeroticism, Pederastic model, Military model.

Plutarch, the Sacred Band of Thebes and Greek homosexuality models

In Pelopidas' *Life*, Plutarch informs us of what became known as the Sacred Band (*hieros lokhos*) of Thebes. According to the biographer, this military group was organized by Gorgidas, who, in the first quarter of the 4th century BC, was said to have recruited 300 men to be trained and supported by the Boeotian city, settle within the citadel of Cadmea and henceforth remain at the service of Thebes. For that reason, this special force would also be known as the City Band or the Band of Cadmea.

The sources suggest that the Greeks considered the Sacred Band of Thebes as an elite troop. However, and still according to Plutarch, the group had another characteristic: it was comprised of lovers and loved ones. That is, the group would be formed by 150 pairs of warriors and each pair consisting of an *erastes* and an *eromenos* (Plu. *Pel.* 18).[2]

More than on a whim, the formation of a military unit based on a method like the one suggested by Plutarch would have meant a well-defined tactical and military objective. Plutarch explains it:

---

[1] This research was conducted within the following projects: UIDB/00196/2020 – Centre for Classical and Humanistic Studies of the University of Coimbra; UIDB/04311/2020 and UIDP/04311/2020 – Centre for History of the University of Lisbon; and UIDB/00019/2020 and UIDP/00019/2020 – Centre for Classical Studies of the University of Lisbon, sponsored by FCT – Fundação para a Ciência e a Tecnologia (Portuguese Foundation for Science and Technology).

[2] Plutarch is one of the few known sources that refer to the Sacred Band of Thebes. However, it is not the only one. The *Anthologia Graeca*, e.g., includes an epigram by Phaedimos, which researchers consider to contain an allusion to the Band (*AP* 13.22). We know other sources, such as Dinarchus, Hieronymos of Rhodes, Dio Chrysostom, Polyaenus, Maximus of Tyre and Athenaeus of Naucratis. Leitao (2002) studies these sources.

a band that is held together by the friendship between lovers is indissoluble and not to be broken, since the lovers are ashamed to play the coward before their beloved, and the beloved before their lovers, and both stand firm in danger to protect each other. Nor is this a wonder, since men have more regard for their lovers even when absent than for others who are present, as was true of him who, when his enemy was about to slay him where he lay, earnestly besought him to run his sword through his breast, 'in order', as he said, 'that my beloved may not have to blush at sight of my body with a wound in the back'. (*Pel.* 18.2-3, trans. B. Perrin).

Plutarch adds, as if to confirm the idea he has just expounded, that this was the case of Iolaus, who, according to mythological tradition, would have fought alongside Heracles, whom he accompanied and whose lover he was. The reference Plutarch makes to Aristotle is intended to make the story of Heracles and Iolaus an aetiological narrative, explaining why, until his time the warrior lovers swore mutual allegiance by the tomb of the young Iolaus (*Pel.* 18.4; cf. Arist. F97 Rose). On the other hand, Plutarch mentions Plato as the authority that would justify the designation of 'sacred' for the band, because, according to the philosopher, a lover was a friend taken by the divine spirit or inspired by divinity (*Pel.* 18.4; cf. Pl. *Smp.* 179a).

Confirming the effectiveness of the method, Plutarch states that the Sacred Band was invincible until the battle of Chaeronea (338 BC., *Pel.* 18.5), when Thebes succumbed to the forces of Philip of Macedon. In the plight, 300 warriors would have perished and the Macedonian king, moved and impressed by the bodies of the fallen men, would have proclaimed: 'Perish miserably they who think that these men did or suffered anything disgraceful' (*Pel.* 18.5, adapt. trans. B. Perrin).[3]

Plutarch also takes the opportunity to make some reflections on pederasty and homoeroticism in Thebes, one not necessarily to be confused with the other. According to the author of the *Lives*, it was not Laius, as was traditionally told in some regions of Greece, who sponsored pederastic relations among the Thebans but their legislators, who encouraged them while introducing the flute as a means of socialising to create an atmosphere of camaraderie and harmony among young Thebans. Through these innovations, it was intended that young people would soften and relax their impetuous character and strong passions (*Pel.* 19.1). The reference to Laius is pertinent, not only being one of the mythical kings of Thebes – to which the Sacred band was duty-bound – but also because, as I have pointed out, some traditions attributed the 'creation' of homosexuality and homoerotic relationships to him. Pseudo-Apollodorus refers to it in his mythography and most likely this was also the theme of Euripides' lost tragedy *Chrysippus*.[4]

In this way, the Band would have formed what is suggested to be a form of civic-military organisation of utopian nature, in which the bonds between individuals were based on *erotike philia*, thus favouring the cohesion of the group members.[5] Plutarch himself supports this by stating that, in the beginning, Gorgidas distributed the members of the Sacred Band among the first rows of the phalanx so as to distribute them and disseminate their presence among the

[3] On the Band's end, see Rahe (1981).
[4] Apollod. *Bib.* 3.5.5. In line with this, see Hyg. *Fab.* 85; 243. Plutarch himself recalls the topic in *Moralia* 313E. Rodrigues (2019) discusses the issue.
[5] On the utopian nature of this institution, see Rodrigues (2009).

remaining soldiers, nullifying the possibility of a concerted attack against them by the enemy. However, Pelopidas, after the battle of Tegyra, where is said each man fought for himself, did not separate the members of the Band again, but treated them as a unit and henceforth always placed them at the head of the Theban troops. Pelopidas would have understood the strength of the Band lay precisely in the affective ties its members had developed between one for another, which consolidated its strength and military effectiveness. Plutarch explains it by using a Homeric simile, albeit with a Platonic tone (cf. Pl. *Phd.* 246a-247e):

For just as horses run faster when yoked to a chariot than when men ride them singly, not because they cleave the air with more impetus owing to their united weight, but because their mutual rivalry and ambition inflame their spirits; so, he thought that brave men were most ardent and serviceable in a common cause when they inspired one another with a zeal for high achievement (*Pel.* 19.4, trans. B. Perrin).

It is inferred from the example that the success of such a military organisation would derive from the Band's homoerotic contribution to group cohesion, not only because the warriors would feel ashamed to be seen by their loved ones doing something perceived as cowardice, but also because the underlying love relationship would raise the men's spirits, leading them to sacrifice themselves for those they loved.[6] J. Davidson refers to them as 'the most visible image of the human city as a single undivided collective'.[7]

One of the questions we should ask about the Sacred Band of Thebes is its factual existence. Had the band actually existed or is it a mere literary creation?[8]

In this regard, it should be noted that in Plutarch's passage we perceive topical elements that disregard the absolute originality of the subject, clearing the way for possible confirmation of its fictional and literary origin and nature. Firstly, the number 300, which also appears in the episode of the Spartan soldiers at Thermopylae (Hdt. 7.201-238) and is associated with another elite Theban contingent, amounted to the war chariot drivers and those who accompanied them only. Diodorus Siculus refers to this group (*heniochoi kai parabatai*, 12.70.1) in the context of the battle of Boeotia between Athenians and Boeotians in 424 BC.[9] The motif of the 300 is further present in a reference by Xenophon to a battalion that took part in the conflicts involving the city of Elis in the 360s (*HG* 7.4.13, 16, 31).[10] Secondly, there is the theme of loving pairs, appearing in Greek literature possibly from its very beginning. This is the case of Achilles and Patroclus in the *Iliad*, even if I share reservations about a conclusively homoerotic character of the relationship between the two warriors.[11] There are also the cases

---

[6] I dealt with this issue in Rodrigues (2009). See also Davidson (2007: 494) and Ogden (1996: 484-495). As we shall see below, this argument is already present in Pl. *Smp.* 178e-179b.

[7] Davidson (2007: 350).

[8] On this discussion, see e.g. Leitao (2002: 143-169). Recently, Romm (2021) offers a comprehensive book of what the author calls 'the Age of the Sacred Band' (p. xvi). Romm stresses the fact that Xenophon practically omits the subject of the Sacred Band, but takes Plutarch's information as accurate and correct, as well as that of other authors, accepting the tradition regarding the Sacred Band as historical.

[9] Maybe the Sacred Band had roots in this other one, mentioned by Diodorus, and is therefore associated with battles of Tegyra (375 BC), Leuctra (371 BC) and Chaeronea (338 BC). See Leitao (2002: 147).

[10] See e.g. Marincola (2016).

[11] There is an extensive amount of literature on this subject, on which we cite just a few examples: Barrett (1977); Buffière (1980); Clarke (1978); Mills 2000.

of Heracles and Hylas, or Iolaus (cited by Plutarch on this subject), Theseus and Pirithous, Orestes and Pylades and, perhaps, even Idomeneus and Meriones.[12] Although mythological constructions, these references may articulate representations of Greek military realities as they always refer to the idea of an elite contingent, the underlying concept of the Sacred Band of Thebes.

Rightfully, one should also mention the military frameworks in which much of the discussion around pederasty and homoeroticism in ancient Greece has been outlined and which create a context of verisimilitude for the institution referred to by Plutarch in the *Life* of Pelopidas.[13] In a controversial study published in 2007, Davidson proposed a new approach to the problem of homoeroticism and homosexuality (insofar as we can use this concept, which did not exist among the ancients), going beyond, and even problematising, the seminal perspectives of Dover and Foucault in the 1970s.[14] Some of the issues raised by Davidson, in particular those we have been underlining, had also been the focus of D. Ogden in 1996.[15] As Ogden had noted and Davidson's study confirmed, it is not methodologically sound to analyse the problem of the Sacred Band of Thebes without taking into account that what is said about this city would not be unique or an isolated case. In fact, they argue that the sources mention other Greek cities and regions where the association between military life and homoeroticism would have been a constant, such as Elis, Sparta, Chalcis and Crete. In some cases, this bond even seems to have been a *sine qua non* condition for the formation of a military group. The aim seems to have been to create bonds of affection between individuals, so that the necessary and desirable unity of a military squad could emerge from them. This is, in fact, what Plutarch himself suggests in the *Life* of Pelopidas, revealing an awareness of the importance of the erotic function in civic and warlike organisation.

Moreover, as Ogden also notes, this historiographical issue must also be distinguished from the so-called 'Greek pederastic model', since the latter was based on homoerotic relations between individuals understood nowadays as adolescents and others, at a minimum, as young adults.[16] The recognition of homoeroticism and consequent homosexuality in a military environment, on the other hand, implies the establishment of relationships between adult individuals, peers, therefore post-pederastic relations, markedly distinct from the previous model. We should also note that the existence of cases of homoeroticism in Ancient Greece outside the pederastic model, and even outside the military model, is well attested by the sources, strongly confirming that this cannot be the only applicable model when approaching this historiographical issue.[17]

---

[12] See e.g. Plu. *Thes.* 30-31; Apollod. *Bib.* 2.4.11; A.R. 1.1207-1272; Theoc. 13; Lucianus, *Am.* 47; *Il.* 2.650-652; 4.251-254; 13.240-344; 16.342-350; 17.620-625; 23.112-114, 860 e 888 (where Meriones is called Idomeneus' *therapon*, squire). Later, historiography on Alexander will compose a similar relationship for the Macedonian general, experienced by himself and Hephaestion. See e.g. Ogden (2009: 210-217) and Rodrigues (2014).

[13] Already Marrou (1948: 55-67) connected pederasty and military context.

[14] Davidson (2007).

[15] Ogden (1996: 484-495).

[16] The 'pederastic model' is also called the 'educational model': Ogden (1996: 132).

[17] See Eubulos' reference to military life in F118 K-A. See also other examples in Leitao (2014: 230-243) and Ogden (1996: 108110). In this enumeration, I essentially follow Ogden, who seems well-grounded as to the coexistence of various models of the practice of (homos)sexuality in ancient Greece. One must underline sources that also give information about the existence of the so-called pederastic model in military environment or context, e.g.: X. *An.* 4.1.14; 4.6.1-3; 5.8.4; 7.4.7-8; *Hell.* 4.8.39; Polyaen. 5.3.4; cf. also Thuc. 1.132.5; X. *Hell.* 5.4.57; *Ages.* 5.4-5; Athen. 603-604;

The testimonies concerning Thebes reveal that the case of the defeated Sacred Band at Chaeronea was not unique. I have already alluded to the Battle of Boeotia, in 424 BC, when, according to Diodorus Siculus, an elite contingent of 300 men again played a key role in the conflict, occupying the front posts of the army they were fighting for. The form described coincides in many ways with testimonies of the Sacred Band without, however, confusing one with the other (D.S. 12.70.1).[18] Perhaps this is the same institution and Diodorus' reference might point to an earlier creation of the Sacred Band that Plutarch refers to. Or maybe Diodorus just got the data mixed up. In any case, even if we take the former hypothesis into account, Diodorus' testimony confirms that the phenomenon associated with the Cadmean Band is not exhausted in Plutarch's reference, clearing the way to a stronger argument regarding its historical existence. In fact, I agree with Leitao when he writes: 'The legend of the Sacred Band seems to have begun in the early fourth century as a fanciful real-world analogy that initially supported and ultimately replaced a utopian proposal to build a city or army on the ennobling bond between lover and beloved.'[19]

There is said to have been a similar institution in the city of Elis, in the Peloponnese, judging from what Xenophon and Plato tell. In his *Symposion*, Xenophon mentions that the soldiers of Elis, like the Thebans, shared beds and stood in pairs in the line of battle; the text suggests the existence of an erotic-affective relationship between the soldiers (8.34). We have also already mentioned the battalion of 300 which, according to Xenophon, was involved in military conflicts in 366 BC and their organisation was supposed to be very similar to that of the Theban battalions (*HG* 7.4).[20]

Another Peloponnesian city in which homoeroticism and consequent homosexuality should be put into practice is Sparta. The segregation and isolation from the feminine universe in which the Spartans found themselves, at least up to the age of 30, should be emphasised.[21] This would certainly be a situation that would favour a homoerotic environment. Some of the information gathered from sources points in the direction of the existence, in Sparta, of mainly a pederastic model (e.g. Plu. *Lyc.* 25.1). But there are also elements that allow us to conclude the presence of the model of homosexual practices between peers, in a military environment, in Sparta: in a passage from Xenophon's *Symposion* the author states that the Lacedæmonians train those they love in courage, never shaming their lovers, even when they are not lined up by the same city as them (8.35). Therefore, the passage suggests that

---

see Hindley (1999) and Leitao (2002: 144).

[18] See Leitao (2002: 147).

[19] Leitao (2002: 162); see also Rodrigues (2009). One must consider the hypothesis of the existence of an actual Sacred Band, as an elite unit, however without any erotic bond between their members.

[20] Ogden (1996: 115), dates the episode, as far as we are concerned correctly, given the context of the passage, to the year 366 BC. The same author presents in this part of his study complementary data regarding the military context of practices of a homosexual nature recognised among the citizens of Elis. As Ogden further suggests, maybe the kissing contests practised in Megara in honour of Diocles were also indicative of the same kind of practices among the Megarians. On these contests known as *Dioclea*, see Theoc. 12.307. According to a scholion on Theocritus, Diocles, perhaps a ruler of Eleusis, fled from Attica to Megara and died in battle defending his *eromenos*. Gow (1973.2: 226-227), however, doubts its historicity and remarks that no mention is made elsewhere of the kissing competition which Theocritus refers to, although another competition of this kind may have existed in at Didyma, as we learn from Varro *ap.* schol. Stat. *Theb.* 8.198. The comic poet Crates also made reference to a kissing game (F 23), but nothing is known of its rules. On the other hand, in a recent study Gherchanoc (2016: 122), accepts the historicity of the *Dioclea*. On Elis, see also Davidson (2007: 344-355). Although not a reference to a kissing contest, see also the references to importance of the kiss in Pl. *R.* 468bc.

[21] Ogden (1996: 118).

such a model would be a normal practice and other texts seem to confirm this (e.g. X. *HG.* 4.8.39, 5.4.25; Ath. 561).[22] A reference by Pausanias, included in his description of Laconia, notes a depiction of a local bearded Hyacinthus (Paus. 3.19.4). Now, judging by Pausanias' annotation, the hero who is often said to be Apollo's *eromenos* and particularly worshipped among the Spartans was also represented not as a youth or adolescent, but as an adult man. The indication of the beard refers to that conceptualization and reinforces the idea that also among the Spartans homosexuality among peers would not only be associated to Apollo and Hyacinthus textual form of the myth but even suggested in iconographic representations. The fact that Pausanias mentions this detail is also pertinent.

Chalcis, possibly in Euboea,[23] is another of the regions of Hellas where this type of practice seems to have been carried out. In the *Erotikos*, against the background of the Lelantine War that opposed Chalcis and Eretria in Euboea, Plutarch states that Cleomachus of Pharsalus, when intervening in the conflict in favour of Chalcis and being in the presence of his beloved, fought with a particularly intense vigour and spirit, confirming the homoerotic affective bond between the general and a young beloved. The type of relationship as described by Plutarch suggests the pederastic model. But the fighting context in which it is set, as well as the allusion to the song that would have become popular among the Chalcidians, strengthen the case for the military and peer homosexuality perspective (Plu. *Moralia* 760e-761d).[24] However, one must underline how difficult is to historically contextualize this story without speculation.

After Boeotia, Peloponnese and Euboea, there was also Crete, where Doric cities were prominent. Aristotle mentions that the organisation of Crete was analogous to that of Sparta and, to prevent overpopulation, the Cretan legislator had allowed homosexual relations there (*Pol.* 1272a).[25] This detail must be just an aetiology without historical substance. Still, the information is relevant since it connects, for the Greeks, Cretan practices with Sparta. Aristotle promises to go back to this issue another occasion, to consider whether it was a bad or a good decision, but he did not fulfil his promise. We know that in some cities on the island, an initiation-type practice – and a clearly pederastic model – would have been followed, as mentioned by Strabo (who quotes Ephorus), according to whom it was customary for older men to 'kidnap' the young men who interested them and initiate them into both (homo)sexual activity and military life (Strb 10.4.20-21 = Ephorus *FGrH* 70 F149). I agree with Ogden when he says that the passage partly implies the practice of the pederastic model, but also suggests that the homoerotic relationship established between the older soldier and the young initiate would later extend into the latter's adult military life, thus, into a relationship between peers.[26]

---

[22] On Sparta, see also Davidson (2007: 315-328, 470). Xenophon depicts a Thessalian commander named Meno, one of the generals leading contingents of Greek mercenaries, as an ambitious youth who while still beardless had a bearded favourite named Tharypas and, after that, became extremely intimate with Arieus (*An.* 2.6.28). This would have occurred in military environment too.

[23] Ogden (1996: 115-116) hypothesises that it is either Chalcis on Euboea or Chalcis in Thrace. Indeed, the sources are not clear as to the exact geographical location. Cleomachus, the general referred to in the passage, was the commander of a Thessalian battalion, and Thessaly was allied with Chalcis in that war. See Plu. *Moralia* 760e-761b.

[24] The context of the passage reinforces the military framework, which goes beyond the pederastic model *stricto sensu*. See also Lucchesi (2013).

[25] Similarly, as Ogden (1996: 154) notes, Plato suggests that it was the Spartans who introduced homosexuality to Athens, Pl. *Prot.* 342bc.

[26] As if homosexuality between peers were understood as an expected and 'normal' postpederastic continuity. In this

Several references alluding to Macedonia allow us to conclude that there, too, both the pederastic model and that of homosexuality between peers, even in a military environment, were a current and regular practice. We highlight a passage from Theopompus' lost *Philippika*, quoted by Polybius, according to which the Macedonian military elite shaved themselves completely, as well as indulging in sexual practices, not only, with male prostitutes accompanying them, but also with their own comrades from the battalion (Plb. 8.9.912 = Theopomp. Hist. FGrH 115 F225a).[27] One might evoke the critical character of the quotation made by Polybius, which is particularly antiMacedonian. Being an elite, his audience would have wanted to hear about stories like this, whether they were true or not. But for it to have an effect and fulfil its rhetorical function, its content should resonate with the audience and, at least, make sense.

Thus, from the general perspective of the sources, the idea we get is that the exception to a widespread existence of a model of peer homosexuality in Greece seems to have been Athens. But was it? In effect, there, the sources stress above all the assumed existence of the pederastic model, constructing the image of a polis that was prudish and reserved regarding homosexual practices between peers. Aristophanic comedy seems to have been paradigmatic in this, satirizing and negatively criticising peer homosexuality. Even philosophical discourse, such as Plato's *Symposion*, and forensic rhetoric point in this direction.[28] However, as we have implied, Athens only is perceived to be the exception, as some other sources also suggest that the Athenian reality should not be very different from what was happening in other Greek regions and poleis. This does not invalidate that the official discourse in Athens valued the pederastic model over or against the peer homosexuality model, considering a certain ideology of polis and citizenship. Among the other sources suggesting the practices and representations of homoeroticism and homosexuality among the Athenians was not limited to pederasty, stands out, again, Plutarch, with a striking passage from the *Life of Alcibiades*.

Plutarch and Alcibiades' *exemplum*

Was Athens really a city of coyness, when compared to other Hellenic realities, where pederastic practices were recognised, associated with an aristocratic elite, but still treated almost tacitly?[29] Would this attitude coincide with the Athenians rejecting and negatively criticising the model of peer homosexuality practices? And, therefore, would it coincide with denial or intolerance towards homosexual practices in a military context?

Indeed, the pederastic model seems to be the one standing out most from the sources that bear witness to the practice of homosexuality either among the Athenians or in Athens.[30]

---

regard, it should be noted that Plutarch's description of the Sacred Band of Thebes is also made with recourse to vocabulary of a pederastic type, as shown by the use of the terms *eromenos* and *erastes*; but the model of the institution would go beyond this. Davidson (2007: 312-315); Ogden (1996: 117). Further data that reinforce the thesis of the military context of this practice are also indicated here. The initiation character of Cretan practice is the subject of particular attention by historians. See e.g. Bremmer (1980). See also Caeiro (2018: 81-82).

[27] Passage also referred to by Ogden (1996: 120). For the whole Macedonian context, see 119-123.

[28] An excellent summary of the problem can be read at Hubbard (2014). See also Ludwig (2002).

[29] On aristocracy and oligarchy as elite groups see Brock, in this volume.

[30] The study of Athenian pederasty has been done by several researchers and the bibliography devoted to it is significant. We highlight only the studies of Buffière (1980); Davidson (2007); Halperin (1990); Hubbard (1998; 2000); Skinner (2010); and, of course, Dover (1989).

But, as already suggested,[31] a deeper analysis of the sources allows us to uncover another part of Athenian reality. It does not deny the pederastic model, but relativizes it, especially concerning its social importance. Such is the case with a passage by Sophocles, belonging to the lost tragedy *Niobe* and passed on by Plutarch. In this context, according to the tragic poet, none of Niobe's sons, in the moment of their death by Apollo's arrows, would have invoked any other help than that of their respective lovers (Plu. *Moralia* 760e).[32] Xenophon also tells how one Episthenes of Olynthus, seeing one of the young combatants about to be executed in battle by the king of the Thracians, asked him to intervene for the boy and offered his own life in exchange (*An.* 7.4.7-10). Xenophon's anecdote alludes much to the pederastic theme, as is readily apparent, but simultaneously points in the direction of a model of homosexuality among soldiers, necessarily entwining young men of an age closer to veteran soldiers, rather than mere adolescents. Such practice would be more in line with the model of peer homosexuality than pederasty.[33]

We also recall that Herodotus and Thucydides, and others, refer to the tyrannicide episode of 514 BC as an event entangling a homoerotic and homosexual relationship (Hdt. 6.123.2; Thuc. 6.54.1-3; and e.g. Pl. *Smp.* 182c).[34] As far as the representation of tyrant slayers themselves is concerned, iconography also seems to support this notion. The second version of the sculpture in honour of Harmodius and Aristogeiton, attributed to Kritios and Nesiotes and of which a Roman replica is preserved in the Archaeological Museum of Naples, suggests this by depicting the two aristocrats as adult men: one younger in appearance than the other, but still both adults.[35] In itself, the sculpture does not necessarily represent a homoerotic relationship. But if we add the information from the texts to it, the conclusions we reach seem pertinent.[36] Plato's *Symposion*, despite being often cited as an example of pederasty in Athens, does not fail to stress the military ambient intrinsic to it. It has, moreover, already been noted, that there are passages in the Platonic dialogue which cannot but be related to the theme of the Sacred Band of Thebes, as Plutarch presents it. Such is the case of Phaedrus' speech, in which we read:

Let me then say that a man in love, should he be detected in some shameful act or in a cowardly submission to shameful treatment at another's hands, would not feel half so much distress at anyone observing it, whether father or comrade or anyone in the world, as when his favorite did; and in the selfsame way we see how the beloved is especially ashamed before his lovers when he is observed to be about some shameful business. So that if we could somewise contrive to have a city or an army composed of lovers and their favorites, they could not be better citizens of their country than by thus refraining from all that is base in a mutual rivalry for honor; and such men as these, when fighting side by side, one might almost consider able to make even a little band victorious over all the world. For a man in love would surely choose to have all the rest of the host rather than his favorite see him forsaking his station or flinging away his arms; sooner than this, he would prefer to die many deaths: while, as for leaving his favorite in the lurch, or not succoring him in his peril, no man is such a craven that Love's

---

[31] E.g. Ogden (1996: 125-131).

[32] According to Athenaeus 601, this tragedy was also known as *Paiderastia*.

[33] See note 17.

[34] On this issue and its sources, see Rodrigues (2018).

[35] Indeed, none of those represented passes for being a teenager or non-adult. On the statue of tyrant slayers, see Azoulay (2014); Brunnsåker (1971); Taylor (1991).

[36] See also Hubbard (2014: 142-146).

own influence cannot inspire him with a valor that makes him equal to the bravest born; and without doubt what Homer calls a 'fury inspired' by a god in certain heroes is the effect produced on lovers by Love's peculiar power (Pl. *Smp.* 178d-179b, trans. H. N. Fowler).

Ogden has already shown how much likelier it is that Plato would have had the Theban case on his horizon, concerning this allusion, when writing the *Symposion*.[37] And, further, it seems clear to that, in turn, Plutarch's reference to the Sacred Band of Thebes in the *Life of Pelopidas* meets the Platonic text.[38]

Our impression is strengthened when, reading the *Life of Alcibiades*, we come across another passage that echoes both Plato's *Symposion* and the reference to the Sacred Band made in the *Life of Pelopidas*.[39] Plutarch states that Alcibiades was still a *meirakion*, a young man, when he took part in the military expedition against Potidaea in Chalcidice (431 BC). On this occasion, the young Alcibiades would have shared the tent with Socrates, a comrade in the same battalion. At some point, Alcibiades was wounded and fell on the battlefield. To defend and protect him, Socrates placed himself between the young man and the enemy, saving him from imminent death. Later, despite deserving to be recognised by the generals for his effort and bravery in battle, Socrates, 'wishing to increase his pupil's honourable ambitions, led all the rest in bearing witness to his bravery, and in begging that the crown and the suit of armour be given to him.' (Plu. *Alc.* 7.3-5, trans. B. Perrin).[40] As if to show the young man's gratitude towards his master and lover, Alcibiades' biographer later recounts another occasion, this time in Delion, in Boeotia (424 BC), when the young man had his chance to show bravery on the battlefield and intercede for Socrates. According to Plutarch, when the Athenians beat a retreat, Alcibiades, who was on horseback, spotted Socrates retreating on foot as part of a small infantry group. It was then Alcibiades' turn to place himself between Socrates and the enemy, protecting him from the attacks he was subjected to (Plu. *Alc.* 7.6).

One must point up that there is no unanimity among scholars about the historicity of these alleged 'facts'.[41] However, it is with the narrative as itself and as it was told we are dealing here. The two episodes gain greater significance once considering that, elsewhere, Plutarch mentions how between Alcibiades and Socrates there was a homophilic and homoerotic relationship (Plu. *Alc.* 4.1-4; 6.1,5), which would most likely also be homosexual, as other sources suggest. Among these, Plato is the most striking (*Smp.* 217a-219e; in addition to the *Symposion,* the passage in which it suggests homosexuality between Socrates and Alcibiades can be found in *Gorg.* 481d; *Prot.* 309a; *Alc.* 103a, in which Socrates defines himself as the *protos erastes* of Alcibiades).[42]

As we have noted and considering the significance of the two passages of the *Life of Alcibiades*, the episodes reported by Plutarch are also reminiscent of Plato's *Symposion*, reinforcing an

---

[37] Ogden (1996: 126-127); see also Rodrigues (2009: 110-111).

[38] This aspect has also been noted by Duff (2009: 37-50), and Lucchesi (2013: 213-214).

[39] Duff (2009: 37-50).

[40] See Vickers (2008: 49, 138, 145; 2015: 81).

[41] Wallace (2015) has demonstrated that the narrative of Socrates as hoplite is possibly a platonic fiction.

[42] On this issue, see Babelon (1935: 52-70); Ellis (1989: 20-21); Littman (1970: 271-275); Renero (1998: 39-47); Rhodes (2011: 22 – in which the author refers to the intimacy between Socrates and Alcibiades – and 26); Romilly (1995: 2830); Stuttard (2018: 33-34); Wallace (2015: 149-150, 156-160).

idea of intertextuality between the two authors regarding a reference to the Sacred Band of Thebes.[43] Thus, in the Platonic dialogue, Alcibiades, one of the characters, delivers a speech in which he reveals his attempts to become Socrates' *eromenos* (*Smp.* 217a-219e). But this same context is used by Plato to integrate into the dialogue the references to the battles of Potidea and Delion, which are equivalent to the mentioned passages of Plutarch (Pl. *Smp.* 219e, 220e-221c). In fact, in reading these passages from the *Life of Alcibiades*, one suspects to be faced with information that Plutarch has gathered *pari passu* from the Platonic dialogue.[44]

Most remarkably is that both in the Platonic dialogue and in Plutarch's *Life*, what is told about Socrates and Alcibiades seems to match what the sources say about the Sacred Band of Thebes and, specifically, Plutarch's comment on the Boeotian institution. As we have seen, the overwhelming majority of sources that provide information about models of homoerotic and homosexual experience among the Greeks other than pederastic are not Athenian. Those from Athens emphasise above all pederasty as a homoerotic and homosexual practice, and are particularly laconic, if not outright hostile, to other models. Ogden and Davidson already noted this, as Ogden writes: 'homosexual licences were sanctioned in Athens, homosexuality remained something that fundamentally belonged to the "other", with the result that the Athenians felt happier describing the homosexual customs to others in preference to themselves.'[45] Evidence of this is, moreover, to be found in the *Symposion* itself, where, through Pausanias, Plato refers to the homoerotic sexual customs of Elis and Boeotia in a disapproving way (182a-b).

In this context, it seems pertinent that Plutarch, himself a Boeotian, refers to two episodes played by two Athenians, Socrates and Alcibiades, in this way. It is a fact that the battles of Potidea and Delion took place in the regions of Chalcidice and Boeotia, which, as we have seen, were associated by the Greeks to with non-pederastic homosexual practices, in a military environment, and therefore tended to be censored by the Athenians. Perhaps in Plato these same references appear as an ill-concealed and even cynical reality, with which the intention is to stress above all the pederastic aspect still perceptible in them. But when he recovers these threads and, by dedicating to them the *exemplum* that he includes in the *Life of Alcibiades*, entangles a thematic coincidence with his comment on the Sacred Band of Thebes in the *Life of Pelopidas*, Plutarch appears to present his readers with another perspective of the Athenians and their sex life, both regarding practices and representations. In fact, the actions carried out by Alcibiades and Socrates in Potidea and Delion, as Plato relates them in the *Symposion* and Plutarch recounts them in his biography of Alcibiades, exemplify in practice how the Sacred Band of Thebes would function.[46] The man who would become an Athenian general had behaved in battle as the model soldier or general of Chalcidean or Boeotian origin would have been expected to act. What differences would there have been between them?

Thus, by recovering these narratives and echoing them intertextually within his own work, Plutarch seemingly and simply wishes to say that the Athenians were not so different from

---

[43] This intertextual relation has already been noted by Duff (2009: 46).

[44] It should be noted that some authors have made serious observations about the coexistence of Socrates and Alcibiades in Potideia, stressing above all that in 431 BC Alcibiades would be too young to be a hoplite. On this discussion, see Ogden (1996: 160, n. 184).

[45] Ogden (1996: 131).

[46] Stuttard (2018: 50) also establishes a relation with the pair Achilles and Patroclus in Troy.

other Greeks after all, such as the Chalcideans, the Cretans, the Macedonians or even the Boeotians, like himself. Perhaps this amounts to a veiled criticism by Plutarch of a certain Athenian arrogance.

Conclusions

Until recently, the study of homosexuality in ancient Greece has mainly been guided by the so-called 'pederastic model', which seems to have been preponderant in Athens.[47] Thus, as in so many other fields, historiography on this subject has been dominated by the Athenian case. However, research inspired and intensified after the publications of Dover and Foucault in the 1970s has concluded that this is not, and cannot be, the only viable model to analyse this subject. Therefore, it has emerged an alternative that we may call the 'peer homosexuality model', which answers other questions raised by the available sources which the 'pederastic model' failed to. Among these issues is that of the practice of homosexuality in military environments.

All the while, the same sources that highlight significant resistance among Athenians to recognize peer homosexuality in Athens, they still do not allow us to rule it out completely.

Plutarch's references in the *Life of Alcibiades* to his subject's courage in protecting his beloved Socrates, and vice versa, point in this direction. Even if fiction, the story was told, as Plutarch testimonies, and that is also significant. Furthermore, the way Plutarch describes the moments in Potidea and Delion seems to fill in as an example for the same allusion Plutarch makes, in the *Life of Pelopidas*, to the Sacred Band of Thebes. This military group seems indicative of the practice of a homosexuality not exclusively pederastic, which the sources locate in Boeotia. By dialoguing intertextually with his own work, Plutarch converts two Athenians, Alcibiades and Socrates, into a model example that could represent the mode of operation of the Boeotian battalion.[48]

In this way, the *exemplum* of Alcibiades becomes evidence of how in Athens they did not stop at the 'pederastic model'. Plutarch thus broadens the scope of Athenian reality regarding sexuality, inscribing Athens among the set of regions of Greece and comparing it to Thebes. One wonders whether, in doing so, Plutarch would tacitly criticise Athens and the Athenians, 'telling' them and others that they too behave like other Greeks and are not so distinct from other poleis, even those they are used to censure and reproach. Showing their hidden behaviour and presenting it as valorous in the field of battle, Plutarch seems to draw the Athenians' attention to their misguided arrogance.

Nevertheless, it also seems to that, in resorting to the issue of the Greeks' attitude towards homosexuality, Plutarch is, above all, contributing to the construction of a model of Greek identity, which places sexual practice and the attitudes related to it alongside language (Greek), myth (e.g. Homer's poems) and games (Olympic). That is: these are all factors of Pan-Hellenic identity among the Greeks. By inscribing the way (homo)sexuality is understood and

---

[47] See e.g. Davidson (2007); Dover (1989); Halperin (1990); Hubbard (1998; 2000); Skinner 2010.

[48] It seems that this conclusion is possible, regardless of whether we know which of the lives, whether Alcibiades' or Pelopidas', was written first.

practised in this set of *ta hellenika*, to quote Herodotus and Pausanias, through the example of Alcibiades, Plutarch reconciles Athens with the broader identity block of all of Hellas.

Plutarch does so not only by integrating the behaviour of the Athenians Alcibiades and Socrates into what would be the practice of peer homosexuality and homoeroticism, but also by characterising the Sacred Band of Thebes with recourse to the vocabulary of the 'pederastic model'. Indeed, let us note how Plutarch refers to the individuals who made up the Sacred Band as *erastai* and *eromenoi*, concepts that are fully associated to that model. Moreover, it seems evident and has been demonstrated that warring pairs would hardly consist of men and young boys (*paidika*) and military environment would be particularly conducive to homoeroticism and even homosexuality. It seems that the comic poet Eubulus allusion to *euryproktoteroi* (F118 K-A)[49] was valid for any context of the same type.

Bibliography

Azoulay, V. 2014. *Les Tyrannicides d'Athène. Vie et mort de deux statues*. Paris: Éditions du Seuil.

Babelon, J. 1935. *Alcibiade 450-404 av. J.-C.* Paris: Payot.

Barrett, D.S. 1977. The Friendship of Achilles and Patroclus. *Classical Bulletin* 54.1: 87-93.

Bremmer, J. 1980. An Enigmatic Indo-European Rite: Paederasty. *Arethusa* 13: 279298.

Brunnsåker, S. 1971. *The Tyrant-Slayers of Kritios and Nesiotes. A Critical Study of the Sources and Restorations*. Stockholm: Svenska Institutet i Athen.

Buffière, F. 1980. *Eros adolescent: la pederastie dans la Gréce antique*. Paris: Les Belles Lettres.

Caeiro, A.C. 2018. *As Constituições perdidas de Aristóteles*. Lisboa: Abysmo.

Clarke, W.M. 1978. Achilles and Patroclus in Love. *Hermes* 106: 381-396.

Davidson, J. 2007. *The Greeks and the Greek Love. A Radical Reappraisal of Homosexuality in Ancient Greece*. London: Weidenfeld and Nicolson.

Dover, K.J. 1989. *Greek Homosexuality*. Updated with a new Postscript. Cambridge, Mass.: Harvard University Press.

Duff, T.E. 2009. Plato's *Symposium* and Plutarch's *Alcibiades*, in J.R. Ferreira et al. (eds), *Symposion and Philanthropia in Plutarch*: 37-50. Coimbra: Classica Digitalia.

Ellis, W.M. 1989. *Alcibiades*. London; New York: Routledge.

Gherchanoc, F. 2016. *Concours de beauté et beautés du corps en Grèce ancienne. Discours et pratiques*. Bordeaux: Ausonius.

Gow, A.S.F. 1973. *Theocritus. A Translations and Commentary*, 2nd ed. Cambridge: Cambridge University Press.

Halperin, D.M. 1990. *One Hundred Years of Homosexuality. And Other Essays on Greek Love*. New York; London: Routledge.

Hindley, C. 1999. Xenophon on Male Love. *The Classical Quarterly* 49.1. 74-99.

Hubbard, T.K. 1998. Popular Perceptions of Elite Homosexuality in Classical Athens. *Arion* 6.1: 48-78.

Hubbard, T.K. 2000. Pederasty in Democracy: The Marginalization of a Social Practice, in T.K. Hubbard (ed.), *Greek Love Reconsidered*: 1-11. New York: W. Hamilton Press.

---

[49] Eubulus, F118 K-A: 'Nor did any of them see a courtesan, but they kneaded themselves for ten years. Bitter was the military service they saw, who, having taken but one city, went away far wider-arsed than the city which they took at the time.' Quoted by Ogden (1996: 111); see also Pinney (1984: 183).

Hubbard, T.K. 2014. Peer Homosexuality, in T.K. Hubbard (ed.), *A Companion to Greek and Roman Sexualities*: 128-149. Oxford; Malden: Wiley Blackwell.

Leitao, D. 2002. The Legend of the Sacred Band, in M.C. Nussbaum, and J. Sihvola (eds), *The Sleep of Reason. Erotic Experience and Sexual Ethics in Ancient Greece and Rome*: 145-151. Chicago; London: The University of Chicago Press.

Leitao, D. 2014. Sexuality in Greek and Roman Military Contexts, in T.K. Hubbard (ed.), *A Companion to Greek and Roman Sexualities*: 230-243. Oxford: Wiley Blackwell.

Littman, R.J. 1970. The Loves of Alcibiades. *Transactions and Proceedings of the American Philological Association* 101: 263-276.

Lucchesi, M.A. 2013. Love Theory and Political Practice: The Amatorius and the Lives of Coriolanus and Alcibiades, in E. Sanders, N. Lowe, C. Thumiger, and C. Carey (eds), *Eros in Ancient Greece*: 209-227. Oxford: Oxford University Press.

Ludwig, P.W. 2002. *Eros and Polis. Desire and Community in Greek Political Theory*. Cambridge: Cambridge University Press.

Marincola, J. 2016. The Historian as Hero: Herodotus and the 300 at Thermopylae. *Transactions of the American Philological Association* 146: 219-236.

Marrou, H.I. 1948. *Histoire de l'éducation dans l'Antiquité. I. Le monde grec*. Paris: Editions du Seuil.

Mills, S. 2000. Achilles, Patroclus and Parental Care in some Homeric Similes. *Greece and Rome* 47.1: 3-18.

Ogden, D. 1996. Homosexuality and Warfare in Classical Greece, in A.B. Lloyd (ed.), *Battle in Antiquity*: 107-168. Swansea: Duckworth, and The Classical Press of Wales.

Ogden, D. 2009. Alexander's Sex Life, in W. Heckel, and L.A. Tritle (eds), *Alexander the Great. A New History*: 203-217. Oxford; Malden; MA: Wiley Blackwell.

Perrin, B. 1955. *Plutarch's Lives. V – Agesilaus and Pompey. Pelopidas and Marcellus*. Cambridge, Mass.; London; Harvard University Press, and William Heinemann Ltd.

Pinney, G.F. 1984. For the Heroes are at Hand. *The Journal of Hellenic Studies* 104: 181-183.

Rahe, P.A. 1981. The Annihilation of the Sacred Band at Chaeronea. *American Journal of Archaeology* 85.1: 84-87.

Renero, V.M. 1998. *Alcibíades. La ambición del poder*. Madrid: Alderabán Ediciones.

Rhodes, P.J. 2011. *Alcibiades. Athenian Playboy, General and Traitor*. Barnsley: Pen and Sword Books.

Rodrigues, N.S. 2009. O Batalhão Sagrado de Tebas, uma utopia platónica?, in M.F. Silva (ed.), *Utopias and Distopias*: 107-111. Coimbra: Imprensa da Universidade de Coimbra.

Rodrigues, N.S. 2014. Alexandre entre paixões femininas e masculinas: Digressões plutarquianas pelo Cinema, in C. Alcalde Martín, and L.N. Ferreira (eds), *O sábio e a imagem. Estudos sobre Plutarco e a Arte*: 153-172. Coimbra; São Paulo: Imprensa da Universidade de Coimbra, and Annablume.

Rodrigues, N.S. 2018. Os Tiranicidas de Atenas: entre a representação aristocrática e a ideologia democrática, in B.B. Sebastiani, D.Leão, L. Sano, M. Soares, and C. Werner, (eds), *A Poiesis da Democracia*: 158186. Coimbra: Imprensa da Universidade de Coimbra.

Rodrigues, N.S. 2019. A violação de Crisipo à luz das ideias de *physis* e *nomos*, in M.F. Silva, M.C. Fialho, and M.G.M. Augusto (eds), *Casas, património, civilização. Nomos uersus physis no Pensamento Grego*: 99-113. Coimbra: Imprensa da Universidade de Coimbra.

Romilly, J. de 1995. *Alcibiade*. Paris: Éditions de Fallois.

Romm, J. 2021. *The Sacred Band. Three Hundred Theban Lovers Fighting to Save Greek Freedom*. New York; London; Toronto; Sydney; New Delhi: Scribner.

Skinner, M.B. 2010. *Alexander* and Ancient Greek Sexuality: Some Theoretical Considerations, in P. Cartledge and F.R. Greenland (eds), *Responses to Oliver Stone's* Alexander. *Film, History and Cultural Studies*: 119-134. Madison: The University of Wisconsin Press.

Stuttard, D. 2018. *Nemesis. Alcibiades and the Fall of Athens.* London; Cambridge, MA: Harvard University Press.

Taylor, M.W. 1991. *The Tyrant Slayers. The Heroic Image in Fifth Century B.C. Athenian Art and Politics.* Salem; NH: Ayer Co. Publishers.

Vickers, M. 2008. *Sophocles and Alcibiades. Athenian Politics in Ancient Greek Literature.* Ithaca; New York: Cornell University Press.

Vickers, M. 2015. *Aristophanes and Alcibiades. Echoes of Contemporary History in Athenian Comedy.* Berlin; Boston: Walter de Gruyter.

Wallace, R.W. 2015. Sokrates as Hoplite and Other Curious Sokratica. How Plato indicates Untruths. *Philosophia* 45: 148-160.

Sailing Directions.
Echoes of Ancient Nautical Knowledge
in the *Periplous of Ps.-Skylax*[1]

Chiara Maria Mauro

Departamento de Prehistoria, Historia Antigua y Arqueología
Universidad Complutense de Madrid (Spain)
cmauro@ucm.es

Abstract

This contribution explores how seafaring was practiced in Antiquity through the analysis of the data contained within the *Periplous of Ps.-Skylax*. Since the *Periplous of Ps.-Skylax* relies on maritime information dated between the 6th and the end of the 4th century BC, all the observations presented here should be mainly referred to pre-Hellenistic seafaring. In particular, the focus will be on the way in which three different kinds of information were possibly disseminated amongst seafarers: what course to steer, how far to sail to reach the desired destination and how to sail (i.e. decisions on hugging the coast or crossing directly from one island to another, or on where and when to stop to refurbish the ships).

Keywords

Periploi, ancient seafaring, Ps.-Skylax, maritime information, nautical practice.

Introduction

Sea travel was fairly convenient in Antiquity: although it was as (in)secure as travelling by land,[2] it was—at least—cheaper and faster. How nautical knowledge was transmitted is, however, still an unresolved issue, for whereas maritime culture deeply permeates all literary genres, no specialised nautical handbook has survived from Antiquity.[3] This state of affairs has led scholars to wonder whether nautical handbooks (at least in the way in which they would be conceived nowadays) ever existed in the first place or, conversely, information of this sort was only orally transmitted.[4] In our opinion, coastal pilot books must have existed and been used at least at some moments in Antiquity;[5] in this regard, telling evidence of this

---

[1] This work was co-funded by the Comunidad the Madrid and the Complutense University under the Grant No. 2018-T2/HUM-10960; it also benefitted from a short research stay kindly offered by the Hardt Foundation. Additionally, I am thankful to the Research Group Eschatia (UCM 930100) and its members for supporting the development of this research project.

[2] In addition to physical hazards (Morton 2001: 67-142), other seafarers also posed a threat (on Graeco-Roman piracy, De Souza 2002).

[3] The sole exception is currently considered to be the *Stadiasmus Maris Magni*, a stratified document that, for the kind of information that it records, as well as in the way in which it is presented, stands out from the rest of the extant texts. The *Stadiasmus* is dated between the 1st and the 3rd century AD (Medas 2008).

[4] On the two different approaches to this topic, see Janni (2002) and Medas (2004), a brief English summary of which can be found in Dunsch (2012: 272).

[5] As a matter of fact, Timosthenes of Rhodes, the admiral and chief helmsman of the fleet of Ptolemy II (285-246 BC), wrote a treatise entitled Περὶ λιμένων (*On harbours*). As the treatise comprised 10 books, it is highly unlikely that it accompanied seafarers on their journeys. Yet, Marcianus (Müller 1855, *GGM* 1.565-566) claims to have written a one-

is provided by a passage written by the Greek poet Crinagoras of Mytilene.[6] However, this aspect of the debate will not be addressed here, because the intention is not to determine how knowledge of the sea was transmitted in the ancient Greek world, but to identify the echoes of the information that ancient *periploi* probably included (regardless of whether it had been transmitted orally or in writing) and to pinpoint its origin. Since the quantity and quality of this information increase from the Hellenistic Age onward, the focus will be placed here on the previous period, running approximately from the 6th to the end of the 4th century BC. Despite having been scarcely examined, this time frame appears to be crucial for understanding the development and transmission of nautical issues, as it was the time when a particular category of geographical-literary documents appeared, viz. the so-called *periploi* (literally, 'circumnavigations').[7]

As already noted, clues to the kind of information recorded and transmitted by seafarers can be inferred from a variety of texts: to a greater or lesser extent, all kinds of documents were, in fact, influenced by previous sea journeys and adventures.[8] Even so, *periploi* appear to be especially enlightening as to how seafaring was conceived and practiced in Antiquity. For this reason, recourse will be made to these *periploi*, and particularly to the *Periplous of Ps.-Skylax*,[9] for the purpose of determining the kind of information that was shared by seafarers before the Hellenistic period.

The ancient *periploi*

The term *periplous* is currently employed to designate a particular category of ancient texts. Even though it has been traditionally assumed that some of them originally had practical purposes[10] and were therefore used to plan sea journeys, the surviving *periploi* should rather be described as geographical works, by and large without any literary pretensions. Unlike other geographical works, however, *periploi* have at least two things in common. Firstly, they focus on the coast and, even though they occasionally contain land descriptions, usually use the sea as a σύμβουλος, viz. as their common thread or guiding principle.[11] Secondly, they frequently repeat the same formulas, employing a limited vocabulary and short main clauses following one another in hypotaxis. These characteristics suggest that—even though in the form in which they have come down to us, they were actually of little use at sea—they might have been based on prior nautical knowledge, thus reflecting real sea journeys.

The advent and dissemination of *periploi* can be plausibly traced back to the 6th century BC. While sea journeys (and travels in general) had been previously depersonalised and ascribed

---

volume summary of Timosthenes' work; this abridged version might have reached a wider audience and, therefore, could have been used for practical purposes (Dunsch 2012).

[6] In the same passage, Crinagoras asks Menippus to write a *periplous* to guide him around the Cyclades: 'I am looking for a guiding *periplous* that will lead me/ around Cycladic Islands as far as old Scheria./ Menippus, my friend, expert in all geography,/ help me a bit by writing a scholarly tour' (Gow and Page 1968: 218).

[7] In Greek, περίπλοι. The origin of the so-called *Periplous of Hanno* and of Rufius Festus Avienius's *Ora Maritima*, for example, can be traced back to the 6th century BC (Medas 2008: 41).

[8] See, for example, Telemachos' journeys from Ithaka to Pylos and back (Hom. *Od.* 15.284-300 and 494-500) and the account of Eumaios' arrival on the island of Ithaka (Hom. *Od.* 15. 474-482).

[9] Shipley's (2011) edition is employed here, adopting the same subdivision of paragraphs, conventions and translations.

[10] See note no. 6.

[11] The expression is borrowed from Strabo 8.1.3.

to heroes or gods,[12] as of the 7th-6th century BC specific sea (and land) expeditions began to feature mere mortals.[13] Such a change was probably brought about by the increase in contacts during this period, which would have accentuated the need for reliable first-hand information based on real journeys.[14] Accordingly, the first strata of the *Periplous of Ps.-Skylax*, the *Periplous of Hanno* and Rufius Festus Avienius' *Ora Maritima* could be attributed to the 6th century BC. Of these three *periploi*, however, it is the *Periplous of Ps.-Skylax* that contains the earliest information, since the extant versions of the *Periplous of Hanno* and the *Ora Maritima* are generally thought to date back to the Hellenistic[15] and Roman periods,[16] respectively. In contrast, a date in the late-4th century BC has been traditionally suggested for the *Periplous of Ps.-Skylax*.[17] Furthermore, many scholars have acknowledged its reliance on nautical knowledge in circulation at the time when it was written, for which reason parts of it could be attributed to an even earlier date.[18] In this connection, the *Periplous of Ps.-Skylax* appears to be the only source capable of allowing us to gain a better understanding of how seafaring was practiced before the Hellenistic period. Additionally, as it presumably draws from previous sources, it can also provide us with clues about the information that earlier *periploi* might have included and transmitted.

A careful reading of the *Periplous of Ps.-Skylax* confirms that it is indebted to practical nautical knowledge, as the majority of its passages contain the three essential information categories that a seafarer would have desired to know before embarking on a sea journey: what course to steer, how far to sail to reach the final destination and what to do along the way (e.g. where to stop over or find shelter). In the following sections, how these indications are offered in the *Periplous of Ps.-Skylax* is examined, since the way in which they are expressed casts some light on how pre-Hellenistic seafaring was practiced, as well as on their origin.

What course to steer?

In Antiquity, there were two different navigation systems: one resorted to objective reference values (such as specific constellations,[19] the position of the sun and the direction of the wind); while the other relied on subjective—and experienced-based—information, like, for example, 'beyond these islands'.[20]

---

[12] Gómez Espelosín 2000: 38.

[13] For instance, Herodotus provides information about the journeys made by Kolaios of Samos to the SW Iberian Peninsula (4.152), by Aristeas to the land of the Issedones (4.13-16) and by Skylax of Karyanda to discover the course of the river Indus (4.44).

[14] Dueck 2012: 52.

[15] The *Periplous of Hanno*, which was originally a Punic report on a Carthaginian expedition, is preserved in a Greek version dated to between the 2nd-1st century BC (Desanges 1978: 83).

[16] The *Ora Maritima* is believed to be a poetic adaptation of an original Massaliote *periplous*, dated to around 525 BC. The Latin poem was composed by Rufius Festus Avienius, a late Roman author (Cary and Warmington 1929: 30).

[17] The *Periplous* is attributed to Ps.-Skylax because it does not match the itinerary allegedly followed by the Skylax of Karyanda mentioned by Herodotus (4.44). On the chronology of this text, see Fabre 1965: 353-366; Marcotte 1986: 166-182; Müller 1855: 44. The seven surviving fragments actually attributed to Skylax of Karyanda can be found in *FGrH* III C 709.

[18] Dilke 1985: 134; Kowalski 2012: 31; Peretti 1979, 1989; Shipley 2008: 283.

[19] Even though there are no examples of the use of astronavigation in the *Periplous of Ps.-Skylax*, there is evidence indicating that night sailing was already common. For references to night sailing in the literary sources, see Hom. *Od.* 2.434, 14.252-258; 15.292-300. On night sailing, Morton 2001: 261-265.

[20] Ps.-Skyl. 58.2: ὑπὸ δὲ ταύταις ἕτεραι νῆσοι.

The first system is certainly closer to the modern conception of navigation, but it is barely employed in the *Periplous of Ps.-Skylax*, being limited to the four cardinal points. The north is identified with the corresponding wind, namely, Boreas,[21] and the south with Notos.[22] On the contrary, the east and the west are always referred to in relation to the position of the sun, viz. 'the dawn'[23] and 'the sun's setting'.[24]

The scant use of information of this kind is not unique to the *Periplous of Ps.-Skylax*, but also has close parallels in later *periploi*.[25] This seems to suggest that—despite their use—resorting to absolute sailing directions was not the most common way of steering an adequate course at sea.

It was apparently more customary to resort to information deriving from actual sea voyages. Although directions such as 'on the left as one sails in'[26] would seem to be more ambiguous to modern readers, they were highly appreciated in Antiquity, as evidenced by the frequency with which they appear.[27] It is important to stress that sailing directions of this type were mainly devised by and for seafarers: in this sense, whoever took a specific sea route based on knowledge transmitted by other seafarers was likely to interpret these directions correctly, however vague they may seem to us. Those sailing on the same route were, in fact, roughly in the same position as the person who had initially provided that information. On the other hand, it is undeniable that these same relative sailing directions, once taken out of their original context, are very hard to understand.

To the two aforementioned navigation systems based on sailing directions should be added another generally known as 'pilotage' or 'environmental navigation'.[28] It consisted in determining the ship's position and course in relation to its destination by following a chain of landmarks identified on previous sea journeys.[29] In this navigation system, both natural (e.g. promontories, mountains, islands, etc.) and artificial (e.g. towers, settlements, temples, etc.) markers could be employed, as long as they were easily recognisable from afar. Besides allowing seafarers to familiarise themselves with the entire sea route in terms of a specific succession of landmarks, this environmental navigation system also allowed them to calculate, to a certain extent, the distance travelled.[30]

---

[21] Ps.-Skyl. 47 *passim*: πρὸς βορέαν.

[22] Ps.-Skyl. 47: πρὸς νότον.

[23] Ps.-Skyl. 47.4: '*Itanos*, the promontory of Crete towards the up-coming sun'; § 55: 'And after Epidauros is the territory of the Korinthioi, [the part] towards the dawn'; § 111.3: 'Past Hermaia Cape towards the upcoming sun, *a long way from* Hermaia, are three small islands by this place'.

[24] Ps.-Skyl. 47.2: '*Krete* extends from the settings of the sun towards the risings of the sun'; 110.9: 'The Gyzantes, a community, and a city beyond (the lake) towards the sun's setting'.

[25] See Medas' considerations on this same topic in relation to the *Stadiasmus Maris Magni* (Medas 2008: 88-93).

[26] Ps.-Skyl. 63.

[27] Janni (1984) refers to sailing directions of this kind in order to demonstrate that, in Antiquity, the perception of space was mainly 'hodological', namely, unidimensional and highly subjective.

[28] McGrail 1991: 86. 'Environmental navigation' depended on the ability not only to determine a ship's position by observing the landscape, but also to identify sounds and smells so as to anticipate approaching dangers.

[29] Morton 2001: 186.

[30] Parker 2001: 36.

The use of navigational instruments being limited to say the least,[31] steering the right course mainly depended on the visibility and recognisability of specific landmarks, for which reason they played a decisive role. This is borne out by the special attention that *periploi*, in general, and the *Periplous of Ps.-Skylax*, in particular, pay to shoreline descriptions,[32] an aspect that has been more or less confirmed by archaeological and documentary evidence. Indeed, the literary sources reveal that the πρωρεύς (or πρωράτης) played a relevant role among the crew members of a ship. The πρωρεύς was a sort of lookout, specifically entrusted with identifying landmarks so as to keep the ship on the right course.[33] As visibility normally increases with height, the lookout was usually stationed on a raised platform in the prow of the ship (Figures 1 and 2).[34] Be that as it may, archaeological finds have revealed that it might also have been placed elsewhere: a sixth-century-BC clay model of a Cypriot merchant ship, for example, was equipped with a sort of crow's nest from which the lookout could scan the horizon.[35]

How far to sail to reach the final destination?

After ascertaining the course that the ship should steer, the next piece of essential information had to do with the distance that should be covered to reach the final destination; in other words, it was desirable to know how far away it was and for how long it was necessary to sail to reach it.

For those who were familiar with the entire sea route as a succession of landmarks heaving into view or passing out of sight, it was already possible to estimate their relative position, at the very least, meaning that they could establish whether they were at the beginning, in the middle or near the end of their journey. However, it was certainly easier to determine, with a certain degree of accuracy, how far away a place was located when distances were provided.

Measuring distances at sea in order to transmit them was surely one of the greatest challenges when recording a sea route.[36] Whereas measuring distances on land without specific instruments was relatively simple by counting steps,[37] this was more complicated at sea, where the simplest way of gauging the distance travelled was by recording the time required to cover it. Time measurements doubtless provided a valuable estimate. As could not be otherwise, they were not always accurate, as the time employed could vary greatly depending on different factors. For example, sailing times could be shorter or longer depending on the type of vessel involved (warships were swifter than merchant ships) and on its seaworthiness,

---

[31] The only attested navigational instruments before the Hellenistic period were the sounding pole (originating from Egypt during the 2nd millennium BC) and the sounding lead and line, described by Herodotus (2.5.2) (McGrail 1991).

[32] For a description of natural landmarks, see Ps.-Skyl. 23.3, 26.3, 109.1, 110.8, 112.1. For artificial landmarks, see Ps.-Skyl. 13.5, 46.1.

[33] See Philostr. *Im.* 2.15; Soph. *Achaion Syllogos*, fr. 142.

[34] Marinatos (1974: 35) suggested adopting the Homeric term ἴκρια to designate the raised platform usually located in the stern of vessels during the LMI/LMII period. However, he was referring to a structure whose purpose was quite different from that of its archaic and classical counterparts: the Minoan ἴκρια was, in fact, a cabin with a seat, which was placed in the stern and which presumably had a ceremonial function (Wedde 2000: 132).

[35] Basch 1987: fig. 546.

[36] Marcianus (*c.* 4th-5th century AD) claimed that in Antiquity there were no instruments capable of measuring distances at sea (Müller 1855, GGM 1.567-568), thus making it necessary to rely on experience and intuition. On distances at sea, see also Medas 2008: 77-81.

[37] This is the case of the *bematistae*, the 'steppers' or 'road-surveyors'.

Fig. 1: Attic black-figure hydria by the Cleimachos painter, depicting an oared ship, with a helmsman in the stern and a lookout in the prow looking sternwards, mid-sixth century BC. Paris, Louvre Museum, inv. n. E735.

Fig. 2: Attic black-figure cup signed by Nicosthenes. In each ship it is possible to identify a helmsman and a lookout, positioned on a raised platform in the prow ('ἴκρια'), late-sixth century BC. Paris, Louvre Museum, inv. n. F123.

the weather and sea conditions encountered along the way and the kind of route chosen.[38] In this regard, it is interesting to note that the *Periplous of Ps.-Skylax* contains an elaborate scale of time units, far more sophisticated than those appearing in other works.[39] Such complex information points to its seafarer origin. From the longest to the shortest unit, this scale includes νυχθήμερον, sailing for a period of 24 consecutive hours,[40] ἡμέρα μάκρα or a long day's sailing, perhaps referring to the length of a day at the summer solstice,[41] ἡμέρα, a normal day of sailing,[42] ἡμέρας ἥμισυ, a half day of sailing,[43] πλοῦς προαριστίδιος, sailing with an arrival before noon,[44] and ἡμέρας τρίτον μέρος, sailing for the third part of a day.[45]

Together with sailing times, the *Periplous of Ps.-Skylax* also offers some distances using a different unit of measurement, to wit, the *stadion*.[46] Notwithstanding the fact that the value of the *stadion* underwent changes over time,[47] this linear measurement was certainly more reliable than sailing times, as well as being less subject to personal interpretations, at least in theory.

In whatever unit they were provided, distances always corresponded to the individual legs of a route, thus making it necessary to add them all together in order to arrive at the overall distance. The appearance of both *stadia* and sailing times in the *Periplous of Ps.-Skylax* suggests that, when it was compiled, both systems were in use.[48] The prevalence of sailing times, furthermore, also points to the fact that, in the pre-Hellenistic period, the nautical information in circulation was closely linked to an empirical perception of space.

What to do along the way?

After having determined the correct course and how long to sail, seafarers still had to make a number of decisions on how to sail (e.g. hugging the coast or crossing directly from one island to another) and where (and when) to stop to refurbish their ships. Obviously, these decisions did not depend solely on the crew, but were also strongly influenced by technical and human considerations. From a technical point of view, the main issues that had to be taken into account were surely the kind of ship employed and its seaworthiness,[49] as well as the quantity, nature and weight of its cargo.[50] As to human considerations, the experience of seafarers and the purpose of their journey might have similarly determined the route, together with the number and location of possible stopovers.

---

[38] Arnaud 1993, 2005: 61-96; Medas 2008: 77; Rougé 1966: 99-101.

[39] Arnaud 1993: 236.

[40] Ps.-Skyl. 20.

[41] Ps.-Skyl. 22.

[42] Ps.-Skyl. 1.

[43] Ps.-Skyl. 11.

[44] Ps.-Skyl. 64.2.

[45] Ps.-Skyl. 7.

[46] Ps.-Skyl. 64.1.

[47] Arnaud (2005: 84-86) has estimated that it varied between 150 and 210m.

[48] A definitive conversion from time to distance took place in the 3rd century BC (Arnaud 2004: 47), so slightly later in date than the *Periplous of Ps.-Skylax*.

[49] While merchant vessels were better suited to open seas and could sail for several days without having to approach the coast, triremes and small boats had to do so with frequency, wherever possible.

[50] Heavy cargoes made ships less buoyant and manoeuvrable, while also reducing their speed.

With regard to the first of the abovementioned decisions—namely, how to sail—the *Periplous of Ps.-Skylax* records at least two different ways of proceeding: the first consisted of sailing from cape to cape (ἐπ'εὐθείας), while the second involved coastal navigation (παρὰ γήν).[51] As a matter of fact, when describing a gulf, the *Periplous* often caters to both those merely sailing past it (providing its overall length)[52] and those who might have planned one or more stopovers there (by listing the landmarks along its shore).[53] This suggests that several possibilities for almost every stretch of coast were known and shared by seafarers: a direct route that allowed for reducing distances and, therefore, the duration of the voyage;[54] and a second route, hugging the coast, which made it possible to find refuge swiftly in the event of adverse weather conditions or other hazards.

The other essential decision was how often and where to break the journey. Although it is reasonable to assume that several stopovers were planned in advance, in the case of sudden and unexpected events, last minute decisions would have had to be made, for which reason it was useful to know where it was possible to seek shelter on a specific stretch of coast.[55]

Based on later *periploi* (e.g. the *Stadiasmus Maris Magni* and what is known of Timosthenes' Περὶ λιμένων) and medieval rutters, information on safe places to shelter was presumably transmitted in the form of lists. On these lists, such locations were recorded in the order in which a ship would have encountered them while sailing along a given route. In the *Periplous of Ps.-Skylax*, their existence is reflected in the long lists of cities, harbours and shelters along the coast. In most cases, the *Periplous* merely records the presence of harbours in certain places,[56] while in others, it provides valuable details, such as specifying the number of harbour basins available[57] and their characteristics.[58] Whereas the most common term for identifying a harbour was λιμήν, other words, including ὕφορμος (anchorage), were occasionally employed.[59]

Conclusions

Despite the fact that no *periplous* produced earlier than the 1st century AD has survived the passage of time, in several written sources it is still possible to discern echoes of nautical knowledge that was shared by seafarers. Indeed, it is *periploi* that drew most directly from previous knowledge and, consequently, provide us with the most valuable insights into how seafaring was practiced in Antiquity.

---

[51] Peretti 1989: 49.

[52] Ps.-Skyl. 68.

[53] Ps.-Skyl. 70.

[54] It also avoided most of the dangers relating to coastal navigation, such as shallow water, sand banks, submerged reefs, etc.

[55] On the specific kind of shelter offered by different topographical features, see Blue 1997; Mauro 2019a, 2019b; Morton 2001.

[56] Ps.-Skyl. 4, 13, 22, 74.

[57] Ps.-Skyl. 53, 57, 86.

[58] Ps.-Skyl. 47.4, 103. On the 14 cases of 'closed harbours' and the possible meaning of this expression, see Mauro and Gambash 2020.

[59] Ps.-Skyl. 108.

In this paper we have chosen to focus on the *Periplous of Ps.-Skylax* due to its chronology: as observed above, of all the extant *periploi* it is the one that might preserve the earliest traces of sailing directions. As such, we have performed an analysis on its content with the aim of gaining a better understanding of the kind of information on sea routes that was possibly transmitted and why. The results show that the *Periplous of Ps.-Skylax* contains, in an embryonic form, all the information that would become commonplace in subsequent documents of this type (i.e. sailing directions, recommendations, distances, etc.) and which nowadays are still essential for seafaring. The way in which it is conveyed, moreover, highlights a knowledge of the sea strongly influenced by an empirical conception of space. In fact, instead of other orientation methods, the coastline marked the route that should be taken. This seems to imply that the environment, with its succession of prominent artificial and natural landmarks, was considered to be a more reliable guide than astronomical indications during this pre-instrumental phase. A similar phenomenon can be observed as regards distances, with sailing times (yet again an experience-based measure) prevailing over distances in *stadia* (the scientific unit).

This state affairs gives rise to two different, but compatible, observations. On the one hand, it might indicate that a scientific awareness of maritime space was *in fieri* at the end of the 4th century BC, thus justifying the coexistence of different methods of orientation and measurement. On the other, it might also point to the origins of the nautical information contained in the *Periplous of Ps.-Skylax*, since its marked pragmatism, combined with detailed knowledge of specific coastal features that it implies, suggest that local seafarers—who regularly embarked on short trading ventures or brief trips along the same stretch of coast[60]—were probably, at this stage, the driving force behind the generation and transmission of a common corpus of nautical knowledge.

Bibliography

Arnaud, P. 1993. De la durée a la distance: l'évaluation des distances maritimes dans le monde gréco-romain, *Histoire and Mesure* 7.3-4: 225-247.

Arnaud, P. 2005. *Les routes de la navigation Antique. Itinéraires en Méditerranée.* Paris: Errance.

Arnaud, P. 2014. Ancient Mariners Between Experience and Common Sense Geography, in K. Geus and M. Thiering (eds) *Features of common sense geography. Implicit knowledge structures in ancient geographical texts:* 39-68. Wien: LIT Verlag.

Basch, L. 1987. *Le musée imaginaire de la marine antique.* Athens: Institute hellénique pour la préservation de la tradition nautique.

Beresford, J. 2012. *The Ancient Sailing Season.* Leiden: Brill.

Blue, L. 1997. Cyprus and Cilicia: the typology and palaeogeography of second millennium harbours, in S.Swiny, R.L. Hohlfelder and H.W. Swiny (eds) *Res Maritimae. Cyprus and the Eastern Mediterranean from Prehistory to Late Antiquity:* 31-44. Atlanta: Scholar Press.

Cary, M. and Warmington, E.H. 1929. *The ancient Explorers.* London: Methuen.

De Souza, P. 2002. *Piracy in the Graeco-Roman World.* Cambridge: Cambridge University Press.

Desanges, J. 1978. *Recherches sur l'activité des Méditerranéens aux confine de l'Afrique.* Rome: École Française de Rome/ De Boccard.

Dilke, O.A.W. 1985. *Greek and Roman Maps.* London: Thames and Hudson.

---

[60] Beresford 2012: 185-190.

Dueck, D. 2012. Descriptive Geography, in D. Dueck (ed.) *Geography in Classical Antiquity*: 20-67. Cambridge: Cambridge University Press.

Dunsch, B. 2012. Arte rates reguntur: Nautical handbooks in antiquity?, *Studies in History and Philosophy of Science Part A* 43.2: 270–283. Doi: 10.1016/j.shpsa.2011.12.024

Fabre, P. 1965. La date de rédaction du périple de Scylax, *Les Études Classiques* 33: 353-366.

Gómez Espelosín, F.J. 2000. *El descubrimiento del mundo. Geografía y viajeros en la antigua Grecia.* Madrid: Akal.

Gow, A.S.F. and Page, D.L. 1968. *The Greek Anthology: The Garland of Philip and Some Contemporary Epigrams, vol. I.* Cambridge: Cambridge University Press.

Janni, P. 1984. *La mappa e il periplo: cartografia antica e spazio odologico.* Rome: L'Erma di Bretschneider.

Janni, P. 2002. Nautica, in I. Mastrorosa and A. Zumbo (eds) *Letteratura scientifica e tecnica di Grecia e Roma*: 395–412. Roma: Carocci.

Kowalski, M. 2012. *Navigation et géographie dans l'Antiquité gréco-romaine. La terre vue de la mer.* Paris: Picard.

Marcotte, D. 1986. Le périple dit de Scylax: esquisse d'un commentaire épigraphique et archéologique, *Bollettino dei Classici* 7: 166-182.

Marinatos, Sp. 1974. *Excavations at Thera, vol. VI.* Athens: Archaiologikē Hetaireia.

Mauro, C.M. 2019a. *Archaic and Classical Harbours of the Greek World. The Aegean and Eastern Ionian contexts.* Oxford: Archaeopress. Doi: 10.2307/j.ctvndv7h2

Mauro, C.M. 2019b. A Bridge to Overseas. Insight into the geomorphology, harbourworks and harbour layouts of the Archaic and Classical Greek harbours, in R. Morais, D. Leão and D. Rodríguez Pérez (eds) *Greek Art in Motion. Studies in honour of Sir John Boardman on the occasion of his 90th birthday*: 377-385. Oxford: Archaeopress.

Mauro, C.M. and Gambash, G. 2020. The earliest "limenes kleistoi": a comparison between archaeological-geological data and the Periplus of Pseudo-Skylax, *Revue des Études Anciennes* 122.1: 55-84.

McGrail, S. 1991. Early sea voyages, *International Journal of Nautical Archaeology* 20.2: 85-93. Doi: 10.1111/j.1095-9270.1991.tb00303.x

Medas, S. 2004. *De Rebus Nauticis. L'arte della navigazione nel mondo antico.* Rome: L'Erma di Bretschneider.

Medas, S. 2008. *Lo Stadiasmo o Periplo del Mare Grande e la navigazione antica* (Gerión Anejos 12). Madrid: Universidad Complutense de Madrid.

Morton, J. 2001. *The Role of the Physical Environment in Ancient Greek Seafaring* (Mnemosyne Supplements 213). Leiden: Brill.

Müller, K. 1855. *Geographi graeci minores, vol. I.* Paris: Didot.

Rougé, J. 1966. *Recherches sur l'organisation du commerce maritime en Méditerranée sous l'Empire Romain.* Paris: S.E.V.P.E.N.

Parker, A.J. 2001. Maritime Landscape, *Landscape* 1: 22-41. Doi: 10.1179/lan.2001.2.1.22

Peretti, A. 1979. *Il Periplo di Scilace. Studio sul Primo Portolano del Mediterraneo.* Pisa: Giardini.

Peretti, A. 1989. Dati storici e distanze marine nel "Periplo" di Scilace, *Studi Classici e Orientali* 138: 13-137.

Shipley, G. 2008. Pseudo-Skylax on the Peloponnese, in C. Gallou, M. Georgiadis and G.M. Muskett (eds) *Dioskouroi: Studies presented to W.G. Cavanagh and C.B. Mee on the Anniversary of Their 30 year joint contribution to Aegean Archaeology*: 281-291. Oxford: British Archaeological Reports.

Shipley, G. 2011. *Pseudo-Skyklax's Periplous. The Circumnavigation of the Inhabited World*. Exeter: Exeter University Press.

Wedde, M. 2000. *Towards a Hermeneutics of Aegean Bronze Age Ship Imagery*. Mannheim: Bibliopolis.

Heraclides' Epitome of the Aristotelian *Athenaion Politeia*

Gertjan Verhasselt

LMU Munich / KU Leuven
gertjan.verhasselt@klassphil.uni-muenchen.de

Abstract

Aristotle's *Constitutions* gathered information on the history and organisation of reportedly 158 Greek states. Of these, only the *Athenaion Politeia* survives more or less in its entirety. Many of the other constitutions are known only through the epitome written by the second-century BC scholar Heraclides Lembus. This paper commemorates P.J. Rhodes by assessing the reliability of Heraclides' text as a witness to the *Athenaion Politeia*. Comparing Heraclides' epitome with the original Aristotelian text sheds light onto the filter through which the other Aristotelian *Constitutions* are now known to us. A major problem is that Heraclides' epitome is itself only preserved through excerpts. Because of this double process of abbreviation and the random cut-and-paste technique of the later excerptor, the epitome is no accurate summary of the original text. It juxtaposes isolated details without much coherence and often connects information with the wrong person. It also heavily focuses on the historical section and reports only few details from the descriptive section of the *Athenaion Politeia*. Furthermore, Heraclides seems to show no interest in Aristotle's main argument, viz. that the constitution goes through various *metabolai*. In its current form, the epitome thus gives a heavily distorted picture of the original.

Keywords

Aristotle, *Athenian Constitution*, *Politeiai*, Heraclides Lembus

Introduction

The *Constitutions* attributed to Aristotle gathered information on the history and organisation of the Greek city-states.[1] Of the 158 constitutions which this vast collection is said to have contained, the *Athenaion Politeia* is the only one to survive almost in its entirety on a papyrus published in 1891 and now preserved in the British Library (P.Lond. 131).[2] All that remains of the other constitutions are fragments, i.e. citations in later writers, and an epitome written by the second-century BC scholar Heraclides Lembus.[3] Heraclides' epitome covers 44 cities and opens with the constitution of Athens. He further also wrote epitomes of Hermippus' works *On Lawgivers*, *On the Seven Sages*, and *On Pythagoras* (P.Oxy. XI 1367), of Satyrus' *Biographies* (*FHG* III, 169 F 6-7), and of Sotion's *Successions of Philosophers* (*FHG* III, 169-71 F 8-17).[4] Apart from

---

[1] In this article, I refer to the author of the *Athenaion Politeia* as 'Aristotle'. The authorship of this work is rejected by many scholars (among others by P.J. Rhodes himself). Because of limitations of space, I cannot discuss the whole debate here. My personal view is that the arguments against Aristotle' authorship are insufficient to refute the authenticity. Regardless, the issue is not crucial for the main argument in this paper, viz. the reliability of Heraclides as a witness to the *Constitutions* in general and the *Athenaion Politeia* in particular.

[2] Another papyrus that preserves a small part of the *Athenaion Politeia* is P.Berol. 5009.

[3] Heraclides' epitome covered not only the *Constitutions* but also Aristotle's *Barbarian Customs*.

[4] For Heraclides' biographical epitomes, see especially Schorn (2018: 288-99).

these epitomes, Heraclides also wrote *Histories* in at least 37 books (*FHG* III, 168-69 F 3-5)[5] and a Λεμβευτικὸς λόγος (D.L. 5.94). In this paper, I shall discuss Heraclides' method and reliability as an epitomist of Aristotle by comparing the section on Athens with the original text of Aristotle.[6] This will shed light onto the filter through which the other constitutions are now known to us.

The *Athenaion Politeia* consists roughly of two parts. In the first part, Aristotle presents a history of Athens from the foundation of the polis down to the fall of the Thirty and the restoration of democracy in 403 BC. The second part consists of a systematic description of the Athenian political system as it existed in Aristotle's time. Heraclides' epitome is important for the reconstruction of the beginning of *Athenaion Politeia*, which is not preserved in the London papyrus and treated history from Ion down to the expulsion of the Alcmeonids (Heraclid. Lemb. *Pol.* 1). In this paper, however, I shall focus on the sections that allow us to make a comparison with the original text.

Before I move on to the discussion of the text, it is important to highlight that the epitome of Heraclides itself is not preserved in its entirety either but only survives as excerpts, as the incipit ἐκ τῶν Ἡρακλείδου περὶ πολιτειῶν in the manuscripts already shows.[7] As a result of this double process of abbreviation, the epitome in its current form often gives isolated details without any coherent transition from one point to the next.

The death of Cylon and the condemnation of the Alcmeonids

> τοὺς μετὰ Κύλωνος διὰ τὴν τυραννίδα[8] ἐπὶ τὸν βωμὸν τῆς θεοῦ πεφευγότας οἱ περὶ Μεγακλέα ἀπέκτειναν. καὶ τοὺς δράσαντας ὡς ἐναγεῖς ἤλαυνον. (Heraclid. Lemb. *Pol.* 2)
>
> Cylon and his supporters had fled to the altar of the goddess but were killed by Megacles and his supporters because of his tyranny. And they banished those who had done this as accursed people.

The preserved text of the *Athenaion Politeia* starts in the middle of the description of the trial of the Alcmeonids (*Ath.* 1). Aristotle appears to have originally described the coup of Cylon, who had tried to seize the acropolis and make himself tyrant *c.* 630 BC. When this attempt failed, Cylon and his supporters took sanctuary at the altar of Athena but were nevertheless killed by the Alcmeonid Megacles (one of the archons) and his followers. The Alcmeonids were therefore considered ἐναγής, i.e. 'accursed' or 'polluted'. Aristotle then seems to have included a flash forward to a later period in which the Alcmeonids were put to trial with Myron of Phlya as prosecutor, which is where the papyrus text begins. This is implied by the fact that Aristotle states that the bones of the dead Alcmeonids were dug up (αὐτοὶ μὲν ἐκ τῶν τάφων ἐξεβλήθησαν). This means that, in Aristotle, the trial must have taken place at

---

[5] Heraclides' *Histories* were in their turn later epitomised by Heron of Athens (cf. Suid. η 552, s.v. Ἥρων: Ἐπιτομὴν τῶν Ἡρακλείδου ἱστοριῶν).

[6] The text of Heraclides quoted in this article is that of Dilts (1971). The *Athenaion Politeia* is quoted after the edition of Chambers (1994).

[7] See especially Polito (2001: 230-33); Verhasselt (2019: 672-74).

[8] Chambers (1990: 436; 1994: 67) deleted the words διὰ τὴν τυραννίδα, but this is unnecessary.

least a generation after the coup.[9] The epitome thus seems to have compressed Aristotle's account, reducing the coup of Cylon and the trial of the Alcmeonids to one episode.[10] This might explain why it does not mention the exhumation of the bones, since this would make little sense if, in Heraclides, the Alcmeonids were convicted immediately after the death of Cylon. Note also that the epitome does not indicate that the subject of the verb ἤλαυνον (i.e. the Athenians) is different from that of ἀπέκτειναν (i.e. Megacles and his supporters). In Aristotle, this is then followed by the statement that Epimenides of Crete purified the city, but this is omitted in the epitome.

Solon's legislation

> Σόλων νομοθετῶν Ἀθηναίοις καὶ χρεῶν ἀποκοπὰς ἐποίησε, τὴν σεισάχθειαν λεγομένην. ὡς δ' ἐνώχλουν αὐτῷ τινες περὶ τῶν νόμων, ἀπεδήμησεν εἰς Αἴγυπτον. (Heraclid. Lemb. Pol. 3)

> Solon, when he gave laws for the Athenians, also made a cancellation of debt, which was called the 'shaking off of burden' (seisachtheia). When some people gave him trouble about his laws, he journeyed to Egypt.

After the discussion of the Cylonian coup, the epitome immediately jumps to the legislation of Solon, skipping the description of the 'ancient' constitution (Ath. 3) and the Draconian constitution (Ath. 4)[11] and omitting the conflict between the demos and the nobility (Ath. 5), which was the historical context for Solon's reforms. Of these reforms, the epitome only mentions the seisachtheia (Ath. 6.1), omitting the introduction of the four property classes (Ath. 7), the description of the officials (Ath. 8), and the reform of weights and measures (Ath. 10). It immediately moves on to Solon's journey to Egypt, which he undertook to evade the people who were questioning him about his laws (Ath. 11.1). The trip to Egypt is hardly the most important point in Aristotle's narrative, but it is nevertheless what the epitomator has preferred to highlight. Heraclides also appears to have omitted the additional motivation for this journey cited by Aristotle, viz. trade and sightseeing (κατ' ἐμπορίαν ἅμα καὶ θεωρίαν). The comparison between the epitome and the original further shows that Heraclides appears to have stayed relatively close to the phrasing of the original here.[12]

Pisistratus and the Pisistratids

> Πεισίστρατος λγ΄ ἔτη τυραννήσας γηράσας ἀπέθανεν. Ἵππαρχος ὁ υἱὸς Πεισιστράτου παιδιώδης ἦν καὶ ἐρωτικὸς καὶ φιλόμουσος, Θεσσαλὸς δὲ νεώτερος καὶ θρασύς. τοῦτον

---

[9] So Rhodes (1993: 83-84; 2002: 119; 2017: 182). See also Kenyon (1892: 1-2; 1895: 1-2 n. 1); Levi (1968: 9-10); Moore (1975: 218); von Fritz and Kapp (1950: 149 n. 1). Plu. Sol. 12 puts the trial in the time of Solon.

[10] Some editors actually separate the phrase καὶ τοὺς δράσαντας ὡς ἐναγεῖς ἤλαυνον as a new excerpt, thus implying that Heraclides originally separated the two episodes as well. So Korais (1805: 205); Schneidewin (1847: 4).

[11] The description of the Draconian constitution in the Athenaion Politeia is usually considered a later insertion. See Chambers (1990: 154); Fuks (1953: 84-101); Rhodes (1993: 53-56, 84-87; 2017: 30, 183); Wallace (1992) with further literature.

[12] Cf. Arist. Ath. 6.1: καὶ <u>νόμους ἔθηκε</u> **καὶ χρεῶν ἀπ[ο]κοπὰς ἐποίησε** καὶ τῶν ἰδίων καὶ τῶν δ[η]μοσίων, <u>ἃς</u> <u>σεισάχθειαν καλοῦσιν</u>, ὡς ἀποσεισάμενοι τὸ βάρος; Ath. 11.1: ἐπειδὴ προσιόντες αὐτῷ **περὶ τῶν νόμων ἐνώχλουν** ... <u>ἀποδημίαν ἐποιήσατο</u> κατ' ἐμπορίαν ἅμα καὶ θεωρίαν **εἰς Αἴγυπτον**.

τυραννοῦντα μὴ δυνηθέντες ἀνελεῖν Ἵππαρχον ἀπέκτειναν τὸν ἀδελφὸν αὐτοῦ. Ἱππίας δὲ πικρότερον ἐτυράννει. (Heraclid. Lemb. *Pol.* 4)

Pisistratus, having ruled as tyrant for 33 years, became old and died. Hipparchus, the son of Pisistratus, was fond of amusement, amorous, and a lover of music. Thessalus was younger and insolent. Since they could not eliminate him, when he was tyrant, they killed his brother Hipparchus. Hippias ruled more bitterly as tyrant.

From Solon the epitome moves on to Pisistratus,[13] indeed the next major political figure treated by Aristotle. It has only preserved Aristotle's concluding remarks about Pisistratus' reign (*Ath.* 17.1), omitting his rise to power with the struggle against Megacles and Lycurgus (*Ath.* 13-15) and the political changes under his rule (*Ath.* 16). Although Heraclides' phrasing is again close to Aristotle's,[14] he has introduced an error here. For he claims that, when Pisistratus died, he had been tyrant for 33 years (λγ´ ἔτη *τυραννήσας*). But Aristotle states that, from the moment he first became tyrant until his death, Pisistratus had *lived* for 33 years (ἀφ᾽ οὗ μὲν κατέστη τὸ πρῶτον τύραννος ἔτη τριάκοντα καὶ τρία *βιώσας*). For he was banished twice. Aristotle specifies that, of those 33 years, Pisistratus ruled for 19 years and was in exile for the remaining years (ἃ δ᾽ ἐν τῇ ἀρχῇ διέμεινεν, ἑνὸς δέοντα εἴκοσι· ἔφε[υ]γε γὰρ τὰ λοιπά). The error probably arose from the fact that Heraclides omitted the specification 'from the moment he had first become tyrant'. Since it would be nonsensical to keep the phrase 'having lived for 33 years' (Pisistratus was obviously older than 33 years when he died), he probably changed it to 'having ruled as tyrant for 33 years'. Yet Aristotle himself might be partly to blame here. For in *Ath.* 19.6, he counts the duration of the tyranny of Pisistratus and his sons as 49 years.[15] Since he adds that Pisistratus' sons ruled for 17 years, the number implies a rule of 32/33 years for Pisistratus.[16]

The epitome then discusses the Pisistratids. Aristotle (*Ath.* 17.3-4) distinguished Pisistratus' sons by his wedded wife (Hippias and Hipparchus) from those by his Argive wife (Iophon and Hegesistratus, who was also named Thettalus). The epitome glosses over this distinction and does not name Iophon, who indeed plays no part in the rest of Aristotle's narrative. It first treats Hipparchus and Thettalus, following Aristotle nearly verbatim.[17] Heraclides only adds the words ὁ υἱὸς Πεισιστράτου, which he supplied from the rest of Aristotle's narrative.

The epitome then states that some unnamed people were unable to kill 'him'. At a first glance, τοῦτον would be taken to refer to the person mentioned in the previous sentence, i.e. Thettalus. However, the original shows that the pronoun τοῦτον refers to Hippias. Aristotle

---

[13] The epitome also omits the long quotations from Solon's poems, adduced by Aristotle as evidence for Solon's legislation (*Ath.* 12).

[14] Cf. Arist. *Ath.* 17.1: **Πεισίστρατος** μὲν οὖν ἐγκατεγήρασε τῇ ἀρχῇ καὶ **ἀπέθανε** νοσήσας ἐπὶ Φιλόνεω ἄρχοντος.

[15] Rhodes (2017: 78, 240) corrected ἑνὸς δεῖ πεντήκοντα (49) to τριάκοντα ἕξ with Sumner (1961: 1941), but this is unnecessary and not palaeographically straightforward. Schol. Ar. *V.* 502d Koster cites Aristotle as counting 41 years (τεσσαράκοντα καὶ ἕν), which is probably an error for 49 (τεσσαράκοντα καὶ ἐν<νέα>). See Haussoullier (1891: 31 n. 1); Kaibel and von Wilamowitz-Moellendorff (1898: 21); Kenyon (1892: 65; 1903: 23); Montana (1996: 156-61); Oppermann (1928: 26); Sandys (1912: 79); Thalheim (1914: 27).

[16] See also Bauer (1891: 52-53); Hude (1916: 28); Kenyon (1892: 65); Maddoli (1975: 29); Sandys (1912: 79); Viano (1955: 376-77 n. 39); von Wilamowitz-Moellendorff (1893: 21).

[17] Cf. Arist. *Ath.* 18.1: ὁ δ᾽ Ἵππαρχος **παιδιώδης καὶ ἐρωτικὸς καὶ φιλόμουσος ἦν**; *Ath.* 18.2: **Θέτταλος** δὲ νεώτερος πολὺ **καὶ** τῷ βίῳ **θρασὺς** καὶ ὑβριστής.

is discussing the conspiracy of Harmodius and Aristogeiton, who intended to kill Hippias at the Panathenaic Festival (*Ath.* 18.3). The epitome omits both the names of the two famous conspirators and the reason for the plot, given in *Ath.* 18.2 (viz. since Harmodius had not reciprocated Thettalus' love for him, the latter had taken revenge by excluding Harmodius' sister from the Panathenaic procession and insulting Harmodius himself as being effeminate). The later excerptor has thus taken the sentence of Heraclides out of its original context without indicating whom the pronoun originally referred to.[18] Moreover, the detail about Thettalus' revenge explains why Aristotle described Thettalus shortly before as 'insolent and violent' (θρασὺς καὶ ὑβριστής). The epitome has only kept this characterisation of Thettalus but has omitted his actions, thus obscuring the relevance of that characterisation in Aristotle. Heraclides' explanation 'since they could not eliminate him, when he was tyrant' is his own paraphrase of the failed attempt at killing Hippias, described in more detail by Aristotle. What Aristotle says in the original text is that, on the day of the assault, the conspirators at one point wrongly thought that one of the accomplices had informed Hippias of their plan, which prompted them to kill Hipparchus instead. Heraclides also supplies τὸν ἀδελφὸν αὐτοῦ after Ἵππαρχον, again based on the rest of Aristotle's narrative.

The epitome omits the subsequent fate of the conspirators (*Ath.* 18.4-6) and only comments that Hippias' rule was bitter (*Ath.* 19.1). The latter is a small modification of what Aristotle said. In Aristotle, Hippias' tyranny was described as 'harsher', while Hippias himself was dubbed 'bitter' (πολλῷ τραχυτέραν εἶναι τὴν τυραννίδα ... πᾶσιν ἦν ἄπιστος καὶ πικρός). Heraclides has compressed this statement so that Hippias' tyranny is dubbed πικρότερον.

Cleisthenes and the introduction of ostracism

> καὶ τὸν περὶ ὀστρακισμοῦ νόμον εἰσηγήσατο, ὃς ἐτέθη διὰ τοὺς τυραννιῶντας. καὶ ἄλλοι τε ὠστρακίσθησαν καὶ Ξάνθιππος καὶ Ἀριστείδης. (Heraclid. Lemb. *Pol.* 49)

> And he introduced the law about ostracism, which was enacted because of those people who had tyrannical ambitions. And several people were ostracised, especially Xanthippus and Aristides.

After the statement about Hippias' tyranny, the epitome immediately adds that 'he introduced the law about ostracism'. Once again, this does not refer to the person mentioned in the previous sentence (i.e. Hippias). Instead, it denotes the lawgiver Cleisthenes.[19] The epitome has omitted the expulsion of Hippias (*Ath.* 19.2-6), the rivalry between Isagoras and Cleisthenes (*Ath.* 20), and the transition to the democratic reforms of Cleisthenes (*Ath.* 21) and does not indicate that the subject of εἰσηγήσατο is different from that of the previous

---

[18] *Pace* von Holzinger (1891: 438), who claimed that τοῦτον referred to Thettalus. Holzinger considered τυραννοῦντα a paraphrase of Aristotle's words ὑβριστής, ἀφ' οὗ καὶ συνέβη τὴν ἀρχὴν αὐτοῖς γενέσθαι πάντων τῶν κακῶν. However, Aristotle does not claim that Harmodius and Aristogeiton were unable to kill Thettalus. The failed assassination obviously refers to Hippias. According to Chambers (1990: 437), τοῦτον does refer to Thettalus and is the result of Heraclides incorrectly paraphrasing Aristotle. Thalheim (1914: 111), in his turn, considered correcting τοῦτον to Ἱππίαν τὸν.

[19] For this reason, Chambers (1990: 437; 1994: 68) and Müller (1848: 209) accepted Simson's correction of καὶ τὸν περί, etc. to Κλεισθένης τὸν περί, etc. See also Thalheim (1914: 111). Gigon (1987: 565) assumed a lacuna before καὶ τὸν περί. Similarly, Polito (2001: 15, 33-35) supplemented ἐτυράννει. <... Κλεισθένης> καὶ τὸν περί, etc. Korais (1805: 206, 350) and Schneidewin (1847: 5, 39) tried to solve the problem by correcting εἰσηγήσατο to εἰσηγήσαντο (sc. οἱ Ἀθηναῖοι).

sentence. The only reform mentioned by the epitome is the law about ostracism (*Ath.* 22.1). The explanation why the law was enacted (viz. mistrust of potential tyrants) is again paraphrased in Heraclides. Cleisthenes' reorganisation of the citizenry into 10 new tribes and the introduction of demarchs (*Ath.* 21.2-6) are omitted. In the *Athenaion Politeia*, Aristotle goes on to describe several people who were ostracised (*Ath.* 22.3-7). The epitome only names the last two mentioned by Aristotle (Xanthippus and Aristides); the other two (Hipparchus and Megacles) are only designated with ἄλλοι. Aristotle also gives the historical context for each ostracism, but this is all omitted by the epitome.

Ephialtes and Cimon

> Ἐφιάλτης τοὺς ἰδίους ἀγροὺς ὀπωρίζειν παρεῖχε τοῖς βουλομένοις, ἐξ ὧν πολλοὺς ἐδείπνιζε. (Heraclid. Lemb. *Pol.* 5)

> Ephialtes offered his own lands to anyone who wished to gather fruits. With this,[20] he gave a dinner for many people.

After mentioning the law about ostracism, the epitome jumps to the politician Ephialtes, skipping the discussion of Aristides and Themistocles (*Ath.* 23-24) for now (cf. below), and states that 'he' allowed everyone to pick the fruits from his fields. However, in Aristotle (*Ath.* 27.3), this story is connected with Cimon, not Ephialtes! Some scholars explain this as due to Heraclides' sloppiness in abbreviating Aristotle's text.[21] Others assume a lacuna and restore the text as Ἐφιάλτης <... Κίμων> τοὺς ἰδίους ἀγροὺς, etc.[22] The most economic solution is probably to follow Holzinger and Kaibel/Wilamowitz in punctuating after Ἐφιάλτης, so that a new excerpt starts in τοὺς ἰδίους ἀγροὺς, etc.[23] This means that Ἐφιάλτης is an empty lemma (see the section on Themistocles and Aristides below), which, in Heraclides' original text, probably contained a discussion of Ephialtes (*Ath.* 25.1). The excerptor has once again taken a sentence out of its context and fails to indicate that the subject is not the same as in the previous sentence.

The epitome also leaves out the context for the anecdote. Aristotle adduced the story to explain the increasing influence of the demagogue Cimon, which prompted his rival, Pericles, who was not as rich, to introduce juror pay. Aristotle's main argument is omitted by the epitome, however. Only the banal details are preserved. In fact, the epitome does not even mention Pericles at all. Furthermore, although Heraclides uses similar vocabulary as Aristotle,[24] his paraphrase is inaccurate here. Aristotle mentions three points regarding Cimon's generosity: (1) Cimon performed the *leiturgiai* magnificently; (2) he gave the fellow demesmen (Laciads)

---

[20] It is also possible that the antecedent of ἐξ ὧν is τοῖς βουλομένοις, in which case the second part could be translated as 'Out of these people, he invited many to dinner'.

[21] So Bloch (1940: 36); Dilts (1971: 8). Schneidewin (1847: 39-40) attributed the confusion of Ephialtes with Cimon to the later excerptor.

[22] Chambers (1990: 267; 1994: 68); Gigon (1987: 565); Kenyon (1903: 88); Mathieu and Haussoullier (1930: 78); Oppermann (1928: 103); Rühl (1892: 702 n. 1); Sandys (1912: 266). Similarly, Thalheim (1914: 111) changed the text to Ἐφιάλτης <...> τοὺς ἰδίους ἀγροὺς, etc.

[23] Kaibel and von Wilamowitz-Moellendorff (1898: 84); von Holzinger (1891: 440). So also Polito (2001: 37, 212, 232, 235). Elsewhere, however, Polito (2001: 14 n. 3; 15) assumes a lacuna after Ἐφιάλτης.

[24] Cf. Arist. *Ath.* 27.3: ἔπειτα τῶν δημοτῶν ἔτρεφε **πολλούς** ... ἔτι δὲ <u>τὰ χωρία πάντα</u> ἄφρακτα ἦν, ὅπως ἐξῇ <u>τῷ βουλομένῳ τῆς ὀπώρας ἀπολαύειν</u>.

who came to his house a modest provision; (3) his fields had no fences, so that anyone was allowed to pick the fruits. Heraclides only mentions the third point but adds that the food of the fields was used to organise a dinner for many people. However, Aristotle nowhere mentions such a dinner and certainly does not state that the fruits which were picked were used for any dinner organised by Cimon. Heraclides' text is probably based on a misinterpretation of Aristotle's words τῶν δημοτῶν ἔτρεφε πολλούς in point (2) as referring to a dinner organised at Cimon's house. What Aristotle means by ἔτρεφε πολλούς is explained in the subsequent sentence in the *Athenaion Politeia* (as is indicated by the particle γάρ): every day, any of the Laciads were allowed to come to him to receive a modest *livelihood* (ἐξῆν γὰρ τῷ βουλομένῳ Λακιαδῶν, καθ' ἑκάστην τὴν ἡμέραν ἐλθόντι παρ' αὐτὸν ἔχειν τὰ μέτρια). A similar error is found in Plutarch (*Cim.* 10.1-2), who also speaks of a dinner.[25] Note also that, in Aristotle, point (2) only extends to Cimon's demesmen, a detail which Heraclides glosses over.

Cleon and the Thirty

> Κλέων παραλαβὼν διέφθειρε τὸ πολίτευμα, καὶ ἔτι μᾶλλον οἱ μετ' αὐτόν, οἳ πάντας[26] ἀνομίας ἐνέπλησαν, καὶ ἀνεῖλον οὐκ ἐλάσσους αφ΄. τούτων δὲ καταλυθέντων Θρασύβουλος καὶ Ῥίνων προειστήκεισαν, ὃς ἦν ἀνὴρ καλὸς καὶ ἀγαθός. (Heraclid. Lemb. *Pol.* 6)

> Cleon took over the government and corrupted it[27], and even more so those who came after him. They filled everyone with lawlessness and eliminated no fewer than 1500 people. When they were deposed, the most prominent men were Thrasybulus and Rhinon, who was an honourable man.

After Ephialtes/Cimon, the epitome jumps to Cleon (*Ath.* 28.3), skipping Pericles and the overview of politicians up to that point (*Ath.* 28.1-2). Heraclides claims that Cleon corrupted the government (διέφθειρε τὸ πολίτευμα). While Aristotle does use the verb διαφθεῖραι, he says something slightly different in the original text. In the *Athenaion Politeia*, it is the *people* who become corrupted (διαφθεῖραι τὸν δῆμον). This discussion is part of an opposition between the notables and the *demos* with their respective champions (a thread throughout the historical part of the *Athenaion Politeia*):[28] Nicias championed the former, and Cleon the latter. The epitome has omitted Nicias and has generalised the corruptive influence of Cleon to the entire political system. Heraclides also adds the verb παραλαβών on the basis of the general context in Aristotle. For in Aristotle, Cleon is Pericles' successor as champion of the *demos*. Heraclides therefore probably originally discussed Pericles as well, but the excerptor has omitted that section, so that, in the current form of the text, it is unclear from whom Cleon took over the position.

---

[25] In Plutarch, the reference to a dinner probably goes back to Theopompus, who seems to be Plutarch's source in *Cim.* 10.1 and who did actually mention such a dinner (*FGrH* 115 F 89 = Ath. 12.533a-c).

[26] The word πάντας should perhaps be corrected to πάντα, as proposed by Heyne *ap.* Koeler (1804: 30). So also Blass (1903: 115); Chambers (1990: 72; 1994: 68); Gigon (1987: 565); Hose (2002: 91); Kaibel and von Wilamowitz-Moellendorff (1898: 84); Kenyon (1903: 88; 1920); Mathieu and Haussoullier (1930: 78); Oppermann (1928: 103); Sandys (1912: 266); Thalheim (1914: 111); von Holzinger (1891: 439).

[27] Alternatively, it is possible that τὸ πολίτευμα means 'the body of citizens'. In that case, it is only the object of διέφθειρε but not of παραλαβών, whose original object (perhaps something like τὴν δημαγωγίαν) was then presumably omitted by the later excerptor.

[28] Aristotle lists the previous champions in *Ath.* 28.2.

The epitome then moves on to 'those who came after him' (οἱ μετ' αὐτόν) and states that these corrupted the system even more. In Aristotle's original text, the pair Nicias/Cleon is followed by the pair Theramenes/Cleophon. However, in *Ath.* 28.3, neither Theramenes nor Cleophon is mentioned for their corrupting influence. In fact, it is the successors of Cleophon who 'wished to be insolent and pander to the masses' (ἀπὸ δὲ Κλεοφῶντος ἤδη διεδέχοντο συνεχῶς τὴν δημαγωγίαν οἱ μάλιστα βουλόμενοι θρασύνεσθαι καὶ χαρίζεσθαι τοῖς πολλοῖς πρὸς τὰ παραυτίκα βλέποντες). It is possible that Heraclides inaccurately spoke of Cleon's successors instead of Cleophon's successors, confusing the similar names. Alternatively, it can be the result of another infelicitous cut-and-paste intervention by the excerptor. However, Heraclides may have also expanded the succession of bad politicians to Cleophon because of what Aristotle later writes in *Ath.* 34.1, viz. that the populace was deceived by Cleophon in rejecting peace negotiations with the Spartans.

The subsequent information is more problematic. The epitome states that 'they filled everyone with lawlessness and eliminated no fewer than 1500 people'. Without external knowledge, we would connect this with the successors of Cleon, who have just been mentioned. However, the elimination of 1500 people refers to the tyranny of the Thirty and closely follows Aristotle's original phrasing.[29] The lawlessness (ἀνομία) is a paraphrase of the injustice of the Thirty, described in more detail by Aristotle (*Ath.* 35.4). Heraclides is unlikely to have considered the Thirty successors of Cleon. Therefore, a new excerpt probably starts with οἳ πάντας ἀνομίας ἐνέπλησαν, in which again the subject is not the same as that of the previous sentence.[30] In this process, Aristotle's discussion of the constitution of the Four Hundred and the Five Thousand (*Ath.* 29-34.1) and the installation of the Thirty (*Ath.* 34.1-3) has also been omitted. The elimination of 1500 people is the only detail mentioned with regard to the tyranny of the Thirty. The actual constitutional changes, particularly the cancellation of the laws of Ephialtes and Solon (*Ath.* 35.1-3) and the enrolment of the Three Thousand (*Ath.* 36), are omitted.

The epitome then immediately skips to the deposing of the Thirty (*Ath.* 38.1), glossing over the execution of Theramenes (*Ath.* 37) and the conflict between the people from the city and the exiles occupying the Piraeus and Munichia (*Ath.* 37.1; 38.1; 38.3). It also omits any reference to the Ten, who were appointed after fall of the Thirty but were removed because they did not do their job; these were subsequently replaced by a new college of Ten (*Ath.* 38.1-3). The epitome next mentions Thrasybulus and Rhinon as 'the most prominent men' (προειστήκεισαν). Although Aristotle uses the same verb, he actually names Rhinon and *Phyllus* (*Ath.* 38.3: προειστήκεσαν δ' αὐτῶν μάλιστα Ῥίνων τε ὁ Παιανιεὺς καὶ Φάυλλος ὁ Ἀχερδούσιος). In fact, he mentions them as the most prominent *among the (new group of) Ten*. Heraclides supplied Thrasybulus from *Ath.* 37.1, where Aristotle states that, under Thrasybulus, the exiles conquered Phyle. However, Rhinon belonged to the other side of the conflict and was sent (together with Phayllus) to negotiate a reconciliation between the exiles and the people from the city. Because there is no reference to the Ten, the epitome can repurpose the verb προειστήκεσαν to denote the most prominent politicians *tout court*. The omission of Phyllus is no real surprise, since only Rhinon is mentioned as an important politician afterwards (*Ath.* 38.4). After mentioning Rhinon, Heraclides adds that he was 'an honourable man', which is a

---

[29] Arist. *Ath.* 35.4: οὐκ ἐλάττους <u>ἀνῃρήκεσαν</u> ἢ χιλίους πεντακοσίους.

[30] See also Polito (2001: 40-41, 207-08). Dilts (1971: 8) held Heraclides himself responsible for not supplying an antecedent for the relative pronoun.

paraphrase of what Aristotle says ('Rhinon and his supporters were praised for their good will towards the people').

Themistocles, Aristides, and the Areopagus

> Θεμιστοκλῆς καὶ Ἀριστείδης. καὶ ἡ ἐξ Ἀρείου πάγου βουλὴ πολλὰ ἐδύνατο. (Heraclid. Lemb. *Pol.* 7)

> Themistocles and Aristides. And the Areopagus council had a lot of power.

From Rhinon the epitome suddenly jumps back to Themistocles, Aristides, and the Areopagus council (i.e. the situation around the second Persian War). This is the only part of the section on Athens that seems out of place in the epitome. Some scholars have therefore inserted it before Ἐφιάλτης, between *Pol.* 4 and *Pol.* 5.[31] It is possible, however, that the current position is due to the excerptor; he may have initially forgotten to excerpt it, adding it later at the end of the historical section.[32]

Most scholars punctuate after Θεμιστοκλῆς καὶ Ἀριστείδης, thus making it an empty lemma.[33] This is probably correct. Note, however, that – just like in the case of Ephialtes – the medieval scribes do not punctuate but consider it part of the same sentence as καὶ ἡ ἐξ Ἀρείου πάγου βουλὴ πολλὰ ἐδύνατο.[34]

It is unclear what sections of the *Athenaion Politeia* the reference to Themistocles and Aristides in the epitome is exactly based on. It could be *Ath.* 23.3 (ἦσαν δὲ προστάται τοῦ δήμου κατὰ τούτους τοὺς καιροὺς Ἀριστείδης ὁ Λυσιμάχου καὶ Θεμιστοκλῆς ὁ Νεοκλέους),[35] especially since the subsequent note on the Areopagus appears to be taken from *Ath.* 23.1 (μετὰ δὲ τὰ Μηδικὰ πάλιν ἴσχυσεν ἡ ἐν Ἀρείῳ πάγῳ βουλή). However, the epitome names them in reverse order (Θεμιστοκλῆς καὶ Ἀριστείδης, not Ἀριστείδης καὶ Θεμιστοκλῆς). Heraclides could have reversed the order, but it is also possible that the names are actually taken from Aristotle's survey of the champions of the *demos* and nobility in *Ath.* 28.2, where Themistocles is indeed named before Aristides (μετὰ δὲ ταῦτα τοῦ μὲν δήμου προειστήκει Ξάνθιππος, τῶν δὲ γνωρίμων Μιλτιάδης, ἔπειτα Θεμιστοκλῆς καὶ Ἀριστείδης).[36] In either case, it appears that the epitome has changed the order of the narrative. For Aristotle first discussed the increased power of the Areopagus before commenting on Aristides and Themistocles.[37]

---

[31] Chambers (1990: 72, 437; 1994: 68); Kenyon (1903: 88; 1920); Mathieu and Haussoullier (1930: 78); Sandys (1912: 265). Schneidewin (1847: 5; 41-42) simply deleted the words Θεμιστοκλῆς καὶ Ἀριστείδης καὶ. However, even if we were to consider this an interpolation, the note on the Areopagus is still out of place.

[32] So Polito (2001: 42-43).

[33] Blass (1903: 116); Bloch (1940: 35); Dilts (1971: 16); Gigon (1987: 565); Kaibel and von Wilamowitz-Moellendorff (1898: 85); Kenyon (1903: 88; 1920); Mathieu and Haussoullier (1930: 78); Polito (2001: 14, 16, 42-43, 212, 232, 235); Rose (1886: 372); Sandys (1912: 265); von Holzinger (1891: 440). Chambers (1990: 72); (1994: 68) assumed a lacuna after Θεμιστοκλῆς καὶ Ἀριστείδης.

[34] So also Oppermann (1928: 104) and Thalheim (1914: 112). Most scribes of the x group of manuscripts (Laurentianus 60.19 fol. 210ᵛ (d), Ambrosianus C 4 sup. fol. 153ʳ (g), Parisinus gr. 1694 fol. 67ʳ (b), Vossianus gr. Q 18 fol. 24ʳ (k)) even write ἐδύναντο instead of ἐδύνατο.

[35] So Chambers (1990: 72); Kaibel and von Wilamowitz-Moellendorff (1898: 85); Oppermann (1928: 104); Rhodes (2002: 165 n. 7); Sandys (1912: 265).

[36] So von Holzinger (1891: 440).

[37] Theoretically, the note on the Areopagus might also be based on Aristotle's survey of the changes in the constitution

Finally, in his paraphrase of the note about the Areopagus, Heraclides has changed an important detail. Aristotle states that the power of the Areopagus increased *again* (πάλιν). For the Areopagus had been powerful before the reforms of Solon (cf. Arist. *Ath.* 3.6; 4.4). Also, the aorist ἴσχυσεν indicates a change with respect to the previous situation.[38] Heraclides has turned this into the bland πολλὰ ἐδύνατο. The epitome also omits the historical context for the increase of the power of the Areopagus. They were able to increase their power, since – according to Aristotle at least – they played a decisive role in the Battle of Salamis: when the generals were all in panic, the Areopagus had been responsible for manning the triremes.

This is where, in the epitome, the historical section ends. It thus omits the regulations after the restoration of democracy (particularly the amnesty law) and the discussion of the politician Archinus (*Ath.* 39-40).

Sortitive functions: the *astynomoi* and the Eleven

> καὶ τῶν ὁδῶν ἐπιμελοῦνται, ὅπως μή τινες ἀνοικοδομῶσιν αὐτὰς ἢ δρυφάκτους ὑπερτείνωσιν. ὁμοίως δὲ καθιστᾶσι καὶ τοὺς ια΄, τοὺς ἐπιμελησομένους τῶν ἐν τῷ δεσμωτηρίῳ. (Heraclid. Lemb. *Pol.* 8)

> And they see to it that nobody constructs buildings that obstruct the streets or extends balconies over them. Similarly, they also appoint the Eleven, who have to take care of those in prison.

Heraclides has now moved on to the descriptive part of the *Athenaion Politeia*. This is where the epitome becomes extremely scant. It omits the discussion of the registration of new citizens (*Ath.* 42), the council and assembly (*Ath.* 43-49), the *athlothetai* (*Ath.* 60), and the courts (*Ath.* 63-69). Of all the officials that are appointed by lot (discussed in *Ath.* 50-54),[39] the epitome only discusses the *astynomoi* (who are not even mentioned by name) and the Eleven. However, the excerptor is once again randomly cutting and pasting and does not specify that the subject of ἐπιμελοῦνται is not the same as that of the previous sentence. This creates the false impression that the people whose tasks are described here are the members of the Areopagus![40]

Of the *astynomoi*'s tasks described by Aristotle, the epitome only mentions the regulations regarding the construction of buildings and balconies (*Ath.* 50.1-2). All the other tasks are omitted: in Aristotle, they are also responsible for keeping the price of hiring pipe-girls, harp-girls, and lyre-girls in check, see to it that dung collectors do not deposit their dung too close to the city, and take up people who die in the streets. Heraclides' description uses vocabulary

---

in *Ath.* 41.2 (ἕκτη δ' ἡ μετὰ τὰ Μηδικά [sc. μεταβολὴ], τῆς ἐξ Ἀρείου πάγου βουλῆς ἐπιστατούσης). So von Holzinger (1891: 441). However, the words πολλὰ ἐδύνατο are more likely to be a paraphrase of ἴσχυσεν.

[38] See also Polito (2001: 43-44, 209-10).

[39] These are the Repairers of Temples (ἱερῶν ἐπισκευασταί), the *astynomoi, agoranomoi, metronomoi, sitophylakes*, Overseers of the Exchange (ἐμπορίου ἐπιμεληταί), the Eleven, *eisagogeis*, the Forty, Road-Builders (ὁδοποιοί), *logistai* and their advocates (συνήγοροι), the secretary by prytany (γραμματεὺς κατὰ πρυτανείαν), the secretary for the laws (γραμματεὺς ἐπὶ τοὺς νόμους), *hieropoioi*, the archon for Salamis (εἰς Σαλαμῖνα ἄρχων), and the demarch for Piraeus (εἰς Πειραιέα δήμαρχος).

[40] Gigon (1987: 565), Hose (2002: 91), and Thalheim (1914: 112) assumed a lacuna before καὶ τῶν ὁδῶν ἐπιμελοῦνται. See also Chambers (1990: 437; 1994: 68); Kenyon (1903: 88; 1920). According to Schneidewin (1847: 42-43), the implied subject of ἐπιμελοῦνται is οἱ Ἀθηναῖοι.

similar to that of Aristotle.[41] Note also that Heraclides has preserved the use of the present tense (ἐπιμελοῦνται[42]) for the descriptive section of the *Athenaion Politeia*. This suggests that, if the epitome uses present tenses in the description of other constitutions, it probably refers to Aristotle's time.[43]

From the *astynomoi* the epitome moves on to the Eleven (*Ath.* 52.1). Heraclides follows Aristotle nearly verbatim here.[44] He only adds ὁμοίως, which probably refers to the way in which they were appointed (i.e. κλήρῳ). This suggests that Heraclides originally discussed more functions chosen by lot, which the excerptor has omitted. Of the tasks performed by the Eleven, the epitome only mentions their responsibility for taking care of the people in prison. The other, more important tasks described by Aristotle (their function as executioners and their task of bringing before the court people accused of robbery, kidnapping, and brigandage as well as a list of confiscated property, and the so-called ἐνδείξεις, i.e. indications against disqualified officials) are omitted.

The nine archons

> εἰσὶ δὲ καὶ θ´ ἄρχοντες, θεσμοθέται ϛ´, οἱ δοκιμασθέντες ὀμνύουσι δικαίως ἄρξειν καὶ δῶρα μὴ λήψεσθαι ἢ ἀνδριάντα χρυσοῦν ἀναθήσειν. ὁ δὲ βασιλεὺς τὰ κατὰ τὰς θυσίας διοικεῖ καὶ τὰ πολέμια. (Heraclid. Lemb. *Pol.* 8)

> There are also 9 archons, 6 thesmothetes; those who[45] have been vetted swear that they will exercise their office justly and will not take bribes, or else they will dedicate a golden statue. The *basileus* administers everything related to the sacrifices and everything related to war.

From the Eleven, the epitome jumps to the nine archons (*Ath.* 55), skipping all the other functions chosen by lot. In its current form, the text gives the impression that Heraclides mentioned the thesmothetes as a separate category alongside the nine archons, which is obviously false. We should probably insert a colon after ἄρχοντες.[46] Like Aristotle, Heraclides probably originally listed all the nine archons (thesmothetes, (eponymous) archon, *basileus*, and polemarch),[47] but the excerptor has only kept the reference to the thesmothetes. The epitome then discusses

---

[41] Cf. Arist. *Ath.* 50.2: καὶ τὰς ὁδοὺς κωλύουσι κατοικοδομεῖν, καὶ **δρυφάκτους** ὑπὲρ τῶν ὁδῶν ὑπερτείνειν.

[42] This is the reading of Parisinus suppl. gr. 352 fol. 132ʳ (V). The manuscripts of the other branch, the x family, however, read ἐπεμελοῦντο.

[43] According to Polito (2001: 218-19), the epitome has sometimes transposed present verbs to past verbs, viz. in the section on Iasus (*Pol.* 74) and Thespiae (*Pol.* 76).

[44] Cf. Arist. *Ath.* 52.1: καθ[ι]στᾶσι δὲ καὶ τοὺς ἔνδεκα κλήρῳ, τοὺς ἐπιμελησομένους τῶν ἐν τῷ δεσμωτηρίῳ. Contrary to Chambers (1994: 46), I print κλήρῳ τοὺς instead of κληρωτοὺς here.

[45] In all likelihood, we should correct οἱ to οἳ, i.e. read the relative pronoun. So also Blass (1903: 116); Chambers (1994: 68); Kaibel and von Wilamowitz-Moellendorff (1898: 85); Kenyon (1903: 88; 1920); Mathieu and Haussoullier (1930: 79); Müller (1848: 209); Oppermann (1928: 104); Rose (1886: 372); Sandys (1912: 266); Schneidewin (1847: 5); Thalheim (1914: 112). I assume that a new excerpted started here. The original antecedent was the nine archons (and not simply the thesmothetes).

[46] So Kenyon (1903: 88; 1920); von Holzinger (1891: 441-42).

[47] Cf. Arist. *Ath.* 55.1: οἱ δὲ καλούμενοι **ἐννέα ἄρχοντες** τὸ μὲν ἐξ ἀρχῆς ὃν τρόπον καθίσταντο, ε[ἴ]ρηται· [νῦν] δὲ κληροῦσιν θεσμοθέτας μὲν ἓξ καὶ γραμματέα τούτοις, ἔτι δ᾽ ἄρχοντα καὶ βασιλ[έ]α καὶ πολέμαρχον κατὰ μέρος ἐξ ἑκάστης φυλῆς.

the oath of the archons (*Ath.* 55.5), skipping Aristotle's lengthy description of their vetting (*Ath.* 55.2-4). Heraclides' phrasing again closely follows Aristotle's.[48]

Of the nine archons, the only one that is explicitly named after this is the *basileus*, and the only function that is mentioned is his administration of 'everything related to the sacrifices' (τὰ κατὰ τὰς θυσίας). The *basileus*' role in public lawsuits (*Ath.* 57.2-4), however, is omitted. The detail about the administration of sacrifices is also imprecise. Aristotle speaks of 'all the *traditional* sacrifices' (τὰς πατρίους θυσίας διοικεῖ οὗτος πάσας), which is a reference to the fact that the *basileus* presides over the mysteries of Eleusis and the Lenaea, as Aristotle explained in the original text (*Ath.* 57.1).

Finally, the epitome surprisingly seems to conclude that the *basileus* also administers 'everything related to war' (καὶ τὰ πολέμια). Most scholars have therefore suggested that this last detail refers to the polemarch, the last of the archons treated by Aristotle (*Ath.* 58).[49] However, Aristotle does not present the polemarch as holding a military function either.[50] Although it is possible that Heraclides incorrectly claimed this, it is more likely that we have one final new excerpt, now from the section on the military functions, described in *Ath.* 61.[51] The excerpt probably goes back to *Ath.* 61.1.[52]

Conclusion

The comparison between the epitome and the original *Athenaion Politeia* shows that Heraclides preserves the order of Aristotle's original text (with the exception of the note on Themistocles, Aristides, and the Areopagus, which may be a secondary excerpt added at the end of the historical section). This means that, for the other constitutions, the epitome probably preserves the original structure as well. However, in its current form, the epitome gives a heavily distorted picture of the original. It is certainly no accurate summary. The text consists of snippets of usually isolated information. A change of subject is often not indicated, and information is juxtaposed without much coherence. This means that we should be careful with the excerpts on other constitutions: information that is seemingly connected with a specific person might have originally concerned a totally different one. In terms of the vocabulary used, Heraclides often stays close to the original, sometimes even following

---

[48] Cf. Arist. *Ath.* 55.5: **δοκιμασθέν<τες>** δὲ τοῦτον τὸν τρόπον βαδίζουσι πρὸς τὸν λίθον ἐφ' ὁ[ῦ] τὰ τόμι' ἐστίν, ἐφ' οὗ καὶ οἱ διαιτηταὶ ὀμόσαντες ἀποφαίνονται τὰς διαίτας καὶ οἱ μάρτυρες ἐξόμνυνται τὰς μαρτυρίας· ἀναβάντες δ' ἐπὶ τοῦτον **ὀμνύουσιν δικαίως ἄρξειν** καὶ κατὰ τοὺς νόμους, **καὶ δῶρα μὴ λήψεσθαι** τῆς ἀρχῆς ἕνεκα, κἄν τι λάβωσι ἀνδριάντα ἀναθήσειν χρυσοῦν.

[49] Kaibel and von Wilamowitz-Moellendorff (1898: 85); Koeler in Volckhausen and Koeler (1801: 9); Koeler (1804: 32-33); Polito (2001: 47-48, 211); Rhodes (2002: 165 n. 8); Schneidewin (1847: 46); von Fritz and Kapp (1950: 207 n. 8). Chambers (1990: 72); (1994: 68), Kenyon (1903: 88; 1920), Mathieu and Haussoullier (1930: 79), and Sandys (1912: 231, 266) supplemented καὶ <ὁ πολέμαρχος> τὰ πολέμια. Similarly, Korais (1805: 206, 350) conjectured <ὁ δὲ πολέμαρχος ταῦτά τε> καὶ τὰ πολεμικά.

[50] The only thing connected to war that is mentioned by Aristotle in reference to the polemarch is the fact that he organises the funeral competition for those who died in war (*Ath.* 58.1). In his description of the 'ancient constitution' (*Ath.* 3.2), however, the polemarch – as the name suggests – appears to have originally had a real military function (δευτέρα δ' ἐπικατέστη π[ολ]εμαρχία διὰ τὸ γενέσθαι τινὰς τῶν βασιλέων τὰ πολέμια μαλακούς). Indeed, in the description of Cleisthenes' reforms (*Ath.* 22.2), the polemarch is still mentioned as the commander of the whole army (τῆς δὲ ἁπάσης στρατιᾶς ἡγεμὼν ἦν ὁ πολέμαρχος).

[51] Note that three manuscripts of the x family (Laurentianus 60.19 fol. 210ᵛ (d), Ambrosianus C 4 sup. fol. 153ʳ (g) and Parisinus gr. 1693 fol. 56ᵛ (a)) punctuate after διοικεῖ.

[52] Cf. Arist. *Ath.* 61.1: χειροτονοῦσι δὲ καὶ τὰς πρὸς τὸν πόλεμον ἀρχὰς ἁπάσας.

Aristotle nearly verbatim. But he sometimes also paraphrases more extensive sections in his own words and seems to have occasionally created inaccuracies.

If we look at the information that is included, the epitome on Athens – in its current form at least – shows a far greater interest in the historical section than in the descriptive section of the *Athenaion Politeia*: 83% of the text is derived from the historical part, while only 17% goes back to the descriptive part. Moreover, the epitome shows no interest in Aristotle's main argument, viz. that the constitution goes through *metabolai*, especially in the conflict between *demos* and aristocracy. The epitome focuses more on the individual politicians. Most of the central politicians discussed by Aristotle are mentioned, but there are a few conspicuous omissions (Miltiades, Pericles, Nicias, Theramenes, and Thucydides). The epitome also often highlights details that, in the grand constitutional scheme, are not that crucial (such as Solon's travels or Cimon's charity) and often omits the important political changes with which these details are connected.

It is not always easy to separate interventions by Heraclides from interventions by the later excerptor.[53] This is why, in this contribution, I have often spoken of 'the epitome' rather than 'Heraclides'. One point which can be attributed to Heraclides with relative certainty is that the text is structured according to lemmas, i.e. personal names are usually put at the start of the section. This is also seen in Heraclides' epitome of Hermippus' biographies (P.Oxy. XI 1367 = *FGrH* 1026 F 3).[54] Comparison with that papyrus fragment also shows that the random cut-and-paste technique, in which information is sometimes (seemingly) connected with the wrong person and some lemmas appear as empty, is due to the excerptor, not Heraclides. Some scholars assume lacunas in the transmitted text, but it rather seems to have been a feature of the excerptor, carelessly chopping up Heraclides' text. In fact, when Heraclides moves on to another section in Aristotle, he often adds contextual information. Thus, he specifies that Hipparchus is Pisistratus' son and Hippias' brother and adds that the Eleven are appointed 'in a similar way' (sc. by lot). So Heraclides cannot be blamed for the excessive decontextualisation of the Aristotelian information. Yet, while the excerptor must be responsible for many omissions, the extreme selectiveness is not always due to him alone. In the epitome of Hermippus, for instance, the only thing which Heraclides has to say about Buzyges is: 'is said to have given laws; he is also mentioned by the poet Lasus' (Βουζύγης· νομο[θετῆ]]σαι· μέμνηται δ' α[ὐτοῦ] | καὶ Λᾶσος ὁ ποιη[τής]).

It is difficult to determine the audience for which Heraclides wrote his epitome. According to Gallo, Heraclides' epitomes were written to be used in schools.[55] Bloch, in his turn, assumed that Heraclides wrote his epitome of Aristotle's *Constitutions* as a preparatory work for his *Histories*.[56] According to Bloch, Heraclides' use of Aristotle's *Constitutions* and/or *Barbarian Customs* in his *Histories* is indicated by a fragment in Festus on the foundation of Rome.[57] However, as I have argued in another article, that fragment is more likely to be a fragment of

---

[53] See especially the discussion in Polito (2001: 229-43).

[54] See Bloch (1940: 34-35); Polito (2001: 234).

[55] Gallo (1975: 28, 30-31).

[56] Bloch (1940: 38). See also Ottone (2002: 72). *Contra* Schorn (2018: 296 n. 59).

[57] Festus 17 p. 329 Lindsay (p. 269 Mueller, p. 364 Thewr) = Heraclid. Lemb. *FHG* III, 168 F 1. So Bloch (1940: 37). Cf. Arist. F 609(1) Rose³ = F 700 Gigon = D.H. 1.72.3-4 and Arist. F 609(2) Rose³ = F 701 Gigon = Plu. *Quaestiones Romanae* 6.265b-d. Heraclides is also cited by Serv. auct. *Aen.* 1.273 and Solin. 1.2.

Heraclides' epitome instead.[58] A new interpretation of Heraclides' epitomes was proposed by Schorn. In his view, Heraclides' main biographical work was his epitome of Sotion,[59] while his epitomes of Hermippus (on the Seven Sages and Pythagoras) and of Satyrus were supplements that offered information not found in Sotion. According to Schorn, Heraclides' epitome of Aristotle's *Constitutions* may have been a similar reference work, to which the epitome of Hermippus' work on lawgivers served as a supplement.[60] However we judge Heraclides' activity as an *epitomator*, it is clear that – unlike his epitome of Sotion[61] – the epitome of the *Constitutions* did not replace the original. There are only two fragments of Heraclides that appear to go back to his epitome of Aristotle,[62] as opposed to the numerous fragments of Aristotle's *Constitutions*.

Finally, the comparison of the epitome with the original text which I have given in this article has left one important aspect of the epitome untouched: the preference for sensational, sexual, and macabre anecdotes. Especially stories about mutilations and adultery seem to have enjoyed some preference. For instance, the only information reported in the section on Elis is that the tyrant Pantaleon castrated ambassadors and forced them to eat their own testicles (*Pol.* 21). This type of information is absent from the extant text of the *Athenaion Politeia*. But in the lost section, the epitome does not neglect to mention the adultery of Limone, daughter of the archon Hippomenes, and the severe punishment by her father (*Pol.* 1). Thus, more so than Aristotle, Heraclides' epitome seems to have been written not only for instruction but also for entertainment.

Bibliography

Bauer, A. 1891. Literarische und historische Forschungen zu Aristoteles Ἀθηναίων πολιτεία. Munich: Beck.

Blass, F. 1903. Aristotelis Πολιτεία Ἀθηναίων (Bibliotheca Scriptorum Graecorum et Romanorum Teubneriana). 4th ed. Leipzig: Teubner.

Bloch, H. 1940. Herakleides Lembos and his Epitome of Aristotle's Politeiai. Transactions of the American Philological Association 71: 27–39.

Chambers, M. 1990. Aristoteles. Staat der Athener (Aristoteles Werke in deutscher Übersetzung 10.1). Berlin: Akademie-Verlag.

Chambers, M. 1994. Aristoteles. Ἀθηναίων πολιτεία (Bibliotheca Scriptorum Graecorum et Romanorum Teubneriana). 2nd ed. Stuttgart - Leipzig: Teubner.

Dilts, M.R. 1971. Heraclidis Lembi Excerpta Politiarum (Greek, Roman and Byzantine Monographs 5). Durham (NC): Duke University.

Fuks, A. 1953. The Ancestral Constitution. Four Studies in Athenian Party Politics at the End of the Fifth Century B.C. London: Routledge and Kegan Paul.

---

[58] Verhasselt (2019: 674-80).

[59] This is suggested by the fact that Heraclides' epitome of Sotion (in six books) was about half as long as the original text (in thirteen books).

[60] Schorn (2018: 294-96).

[61] See Schorn (2018: 298-99).

[62] The other text – apart from the fragment on the foundation of Rome (cf. n. 55) – that might be a fragment of Heraclides' epitome of Aristotle is found in Ath. 13.566a (= *FHG* III, 168 F 2) and deals with the beauty of Spartan men and women (with an anecdote about king Archidamus II). See my discussion in Verhasselt (2019: 281-82).

Gallo, I. 1975. Frammenti biografici da papiri. Vol. I. La biografia politica (Testi e commenti 1). Rome: Edizioni dell'Ateneo.

Gigon, O. 1987. Aristotelis Opera. Vol. III. Berlin - New York: de Gruyter.

Haussoullier, B. 1891. Aristote. Constitution d'Athènes traduite (Bibliothèque de l'École des hautes études. Sciences philologiques et historiques 89). Paris: Émile Bouillon.

Hose, M. 2002. Aristoteles. Die historischen Fragmente (Aristoteles Werke in deutscher Übersetzung 20.3). Darmstadt: Wissenschaftliche Buchgesellschaft.

Hude, K. 1916. Aristoteles. Der Staat der Athener. Für den Schulgebrauch erklärt (Griechische und lateinische Schriftsteller. Ausgaben mit Anmerkungen). 2nd ed. Leipzig - Berlin: Teubner.

Kaibel, G. and von Wilamowitz-Moellendorff, U. 1898. Aristotelis Πολιτεία Ἀθηναίων. 3rd ed. Berlin: Weidmann.

Kenyon, F.G. 1892. Ἀθηναίων πολιτεία. Aristotle on the Constitution of Athens. 3rd ed. Oxford: Clarendon.

Kenyon, F.G. 1895. Aristotle on the Athenian Constitution. Translated with Introduction and Notes. 2nd ed. London: George Bell and Sons.

Kenyon, F.G. 1903. Aristotelis Res publica Atheniensium (Supplementum Aristotelicum 3.1). Berlin: Reimer.

Kenyon, F.G. 1920. Aristotelis Atheniensium respublica (Scriptorum classicorum bibliotheca Oxoniensis). Oxford: Clarendon.

Koeler, G.D. 1804. Heraclidae Pontici fragmenta de rebus publicis. Halle: Officina Rengeriana.

Korais, D. 1805. Πρόδρομος Ἑλληνικῆς βιβλιοθήκης, περιέχων Κλαυδίου Αἰλιανοῦ τὴν ποικίλην ἱστορίαν, Ἡρακλείδου τοῦ Ποντικοῦ, Νικολάου τοῦ Δαμασκηνοῦ, τὰ σωζόμενα. Paris: Didot.

Levi, M.A. 1968. Commento storico alla Respublica Atheniensium di Aristotele (Testi e documenti per lo studio dell'antichità 19). Milan - Varese: Istituto editoriale cisalpino.

Maddoli, G. 1975. Cronologia e storia. Studi comparati sull' "Athenaion Politeia" di Aristotele (Pubblicazioni degli Istituti di Storia della Facoltà di Lettere e Filosofia). Perugia: Tipografia Porziuncola.

Mathieu, G. and Haussoullier, B. 1930. Aristote. Constitution d'Athènes. Texte établi et traduit (Collection des Universités de France). 2nd ed. Paris: Belles Lettres.

Montana, F. 1996. L'Athenaion Politeia di Aristotele negli scholia vetera ad Aristofane (Biblioteca di studi antichi 80). Pisa - Rome: Istituti editoriali e poligrafici internazionali.

Moore, J.M. 1975. Aristotle and Xenophon on Democracy and Oligarchy. Aristotle's The Constitution of Athens. The Constitution of the Athenians Ascribed to Xenophon the Orator. Xenophon's Politeia of the Spartans. The Boeotian Constitution from the Oxyrhynchus Historian. Translated with Introductions and Commentary. Berkeley - Los Angeles: University of California Press.

Müller, K. 1848. Fragmenta Historicorum Graecorum. Vol. II. Paris: Didot.

Oppermann, H. 1928. Aristoteles. Ἀθηναίων πολιτεία (Bibliotheca Scriptorum Graecorum et Romanorum Teubneriana). Leipzig: Teubner.

Ottone, G. 2002. Libyka. Testimonianze e frammenti (I frammenti degli storici greci 1). Tivoli: Edizioni TORED.

Polito, M. 2001. Dagli scritti di Eraclide sulle costituzioni. Un commento storico (Università degli studi di Salerno. Quaderni del Dipartimento di scienze dell'antichità 26). Naples: Arte Tipografica.

Rhodes, P.J. 1993. A Commentary on the Aristotelian Athenaion Politeia. 2nd ed. Oxford: Clarendon.

Rhodes, P.J. 2002. Aristotle. The Athenian Constitution. Translated with Introduction and Notes (Penguin Classics). 2nd ed. London: Penguin Books.

Rhodes, P.J. 2017. The Athenian Constitution Written in the School of Aristotle with an Introduction, Translation and Notes (Aris and Phillips Classical Texts). Liverpool: University Press.

Rose, V. 1886. Aristotelis qui ferebantur librorum fragmenta (Bibliotheca scriptorum Graecorum et Romanorum Teubneriana). Leipzig: Teubner.

Rühl, F. 1892. Der Staat der Athener und kein Ende, in Jahrbücher für classische Philologie. Supplementband 18: 673–706. Leipzig: Teubner.

Sandys, J.E. 1912. Ἀριστοτέλους Ἀθηναίων πολιτεία. Aristotle's Constitution of Athens. A Revised Text with an Introduction, Critical and Explanatory Notes, Testimonia and Indices. 2nd ed. London: Macmillan and Co.

Schneidewin, F.G. 1847. Ἐκ τῶν Ἡρακλείδου περὶ πολιτειῶν. Heraclidis politiarum quae extant. Göttingen: Vandenhoeck and Ruprecht.

Schorn, S. 2018. Studien zur hellenistischen Biographie und Historiographie (Beiträge zur Altertumskunde 345). Berlin - Boston: de Gruyter.

Sumner, G.V. 1961. Notes on chronological problems in the Aristotelian Ἀθηναίων πολιτεία. Classical Quarterly 11: 31–54.

Thalheim, T. 1914. Aristotelis Ἀθηναίων πολιτεία (Bibliotheca scriptorum Graecorum et Romanorum Teubneriana). 2nd ed. Leipzig: Teubner.

Verhasselt, G. 2019. Heraclides' epitome of Aristotle's Constitutions and Barbarian Customs: Two neglected fragments. Classical Quarterly 69: 672–83.

Wallace, R.W. 1992. Aristotelian politeiai and Athenaion Politeia 4, in R.M. Rosen and J. Farrell (eds), Nomodeiktes. Greek Studies in Honor of Martin Ostwald: 269–86. Ann Arbor: University of Michigan Press.

Viano, C.A. 1955. Politica e Costituzione di Atene di Aristotele (Classici politici 9). Turin: Unione Tipografico.

Volckhausen, A. E. and Koeler, G. D. 1801. Die übrig gebliebenen Auszüge aus Heraclides des Pontikers Schrift über die Staaten nebst der deutschen Uebersetzung von A.E.V. und kritischen und erklärenden Anmerkungen von G.D.K. Lemgo: Meyer.

von Fritz, K. and Kapp, E. 1950. Aristotle's Constitution of Athens and Related Texts (The Hafner Library of Classics 13). New York: Hafner Publishing Company.

von Holzinger, C. 1891. Aristoteles' athenische Politie und die Heraklidischen Excerpte. Philologus 50: 436–46.

von Wilamowitz-Moellendorff, U. 1893. Aristoteles und Athen. Vol. I. Berlin: Weidmann.

This project has received funding from the European Union's Horizon 2020 research and innovation programme under the Marie Sklodowska-Curie grant agreement No 796992.

A bastard Pharaoh: Why Ptolemy XII Auletes was not the Son of a Ptolemaic Princess[1]

Antony Keen

University of Notre Dame (USA) in England
akeen1@nd.edu

Abstract

The idea that the Egyptian Pharaoh Ptolemy XII Auletes and his brother Ptolemy of Cyprus should be identified with two sons of Ptolemy IX Lathyros and Cleopatra Selene mentioned by Justin in his *Epitome of Pompeius Trogus* was first proposed in the nineteenth century by Rachel Evelyn White. Though many standard works on the period do not accept the identification, it has recently acquired some scholarly traction, being promoted by the Egyptologist Christopher Bennett, and subsequently being adopted by the Wikipedia entry on Ptolemy Auletes. Bennett further identifies the mother of the children mentioned by Justin not with Selene, but with her sister Cleopatra IV. This chapter argues that this identification is historically problematic, and contradicts what little is known about the circumstances of Ptolemy's birth, and has no better justification than wanting to reduce the number of Ptolemies about. The orthodoxy, that treats these four individuals as separate from each other, is correct. Auletes' mother was neither Cleopatra Selene nor Cleopatra IV, but an unknown woman of unknown origin.

Keywords

Ptolemy Auletes, Ptolemy XII, Ptolemaic Egypt, Hellenistic history

In '100 BC', episode 4 of the 1983 BBC television series *The Cleopatras*,[2] the audience is introduced to Irene (played by Lois Baxter), mistress of Ptolemy 'Chickpea' (Ptolemy IX Lathyros, played by David Horovitch), and mother of his illegitimate children, one of whom will grow up to be Ptolemy 'Fluter' (Adam Bareham), next-but-one king of Egypt. All have arrived from Cyprus, where Lathyros was king while in exile from Egypt.

In historical reality, it is just not known for certain who was the mother of Ptolemy XII Auletes ('Fluter').[3] This is not surprising; our sources for later Ptolemaic Egypt are often patchy. It is

---

[1] I am delighted to be part of this volume honouring Peter Rhodes. Besides his high standing as a scholar, thirty years ago, at the start of my career as an academic, Peter was kind and generous and welcoming to me. I hope he will forgive this straying outside his usual historical interests (it's straying outside mine!). My thanks are due to John J. Johnston, who organised the Twitter viewing between May and June 2020 of *The Cleopatras*, #CleoWatch, that led me to thinking about Ptolemy Auletes' parentage, and for his subsequent comments on this chapter. I thank also the anonymous reader for this volume. Unfortunately, Llewellyn-Jones and McAuley 2022 was not available to me when I wrote this piece.

[2] The only onscreen title to appear is 'Episode 4'. The title '100 BC' is taken from the *Radio Times* (issue 3091, 3 February 1983: 47)—this was clearly only intended as indicating the date when the episode begins, as were the dates attached to other episodes. However, these dates have become semi-official episode titles, and are used, for example, by the Internet Movie Database. Mackie novelised the story (1983); this scene is at 122-23.

[3] In this chapter, 'Auletes' = Ptolemy XII Neos Dionysos Auletes; 'Lathyros' = Ptolemy XI Soter II Lathyros, Auletes' father; 'Alexander I' = Ptolemy X Alexander I, Lathyros' brother; 'Alexander II' = Ptolemy XI Alexander II, Alexander I's son; 'Selene' = Cleopatra Selene I, Lathyros' second wife, and later Cleopatra II of Syria; 'Berenike III' = Cleopatra Berenike III, Lathyros' daughter; 'Tryphaina II' = Cleopatra Tryphaina II, Auletes' wife; 'Physkon' = Ptolemy VIII Euergetes II Physkon, father of Lathyros, Alexander I, and Selene I. Other Ptolemies and Cleopatras are referred to by

only really when Julius Caesar arrived in Alexandria in 48 that some of the concealing fog is lifted.

What is known, however, is that Auletes is described as a *nothos*, 'bastard', by Pompeius Trogus (*Prologoi* 39; he Latinises the term as *nothus*). Hence it is commonly assumed that his mother was some royal concubine.

Irene is an invention of Mackie, but she fits in the picture of the mother found in the works of modern scholars such as Edwyn Bevan, who says of Auletes' mother, somewhat floridly, that she was 'in all probability an accomplished and beautiful woman from some city of the Greek world'; or Michael Grant, who says she was 'quite likely to have been a Syrian', and possibly 'partly Greek' (Bevan 1927: 344; Grant 1972: 5). Others, however, have suggested that she was an aristocratic Egyptian (Reymond and Barns 1977: 24; Sullivan 1990: 92-93). Grant dismisses this idea, on the grounds that only one other Egyptian mistress of a Ptolemaic king is known, Didyme, the mistress of Ptolemy II Philadelphus (Athenaeus, *Deipnosophists* 13.37 [576e-f]; Grant 1972: 5; cf. Bevan 1927: 77). Given how random it is that we know of Didyme at all, and the general state of the sources, this is not as strong an argument as Grant believes.[4]

There is, of course, an element of racist assumption in the desires of some to see Auletes' mother as Greek and not Egyptian, bound up with the highly contentious ethnicity of the famous Cleopatra, Cleopatra VII, Auletes' daughter, and whether she should be considered wholly Macedonian Greek, or partly Egyptian. This chapter does not intend to enter into that debate (on which see Blouin, Gad and Kennedy 2020a and 2020b). I am not concerned with demonstrating that Auletes' mother was, or was not, Egyptian, or Greek, or Syrian. My objective is to show who she definitely was not, i.e. not one of two particular members of the Ptolemaic royal house.

The suggestion that Auletes' mother was in fact a Ptolemaic princess was first advanced by Rachel Evelyn White in 1898, who identified Auletes and his brother Ptolemy of Cyprus with two sons of Lathyros and Selene attested to in Justin (39.4.1);[5] they are mentioned in the context of Lathyros' forced exile from Egypt in 107, when he fled to Syria, before taking control of Cyprus in 105, where he ruled until he was able to return to Egypt (Josephus, *Jewish Antiquities* 13.12.2 [328]). This has been taken up by others, such as Christopher Bennett (2001-2012). Bennett's idea, that Auletes was the son of Cleopatra IV, has gained considerable purchase, being accepted by, e.g., Peter Nadig (2012), and Adrian Goldsworthy (2011: 69-70), in spite of the scepticism of others (e.g. Huss 2001: 672 n. 3; Llewellyn-Jones 2012a). So popular is the idea that the Wikipedia article on Auletes currently gives his date of birth as 117/116 (2021e). This chapter aims at reiterating the reasons why the sceptics are right, and this theory is implausible.

---

regnal numbers, where appropriate. For the regnal numbers, see the note at the end of the text. All dates for events in Ptolemaic and Roman history are BCE, unless otherwise indicated.

[4] There is also the possible intermarriage between the Ptolemies and the family of the high priests of Memphis (Vienna stele no. 82, discussed, e.g., at Sullivan 1990: 83, and Ogden 1999: 92). But, however one interprets this document, there is no suggestion that Auletes was a result of this marriage, and it only supplies comparative data about the possible origins of Auletes' mother. Since it is not my intention here to advance a case for who Auletes mother was, but rather to demonstrate who she was not, the stele's testament is not really relevant.

[5] These sons may further to be identified with the 'children' mentioned in a dedication to Cleopatra III, Lathyros and Selene; Massar 2016: 98.

If Auletes' mother is to be a Ptolemaic princess, there are only two candidates; one is Cleopatra Selene I, daughter of Ptolemy VIII Physkon and Cleopatra III, and second wife of Ptolemy IX Lathyros, and the other is Cleopatra IV, eldest daughter of the same parents, and first wife of Lathyros.[6]

There are essentially two separate propositions put forward. The first is that Auletes and his brother Ptolemy of Cyprus are to be identified with the sons of Lathyros mentioned by Justin. The second, which only comes into play if Cleopatra IV is advanced as Auletes' mother, is that Selene was not the biological mother of those two sons. It is best to address them separately.

To take the second argument first, it is proposed, for instance by Bennett (2001-2012), that, although Justin says that the two sons were those of Lathyros and Selene, one or both of them were in fact the sons of Lathyros and Cleopatra IV, to whom he was first married, before his mother, Cleopatra III, forced him to divorce Cleopatra IV and marry Selene, probably in 115 (Justin 39.3.2). It is argued that Selene could still represent herself as 'mother' to these children, even if she was only stepmother or adoptive mother.

It is certainly true that 'mother' might not mean a biological connection (so Ptolemy III is found making offerings to his 'parents' Ptolemy II and Arsinoe II, of whom only the former was his natural parent; Bennett 2001-2012 provides other examples). The problem is with what Justin actually says. He writes that the sons were *ex Selene*, 'out of Selene', which naturally implies a biological relationship. Moreover, he is writing about the forced divorce of Lathyros from Selene, and says that the divorce was made *indignius*, 'more insulting', because of the existence of the sons. If Selene was merely the stepmother or adoptive mother of these sons, it seems to me that Justin's text is robbed of its emotional weight. Why should being separated from the stepmother of one's children be such an insult? Would not the insult in that case be when Lathyros was divorced from Cleopatra IV, which Justin has already discussed (39.3.2)?

One possible reading of Justin's *indignius* is that the treatment of Lathyros was that much more insulting because he was, when exiled, forced to leave his sons behind him. This seems to be the inference drawn by those who report that the sons remained in Egypt while Lathyros fled (e.g. Bennett 2001-2012), though I have found no-one be explicit about this. The problem, again, is that this is not what Justin says. He clearly attaches *indignius* to the divorce, and says nothing about what happened to Lathyros' sons. That they stayed in Egypt is an inference from Josephus' report that Cleopatra III subsequently sent 'grandsons' to Cos for safety (*Jewish Antiquities* 13.13.1 [349]; for the inference see Bevan 1927: 330, citing Bouché-Leclerque 1904: 100 n. 3).

Nor is it tenable that one of the sons is by Cleopatra IV and one by Selene. If that were the case, one would expect Justin only to mention one son. Also, the link of the elder of these sons with Auletes requires that the children of Lathyros and Cleopatra IV were rendered illegitimate by the cancellation of their parents' marriage, in order to explain Auletes' epithet of *Nothos*, 'bastard' (see below). But if that was the case, then the younger son by Selene, being legitimate, would have a prior claim to the throne over the son of Cleopatra IV. This would

---

[6] Fogel's identification (2002) of Cleopatra Tryphaina II (whom he calls Cleopatra V Tryphaena) as Auletes' 'mother' is presumably an error for 'wife'; similarly, he calls Berenike IV Auletes' sister, rather than daughter. Neither error comes from Siani-Davies 2001.

mean Ptolemy of Cyprus ought to have ascended the Egyptian throne, not Auletes, assuming that Ptolemy of Cyprus was the younger brother of Auletes. That Ptolemy of Cyprus was younger is not, however, stated explicitly in the sources that mention him (Appian, *Civil Wars* 2.23; Dio 38.30.5, 39.22.2; Plutarch, *Cato Minor* 34.2-36.1; *Brutus* 3.1-2; Strabo 14.6.6; Valerius Maximus 9.4, ext. 1; Velleius Paterculus 2.45.4-5). It is, therefore, possible that Auletes was actually the younger brother, and had precedence over Ptolemy of Cyprus because Ptolemy of Cyprus was illegitimate. Alternatively, the marriage of Lathyros and Selene may also have been invalidated, but it would have to be for different reasons from those proposed for the invalidation of the marriage of Lathyros and Cleopatra IV, which are that the marriage took place and the children were born before Lathyros become king in 116 (see below). But this is all speculation.

Justin does make errors, of course. He suggests that the (alleged) murder of Cleopatra III by Ptolemy X Alexander I took place shortly after the exile of Lathyros (39.4.5), and that Alexander I's own exile followed shortly thereafter (39.5.1). In fact, we know from documentary evidence that Alexander I became king in 107 (*pGrenf.* 2.23a, the earliest dated document for Alexander I), that his mother died *c.* 101 (*pAdler* 11, the last dated document for Cleopatra III), and that Alexander I was not driven out of Egypt until 88 (*pAmherst* 2.51, the last dated document for Alexander I).[7] It is therefore entirely possible that Justin (or Trogus) has misunderstood what the description of Selene as 'mother' meant. But is it necessary to believe that?

Bennett (2001-2012) notes that a Ptolemy, son of Lathryos, is attested on two documents of 108, on a papyrus as eponymous priest (*pdem Brooklyn* 37.1796 = *pdem Recueil* 6), and on a letter to the Cyrenaeans (*Supplementum Epigraphicum Graecum* IX.5). Neither document states the age of the son. Bennett argues that, in accordance with standard Ptolemaic practice, he would have been eight when appointed to the post of eponymous priest, and hence born 117/116, a year or so before Lathryos married Selene, and before Lathyros become king. In order to equate this Ptolemy with Auletes, Bennett postulates that the reason for this marriage and the children being considered illegitimate was that the marriage took place and the children were born before Lathyros was king.

One problem, however, is that the Ptolemy attested in 108 clearly was not considered illegitimate at the time, since he is evidently being treated as Lathyros' heir. It seems strange that the marriage and children would not be declared illegitimate at the time of Lathyros' divorce from Cleopatra IV, rather than being delayed until after 108. Another issue is that Bennett's 'standard practice' is something of a chimaera; all he can say is that when other sons of Ptolemaic pharaohs were presented as eponymous priests, there is 'reason to believe' that they were eight, or they 'may' have been eight or nine (Bennett 2001-2012). The argument that this Ptolemy must have been eight seems weak. It seems more likely that, for some reason, Lathyros advanced the career of his eldest son by Selene. This might perhaps be connected with the dynastic struggles with his mother, who had already tried at least once to put his brother Alexander I on the throne.

---

[7] Both Pausanias 1.9.3, and Justin say that Alexander I was exiled once his murder of his mother was discovered. It is possible that what both elide is twelve years passing between the death of Cleopatra III and the revelation of Alexander's responsibility for it, though that seems implausible.

sources in order to combine individuals. In this case, there is a clear reason to read the sons of Selene and Auletes and Ptolemy of Cyprus as separate people. The sons mentioned by Justin were clearly born in wedlock, when Lathyros and Selene were married. In contrast, Auletes was, so Trogus says, a *nothos.*

Nothos, in its basic meaning, is a term applied to children born of relationships that were not formalised into marriage (Odgen 1996: 15-17, partially correcting Patterson 1990). It is commonly used for a child born of a concubine, and Ogden (1999: 92), in connection with Ptolemy Apion of Cyrene, thinks that for the Ptolemies it means that the son was not born of two Ptolemaic parents. *Nothos* can be found applied to one who was born as legitimate, but subsequently made illegitimate (at least in some people's eyes) by an additional marriage; Alexander the Great accused Attalus of suggesting that he, Alexander, was a *nothos*, after Philip II had married Attalus' daughter Cleopatra Eurydice (but not divorced Alexander's mother Olympias; Plutarch, *Alexander* 9.8).

Moreover, it is true that, in other cultures, illegitimacy arising out of the dissolution of a once legitimate marriage could be transient and reversible. Two examples from English history will demonstrate this. When Queen Anne Boleyn's marriage to Henry VIII was dissolved, her daughter Elizabeth was declared illegitimate (Somerset 2003: 10). Yet, that was later reversed, so that Elizabeth could succeed to the English throne (though many of her enemies still saw her as illegitimate). Similarly, Elizabeth's grandmother, Elizabeth of York, was rendered illegitimate when the marriage of her father Edward IV and Elizabeth Woodville was declared invalid, a device allowing her uncle Richard to set aside Elizabeth's brother Edward V and ascend the throne himself as Richard III (Okerlund 2009: 21-32). Yet, the law to this effect was explicitly revoked when Henry Tudor became king, in order that he could marry her and have children that would be legitimate descendants of the House of York.

Could something similar not have happened with Auletes? If he was the son of Lathyros from a marriage which was legitimate at the time, would his ascending the throne not mean that his parents' marriage was effectively re-legitimised? Yet there is little trace of a tradition to this effect in the sources.

The best signs are in the contemporary literature (i.e. Cicero), but even those are not good. In his mention of the Antiochid claim to the Egyptian throne (*Verrines* 2.4.61), Cicero is not clear whether he thinks the claim was valid or not, though he pairs it with their inheritance of the Syrian throne, which he clearly does think is legitimate. In any case, Cicero is concerned to gain the sympathy of the jury for one of these children, the Syrian King Antiochus XIII, who had been robbed by Gaius Verres, the Roman governor of Sicily, while Antiochus was in Verres' province (*Verrines* 2.4.62-67). So, Cicero is unlikely to have said anything that would undermine support for Antiochus.

Then, there is the fragmentary *de rege Alexandrino*; it goes without saying that many of the questions addressed in this paper would be answered if we had this speech intact. Sadly, it survives only in a few quotations in an incomplete commentary on the speech in the *Scholia Bobiensia*, and a few other *testimonia* (e.g. Strabo, 17.1.13). The king concerned is unnamed, but must be Auletes, since Cicero's description of the death of the king's predecessor (F10) clearly matches the details of the deaths of Berenike III and Alexander II, as recorded in other sources (Porphyry, F2).

It is unclear when the speech was delivered; some (e.g. Siani-Davies 2001: 9; Narducci 2009: 143) argue for 65, in the context of Marcus Licinius Crassus' attempt to annex Egypt as a Roman province (Plutarch, *Crassus* 13.1), which Cicero is assumed to have opposed. The date of this attempt is known because it took place during Crassus' holding the office of censor. Others (e.g. Hollings 1839: 232-33) place the speech in 56, and see it as an oration intended to ensure that Cicero's friend Publius Cornelius Lentulus Spinther, at that point proconsul in Cilicia, would get the command to restore Auletes to the throne of Egypt, from which Auletes had been forced in 58.[15] Spinther did get the command, as we know from Dio (39.12.2). However, subsequent omens and readings from the Sibylline Books meant that no action was taken (Cicero, *ad familiares* 1.1, 1.2, 1.7; Dio 39.14). After that point, Cicero continued to agitate for the command still to remain with Spinther, though Auletes' restoration was finally achieved by Aulus Gabinius.

My own inclination is towards the earlier date for *de rege Alexandrino*. Not only does the speech contain direct references to Crassus and, in the view of the scholiast, a disguised attack on his character, but also Cicero's pleas for the Roman state to be motivated by decency and restraint, rather than profit and naked self-interest, better fit arguing a case against the annexation of Egypt rather than a case for a particular individual to be placed in charge of an expedition there. However, this does not actually matter for the argument I am making here.

What is important is that Cicero makes no comment either in support or denial of the king's illegitimacy. In what survives, Cicero is principally concerned to exonerate Auletes from charges of involvement in the death of Alexander II. Either this is to demonstrate that there is no moral argument to justify removing the king, or that there is no moral argument to prevent Rome from restoring him to the throne.

In the *de lege agraria* of 62, Cicero does admit that 'almost everybody' (*inter omnia fere*) agreed with Philippus that Auletes was unfit by birth and spirit to be king (2.42). But Cicero is irritatingly vague here. It is impossible to tell whether it was the comment about Auletes' birth or spirit or both that a few people disagreed with, or precisely what he means by 'unfit by birth'. In any case, Cicero seems much less concerned about a contrary view on this issue than he is with those who asserted that there existed no will of Ptolemy Alexander leaving Egypt to Rome.[16]

---

[15] That Cicero and Spinther were friends is demonstrated by Cicero's letters to him, e.g. *ad familiares* 1.1, 1.2, 1.4, 1.5, 1.6, 1.7, 1.8, 1.9. Of these, all except 1.8 and 1.9 date to 56, and show Cicero acting for Spinther in the matter of the restoration of Auletes.

[16] Which Ptolemy Alexander, Alexander I or Alexander II, is unclear. The arguments are set out in Badian 1967, for Alexander I, Braund 1983: 24-28, for Alexander II, and Bennett 2001-2011c, for Alexander I. In the nineteenth century the will was linked to a non-existent Ptolemy Alexander III (Badian 1967: 179). I remain undecided, but fortunately it does not matter for my argument here. Some modern accounts (e.g. Aneni 2016: 161, 162) state that both Alexanders left wills naming Rome. I think that is going beyond the evidence, though as naming Rome in a will was a frequent practice of late Hellenistic monarchs (Ptolemy Physkon did it in 155 when ruler of Cyrenaica; *Supplementum Epigraphicum Graecum* IX.7), it is not impossible. There seems to be no ancient evidence to support the assertion of Wikipedia 2021d and Aneni 2016: 162, that Sulla published the will of Alexander I in order to impose Alexander II; it would be unlikely that a document made public in 81 could have its very existence questioned in 65.

Cicero does again discuss Auletes' lineage in the *pro Sestio*, delivered in 56. Cicero is busy condemning a whole series of decisions of the Roman state taken in 58 (which includes the decision to exile him). One of these is the annexation of Cyprus. Here Cicero says that Auletes' brother, Ptolemy of Cyprus, was 'of the same family and same ancestors' (*erat eodem genere eisdemque maioribus*) as Auletes (*pro Sestio* 26.57). This is not, however, necessarily a reversal of Cicero's earlier position in the *de lege agraria*, though it has been taken as such (Bennett 2001-2012). Cicero may not be saying that the deposing of Ptolemy of Cyprus was unjust, because he was as legitimate a monarch as his brother, whom Rome restored. Rather, he may be implying that Ptolemy of Cyprus was just as illegitimate as Auletes (so taken by Ogden 1999: 95). Hence, the injustice in deposing Ptolemy of Cyprus came not from the fact that he was the legitimate king, but from the inconsistency shown by Rome through deposing one illegitimate king and restoring another.

In the *pro Rabirio Postumo* in 54, a speech defending Rabirius Postumus from a charge of extortion arising out of his dealings with Auletes, Cicero is keen to perform a character assassination on the king. But he does not, evidently, see the need to bring up Auletes' legitimacy.

Before moving on from Cicero, we must note that *de lege Alexandrino* contains one further point that is very important for the alleged identification of Auletes with one of the sons of Lathyros and Selene; Cicero does provide some evidence for Auletes' age. He states that Auletes was a *puer* ('boy') when he ascended the throne *c.* 80 (F9). *Puer* strictly speaking means up to the age of seventeen (see Lewis and Short 1879: *s.v. puer*). It could often be used for older (but still comparatively young) men; Cicero, for instance, uses it of the nineteen-year-old Octavian (e.g. *ad familiares* 2.1.2). But the eldest of the sons of Lathyros and Selene would have been, at the youngest, nearly 30 in 80, which seems to stretch the definition of *puer*.[17] Bennett's postulated son of Cleopatra IV would have been in his mid-30s, old enough to be a member of the Roman Senate.

Bennett's solution to this (2001-2012) is that F9, which says that Auletes was a *puer* when a king died, and F10, which describes the death of a king who can only be Alexander II, should not be taken together, that the king in F9 is in fact Alexander I, who died some seven years before Alexander II, and that the *puer* in F9 is in fact not Auletes, but Alexander II. It is true that we do not know that the scholiast was commenting on consecutive passages. But both passages are concerned with defending someone against a charge of having killed a king, as the scholiast explains, and to take the two passages as referring to two separate kings and two separate people being defended, without the scholiast telling us so, is to weave a rather complicated narrative in order to avoid taking the sources at face value.

Pausanias' statement that Berenike III was Lathyros' only legitimate daughter is important. This means that she cannot have had the same parents as Auletes. Unfortunately, Pausanias only gets us so far, as we do not know who Berenike's mother was. Scholarship once tended towards Cleopatra IV (and some, such as Llewellyn-Jones 2012c, still advance that as the most likely option). Bennett (2001-2011a) rejects that in favour of Selene, allowing him to have Cleopatra IV as the mother of Auletes.

---

[17] Sullivan 1990: 92, sees *puer* as simply being used in a contemptuous fashion.

A further question that arises if Auletes was one of the sons of Selene, or of Cleopatra IV, is, where was he when Alexander II was placed on the throne? Of course, Alexander II was the chosen candidate of Sulla, at that point dictator of Rome, who knew Alexander well (Appian, *Civil Wars* 1.102).[18] But there had been a brief period when Berenike III ruled alone. Would that even have been feasible had there been available an adult son of Lathyros by a Ptolemaic princess? One might expect at least that Auletes' candidature would be advanced, or even that Lathyros would have summoned Auletes towards the end of his reign. Of this, there is no trace in the sources, though again, it must be admitted that the sources are very poor (Mackie 1983: 123, for dramatic reasons, has Auletes come to Egypt shortly after Lathyros is restored in 88). That absence is perhaps even more notable if Alexander II was himself a *nothos*, i.e. not of Ptolemaic parentage on both sides (see Ogden 1999: 96). Unfortunately, it is unclear who Alexander II's mother was. Mackie in his fictionalised version (1983: 106) makes her a wife of Alexander I from Cyprus. It has more recently been suggested that Alexander II's mother was Cleopatra Selene I, briefly married to Ptolemy I Alexander I before being packed off to Syria to marry Antiochus VIII Grypus (see Llewellyn-Jones 2012b, though he admits this only as a remote possibility).

One explanation of Auletes' absence from the early part of the dynastic crisis of 81-80 is that Auletes was at the time a hostage at the court of Mithradates VI of Pontus. This notion is based on the information that two daughters of Mithradates, Mithridatis and Nyssa, who committed suicide along with their father in 63, were engaged to Auletes and Ptolemy of Cyprus (Appian, *Mithradatic Wars* 16.111 [536]). It is not explicit who was betrothed to whom, but assuming that the potential husbands are mentioned in the same order as the daughters, Auletes was probably betrothed to Mithridatis. Appian describes them as being in 63 *korai*, 'girls', so perhaps they were then under 20.

The problem is that we do not know when these betrothals were made. The natural inference would be that they took place in the 60s. This is rejected by Bennett (2001-2012), on the grounds that Mithradates, driven out of Pontus in 66, and in exile in the Crimea, was in no position to be building alliances that include Egypt and Cyprus, and a marriage alliance would have jeopardised Auletes' attempts to get recognition from Rome as a friend and ally of the Roman people. The 70s are rejected because Auletes was married to Cleopatra V Tryphaina II from 80 to 69.

Hence some (e.g. Bevan 1927: 344-5; Bennett 2001-2012) place the betrothals before 80. The story is that the sons of Selene were sent, with the future Alexander II, to the island of Cos for safety. There they were captured by Mithradates, who, while they were under his control, had them betrothed to his daughters. Their return to Egypt on the death of Alexander II was then sponsored by Mithradates.

This story, though taken as fact by many (e.g. Green 1990: 553), is a highly speculative modern invention. It is the case that Cleopatra III sent grandsons in the plural to Cos (Josephus, *Jewish Antiquities* 13.13.1 [349]),[19] and that the future Alexander II was captured there by Mithradates

---

[18] Appian's account, along with that of Porphyry (F2) could be read as implying that Berenike III actually asked for Alexander II, rather than having him imposed upon her, but we cannot know what pressures were brought to bear.

[19] Contrary to Whiston 1737 *ad loc*, the Cos from where Alexander II was seized from cannot be a city on, or island off, the coast of Egypt, which would be well beyond Mithradates' grasp, but must be the more famous Aegean island.

in 88 (Appian, *Civil Wars* 1.102; *Mithradatic Wars* 4.23). It is not clear, however, that Alexander had spent the entire intervening period on Cos, and there is possible evidence (in *pdemTurin Botti* 34, 36, 37) that he did not. Moreover, we lack evidence for who else, apart from Alexander, was sent to Cos. However, perhaps it is best to assume that the sons of Selene were sent, in order not to invent at least one otherwise unattested grandson of Cleopatra.[20]

We also have no direct evidence that anyone else apart from Alexander was captured in Cos by Mithradates. There is no direct evidence that the sons of Lathyros and Selene were ever at the court of Mithradates. Nor is there any evidence Auletes and Ptolemy of Cyprus were there, other than by inference from Appian. Auletes does seem to have been in Syria when Alexander II was killed, and still there when he was summoned by the Alexandrines (Cicero, *de rege Alexandrino* F9). According to conventional chronology, at the time Syria was under the control of Mithradates' ally, Tigranes II of Armenia, but there is no evidence that Auletes had come to Syria from Pontus. The connection becomes even more tenuous if Oliver Hoover's redating of Tigranes' invasion of Syria to 74/73 is accepted (2007: 296-7), since Auletes would then have been summoned from a Syria not at all under the control of a Mithradatic ally. Why Auletes was in Syria must remain a mystery.[21]

This story of the Mithradatic imprisonment does not just support the idea that Auletes and Ptolemy of Cyprus were the sons of Selene; it all but demands it, and so is rather circular. It is true that, if Mithradates had possession of Auletes and Ptolemy of Cyprus, he might have recognised that they were important as royal bastards, even if they were not sons of Selene, and had them betrothed to daughters of roughly the same status, but the idea is much more attractive if they were Selene's children.

However, if Mithradates' daughters' betrothal to the Ptolemies is to be dated to before 80, they must have been betrothed to the Ptolemies at a very young age. And they seem not to have married or been betrothed to anyone else before their deaths in 63, despite Auletes obviously reneging on the deal. This also seems unlikely. In the 60s, Mithradates sent some of his daughters to Scythian leaders as wives (Appian, *Mithradatic Wars* 16.108 [516]), yet evidently Mithridatis and Nyssa were not among them. This might mean that at the time they were younger than their sisters, i.e. old enough to be betrothed, but not yet old enough to be married.

There is no good reason to reject the 60s for such a marriage alliance. Mithradates was trying to build forces to retake and secure his Pontic kingdom, first from exile in Armenia, and then from the Crimea. It is not impossible that, at this point, he would have reached out to two other independent powers in the eastern Mediterranean, both very rich, seeking to build

---

The suggestion of Marcus (1943: 401 n. 8) that the grandsons were housed in the Asclepeion on Cos is plausible, but without evidence in the sources.

[20] Ogden 1999: 94, thinks it unlikely that the sons of Selene were sent to Cos, since the purpose of sending the grandsons to Cos was to protect them from Lathyros; this would have been unnecessary for his own sons. However, Josephus does not say that the object was to protect the grandsons; this is inferred from the fact that Cleopatra III sent much of her money and her will there, which will have been to protect them. It may well be that the sons of Selene were being used as hostages, and the point of sending them to Cos was to put them out of Lathyros' grasp.

[21] At a guess, but only a guess, he was in the northern part of Syria, controlled, on Hoover's chronology, by Philip I, rather than in that part controlled by Selene, who might have taken action against him to further the claims of her Antiochid sons. It is assumed that Ptolemy of Cyprus was with him, but there is no direct evidence.

a coalition. Nor is it impossible that Auletes and Ptolemy would have responded positively. Rome had failed to recognise Auletes as a friend and ally of the Roman people, and was constantly threatening to annex Egypt, according to the terms of the alleged will of Ptolemy Alexander. In the *Scholia Bobiensia* on *de rege Alexandrino*, the scholiast says that Crassus had tried on a number of previous occasions to get Egypt taken over. If the speech is correctly dated to 65, these attempts will have taken place in the early 60s, if not earlier. Under those circumstances, Auletes might well consider an alliance with Mithradates as an alternative to trying to get recognition from Rome. This might well have looked particularly attractive in the aftermath of Mithradates' victory over the Romans at Zela in 67, and his subsequent reoccupation of Pontus. Auletes eventually turned against the idea; in 63 he offered to fund Pompey's attack on Judea and supply troops (Appian, *Mithradatic Wars* 17.114; Josephus, *Jewish Antiquities* 14.3.1 [35]; Pliny, *Natural History* 33.48.136).

A complicating factor here is whether Auletes was still married to Tryphaina II at this point, and indeed whether she was still alive. At one point it was thought that Cleopatra Tryphaina II, wife of Auletes, died in 69/68.[22] The Cleopatra Tryphaina who later usurped Auletes[23] and briefly ruled Egypt with his daughter Berenike IV, before dying and leaving Berenike to rule on her own, was considered a different person, Cleopatra VI Tryphaina III (Grant 1972: 4). It is now more generally thought that the wife of Auletes and the co-ruler with Berenike were the same person (Llewellyn-Jones 2012d). However, Porphyry (F2), the only source to mention the later Tryphaina, explicitly states that she was the daughter of Auletes, and repeats this at F32, where he identifies those who were ruling in Auletes' absence as 'daughters of Ptolemy'. This is disregarded, on the grounds that Strabo does not seem to know of her; he mentions three daughters of Auletes, without naming them, of which the first is definitely Berenike IV, and the other two are presumably Cleopatra VII and Arsinoe (17.1.11). Moreover, the joint rule of two sisters is otherwise unprecedented in Egyptian or Greek thought (Macurdy 1932: 178; Whitehorne 1994: 183; Ashton 2003: 68).

But Strabo also does not mention that Berenike IV had a co-ruler (indeed, no other literary source other than Porphyry does), yet we know from a papyrus record (*BGU* 8.1762.3-4) that she did.[24] Hence we cannot say that if something is not in Strabo, it is not historical, and so a putative younger Tryphaina's absence from Strabo's list of Auletes' daughters cannot be a conclusive point against her existence. As for the rule of two sisters, unprecedented does not mean impossible, especially in the volatile environment of first-century Alexandria, and we should be careful not to overrule what the sources actually say with what we think they ought to say. The argument advanced by Bennett (2001-2012) that Berenike IV's co-ruler must be Auletes' wife, because it is known that Auletes' wife survived past 69, because she ruled with Berenike IV, is, of course, wholly circular.[25]

---

[22] The latest mention of her is in *Orientis graeci inscriptiones selectae* I 185, of August 69. Her name is already missing in *pdem Ashm.* (Reymond 1973) 16/17, a document of November 69.

[23] A good discussion of what the sources say about Auletes' loss of power and departure for Rome in 58 is to be found at Siani-Davies 2001: 14-20. Most of the details do not matter for my argument here.

[24] Ogden 1999: 100, interprets the sequence of events as Auletes leaving Berenike IV and Tryphaina in charge in Egypt while he went to Rome to press his claim for recognition, and Berenike IV only usurping her father after Tryphaina's death. This would render moot my point about Strabo's omission, but this seems to me to be a tenuous reading of Porphyry's text, which reads more naturally as if the two deposed Auletes in his absence.

[25] Siani-Davies 2001: 22, takes a demotic graffito from Dendera of January 55, dated to year 26 of Ptolemy and year 3 of Cleopatra, as indicating that, contrary to Porphyry, Tryphaina was still alive in 55. This seems implausible, and the

So it may well be that Auletes was free to be betrothed to Mithridatis in the mid-60s. Alternatively, if Auletes' wife was still alive in the mid-60s, he either had divorced her (which might explain her disappearance from the historical record after 69), or the betrothal to Mithridatis was not considered a full marriage. Or it is just possible, from a reference to 'wives', on a sepulchral stele now in the British Museum (no. 886), that Auletes was polygamous.[26] In any case, there is not enough of a case in the evidence to move Auletes' betrothal to Mithridatis to before 80. Hence there is no reason to believe that Mithridates saw Auletes and his brother as important before they became kings, or to invent a Pontic sojourn for them.

The main objection to separating Auletes and his brother from Justin's sons of Selene is that it then becomes necessary to account for what happened to the sons of Selene. Leaving aside that identifying Auletes and a son of Selene, as we have seen, raises rather more questions than this, the answer to this objection is obvious. They died.

This might have simply been the sort of infant deaths that affected the ancient world.[27] Another possible occasion for their deaths is the point at which Lathyros was driven off the Egyptian throne. The sons of Lathyros would become potential further rivals for the throne, a threat to the line of descent through Alexander I and his son, the future Alexander II. If the sons did not leave Egypt with their father (and, as noted, no ancient source says whether they did or not), then, perhaps after being sent to Cos for safety, they might well have suffered the fate of Ptolemy Memphites, murdered by Ptolemy Physkon when he was in exile and challenging Memphites' mother, Cleopatra II, for rule of Egypt; Physkon wanted to focus the line of succession upon his children with Cleopatra III (Justin, 38.8.13-15, Diodorus, 34/35.14; Livy, *Perochiae* 59.14; Orosius, *History Against the Pagans* 5.10.6).

But my story of the deaths of the sons of Selene is no less invention than the story that they went to Cos and ended up with Mithradates. What evidence there exists is slim, but it may suggest that they survived longer. Two Cypriot inscriptions (*iKition* [= Yon *et al.* 2004] 2003, and *Report of the Department of Antiquities, Cyprus* 1968: 74.4), both of which in all probability date to after 105, mention Laythros' children, at a time when Lathyros was ruling in Cyprus. I agree with Bennett (2001-2012) that these children are almost certainly the sons mentioned by Justin, and that they were alive at the time of the inscriptions. But I also suspect that the fact that both documents are dedications on behalf of Lathyros and his children means that the children were present with him on Cyprus at the time of the inscriptions, and not in the control of Cleopatra III.[28] This does not necessarily mean that they were not sent to Cos by Cleopatra III; merely that at some point after this, they had left and gone to Cyprus. It is even possible that the 'youthful Ptolemy' who met Lucius Licinius Lucullus in Egypt in 86 (Plutarch, *Lucullus* 2.5) was not, as generally assumed, Lathyros himself, then in his fifties, but one of

---

reference in the graffito must surely be to Berenike IV. There is no other evidence that Berenike also had the name Cleopatra, but given Ptolemaic naming practices, it seems entirely possible that she did, at least when acting as ruling queen.

[26] This is dismissed by Grant 1972: 4, on the grounds that polygamy is not otherwise attested amongst the Ptolemies, and it must be said that the status of Auletes' 'wives' in this inscription is most unclear. The context was once thought to be 76 (Bevan 1927: 346), though this is now doubted (Bennett 2001-2020). A translation of the stele appears at Bevan 1927: 347-48.

[27] So Ogden 1999: 94, who adduces in support of this the lack of any mention of their fate in Justin, a writer very interested in dynastic murder. But this sort of argument from Justin's silence is dangerous.

[28] Ogden 1999: 90, however, notes that references to unspecified plural children might be 'formulaic and hypothetical'.

these sons.[29] As noted already, we do not know enough about Egypt in the late second and early first centuries, and the fates of these sons could easily have disappeared from the record. All that can be said for certain is that these sons of Lathyros were dead by 81, when Berenike III succeeded her father.[30]

In conclusion, it is reasonable to believe that Ptolemy XII Auletes was the illegitimate son of Ptolemy IX Lathyros, by an unknown mother. He was probably born in the early to mid-90s, since he was probably seventeen at the eldest when he ascended the Egyptian throne in 80. At the time of Auletes' birth, his father Lathyros was exiled from Egypt and ruling in Cyprus (Josephus, *Jewish Antiquities* 13.12.2 [328]), so it is perhaps more likely that Auletes' mother was Greek, rather than Egyptian; but no definite evidence exists.

But if Auletes' parentage is uncertain, what can more firmly be asserted is that we should not identify Auletes and his brother with the two sons of Lathyros and Cleopatra Selene mentioned in Justin. Hence Auletes' mother was not a Ptolemaic princess or queen. To reject the identification does require an explanation for what happened to those two sons, but accepting the identification asks far more questions of the sources, and requires an intricate and speculative reconstruction of events that needs several of the ancient sources not to be saying what they appear at first reading to be saying.

There is consequently no need to read Auletes' epithet *nothos* as deriving from a once legitimate marriage subsequently invalidated, nor that it was simply an accusation thrown about by his enemies (so Sullivan 1990: 93). Rather, Auletes' bastardy was irreversible and undeniable, like that of the eleventh century AD Duke William the Bastard of Normandy. Like William, all Ptolemy Nothos could do was hope that eventually a less unflattering nickname would take over (William the Bastard, of course, became better known as William the Conqueror).

A note on Ptolemaic regnal numbering

Ptolemaic regnal numbering is not an ancient convention. As a result of the unreliability of the evidence for the Ptolemies, regnal numbers have varied over the years, as it is never quite clear who should, or should not, be included in the list of Ptolemaic kings. Older works may give a regnal numbering one higher or one lower than that currently generally employed. Ptolemy Physkon, for instance, who is generally considered Ptolemy VIII, appears in some works as Ptolemy VII (cf. Ogden 1999: 105 n. 1), and in others as Ptolemy IX (e.g. Mahaffy 1895: 377), whilst Auletes appears in the introduction to the Loeb translation of Cicero's *pro Sestio* as Ptolemy XI (Gardner 1958: 27). The regnal numbering for the Ptolemies has largely settled down now, and most people adopt the numbers currently employed in *Brill's New Pauly* (Ameling *et al.* 2006), as do I.

---

[29] The Ptolemy who subsequently refused to commit to the Mithradatic War (*Lucullus* 3.1), must have been Lathyros. I believe that Lathyros' reluctance had less to do with fear of reprisals from Mithradates (and certainly nothing to do with any fear for sons held hostage by Mithradates), and more to do with not wanting to pick sides in the as yet unresolved Roman civil war (Green 1990: 553, notes that Sulla's status at the time was hardly clear; he was in command in the east, but his enemy Lucius Cornelius Cinna was in command at Rome, and Sulla was officially in exile).

[30] Ogden 1999: 94, thinks that they 'evidently' died in infancy, but this is to place too much weight on our not definitely hearing about them later.

The situation remains much more fluid for the Cleopatras, largely because of the issue over Cleopatra V and Cleopatra VI discussed in my main text. This raises a question of what to do about the famous Cleopatra, daughter of Auletes. Conventionally she has been referred to as Cleopatra VII, and there is a reluctance to renumber her. As a result, various other solutions have been employed. The *New Pauly* (Prescendi *et al.* 2006) records the second wife of Lathyros, Selene, as Cleopatra V, and the wife of Auletes as Cleopatra VI. Édouard Will (1979-1982) and Lloyd Llewellyn-Jones (2012c), with some justification, choose to make Berenike III Cleopatra V. For Wikipedia, Selene (2021c) is not part of the sequence of Egyptian Cleopatras (her regnal number II is as queen of Syria), Auletes' wife is Cleopatra V (2021a), and Cleopatra VI exists simply as a marker used for a person no longer thought to exist (2021b). However, as indicated in my main text, I am sympathetic to Cleopatra VI Tryphaina III actually having existed separately from the wife of Ptolemy Auletes. (I also believe that the ruling queen Berenike IV was another Cleopatra.)

Bibliography

Ameling, W. *et al.* 2006. Ptolemaeus, in *Brill's New Pauly*, viewed 1 March 2021, <http://dx.doi. org.proxy.library.nd.edu/10.1163/1574-9347_bnp_e1012900>.

Aneni, M.O. 2016. Politics of the Ptolemaic Dynasty. *OGIRISI: A New Journal of African Studies* 12: 146–69.

Ashton, S.-A. 2003. *The Last Queens of Egypt*. Harlow and London: Pearson.

Badian, E. 1967. The Testament of Ptolemy Alexander. *Rheinisches Museum für Philologie* 110: 178–92.

Bennett, C. 2001-2011a. Berenice III, *Ptolemaic Dynasty*, viewed 27 February 2021, <http://www. instonebrewer.com/TyndaleSites/Egypt/ptolemies/berenice_iii.htm>.

Bennett, C. 2001-2011b. Berenice IV, *Ptolemaic Dynasty*, viewed 1 June 2021, <http://www. instonebrewer.com/TyndaleSites/Egypt/ptolemies/berenice_iv.htm>.

Bennett, C. 2001-2011c. Ptolemy X, *Ptolemaic Dynasty*, viewed 27 February 2021, <http://www. instonebrewer.com/TyndaleSites/Egypt/ptolemies/ptolemy_x.htm>.

Bennett, C. 2001-2012. Ptolemy XII, *Ptolemaic Dynasty*, viewed 27 February 2021, <http://www. instonebrewer.com/TyndaleSites/Egypt/ptolemies/ptolemy_xii.htm>.

Bevan, E.R. 1927. *The House of Ptolemy: A history of Hellenistic Egypt under the Ptolemaic Dynasty*. London: Methuen.

Blouin, K., U. Gad and R.F. Kennedy. 2020a. Casting Cleopatra: It's All About Politics: Part I, *Society for Classical Studies Blog*, viewed 27 February 2021, <https://classicalstudies.org/scs-blog/three-ancient-historians/blog-part-i-casting-cleopatra-it's-all-about-politics>.

Blouin, K., U. Gad and R.F. Kennedy. 2020b. Casting Cleopatra: It's All About Politics: Part II, *Society for Classical Studies Blog*, viewed 27 February 2021, <https://classicalstudies.org/scs-blog/three-ancient-historians/blog-part-ii-casting-cleopatra-it's-all-about-politics>.

Bouché-Leclerque, A. 1904. *Histoires des Lagides, II:* Décadence et fin de la dynastie (181–30 av. J.-C.). Paris: Ernest Leroux.

Braund, D.C. 1983. Royal wills and Rome. *Papers of the British School at Rome* 51: 16–57.

The Cleopatras. 100 BC (episode 4). UK, TV, dir. John Frankau, scr. Philip Mackie, starring Michelle Newell. BBC, 9 February 1983.

Crawford, J.W. (ed.) 1994. *M. Tullius Cicero: The fragmentary speeches*. 2nd edn. Atlanta, GA: Scholars Press.

Fogel, J. 2002. Cicero's Speech: *Pro Rabirio Postumo*, translated with introduction and commentary (review of Siani-Davies 2001). *Bryn Mawr Classical Review* 2002.04.12, viewed 26 February 2021, <https://bmcr.brynmawr.edu/2002/2002.04.12/>.

Gardner, R. (tr.) 1958. *Cicero, XII. Orations: Pro Sestio; In Vatinam*. Cambridge, MA, and London: Harvard University Press.

Goldsworthy, A.K. 2011. *Antony and Cleopatra*. London: Phoenix.

Grant, M. 1972. *Cleopatra: A biography*. London: Weidenfeld and Nicolson.

Green, P. 1990. *Alexander to Actium: The Historical Evolution of the Hellenistic Age*. Berkeley and Los Angeles, CA: University of California Press.

Greenwood, L.H.C. (tr.) 1935. *Cicero. VIII: The Verrine Orations II*. Cambridge, MA, and London: Harvard University Press.

Hölbl, G. 1994. *Geschichte des Ptolemäerreiches: Politik, Ideologie und religiöse Kultur von Alexander dem Grossen bis zur römischen Eroberung*. Darmstadt: Wissenschaftliche Buchgesellschaft.

Hölbl, G. 2001. *A History of the Ptolemaic Empire*. London: Routledge.

Hollings, J.F. 1839. *The Life of Marcus Tullius Cicero*. London: Thomas Tegg.

Hoover, O.D. 2005. Dethroning Seleucus VII Philometor (Cybiosactes): Epigraphical Arguments Against a Late Seleucid Monarch. *Zeitschrift für Papyrologie und Epigraphik* 151: 95–99.

Hoover, O.D. 2007. A Revised Chronology for the Late Seleucids at Antioch (121/0-64 BC). *Historia* 56: 280–301.

Huss, W. 2001. *Ägypten in hellenistischer Zeit 323-30 v. Chr.* Munich: Beck.

Jones, H.L. (tr.) 1949. *The Geography of Strabo, VIII*. Cambridge, MA: Harvard University Press.

Kritt, B. 2002. Numismatic Evidence for a New Seleucid King: Seleucus (VII) Philometor. *The Celator* 16.4: 25–36.

Lewis, C.T. and C. Short. 1879. *A Latin Dictionary*. Oxford: Clarendon Press.

Llewellyn-Jones, L. 2012a. Cleopatra IV, in *The Encyclopedia of Ancient History*, viewed 26 February 2021, <10.1002/9781444338386.wbeah07027>.

Llewellyn-Jones, L. 2012b. Cleopatra Selene, in *The Encyclopedia of Ancient History*, viewed 26 February 2021, <10.1002/9781444338386.wbeah07028>.

Llewellyn-Jones, L. 2012c. Cleopatra V Berenike III, in *The Encyclopedia of Ancient History*, viewed 26 February 2021, <10.1002/9781444338386.wbeah07019>.

Llewellyn-Jones, L. 2012d. Cleopatra VI Tryphaina, in *The Encyclopedia of Ancient History*, viewed 27 February 2021, <10.1002/9781444338386.wbeah07029>.

Llewellyn-Jones, L. and A. McAuley 2022. *Sister-Queens in the High Hellenistic Period: Kleopatra Thea and Kleopatra III*. London: Routledge.

Mackie, P. 1983. *The Cleopatras: A Novel*. London: BBC Books.

Macurdy, G.H. 1937. *Hellenistic Queens: A study of woman-power in Macedonia, Seleucid, Syria, and Ptolemaic Egypt*. Baltimore: John Hopkins Press.

Mahaffy, J.P. 1895. *The Empire of the Ptolemies*. Cambridge: Cambridge University Press.

Marcus, R. (tr.) 1943. *Josephus VII: Jewish Antiquities, Books XII–XIV*. Cambridge, MA, and London: Harvard University Press.

Massar, N. 2016. Trois inscriptions ptolémaïques: dédicaces en l'honneur des souverains lagides. *Cahiers de Mariemont* 40: 86–103.

Nadig, P. 2012. Ptolemy XII Neos Dionysos Auletes, in *The Encyclopedia of Ancient History*, viewed 27 February 2021, <10.1002/9781444338386.wbeah07091.pub2>.

Narducci, E. 2009. *Cicerone. La parola e la politica*. Rome and Bari: Laterza.

Ogden, D. 1996. *Greek Bastardy*. Oxford: Clarendon Press.

Ogden, D. 1999. *Polygamy, Prostitutes and Death: The Hellenistic dynasties*. London: Duckworth with the Classical Press of Wales.

Okerlund, A. 2009. *Elizabeth of York*. New York: Palgrave Macmillan.

Patterson, C.B. 1990. Those Athenian bastards. *Classical Antiquity* 9.1: 39–73.

Prescendi, F. *et al.* 2006. Cleopatra, in *Brill's New Pauly*, viewed 1 March 2021 <http://dx.doi.org.proxy.library.nd.edu/10.1163/1574-9347_bnp_e616480>.

Reymond, E.A.E. 1973. *Catalogue of Demotic Papyri in the Ashmolean Museum*. Oxford: Griffith Institute.

Reymond, E.A.E. and J.W.B. Barns. 1977. Alexandria and Memphis: Some historical observations. *Orientalia* 46: 1–33.

Schottky, M. 2006. Tigranes, in *Brill's New Pauly*, viewed 1 June 2021 <http://dx.doi.org.proxy.library.nd.edu/10.1163/1574-9347_bnp_e1214050>.

Siani-Davies, M. (tr.) 2001. *Marcus Tullius Cicero: Pro Rabirio Postumo*. New York and Oxford: Clarendon Press.

Somerset, A. 2003. *Elizabeth I*. London: Anchor Books.

Sullivan, R.D. 1990. *Near Eastern Royalty and Rome, 100-30 BC*. Toronto: University of Toronto Press.

Thompson, D.J. *et al.* 2016. Ptolemy (1), in *The Oxford Classical Dictionary*, viewed 28 February 2021, <https://doi-org.proxy.library.nd.edu/10.1093/acrefore/9780199381135.013.5423>.

Whiston, W. (tr.) 1737. *The Genuine Works of Flavius Josephus the Jewish Historian*. London.

White, R.E. 1898. Women in Ptolemaic Egypt. *Journal of Hellenic Studies* 18: 238–66.

Whitehorne, J.E.G. 1994. *Cleopatras*. London: Routledge.

Wikipedia 2021a. Cleopatra V, viewed 1 June 2021, <https://en.wikipedia.org/wiki/Cleopatra_V>.

Wikipedia 2021b. Cleopatra VI, viewed 1 June 2021, <https://en.wikipedia.org/wiki/Cleopatra_VI>.

Wikipedia 2021c. Cleopatra Selene of Syria, viewed 1 June 2021, <https://en.wikipedia.org/wiki/Cleopatra_Selene_of_Syria>.

Wikipedia 2021d. Ptolemy XI Alexander II, viewed 1 June 2021, <https://en.wikipedia.org/wiki/Ptolemy_XI_Alexander_II>.

Wikipedia 2021e. Ptolemy XII Auletes, viewed 1 June 2021, <https://en.wikipedia.org/wiki/Ptolemy_XII_Auletes>.

Will, É. 1979–1982. *Histoire politique du monde hellénistique (323-30 av. J.-C.)*. Nancy: du Seuil.

Yon, M. *et al.* 2004. *Kition-Bamboula, V: Kition dans les textes. Testimonia littéraires et épigraphiques et corpus des inscriptions*. Paris: Éditions recherche sur les civilisations.

Yonge, C.D. (tr.) 1851. *The Orations of Marcus Tullius Cicero. I: Orations for Quinius, Sextus Roscius, Quintus Roscius, Against Quintus Cæcilius, and Against Verres*. London: George Bell and Sons.

Part II - Law

Aristophanes on Solon and His Laws

Delfim Leão

University of Coimbra
Centre for Classical and Humanistic Studies
leo@fl.uc.pt

Abstract

In Aristophanes work, the references to the laws of Solon are relatively scarce: there are two allusions in *Birds* (*Av.* 1353-57; 1660-64), one in *Clouds* (*Nub.* 1178-95), and a fragment from the lost comedy *Banqueters* (*Dait.* fr. 233 Kassel and Austin). An equal number can be found in four *scholia* to passages: again from *Birds* (*Av.* 1354; 1541) and *Clouds* (*Nub.* 37), and another from *Knights* (*Eq.* 658). Despite this relative paucity, those occurrences prove that Aristophanes was familiar with Solon's laws, which he uses mainly for parodic purposes. The aim of this paper is to analyse those passages in their proper context and in comparison with passages from other authors, in order to discuss their validity as sources for the study of Solon's laws.

Keywords

Aristophanes, Solon, Greek law, comedy

The edition of *The Laws of Solon*[1] that I had the honour of preparing with P.J. Rhodes constitutes a work that I place, without hesitation, among the types of scholarly production that I have most enjoyed and profited from. This is justified, firstly, because the figure of Solon qua legislator, poet and *sophos* has been one of my preferred subjects of study for more than twenty years. However, to this reason I must add another, which makes all the difference: the privilege of being able to work, over several years, with P. J. Rhodes, a personal and academic experience that has marked me deeply, whose multiple benefits I feel daily and for which I will never be able to give adequate thanks, however often I acknowledge it. Still, I would like to begin this brief study by again publicly attesting to this feeling of gratitude on my part.

This edition of Solon's laws reunites and provides analysis for a total of 318 fragments concerning the legislation of the most paradigmatic Athenian statesman. In preparing this edition, 43 new fragments were identified that had not been included in Ruschenbusch's earlier publications.[2] The material used for the reconstitution of Solon's legislation derives from almost sixty authors, from different times and sources, and of an equally varied nature, ranging from the time of Herodotus to the *Suda*, thus raising complex problems of interpretation and determination of authenticity. Indeed, even when the original text of a given law is not

---

[1] Leão and Rhodes (2015). The 2nd revised paperback edition (2016) is used as the reference. The Greek text, translation and numbering of the fragments of Solon's laws (= Fr.) used in this study correspond to those fixed for that edition. This paper is a revised and updated version of a work originally published in Portuguese by Leão (2018), to whose editors and publisher I would like to thank for allowing me to reuse that study as the basis of the argument now proposed. I want to thank as well David Wallace-Hare and the anonymous reviewer, who read an earlier version of this paper, and whose comments helped me to improve it, especially at the linguistic level. The research presented is framed within the UID/ELT/00196/2019 project, funded by FCT - Foundation for Science and Technology.
[2] Ruschenbusch (1966, 2010).

available, this does not necessarily imply that the marks of a certain "Solonian kernel" cannot be identified in it.[3] Solon was active in the Archaic Period (at the turn of the 7th to the 6th century BC), but the most important source for his legislation (providing information for fifty-seven fragments[4]) is the biographer Plutarch, who lived many centuries later. This implies that Plutarch alone provides about a fifth of the entire *corpus* of Solon's laws.[5] By comparison, only Demosthenes (or Pseudo-Demosthenes) comes close to him in magnitude, providing data for forty-eight fragments (plus two other *scholia* references), followed in third place by the Aristotelian *Athenaion Politeia*, which has twenty-four references.

A quite different scenario, however, at least in terms of the abundance of material, is found in other sources, in particular in the comic writer Aristophanes, who constitutes the most direct focus of this study. Indeed, only three references to Solon's laws occur in his extant works, two in *Birds* (*Av.* 1353-57 = Fr. 55a; *Av.* 1660-64 = Fr. 50a) and one in *Clouds* (*Nub.* 1178-95 = Fr. 123a), in addition to a fragment from the lost comedy *Banqueters* (*Dait.* fr. 233 Kassel and Austin, *apud* Gal. *Linguarum Hippocratis Explicatio, prooemium,* xix. 66 Kuhn = Fr. 41a), and 4 others in *scholia*, concerning *Birds* (*Av.* 1354 = Fr. 85c; *Av.* 1541 = Fr. 79/b), *Knights* (*Eq.* 658 = Fr. 64b), and *Clouds* 37.[6] Since this is a rather small set of fragments, it is justified to approach them on a case-by-case basis, providing a brief contextualisation of the areas of Solon's legislative activity in which they fall.

Aristophanes and Solon's laws

The first of the passages to be analysed concerns certain obligations arising from the right of *anchisteia*, a term used to refer to the direct relatives of a deceased, although relatives in the broad sense could also be designated by the word *syngeneia*. However, the former term was more restrictive, as it did not include relatives beyond the degree of 'sons of cousins'.[7] The *anchisteia* guaranteed the relatives covered by it the possibility of applying to inherit the estate of a deceased relative. This prerogative was, however, accompanied by certain obligations, such as ensuring the application of justice (in case the deceased had been a victim of homicide), as well as ritual duties, especially those concerning the cult of the dead. But even before the death of the relative, his most direct descendants were obliged to provide for the members of the *oikos* in old age (*gerotrophia*), a principle that was, moreover, compensation for the fact that parents had made a similar effort with regard to their children (*paidotrophia*), when they were still too young to provide for themselves. It is to this reality, already foreseen in Solon's code, that Aristophanes refers, in parodic terms (*Av.* 1353-57 = Fr. 55a):

> ἀλλ' ἔστιν ἡμῖν τοῖσιν ὄρνισιν νόμος
> παλαιὸς ἐν ταῖς τῶν πελαργῶν κύρβεσιν·

---

[3] The expression "Solonian kernel" is taken from the stimulating study of Scafuro (2006: 179). For an overview of the main problems concerning the correct identification of Solon's laws, see Leão and Rhodes (2016: 1-9).
[4] A small part of them (11) comes from the *Moralia*, without there being a predominance of any particular work. In fact, although Solon is the most important character in the *Banquet of the Seven Wise Men*, there is only one legislative reference in this work, concerning pederasty (*Sept. sap. conv.* 152 D = Fr. 74c). Information on the other fragments occurs in the *Vitae*, with special relevance, as might be expected, to the *Life of Solon*.
[5] Even taking into consideration that not all of them can be considered genuine. See Leão (2016a), who expands and discusses in detail these considerations regarding Plutarch's testimony.
[6] Not previously registered in Leão and Rhodes (2016).
[7] In other words, not all *syngeneis* were *anchisteis*, although all *anchisteis* were *syngeneis*. On this question, see Harrison (1968-1971: I.143-48).

"ἐπὴν ὁ πατὴρ ὁ πελαργὸς ἐκπετησίμους
πάντας ποήσῃ τοὺς πελαργιδέας τρέφων,
δεῖ τοὺς νεοττοὺς τὸν πατέρα πάλιν τρέφειν."

But there is among us, the birds, this ancient law written in the *kyrbeis*[8] of the storks: 'When the father stork has brought up his storklings and made them ready to fly, then must those young support the father in their turn.'

While recognising the obvious comic perspective of this passage, it is equally true that Aristophanes' verses express the gist of the law on the obligation of children to feed their parents in old age (δεῖ τοὺς νεοττοὺς τὸν πατέρα πάλιν τρέφειν), which expressed a kind of principle of reciprocity, arising from the effort made by the parents to raise them from a young age.[9] However, this norm could suffer some restrictions. Indeed, Plutarch (*Sol.* 22.1 = Fr. 56/a) reports that the legislator made *gerotrophia* dependent on the obligation of the parents themselves to teach in advance their children a *techne*. This clause has been correctly related to a concern to encourage trade and industry, at a time when the economy of Attica needed a strong stimulus to counteract the situation of widespread debt discussed in our sources. Among other measures, the statesman is said to have sought to attract outsiders to Athens, especially those who were in a position to exercise a trade. He also urged citizens to engage in such manufacturing occupations, since the poor soil of Attica was not capable of feeding a very large population. Therefore, strengthening the economy in these areas would create a surplus of production that would favour trade and the exchange of manufactured goods for basic necessities. In this spirit of stimulating production, it is thus particularly significant that the legislator made *gerotrophia* conditional on the obligation of parents to teach their children a craft.[10] In another passage of Plutarch (*Sol.* 22.4 = Fr. 57/a), it is made clear that the obligation to support one's parents in old age only applied to legitimate children. This is a balanced measure, since illegitimate children were penalized in terms of legal prerogatives.[11] At the same time, however, this norm accentuated the legal gap that had been established between *gnesioi* and *nothoi* offspring. In a sense, by prohibiting debt slavery (by not allowing loans that took personal freedom as collateral), Solon had already set in motion a similar process that would lead to the reinforcement of the more exclusive character of citizenship status: since a citizen could not become a slave except in especially serious cases (when he had directly put at risk the security of the state), then the reverse hypothesis also became true, since it would now be much more difficult for a slave to cross the threshold that separated him from a citizen.[12]

---

[8] On the nature and functions of the *axones* and *kyrbeis*, see Leão (2001: 329-40), with bibliography. In *Nub.* 448, Aristophanes mentions the *kyrbis*, but despite the implicit allusion to Solon, no specific law is implied. See Steiner (2020: 253-54).
[9] Incidentally, concern for *gerotrophia* was one of the motivations for adopting someone, but only in the *inter vivos* variant, for obvious reasons. On the attribution of this law to Solon, see Weeber (1973); Stroud (1979: 5).
[10] Somehow, it seems to have been in the mind of the legislator that *paidotrophia* would not have been properly conducted if the parents had not taught their children a trade that would enable them to earn a living in the future. Consequently, in such a situation the principle of reciprocity binding the mutual obligations of *paidotrophia* and *gerotrophia* would no longer apply. For a more extended discussion of the principle of reciprocity between *paidotrophia* and *gerotrophia*, see Leão (2011); Cantarella (2016), with a response by Leão (2016b).
[11] Cf. Demosthenes 43.51 (= Fr. 50b), together with the commentary by Leão and Rhodes (2016: 85).
[12] Lape (2002/03: 129-35) understands this measure as a kind of first test of the law of citizenship (instated by Pericles in 451/0), which would aim to limit the privileges of the aristocracy, since it was mainly the latter who possessed resources that allowed them to keep illegitimate children. For a complete list of other sources that refer to the same law of Solon and their discussion, see Leão and Rhodes (2016: 92-7).

A second passage of Aristophanes, also from *Birds*, concerns already a different, though complementary, reality in the same area of family law, more specifically the right of inheritance (*Av.* 1660-64 = Fr. 50a):

> ἐρῶ δὲ δὴ καὶ τὸν Σόλωνός σοι νόμον·
> "νόθῳ δὲ μὴ εἶναι ἀγχιστείαν παίδων ὄντων
> γνησίων· ἐὰν δὲ παῖδες μὴ ὦσι γνήσιοι, τοῖς
> ἐγγυτάτω γένους μετεῖναι τῶν χρημάτων."

> I will then cite for you the law of Solon: 'An illegitimate child shall not have right of inheritance, if there are legitimate children; and if there are no legitimate children, the property shall pass to those most closely related.'

The official recognition of a legitimate son, apart from being essential to guarantee his future citizenship, was also a prerequisite for his qualification as an heir to the paternal *oikos* (in the sense of 'property'). Correlative to this reality is also the capacity for the holder of an estate to be able to make a will. Plutarch (*Sol.* 21.3-4 = Fr. 49b) states that Solon was responsible for this innovation. In fact, according to the biographer, before Solon's legislation, making wills was not allowed. For this reason, the deceased's property would pass to his immediate family. By instituting the law on wills, Solon would have granted the owner the right to dispose of his property. However, Plutarch's perspective has been questioned by those who argue the contrary, viz. that Solon may have only been officialising an already common practice, with the aim of overcoming controversies and problems derived from its practical implementation.[13] In any case, the option for a will was dependent on the lack of natural children, as only those who were in that situation could transmit their property. Moreover, it should be guaranteed that the testator made the will of his own free will and in full use of his faculties, therefore without the pressure of illness, nor under the effect of drugs, nor by coercion nor even at the suggestion of a woman.[14] Plutarch, in the passage mentioned above, mentions these various conditions, but omits another that was equally central: the requirement that children must be legitimate (*gnesioi*). This essential detail is clearly expressed in [Demosthenes] (46.14 = Fr. 49a: ἂν μὴ παῖδες ὦσι γνήσιοι ἄρρενες), making it clear that the practice of adoption was ultimately aimed at preventing the extinction of the testator's *oikos*. However, a man could die without a will and without having the most direct heirs of legitimate birth: a child, a grandchild or a great-grandchild. This is the case referred to in the rule mentioned by Aristophanes, who maintains that, in such circumstances, the law of Solon determined that 'property shall pass to those most closely related'. A more complete version of the law can be found in Demosthenes (43.51 = Fr. 50b) and, in essence, it should correspond to Solon's provisions, though revised in the meantime, as illustrated by the information that the norm was (re)published in 403-2, during the archonship of Euclides.[15]

---

[13] Thus Ruschenbusch (1962). Without going into detail, Rubinstein (1993: 10-11) argues in the same sense. Gagliardi (2002), while recognizing the ambivalence of the sources, maintains that the so-called 'testamentary law' would aim at covering not only wills, but rather disciplining universal successions and therefore also adoptions, whether performed *inter vivos* or by testamentary means. For an overview of the sources and their main interpretations, see Leão and Rhodes (2016: 78-83). Humphreys (2018: 64) argues that another of the practical consequences of Solon's law on wills was that it encouraged relatives to question wills in which testators favoured candidates with whom they were associated or attached, to the detriment of candidates' next-of-kin.

[14] In the *Moralia* (265e = Fr. 49c), Plutarch also underlines this clause.

[15] See Arnaoutoglou (1998: 3). Buis (2014: 326-7) acknowledges the parody of Solon's legislation, even if the terms of

Solon's code included several provisions concerning agricultural activity, in particular those governing certain conflicts that could arise between neighbours, such as the distance to be observed between plantations on neighbouring properties, rules for sharing water or even the use of natural fertilisers.[16] Although, in agricultural societies, the importance of such details could be a source of heated dispute, the levity of lawsuits instituted over banalities such as the theft of excrement seems to have given rise to the proverbial expression 'dung suit' (*bolitou dike*). Two brief testimonies refer to this reality:

Paroemiogr. Appendix I. 58 (i. 388) (= Fr. 64a)

> ΒΟΛΙΤΟΥ ΔΙΚΗΝ· πρὸς τοὺς ἀξίους καὶ ἐπὶ μικροῖς τιμωρίαν ὑπέχειν. ἐν γὰρ τοῖς Σόλωνος ἄξοσιν ὁ νόμος καὶ τοὺς βόλιτον ὑφελομένους κολάζει.

> *DUNG SUIT*: [a proverb] coined for those who suffer deservedly even because of trifles. For in the *axones* of Solon the law punishes also those who have stolen dung.

Schol. Aristophanes, *Eq.* 658, *Suda* β 367 (= Fr. 64b)

> ΒΟΛΙΤΟΥ ΔΙΚΗΝ· πρὸς τοὺς ἐπὶ μικροῖς δίκας ὑπέχοντας. ὁ γὰρ Σόλωνος νόμος καὶ τοὺς βόλιτον ὑφελομένους κολάζει.

> *DUNG SUIT*: [a proverb] coined for those who face justice just because of trifles. For the law of Solon punishes also those who have stolen dung.

The fact that the *axones* of Solon are expressly mentioned in Fr. 64a is a sign that this matter could indeed have been dealt with in the legislator's code. Although this detail is absent from Fr. 64b, it is in any case unequivocal that it refers to the same reality. The comment occurs in a *scholium* to Aristophanes' *Knights* (v. 658: τοῖς βολίτοις ἡττημένος), at a time when the character Sausage-Seller refers to the opponent Paphlagon as being a 'piece of dung' who was outdoing him in the debate, prompting him to react by making supplementary promises to the *boule*. The term βόλιτον designates in particular 'ox dung' (cf. Pollux 5.91), and so it is possible that the norm began by referring to anyone who possessed or was responsible for this type of livestock. Over time, the expression βολίτου δίκη would evolve from the literal sense ('dung private suit') to a more generic usage, emphatically expressing penalties arising from trifling contentions.

One of the traits of Solon's legislative action in religious matters would have been the organization of an official calendar of sacrifices, although it is doubtful whether he created them for the first time or if, on the contrary, he limited himself to systematizing already existing regulations. Among the innovations at this level is the reformulation of the *Genesia*, a celebration in honour of the dead that, initially, would have belonged to the private domain of aristocrats, whose influence Solon would have sought to curtail. Therefore, the decision

---

the law do not entirely coincide with the norms referred to by Demosthenes 43.51. Martin (2015: 78-9) admits the parody of Solon's law, but is more favourable to the interpretation that the target is Pericles' law of citizenship. Melis (2020: 81-85) thinks that the play echoes the complaints of Athenian citizens targeting the 'falsi cittadini' who did not meet the conditions laid down in Pericles' law, by not being directly descended from Athenian citizens on both sides.
[16] See Leão and Rhodes (2016: 103-6).

to pass the *Genesia* to the domain of official festivals would have been a contribution to this strategy.[17] In this context, Aristophanes is also evoked, with reference to a *scholium* to the passage of *Birds* discussed earlier (fr. 55a), arguing in favour of Cretan influence in this type of legislation:

Schol. Aristophanes, *Av.* 1354 (Fr. 85c)

ΕΝ ΤΑΙΣ ΤΩΝ ΠΕΛΑΡΓΩΝ ΚΥΡΒΕΣΙΝ· ἀπὸ τῶν κορυβάντων. ἐκείνων γὰρ εὕρημα, ὥς φησι Θεόφραστος ἐν τῷ περὶ εὐσεβείας.

IN THE *KYRBEIS* OF THE STORKS: from the Corybantes. The invention is theirs, as Theophrastus says in his *On Piety.*

The most distinctive aspect of this short fragment is the establishment of a relationship between the religious regulation of Athens (in particular that concerning sacrificial practices) and the influx of the Corybantic rite from Crete. This information is supported by two further sources: Theophrastus (*De Piet. apud Porphyry Abstin.* II. 20-1 = Fr. 85a) and Photius (κ 1234 Theodoridis = Fr. 85b). Plutarch also points in the same direction (*Sol.* 12.7-9), by maintaining that Epimenides of Crete inspired Solon's funerary laws.

In a final *scholium* to the comedy *Birds*, which thus proves to be a very fruitful source for Solon, one finds some information about the *naukrariai* (and their *naukraroi*), an unclear political institution, possibly abolished in the early 5th century:

Schol. Aristophanes *Av.* 1541 (= Fr. 79/b = Androtion *FGrH* 324 F 36)

Ἀνδροτίων γράφει οὕτως· "τοῖς δὲ ἰοῦσι Πυθῶδε θεωροῖς τοὺς κωλακρέτας διδόναι ἐκ τῶν ναυκραρικῶν ἐφόδιον ἀργύρια, καὶ εἰς ἄλλο ὅ τι ἂν δέῃ ἀναλῶσαι".

Androtion writes as follows: 'To the *theoroi* going to Delphi the *kolakretai* shall give silver from the naucraric funds for their travelling expenses, and for anything else which they need to spend'.

It is likely that the *naukrariai* performed a role involving the provisioning of ships, but this *testimonium* suggests that they might also have had other functions, such as financing the official envoys to Delphi (*theoroi*), with pieces of metal (i.e. silver) to guarantee payment of expenses at a time when there was no coinage in Athens. Although brief, this *scholium* thus provides an important contribution to our understanding of a particularly obscure question of the financial organisation of Athenian society in the Archaic Period.[18] The *scholium* to the passage from Aristophanes' comedy is prompted by the occurrence of the term κωλακρέτης in v. 1541; consequently, there is no express reference to Solon's legislation. However, this relationship is clearly established by the *Constitution of the Athenians* (*Ath. Pol.* 8.3 = Fr. 79a), which holds that references to this institution occurred frequently 'in the laws of Solon which

---

[17] For a discussion of the main strands of the debate, see Blok (2006: 235-7). On the testimonies pertinent to this question, see Leão and Rhodes (2016: 140-3).
[18] For the other fragments, see Leão and Rhodes (2016: 135-6). For more details regarding *naukrariai* and *naukraroi* in the Archaic Period, see Leão (2001: 214-21).

are no longer in use' (ἐν τοῖς νόμοις τοῖς Σόλωνος οἷς οὐκέτι χρῶνται).[19] In a *scholium* to Aristophanes' *Clouds* 37 (*SA* 1.3.1.256.11-20 Koster), the institution of the *nauklaroi* is credited to Solon or even to an earlier period, and a testimony from Demetrius of Phalerum is cited, who speaks about the appointment of *demarchoi* by Solon.[20]

Another reference to Solon's legislation occurs in the now lost comedy *Banqueters* (*Daitaleis*), referring to the field of evidence, namely the presentation of witnesses.

Daitaleis (fr. 233 Kassel and Austin), *apud* Gal. *Linguarum Hippocratis Explicatio, prooemium* (xix. 66 Kuhn) = Fr. 41a

> νομίζω δέ σοι τὰ ὑπὸ Ἀριστοφάνους ἀρκέσειν τὰ ἐκ τῶν Δαιταλέων ὧδέ πως ἔχοντα·
> "πρὸς ταῦτα σὺ λέξον Ὁμηρείους γλώττας, τί καλοῦσι κόρυμβα (Hom. *Il.* 9.241);"
> προβάλλει γὰρ ἐν ἐκείνῳ τῷ δράματι ὁ ἐκ τοῦ δήμου τῶν Δαιταλέων πρεσβύτης τῷ
> ἀκολάστῳ υἱεῖ πρῶτον μὲν τὰ κόρυμβα τί ποτ᾽ ἐστὶν ἐξηγήσασθαι. μετὰ δὲ τοῦτο·
> "τί καλοῦσιν ἀμενηνὰ κάρηνα (Hom. *Od.* 10.521, etc.);"
> κἀκεῖνος μέντοι ἀντιπροβάλλει τῶν ἐν τοῖς Σόλωνος ἄξοσιν γλῶτταν εἰς δίκας
> διαφερούσας ὡδί πως·
> "ὁ μὲν οὖν σὸς, ἐμὸς δὲ οὗτος ἀδελφὸς φρασάτω, τί καλοῦσιν ἰδυίους;"
> εἶτ᾽ ἐφεξῆς προβάλλει·
> "τί ποτέ ἐστιν ὀπυίειν (fr. 52c);"
> ἐξ ὧν δῆλον ὡς ἡ γλῶττα παλαιόν ἐστιν ὄνομα τῆς συνηθείας ἐκπεπτωκός.

> κόρυμβα Poll. II. 109: κόρυβα Galen. τὸ ὀπυίειν Dindorf: τὸ εὐποιεῖν Galen.

I think what is said by Aristophanes in the *Banqueters* will be sufficient for you, which runs like this:
'In addition to this you must expound Homeric expressions: what do they mean by *korymba* ["high point"]?'
For in that drama the old man from the deme Daitaleis challenges his dissolute son first to explain what *korymba* means. After that:
'What do they mean by *amenena karena* ["fleeting heads"]?'
He then challenges him in turn on expressions in Solon's *axones* relating to various lawsuits, like this:
'Your son and my brother, tell me, what is meant by *idyioi* ["witnesses"]?'
Then he challenges next:
'What is *opyiein* ["marry"]?'
From which it is clear that the expression is an ancient name which has fallen out of currency.

Aristophanes' fragment lends credence to the possibility that the words under dispute would occur in Solon's *axones*, thus reinforcing their authenticity. It could possibly be argued that the reference to the material support of Solon's laws and to terms like *idyioi* and *opyiein* would serve only the purpose of giving verisimilitude to a legislative forgery imagined by the

---

[19] For further discussion on this passage, see Rhodes (1981: 151-3).
[20] This (new) fragment was not registered by Leão and Rhodes (2016). For the full text of the *scholium*, with a short commentary, see Fortenbaugh and Schütrumpf (2000: 176-9).

playwright.[21] However, the likely occurrence of these terms in the *axones* is strongly indicated by other sources as well,[22] and is also consistent with the recourse to legal imagery with which an audience of *theatai/politai* would be well familiar. Technical terms should therefore be used correctly and as such recognised by the spectators, so that the parody could be apprehended and prove successful on stage.[23]

Finally, the most expressive and direct reference to Solon in Aristophanes' work occurs in the *Clouds*, at a moment when Pheidippides, already initiated in sophistic rhetoric and dialectic, displays his argumentative capacity before his father, Strepsiades, who is overwhelmed by the approach of the day when he must pay his debts. Despite its length and evident comic efficacy, the passage nevertheless represents the case in which a relationship with Solon's actual regulation will be least likely (*Nub.* 1178-95 = Fr. 123a). It is therefore not necessary to quote it in full here, because it will suffice to recall the essence of what is at stake. This passage from the *Clouds* joins a group of fragments that address the question of how to interpret the dictum ἔνη τε καὶ νέα ('the old and new [day]', i.e. the last one of the Attic month), which was actually a current expression that the Aristophanic character presents as a legal archaism of Solon to which he resorts in order to give an age-old authority to an interpretation of the law that would be favourable to him. In fact, he even considers that "Solon, that man of antiquity, was by nature a friend of the people" (v. 1187: ὁ Σόλων ὁ παλαιὸς ἦν φιλόδημος τὴν φύσιν).[24] The term *philodemos* could be taken as an indication that the statesman was seen as being favourable to democracy (thus anticipating the propagandistic image of Solon in the light of the *patrios politeia* theme), but it is too vague to provide secure support for this hypothesis. At any rate, despite the fact that other ancient sources tend to identify in the expression ἔνη τε καὶ νέα an aphorism devised by Solon,[25] possibly linked to the reform of the Attic calendar, it is more likely to be merely a comic invention, intended to demonstrate the sophistical skillfulness of Pheidippides.[26] The fact that it is echoed in other authors argues in favour of Aristophanes' prestige as a playwright, but it does not really contribute to the reconstitution of Solon's code of laws.

---

[21] Martin (2015: 80) argues along these lines, seeking to draw a parallel with the rhetorical practice of 4th-century orators. Loddo (2018: 61-64) underlines the importance of this reference for witnessing the memorisation of Homeric and Solonian *glossae* at school, in this case in an educational programme that would oppose old and new teaching methods, possibly along with the lines of what is caricatured in *Clouds*.

[22] See Leão and Rhodes (2016: 70-3).

[23] A position openly held by MacDowell (2010: 156), who states: "since the spectators were knowledgeable about the law, Aristophanes had to get his facts right, and that means that his comments about the law, though of course they are very incomplete, can, as far as they go, be used by us as historical evidence to supplement the information that we have from other sources".

[24] For more details respecting the reconfiguration of Solon through the lens of the *patrios politeia*, see Leão (2001: 43-72, at p. 61 on this passage). Martin (2015: 77) translates the passage as 'Solon of old was *demos*-loving by nature', but again this does not imply necessarily that Aristophanes saw the legislator as a proto-democrat. Loddo (2018: 65-6) argues that it is in the very 'obscurity' of archaic laws that Pheidippides sees the mark of Solon favouring the *demos* and, as a consequence, that the term *philodemos* could be a sign that "Solone nelle *Nuvole* sia associato con un modo demagogico di fare politica". In fact, in *Ath. Pol.* 9.2 (= Fr. 47a), Solon's law on inheritances and heiresses (*epikleroi*) is presented as an example of an 'obscure' norm, but what seemed not clear enough to a late-fifth-century audience was not necessariy intended as such by Solon. For further details, see Rhodes (1981: 440-1); Leão and Rhodes (2016: 75).

[25] Plutarch *Sol.* 25.4-5 (= Fr. 123b); Diogenes Laertius 1.57-8 (= Fr. 123c); *Lex. Rhet. Cant.* (75.11-12 *Lexica Graeca Minora* = Fr. 123d). See also Leão and Rhodes (2016: 182-4).

[26] See Ruschenbusch (1966: 46); Sommerstein (1982: 218); Manfredini and Piccirilli (1998: 262-3).

Final considerations

At this point in the analysis, there are already enough elements to make a more concrete appreciation of the presence of Solon's laws in Aristophanes' comedy. The most fruitful occurrences undoubtedly occur in the *Birds*, in which there are two allusions to the laws concerning *gerotrophia* and the right of inheritance. Despite its evident parodic nature, Solon's influence on these regulations is easily detected. The same comedy also motivates two *scholia* with references to the regulations established by Solon: one concerning the possible influence of the Corybantic rite of Crete on the legislation on sacrifices and the other on the functions of the *naukrariai* (a topic approached as well in a *scholium* to *Clouds*). There is also another *scholium* to *Knights*, concerning the proverbial expression *bolitou dike*, referring to cases of negligible importance, as well as a fragment of *Banqueters*, in which the archaic and technical use of Solonian *glossae* are under scrutiny. It should be stressed that, in all these cases, the implicit or explicit reference to Solon is confirmed by other sources, in such terms that support the reliability of Aristophanes' testimony.

The same is not true, however, of the more extensive occurrence, in *Clouds*, concerning the saying ἕνη τε καὶ νέα, analysed last. Although it is attested in other ancient sources, it corresponds more probably to a phrase in common usage, which the ambience of comedy (and not necessarily Aristophanes) would end up connecting to the most paradigmatic Athenian legialator.

Still, despite the fact that Aristophanes' contribution is very different in scope and nature from Plutarch's (as briefly evoked at the beginning of this study), the playwright turns out to be a very pertinent source in the skilful way he weaves into his work allusions to the ancient Athenian statesman. Apart from the relative weight that may be attributed to his work for the reconstruction of Attic legal activity, this situation, in particular, provides a very revealing analysis of the way in which the greatest Athenian comic writer knew how to use, for comic effect, a legal imaginary with which the average Athenian *theates/polites* could easily identify.

Bibliography

Arnaoutoglou, I. 1998. *Ancient Greek Laws. A Sourcebook*. London: Routledge.
Blok, J.H. 2006. Solon's funerary laws: questions of authenticity and function, in J.H. Blok and A.P.M.H. Lardinois (eds), *Solon of Athens. New Historical and Philological Approaches*): 197-247. Leiden: Brill.
Buis, E.J. 2014. Law and Greek comedy, in M. Fontaine and A.C. Scafuro (eds), *The Oxford Handbook of Greek and Roman Comedy*: 321-339. Oxford: Oxford University Press.
Cantarella, E. 2016. *Gerotrophia*: a controversial law, in D.F. Leão and G. Thür (eds), *Symposion 2015. Akten der Gesellschaft für griechische und hellenistische Rechtsgeschichte*: 55-66. Wien: Verlag der Österreichischen Akademie der Wissenschaften.
Fortenbaugh, W.W. and E. Schütrumpf. 2000. *Demetrius of Phalerum. Text, Translation and Discussion. Rutgers University Studies in Classical Humamities, vol. IX*. New Brunswick: Transaction Publishers.
Gagliardi, L. 2002. Per un'interpretazione della legge di Solone in materia sucessoria. *Dike* 5: 5-59.
Harrison, A.R.W. 1968-1971. *The Law of Athens*. II vols., Oxford: Oxford University Press.

Humphreys, S.C. (2018). *Kinship in Ancient Athens. An Anthropological Analysis.* Vol I. Oxford: University Press.

Lape, S. 2002/03. Solon and the institution of the 'democratic' family form. *Classical Journal* 98.2: 117-39.

Leão, D. F. 2001. *Sólon. Ética e política.* Lisboa: Fundação Calouste Gulbenkian.

Leão, D. F. 2011. *Paidotrophia* et *gerotrophia* dans les lois de Solon. *Revue historique de droit français et étranger* 89.4: 457-472.

Leão, D.F. 2016a. Consistency and criticism in Plutarch's writings concerning the laws of Solon, in J. Opsomer, G. Roskam and F.B. Titchener (eds), *A Versatile Gentleman. Consistency in Plutarch's Writing*: 243-254. Leuven: Leuven University Press.

Leão, D.F. 2016b. *Gerotrophia*: a controversial law — Response to Eva Cantarella, in D. F. Leão and G. Thür (eds), *Symposion 2015. Vorträge zur griechischen und hellenistischen Rechtsgeschichte*: 75-82. Wien: Verlag der Österreichischen Akademie der Wissenschaften.

Leão, D.F. 2018. Aristófanes e as leis de Sólon, in C.N. Fernández, J.T. Nápoli and G.C. Zecchin de Fasano (eds), *[Una] nueva visión de la cultura griega antigua en el comienzo del tercer milenio: perspectivas y desafíos*: 213-233. La Plata: Editorial de la Universidad de La Plata.

Leão, D.F. and P.J. Rhodes 2016. *The Laws of Solon. A New Edition with Introduction, Translation and Commentary.* London: I.B.Tauris. [2nd revised paperback edition; 1st hardback edition 2015]

Loddo, L. 2018. *Solone demotikotatos. Il legislatore e il politico nella cultura democratica ateniese.* Milano: LED.

MacDowell, D.M. 2010). Aristophanes and Athenian Law, in E. Harris, D. Leão, and P.J. Rhodes (eds), *Law and Drama in Ancient Greece*: 147-157. London: Duckworth.

Manfredini, M. and L. Piccirilli 1998. *Plutarco. La vita di Solone,* Milano: Mondadori. (5th ed.)

Martin, R.P. 2015. Solon in Comedy. *Trends in Classics* 7.1: 66-84.

Melis, V. 2020. Le leggi del diritto attico su eredità e cittadinanza negli *Uccelli* di Aristofane. *Rivista di Filologia e di Istruzione Classica* 148.1: 69-90.

Rhodes, P.J. 1981. *A Commentary on the Aristotelian Athenaion Politeia.* Oxford: Oxford University Press.

Rubinstein, L. 1993. *Adoption in IV. Century Athens.* Copenhagen: Museum Tusculanum.

Ruschenbusch, E. 1962. διατίθεσθαι τὰ ἑαυτοῦ: Ein Beitrag zum sogenannten Testamentsgesetz des Solon. *Zeitschrift der Savigny-Stiftung für Rechtsgeschichte: Romanistische Abteilung* 79: 307- -11.

Ruschenbusch, E. 1966. *Σόλωνος νόμοι: Die Fragmente des solonischen Gesetzeswerkes mit einer Text- und Überlieferungsgeschichte. Historia Einzelschriften ix.* Wiesbaden: Franz Steiner.

Ruschenbusch, E. 2010. *Solon: das Gesetzeswerk — Fragmente: Übersetzung und Kommentar* (ed. By K. Bringmann). *Historia Einzelschriften ccxv.* Stuttgart: Franz Steiner.

Scafuro, A.C. 2006. Identifying Solonian Laws, in J.H. Blok and A.P.M.H. Lardinois (eds), *Solon of Athens. New Historical and Philological Approaches*: 175-196. Leiden: Brill.

Steiner, D. 2020. Inscribing Athenians: the Alphabetic Chorus in Aristophanes' *Babylonians* and the Politics and Aesthetics of Inscription and Conscription in Fifth-Century Athens, in R.M. Rosen and H.M. Foley (eds), *Aristophanes and Politics. New Studies*: 248-272. Leiden: Brill.

Sommerstein, A.H. 1982. *Aristophanes. Clouds.* Warminster: Aris and Phillips.

Stroud, R. 1979. *The Axones and Kyrbeis of Drakon and Solon.* Berkeley: University of California Press.

Weeber, K.-W. 1973. Ein vernachlässigtes solonisches Gesetz. *Athenaeum* 51: 30-33.

Legal Theory, Sophistic Antilogy:
Antiphon's *Tetralogies*[1]

Davide Napoli

Harvard University
davidenapoli@g.harvard.edu

Abstract

The paper argues that Antiphon's *Tetralogies* are not a handbook or a school exercise, as often assumed, but a sophisticated reflection on the underpinnings of Athenian law. The common view about the lack of legal theory in Athens is thus questioned and revised. The notion of "problematization" is used to describe and analyze the purpose of Antiphon's work: the starting point is a consideration of the mimetic and antilogical form of the *Tetralogies*, which is set against other contemporary texts. The paper examines some of the techniques deployed in the *Tetralogies* to problematize Athenian law, as for example the manipulation of widespread forensic *topoi* and the exploitation of the instability of legal language. Finally, the theoretical enterprise of the *Tetralogies* is framed within the concerns of the sophistic movement, thus showing how the work can contribute to expand and modify our understanding of sophistic modes of theorizing.

Keywords

Athenian law – Sophistic movement – *topoi* – oratory

Antiphon's *Tetralogies* are, in many ways, a marginal work. Not only do they stand isolated in the panorama of classical literature,[2] but they also read as a foreign body in the corpus of Athenian oratory. In fact, within said corpus, they are the earliest work;[3] they contain the only fictional speeches;[4] they were uniquely designed to be read;[5] and they provide the only legal cases for which four speeches are extant.[6] Since each point I just touched upon is fraught with controversies (starting from my first words: 'Antiphon's [?] *Tetralogies*'), for the sake of convenience I will rely on the balanced treatment offered by Michael Gagarin in his fundamental study of Antiphon's work (2002: 103–34). My contribution will be centered on the method and purpose of the *Tetralogies*, and their connection to the sophistic reflection on language and law.

Athenian law has been traditionally denied self-reflexivity: since in Athens there are no legal experts – so the common view goes – there can be no expert reflection on the principles of

---

[1] I would like to thank Adriaan Lanni, Joel Mann, Christopher Moore and Mark Schiefsky for helpful comments on earlier drafts of the paper.

[2] As already remarked by Blass 1887-98: 1.149.

[3] E. g. Dover 1950; Usher 1999: 355–9.

[4] Schmitz 2000: 52–9.

[5] As opposed to non-fictional speeches, delivered orally: see Gagarin 1999 and Vatri 2017.

[6] Two speeches (plaintiff, defendant) were probably the norm in public cases (*graphai*), four (plaintiff, defendant, plaintiff, defendant) in private ones (*dikai*): see AP 67.2 with Harrison 1968-71: 2.160–1; MacDowell 1963: 113–4; Rhodes 1993 *ad loc*. We have no extant legal case for which four speeches survive, and only a handful cases for which two of them are extant (listed in Siron 2019: 26).

law.[7] This conclusion can be questioned by a reexamination of Antiphon's *Tetralogies*: as it will turn out, the failure to countenance the diverse textual forms that theory could take on in the fifth century has hindered our understanding of the *Tetralogies* in their sophistic context, and consequently their contribution to Athenian (and sophistic) legal theory.[8]

Before starting the discussion, let me clarify why I use the concept of 'legal theory' (instead of, say, 'philosophy of law'). With 'theory' I do not mean a systematic, unified, comprehensive 'grand theory'. Instead, I use 'theory' as a shorthand for a sustained inquiry into the unspoken assumptions of a social practice (namely Athenian law), exposing its implicit blind spots, virtual pitfalls and potential consequences.[9] In the *Tetralogies* such inquiry is not formalized into a prose treatise,[10] but rather conducted in a mimetic fashion by staging a trial.[11] The form of the *Tetralogies* is thus peculiarly embedded in its own subject matter, the lawcourt: to appreciate Antiphon's bold project, then, we first have to briefly touch on its formal features.

Form: what the *Tetralogies* are

Formally, the *Tetralogies* participate in two cultural fields: Athenian law and sophistic antilogy. As for the former, the unfolding of four speeches in the *Tetralogies* mirrors the standard procedure for homicide cases (above, n. 6). More specifically, the *Tetralogies* partake in Athenian law by sharing numerous forms of argument with forensic oratory.[12] Even so, for some of these arguments it is hard to demarcate their entanglement with Athenian law from their affinity to sophistic display pieces (*epideixeis*) – predictably so, since *epideixeis* often make use of the same arguments of Athenian courts.[13]

---

[7] In ancient terms, no τεχνῖται, no τέχνη (see Hippocr. *VM* 4.1). This is, of course, an oversimplification of the common view (on which see Todd 1993: 21–3; cf. Hansen 1991: 180, 308–9; *contra* Rossetti 2004): elements of legal theorizing are often acknowledged to be present here and there in Athenian oratory (e. g. Dem. 54). However, my contention will be that the *Tetralogies* offer a sustained, if not systematic, discussion of the underpinnings of Athenian law. On legal expertise in Athens see Todd 1996. On Athenian expertise more generally (especially political) see Bertrand 2001; Ismard 2015; Ober 2008; Sobak 2015; cf. Harris 2002. On the topical denial of expertise in oratory see Hesk 2000: 202–41; Ober 1989: 170–9, and Siron 2019: 291–309.

[8] For some examples of different modes of theorizing see Schiappa 1996: 79–85 and Velardi 2011: 117. On fifth-century vs. fourth-century theorizing of rhetoric see Cole 1991. A cursory scan of modern European philosophy is enough to show the multiformity of philosophical communication: compare e. g. Pascal's *Pensées*, Nietzsche's *Also sprach Zarathustra* and Derrida's *Glas*.

[9] This unsystematic sense of 'theory' is close to both fifth-century sophistic practice (Striker 1996: 3–21; cf. Bonazzi 2021: 59–61) and contemporary uses of the word (e.g. 'French theory', 'cultural theory': see Culler 2011: 1–18). *Contra* Decleva Caizzi 1969: 69–71 and *passim*, who claims that the *Tetralogies* express a systematic and coherent theory of law.

[10] On the development of early philosophical prose treatises see Kahn 2003.

[11] Wohl 2010: 119 aristotelically calls it 'theoretical *mimesis* of legal *praxis*'.

[12] See Carawan 1993; cf. also Vatri 2017 on linguistic similarities. For shared arguments see e. g. the reminding of the judicial oath (Ant. 4.4.1 with Siron 2019: 258); self-speaking facts (Ant. 2.4.8 and 4.3.3 with Siron 2019: 271, 273); the lack of preparation or expertise (Ant. 3.2.1–2 with Siron 2019: 292 and Ober 1989: 170–9). Compare also the common argument from precedent (Rubinstein 2007: 362 n. 7) with Ant. 2.4.10 (a very close parallel to Antiphon's formulation is in Dem. 54.43). *Contra* Innes 1991, arguing that the cases of the *Tetralogies* are not set in Athens but in a generic 'Sophistopolis'.

[13] On *epideixeis* see Demont 1993 and Thomas 2003. Cf. Cole 1991: 79–80; Mann 2012b: 8–20; and Pendrick 2002: 45 n. 85 for older bibliography. For the same arguments in *epideixeis* and lawcourts compare e. g. Ant. 4.2.3 with Hippocr. *VM* 17.1, *Flat.* 6.2, 10.1 and *Art.* 5.1 (with Lloyd 1979: 86 n. 144); Ant. 2.2.7 with Gorg. LM D 26.11 (evaluation of the slaves' testimonies); Ant. 2.1.4 with Gorg. LM D 26.7–8 (apagogic method: cf. Spatharas 2001: 405–6); Ant. 2.2.3 with Hippocr. *Art.* 8.4–5 (use of *eikos* arguments). See further Cassin 1997; Notomi 2012: 194–8; Denyer 2008: 159 *ad* 343b3 (on rhetorical questions).

This brings us to the second cultural field traversed by the *Tetralogies*: sophistic antilogy. In the fifth century, the antilogical form spans texts well beyond what we would strictly categorize as sophistic works (e. g. dramatic *agones*, the historians' speeches, medical debates).[14] At the same time, thinkers like Protagoras seem to have harnessed the philosophical potential of antilogy.[15] In fact, the antilogic form is well suited to treating human affairs in which a single, unanimous truth is out of reach (de Romilly 1988: 129). Athenian law and politics, as social practices in which the putative final word (the decisions taken in the lawcourts or in the assembly) often undergoes revision or engenders contradictions, constitute ideal subject matters for antilogy.[16] In addition, the antilogic form is intrinsic to Athenian law, which operates with paired and opposed speeches and no independently authoritative sources of evidence:[17] the happy coincidence of legal and sophistic form becomes in Antiphon's hands a powerful tool of inquiry, ideally suited to a crossbreeding of these two intersecting cultural fields, as we now turn to discuss.

Method: what the *Tetralogies* do

The theoretical procedure followed by the *Tetralogies* can be defined as *problematization*. With problematization I designate the diagnosis of gaps or contradictions in juridical argumentative practices, and the act of making such gaps available for critical investigation by drawing the readers' attention to them.[18] The diagnosis becomes especially difficult, and thus even more important, in the case of stock argumentative tools (*topoi*),[19] so naturalized as to usually go without saying in Athenian courts.

The textual joints where we can see problematization in action are the points identified by several scholars as deviations from Athenian law (see below, n. 45). It will be argued that Antiphon deviates from established Athenian legal practice in order to draw attention to problems that are already implicit (but unacknowledged) in Athenian law. To approach Antiphon's technique, we can start with a deviation that has received less attention than others, but carries a substantial theoretical potential. In Athenian courts, the defense speech is not supposed to be a reply to the plaintiff's narrative, but a different narrative in its own right.[20] This convention is consistently flouted in the *Tetralogies*, in which the litigants show

---

[14] See Demont 1994 and Kraus 2006.

[15] See Kerferd 1981: 59–67 on the similarities between sophistic antilogy, Socratic *elenchos* and Platonic dialectic; cf. Farrar 1988: 63–4.

[16] Revision: Ant. 5.69–71, 5.94, 6.69–70, 6.91 (court decisions); Thuc. 3.36 (assembly decision); And. 1.76 (repeal of a decree). Contradictions: Lys. 30.3, Dem. 24.35. Cf. also Hippias, LM D 18c. Admittedly, in the rhetoric of the courts and of the assembly the audience, as expression of the timeless, unchanging *demos*, is often depicted as infallible, while the mistakes are attributed to evil, misleading *rhetores* (see Wolpert 2003; but on the difference between assembly and lawcourt rhetoric of *demos* cf. Hansen 1991: 154–5): see Ant. 6.91, And. 2.27.

[17] See Cohen 2003 and Todd 1993: 54–60 on the rhetorical use of statutes (including laws) in Athenian law.

[18] My concept of problematization is indebted to the work of Michel Foucault (on problematization as the main axis of Foucault's work see Koopman 2013: 44–8). I consider 'problematization' a more accurate characterization of Antiphon's critical method in the *Tetralogies* than the notions of 'metadiscourse' (Gagarin 2002: 115 and *passim*; cf. Wohl 2010: 119) and 'reversal' (Carawan 1993: 266). Problematization of legal *topoi* occasionally surfaces in real speeches too: see Hesk 2000: 227–31.

[19] Cf. Ober 1989 on *topoi* (Ober 1989: 44: 'symbols, in the form of modes of address and metaphors, that derived from and referred to the common ideological frame of reference of his listeners'). On the meaning and possible origin of *topos* see Cole 1991: 88–9.

[20] See Lys. 12.38, Aes. 1.178–9; Lavency 1964: 140–9; Johnstone 1999: 54–60. This convention might be due to the process of drafting the speech (or having it drafted by a logographer) ahead of the trial, when it could be hard to know

an exceptional willingness to respond to the opponent's arguments, or more generally to speak on the opponent's terms – we can call this practice 'dialectic engagement.'[21] Deviating from the courts' conventions, dialectic engagement allows Antiphon to demonstrate that no argument is safe from antilogy: in other words, every argument can be used by a skilled speaker to support either side of the debate.

Although it is impossible here to discuss all the cases of deviation-as-problematization in the *Tetralogies*, a few more examples will hopefully prove the main point. One way in which Antiphon draws our attention to unacknowledged legal problems is by providing extreme version of common forensic arguments. What is exceptional here is the demonstration that even such *topoi*, which are usually the safest cards to play in a court, are not beyond the suspicion of a critical eye. Take a *topos* mostly used by defendants, the mention of the past services rendered to the city. As Steven Johnstone highlights (1999: 96–7), this *topos* can work only by assuming the stability of a person's character: if I have been generous towards the city in the past, it is unlikely that I would ever commit a crime against it. This argument is very frequent in forensic oratory and usually goes unchallenged.[22] It would then probably escape the notice of an Athenian reading the first Tetralogy; but in the first defense speech, Antiphon introduces a version of the argument so extreme that it is hard to overlook:

If you consider everything I have done, you will know that I didn't make plots or seek anything improper. On the contrary, I have contributed generously to many special levies, outfitted many triremes, produced splendid choral performances, loaned money to many friends, and guaranteed many large debts as well. (Ant. 2.2.12)[23]

There is no parallel in forensic oratory for a similar exaggeration of the *topos*.[24] This particular form of the argument is all the more striking because, while the *topos* is strongly based on individual character,[25] it is here applied to a non-character – the fictional defendant is a better citizen than any real Athenian.[26]

Even more surprisingly, the plaintiff fires back against the *topos* – another move that has no parallels in forensic oratory:[27]

all of the opponent's arguments in detail (see Dorjahn 1935; Thür 2008).

[21] On my use of 'dialectic' cf. Kerferd 1981: 59–67. Dialectic engagement in the *Tetralogies*: Ant. 2.1.4, 2.2.5, 2.3.2 (who is the killer?); 2.1.9, 2.2.7, 2.3.4, 2.4.7 (the slave's testimony); 3.2.8, 3.3.6, 3.4.5 (only a mistake justifies punishment); 4.2.4, 4.3.5 (the doctor is the actual killer). See also the explicit declarations of dialectic engagement in 2.2.4, 2.3.9, 3.3.10, 3.3.11, 4.3.1 (cf. also 3.4.1). Cf. Decleva Caizzi 1969: 40, 44 (on the use of different *nomoi*). While absent from court procedure, dialectic engagement was probably a feature of pretrial procedures (Thür 2008, 55) and connotes several tragic *agones* (see e. g. Hecuba's rebuttal of all of Helen's arguments in Eur. *Tro.* 969–1032.).

[22] See Johnstone 1999: 94–97; Lavency 1964: 167; Ober 1989: 226–37.

[23] All translations are from Gagarin and MacDowell 1998.

[24] Gagarin (2002: 114) glosses: 'the defendant has performed every possible service more splendidly than anyone else ever.'

[25] See Carey 1994: 36 for a framing of this argument within other character-arguments.

[26] Cf. Wohl 2010: 115–54 on the minimal characterization of speakers in the *Tetralogies*.

[27] The closest we get is Lys. 30.1, which however, while recognizing the *topos* as such, uses it to its own advantage.

The special levies and choral productions are a good indication of his prosperity but not of his innocence. On the contrary, fear of losing prosperity makes it likely that he committed this unholy murder. (Ant. 2.3.8)

This is at the same time an instance of the antilogic drive of the *Tetralogies* (the very same argument can be taken in two opposite directions by the two speakers) and a challenge to one of the fundamental pieces of legal rhetoric. The same critique could be in fact levelled against any other instance of the *topos*, not just against the exaggerated version adopted by the defendant. But such exaggeration is conducive to theoretical reflection: it prompts us to pay attention to a conventional argument and prepares us for its questioning in the following speech. If Antiphon makes his audience reconsider the validity of common arguments, we can hardly deny the theoretical import of his critical inquiry.[28]

A further element that is taken to the extreme in the first Tetralogy is the testimony of the slave. Nicolas Siron has recently demonstrated that witnesses are central to the *dispositif de vérité* operating in Athenian lawcourts:[29] but the first Tetralogy presents a testimony so fraught with problems that, far from becoming an alternative to the arguments based on likelihood, it can be subject to the same procedure of probabilistic assessment (cf. Cassin 1995, 167–8). The testimony is introduced by the plaintiff in his first speech:

As for witnesses, if many had been present (*paregenonto*), we would have presented many here. But since only his attendant was present (*paragenomenou*), those who heard him speak will testify. For he was still breathing when we picked him up and questioned him, and he said he recognized this man alone among those who attacked[30] them. (Ant. 2.1.9)

Antiphon uses for the slave the verb *paragignomai*, which regularly designates eyewitnesses in Athenian courts (Siron 2019: 188–93).[31] The testimony of the eyewitness is a trusted, fundamental source of evidence in Athenian trials: so much so that in his first oration Antiphon can have his client asking 'how could someone be quite certain of something that happened when he wasn't there himself (*paregeneto autos*)?' (Ant. 1.28; cf. also Ant. 6.28–9). However, the testimony of the eyewitness is here tainted by several complications: first, the text underlines that there is unfortunately only one *paragenomenos* available. Second, the *paragenomenos* is by now dead: it will not be him who testifies, but – flouting Athenian procedure – some people who 'heard him speak' before he died.[32] Third, the single eyewitness is a slave: in Athens the testimony of a slave could be adduced only if obtained through torture (*basanos*),[33] which here, since the slave is dead, is clearly impossible. Fourth, accepting Gagarin's text (see n. 29), there

---

[28] In fact, in the *Against Eratosthenes* Lysias explicitly exhorts the jurors to be skeptical of such arguments (Lysias 12.38): Antiphon's reflection is thus close to the concerns voiced by legal practice (cf. below, n. 34).

[29] Siron 2019 (cf. Zinsmaier 1998, 400). See e. g. Ant. 4.1.1 and Ant. 44(c)I Pendrick.

[30] Gagarin, like other editors (most recently Dilts and Murphy 2018), accepts Bekker's conjecture παιόντων for the ms. παρόντων (see Gagarin 1997 *ad loc.*; *contra* Decleva Caizzi 1969 *ad loc.*).

[31] Siron is rightly cautious about equating these different ways of defining 'presence' on the crime scene (emphasis on body presence vs. autopsy). On the importance of 'presence' for witnesses and proofs in Athens cf. Foucault 2012: 47–70.

[32] Testimony from hearsay was not allowed in Attic trials (Harrison 1968-71: 2.145-7 and Siron 2019: 169–73). See however Gagarin 1997, 129 *ad* 2.1.9.

[33] There might have been a few exceptions to this rule: see Gagarin 1996: 1, n. 1. On the use of *basanos* as evidence see Thür 1977, esp. 205–14.

were several attackers, but only one was recognized by the slave – the others seem, due to the lack of other witnesses, beyond the reach of the law.

These complications change the nature of what should be the only piece of evidence not based on *eikos*. In fact, the testimony is challenged by the defendant in 2.2.7: he indicates that the absence of *basanos* makes the testimony unreliable (an argument repeated in his last speech, 2.4.7), and that fear induced the half-dead slave to answer positively to the identification of the killer (cf. Ant. 5.32). However, in 2.3.4 the plaintiff has a surprising counterargument to the absence of *basanos*: he presents *basanos* not as a means to get to the truth, but as a punishment for bad slaves – in this case, the importance of the testimony rendered by the slave should have set him free, rather than making him undergo torture.

Of the four complications identified in the construction of the testimony, the opponent takes advantage of only one, the absence of *basanos*. But the other complications have an important, if implicit, role to play: the testimony crafted by Antiphon would not be admissible in a real court, and yet it is the only source of evidence enabling the speakers to discuss the case. Athenian law, therefore, would not be able to solve a similar case. The extreme version of the testimony, like the extreme version of the liturgies seen above, throws into relief the limits of Athenian law.[34]

If we turn to the second Tetralogy, we can see problematization operating on a more general level: not addressing individual *topoi*, but rather running through the entire argumentative structure of the speeches.[35] The central issue of the Tetralogy is the attribution of causality and legal responsibility (*aitia*):[36] a boy, while training, has been hit by a javelin thrown by one of his companions. The companion (which, following Gagarin and MacDowell 1998, we will call 'young man' to distinguish him from the dead boy) was aiming for the target, not for the boy, but the boy ran in the trajectory of the javelin. Is the young man to be convicted of unintentional homicide? Put in these terms, the case raises important legal and ethical questions. But Antiphon ties these broad questions to a specific linguistic ambiguity: the verb βάλλω, meaning both 'to throw' and 'to hit (by throwing)' in the aorist tense.[37] The litigants seem to agree from the beginning on how to characterize what happened: 'I think even the defendant will not disagree with me; for my boy, struck in the side on the training field by a javelin thrown by this young man, died on the spot' (3.1.1). Nonetheless, with the introduction of the verb βάλλω the dispute becomes one of linguistic normativity, or of interpretation of reality through language. In 3.2.3 the defendant argues that 'the young man [...] threw his javelin but did not kill anyone' (ἔβαλε μὲν, οὐκ ἀπέκτεινε δὲ οὐδένα). The defendant agrees that the javelin was thrown, but, he claims, the responsibility stops there: what happened afterwards is not the young man's fault, but the boy's, who, by his own mistake, ran in the trajectory of the javelin (3.2.4). The contrast becomes explicit in 3.3.5, where the plaintiff states: 'he has the audacity and the insolence to claim that his son, who both threw and killed, did not wound or kill' (τὸν μὲν βαλόντα καὶ ἀποκτείναντα οὔτε τρῶσαι οὔτε ἀποκτεῖναί φησι).

---

[34] Real speeches too express concerns about testimonies rendered by slaves (e. g. Ant. 5.49, 6.25): cf. above, n. 28.

[35] Cf. Mann 2012a, who concludes (p. 18): 'Antiphon supplies the philosophical artillery needed to destroy the credibility of the very institution in which his tetralogy is set.'

[36] See more in detail Mann 2012a; cf. Mann 2020.

[37] See de Boel 1987. Cf. also the ambiguity of ἀδικέω in Antiphon fr. 44(c)I.15–21 Pendrick (with Pendrick 2002: 371 *ad* 15–21).

The opposition works at the micro-level of grammar: in the passage quoted above (3.2.3) the actions of 'throwing' and 'killing' were disjuncted by the defendant through the particles μέν ... δέ, while here the plaintiff nonchalantly connects the same verbs with a καί and attributes the move to the defendant. By cashing in on the ambiguity of βαλεῖν the plaintiff can misrepresent the defendant's position, who in fact did not deny that his son 'threw' (3.2.3 ἔβαλε μὲν), but only that this throw was not to be connected to the outcome – the young man's death (3.2.3 οὐκ ἀπέκτεινε δὲ οὐδένα).

Antiphon draws out the extreme consequences of Athenian court procedure, in which the speakers' words, always open to interpretation and misunderstanding, are the sole means of communication – no further ontological level beyond language is available.[38] Interestingly, the defendant himself makes this point at the outset of his last speech:

My opponent was probably thinking about his own prosecution speech and didn't understand my defense, but your task is to recognize that we litigants judge a matter from our own point of view, and we each naturally assume our own case is just. You, however, must consider the things that have been done (πραχθέντα) impartially, for the truth of these must be examined from the things said (ἐκ τῶν λεγομένων γὰρ ἡ ἀλήθεια σκεπτέα αὐτῶν ἐστίν) (Ant. 3.4.1)[39]

The defendant argues that the plaintiff has failed to understand some of his arguments. Among them, we can infer, there is also the use of βαλεῖν, which represents the most consequential instance of miscommunication between the two. The traditional antithesis of *logos* and *ergon*, so widely accepted in the fifth century,[40] is here questioned: the *legomena*, 'things said', are said to be the only medium available to access the *prakhthenta*, 'things done'. Words and deeds are not opposed, but the latter depends on the former to be communicable – a thesis that presents remarkable similarities with Gorgias' views on language.[41] This epistemological thesis would defy the pretense, common in forensic oratory, of showing the unadorned, pure facts (*erga*) as opposed to mere words (*logoi*).[42] The importance attributed by the litigants to a single word, βαλεῖν, is warranted if we accept the relationship of dependence between *logos* and *ergon* put forward by the defendant: a word, βαλεῖν, is our only means to access the reality of what happened between the young man and the boy. We will shortly see how the philosophical import of the case constructed by Antiphon is perfectly at home in the environment of sophistic thought.

Purpose: what the *Tetralogies* are for

Having examined what the *Tetralogies* do, we are now in a good place to discuss their purpose. Many scholars have deemed this work a 'school exercise', intended to be studied and imitated

---

[38] Cf. Ant. 6.18; Ant. F44(a)VI.25–33 Pendrick (textually problematic); *Dissoi Logoi* 4.3–5, 8–9; Johnstone 1999: 90. See further Cassin 1995: 171–5 and Cohen 2003, 92. Contrast the powerful reversal of this idea in Eur. *Hipp.* 1077 and 1091.

[39] The translation of the last sentence is slightly adapted to be closer to the Greek, because the precise formulation matters for our purposes.

[40] E. g. Ant. 5.84; see Parry 1981: 15–61. This rhetorical move is present in the *Tetralogies* too (see e. g. 3.3.1).

[41] See Gorg. LM D 27.21–5; cf. Cassin 1995: 23–65 and Gorg. LM D 26.35.

[42] See e. g. Ant. 5.5, 6.47; cf. Ant. 6.2 (*nomos* vs. *logos*). The pretense is not absent from the *Tetralogies*: see Ant. 2.4.1 and 3.2.3; see further Zinsmaier 1998.

in order to learn forensic rhetoric (a handbook)[43] or argumentative techniques in general (a *techne*).[44] An important opponent of the former view was Dittenberger, who, tracing all the points where the *Tetralogies* deviate from Athenian practice, argued that they would be useless for teaching Athenian law, and therefore they must be a purely theoretical text.[45] As we have seen in the previous section, deviations constitute a real problem only if we maintain a narrow definition of 'useful for legal practice': in fact, deviations increase our reflective awareness of Athenian law by alienating familiar *topoi* and allowing us to question their legal foundations. Moreover, some of the problematization of legal practice undertaken by the *Tetralogies* is paralleled in forensic speeches,[46] suggesting that, even from a narrowly practical point of view, theoretical awareness can have far-reaching consequences in forensic argumentation.[47]

Between the two extreme views of the *Tetralogies* as a practical handbook or as a purely theoretical text, a third option has been explored in different ways by Edwin Carawan (1993) and Victoria Wohl (2010), who situate them halfway between theory and practice.[48] Following a similar line of thought, I now hope to elaborate on the aims of the *Tetralogies* by framing them within the contemporary sophistic speculation. The novelty of the *Tetralogies* is firmly grounded in sophistic thought, which had elected the domain of justice and law as a privileged field of inquiry.[49] More importantly, many sophistic writings are characterized by the same attitude, problematization, deployed by the *Tetralogies* in confronting Athenian law.[50] For example, the second Tetralogy, exploring the consequences of the instability of language (the ambiguity of βαλεῖν), contributes to the contemporary debate about the 'correctness of names' (ὀρθότης τῶν ὀνομάτων), a topic pursued by many prominent thinkers in the late fifth century.[51] In fact, semantic ambiguity was a matter of special interest for Prodicus of Ceos;[52] Protagoras was said to have discussed with Pericles a case that bears a very close resemblance to that of the second Tetralogy (31D30 LM);[53] and Antiphon himself, in his *On Truth*, exploited the ambiguity of the verb ἀδικέω ('to commit injustice', but also 'to harm') to problematize

---

[43] Gagarin 1997: 8. Gagarin has later somewhat revised this idea, countenancing a broader readership with broader interests (Gagarin 2002: 105).

[44] Cole 1991: 75–8; Kerferd 1981: 80–1. On sophistic *technai* see Cole 1991: 80–112; Velardi 2011. Cf. Mann 2012b: 1–7.

[45] Dittenberger 1896 and Dittenberger 1897 (Dittenberger 1897: 23 'aus einem rein theoretischen... Interesse hervorgegangen sind'). Many of the deviations identified by Dittenberger were challenged by Lipsius 1905; cf. also Dittenberger 1905. A balanced assessment of the debate can be found in Gernet 1954: 6–16.

[46] Above, nn. 18, 28, 34 and below, n. 55.

[47] Hence, the *Tetralogies* could be appealing to different audiences: cf. Ford 2001: 94; Gagarin 2002: 105.

[48] See Carawan 1993: 265–6 and Wohl 2010: 119.

[49] See e. g. Ant. LM D 38, *Anonymus Iamblichi* 6–17, *Dissoi Logoi* 3, 4.3–5, 8–9, Thrasymachus LM D 17 and 21, Hippias LM D 18, Lycophron LM D 3. See Bonazzi 2021: 65–95; Noël 2003; Rossetti 1989; de de Romilly 1988: 181. The legal environment is also salient in the extant sophistic judiciary speeches with mythical characters (Gorgias' *Palamedes*, Antisthenes' *Ajax* and *Odysseus*, Alcidamas' *Odysseus*: on these speeches see Ahern Knudsen 2012). Moreover, Protagoras' interest in *nomoi* is suggested by his role as the lawgiver of the newly founded Athenian colony of Thurii, if we believe the testimony of Diogenes Laertius (LM P 12). The sophistic reflection on law and justice is to be connected to their involvement in and the promotion of democratic practices in Athens and beyond (Robinson 2007).

[50] Cf. Bonazzi 2021, 9: 'what might be regarded as the sophists' most important contribution [is] their acknowledgement of the fact that reality is "problematic"'.

[51] See Bonazzi 2021: 44–69; Kerferd 1981: 61–77.

[52] See Dorion in Pradeau 2009, 531 n. 22.

[53] On this testimony and its relationship with the second Tetralogy see Carawan 1993: 239–40 and Rossetti 1989: 324–7. Cf. also Herodotus' account of Croesus' son Atys (Her. 1.34–45): his guest Adrastus, throwing a spear to kill a boar, 'missed the boar, but hit the son of Croesus' (Her. 1.44.2; thanks to Mirjam Kotwick for pointing out this parallel to me).

conventional definitions of justice (above, n. 37). Moreover, the position expressed (3.4.1, quoted above) and explored in the second Tetralogy – namely that *logos*, far from being the alternative to *ergon*, is our only point of access to it – is close to what has been often regarded by later authors as characteristic of sophistic philosophy: the interest in *logos* divorced from its referent.[54] The *Tetralogies* demonstrate how linguistic discussions of this sort, dismissed by many contemporaries too as the idle disputes of savants (e. g. Aristophanes, *Clouds* 658–93), can have a profound impact on our construction of reality: setting the problematization of language in a high-stakes environment (a trial for homicide), Antiphon harnesses the legal setting to explore the conceptual power of sophistic *orthoepeia*.[55]

A distinguishing pedagogical method introduced by the sophists, especially in the Athenian context, was the application of theoretical reflection to practical aims,[56] such as teaching one how to be a virtuous democratic citizen (Protagoras' *euboulia*).[57] The picture that emerges from one of the very few fully preserved texts written within the sophistic environment, Antiphon's *Tetralogies*, affords us a glimpse into a related but subtly different method. Antiphon does not deploy a theoretical discussion (say, poetic criticism) for practical purposes either (say, to teach rhetoric).[58] Instead, the *Tetralogies* use a legal form to problematize legal principles, and thus have Athenian legal practice exhibit its own limitations. Read in this way, the *Tetralogies* might help us redraw the boundaries of theory and practice in sophistic thought.[59]

Bibliography

Ahern Knudsen, R. 2012. "Poetic speakers, sophistic words." *AJP* 133 (1):31-60.

Balaudé, J.-F. 2006. "Hippias le passeur." In *La costruzione del discorso filosofico nell'età dei Presocratici = The construction of philosophical discourse in the age of the Presocratics*, edited by Maria Michela Sassi, 287-304. Pisa: Edizioni della Normale.

Bertrand, J.-M. 2001. «Réflexions sur l'expertise politique en Grèce ancienne.» *Revue Historique* 125 (4):929-964.

Blass, F. 1887-98. *Die attische Beredsamkeit*. 2nd ed. Leipzig: Teubner.

Bonazzi, M. 2021. *The Sophists*. Cambridge ; New York: Cambridge University Press.

Carawan, E. 1993. "The Tetralogies and the Athenian homicide trials." *AJP* 114:235-270.

Carey, C. 1994. "«Artless» proofs in Aristotle and the orators." *BICS* 39:95-106.

Cassin, B. 1995. *L' effet sophistique*. Paris: Gallimard.

---

[54] The first critics to follow this line of thought are Plato and Aristotle: see Bonazzi 2021: 7–8 and 61–2; Cassin 1995: 334–65. Cf. also Cassin's notions of *logologie* and *effet-monde* (as opposed to ontology: Cassin 1995: 13, 70–4).

[55] Lysias 10 presents a comparable case – but a real one – where linguistic reflection (the distinction between *onoma*, 'word', and *dianoia*, 'meaning': Lys. 10.7) provides the basis of the argumentation.

[56] See Balaudé 2006; Ford 2001; Heinimann 1961. Cf. Farrar 1988: 12–3.

[57] See Plato, *Prot.* 318e–319a with Woodruff 2013 (cf. de Romilly 1988: 64). For other examples of the practical aims of sophistic teaching (e. g. *euepeia*, *alupia* etc.) see Heinimann 1961: 120–1. The 'practical purposes' were, as Ford 2001: 94 rightly stresses, not narrowly practical: 'even if their students did not get elected generals or win every law suit, they would emerge as polished gentlemen able to act and speak impressively on a wide variety of social occasions' (cf. Ford 2001: 108).

[58] See Rademaker 2013 on Protagoras' rhetorical application of poetic criticism.

[59] Cf. Cole 1991: 92–4, arguing that fifth-century pedagogy, proceeding with examples rather than formulating general rules, lacks the theoretical depth of the following rhetorical tradition (*contra* Schiappa 1996: 79). The *Tetralogies*, read as problematization of the very legal matter they are made of, might offer a challenge to Cole's view of what model-speeches can do (cf. also Striker 1999: 3–21).

Cassin, B. 1997. «Procédures sophistiques pour construire l'évidence.» In *Dire l'évidence: (philosophie et rhétorique antiques)*, edited by Carlos Lévy and Laurent Pernot, 15-29. Paris ; Montréal (Québec): L'Harmattan.

Cohen, D.J. 2003. "Writing, law, and legal practice in the Athenian courts." In *Written texts and the rise of literate culture in ancient Greece*, edited by Harvey Yunis, 78-96. Cambridge ; New York: Cambridge University Press.

Cole, T. 1991. *The origins of rhetoric in ancient Greece*. Baltimore (Md.): Johns Hopkins University Press.

Culler, J.D. 2011. *Literary theory : a very short introduction*. 2nd ed. Oxford ; New York: Oxford University Press.

de Boel, G. 1987. "Aspekt, Aktionsart und Transitivität." *IF* 92:33–57.

de Romilly, J. 1988. *Les grands sophistes dans l'Athènes de Périclès*. Paris: de Fallois.

Decleva Caizzi, F., ed. 1969. *Antiphontis Tetralogiae*. Milan.

Demont, P. 1993. «Die Epideixis über die Techne im V. und IV. Jh.» In *Vermittlung und Tradierung von Wissen in der griechischen Kultur*, edited by Wolfgang Kullmann and Jochen Althoff, 181-209. Tübingen: Narr.

Demont, P. 1994. «Notes sur l'antilogie au cinquième siècle.» In *La rhétorique grecque: actes du colloque « Octave Navarre » : troisième colloque international sur la pensée antique organisé par le CRHI (Centre de recherches sur l'histoire des idées) les 17, 18 et 19 décembre 1992 à la Faculté des Lettres de Nice*, edited by Jean-Michel Galy and Antoine Thivel, 77-88. Paris: C.I.D. Diffusion.

Denyer, N., ed. 2008. *Plato: Protagoras, Cambridge Greek and Latin Classics*. Cambridge ; New York: Cambridge University Press.

Dilts, M.R., and D.J. Murphy, eds. 2018. *Antiphontis et Andocidis Orationes*. Oxford: Oxford University Press.

Dittenberger, W. 1896. "Antiphons Tetralogien und das attische Criminalrecht." *Hermes* 31 (1):271-277.

Dittenberger, W. 1897. "Antiphons Tetralogien und das attische Criminalrecht II. III." *Hermes* 32 (1):1-41.

Dittenberger, W. 1905. «Zu Antiphons Tetralogien.» *Hermes* 40 (3):450-470.

Dover, K.J. 1950. "The Chronology of Antiphon's Speeches." *CQ* 44 (1-2):44-60.

Farrar, C. 1988. *The origins of democratic thinking. The invention of politics in classical Athens.* Cambridge ; New York: Cambridge University Press.

Ford, A.L. 2001. "Sophists without rhetoric: The arts of speech in fifth-century athens." In *Education in Greek and Roman Antiquity*, edited by Yun Lee Too, 85-109. Leiden ; Boston: Brill.

Foucault, M. 2012. *Du gouvernement des vivants : cours au Collège de France, 1979-1980*. Paris: Seuil.

Gagarin, M. 1996. "The Torture of Slaves in Athenian Law." *CP* 91 (1):1-18.

Gagarin, M., ed. 1997. *Antiphon: The Speeches, Cambridge Greek and Latin Classics*. Cambridge ; New York: Cambridge University Press.

Gagarin, M. 1999. "The orality of Greek oratory." In *Signs of orality: the oral tradition and its influence in the Greek and Roman world*, edited by Elizabeth Anne Mackay, 163-180. Leiden ; Boston: Brill.

Gagarin, M. 2002. *Antiphon the Athenian: oratory, law, and justice in the age of the Sophists*. Austin, TX: University of Texas Press.

Gagarin, M., and D.M. MacDowell, eds. 1998. *Antiphon and Andocides*. Vol. 1, *The Oratory of Classical Greece*. Austin, TX: University of Texas Press.

Gernet, L., ed. 1954. *Antiphon, Discours, suivis des Fragments d'Antiphon le Sophiste / éd. and trad. Gernet L, Collection Guillaume Budé*. Paris: Les Belles Lettres.

Hansen, M.H. 1991. *The Athenian democracy in the age of Demosthenes : structure, principles and ideology / transl. by Crook J. A*. Oxford: Blackwell.

Harris, E.M. 2002. "Workshop, marketplace and household: the nature of technical specialization in classical Athens and its influence on economy and society." In *Money, labour and land: approaches to the economies of ancient Greece*, edited by Paul Cartledge, 67-99. London: Routledge.

Harrison, A.R.W. 1968-71. *The Law of Athens*. Oxford: Clarendon Press.

Heinimann, F. 1961. "Eine vorplatonische Theorie der τέχνη." *Museum Helveticum* 18 (3):105-130.

Hesk, J. 2000. *Deception and democracy in classical Athens*. Cambridge ; New York: Cambridge University Press.

Innes, D.C. 1991. "Gorgias, Antiphon and Sophistopolis." *Argumentation* 5 (2):221-231.

Ismard, P. 2015. *La démocratie contre les experts: les esclaves publics en Grèce ancienne*. Paris: Éd. du Seuil.

Johnstone, S. 1999. *Disputes and democracy : the consequences of litigation in ancient Athens*. 1st ed. ed. Austin, TX: University of Texas Press.

Kahn, C.H. 2003. "Writing philosophy: prose and poetry from Thales to Plato." In *Written texts and the rise of literate culture in ancient Greece*, edited by Harvey Yunis, 139-161. Cambridge ; New York: Cambridge University Press.

Kerferd, G.B. 1981. *The sophistic movement*. Cambridge ; New York: Cambridge University Press.

Koopman, C. 2013. *Genealogy as critique : Foucault and the problems of modernity*. Bloomington: Indiana University Press.

Kraus, M. 2006. "Antilogia: zu den Grundlagen sophistischer Debattierkunst." *Rhetorik* 25:1-13.

Lavency, M. 1964. *Aspects de la logographie judicaire attique*. Louvain: Bureaux du recueil, Bibliothèque de l'Université.

Lipsius, J.H. 1905. «Über Antiphons Tetralogien.» *Berichte Über die Verhandlungen der Königlich Sächsischen Gesellschaft der Wissenschaften Zu Leipzig. Philologisch-Historische Klasse* 56 (4):191.

Lloyd, G.E.R. 1979. *Magic, reason, and experience. Studies in the origin and development of Greek science*. Cambridge ; New York: Cambridge University Press.

MacDowell, D.M. 1963. *Athenian Homicide Law in the Age of the Orators*. Manchester: University Press.

Mann, J.E. 2012a. "Causation, agency, and the law: on some subtleties in Antiphon's second tetralogy." *JHPh* 50 (1):7-19.

Mann, J.E., ed. 2012b. *Hippocrates: On the art of medicine*. Vol. 39. Leiden ; Boston: Brill.

Mann, J.E. 2020. "Responsibility Rationalized: Action and Pollution in Antiphon's Tetralogies." In *Early Greek Ethics*, edited by David Conan Wolfsdorf, 132-148. Oxford ; New York: Oxford University Press.

Noël, M.-P. 2003. «La place du judiciaire dans les premières τέχναι λόγων.» In *Ars/Techne: il manuale tecnico nelle civiltà greca e romana : atti del convegno internazionale, Università « G. D'Annunzio » di Chieti-Pescara, 29-30 ottobre 2001*, edited by Maria Silvana Celentano, 1-15. Alessandria: Ed. dell'Orso.

Ober, J. 1989. *Mass and elite in democratic Athens : rhetoric, ideology, and the power of the people*. Princeton, N.J.: Princeton University Press.

Ober, J. 2008. *Democracy and knowledge: innovation and learning in classical Athens*. Princeton (N. J.) ; Oxford: Princeton University Press.

Parry, A.M. 1981. *Logos and ergon in Thucydides*. New York: Arno Press.

Pendrick, G.J. 2002. *Antiphon the Sophist: The Fragments.* Cambridge ; New York: Cambridge University Press.

Pradeau, J.-F., ed. 2009. *Les sophistes.* Paris: Flammarion.

Rhodes, P.J. 1993. *A commentary on the Aristotelian Athenaion politeia.* Oxford: Clarendon Press.

Robinson, E.W. 2007. "The Sophists and Democracy Beyond Athens." *Rhetorica* 25 (1):109-122.

Rossetti, L. 1989. "La filosofia penale di Ippodamo e la cultura giuridica dei sofisti." *Rivista Internazionale di Filosofia del Diritto* LXVI:315-335.

Rossetti, L. 2004. "Materiali per una storia della letteratura giuridica attica." In *Nomos: direito e sociedade na Antiguidade Clássica = derecho y sociedad en la Antigüedad Clásica,* edited by Delfim Ferreira Leão, Livio Rossetti and Maria do Céu Zambujo Fialho, 51-73. Madrid: Ed. Clásicas.

Rubinstein, L. 2007. "Arguments from Precedent in the Attic Orators." In *Oxford Readings in Classical Studies,* edited by Edwin Carawan, 359-371. Oxford ; New York: Oxford University Press.

Schiappa, A.E. 1996. "Toward a predisciplinary analysis of Gorgias' « Helen »." In *Theory, text, context: issues in Greek rhetoric and oratory,* edited by Christopher Lyle Johnstone, 65-86. Albany (N. Y.): State University of New York Pr.

Schmitz, T.A. 2000. "Plausibility in the Greek Orators." *AJP* 121 (1):47-77.

Siron, N. 2019. *Témoigner et convaincre : le dispositif de vérité dans les discours judiciaires de l'Athènes classique.* Paris: Éditions de la Sorbonne.

Sobak, R. 2015. "Sokrates among the shoemakers." *Hesperia: The Journal of the American School of Classical Studies at Athens* 84 (4):669-712.

Spatharas, D.G. 2001. "Patterns of argumentation in Gorgias." *Mnemosyne: Bibliotheca Classica Batava* Ser. 4, 54 (4):393-408.

Striker, G., ed. 1996. *Essays on Hellenistic epistemology and ethics.* Cambridge ; New York: Cambridge University Press.

Thomas, R. 2003. "Prose performance texts: ἐπιδείξις and written publication in the late fifth and early fourth centuries." In *Written texts and the rise of literate culture in ancient Greece,* edited by Harvey Yunis, 162-188. Cambridge ; New York: Cambridge University Press.

Thür, G. 1977. *Beweisführung vor den Schwurgerichtshöfen Athens. Die Proklesis zur Basanos.* Wien: Verlag der Österreichischen Akademie der Wissenschaften.

Thür, G. 2008. "The principle of fairness in Athenian legal procedure: thoughts on the « echinos » and « enklema »." *Dike* 11:51-73.

Todd, S.C. 1993. *The shape of Athenian law.* Oxford ; New York: Oxford University Press.

Todd, S.C. 1996. "Lysias against Nikomachos: the fate of the expert in Athenian law." In *Greek law in its political setting: justifications not justice,* edited by Lin Foxhall and Andrew D. E. Lewis, 101-131. Oxford ; New York: Oxford University Press.

Usher, S. 1999. *Greek oratory : tradition and originality.* Oxford ; New York: Oxford University Press.

Vatri, A. 2017. "Public performance and the language of Antiphon's speeches." In *The theatre of justice : aspects of performance in Greco-Roman oratory and rhetoric,* edited by Sophia Papaioannou, Andreas Serafim and Beatrice da Vela, 304-319. Leiden ; Boston: Brill.

Velardi, R. 2011. "Metodi di insegnamento nelle scuole di retorica in Grecia, tra V e IV secolo a.C." In *L' insegnamento delle « technai » nelle culture antiche: atti del convegno, Ercolano, 23-24 marzo 2009,* edited by Amneris Roselli and Roberto Velardi, 109-124. Pisa: Serra.

Wohl, V.J. 2010. *Law's cosmos: juridical discourse in Athenian forensic oratory.* Cambridge ; New York: Cambridge University Press.

Wolpert, A.O. 2003. "Addresses to the jury in the Attic orators." *AJP* 124 (4):537-555.

Woodruff, P. 2013. "Euboulia as the Skill Protagoras Taught." In *Protagoras of Abdera: The Man, His Measure*, edited by Johannes M. van Ophuijsen, Marlein van Raalte and Peter Stork, 179-193. Leiden: Brill.

Zinsmaier, T. 1998. "Wahrheit, Gerechtigkeit und Rhetorik in den Reden Antiphons: zur Genese einiger Topoi der Gerichtsrede." *Hermes: Zeitschrift für Klassische Philologie* 126 (4):398-422.

Demosthenes, *Against Aristogeiton.*
Νόμος and Φύσις in 4th Century BC Athens

Lorenzo Sardone

Scuola Superiore di Studi Storici
Università di San Marino
lorenzosardone@hotmail.it

Abstract

In the Greek political and philosophical reflection there is an irremediable conflictual relationship between nature and law. Antiphon, the oligarch who orchestrated the *coup d'état* of 411 BC, takes position in defense of φύσις, against νόμος, arguing that laws are constraints and chains for nature. Antiphon's ideas are not isolated voices but are part of a larger debate about law legitimacy, which was still alive in the second half of the 4th century BC. An interesting text is speech XXV, an oration written by Demosthenes (325/324 BC) against Aristogeiton, a marginal political figure, probably a sycophant, with good oratory skills. The impetuous Demosthenic accusation includes an articulated theoretical reflection, which resumes and overturns the antinomy between νόμος and φύσις. Our orator reshapes the terms: on the one hand, nature, undisciplined, irregular, individual and source of lawlessness; on the other hand, law, guarantor of what is beautiful, good and right in society, a brake against a beastly way of living.

Keywords
Demosthenes, Aristogeiton, Greek oratory

In 1883 Richard Wagner proposed a dissertation for the Rostock University academic year inauguration about the oration *Against Aristogeiton*.[1] The opening words are eloquent and curious: *De nulla fere oratione inter Demosthenicas nobis tradita tam multae tamque diversae a viris doctis prolatae sunt sententiae quam de vicesima quinta.*[2] Today, the attribution to Demosthenes is still hotly debated. Therefore, a re-examination of some crucial themes can highlight new elements about the orator and the historical, political and cultural background of 4th century BC Athens.[3]

---

[1] These are the orations XXV and XXVI in the traditional order of the *Corpus Demosthenicum*, as transmitted by Marc. gr. Z 416 (F), which reports 61 orations, 56 proems and 6 letters. Speech XXVI remains excluded from our examination: for its brevity and for the poorness of its content and style, it is perhaps a rhetorical exercise or a short speech by a third anonymous accuser. On the two orations *Against Aristogeiton* see Wagner 1883, and cf. Blass (1893: 408-418); Mathieu (1947: 129-139); MacDowell (2009: 298-313).

[2] Wagner (1883: 1).

[3] Demosthenes, an excellent model of style imitated in schools of rhetoric from the Hellenistic age to the Byzantine period, has an importance that transcends his literary *status*. In fact, as a consequence of the loss of contemporary historical works, the *Corpus Demosthenicum* – with other orators, with Aristotle's *Respublica Atheniensium* and with Attic inscriptions – it represents the main source for reconstructing the central years of the 4th century BC, approximately 355-322. Cf. Hansen (1991); Lehmann (2004); Sealey (1993); Worthington (2013).

There remains little information about Aristogeiton[4] and his oratorical and political activity.[5] The affair related to the pronouncement of the speech *Against Aristogeiton* is long and complex, but Libanius meticulously describes the events in the *hypothesis* 24 [XXV+XXVI] oration.[6] Aristogeiton was condemned twice, due to his false accusations against Hierocles and Hegemon. He was fined up to a thousand drachmas and because of insolvency the amount of the debt was doubled and his name was written among the public treasure debtors. For this reason, he lost his citizens' rights and stayed out of public life for five years. In order to pay the debt, Aristogeiton sold an estate to his brother, Eunomus, who had to pay installments to the public treasury. However, only two installments were paid, not the total amount. Aristogeiton claimed that now the State-debtor was Eunomus, and he proceeded to exercise his citizens' rights as usual. For this reason, Lycurgus and Demosthenes accused Aristogeiton of usurping the right of speech. The latter defended himself with a harangue entitled *Defence against the accusation of Demosthenes and Lycurgus* (Phot. *Bibl.* 265).

The trial can be dated either to 325, or the beginning of 324 BC. Indeed, *termini ante quem* are the death of Lycurgus (324) and a quote from Dinarchus (II.13), who considered this episode the last *performance* of Aristogeiton before the Harpalic trial.[7]

The authenticity of the first speech *Against Aristogeiton* transmitted within the *Corpus Demosthenicum*[8] has been discussed since antiquity. Dionysius of Halicarnassus (*De Dem.* 57) disputed that the author was Demosthenes: he thought that the language and style were far too hateful and violent. On the contrary, Pliny the Younger (*Ep.* IX.26), Plutarch (*Dem.* 15), Ps. Longinus (XX.3) and others defended the authenticity and considered this speech as one of the most beautiful orations of Demosthenes.[9] In modern times, conflicting opinions coexist: Schaefer detected a lack of legal arguments and a redundant style, dating the speech to the Hellenistic period.[10] Lipsius highlighted an inadequate knowledge of Attic law,[11] in

---

[4] Cf. PAA 168145; PA 1775. Aristogeiton, of humble origin, son of Cidimacus of Afidna, did not have any compunction in leaving his father unburied, who died in prison or in exile because of a public debt (Suda s.v. Ἀριστογείτων; Din. II.18). He did not hesitate to sell his sister into slavery and to use violence against his mother. During one of his imprisonments, he stole a register of his cellmate and, once the theft was discovered, he bit off his cellmate's nose (Suda s.v. Ἀριστογείτων). Among the many sordid acts, he demonstrated deep ingratitude towards Zobia (Dem. XXV.58), who hosted him, denouncing her for not having paid the metic tax. Despite all these crimes, Aristogeiton was undoubtedly a relevant popular leader in Athens: he was elected ἐπιμελητὴς τοῦ ἐμπορίου (Din. II.10) and he took part in numerous trials. After the battle of Chaeronea, he unsuccessfully submitted a γραφὴ παρανόμων against Hypereides, for his emergency decree containing extraordinary measures (Dem. XXVI.11; Lyc. 36-37; Ps. Plut. *V.X Or.* 848f-849a). Lastly, there was the Harpalic trial (Din. II), in which paradoxically Demosthenes was condemned, while Aristogeiton was acquitted (Dem. *Ep.* III.37, 42). Cf. also Plut. *Phoc.* 10.2-9.

[5] According to ancient sources, his oratorical production – currently lost in its entirety – was worthy of appreciation. Quintilian mentions him among Lycurgus, Isaeus and Antiphon (*Inst. Or.* XII.10.22). In accordance with Ps. Plut. *V.X Or.* 850e, some of the 64 Dinarchus' orations may be attributed to Aristogeiton; besides, Suda (s.v. Ἀριστογείτων) reports 7 titles of speeches attributed to him. On this figure cf. also Christ (1998: 56-59) and Sealey (1960: 33-43).

[6] Cf. Foerster (1915: 642-645).

[7] Cf. Blass (1893: 416).

[8] Concerning the *Corpus Demosthenicum* birth, cf.: Drerup 1923; (1923); Canfora (1974: 9-98; 2020: 5-39).

[9] For what concerns the ancient direct tradition, the oration is testified by 5 papyri: P.Oxy. LXXVIII 5148 (1st BC/1st AD; TM 171894; MP³ 323.010), P.Oxy. LXXVIII 5150 (1st AD; TM 171896; MP³ 324.010), P.Yale I 23 (2nd AD; TM 59580; MP³ 324), P.Lond.Lit. 125 (5th AD; TM 59653; MP³ 325), P.Oxy. LXXVIII 5149 (7th AD; TM 171895; MP³ 323.020). In general, about Demosthenes' papyri cf.: Hausmann (1978; 1981); De Robertis (2015); Sardone (2021).

[10] Cf. Schaefer (1858: 113-129).

[11] Cf. Lipsius (1883: 317-331).

conflict with Weil, who firmly defended the genuineness of the legal aspects.[12] Blass, initially among the detractors of the authorship, upon re-evaluation of the content and the prose rhythm, attributed the work to Demosthenes, although considering it as a μελέτη,[13] not as a true forensic speech. Treves[14] judged the oration spurious and ascribed it to a skilled unknown orator, a contemporary of Demosthenes, while Sealey[15] attributed it to two different anonymous Hellenistic rhetors. By contrast, for Paoli[16] and Hansen[17] the oration was authentic because of the correctness of the legal arguments. Mathieu[18] considered the oration 'plaine d'esprit démosthénien' and finally MacDowell[19] stood in favor of the Demosthenic paternity.

This re-examination primarily focuses on several particular content and stylistic aspects,[20] that have certainly contributed to make this speech *remarkable*, animating the debate about its authenticity, which ultimately seems undeniable.

First and foremost, the alleged argumentative freedom with which Demosthenes led his accusation speech should be reconsidered. As stated, some scholars were suspicious of the lack of legal arguments. However, we have to take into account that the speech was a *deuterology*, namely the second prosecution harangue pronounced in court. In fact, Lycurgus was Demosthenes' colleague and, as the elder of the two, he presented the first accusation[21] and outlined all the charges against Aristogeiton, as Demosthenes says in chap. 14: 'Now as regards the laying of the injunction and the legal points, I considered that Lycurgus would deal adequately with them; and I also saw that he was producing witnesses to the wickedness of the defendant.' Furthermore, Demosthenes declares his different aim, stating: 'I resolved to devote my speech to those points which ought always to be considered and examined by those who are deliberating in the interests of the State and of the laws.' The orator himself speaks about the freedom with which he intended to conduct the speech, emphatically saying: 'In Heaven's name grant me the privilege of addressing you on these topics in the way that suits my natural bent and the scheme of my speech, for indeed I could not speak in any other way.' Therefore, it is no surprise that a tight prosecution is not recognizable, given that this would have mainly been Lycurgus' task.

---

[12] Cf. Weil (1887: 17-25).

[13] Cf. Blass (1893: 415): 'Es ist übrigens allgemein eine solche Kraft und Mächtigkeit in der Rede, dass es wirklich schwer wird, einem andern als dem Demosthenes solche Leistung zuzutrauen.'

[14] Cf. Treves (1936: 252-258).

[15] Cf. Sealey (1967: 254-255; 1969: 33; 1993: 237-239). Sealey (1993: 239): 'Speech 25 is not one exercise by a later rhetorician but two.'

[16] Cf. Paoli (1956: 224).

[17] Cf. Hansen (1976: 144-152).

[18] Mathieu (1947: 138). *Contra* cf. Vince (1935: 515): 'No one familiar with Demosthenes will doubt the spuriousness of these speeches. They read like rhetorical exercises and, though in places the rhetoric is good of its kind, they are often both obscure and tedious. They contain many expressions not found in Demosthenes' admitted speeches and some scurrility which is far beneath him.'

[19] Cf. MacDowell (2009: 310-313) and Faraguna (2011: 75-77, esp. 75).

[20] Regarding stylistic features, it is always useful to remember Wilamowitz (1923: 69): 'Und vom Stil aus zu sagen: dies muß Demosthenes sein, scheint mir verwegen; dies kann Demosthenes sein, ist schon viel.' In regards to Demosthenes' style, cf. Dionysius of Halicarnassus' treatises *De Demosthene* and *De compositione verborum*; Ps. Longinus *De Sublitate* 34 (style), 39 (rhythmic patterns). Among modern studies, cf.: Adams (1927: 74-96); Mathieu (1948: 174-179); MacDowell (2009: 398-407); Norden (1986: 125-131); Ronnet (1951). On stylistic criteria used to solve problems of authenticity, cf. Sardone (2020: 194-201).

[21] Only fragments survive of Lycurgus' harangue; cf. Conomis (1970: 92-96).

Moreover, Demosthenes himself declares in his opening words the peculiarities of this trial: 'ὁ παρὼν ἀγών seems to me quite different from all others' (chap. 3), justifying his choice later: 'You who are to give the verdict have come here knowing better than we, the accusers, that this man, since he is a State-debtor and, as registered as such in the Acropolis, has no right to speak at all; so that each of you is in the position of an accuser, knowing the facts and not needing to be told them' (chap. 4). Consequently, Demosthenes underlines, with great rhetorical emphasis, how unnecessary the addition of new charges would have been: first of all, because Lycurgus had already exposed them, but also because Aristogeiton's faults were known to all. This declaration is useful as it suggests new evidence: Demosthenes points out the crimes of Aristogeiton on a more general level, with an ethical, philosophical and political focus.

According to the *hypothesis* of Libanius, in this speech the tone of the orator is φιλοσοφώτερον. Max Pohlenz, probably influenced by this ancient judgment, assumed that this oration was the result of a contamination between a philosophical treatise Περὶ Νόμων and a real forensic speech.[22] Beyond this intriguing – but very cumbersome – reconstruction, it is certain that some chapters in the text disclose their remarkable philosophical nature. In fact, these passages seem to sketch out elements and themes of the 5th and 4th century BC socio-political theories. For instance, in chaps. 15-16 the orator says: 'The whole life of men, Athenians, whether they dwell in a large state or a small one, is governed by nature and by the laws. Of these, nature is something irregular and incalculable, and peculiar to each individual; but the laws are something universal, definite, and the same for all. Now nature, if it be evil, often chooses wrong [...]. But the laws desire what is just and honourable and salutary; they seek for it, and when they find it, they set it forth as a general commandment, equal and identical for all. The law is that which all men ought to obey for many reasons [...]'.[23] Demosthenes, in these lines, is no longer just the accuser of Aristogeiton, but he is also the main actor of the recent Athenian political scene. In his opinion, human existence – seen as civil existence – is based on φύσις and on νόμος. Their properties are diametrically opposed: φύσις represents all that is ἄτακτον and κατ' ἄνδρ' ἴδιον; on the contrary, νόμος is κοινόν, τεταγμένον, ταὐτὸ πᾶσιν. Human nature inclines towards evil and this explains crimes. By contrast, the law ensures all that is fair and legal, or, to quote Demosthenes, 'everything that is δίκαιον, καλόν and συμφέρον'. Blind obedience to the law is due to the fact that it is considered 'an invention and a gift of the gods, a tenet of wise men, a corrective of errors voluntary and involuntary, and a general covenant of the whole State' (chap. 16). Keeping this in mind, the opening invocation to Ἐυνομία and Δίκη, 'Goddesses of the Order' protecting the civil society[24] (chaps. 10-11), becomes even more crucial.

Afterward, the orator explains why Aristogeiton was responsible for the disruption and ruin of this civic κόσμος (chap. 19). He illustrates to his fellow-citizens the threat caused by the

---

[22] Cf. Pohlenz (1924: 19-37).

[23] Cf. Dem. XXV.15-16: Ἅπας ὁ τῶν ἀνθρώπων βίος, ὦ ἄνδρες Ἀθηναῖοι, κἂν μεγάλην πόλιν οἰκῶσι κἂν μικράν, φύσει καὶ νόμοις διοικεῖται. τούτων δ' ἡ μὲν φύσις ἐστὶν ἄτακτον καὶ κατ' ἄνδρ' ἴδιον τοῦ ἔχοντος, οἱ δὲ νόμοι κοινὸν καὶ τεταγμένον καὶ ταὐτὸ πᾶσιν. ἡ μὲν οὖν φύσις, ἂν ᾖ πονηρά, πολλάκις φαῦλα βούλεται [...] οἱ δὲ νόμοι τὸ δίκαιον καὶ τὸ καλὸν καὶ τὸ συμφέρον βούλονται, καὶ τοῦτο ζητοῦσιν, καὶ ἐπειδὰν εὑρεθῇ, κοινὸν τοῦτο πρόσταγμ' ἀπεδείχθη, πᾶσιν ἴσον καὶ ὅμοιον, καὶ τοῦτ' ἔστι νόμος. ᾧ πάντας πείθεσθαι προσήκει διὰ πολλά [...].

[24] On Demosthenes' religiousness, cf. Martin (2009) and Willey (2019: 271-282). About Ἐυνομία, a contemporary political charged term, cf. Faraguna (2011: 76).

of his real faults – deserves a punishment even worse than death.[34] On the other hand, it is undeniable that this speech is characterized by a singular ferocity[35] (τὸ φορτικόν), that sounds almost like a kind of counterpart to its theoretical political-philosophical reflections.

Indeed, the orator resorts to several vivid metaphors: Aristogeiton is depicted as a slave (chap. 78), a θηρίον μιαρόν and ἄμεικτον (chap. 58), an impure abominable being who is rejected by society. In addition to this, he is compared with a viper (ἔχις), or with a scorpion (σκορπίος), that runs through the agora with the raised sting, trying to inflict damage, slander or sickness (chap. 52). He is 'the thrice-accursed, the common foe, the universal enemy, against whom one prays that the earth may neither yield him fruit, nor receive him after death' (chap. 82); he is compared with a cancer or with an ulcer that needs to be extirpated and burnt (chap. 95); he should be killed at first sight like a tarantula (chap. 96). But the best metaphor used by Demosthenes to depict Aristogeiton remains κύων τοῦ δήμου:[36] a dog that does not bite the wolves but is capable of devouring the sheep that he should protect. And mainly these metaphors give us other elements about the authorship quarrel: as demonstrated by P.Oxy. IX 1176[37] (fr. 39 col. VIII), Satirus of Callatis in the second part of the 3rd century BC knew and quoted this passage of the oration *Against Aristogeiton* (chap. 40) in his *Vita Euripidis*. So, once again, it seems unlikely to believe that this speech would have already been forged and also in the learned *milieu* of Alexandria firmly included in the *Demosthenic Corpus*, less than a hundred years after the death of our orator.

Despite these figurative representations, Demosthenes anyway offers an interesting multifaceted profile of his enemy: a sycophant, a popular leader, philo-Macedonian partisan, friend of Philocrates (chap. 44) and 'full of hereditary hate towards democracy' (chap. 32). On one side, he seems to have been a demagogue, a bulwark and a defender of the common people's rights. In this light, it is easy to understand his accusation against Hypereides, who proposed extraordinary measures post-Chaeronea that would have threatened the privileges of the δῆμος. On the other hand, he is presented as an agitator in the assemblies and as a sycophant in the courts (chap. 9). According to Demosthenes, Aristogeiton acted like the leader of an ideal popular mass, but then he raged against individuals and especially against the most marginalized, acting as a 'betrayer of those who resemble him [...], enemy by instinct and by inheritance of good men' (chap. 48). And also: 'In the Assembly he recklessly abuses and attacks all alike, and for all the misrepresentations that he thus foists upon you collectively, he gets his remuneration from each of you separately, when he descends from the platform, by threatening prosecution and by demanding and extorting money. Not from the orators, you may be sure: they know how to throw mud back at him, but from the inexperienced private citizens' (chap. 41).

Aristogeiton's profile depicted by Demosthenes is substantially the same as that found in Dinarchus' second speech,[38] written against Aristogeiton on the occasion of the Harpalic

---

[34] In this oration, cf. XXV.59. It is much rarer to find any form of respect for the opponent. In the *Corpus Demosthenicum* an isolated example is provided by the oration *Against Leptines* (XX). About this, cf. MacDowell (2009: 156-167, esp. 167).

[35] Cf. Worman (2008: 230-232).

[36] Cf. Canfora (2000: 441 and n. 5).

[37] TM 62717; MP³ 1456.

[38] Furthermore, this discourse gives us the important notice that in the trial against Demosthenes and Lycurgus,

trial. It is likely that Dinarchus had in-depth knowledge of the Demosthenic discourse,[39] as demonstrated by the common discrediting strategy[40] and the final (surviving) paragraph of the oration. Here, after speaking about Arthmius[41] and quoting from Demosthenes' *Third Philippic*, he concludes saying that Aristogeiton would be 'a man who was not Greek in birth or character' (Din. II.26: ἀλλότριον καὶ τῷ γένει καὶ τῇ φύσει τῆϲ Ἑλλάδοϲ), where the use of the term φύϲιϲ seems to recall the opposition with νόμοϲ, as seen frequently used by Demosthenes (XXV).

It is certain that the virulence of the attack is justified by a personal hate. Demosthenes himself, indeed, specifies that he had already been accused nine times by Aristogeiton (chap. 37). Furthermore, an elitist class hate is tangible against this popular leader, who remained outside the prestigious party of the ῥήτορεϲ because of birth, resources, conduct and perhaps choice too. If their political actions are presented as the product of deep and accurate reflections (νοῦ καὶ φρενῶν ἀγαθῶν καὶ προνοίαϲ πολλῆϲ [chap. 33]), Aristogeiton, on the other hand, acts only for his personal interests and talks to people only to please them, repeating: 'I, only I, am your sincere well-wisher. All these others are in a cabal. You are betrayed. My patriotism is all you have left' (chap. 64). In particular in this passage the contrast between the two political behaviors is evident, because Demosthenes proudly says that has always pursued the good for the δῆμοϲ and never his blind and ephemeral complacency.[42]

Thus, the accusation against Aristogeiton leads to a more general discussion about the paradoxes of a personal and extremist declination of democracy. Indeed, Demosthenes said: 'If everyone in the city copied the audacity and shamelessness of Aristogeiton and argued in the same way he did, that in a democracy a man has an unlimited right to say and do whatever he likes [...], that the citizen rejected at the ballot or at the election should put himself on an equality with the chosen citizen; if, in a word, neither young nor old should do his duty, but each man, banishing all discipline from life, should regard his own wish as law, as an authority, as all in all – if, I say, we should act like this, could the government continue to be carried on? Would the laws be any longer valid?' (chaps. 25-26). Demosthenes claims that in this catastrophic scenario, people can save themselves only thanks to νόμοϲ, intended as a limit to the blind single will (βούληϲιϲ) that is typical of the individual, of the mass and of the most extreme political parties, of which Aristogeiton is symbol and chief. They do not submit to the 'wise' leadership of the ῥήτορεϲ and dangerously usurp the faculty of speech (chap. 30).

In addition to this, the orator subtly criticizes the judges, and this fact confirms that the discussion focuses on the democratic life foundations. He says: 'While Aristogeiton is on his trial, it is your character that is being tested, your reputation that is at stake' (chap. 6). And he adds: 'We who seem to accuse Aristogeiton may be found to be accusing you' (chap. 12). In fact, if his fellow-prisoners judged him guilty of the worst crimes, could honest Athenians judges ever have the courage to absolve him? Finally, the austere *explicit* is evocative. In this

---

Aristogeiton was found guilty; cf. Din. II.13.

[39] *Contra* cf. Worthington (1992: 311-312).

[40] Cf. the passages that define Aristogeiton as the worst man ever existed (Din. II.3); the statement that is unnecessary to list all his crimes because they are well-known to all (Din. II.6, 19); the use of the term θήριον (Din. II.10); his impious conduct towards his father and his cellmates (Din. II.8, 10).

[41] The episode of Arthmius is also quoted by Dem. XIX.271, Aesch. III.258, Plut. *Them.* 6.4. See Nouhaud (1982: 239-242).

[42] Cf. Dem. IX.2, III.22. See also Canfora (1974: 47, 52-53).

passage the orator imagines that once the trial is over, every judge who voted for Aristogeiton's absolution will be considered a betrayer of the laws (chap. 98). We have already mentioned the potential criticism of Antiphon against the court system. The critical opinion of Demosthenes is interesting too: he is a politician, perfectly integrated into the democratic system, who fights a never-ending ideological battle against the individualistic, emotive and irrational drifts that in assembly and court can inflame the popular souls, distracting them from the pursuit of their own common good.[43]

If this interpretation is correct, in conclusion a question arises: do the deep socio-political and philosophical reflections contained in the oration *Against Aristogeiton* occur too late? Actually, the defeat of Chaeronea, more than a decade before, opened a starkly different scenario, in which Athens had lost the greatest part of its autonomy and was subjugated to the Macedonians' reign, now a huge, multi-ethnic, empire.[44] Such a rethinking about democracy during a period of absolutism does not seem to be isolated in those years in which Athens was guided by Lycurgus.[45] It is well-known, in fact, that at that time many political, economic, urban and religious reforms took place, but it is possible to follow the traces of a critical and self-critical debate about civic history, institutions and behaviors too. These traces are evident in some of the surviving δημόσιοι. Indeed the violent tone in Demosthenes' *Against Aristogeiton* (325/324 BC) is as virulent as the attacks of Lycurgus in *Against Leocrates* (330 BC) and the one of Demosthenes himself in *On the crown* speech (330 BC).[46] These three discourses – and it should perhaps be mentioned Aeschines' *Against Ctesiphon* too – have in common the fact that the awful depiction of the enemy transcends the simple personal hostility and aims to furnish *e contrario* a lesson in civic education. In this sense, the scope of such speeches[47] goes beyond mere court success, inviting the community to reflect on the foundations of democratic life post-Chaeronea. In order to achieve this goal, the orators make use of literary and philosophical references, in an elitist attempt to instruct and orient the court and, more generally, the Athenian δῆμος. Even though 4th century BC Athenian society was still largely oral, the circulation of written text was becoming increasingly common and subtle allusions or explicit quotes were useful, precious didactic devices for the orators.[48] Consequently, as has been seen, Demosthenes' oration XXV probably refers to Antiphon's Περὶ ἀληθείας and at the very least to the philosophical debate around nature and law. In the same way, the

[43] It is perhaps interesting to note that Din. I.66 seems explicitly to imitate Demosthenes in this oratorical strategy, that covertly threat the judges in the case in which they would absolve Aristogeiton: τί γὰρ ἐροῦμεν ὦ Ἀθηναῖοι πρὸς τοὺς περιεστηκότας ἐξελθόντες ἐκ τοῦ δικαστηρίου, ἐάν, ὃ μὴ γένοιτο, παρακρουσθῇθ' ὑπὸ τῆς τούτου γοητείας; τίσιν ὀφθαλμοῖς ἕκαστος ὑμῶν τὴν πατρῴαν ἑστίαν οἴκαδ' ἀπελθὼν ἰδεῖν τολμήσει [...]. Cf. Dem. XXV. 98-99: ἔξιτ' αὐτίκα δὴ μάλ' ἐκ τοῦ δικαστηρίου, θεωρήσουσι δ' ὑμᾶς οἱ περιεστηκότες καὶ ξένοι καὶ πολῖται, καὶ κατ' ἄνδρ' εἰς ἕκαστον τὸν παριόντα βλέψονται καὶ φυσιογνωμήσουσι τοὺς ἀπεψηφισμένους. τί οὖν ἐρεῖτ', ὦ ἄνδρες Ἀθηναῖοι, εἰ προέμενοι τοὺς νόμους ἔξιτε; ποίοις προσώποις ἢ τίσιν ὀφθαλμοῖς πρὸς ἕκαστον τούτων ἀντιβλέψεσθε [...]. Furthermore, in Lycurgus too the courts and judges' role is underlined in an attempt to civic re-organization (likely influenced by Platonic teaching): cf. chap. 4 and Renehan (1970: 219-231).

[44] It is obvious that the defeat of 338 BC did not mark a sharp *caesura* in Athenian history and the consequences of this event were spread over a longer period of time. About this aspect, cf. Cawkwell (1996: 98-121). About Demosthenes' and Aeschines' historical perception and oratorical usage of the Chaeronea defeat, cf. Westwood (2020: 281-282 and note 34).

[45] Cf. Faraguna (1992; 2011: 67-86).

[46] On the date of this trial, cf. Wankel (1976: 25-37) and Sardone (2021: 12-15).

[47] Or of their *post eventum* written reworkings, which success, in the case of Demosthenes and Aeschines, is largely testified by a great number of Egyptian papyri.

[48] About Lycurgus' didactic intents, well testified by the ephebic reform too, cf. Sawada (1996: 57-84, esp. 77-78).

speech *Against Leocrates* furnished a large quantity of literary references: for example, the long *rhesis* from Euripides' *Erecteus*[49] (chap. 100), *Iliad* XV.494-499 (chaps. 102-103) and Tyrtaeus' paraenetic poetry (chaps. 106-107).[50] More specifically, the conjunction of the terms νόμος and φύσις here becomes a frequent argument to underline the elitist position of eminent politicians like Demosthenes and Lycurgus to the detriment of their enemies: it is constantly present in the prosecution against Aristogeiton and recurs also to depict Aeschines' behavior in *On the crown* 275[51] and to condemn the hapless deserter in *Against Leocrates* 131.

In light of this, and considering the comparative evidence between these speeches, it is clear that the first oration *Against Aristogeiton* is therefore a precious source, 'ein Dokument für eine Zeit der attischen Litteratur' as sustained by Wilamowitz.[52] *A fortiori*, if there are several elements to corroborate the authenticity, the oration becomes an interesting proof of Demosthenes' post-Chaeronea political action.

Bibliography

Adams, C.D. 1927. *Demosthenes and his influence*. New York: Longmans, Green.

Blass, F. 1893. *Die attische Beredsamkeit*, III.1, *Demosthenes*. Leipzig: Teubner.

Blass, F. 1887. Ad Henricum Weil epistula de oratione in Aristogitonem priore. *Revue de Philologie, de Littérature et d'Histoire Anciennes* 11: 129-141.

Canfora, L. 1974. *Discorsi e Lettere di Demostene*, I, *Discorsi all'assemblea*. Torino: UTET.

Canfora, L. 2000. *Discorsi e Lettere di Demostene*, II.2, *Discorsi in Tribunale*. Torino: UTET.

Canfora, L. 2020. La ricezione greca di Demostene. *Quaderni di Storia* 92: 5-39.

Cawkwell, G.L. 1969. The Crowning of Demosthenes. *Classical Quarterly* 19: 163-180.

Cawkwell, G.L 1996. The End of Greek Liberty, in R.W. Wallace and E.M. Harris (eds), *Transitions to Empire: Essays in Greco-Roman History, 360-146 BC, in Honor of E. Badian*: 98-121. Norman: University of Oklahoma Press.

Christ, M.R. 1998. *The litigious Athenian*. Baltimore; London: Johns Hopkins University Press.

Conomis N. (ed.) 1970. *Lycurgi oratio in Leocratem, cum ceterarum Lycurgi orationum fragmentis*. Leipzig: Teubner.

De Robertis, F. 2015. *Per la storia del testo di Demostene*. Bari: Dedalo.

Drerup, E. 1923. *Demosthenes im Urteile des Altertums. Von Theopomp bis Tzetzes: Geschichte, Roman, Legende*. Würzburg: Becker.

Faraguna, M. 1992. *Atene nell'età di Alessandro. Problemi politici, economici, finanziari*, Roma: Atti della Accademia Nazionale dei Lincei.

Faraguna, M. 2011. Lykourgan Athens?, in V. Azoulay and P. Ismard (éds), *Clisthène et Lycurgue d'Athènes. Autour du politique dans la cité classique*: 67-86. Paris: Publications de la Sorbonne.

Foerster, R. (ed.) 1915. *Libanii Opera*, VIII. *Progymnasmata, Argumenta Orationum Demosthenicarum*. Lipsiae: Teubner.

Gotteland, S. 2010. Conseiller et persuader: quelques échos thucydidéens dans les Harangues de Démosthène, in V. Fromentin, S. Gotteland, and P. Payen (éds), *Ombres de Thucydide. La réception de l'historien depuis l'Antiquité jusqu'au début du XXe siècle*: 35-50. Paris: De Boccard.

---

[49] Fr. 360 Kannicht.

[50] Fr. 6 Gentili-Prato.

[51] Cf. Wankel (1976: 1187-1191).

[52] Wilamowitz (1893. II: 402).

Hansen, M.H. 1976. *Apagoge, Endeixis and Ephegesis against kakourgoi, atimoi and pheugontes: a study in the Athenian administration of justice in the fourth century BC*. Odense: Odense University Press.

Hansen, M.H. 1991. *The Athenian Democracy in the Age of Demosthenes: Structure, Principles, and Ideology*. Oxford; Cambridge: Blackwell.

Hausmann, B. 1978-1981. *Demosthenis Fragmenta in Papyris et Membranis Servata*. Diss. Leipzig 1921, ed. by R. Pintaudi, *Pars Prima, Pars Secunda*; P. Mertens, *Appendice di aggiornamento. Papyrus et Parchemins d'origine égyptienne édités après la Dissertation de B. Hausmann. Pars Tertia*. Firenze: Gonnelli.

Heinimann, F. 1945. *Nomos und Physis: Herkunft und Bedeutung einer Antithese im griechischen Denken des 5. Jahrhunderts*. Basel: Reinhardt.

Hernández Muñoz, F.G. 1994. Tucídides y Platón en Demóstenes. *Cuadernos de Filología Clásica. Estudios Griegos e Indoeuropeos* 4: 139-160.

Labriola, I. (ed.) 1992. *Antifonte. La verità*. Palermo: Sellerio.

Lehmann, G.A. 2004. *Demosthenes von Athen: Ein Leben für die Freiheit*. München: Beck.

Lipsius, J.H. 1883. Über die Unechtheit der ersten Rede gegen Aristogeiton. *Leipziger Studien zur classischen Philologie* 6: 317-331.

MacDowell, D.M. 2009. *Demosthenes, the Orator*. Oxford: Oxford University Press.

Martin, G. 2009. *Divine Talk, religious argumentation in Demosthenes*. Oxford: Oxford University Press.

Martin, G. (ed.). 2019. *The Oxford Handbook of Demosthenes*. Oxford: Oxford University Press.

Mathieu, G. (ed.) 1947. *Démosthène, Plaidoyers Politiques*, IV, *Sur la Couronne, Contre Aristogiton I et II*. Paris: Les Belles Lettres.

Mathieu, G. 1948. *Démosthène. L'homme et l'œuvre*. Paris: Boivin.

Norden, E. 1898. *Die antike Kunstprosa vom VI. Jahrhundert V. Chr. bis in die Zeit der Renaissance*. Leipzig: Teubner. Italian ed. B. Heinemann Campana 1986. *La prosa d'arte antica: dal VI secolo a.C. all'età della Rinascenza*. Roma: Salerno.

Nouhaud, M. 1982. *L'utilisation de l'histoire par les orateurs attiques*. Paris: Les Belles Lettres.

PA = Kirchner, I. 1901-1903. *Prosopographia Attica*. Berolini: Reimer.

PAA = Traill, J.S. 1994-2011. *Persons of Ancient Athens*. Toronto: Athenians.

Paoli, U.E. 1930. *Studi di diritto attico*. Firenze: Bemporad.

Pohlenz, M. 1924. *Anonymus περὶ νόμων*. Nachrichten von der Gesellschaft der Wissenschaften zu Göttingen, Phil.-Hist. Klasse: 19-37.

Renehan, R.F. 1970. *The Platonism of Lycurgus. Greek, Roman, and Byzantine Studies* 11: 219-231.

Ronnet, G. 1951. *Étude sur le Style de Démosthène dans les Discours Politiques*. Paris: de Boccard.

Schaefer, A. 1858. *Demosthenes und seine Zeit*, III.2. Leipzig: Teubner.

Sealey, R. 1960. Who was Aristogeiton? *Bulletin of the Institute of Classical Studies* 7: 33-43.

Sealey, R. 1967. Pseudo-Demosthenes XIII and XXV. *Revue des Études Grecques* 80: 250-255.

Sealey, R. 1993. *Demosthenes and his Time: a study in Defeat*. New York; Oxford: Oxford University Press.

Sardone, L. 2020. Nuove prospettive ecdotiche per la retorica demostenica. *Rhesis* 11.1: 194-201.

Sardone, L. 2021. *I Papiri del* De Corona *di Demostene. Storia e critica del testo*. Bari: Edipuglia.

Sawada, N. 1996. Athenian Politics in the Age of Alexander the Great: A Reconsideration of the Trial of Ctesiphon. *Chiron* 26: 57-84.

Treves, P. 1936. Apocrifi demostenici. *Athenaeum* 14: 152-174, 233-258.

Untersteiner, M. 2008. *I sofisti*. Milano: Mondadori.

Vince, J.H. (ed.) 1935. *Demosthenes, III. Against Meidias, Androtion, Aristocrates, Timocrates, Aristogeiton.* Cambridge: Harvard University Press; London: Heinemann.

Wagner, R. 1883. *De priore quae Demosthenis fertur Adversus Aristogitonem oratione.* Cervimontii: Diss. Rostock University.

Wankel, H. 1976. *Demosthenes, Rede für Ktesiphon über den Kranz.* Heidelberg: Winter.

Weil, H. 1887. L'auteur du premier discours contre Aristogiton est-it bien informé des institutions d'Athènes?, in *Mélanges Renier*: 17-25. Paris: Vieweg.

Westwood, G. 2019. Views on the Past, in G. Martin (ed.), *The Oxford Handbook of Demosthenes*: 179-189. Oxford: Oxford University Press.

Westwood, G. 2020. *The Rhetoric of the Past in Demosthenes and Aeschines: oratory, history, and politics in classical Athens.* Oxford: Oxford University Press.

Wilamowitz-Moellendorff, U. von 1893. *Aristoteles und Athen.* Berlin: Weidmann.

Wilamowitz-Moellendorff, U. von 1923. Lesefrüche. *Hermes* 61: 57-86.

Willey, H. 2019. Religion, in G. Martin (ed.), *The Oxford Handbook of Demosthenes*: 271-282. Oxford: Oxford University Press.

Worman, N. 2008. *Abusive Mouths in Classical Athens.* Cambridge: Cambridge University Press.

Worthington, I. 1992. *A Historical Commentary on Dinarchus.* Ann Arbor: University of Michigan Press.

Worthington, I. 2000. Demosthenes' (in)activity during the reign of Alexander the Great, in I. Worthington (ed.), *Demosthenes. Statesman and orator*: 90-113. London; New York: Routledge.

Worthington, I. 2013. *Demosthenes of Athens and the Fall of Classical Greece.* Oxford: Oxford University Press.

Worthington, I., Cooper, C.R., Harris E.M. (eds) 2001. *Dinarchus, Hyperides, and Lycurgus.* Austin: University of Texas press.

Yunis, H. 2001. *Demosthenes, On the Crown.* Cambridge: Cambridge University Press.

The Search for Consistency in Legal Narratives: The Case of the 'Good Lawgiver'

Ália Rodrigues

University of Coimbra
Centre for Classical and Humanistic Studies (CECH)
alia.rosa.rosa@gmail.com

Abstract

In this paper, I examine the ways in which the figure of the *nomothetēs* was characterised in fourth-century BC legal narratives. My argument is twofold: firstly, I argue that a well-circumscribed and coherent representation of the *nomothetēs* is present in different types of legal narratives. These include accounts about the creation of constitutions (theoretical or historical) in philosophical, historical, and legal discourses in which the lawgiver is the central figure. Secondly, I show that the uniformity of the representation of the *nomothetēs* was maintained through the language used to describe the lawgiver and his activity. In so doing, I wish to show how the idea of legislative intent, along with the sense of structural wholeness that these laws conveyed, was constructed as much inside as outside the courts.

Keywords

Nomothetēs, legislative intent, demiurge, Plato, goodness, legal coherence, creation narrative.

The search for consistency played a key role in the perception of the Athenian rule of law. The procedures and practices introduced at the end of the fifth century suggest that there was a structure in place to ensure that this consistency could be realised in practice. The first step to legal reform was the republication of the laws of Solon. This began in 410 BC, after the fall of the first oligarchic coup, when a panel of *anagrapheis* was appointed to gather all valid existing laws of Solon and Draco, which would be ratified by the *demos* and published in the *Stoa Basileos* (Lys. 30.2-5, And. 1.81).[1] After being disrupted by the oligarchic coup of the Thirty Tyrants in 404 BC, this panel was appointed once again and completed its task in 400/399 BC.[2]

In the midst of this democratic restoration, another board of *nomothetai* composed of 500 members and elected by the *demos* was created in order to introduce new laws aimed at making the system of judicial review more robust and to avoid legal inconstancies or contradictions.[3] These new measures included: the distinction between *nomoi* (laws) and *psephismata* (decrees) whereby the former would always prevail (And.1.87);[4] the prohibition, under any circumstances, against the use of unwritten laws or indeed decrees (And. 1.85, 87); a definition for law (*nomos*) according to which 'No law shall be directed against an individual

---

[1] On material organisation of the Solon's laws, see Rhodes (1991; 2006) and note 17 below.

[2] Also called *nomothetai* by Thucydides (8.97.2), and Andocides (*On the Mysteries* 82). On the second term, see Rhodes (1991: 95-100).

[3] The main source here is the decree of Teisamenos quoted by Andocides (*On the Mysteries* 83-84). See MacDowell (1989 [1962]: 194-119). On the authenticity of this document, see Hansen (2006), who argues that there is no doubt that it is genuine, though Canevaro and Harris (2012) argue that it is a later forgery.

[4] Also mentioned in Demosthenes *Against Aristocrates* 87 and *Against Timocrates* 30.

without applying to all citizens alike, unless an Assembly of six thousand so resolve by secret ballot according to which it could only be considered 'law'";[5] and finally a law preventing the use of retroactive laws (Dem. 24.42).[6] This system was also enforced with penalties for whoever tried to initiate a legal change without following the stablished procedure or if it failed to persuade the jurors. Whereas the *graphe nomon me epitedeion theinai* concerned *nomoi* and prevented illegal changes (Dem. 24.32), the previous *graphe paranomon* dealt with new decrees.[7] Aeschines, for instance, was fined and lost his career as a prosecutor for failing to get one fifth of the votes in the case *Against Ctesiphon*.[8] This complex system of *nomothesia*[9] sought not only to regulate legal change but also to discourage casual changes.[10]

In addition to these procedural measures, the search for consistency was also visible in rhetorical practices employed by Athenian orators in the narrative of legal arguments at court. Such practices included the use of legal precedent[11] and the intent of the lawgiver. Harris (2007) provided a comprehensive analysis about the former in which he showed that whenever orators cited precedents, they tended to rely on public memory of recent trials or precedents that could be supported by written documents. As to the second practice – the intent of the lawgiver – Harris (2007: 364) defines this as 'a fictitious figure to some extent, but a fiction that the Athenians believed in.' Elsewhere, Johnstone (1999: 26) described the latter as 'a fiction' while Thomas (1994: 124) saw it as 'an extra-legal argument'. The characterisation of 'legislative intent' among scholars of modern constitutional theory is more sceptical: 'absurd fiction' (Max Radin, 1930), 'deception' (Australian Justice, 2003) or, as the late United States Supreme Court Justice Scalia (2018 [1997]: 14) put it: 'It is the law that governs, not the intent of the lawgiver'.[12] Ekins (2013: 16) examined these sceptical arguments and showed that scholars' and judges' mistrust towards this interpretative tool relies mostly on the fact that 'modern legislature is a group of legislators', and therefore the idea of 'intention' cannot have a place in legal interpretation. In a recent contribution to this debate, Ekins (2019) is similarly confident about the centrality of legislative intent, particularly based on the fact

---

[5] Translated by Maidment (2014). See also Rhodes (1991: 93).

[6] Also called 'the law of Diocles'. See Canevaro (2015: 25).

[7] On these two procedures, see Canevaro (2015: 28). For a detailed discussion on the procedure *graphe nomon me epitedeion theinai*, see Rhodes (2003: 125-126).

[8] Harris (2006: 407-408). Furthermore, Andocides, *On the Mysteries* 1.33; Demosthenes, *Against Aristogiton 2* 26.9. Another attempt at introducing consistency in law is cross-referencing. This practice can be found in the Gortyn law and in other cities of Crete. As Gagarin showed (2008: 142): 'At Gortyn, there more than two dozen cross-references are scattered throughout the fifth-century texts other than the Code, and there are many more there. All these references occur in one of two contexts, procedural or penal'. The first text to attest this element dates to the end of the sixth-century and comprises a law concerning land regulation for a colony (ML 13 1.44, *Nomima* I.44, *IGT* 47) in which the punishment for civil unrest caused by the division of land is equated with the same penalty already established for homicide: 'he himself and his family shall be cursed for all time, his property shall be confiscated and his house demolished just as under the law (*tethmos*) about homicide' (lines 13-14). See Gagarin (2008: 60-61).

[9] For different interpretations of the reconstruction of this system, see Rhodes (1980; 2003), Hansen (1985), and Canevaro (2013; 2015).

[10] The idea that constant change weakens the law is also discussed by Plato (*Leg.* 7.788b-c) and Aristotle (*Pol.* 2.1269a13). As the latter put it: 'The law has no other source of strength through which to secure obedience apart the habit. But habit can be created only by the passage of time'. Translated by Barker (2009 [1995]).

[11] See Harris (2007). Cf. Lanni (1999).

[12] Apart from Scalia, all quotations are based on Ekins (2013: 3-4), who added that other judges in the United Kingdom and New Zealand also expressed their concerns regarding legislative intent.

that legislators were able to make 'reasoned choices together' in order to protect a 'common good' specific to time and place.[13]

In the context of fourth-century Athens, especially after the creation of the *nomothetai* board composed by 500 members (or even 1,001 members),[14] the figure of the single *nomothetēs* continued to coexist with this new institutional reality[15] as if it belonged to a parallel historical realm. The underlying narrative of fourth-century Athenian legal reforms is that a single individual enacted laws that were meant to remain forever valid. This representation of the past was amplified, politicised and radicalised further by conflicts between oligarchs and democrats who associated themselves with Solon's legacy.[16] Several legal scholars have already shown how Athenians perceived their laws to be the result of a coherent and rational system of laws enacted by an ancient lawgiver.[17]

In this chapter, I examine further how the figure of the *nomothetēs* is characterised in fourth-century philosophical and historical discourse. In so doing, I wish to show how the idea of legislative intent along with the sense of wholeness of the laws was constructed as much inside as outside the courts. Firstly, I will argue that a defined and coherent representation of the *nomothetēs* existed in different fourth-century literary contexts. Secondly, I will show this uniformity was maintained through language used to describe the lawgiver and his activity.

But before addressing aspects of this legal discourse, I will explore the scope of the concept of the *nomothetēs* outside the legal sphere in order to identity the semantic layers which made this 'fiction' such a powerful legal expedient in legal narratives. Legal narratives are broadly conceived here to include accounts about the creation of constitutions (theoretical or historical) in philosophical, historical or legal discourses in which the lawgiver is the main figure and agent. I will argue that these narratives, despite belonging to different genres, share a common language and follow a stable linguistic pattern when describing the role of the lawgiver.[18] Thus, the fourth-century process of humanising the figure of the *nomothetēs* is not only a manifestation of the rhetoric of the past as many have argued.[19] Rather, it also contributed to the use of legislative intent as a tool to achieve consistency in legal narratives. I will begin by addressing Plato and Aristotle's characterisation of the lawgiver as well as the creationist model used to describe his activity. I will also demonstrate how this Plato-Aristotelian language occurs both in historical discourse, especially when it comes to constitutional storytelling, as well as in the legal narratives of orators. In doing so

---

[13] As he (2019: 139) put it: 'Interpreters can and should infer the legislature's intentions in enactments and skepticism about the relevance of legislative intentions to statutory interpretation is unwarranted'. Cf. Dolcetti (2019).

[14] See Rhodes (2003: 125).

[15] The same coexistence can be found in Plato's *Laws*. See further, p. 5.

[16] See Canevaro (2015: 22).

[17] Johnstone (1999), Hölkeskamp (1999), and Harris (2007). As to the material evidence, Rhodes (1991, 2006; Leão and Rhodes 2017) has demonstrated how ancient sources, namely the *Athenaion Politeia*, offers a solid and reliable reconstruction of what an Athenian compilation of laws could look like. As Rhodes (2006: 250) points out elsewhere: 'Plutarch and others were able to cite Solon's laws from numbered *axones* (...) indeed, one list of Aristotle's works includes a treatise in five books "on the *axones* of Solon"'.

[18] Szegedy-Maszak (1978) and Kivilo (2010) have already identified a consistent pattern of *topoi* in biographical accounts of lawgivers.

[19] See further p. 10.

I will explore the use of the *nomothetēs topos* in two speeches – *Against Timarchus* and *Against Ctesiphon* by Aeschines – in which the occurrence of this term is particularly frequent.

The first author to make extensive use of the term *nomothetēs* was Plato, especially in the *Laws*. The Platonic focus on this concept led Daniele Allen (2010) to argue that Plato's influential teachings explain the migration of the concept of *nomothetēs* from philosophical to Athenian legal discourse. Although this argument is debatable in the sense that other contemporaneous circumstances may also help to explain the emergence and political relevance of this term, Plato's contribution is essential not only in understanding the political-legal narrative of the *nomothetēs* but also to establish its characterisation, since no other source uses it with such frequency.

In Plato's dialogues, *The Republic* and in *The Laws*, the description of the lawgiver's activity is bound up with the construction of an imaginary city.[20] In both dialogues, the interlocutors appoint an imaginary lawgiver who is expected to frame a rationally structured constitution and establish a new way of life, such that each city is designed according to a single mindset. In the *Republic*, as in the *Laws*, the lawgiver is consistently characterised in a positive way, being referred to as ἀγαθός ('good', *Resp.* 564c1, 599e2; *Leg.* 671c3; 688a1; 742d4; 922a4) and ἀληθινός ('truthful', *Resp.* 4.427a4).[21] As such, the figure of the lawgiver was an abstract entity whose construction is based on an idealistic projection of early legislators (*Resp.* 10.599e; *Leg.* 9.853c and *Leg.* 1.625e; 1.626a; 1.631d-e). By the end of the third book of the *Laws*, after reflecting on the lawgiver's aims and role, Cleinias (3.702a) mentions that he had been invited, together with nine other parties, to draft laws for Knossos' new colony, Magnesia. The other two interlocutors join him in this enterprise and the imaginary construction of the new city begins. Soon, this group of legislators 'disappears' and is substituted by the same individual and abstract lawgiver mentioned at the beginning (4.709d; cf. 1.631d, 632c; 633a). At this point, however, since the commission of ten lawgivers for the new colony had already been mentioned, it becomes incongruous to refer to a *nomothetēs* in the singular because it deepens the difference between the city outlined in discourse and the objective conditions in which a colony was supposedly founded.[22]

The founding of this new city between the fourth book and the twelfth could be described as a lengthy creation narrative with the *nomothetēs* at its centre. The 'good lawgiver' always has the well-being of the city in mind in order to make the city happy (εὐδαιμονεστάτης, *Leg.* 5.742d) and good (ἀρίστη) as much as possible. Thus, the main intention (βούλησις, *Leg.* 5.742d)

---

[20] Several works by Plato refer to the figure of the lawgiver, but the *Laws* contains the greatest number of occurrences of the term *nomothetēs* in singular form (c. 150 times in the singular, c. 50 in the plural). This work is then followed by *Cratylus*, which also contains more occurrences of term in the singular. This dialogue, which is concerned with language and the naming of things, describes the *nomothetēs* as a 'craftsman (δημιουργός) most rarely found among human beings' (389a, translated by Reeve 1998). In other words, the *nomothetēs* is the 'rule-setter' or the one who defines the rules which enable the creation of names and their meanings. Even though *Cratylus* does not address constitution-making, it presents the main traits of the *nomothetēs*: he is 'rare', and he is also responsible for framing the limits of reality.

[21] Further attributions of ἀγαθός to the *nomothetēs* occur in other works by Plato: *Cra.* 431e7, *Plt.* 309d1, *Prt.* 326d6, [Pl.], *Minos* 318c2, 321c5, 321d2; [*Epistulae*] 354b (as an attribute of Lycurgus). Sometimes the adjective ἀγαθός occurs alongside παλαιός: *Prt.* 326d, *Minos* 318b3. For instances of the attribution of ἀγαθός to the *nomothetēs* in Aristotle and by Aeschines, see above pp. 6-7 and p. 10 respectively.

[22] In addition to this reference in the plural, we find roughly 50 more instances of *nomothetai* throughout the dialogue, either referring to themselves as the lawgivers (e.g. *Leg.* 4.702e), or to past legislators (e.g. *Leg.* 9.853c).

of the lawgiver was to organise a constitution in a way that allows its citizens to develop 'the goodness as a whole'[23] (πᾶσα ἀρετή, *Leg.* 1.630e; 3.688b; 4.704d). This sense of legal coherence is conveyed by various entanglements between the expression of the lawgiver's intention and the law-making process, as the following examples show: 'To sum up, the lawgiver enumerates and lays down what is disgraceful and evil, and conversely what is fine and good' (5.728a);[24] 'The good lawgiver's intention, they would say, must be for the city whose well-being he had in mind, and of which he is the lawgiver, to be great as possible and as wealthy as possible'[25] (5.742d); 'The lawgiver needs to have an eye to all these, and make it a requirement for all the citizens, whatever they do, not to abandon this discipline of number'[26] (5.747a). Take, for instance, the lawgiver's regulation regarding limits to the accumulation of property described in the fifth book (5.744e-745a). Here, everyone is permitted an allocation of land, which may be increased by four times the initial amount. Any additional property above this limit would have to be given to the city. The intention behind this law was to prevent poverty and, subsequently, the threat of civil unrest.

Another distinctive feature of this legislative creative process is the fact that both time and necessity are absent from this discussion, as this is mainly a discourse about the best method of establishing a new constitution (*Leg.* 5.746 b-d; 9.858b).[27] Therefore, no ambiguity is expected in the lawgiver's teachings. For as the Athenian Visitor declares: "He cannot give two different answers to a single question" (*Leg.* 4.719d).[28] That the Platonic lawgiver is acting outside history[29] gives him the freedom to legislate in a methodological way and therefore to envisage the founding of the constitution as a reconstruction of the demiurgic act creation.[30]

Both Plato's *Republic* and *Laws* are reviewed by Aristotle in the second book of the *Politics*. After criticising Plato's constitutional proposals on several fronts,[31] Aristotle carries on examining ideal models of constitutions, namely, the constitutions of Sparta, Crete, and Carthage. However, in order to carry out this task, Aristotle follows the same Platonic discursive structure by placing the lawgiver at the centre of the narrative. Furthermore, like Plato,

---

[23] Translation by Tom Griffith (2016).

[24] Greek text: ὡς δὲ εἰπεῖν συλλήβδην ὃς ἅπερ ἂν νομοθέτης αἰσχρὰ εἶναι καὶ κακὰ διαριθμούμενος τάττῃ καὶ τοὐναντίον ἀγαθὰ καὶ καλά (ed. Des Places 1951).

[25] Greek text: οὐχ ἥπερ ἂν οἱ πολλοὶ φαῖεν, δεῖν βούλεσθαι τὸν ἀγαθὸν νομοθέτην ὡς μεγίστην τε εἶναι τὴν πόλιν ᾗ νοῶν εὖ νομοθετοῖ, καὶ ὅτι μάλιστα πλουσίαν.

[26] Greek text: πρὸς γὰρ ταῦτα πάντα δεῖ βλέψαντα τόν γε νομοθέτην προστάττειν τοῖς πολίταις πᾶσιν εἰς δύναμιν τούτων μὴ ἀπολείπεσθαι τῆς συντάξεως.

[27] Other instances: *Leg.* 5.746 b-d; 5.742c-744a. See Griffith (2016: 195 n. 53), Rowe (2000: 41), and Lane (2012: 112).

[28] The main concern of this exposition is consistency says the Athenian Visitor: 'Anybody making anything – however mundane – needs to make sure, if he is going to be taken seriously, that it is in every way consistent with itself' (*Leg.* 5.746d).

[29] A similar point is made by Lane (2013: 13).

[30] The platonic idealisation of the lawgiver recalls Kelsen's (2015 [1919]: 13) characterisation of the legislator as 'almighty' in the sense that he was mainly concerned with regulating human conduct and tying legal consequences to them.

[31] Regarding the *Republic*, Aristotle criticises the lack of social differentiation which is essential to the self-sufficiency of the city (2.1260b27-1260b36); the community of women and children would lead to general apathy between parents and children not to collective responsibility (2.1261b16-12621a1); communal ownership of property would make the ruling class unhappy and create problems for farmers (1262b39-1264b24). As for the *Laws*, he says that Plato failed to establish a balanced government and to regulate foreign relations (1264a26-1266a28). One of these critiques are unwarranted, namely that Plato did not stipulate limits to the acquisition of property in the *Laws* (5.744e-745a).

Aristotle describes this lawgiver's expertise as 'good' (ἀγαθός, *Pol.* 1288b27, 1333b19).[32] Also, as in Plato, Aristotle represents the lawgiver as a powerful craftsman who is able to work his material and transform it into something different which, in this case, is taken to mean that he is able to influence people's behaviours. For instance, when he suggests that one way to encourage citizens to practise regular exercise is to make compulsory daily pilgrimages to the shrines of the goddess that presided over their births (7.1335b11). Other examples can be found throughout the *Politics*, such as: 'Anxious (βουλόμενος) for the Spartans to be as numerous as possible, the legislator encouraged (προάγεται) citizens to have as many children as possible'[33] (2.1270b6); 'The task of the good lawgiver is to see how any city or race of men or society with which he is concerned may share in a good life and in whatever form of happiness is available to them'[34] (7.1325a5); 'It follows on this that the legislator must labour to ensure that his citizens become good men (...)' (7.1333a11),[35] among others.

The idea that the agency of one individual was responsible for the creation of a rational order out of chaos also led to inevitable parallels between the lawgiver and *Timaeus'* 'good' demiurge (*Ti.* 29a) in Plato and Aristotle:[36] 'Well, if this universe of ours is beautiful (καλός) and if its craftsman was good (ἀγαθός), it evidently follows that he was looking at an eternal model (...)'[37] (*Ti.* 29a).

Thus, the *nomothetēs'* centrality in narratives about (constitutional) beginnings contributed to his characterisation as a god-like figure and a being who was intrinsically 'good' – a theme which is also found in legal oratory, as we will see further.[38] However, neither the human legislator in Plato and Aristotle nor the divine demiurge in the *Timaeus* has absolute control over the future consequences of their creations. This worry is expressed by Plato in the *Republic* (6.497d) when he acknowledges the need to introduce a permanent 'element which embodies the principles underlying the regime – the same principles on which you, the lawgiver, based the laws',[39] in order to regulate legal change while preserving the initial purpose of former constitutional arrangements. This anxiety appears to have been resolved in the *Laws* with the creation of the Guardians of the Laws (6.772b) and the Council (12.961a-c), which would ensure that the initial intention of the lawgiver remained alive and permanently present in the city (12.960d). The nature of the political constitution, as the Athenian Visitor (12.960b-d) pointed out, is that of a 'living creature' that requires a structure in place to guarantee

---

[32] Other occurrences of the term *nomothetēs*, combined with ἀγαθός, include *Protrepticus* 46.6, 49.6. Interestingly, Aristotle also characterised the Unmoved mover (the divine entity in his *Physics*, *De Caelo* and *Metaphysics* who is the cause of motion and therefore causation and change in the universe), as 'good' in the superlative form (e.g., *Metaph.* 1072b10-11).

[33] Translated by Barker (2009).

[34] Greek text: τοῦ δὲ νομοθέτου τοῦ σπουδαίου ἐστὶ τὸ θεάσασθαι πόλιν καὶ γένος ἀνθρώπων καὶ πᾶσαν ἄλλην κοινωνίαν, ζωῆς ἀγαθῆς πῶς μεθέξουσι καὶ τῆς ἐνδεχομένης αὐτοῖς εὐδαιμονίας'. (ed. Ross, 1964 [1957])

[35] Greek text: τοῦτ' ἂν εἴη τῷ νομοθέτῃ πραγματευτέον, ὅπως ἄνδρες ἀγαθοὶ γίγνωνται (...)'.

[36] E.g. *Leg.* 2.671c. On the comparison between *nomothetēs* and the demiurge in *Cratylus*, see below note 20. The same parallel was also identified by Plutarch's *Life of Lycurgus* (29.1).

[37] Translation by Waterfield (2008). This aspect has been explored by Morrow (1954), Laks (1990, 2000) and Brisson (1994, 2000).

[38] The association of the activity of lawgiving with the gods is also deeply rooted in Greek legal traditions as attested to by the biographies of early legislators. The Platonic dialogue *Laws* itself begins with the word 'God' in order to emphasise the divine origin of both Cretan and Spartan legal codes as opposed to the Athenian one, which seems to be the only one thought to be of human origin.

[39] Translated by Tom Griffith (2015).

its continuous existence. In Aristotle, this is especially relevant in the case of the criticism directed against Lycurgus and the Spartan Constitution: 'The natural result is the very opposite of legislator's *intention* (προαίρεσις)' (2.1271a),[40] 'The legislator who made the Spartan code *intended* (βουλόμενος) to make the whole citizen body hardy; but if he fulfilled that intention, as he obviously did, in the regard to the men, he has wholly neglected to achieve it in regard to the women' (2.1269b). A similar point is also made regarding the *unintended* consequences of Solon's reforms, in particular, the increase of the democratic element: 'This, however, appears to be due to accident rather than to any deliberate design (προαίρεσις) on the part of Solon' (2.1273b35).[41] These are only some of the most representative examples of the language of intention and purpose associated with founders of constitutions (3.1274b32) in Aristotle.[42]

Before addressing the legal discourse, I would like to draw attention to the work of a contemporary of Plato: *The Spartan Constitution* by Xenophon. Despite emphasising Lycurgus' authorship of the constitution, Xenophon does not use the term *nomothetēs* to refer to Lycurgus' position.[43] The same applies to Herodotus who, despite ascribing all Spartan institutions to Lycurgus, does not, however, refer to Lycurgus as the *nomothetēs*.[44] Ducat (2006: 6) compares and analyses all the available sources on Lycurgus and noticed that Xenophon added a feature which is absent from other sources: 'justification'.[45] This element manifested in language, with the use of 'interior deliberation' and verbs expressing volition throughout the *Spartan Constitution* as the following examples show: ὁ δὲ Λυκοῦργος (...), 'ἐποίησε', 'ἔθηκε', 'ἔταξεν', 'ὁρῶν' (1.7), 'ἐνόμισε' (1.7), 'ἐποίησεν' (1.7), 'ἐπιθυμοίη' (1.8), 'ἐποίησεν' (1.8), 'συνεχώρει' (1.9), 'ἀπετέλεσεν' (1.10), 'ἐπέστησε', 'ἔταξεν' (2.3), 'νομίζων' (2.3).[46] The authorship of the *Spartan Constitution* is thus emphatically attributed to Lycurgus in order to characterise it as rational, structured and deliberate constitutional framework (4.7, 5.1, 5.5) as if it were a product of teleological foresight. David (2007: 124) sees Xenophon's representation of Lycurgus as a result of a 'process of Solonisation', whereby the Spartan lawgiver was appropriated as 'an anti-democratic propaganda symbol' just like Solon.[47] For this to happen, Lycurgus needed to be humanised and filled with purpose and volition.[48]

---

[40] For more criticism, see here 7.1333b5-1333b27.

[41] This is also the view in the *Athenian Constitution* 9.2. See Rhodes (2017: 10-11) on this point.

[42] Although the *Politics* is the work featuring more occurrences of the term *nomothetēs*, other works by Aristotle also have meaningful references to this concept, especially within the context of legal philosophy and rhetoric which I am unable to explore fully here. In particular, those in the *Nicomachean Ethics* (eight instances in the singular; six in the plural) and *Rhetoric* (seven instances in the singular; four in the plural).

[43] However, this term is mentioned twice in Xenophon's *Memorabilia* (1.2.31; 4.4.24).

[44] On the emergence of *nomothetēs* as a relevant political concept, see p. 9.

[45] As he explains: 'The attribution, repeated every time, of each custom to Lycurgus already functions as a justification in itself, by presenting it as an element in a planned and considered work (...)'. For a comprehensive analysis of Xenophon's literary and political motivations, see David (2007).

[46] On this enumeration, Lipka (2002: 32) makes the following observation: 'Normally this is not discussed by X. with reasons for and against, but listed without any discussion, as if their excellence is beyond doubt'. Greek Text and English translation were taken from Lipka's edition (2002: 74-75). The parallelism found throughout Xenophon's work recalls the structure of the beginning and creation narratives (*Gen.* 1: 1-2: 4A).

[47] See also Leão (2020), who presents a detailed examination of how the myth of Lycurgus was amplified in a context of a pro-Spartan Athenian ideology focused on the figure of a founding hero. Also David (2007a). For more on the fourth-century construction of Lycurgus, see Gatto in this volume.

[48] For more details about this reading, see Rodrigues (forthcoming).

The positive characterisation of the lawgiver and his comparison to a divine being established a means of expressing his activity. These associations are more visible in Plato's dialogues and Aristotle's writings, but are also found in Greek orators and in subsequent Greek and Greco-Roman thinkers who were more deeply influenced by Plato, namely Philo, Josephus and Plutarch.[49]

In the beginning of the previous section, I mentioned Allen's argument that Plato was responsible for the migration of the concept of the *nomothetes* from philosophical discourse to a political and legal lexicon. Other elements, however, must be taken into account when considering the emergence of the *nomothetes* as a meaningful political concept in the fourth century, namely the shift from *thesmos* and *nomos* (Ostwald 1979 [1969]), which occurred between 511/10 and 494/3 BC, and the fact that references to the *nomothetes* can also be found in the legal oratory prior to Plato's work (i.e. before 399 BC).[50] Regarding the former – the progressive substitution of *thesmos* by *nomos* – Ostwald (1979: 55) thought that this shift was probably motivated by Cleisthenes' reforms, which contributed to the change in perception of the law from an imposition derived from an external and superior agency to the idea of law as an obligation that results from a horizontal consensus. It is thus in the context of *nomothetein* that the concept *nomothetes* and *nomothesia* began to be systematically used.[51] Moreover, the concept of *nomothetes* is already attested in the speeches of first-generation orators with the same language of intentionality and agency.[52] Allen (2010: 192, n.14) points out that the frequency of the use of *nomothetes* between the first and second generation shows Plato's influence in Athenian political discourse, especially after his death (348/7 BC). Among these second-generation orators, Allen (2010: 102) stresses Aeschines' 'unusual emphasis' on the term *nomothetes* to refer to Solon.[53] Clarke (2009: 257), who compared different representations of the pasts by orators, observes that Aeschines also refers to a much more distant and timeless past: 'Historical events of the fourth century, besides the ones which actually form the speeches, are virtually absent'.

The speeches in Athenian legal oratory that contain the most occurrences of the term *nomothetes* in the singular are Aeschines' *Against Timarchos* (346/5 BC) and *Against Ctesiphon* (330 BC), with fourteen and twenty-one instances respectively, in addition to six references to Solon in the speech *Against Timarchos* and four in the speech *Against Ctesiphon*. In addition

---

[49] Both Philo and Josephus use the term *nomothetes* to describe Moses. In Philo, the most common title for Moses is *nomothetes*, while Josephus usually refers to Moses as *nomothetes* without naming him. For further discussions of the reception of this concept in Graeco-Roman Jewish literary contexts, see Feldman (1998: 399; 2006; 2007). For Plutarch, see Rodrigues (forthcoming).

[50] According to Grote (2009 [1865]: 204) and Kraut (2005: 3, 33n.7), Plato did not compose dialogues during Socrates' lifetime.

[51] Ostwald (1979: 92). On the relatively 'late' (i.e. 450's) attestation of the term *thesmothetes*, see Ostwald (1986: 25).

[52] The following are the instances of *nomothetes* in the singular among the first-generation orators: Antiphon (one instance, 1.15); Lysias (eight instances, 1.31, 10.7, 30; 11.4, 11; 30.2, 27; 31.27). There are also other instances in the plural: Thucydides (one instance, 8.97.2), Andocides (three instances, 1.82, 83, 84). The distinction between 'first generation orators' and 'second generation orators' is based on Allen's approach. While the 'first generation' (Antiphon, Andocides, Lysias) lived too early to have been influenced by Plato, members of the 'second generation', such as Aeschines, Lycurgus, Demosthenes, and Hyperides, may have been taught by him. For more on this distinction, see Allen (2010: 192 n.14). The same has been noted by David Murphy (2011).

[53] Apart from Aeschines, Demosthenes' *corpus* is the second to gather more instances of the *nomothetes* concept. However, as Allen (2010: 196 n.42) rightly observed: 'Although Demosthenes number of cases is close to Aeschines', Demosthenes' *corpus* is at least five times the size of Aeschines' *corpus*'.

to these, *nomothetēs* is also the implicit subject in several paragraphs (e.g. *In Tim.* 28, 29; *In Ctesiphon* 6, 9). Furthermore, the majority of the references to the *nomothetēs* in these two speeches are in the nominative case, emphasising its role as an agent filled with purpose and intentionality, just as we saw in examples by Plato, Aristotle and Xenophon. As in the lawgiver's characterisation in Plato and Aristotle, Aeschines also applies similar attributes to characterise the lawgiver: ἀγαθός ('good', *In Ctes.* 257. 7); παλαιός ('old', *In Tim.* 6.7; *In Ctes.* 175.6)',[54] σοφός ('wise', *In Tim.* 6.7. 46.7). As previously observed in Plato, in both speeches, references to the *nomothetēs* in the singular occur alongside references to the *nomothetai* (*In Tim.* 139, 176; *Ctesiphon* 39, 40).

In both of the above speeches, the fact that the instances of the *nomothetēs* are concentrated in the preliminary sections (*In Tim.* 6-36; *Ctesiphon* 9-48) highlights the ways in which Aeschines' main rhetorical strategy establishes a historical account of the law(s) in order to construct a continuity between the lawgiver's alleged intention and his own interpretation.[55] Aeschines replicates the same type of polarisation in both speeches. While in the speech *Against Timarchos* the dichotomy is between the *nomothetēs*/ancient *nomothetai* (6.7) and Timarchos, who supposedly did not meet the minimum standards of decency to participate in political life, in the speech *Against Ctesiphon*, the dichotomy is between the *nomothetēs* and Ctesiphon, who allegedly made a false statement in a public document[56].

In the speech *Against Timarchos*, the strategy of identification between himself and the *nomothetēs* is clear from the start: '8. I would like now to develop my argument in the same manner (τὸν αὐτὸν τρόπον) which the lawgiver used in his laws'.[57] The presence of the *nomothetēs* in the preliminary part (6-36) is so overwhelming that it seems Aeschines was substituted by Solon and became his actual prosecutor:

11: These laws will be read to you, so that you may know that the *lawgiver believed* (ἡγήσατο) that it was the well-brought-up boy who became the man useful to the city; (...) he thought (ἡγήσατο) that the result of such badly brought-up boys would be citizens similar to the defendant, Timarchos.

18.3: But as soon as anyone is registered on the list of citizens, and knows the laws of the city, and is, by now, able to distinguish what is right and what is not, *the lawgiver no longer addresses another person, but the man Timarchos himself.* (οὐκέτι ἑτέρῳ [νομοθέτης] διαλέγεται, ἀλλ᾽ ἤδη αὐτῷ, ὦ Τίμαρχε)

Solon, however, is not the *only* ancient lawgiver to prosecute Timarchos, as Aeschines makes clear: 'Consider, men of Athens, how much concern was shown for moral control (σωφροσύνης) by Solon, our ancient lawgiver, and by Drakon and *the other lawgivers of those*

---

[54] The same attribute is found in the following Platonic texts: *Prt.*, 326d, *Leg.* 853c4, [Pl.] *Minos* 318b3.

[55] Indeed, as Carey (2000: 90) pointed out, this plays a fundamental role in both speeches of Aeschines: 'As with the prosecution of Timarchus, Aeschines relies heavily on narrative. The effect of this, together with a tendency to treat allegations in chronological order, is once more to make neat classification of the different components of the speech difficult.'.

[56] Gagarin's (2020) recent contribution highlights another type of polarisation which is also found in Athenian forensic speeches: the opposition between the lawgiver or lawgivers of the past and the 'contemporary lawgiver" who is "always self-serving and harmful to the city' (p. 33).

[57] Translated by Fisher (2001).

times (οἱ κατὰ τοὺς χρόνους ἐκείνους νομοθέται). (7) First of all, they legislated about the moral control of our boys; (...)'. Thus, besides assuming the unity of the laws through the creation of a single author, Aeschines also ascribes a monolithic intention to different lawgivers in order to create the idea that there is a sort of universal, predictable and unanimous approach to the point under discussion, namely the legislation regarding the upbringing of free-born boys and the development of *sophrosyne*, which Timarchos allegedly failed to show.[58]

In the speech *Against Ctesiphon*, the reference to the lawgiver's intention is also more frequent in the part that precedes the main argument and in which Aeschines addresses two objections to Ctesiphon. The first (9-31) was that Demosthenes was not eligible to receive the crown as he was yet to be submitted to the *euthynai*. The second (32-48) was that, according to the law, it was not permitted to crown Demosthenes in the theatre of Dionysius, only in the Assembly. Here, the intention of the lawgiver is expressed through the same language of foresight, emotions and volition already found in the sources previously discussed. In fact, as often in Demosthenes,[59] Aeschines also equated this intention with the idea of democracy itself:

> 6. This is why the legislator made (ἔταξεν) this the first clause in the jurors' oath: 'I shall vote according to the laws.' He was well aware (εὖ εἰδὼς) that when the laws are protected for the city, the democracy, too, is preserved.

> 11. A legislator noticed this (κατιδὼν) and passed (τίθησι) a law, and a very good one (καὶ μάλα καλῶς), explicitly forbidding the crowning of men who are subject to audit. And though the legislator has taken this sensible precaution (εὖ προκατειληφότος), arguments have been invented to subvert the law;

> 20. Second, the legislator has made the Council of Five Hundred subject to audit, [21] and so strong is his distrust (καὶ οὕτως ἰσχυρῶς ἀπιστεῖ) of men facing audit that right at the beginning of the laws he says: 'An official subject to audit is not to leave the city.'

The orator also has the power to relate laws whose connection was not envisaged by the legislator, thereby reinforcing the idea of legislative intent, as the following example from Aeschines shows: 'Observing this situation, a legislator drafted a law entirely unconnected with the one dealing with individuals crowned by the people. He neither annulled the latter (...), nor did he enact a law opposed to the pre-existing ones (...).'

Despite the rhetorical similarities, these speeches produced two different outcomes. While the former, *Against Timarchos*, resulted in Timarchos' disfranchisement, the second failed to persuade the court, which resulted in Aeschines' losing his right to prosecute public cases.[60] However, this failure did not stop Aeschines from publishing his speech, which became a source of inspiration for others such as Hyperides and Dinarchos.[61] The two speeches here mentioned are just two examples among many that make use of the legislative intent to structure their legal narratives. In other cases, legislative intent and the unity of the laws is

---

[58] The same idea is also mentioned in Dinarchos *Against Aristogiton* 2.16.2 and in Lycurgus' *Against Leocrates* 9.7.

[59] E.g. Demosthenes, *Against Timocrates* 75-76. See Johnstone (1999: 31, 38).

[60] See Harris (2006: 405-422) and p. 2.

[61] See Carey (2000: 166).

also assumed without referring to the concept of the *nomothetēs*, such as in the Demosthenes' *Against Midias* (56-57) or Hyperides (*Against Athenogenes* 21-22).[62]

Despite the intense political colouring of Aeschines' two speeches, the use of the concept of the *nomothetēs*, or 'legislative intent' *per se*, does not necessarily produce a misleading argument from the outset. When referring to the use of this *topos* in Athenian legal practice, Johnstone (1999: 26) defined it simply as persuasive 'interpretative protocol', while Harris (2007: 346) describes it as a legitimate path to achieve legal consistency. The prevailing view is that the lawgiver *can do no* wrong and that the law is never ill-conceived, since it is perceived as a fabric woven by a godlike entity.

In this paper, I have argued that a relatively well defined and coherent representation of the *nomothetēs* can be found in different fourth-century literary contexts, from philosophical discourse (Plato and Aristotle) to history (Xenophon) and legal oratory (Aeschines). I have also showed that this conformity was maintained by the language used to describe the lawgiver and his activity, which is part of a broader process of humanisation which explains the systematic attribution of consciousness and intentionality. While I do not think that Plato's influence alone can explain the use of the *nomothetēs* in legal oratory, I believe that the examination of this concept in Plato can help us to understand the attributes of the *nomothetēs* and his role. Furthermore, I have showed that this characterisation influenced the constitutional storytelling or legal narratives found in both philosophical and historical discourse in general as well as legal reasoning in the context of legal oratory.

Although I have been unable to expand on this demonstration, I believe that the examples presented here are representative and persuasive enough to show that there existed a clear linguistic pattern employed to portray the lawgiver as a figure possessing agency, able to act as a legislative demiurge and to actively shape history. The discourse about the lawgiver was as much a manifestation and memory of past rhetoric as it was a reflection about the present and indeed the future. For instance, the whole dialogue of the *Laws* can be seen as a philosophical commentary on the challenges posed by fourth-century legal reform in search of greater consistency. The sense of the laws' coherence as a code was essential not only for portraying the laws as unchangeable ethical commands but also for making sense of them. The assumption of the laws' unity through the creation of a single author is just part of the changing legal landscape, which was crucial to the political narrative that the Athenians told themselves.

Modern debates about the legislative intent must be understood in a broader context of democratic framework(s) and specific legal traditions. However, the underlying narrative is very similar in the sense that it is also a discourse about time or, in other words, an articulation of past and present notions of common good. This is based on the assumption that the legislator is 'good' and 'reasonable', and that he is rationally committed to protecting the common good.

---

[62] Other examples in which the concept of the *nomothetēs* is mentioned in order to appeal to legislative intent are Demosthenes (*Against Leochares* 57-58) and Isaeus (*Menecles* 13). For the use of legislative intent in Lysias' *Against Theomnestus*, Demosthenes' *Speeches Against Leochares*, *Against Androtion* and Isaeus' *Menecles*, see Johnstone (1999: 25-33), and in Hyperides' *Against Athenogenes* speech, see Harris (2007: 264-265) and Johnstone (1999: 29).

Bibliography

Allen, D. 2010. *Why Plato wrote?* Oxford: Wiley-Blackwell.

Barker, E. and R.F. Stalley 2009. Aristotle. *Politics*. Oxford: Oxford University Press (1st edition 1995).

Brisson, L. 2000. Les préambules dans les *Lois*, in *Lectures de Platon*: 235-262. Paris: Librairie philosophique J. Vrin.

Brisson, L. ²1994. *Le même et l'autre dans la structure ontologique du* Timée *de Platon: un commentaire systématique du* Timée *de Platon*. Paris: Klincksieck (1st edition 1974).

Des Places, E. 1951. Plato. *Ouevres Complètes* vol. 11.1-2 *Les Lois* (l-6). Paris: Les Belles Lettres.

Canevaro, M. 2013. *Nomothesia* in classical Athens: What sources should we believe? *Classical Quarterly* 63.1: 139-60.

Canevaro, M. 2015. Making and changing laws in ancient Athens, in M. Canevaro and E. Harris (eds) *Oxford Handbook of Ancient Greek Law*. Oxford University Press: Oxford.

Canevaro, M. and E. Harris 2012. The documents in Andocides' *On the Mysteries*. *Classical Quarterly* 62.1, 98-129.

Carey, C. 2000. *Aeschines*. Austin: University of Texas Press.

Clarke, K. 2009. *Making time for the past. Local History and the polis*. Oxford: Oxford University Press.

David, E. 2007. Xenophon et le myth de Lycurgue. *Ktema* 32: 297-310.

David, E. 2007a. Myth and historiography: Lykourgos. in G. Herman and I. Shatzman (eds) *Greeks between East and West: essays in Greek literature and history in memory of David Asheri*: 115-35. Jerusalem: Israel Academy of Sciences and Humanities.

Dolcetti, A. 2019. The Central Case Method in *The Nature of Legislative Intent. The American Journal of Jurisprudence* 64: 41-60.

Ducat, J. 2006. *Spartan Education: Youth and Society in the Classical Period*. Swansea: Classical Press of Wales.

Ekins, R. 2013. *The Nature of Legislative Intent*. Oxford: Oxford University Press.

Feldman, L.H. 1998. *Josephus' interpretation of the Bible*. Berkeley: University of California Press.

Feldman, L.H. 2004. Flavius Josephus. *Judean Antiquities*. Translation and commentary (vol. 1-4). Leiden-Boston: Brill.

Feldman, L.H. 2006. Parallel lives of two lawgivers: Josephus' *Moses* and Plutarch's *Lycurgus*, in L.H. Feldman (ed.) *Judaism and Hellenism reconsidered*: 523-556. Leiden: Brill.

Feldman, L.H. 2007. *Philo's Portrayal of Moses in the Context of Ancient Judaism*. Notre Dame, IN: University of Notre Dame Press.

Fisher, N. 2001. Aeschines. *Against Timarchos*. Oxford: Oxford University Press.

Gagarin, M. 2008. *Writing Greek Law*. Cambridge: Cambridge University Press.

Gagarin, M. 2020. Storytelling about the Lawgiver in the Athenian Orators, in *Cahiers des études anciennes* LVII, 2020, 33-44.

Griffith, T. and G.R.F. Ferrari 2015. Plato. *The Republic*. Cambridge: Cambridge University Press.

Griffith, T. and M. Schofield 2016. Plato. *Laws*. Cambridge: Cambridge University Press.

Grote, G. 2009. *Plato, and the Other Companions of Sokrates* (vol. 1). Cambridge: Cambridge University Press (1st edition 1865).

Harris, E. 2006. The Penalty for Frivolous Prosecution in Athenian Law, in *Democracy and the Rule of Law in Classical Athens: Essays on Law, Society, and Politics*: 405-422. Cambridge: Cambridge University Press.

Harris, E. 2007. Did the Athenian Courts Attempt to Achieve Consistency? Oral Tradition and Written Records in the Athenian Administration of Justice, in C. Cooper (ed.), *Politics of Orality*: 343-370. Boston: Brill.

Hölkeskamp, K.-J. 1999. *Schiedsrichter, Gesetzgeber und Gesetzgebung im archaischen Griechenland.* Stuttgart: Steiner.

Johnstone, S. 1999. *Disputes and Democracy: The Consequences of Litigation in Ancient Athens.* Austin: University of Texas Press.

Kelsen, H. 2015. On the Theory of Juridic Fictions. With Special Consideration of Vaihinger's Philosophy of the *As-If* (translated by Christoph Kletzer), in M. Del Mar and W. Twining (eds) *Legal Fictions in Theory and Practice*: 3-22. Cham Switzerland: Springer [Original: 1919, Zur Theorie der Juristischen Fiktonen: Mit besonders Berücksichtigung von Vaihingers Philosophie des Als Ob, *Annalen der Philosophie* 1: 630-658].

Kivilo, M. 2010. *Early Greek Poets Lives: the shaping of the tradition.* Leiden: Brill.

Kraut, R. 1992. *The Cambridge Companion to Plato.* Cambridge: Cambridge University Press.

Laks, A. 2000. The *Laws*, in C.J. Rowe and M. Schofield (eds) *The Cambridge History of Greek and Roman Political Thought*: 258-292. Cambridge: Cambridge University Press.

Laks, A. 1990. Legislation and Demiurgy: On the Relationship between Plato's *Republic* and *Laws. Classical Antiquity* 9: 208-229.

Lane, M. 2013. Founding as legislating: the figure of the lawgiver in Plato's *Republic*, in L. Brisson and N. Notomi (eds) *Plato's* Politeia. *Proceedings of the IX Symposium Platonicum.* Sankt Augustin, pp. 104-114.

Lanni, A. 1999. Precedent and Legal Reasoning in Classical Athenian Courts: A Noble Lie? *American Journal of Legal History* 43.1: 27-51.

Leão, D.F. 2020. Plutarch on Lycurgus: outline of the mythical founder of the Spartan constitution, in J. A. Clúa Serena (ed) *Mythologica Plutarchea. Estudios sobre los mitos en Plutarco*: 203-214. Madrid: Ediciones Clásicas.

Leão, D.F. and P.J. Rhodes 2017. *The Laws of Solon: A New Edition with Introduction, Translation and Commentary.* London: IBTauris.

Lipka, M. 2002. Xenophon's *Spartan Constitution*: Introduction. Text. Commentary. Berlin, Boston: De Gruyter.

Maidment, K.J. 2014. *Minor Attic Orators*, Volume I: Antiphon. Andocides. Cambridge, MA: Harvard University Press (1st edition 1941).

Martin, V. and G. de Budé 1962. Eschine. *Discours*, vol. 1-2. Paris: Les Belles Lettres (1st editions 1927, 1928).

Morrow, G.R. 1954. The Demiurge in Politics: The *Timaeus* and the *Laws. Proceedings and Addresses of the American Philosophical Association* 27: 5-23.

Murphy, D. 2011. Review: Danielle S. Allen, *Why Plato Wrote*. Blackwell Bristol lectures on Greece, Rome and the classical tradition. Chichester; Malden, MA: Wiley-Blackwell, 2010. xii, 232. *Bryn Mawr Classical Review* 11.44. https://bmcr.brynmawr.edu/2011/2011.11.44/, viewed on the 1st of February, 2021.

Ostwald, M. 1986. *From Popular Sovereignty to the Sovereignty of Law: Law, Society, and Politics in Fifth-Century Athens.* Berkeley: University of California Press.

Ostwald, M. 1979. *Nomos and the Beginnings of the Athenian Democracy.* Westport, Conn.: Greenwood Press (1st edition 1969).

Reeve, C.D.C. 1998. Plato. *Cratylus.* Indianapolis: Hackett PubCo.

Rhodes, P.J. 1980. Athenian Democracy after 403 B.C. *Classical Journal* 75. 4: 305-23.

Rhodes, P.J. 1991. The Athenian Code of Laws, 410-399 B.C. *The Journal of Hellenic Studies* 111: 87-100.

Rhodes, P.J. 2003. Sessions of *Nomothetai* in Fourth-Century Athens. *Classical Quarterly* 53.1: 124-29.

Rhodes, P.J. 2006. The Reforms and Laws of Solon: An Optimistic View, in J. Blok and A.P.M.H. Lardinois (eds) *Solon of Athens: New Historical and Philological Approaches*: 248-260. Leiden/Boston: Brill.

Rodrigues, A. Plutarch's *Life of Lycurgus*: Constructing Spartan Exceptionalism, in J. Mossman and Ph. Davies (eds) *Plutarch and Sparta*. Classical Press of Wales: Swansea. (forthcoming)

Ross, W.D. 1964. *Aristotelis politica*. Oxford: Clarendon Press (1st edition 1957).

Scalia, A. 2018. *A Matter of Interpretation: Federal Courts and the Law*. Princeton: University Press (1st edition 1997).

Szegedy-Maszak, A. 1978. Legends of the Greek Lawgivers. *GRBS* 19.3: 199-209.

Thomas, R. 1994. Law and the lawgiver in the Athenian Democracy, in R. Osborne and S. Hornoblower (eds) *Ritual, Finance and Politics: Athenian democratic accounts presented to David Lewis*: 119-133. Oxford, Clarendon Press; New York: Oxford University Press.

Waterfield, R. and A. Gregory 2019. Plato. *Timaeus and Critias*. Oxford: Oxford University Press.

epikleroi,[15] orphans, empty *oikoi*, and pregnant widows. The 'Solonian kernel' of the law is probably to be identified with the procedure of legally involving the archon in the enforcement of the obligation to protect those persons against acts of arrogance and attacks on their honour, and in the very nature of the offence.'[16]

That explanation makes good sense in relation to the protection of orphans, pregnant widows, and *epikleroi*, but the addition of *oikoi exeremoumenoi* seems somewhat anomalous: an *oikos*, unlike the other entities listed, is not a person, and cannot be a victim of *hybris*.[17]

The wording of the law is reflected in a passage from the Aristotelian *Athenaion Politeia* (*Ath. Pol.*, c. 329-325 BC) describing the functions of the archon:

> [The archon] takes care [ἐπιμελεῖται] also of orphans, of heiresses and of those widows who after the death of their husbands claim to be pregnant. He has the full authority to fine anyone offending against them or to bring them to court. He lets out the estates of orphans and heiresses until they come to the age of fourteen, and receives the securities [provided by the lessees]. And if the guardians do not provide the maintenance due to the orphans, the archon extracts it from them. (*Ath. Pol.* 56. vii; Leão and Rhodes 2016: fr. 51/d)

The *Ath. Pol.*'s account of the archon's duties transposes the imperative of the law (*epimeleistho*) into the indicative mood (*epimeleitai*), not prescribing what should happen but describing what actually did happen in the late 4th century.[18] But there are also some substantive differences between the wording of the law and the paraphrase in *Ath. Pol.* On the one hand, *Ath. Pol.* gives more specific details of the archon's responsibilities in relation to the leasing of orphans' estates (of which there is ample corroborative evidence from other fourth-century sources).[19] On the other hand, it makes no mention of *oikoi exeremoumenoi*.[20] The reason for this omission is uncertain: it may have been deliberate, indicating that this part of the law had fallen into disuse by the 320s, or it could be simply an authorial or scribal error.

What was an *oikos eremos*?

The phrase *oikos eremos* may be translated in various ways, reflecting the different meanings, literal or figurative, of both words. According to context *oikos* may mean literally 'house' (a physical building, equivalent to *oikia* in Greek), 'family' (a 'house' in the figurative sense, such as 'the house of Atreus' or 'the house of Windsor'), or 'property' (equivalent to *kleros*), and sometimes two, or even all three of these senses overlap.[21] The adjective *eremos*, too, could be used either literally ('empty') or figuratively ('deserted', 'abandoned', 'extinct'). In relation to an inheritance, at least two interpretations of *oikos eremos* are potentially relevant: the

---

[15] See n. 5, above.

[16] Leão and Rhodes 2016: 90-91.

[17] Cf. MacDowell 1989:19-20: 'When Isaios says that an *oikos* is 'left empty', he means that a family has no male member left alive. But this law cannot mean that the arkhon is to care for non-existent sons.'

[18] Cf. Rhodes 1981: 34 and 633-34.

[19] See, especially, Isa. 6. 36-37.

[20] This omission is not discussed by either Rhodes 1981 or Leão and Rhodes 2016.

[21] On the definition of *oikos*, and its overlapping meanings, cf. MacDowell 1989:10.

property or estate left by a dead man may become 'empty' if it is left temporarily without a new owner, and his family may die out, or become 'extinct' if he leaves no descendants, natural or adopted.

The Solonian laws discussed above are known to modern scholars primarily from the two forensic speeches in which they are cited ([Dem.] 43 and [Dem.] 46), both of which date from around the middle of the 4th century. We know extremely little about the development of the Athenian legal system (particularly in relation to inheritance) during the late archaic and early classical periods. We need, therefore, to bear in mind that both the meaning of these specific words and the broader interpretation of Solon's laws may differ from their original 6th century context.[22]

MacDowell, pointing out that there are no attested examples of *oikos* in the sense of 'family' before the 5th century, concludes that 'in the texts of Athenian laws, *oikos* means "property" or "house"'. In the specific context of the law prescribing the duties of the archon: 'I believe therefore that τῶν οἴκων in this law does not mean "families"; it means "properties" left with no man in control. Or possibly it may even have the more primitive sense of "houses" left with no male inhabitant; certainly the sense of "houses" seems quite appropriate for the pregnant wives who remain ἐν τοῖς οἴκοις.'[23]

The 'empty *oikos*' topos in the forensic speeches

Whatever the original scope and intention of the law cited at [Dem.] 46.14, it was interpreted by fourth-century litigants as bestowing the right to 'bequeath'(*diathesthai*) their property by adopting a son and heir, either *inter vivos* or by will.[24] Concern about the potential consequences of one's death was, naturally enough, a strong motive for testamentary adoption: according to the speaker of Isa. 6 (354 BC), Philoctemon of Cephisia decided to make a will adopting his nephew 'so as not to leave his family without an heir [μὴ ἔρημον καταλίπῃ τὸν οἶκον]' if he should die while abroad on military service (Isa. 6.5).[25] An Athenian who had more immediate concerns about the need for companionship or for help with the management of his financial affairs was more likely to adopt a son *inter vivos*. For example, the speaker of Isa. 2 (c. 354/3 BC) says that when Menecles chose to adopt him 'His main motivation was his loneliness [μάλιστα μὲν ὑπὸ τῆς ἐρημίας]' (2.20). Thrasyllus, the speaker of Isa. 7 (c. 354 BC) describes how his uncle, Apollodorus, adopted him: 'he immediately took me home with him and entrusted me with the management of all his affairs, saying that he could no longer do any of this himself, but I would be able to do all of it' (7.15).

But in these speeches, too, we find the wish to avoid leaving the dead man's *oikos* empty as a motive for adoption (or as a reason for the judges to uphold an adoption). In Isa. 2,

---

[22] Cf. MacDowell 1989: 19: 'The law is undated, and it is possible, or even probable, that it is one of the early laws defining the functions of the arkhon, to be attributed perhaps to Solon; we must therefore not take for granted that its use of terminology is the same as that of the orators.'

[23] MacDowell 1989: 20.

[24] The law is mentioned, though not cited verbatim, in support of an adoption *inter vivos* in Isa.2 and 7, and in support of a testamentary adoption in Isa. 4 and 6. The validity of the law is also acknowledged by the speaker of Isa. 9, who opposes a testamentary adoption.

[25] All translations from the speeches of Isaeus are those of Edwards 2007.

Menecles's adopted son accuses his opponent (Menecles's brother) of insulting Menecles and trying to make his *oikos* empty by challenging the adoption (2.15, 35). Both of these speakers also emphasize the adoptive father's concern to ensure that *ta nomizomena* would be properly carried out for him: 'Menecles began to consider how not to remain childless but instead to have someone to look after him in his old age and bury him when he died, and afterwards perform the customary rites (*ta nomizomena*) for him' (2.10). Thrasyllyus puts this in more general terms, claiming that *everyone* who is about to die takes precautions not to leave his *oikos* empty, by adopting a son who will carry out *ta nomizomena* on his behalf.[26] Similar argumentation in Isocrates's *Aegineticus* suggests that such concern was not confined to Athens: the speaker (who claims the estate of Thrasylochus as his son by testamentary adoption) denounces his opponent for trying to annul Thrasylochus' will and leave his *oikos* empty (Isoc. 19.3).

The speakers of Isa. 2 and 7 (and Isoc. 19), who were claiming an estate as the dead man's adopted son, conceived of an *oikos* as becoming 'empty' if its *kyrios* died leaving no direct male heirs (natural or adopted legitimate sons or grandsons) who would not only inherit his property but also take on the responsibility for *ta nomizomena*. They were clearly not concerned with an 'empty house' in the literal sense of a dwelling with no occupants. Neither can they have been talking about a property left vacant in the sense that it no longer had an owner, because the dead man's estate would go to his next of kin (that is to say, the speaker's opponent) if the adoption were found to be invalid. That, of course, was precisely what the speakers wanted to avoid – and, as they claim, precisely what their adoptive fathers had wanted to avoid, because collateral relatives could not be relied on to assume the responsibility for carrying out the funeral rites and commemorative rituals for their deceased kinsman. By emphasizing the religious dimension of inheritance, these speakers probably hoped to convince the judges that their motivation for claiming the estate was not purely mercenary. But, even if their concern about *ta nomizomena* was exaggerated, it shows that, for them and their contemporaries, an *oikos eremos* was not merely a property deprived of its owner but a family at risk of 'dying out' or 'becoming extinct'.

Posthumous adoption

Even if a dead man left no direct heirs, natural or adopted, there was an alternative way of preventing the extinction of his *oikos*: giving him a son by posthumous adoption – an obscure procedure which had probably developed as a matter of custom rather than law.[27] A posthumous adoption was negotiated among the surviving family members, sometimes (but not necessarily) following the expressed wishes of the 'adoptive father' himself, and it might even take place some years after his death.

The sources tell us little about the process of posthumous adoption, except that the adoptee would be introduced into the father's phratry (as was the case with the other forms of adoption). Given the requirement for claims based on testamentary adoption to be registered with the archon, it seems reasonable to suggest that he may also have had some role in the

---

[26] Isa. 7.30, discussed at p. 168 below.
[27] Cf. Griffith-Williams 2013: 204.

approval of a posthumous adoption, especially in the event of a dispute.[28] In the absence of direct evidence of any official intervention by the *polis*, that remains pure conjecture; but, according to a theory put forward by some late nineteenth-century scholars, the archon in fact had a more active role, even to the extent that he could take the initiative in appointing a successor by posthumous adoption. That theory has, rightly, been discredited, but it is worth reviewing the evidence.[29]

Sositheus, the speaker of [Dem.] 43 (one of two surviving speeches from the long-running dispute over the estate of Hagnias)[30] claims to have given his son (Eubulides III) by posthumous adoption to his father-in-law Eubulides II, making Eubulides III *de jure* a first cousin once removed to the deceased Hagnias. Sositheus's account of the posthumous adoption emphasizes the wishes of the deceased Eubulides II to avoid leaving his *oikos* (and, by extension, that of Hagnias) empty:

> I introduced him to Hagnias's phratry as the [adopted] son of Eubulides [II], the boy's maternal grandfather, so that the house might not become extinct [ἵνα μὴ ἐξερημωθῇ ὁ οἶκος]. For that dear man, judges, Eubulides [II] ... used to pray to the gods that, above all else, a son might be born to him just as a daughter had been, the mother of this boy. But when his prayers failed and no male child was born, not even one, then he earnestly desired that a son of his daughter be adopted into his own house and Hagnias' and that the son be introduced to the latter's phratry. He thought, judges, that the boy would be closest to him of all his surviving kinsmen and that their house would in this way be preserved and would not become extinct [καὶ οὕτως ἂν μάλιστα τὸν οἶκον τὸν ἑαυτῶν διασῴζεσθαι καὶ οὐκ ἂν ἐξερημωθῆναι]. [Dem.] 43.11-12.[31]

Towards the end of the speech, after some lengthy, complex, and sometimes apparently irrelevant argumentation, Sositheus cites the law on the archon's responsibilities (Leão and Rhodes 2016: fr. 51/c, p.163 above) before launching an attack on his opponents for trying to make the *oikos* of Hagnias empty. He apparently thinks the law will support his case by underlining the illegality of the opponents' claim to Hagnias's estate, but its relevance to the adoption of Eubulides III is not immediately obvious.[32] The citation of the law in the context of a posthumous adoption might, nevertheless, suggest that the archon was in some way

---

[28] Cf. Harrison 1968: 92.

[29] For a summary of the earlier debate, and the argument against it, see Harrison 1968: 92-93, and cf. Rubinstein 1993: 106-09.

[30] The other is Isa. 11.

[31] Trans. Scafuro 2011. In her introduction to the speech, Scafuro explains her strategy in translating the word *oikos*, referring to the three meanings identified by MacDowell (n. 21, above): 'I have translated it as "house" throughout the speech because I think the speaker wants the judges to visualize the different families as "houses". That is, he uses "house" as a metaphor for "family", although (...) he sometimes uses it of a "family" of a special sort.' Scafuro 2011: 133.

[32] Cf. Arnaoutoglou 1998: 6: 'It is unclear to a modern reader how this law can support the argument advanced.' According to MacDowell 1989: 18-19, Sositheus 'was desperately trying to find some way of maintaining that the young Euboulides was more closely related to Hagnias than Makartatos was, and he thought that a claim to membership of the same *oikos* would be effective with the jury.' He, therefore, 'made an exhaustive search' for Athenian legal texts using the term *oikos* in the sense of 'family', and the law on the archon's responsibilities was the only one he could find.

argument on this point persuasive) then these speakers' interpretation of Solon's law was (perhaps unwittingly) anachronistic.

We cannot definitively rule out the possibility that the archon at some time had an active role in the arrangement of posthumous adoptions, but in the light of the available evidence that is most unlikely to have been the case in the mid-fourth century or later. And if the archon's legal duty was not concerned with the continuity of Athenian families, but with the supervision of estates left vacant after the last owner had died leaving no direct heir, that would be entirely consistent with his administrative functions of registering claims to such estates and bringing contested cases to court.

Bibliography

Arnaoutoglou, I. 1998. *Ancient Greek laws: a sourcebook.* London: Routledge.

Canevaro, M. 2013. *The documents in the Attic orators.* Oxford: Oxford University Press.

Edwards, M. (trans.) 2007. *Isaeus.* Austin: University of Texas Press.

Gagarin, M. and P. Perlman 2016. *The laws of ancient Crete c.650-400 BCE.* Oxford: Oxford University Press.

Griffith-Williams, B. 2012. Oikos, family feuds and funerals: argumentation and evidence in Athenian inheritance disputes. *Classical Quarterly* 62: 145-162.

Griffith-Williams, B. 2013. *A commentary on selected speeches of Isaios.* Leiden: Brill.

Harrison, A.R.W. 1968. *The law of Athens, volume 1: The family and property.* Oxford: Oxford University Press.

Hodkinson, S. 2000. *Property and wealth in classical Sparta.* Swansea: The Classical Press of Wales.

Leão, D.F. and P.J. Rhodes. 2016. *The laws of Solon: a new edition with introduction, translation and commentary.* London: Tauris.

MacDowell, D.M. 1986, *Spartan law.* Edinburgh: Scottish Academic Press.

MacDowell, D.M. 1989. The oikos in Athenian law, *Classical Quarterly* 39: 10-21.

Rhodes, P.J. 1981. *A commentary on the Aristotelian Athenaion Politeia.* Oxford: Clarendon Press.

Roussel, P. (ed. and trans.) 1926. *Isée: Discours.* Paris: Les Belles Lettres.

Rubinstein, L. 1993. *Adoption in IV. century Athens.* Copenhagen: Museum Tusculanum Press.

Scafuro, A.C. (trans.) 2011. *Demosthenes, speeches 39-49.* Austin: University of Texas Press.

The Semantic Overlap of Ἀδικία and Ἀσέβεια in the Amphiareion at Oropos[1]

Aikaterini-Iliana Rassia

Department of Classics
King's College London
aikaterini-iliana.rassia@kcl.ac.uk

Abstract

It can be argued that in the works of ancient Greek historians as well as in inscriptions, especially sacred regulations, one can find the notions of ἀδικία (injustice) and ἀσέβεια (impiety) used seemingly interchangeably. Both being notions which qualify some kind of human transgression, they give the impression of being used as synonymous notions. Part of the confusion of the semantic overlap between ἀδικία and ἀσέβεια is that both notions can be indistinguishably applied in both secular (e.g. περὶ δὲ ἀνθρώπους ἀδικίαν, Xen. *Cyr.* 8.8.7) and religious matters (e.g. Ἂν δέ τις ἀδικεῖ ἐν τοῖ ἱεροῖ, *LSCG* 69.9). However, how we choose to interpret this semantic overlap, often affects our broader understanding of the value terms of injustice and impiety in relation to social and religious matters. The focus of this paper is placed on the analysis of the semantic overlap of ἀδικία and ἀσέβεια attested in the sacred regulation (*LSCG* 69) of the Amphiareion at Oropos, one of the most important healing sanctuaries of ancient Greece. My aim in this paper is to give a comprehensive outline of the range of the overlap's use in *LSCG* 69.

Keywords

Amphiareion, Oropos, sacred regulations, injustice, impiety.

LSCG 69 as a medium for inculcating εὐσέβεια

The sacred regulation that helps us most to understand the semantic overlap between ἀδικία and ἀσέβεια is surely *LSCG* 69, and it may be instructive to look at it in this light. The pertinent regulation (Figure 1) was discovered at the Amphiareion at Oropos, a sanctuary located on the east coast of the Greek mainland on the borderland between Attica and Boeotia.[2] To begin with a general remark, the aim of sacred regulations was to remind the ancient worshipper on what he was not allowed to do within a sacred area.[3]

---

[1] I am very grateful to the Executive Committee, in particular, Daniela Ferreira, Delfim Leão, Nuno Rodrigues and Rui Morais, who initiated and executed the volume and conference in honour of Peter J. Rhodes. I would also like to thank Davide Napoli and the anonymous reviewer for their valuable comments that helped me to improve the paper.
To the distinguished honorand of this volume, professor Peter J. Rhodes, I would like to offer this paper in admiration and respect for his inspiring and influential studies that have deepened our knowledge and understanding of the ancient Greek historical sources as well as political and social history.

[2] Petrakos (1984: 310).

[3] In this paper, I employ the term 'sacred regulation' instead of the term 'sacred law'. On this loan-term, see Leonardos (1885: 93-94) who first applied the term "regulation" in reference to *LSCG* 69 (e.g. "Κανονισμὸς τοῦ ἱεροῦ τοῦ Ἀμφιαράου). In a similar way, decades later, Petrovic and Petrovic (2014: 30, n. 6) will use the term 'regulation' instead of 'law'. For a critique and the problems surrounding the use of the term 'sacred law' and for any inscription concerning the observation of rituals, see Pirenne-Delforge and Carbon (2012: 163-182). On the problems of defining 'sacred laws', see Naiden (2008: 125- 127) and Parker (2004: 57-70). For a concise historical overview of the emergence and the conventional use of the nomenclature of 'sacred laws' or *leges sacrae* in the discipline of Classics, see Petrovic

Figure 1. Sacred regulation (LSCG 69) on the administration of the Amphiareion.
Photo: Petrakos (1997), plate 18.

The sacred regulation (*LSCG* 69) under examination currently located in the museum of the Amphiareion[4] is a tapered fragmented stele (Height: 1.49, Width: 0.30, Thickness: 0.095) of fine white Pentelic marble crowned by a cymatium.[5]

The special message of the text (*LSCG* 69) on stele needs to be understood in the light of its original context: where this sacred regulation was originally displayed in the sanctuary. Unfortunately, the stele was found broken. Only three fragments of the stele have been found alongside the ancient drain that runs north to the sacred spring and the altar of the sanctuary.[6] Nevertheless, considering the purpose of the text to remind the worshippers of behaving with the utmost propriety inside the sanctuary, it is not unreasonable to assume that *LSCG* 69 might have stood inside the sanctuary and very close to the great altar of the sanctuary so as to be seen on time (i.e. before the sacrifice). It was not uncommon to set up sacred regulations within the sanctuary in the vicinity of one or more altars.[7] In terms of date, the fourth century sacred regulation (*LSCG* 69) is classified within the period of Oropos' independence, between 387 and 377 BC.[8] It can be fairly assumed that the regulation must have been in force shortly around after the independence of Oropos.

We often know little about the motives surrounding the enactment of sacred regulations. Nonetheless, at Oropos, the enactment of *LSCG* 69 not only reveals how the polis cemented the sanctuary's independence but also discloses the objective of the state authorities to inculcate in their cultic personnel as well as worshippers a normative behaviour for Amphiaraos.[9] The following four modes of thinking can also be detected behind the enactment of *LSCG* 69. First, the setting up of the inscribed sacred regulation that defined the rules for normative behaviour might be explained as a fear of pollution (*miasma*). Second, it was the only secure way to inform each newly appointed religious officer of its role and religious duties. Third, it was a way to cement and ensure that the Amphiareion could meaningfully be treated as independent based on its own legal regulations as well as administration. Fourth, it was an expedient way to inculcate in each pilgrim a normative behaviour towards the god and his sanctuary. All the aforementioned prefatory remarks are essential, if we are to examine the function of *LSCG* 69 in its true perspective. An aspect that has not yet been addressed is the significance of the function of this sacred regulation in expressing and reinforcing ethical concerns, in our case, the semantic overlap of *adikia* and *asebeia*, as we shall next discuss.

---

[4] (2015: 339-352).
[4] Inv. No: A 236; Rhodes and Osborne (2003: 128).
[5] Petropoulou (1981: 42; 1997: 178).
[6] For the first commentaries of *LSCG* 69, see Leonardos (1885: 93-98) and Wilamowitz-Möllendorff (1886: 93-115). For a brief description of the findspot of the stone, see Leonardos (1885: 95-96); Petrakos (1997: 178) and Petropoulou (1981: 42).
[7] For instance, see *LSCG* 21 A. 14-17.
[8] *IG* VII 235; *SIG* 1004; *LSCG* 69. For a thorough epigraphic commentary of this decree, the reader should turn to the article by Petropoulou (1981: 42-52); *SEG* 31.416; Petrakos (1997: 177) accepts the date of Petropoulou; *LSCG* 69 is dated to 386-374 BC by Rhodes and Osborne (2003. no. 27); *SEG* 53.465. For a brief discussion of the inscription under consideration, see Lupu (2005: 321-323).
[9] Rhodes and Osborne (2003: 132).

Inculcating εὐσέβεια: Cultic Personnel

Θεοί.

Τὸν ἱερέα τοῦ Ἀμφιαράου φοιτᾶν εἰς τὸ ἱερό-
ν, ἐπειδὰν χειμὼν παρέλθει μέχρι ἀρότου ὥρ-
ης, μὴ πλέον διαλείποντα ἢ τρεῖς ἡμέρας καὶ
μένειν ἐν τοῖ ἱεροῖ μὴ ἔλαττον ἢ δέκα ἡμέρα-
ς τοῦ μηνὸς ἐκ[[σ]]στο : καὶ ἐπαναγκάζειν τὸν ν-
εωκόρον τοῦ τε ἱεροῦ ἐπιμελεῖσθαι κατὰ τὸ-
ν νόμον καὶ τῶν ἀφικνεμένων εἰς τὸ ἱερόν·

Gods.

The priest of Amphiaraus is to frequent the
sanctuary from when winter has ended until the
season of ploughing, not being absent for more than
three days, and to remain in the sanctuary for not less
than ten days each month. He (the priest) is to compel the temple-warden
to look after both the sanctuary and those who come to the sanctuary,
in accordance with the regulation.

As Peter Rhodes and Robin Osborne have argued, the text of *LSCG* 69 gives a rare glimpse into the functioning and the administration of the Amphiareion.[10] In particular, *LSCG* 69 reflects a quite careful division of administrative duties among three religious officials (i.e. the priest, the *neokoros* and the temple-treasurer). While *LSCG* 69 does not inform us about the selection criteria under which each religious official was appointed, nonetheless, it does tell us about their duties in respect to the maintenance of a good order inside the sanctuary.[11] At his presence in the sanctuary, not only did the priest have the supreme religious power (ll. 25-29) but also a distinct judicial power to deliver justice (*LSCG* 69.9-20) in cases of any misconduct either by a worshipper as well as by a member of the cultic personnel.[12] This can be affirmed by the following instruction.

According to *LSCG* 69.6-8, each appointed priest had the right to exercise a coercive power over the *neokoros* (temple-warden) by compelling (ἐπαναγκάζειν) him not to overlook his religious duties during the tenure of his office.[13] The presence of ἐπαναγκάζειν was not only a functional device but also a restrictive measure. By employing the infinitive ἐπιμελεῖσθαι as shorthand, the lawgiver(s) forewarned each *neokoros* to strictly and diligently (ἐπιμελεῖσθαι) perform his duties in accordance with the prescriptive rules of the regulation (κατὰ τὸν νόμον, ll.7-8).[14] Additionally, every newly appointed *neokoros* had to exercise vigilance and care towards the sanctuary as well as to oversee the conformity to the sanctuary's rules by each incoming worshipper. As concerns the latter, the *neokoros* had to oversee the payment of

---

[10] Rhodes and Osborne (2003: 132).
[11] On the annual office of the priest of the Amphiareion, see Petrakos (1997: 181).
[12] Stavrianopoulou (2006: 138-139).
[13] Sourvinou-Inwood (2000: 39).
[14] Petrakos (1997: 181).

the compulsory pre-incubatory fee, known as ἐπαρχή of nine obols (ll. 20-4). This monetary fee was an essential precondition for any worshipper's permission to incubation. This reasoning is best exemplified, for instance, at *LSCG* 69. 23-24, which imparts the following message: each prospective incubant had to pay the pre-incubatory fee at the presence (παρεόντος) of *neokoros*. Most probably, the deposit of the tariff would have taken place near the entrance of the sanctuary, where the treasury and the offices of priest and *neokoros* were located.[15] This discloses that the polis-authorities of Oropos who enacted the prescribed rules of this sacred regulation (*LSCG* 69) wanted to ensure that each visitor would have internalized a basic sense of piety (εὐσέβεια) towards the god and his sanctuary (i.e. sacred property).

Inculcating εὐσέβεια: Ailing Worshippers

It is doubtless that a worshipper had to demonstrate piety towards Amphiaraus and his sanctuary.[16] Considering the great number of worshippers who visited the sanctuary, one can sensibly assume that it would have been difficult for the three religious officials to oversee the behaviour (i.e. submission to the rules of the sanctuary) of each visitor. Therefore, if a worshipper's misconduct was detected, the priest was empowered by the regulation (*LSCG* 69) to levy a monetary penalty upon him in accordance to the level of his religious offence. This can be best seen in the following extract that reads (*LSCG* 69.9-20):[17]

Ἂν δέ τις ἀδικεῖ ἐν τοῖ ἱεροῖ ἢ ξένος ἢ δημότ-
ης, ζημιούτω ὁ ἱερεὺς μέχρι πέντε δραχμέων   10
κυρίως καὶ ἐνέχυρα λαμβανέτω τοῦ ἐζημιωμένου, ἂν δ' ἐκτίνει τὸ ἀργύριον, παρεόντος τοῦ
ἱερέος ἐμβαλέτω εἰς τὸν θησαυρόν : δικάζει-
ν δὲ τὸν ἱερέα, ἄν τις ἰδίει ἀδικηθεῖ ἢ τῶν ξένων ἢ τῶν δημοτέων ἐν τοῖ ἱεροῖ μέχρι τριῶν   15
δραχμέων, τὰ δὲ μέζονα, ἤχοι ἑκάστοις αἰ δίκαι ἐν τοῖς νόμοις εἰρῆται ἐνταῦθα γινέσθων·
προσκαλεῖσθαι δὲ καὶ αὐθημερὸν περὶ τῶν ἐ-
ν τοῖ ἱεροῖ ἀδικιῶν, ἂν δὲ ὁ ἀντίδικος μὴ συνχωρεῖ εἰς τὴν ὑστέρην ἡ δίκη τελείσθω :   20

If anyone commits an offence in the sanctuary, either
a foreign or a member of the community, let the priest
have power to inflict punishment of up to five drachmai
and let him take guarantees from the man who is punished,
and if he pays the money let him deposit it into the treasury
when the priest is present. The priest is to give judgment
if anyone, either a foreign or a member of the community,
is wronged privately in the sanctuary, up to a limit of three
drachmai, but let larger cases take place where it is stated in
the regulations for each. Summons to be issued on the same day
in the case of offences in the sanctuary, but if the defendant

---

[15] Petrakos (1997: 182).
[16] For piety as duty, see Dover (1974: 246-250) and Burkert (1985: 254-257, 274-275).
[17] Translated by Rhodes and Osborne (2003: no. 27).

does not agree let the case be completed on the following day.

After reading the above extract of *LSCG* 69, each visitor would have been aware that the priest of the Amphiareion had a judicial power (δικάζειν, ll.13-14) and would not condone any offensive behaviour within the sanctuary.[18] The judicial power of the priest to attribute justice on both native and foreign worshippers is a rare case.[19] This point is clarified in some detail through the announcement of the following two sanctions. The first sanction was reserved for any person who would defile the sanctity of the Amphiareion. Regardless if he was an Oropian or a foreign worshipper, the wrongdoer who would desecrate the Amphiareion would be liable to a monetary penalty of up to five drachmai (ll. 9-11). Under the priest's surveillance, any wrongdoer had to deposit the punishment fee within the sanctuary's treasury-box (παρεόντος του ἱερέος ἐμβαλέτω εἰς τὸν θησαυρόν, ll.12-13).

The second sanction of *LSCG* 69 was reserved for the cases where the injured party was not directly the god or his sanctuary, but another human. More specifically, if a foreign or Oropian citizen was privately wronged within the area of the sanctuary by another person (e.g. aggressive behaviour, physical or verbal abuse) the priest had to dispense justice by imposing a fine up to three drachmai to the wrongdoer (ἄν τις ἰδίει ἀδικηθεῖ ἢ τῶν ξένων ἢ τῶν δημοτέων ἐν τοῖ ἱεροῖ μέχρι τριῶν δραχμέων, ll.14-16). What is not specified, however, is whether the monetary penalty was to compensate the person who was wronged or the sanctuary (i.e. the place where the wrongdoing occurred). This interpretive problem is beyond our capacity to answer and the epigraphic silence makes it virtually impossible to ascertain to what injured party the penalty was given.

From the two sanctions considered so far, it is evident, that there existed in *LSCG* 69 not a fixed monetary penalty but several, each one calibrated by the priest to indicate a different level of religious offence. Perhaps the priest would have distinguished the type of transgression: whether it was a deliberate (ἐκ προνοίας) or an unwilling misconduct. One cannot fail to notice that *LSCG* 69 was slightly flexible in the payment of monetary penalties. This flexibility is best observed in the following stipulation: if the wrongdoer could not pay his penalty fee, the priest would take a pledge from him (ἐνέχυρα λαμβανέτω τοῦ ἐζημιωμένου, ll.11- 12). On the whole, the monetary penalties in force were conditioned by the priest's discretion and judgment concerning the nature of the breach of the regulation (*LSCG* 69.11-20). However, in the case of a major religious offence, it is clear that justice would be dispensed in the public courts of each wrongdoer (τὰ δὲ μέζονα, ἤχοι ἑκάστοις αἱ δίκαι ἐν τοῖς νόμοις εἰρῆται ἐνταύθα γινέσθων· ll.16-17).

As Wilhelm observed, 'ἑκάστοις is dative of respect referring not to μέζονα (ἀδικήματα) but to the courts either for foreign pilgrims or for native citizens (τῶν ξένων ἢ τῶν δημοτέων, ll.14-15)'.[20] It can be inferred that this stipulation sheds light on the existence of special courts for foreign worshippers.[21]

---

[18] *I. Oropos* 277.9-13; Papazarkadas (2011:89). On a practical level, the immediate punishment of any transgressor is a common practice that is also attested in other regions. See Petropoulou (1981: 52, n. 31).
[19] Petrakos (1997: 182).
[20] Wilhelm (1915: 6-8).
[21] Petropoulou (1981: 52).

The temporal adverb αὐθημερόν (i.e. on the same day) indicates the urgency of the administration of justice (προσκαλεῖσθαι δὲ καὶ αὐθημερόν περὶ τῶν ἐν τοῖ ἱεροῖ ἀδικιῶν, ll.18-19). If, however, a wrongdoer would contest the validity of the priest's verdict, then, his case would be reconsidered on the next day (ἂν δὲ ὁ ἀντίδικος μὴ συνχωρεῖ εἰς τὴν ὑστέρην ἡ δίκη τελείσθω, ll.19-20). As Petrakos has aptly remarked, the meticulous provision and care for the timely and fair resolve of various conflicts that arose in the sanctuary alludes to the efficiency of the sanctuary's own judicial system. The sanctuary attracted an increasing[22] and diverse number of worshippers from the fourth century BC onwards.[23]

Another feature that deserves notice is the fairness of *LSCG* 69, best detected in lines 9-10 and 13-17. These lines explicitly convey the information that the priest stands apart from both the local and foreign visitors of the sanctuary and in case of a worshipper's misconduct, irrespective of his origin he would act as an impartial arbiter. This visible impartiality of the sanctuary's own judicial power ensured the following two inter-related objectives: first, to preclude any special regard of the priest either towards his friends or enemies. Second, to reassure every visitor of the sanctuary about the sanctuary's judicial equity. This was a precautionary measure that aimed to promote and reinforce the idea that the priest of the Amphiareion would not make any sort of discriminations between the foreign and Oropian citizens.

At this juncture, it is worth returning to the first sanction of a regulation expressed through the following conditional clause: 'If anyone commits an offence in the sanctuary (ἂν δέ τις ἀδικεῖ ἐν τοῖ ἱεροῖ, *LSCG* 69.9)'. What is meant by the clause ἀδικεῖ ἐν τοῖ ἱεροῖ is difficult to pin down, as there is no defined content in terms of what precise kind of injustice (ἀδικία) in the sanctuary would cause a person's indictment for sacrilege and would trigger the monetary penalties exacted from the priest. Whenever the verb ἀδικέω-ἀδικῶ is applied in areas directly associated with gods, it denotes a religious offence (Pl. *Leg.* 9.854e).[24] As a result, the following question may be raised: what kind of activities would define someone as a wrongdoer in the sanctuary of Amphiaraus?

From the scanty literary sources that we can muster, the following are certainly some indicative instances of the most common offences occurred within a sanctuary: (i) the physical damage of a sanctuary (Lys. 7.24-5; Xen. *Hell.* 7.4.31), (ii) the profane use of a sacred precinct (Thuc. 4.97-98), (iii) the mutilation of divine statues or the theft of votive dedications as well as other sacred objects belonging to a sanctuary,[25] (iv) a temple-robbery (τῷ ἀδικοῦντι... περὶ ἱερῶν κλοπὰς, Plat. *Euthphr.* 5d),[26] (v) a person's misconduct during a god's festival (περὶ τὴν ἑορτὴν

---

[22] Rhodes and Osborne (2003: 133) have aptly remarked that 'the concern with good order among the visitors may reflect their increasing numbers at the time this law was made'.

[23] Petrakos (1997).

[24] LSJ⁹ s.v. ἀδικέω-ἀδικῶ.

[25] As Van Straten (2000: 214) remarks: 'votive offerings, once they were placed in a sanctuary, were the property of a god, and there could be no doubt about their inalienability'.

[26] As Xenophon informs the reader, in Attica, the person who would commit temple-robbery was subject to the most harsh penalty that could be inflicted: 'to judge under the following law, which applies to temple-robbers and traitors: namely, if anyone shall be a traitor to the state or shall steal sacred property, he shall be tried before a court, and if he be convicted, he shall not be buried in Attica, and his property shall be confiscated.' (κατὰ τόνδε τὸν νόμον κρίνατε, ὅς ἐστιν ἐπὶ τοῖς ἱεροσύλοις καὶ προδόταις, ἐάν τις ἢ τὴν πόλιν προδιδῷ ἢ τὰ ἱερὰ κλέπτῃ, κριθέντα ἐν δικαστηρίῳ, ἂν καταγνωσθῇ, μὴ ταφῆναι ἐν τῇ Ἀττικῇ, τὰ δὲ χρήματα αὐτοῦ δημόσια εἶναι. Xen. *Hell.* 1.7.22). Transl. adapted from Carleton L. Brownson. Loeb Xenophon of Athens *Hellenica*, LCL 88, pp.76-77.

ἀδικήματα, Dem. 21.26) or (vi) a person's violent behaviour against another person within a sanctuary (*LSCG* 69.14-16)[27], or (vii) the removal of a suppliant from an altar (*CGRN* 71, 7-14). Additionally, equally unacceptable was the fornication inside a sanctuary.[28] As, it is evident, lawgivers as well as authors writing in different genres and in different places of Greece, may not all have meant quite the same thing by ἀδικία in relation to a religious context.[29]

It can also be said that how a man behaves towards other men may be indicative of his behaviour towards the gods. On this view, for instance, an unjust man (ἄδικος) did not have the right to touch the altars of the gods (e.g. τοὺς μὲν γὰρ ἀδίκους βωμὸν οὐχ ἵζειν ἐχρῆν, Eur. *Ion* 1312-1319). By extension, a wrongdoer whether towards men or gods who would offer sacrifices to the gods could not be qualified as pious. In order to clear some confusion in our mind, allow me to reiterate that the notions of ἀδικία and ἀσέβεια might be in places synonymous and overlapping in terms of their meaning. It is the context that reflects their semantic overlap.

As we have raised elsewhere, the semantic overlap between ἀδικία (injustice) and ἀσέβεια (irreverence) can be interpreted more broadly as a person's inappropriate behaviour. One may reasonably assume that it would have been impossible to include in the regulation all the possible religious offences. This non-specificity in terms of what the Oropian authorities understood as wrongdoings towards the sanctuary or other worshippers within the sacred precinct draws upon the existing knowledge of worshippers. All kinds of violations could occur inside a sanctuary,[30] revealed either through a worshipper's offensive sayings or offensive acts (e.g. Lysias, *Against Andocides* 6.17). Whether these transgressions were intentional or unintentional would have left to the priest to judge and announce his verdict.

Despite the reticence of *LSCG* 69 to reveal what kinds of transgressions would have been perceived as religious offences, I would suggest that another prescription in the same regulation sheds some useful light concerning the overlap between ἀδικία (injustice) and ἀσέβεια (irreverence). In the lines 43-47, we read that during the incubation the ailing men worshippers had to sleep eastwards of the altar, whereas women patients would sleep westwards (ἐν δὲ τοῖ κοιμητηρίοι καθεύδειν χωρὶς μὲν τὸς ἄνδρας, χωρὶς ᵛᵛᵛ δὲ τὰς γυναῖκας, τοὺς μὲν ἄνδρας ἐν τοῖ πρὸ ἠ[ο̄]ς τοῦ βωμοῦ, τὰς δὲ γυναῖκας ἐν τοῖ πρὸ ἡεσπέρης, *LSCG* 69.43-47). In fact, an interior Ionic column of the stoa functioned as a barrier that prevented men's access to women's dormitory space.[31] Considering this restrictive measure, it seems reasonably to infer that fornication was forbidden and would have been considered as a grave religious wrongdoing within the sacred precinct of the Amphiareion.

---

[27] For more instances on the sanctity of sacred precincts and properties of the gods, see Parker (1983: 168, n. 133).
[28] See Osborne (2015: 18), with further references.
[29] For different scholarly treatments of the overlap of injustice and impiety, see the following (e.g.): (i) for the presence of the overlap of injustice and impiety in Herodotus, see Harrison (2000: 108-109), with further references in notes 23-25. (ii) For a linguistic approach to the overlap of *dikaios* and *hosios* with a focus on supplication, see Peels (2016: chap. 4). (iii) For a study of the attestations of *eusebeia* and *hosios* in Euripides, see Calderón Dorda (2015: 41-66). In particular, Calderón Dorda (2015: 64) puts forward the idea that the notion of impiety in Euripides has more to do with attitudes against piety than with the absence of faith.
[30] As Harrison (2000: 109) points out: 'The category of actions likely to receive retribution is broader (potentially, at least) than just the narrow class of acts of sacrilege'.
[31] The mention of the *stoa* in *LSCG* 69.43 indicates the first *stoa* dated to the fifth century BC of which hardly anything survives. A second *stoa* which was three times larger as the first, was built east of the first *stoa* in 359/358 BC. See Petropoulou (1981: 56, n. 57, 58).

A further less-discussed but related aspect for the worshipper's internalization of piety towards the god Amphiaraus is revealed in lines 36-39. Regardless of the lacunae among these lines, it appears that one of the cardinal points of the regulation is the following culminating clause of the line 39, which is relatively intact:

> The person in need of the god shall incubate (ἐγκαθεύδειν δὲ τὸν δειόμενο-[[ν]]... (under the condition) that he submits to the rules (πειθόμενον τοῖς νόμοις·).

The overriding ethical responsibility of each worshipper to submit to the rules of the sacred regulation of the Amphiareion is eloquently summed up by the compelling phrase: πειθόμενον τοῖς νόμοις (*LSCG* 69.39) translated as 'to submit/to abide by the rules.' This is a standard formulaic expression that had become an integral part of legal thought during the fifth and fourth centuries BC.[32] For instance, Plato stipulates that whoever would not comply with the norms of the polis would be liable to the crime of ἀσέβεια (τοῖς δὲ μὴ πειθομένοις ἀσεβείας ὅδε ἔστω πέρι νόμος, *Leg.* 10.907d). Similarly, MacDowell asserts that a violation of a law (νόμος) relating to a sanctuary was ipso facto an act of ἀσέβεια.[33] In *LSCG* 69.39, τοῖς νόμοις is an inclusive word that encapsulates all the norms and sanctions of the sacred regulation (*LSCG* 69).[34] Further, this might be the reason why the lawgiver might have inserted the small *vacat* after τοῖς νόμοις. As Petropoulou prudently observes: 'of particular interest to students of epigraphy is the punctuation of the text (*LSCG* 69) by dots and vacats'.[35] In siding with this observation, I would further suggest that the presence of a vacat in the line 39 is not completely accidental. The small *vacat* indicates a short pause that aimed to assist the viewer to ponder more carefully over the rules of the sacred regulation. It is one of the many and subtle ways that the lawgiver has invented in order to coerce the viewer to internalize the rules (τοῖς νόμοις) of the sanctuary.[36]

The selection of the wording of *LSCG* 69 and its overall tone bespeaks a concern to instill a normative behaviour within the sanctuary in order to maintain a good order and ambience, possibly due to the increasing numbers of the worshippers at that period.[37] In this respect, the priest's power of jurisdiction was an effective medium at the hands of the polis authorities to inculcate and instill in the ancient worshippers some basic sense of piety (εὐσέβεια) for the god and his sanctuary. Of note is that no punitive measure is explicitly clarified for the cultic personnel. It appears, therefore, that the state authorities were more concerned about the visitors' behaviour. Although the sacred regulation under discussion does not precisely employ the terms piety (εὐσέβεια) and impiety (ἀσέβεια), it is clear that the entire set of regulations and sanctions is grounded on the premise of these two notions. I would however end with the following caution, that ἀδικία and ἀσέβεια are not identical terms. Both notions can be addressed to both humans and gods. Both are broad semantic categories that depending

---

[32] On the importance of a person's obedience to his city's laws, see Xenophon (ἵνα τοῖς νόμοις πείθωνται, *Mem.* 4.4.16), and Demosthenes (24.215-6)

[33] MacDowell (1978) 17.

[34] As Petropoulou (1981: 56) has insightfully observed, 'in epigraphic use νόμοι can denote regulations of a single law.'

[35] Petropoulou (1981) 43.

[36] This alludes to Xenophon's counsel of Euthydemus that 'there are regulations to be observed in the worship of the gods (ἀλλὰ νόμοι εἰσὶ καθ' οὓς δεῖ τοὺς θεοὺς τιμᾶν, *Mem.* 4.6.2).'

[37] Similar concerns over the keeping of good order in a sanctuary are attested in other sacred regulations (e.g. *LSCG* 83, a sacred regulation of Apollo Coropaeus, c.100 BC).

on their context, they can reflect both legal and religious-ethical implications. For instance, in Antiphon (2.1.3), the meaning of the word ἀσέβημα has both legal and irreligious nuances:

σαφῶς γὰρ οἴδαμεν ὅτι πάσης τῆς πόλεως μιαινομένης ὑπ᾽ αὐτοῦ, ἕως ἂν διωχθῇ, τό τ᾽ ἀσέβημα ἡμέτερον γίγνεται, τῆς θ᾽ ὑμετέρας ἁμαρτίας ἡ ποινὴ εἰς ἡμᾶς τοὺς μὴ δικαίως διώκοντας ἀναχωρεῖ.

We know very well that as the whole city is defiled by the criminal until he is brought to justice, the sin becomes ours and the punishment for your error falls upon us, if our prosecution is misdirected.

Likewise, as Leite has aptly remarked, in the Athenian society of the Classical period, the usual formula ἄδικος καὶ ἀσεβής reflects the transgression of not only the civic but also the divine norms, suggesting that the political,[38] the judicial and the religious were closely intertwined.[39] For instance, in Lysias (6.4), we read that the Eleusinian Mysteries were supervised by the *archon basileus* in order to deter anyone from committing an injustice or demonstrating impiety towards the sacred things:

φέρε γάρ, ἐὰν νυνὶ Ἀνδοκίδης ἀθῷος ἀπαλλαγῇ δι᾽ ὑμᾶς ἐκ τοῦδε τοῦ ἀγῶνος καὶ ἔλθῃ κληρωσόμενος τῶν ἐννέα ἀρχόντων καὶ λάχῃ βασιλεύς, ἄλλο τι ἢ ὑπὲρ ὑμῶν καὶ θυσίας θύσει καὶ εὐχὰς εὔξεται κατὰ τὰ πάτρια, τὰ μὲν ἐν τῷ ἐνθάδε Ἐλευσινίῳ, τὰ δὲ ἐν τῷ Ἐλευσῖνι ἱερῷ, καὶ τῆς ἑορτῆς ἐπιμελήσεται μυστηρίοις, ὅπως ἂν μηδεὶς ἀδικῇ μηδὲ ἀσεβῇ τὰ ἱερά;

I would ask you, if you allow Andocides to get off now unscathed from this trial, and to attend for drawing the lots for the nine archons, and to be elected king-archon, shall we not see him performing sacrifices and offering prayers on your behalf according to ancestral custom, sometimes in the City Eleusinion here, sometimes in the temple at Eleusis, and overseeing the celebration of the Mysteries, to prevent the commission of any offence or impiety concerning the sacred things?

In particular, in the sacred regulation of the Amphiareion, the inscribed phrase ἂν δέ τις ἀδικεῖ ἐν τοῖ ἱεροῖ, *LSCG* 69.9 has both legal and ethical implications. The legal implications of the regulation recall what Demosthenes mentions about the power of law; that the law has the power to improve the ethics of a society by establishing two things: 'to deter everyone from doing anything wrong and to punish wrongdoers to the edification of others (25.17)'.[40] With respect to the metaphysical power of *LSCG* 69, any wrongdoing (ἀδικία) occurring inside a sacred precinct had ethical and metaphysical consequences. By imposing sanctions upon visitors' wrongdoings, the state authorities hoped to limit the risks of a potential 'pollution' (*miasma*) that would threaten the maintenance of a good relationship with both humans and the god.

---

[38] See Vergara Recreo (2018-2019: 360-361) who observes that ἀδικέω and its cognates, when combined with words that denote an impious behaviour, 'are infected by their semantic spectrum' and specify transgressions that threaten both the political and the religious spheres.

[39] Leite (2014: 256).

[40] Transl. Herman (2006: 196).

From the combined evidence, it is not hard to gauge that after an attentive reading of *LSCG* 69, most of the ailing worshippers would have calculated the risks of law-breaking and would not have dared to put themselves into a flimsy relationship with the god (metaphysical level) as well as with the cultic personnel and the other worshippers (mundane level). The thread of my argument lies on the following reasoning. Ailing pilgrims who sought to find cure at the Amphiareion would have suffered from serious and often incurable illnesses and diseases. As a general rule, an ailing person who undergoes a physical suffering feels vulnerable and insecure. Often, in antiquity, the cure of some illnesses and diseases was indeterminate in human capacity. In those cases, the ailing person would have acquired a heightened awareness of his own feebleness and mortality. From a metaphysical perspective, these distressed conditions would have generated a greater feeling of hope and trust in the help of a healing deity.

It can be suggested that the ancient worshipper in need of the redemptive epiphany of Amphiaraus was entrusted to his divine help in order to receive a cure at his illness or disease. The efficacy of the latter would have been strongly dependent on the worshipper's ethical conformity with the rules of the sanctuary, which were the essential conditions for each worshipper's successful incubation. All things considered, *LSCG* 69 aimed to cement and shield in concrete terms the sanctity of the Amphiareion by creating a self-enforcing incentive of the adoption of a religious-ethical behaviour not only in the cultic personnel but also in every worshipper.

Bibliography

Burkert, W. 1985. *Greek Religion*. Translated by John Raffan. Cambridge: Harvard University Press.

Calderón Dorda, E. 2015. *El homo religiosus euripídeo*. *Prometheus* 61: 41-66.

Carbon, J.-M., S. Peels and V. Pirenne-Delforge (eds) 2021. *A Collection of Greek Ritual Norms (CGRN)*. Liège.

Dover, K. 1974. *Greek Popular Morality in the Time of Plato and Aristotle*. Berkeley; Los Angeles: University of California Press.

Harrison, T. 2000. *Divinity and History: The Religion Of Herodotus*, Oxford: Oxford University Press.

Herman, G. 2006. *Morality And Behaviour In Democratic Athens: A Social History*, Cambridge: Cambridge University Press.

Leite, P.G. 2014. *Ética e retórica forense: asébeia e hýbris na caracterização dos adversários em Demóstenes*. Coimbra: Imprensa da Universidade de Coimbra.

Leonardos, B. 1885. Ἀμφιαρείου Ἐπιγραφαί. *ΑΡΧΑΙΟΛΟΓΙΚΗ ΕΦΗΜΕΡΙΣ*: 93-110.

Lupu, E. 2005. *Greek Sacred Law: A Collection of New Documents*. Leiden: Brill. [*NGSL*]

MacDowell, D.M. (1978) *The Law in Classical Athens*, London: Thames and Hudson.

Naiden, F.S. 2008. Sanctions In Sacred Laws, in Harris, E.M. and G. Thür (eds), *Symposion 2007: Vienna: Österreichischen Akademie der Wissenschaften*: 125-138. Vienna: Verlag der Osterreichischen Akademie der Wissenschaften.

Osborne, R. 2015. Unity Vs. Diversity, in Eidinow, E. and J. Kindt (eds), *The Oxford Handbook of Ancient Greek Religion*: 11-19. Oxford: Oxford University Press.

Papazarkadas, N. 2011. *Sacred and Public Land in Ancient Athens*. Oxford: Oxford University Press.

Parker, R. 1983. *Miasma: Pollution and Purification in Early Greek Religion*. Oxford: Oxford University Press.

Parker, R. 2004. What are sacred laws, in Harris, E.M. and L. Rubinstein (eds), *The Law and the Courts in Ancient Greece*: 57-70. London: Duckworth.

Peels, S. 2016. *Hosios: A Semantic Study of Greek Piety*. Leiden: Brill.

Petrakos, B. 1984. Η επιγραφική του Ωρωπού και του Ραμνούντος, in Πελεκίδης, Χ., Ν. Πέππα-Δελμούζου, and Β. Πετράκος (eds), *Πρακτικά του Η' Διεθνούς Συνεδρίου Ελληνικής και Λατινικής Επιγραφικής: Αθήνα, 3-9 Οκτωβρίου 1982*, Αθήνα: Υπουργείο Πολιτισμού και Επιστημών.

Petrakos, B. 1995. *The Amphiareion of Oropos*. Athens: Clio Editions.

Petrakos, B. (1997) *Οι επιγραφές του Ωρωπού*, Αθήνα: Βιβλιοθήκη της εν Αθήναις Αρχαιολογικής Εταιρείας 170, Ἀθῆναι : Ἀρχαιολογικὴ Ἑταιρεία.

Petropoulou, A. 1981. The eparche documents and the early oracle at Oropos. *Greek, Roman and Byzantine Studies* 22: 39-63.

Petrovic, A. and I. Petrovic 2014. On Ritual Pollution by Seeing: *I.Lindos* II 487.1- 3 and Hdt. 2.37.5. *Gephyra. Journal for the Ancient History and Cultures of the Eastern Mediterranean* 11: 29-36.

Petrovic, A. 2015. Sacred Law, in Eidinow, E. and J. Kindt (eds), *Oxford Handbook of Ancient Greek Religion*: 339-352. Oxford: Oxford University Press.

Pirenne-Delforge, V. and J.-M. Carbon 2012. Beyond Greek Sacred Laws. *Kernos* 25: 163-182.

Rhodes, P.J. and R. Osborne 2003. *Greek Historical Inscriptions 404-323 BC*. Oxford: Oxford University Press.

Sourvinou-Inwood, C. 2000. Further Aspects of Polis Religion, in R. Buxton (ed.), *Oxford Readings in Greek Religion*: 38-55. Oxford: Oxford University Press.

Stavrianopoulou, E. 2006. Normative Interventions in Greek Rituals, in *Ritual and Communication in the Graeco-Roman World. Kernos* 1 Suppl. 16: 131- 148.

Van Straten, F. T. 2000. Votives And Votaries In Greek Sanctuaries, in Buxton R. (ed), *Oxford Readings in Greek Religion*: 191-221. Oxford: Oxford University Press.

Wilamowitz-Möllendorff U. 1886. Oropos und die Graer. *Hermes* 21: 91-115.

Vergara Recreo, S. 2018-2019. Ateísmo, retórica y política: el léxico irreligioso en *Contra Andócides* por impiedad de Lisias. *SALDVIE* 18-19: 359-362.

Wilhelm, A. 1915. Neue Beiträge zur griechischen Inschriftenkunde. *Akad. der Wissensch. in Wien, Phil.-hist. Klasse, Sitzungsb.* 214.4: 6-8.

Sacred Laws (*hieroi nomoi*) and Legal Categories in Hellenistic Crete

Michael Gagarin

University of Texas at Austin
gagarin@austin.utexas.edu

Abstract

This paper explores what the expression 'sacred laws' (*hieroi nomoi*) might have meant in Hellenistic Crete. I first examine two inscriptions from Itanos (*IC* 3.4.8 and 9) which show that *hieroi nomoi* designated a category or group of laws. I then examine other categories of *nomoi* in Hellenistic Cretan inscriptions and argue that they all designate a loose grouping of laws on a particular but not well-defined subject. I conclude that the Greeks never tried to define precisely which laws were *hieroi nomoi*, nor did they ever gather them together into one collection.

Keywords

Sacred, Laws, Crete, *Nomoi*, Inscriptions

Ever since Greek "sacred laws" were first collected more than a century ago, scholars have sought clear guidelines for deciding what should be included in such collections and have noted the absence of adequate guidelines from the collections in question.[1] Furthermore, 'scholars are in agreement that there is in fact very little correlation between modern "sacred laws" and any recognizable ancient category of texts, particularly since the words "sacred" and "law" are notoriously problematic when applied to such documents.'[2] Moreover, although the Greeks occasionally used the expression 'sacred laws' (*hieroi nomoi*), 'it is not established that any individual city brought them together into a single classification.'[3] Thus, if no Greek city ever collected its 'sacred laws', then antiquity clearly offers no guidance on how to assemble such collections today.

My aim in the present paper is not to challenge these conclusions, but rather to explore what some Greeks – those living in Crete in the Hellenistic period[4] – may have meant by the expression 'sacred laws' and how they may have thought about legal classification. My starting point is two inscriptions from Hellenistic Crete, *IC* 3.4.8 and *IC* 3.4.9, neither of which

---

[1] The main collections are Von Prott and Ziehen (1896-1906) and Sokolowski (1955; 1962; 1969), supplemented by Lupu (2005). The content of these collections is reviewed most recently in Gawlinski (2021).

[2] There is now an online database of "ritual norms" (Carbon et al. 2016-) but it is not clear whether 'ritual norms' avoids all the problems raised by 'sacred laws'.

[3] Parker (2004: 67).

[4] I focus on Crete because together with my colleague Paula Perlman I have spent more than fifteen years working with the inscribed laws from this island and we are preparing an edition of the Hellenistic laws from Crete to follow our edition of the archaic and classical laws, and also because some of the texts from Crete that may shed light on this question have been overlooked in other discussions. I focus on the Hellenistic period here because *nomos* is not used in archaic or classical texts from Crete, where laws are designated by some form of the expression "what is written" (*ta gegrammena*), which is almost always a reference to a specific text.

is itself a sacred law, and which have scarcely been mentioned in discussions of the subject.[5] These texts indicate that at least one Greek polis not only recognized a category of 'sacred laws' (*hieroi nomoi*) but also defined this category in much the same fuzzy way as modern collections do, namely as 'a heterogeneous group of texts codifying religious practice in various locations.'[6] This conclusion will not provide any further guidance on ways to organize a modern collection, but may help reassure us that in forming such collections we are not radically departing from the Greek notion of sacred laws.

The texts in question come from Itanos, a polis in the north-eastern corner of the island. *IC* 3.4.8, dated to the third century BCE, records a loyalty oath to be sworn by all the citizens of Itanos; it shows that the Itanians could think of their laws in terms of different categories, among which were a group of laws concerning religious practices in their city. *IC* 3.4.9, dated to 139 BCE, is a long account of the arbitration of a border dispute; it shows that the Itanians could categorize this group of laws as *hieroi nomoi*.

I begin with *IC* 3.4.9, the simpler of the two, which records the decision of an arbitration panel from the city of Magnesia regarding a dispute that arose between Itanos and nearby Hierapytna, primarily concerning territorial boundaries. It is hard to be sure of the details because parts of the text are fragmentary,[7] but one issue concerns the boundaries of a sacred precinct of Zeus. To counter the Hierapytnian claim that a certain piece of land was part of this precinct, the Itanians presented documents (*grammata*) showing that the land had been in cultivation and was therefore not sacred and untilled. The text continues (lines 81-82):

νόμοις γὰρ ἱεροῖς καὶ ἀραῖς καὶ ἐπιτίμοις ἄνωθεν διεκεκώλυτο ἵνα μηθεὶς ἐν τῷ ἱ- | ερῶι τοῦ Διὸς τοῦ Δικταίου μήτε ἐννέμηι μήτε ἐναυλοστατῆι μήτε σπείρηι μήτε ξυλεύηι.

For from the beginning sacred laws and curses and penalties have prohibited anyone from pasturing or building a shelter or sewing crops or cutting wood in the sacred precinct of Zeus Diktaios.

In other words, sanctuary regulations, which are a common part of modern collections of sacred laws, were apparently among the documents presented by the Itanians, which were classified by them as 'sacred laws'.

Another indication of the nature of this category of sacred laws is provided by the loyalty oath in *IC* 3.4.8. It contains many provisions that one would expect of such an oath and ends with the standard wish that blessings might come for those who abide by the oath and evils for those who do not. In the middle of the text we find the following sentence (lines 27-36):

οὐδὲ βουλευσέω περὶ τᾶ-
[ς πόλ]ιος κακὸν οὐδέν, πολιτεο-
[σέομ]αι δὲ ἐπ' ἴσαι καὶ ὁμοίαι καὶ θί[ν]-

Nor will I engage in any deliberations concerning harm to the polis, but I will conduct myself as a citizen equally and

---

[5] *IC* 3.4.9 is briefly mentioned in Carbon-Pirenne (2017: 150-51), but to my knowledge no one has brought *IC* 3.4.8 into the discussion.
[6] Carbon (2005).
[7] A large fragment of this text was found at Magnesia and another large fragment at Itanos; presumably a third copy was displayed in Hierapytna.

30 [ων κ]αὶ ἀνθρωπίνων πάντων κα-
[τὰ τ]οὺς νόμους τοὺς προϋπά-
[ρχ]οντας ὅσσοις χρεώμεθα πε[ρὶ]
[τὰ] θῖνα καὶ τοὺς νῦν ἐθέμεθα κ[αἴ]
[κά] τινας ἄλλους ὕστερον θεώ-
35 [μ]εθα ἢ πε[ρὶ τὰ -- c.5 --] ἢ περὶ τὰ πολ[ι]-
[τι]κά·

fairly in all matters sacred and secular,
according to the pre-existing
laws that we use concerning sacred
matters and those we have now enacted
and any others that we might later enact
either concerning [?] or concerning
public matters.

In the first part of this passage the citizen pledges to conduct himself properly in all matters, 'both sacred and secular' (kai thina kai anthropina). This is a very common pairing in Cretan texts, occurring (sometimes with variants such as theia for thina) as early as the Spensithios decree (SEG 27.631, c. 500 BCE). It is especially common in agreements between cities offering full or partial isopoliteia, when citizens of each city are given the right to participate in all the affairs of the other city 'both sacred and secular'.[8] In other words, it was common for Cretans to think of their public activities as consisting of two different groups, sacred and secular.

The loyalty oath then specifies the expectation of proper conduct as follows: 'according to the pre-existing laws (tous prohyparchontas nomous) that we use concerning sacred matters (peri ta thina) and those we have now enacted and any others that we might later enact either concerning [text now lost] or concerning public matters (peri ta politika).' This clause demonstrates that the Itanians could think about at least some of their laws as forming groups, pre-existing laws about sacred matters, laws about public (or polis) matters, and perhaps a third group, regrettably now lost.[9]

Now, although one might be tempted to argue that the expression 'the pre-existing laws' designates (unwritten) traditional practices and customs as opposed to written statutes, other examples of the participle prohyperchontes with nomoi indicate otherwise. A TLG search for the participle with the noun nomos reveals that although they do not occur together in any of the other surviving Cretan inscriptions,[10] hoi prohyparchontes nomoi occurs four times in classical and Hellenistic authors, once of a new regime temporarily using the previous laws (Aristotle, Politics 1292b20), once of Timoleon revising the existing laws of Syracuse (Diodorus Siculus 16.82.6.1), and once of those who continually revise the existing laws (Diodorus Siculus 12.17.1), thereby weakening their authority.

The fourth occurrence, in Demosthenes 21.35, is worth a closer look. In the course of his prosecution speech, Demosthenes maintains that Meidias has violated many laws.

> A law about damage (blabe) has been in effect for a long time, as has one about assault (aikia), and another about outrage (hybris). If it were sufficient for those who commit one of these offenses during the Dionysia to pay the penalty according to these laws, there would be no additional need for this law. But it is not sufficient. Here is the proof: you have established a sacred law (hieron nomon) for the god himself about the

---

[8] See, e.g., IC 3.4.6, line 3 (Itanos), IC 3.3.3B, line 14 (Hierapytna), IC 1.16.5, lines 12 and 14 (Lato).

[9] Suggestions for filling the lacuna in line 35 include πε[ρὶ τὰ [θῖνα] (i.e. newly enacted sacred laws) and πε[ρὶ τὰ [ἴδια].

[10] The simpler hoi hyparchontes nomoi (the existing laws) occurs twice in the Cretan texts (IC 3.3.18, SEG 26.1049.22-23), each time clearly designating the existing statutes.

Lupu, E. 2005. *Greek Sacred Law: A Collection of New Documents (NGSL)*. Leiden: Brill.

Parker, R. 2004. What Are Sacred Laws?, in E.M. Harris and L. Rubinstein (eds), *The Law and the Courts in Ancient Greece*: 7-70. London: Duckworth.

Rhodes, P.J. 2009. State and Religion in Athenian Inscriptions. *Greece and Rome* 56: 1-13.

Rubinstein, L. 2010. Praxis: The Enforcement of Penalties in the Late Classical and Early Hellenistic Periods, in G. Thür (ed.), *Symposion 2009. Akten der Gesellschaft für griechische und hellenistische Rechtsgeschichte*, vol. 21: 193-215. Vienna: Austrian Academy.

Sokolowski, F. 1955. *Lois sacrées de l'Asie mineure*. Paris: de Boccard.

Sokolowski, F. 1962. *Lois sacrées des cités grecques. Supplement*. Paris: Ecole française d'Athènes.

Sokolowski, F. 1969. *Lois sacrées des cités grecques*. Paris: Ecole française d'Athènes.

von Prott, H. and L. Ziehen. 1896-1906. *Leges Graecorum Sacrae*. 2 vols. Leipzig: Teubner.

The Phrase καθάπερ ἐκ δίκης in Greek and Hellenistic Documents

Gerhard Thür

Austrian Academy of Sciences
gerhard.thuer@oeaw.ac.at

Abstract

When, in papyrus contracts of the Ptolemaic and imperial era, a καθάπερ ἐκ δίκης formula was inserted inside a πρᾶξις-clause, enforcement (*praxis*) apparently could be carried out "as if a verdict was pronounced." This legal fiction would therefore suppose that the creditor could act as if a law court had already rendered a judgment (*dike*) in his favor, and therefore he would be entitled to seize the properties of the debtor without having to turn to a judge first: without a verdict. However, Wolff (1970) considered that the expression would mean: "(enforcement shall take place) following the rules of the *dike*" — and was of no practical legal relevance. For outside Egypt Meyer-Laurin (1975) claimed executive force in Dem. 35.10-13 and in several Hellenistic inscriptions, followed by Rodríguez Martín (2019), who furthermore disputed Wolff. Concentrating on sources beyond the Graeco-Egyptian papyri, in this paper I will show that the phrase had a great variety of meanings, depending on the context: from full executive force down to legal irrelevance (the latter in Ptolemaic papyrus documents and in Hellenistic funerary inscriptions as well).

Keywords

Enforcement, judicial sentence, papyri, inscriptions, honor and shame

The Problem[1]

When a lawyer of our times encounters the clause ἡ πρᾶξις ἔστω καθάπερ ἐκ δίκης ('enforcement shall take place just as following from a judicial sentence', or better, 'from a court procedure') in a papyrus document he or she straightforwardly will associate it with a provision bestowing right of immediate enforcement: that means the creditor would be enabled to execute his title directly, without a judicial sentence against the debtor. Since Wachsmuth (1885) this was orthodoxy until disputed by Wolff (1970).[2] Based on his study on the judicial system of the Ptolemies, Wolff suggested that the phrase καθάπερ ἐκ δίκης was *de iure* meaningless.

In a *diagramma* enacted some years before 263 BC, Ptolemy II Philadelphos installed *dikasteria* for the Greek population.[3] From that date on, in contract deeds an enforcement clause κατὰ τὸ διάγραμμα was used ('according to [the judgement of a court installed through] the

---

[1] In a different context a similar topic is alluded to in my contribution "Gewalt, Zwangsvollstreckung und Rechtsstaatlichkeit im Achäischen Bund" (in S. Freund, ed., *Hamburger Studien zu Gesellschaften und Kulturen der Vormoderne*, Franz Steiner Verlag, Stuttgart, in German, forthcoming).

[2] Wachsmuth (1885: 195) spoke of *Exekutivurkunde*; for nearly one century followed by the most prominent scholars on juristic papyrology quoted by Wolff (1970: 527 n. 2 and 3).

[3] Wolff (1962: 37–48).

diagramma'), referring in no way to immediate enforcement but rather to a sentence that had been actually delivered.[4] When, in the beginning of the second century BC, the *dikasteria* had ceased functioning, contemporaneously, the *diagramma* phrase was replaced by καθάπερ ἐκ δίκης.[5] This clause survived up to Roman times, and was included in the overwhelming majority of private contract deeds. Thus, already the strict rules governing enforcement[6] speak against an executive force of the clause, and there are a lot of cases, also of considerable economic importance, where the καθάπερ phrase is omitted in the *praxis* provision; it is impossible to detect any principle in that.[7] Creditors had no advantage in using the clause; herewith the notaries just ensured them that a sentence rendered by the *chrematistai*, now replacing the *dikasteria*, had the same validity as a former one.[8] The notaries simply adapted the deeds to the procedural mutations; technically, they made use of transferring the legal consequences from the old situation to the new one (*Rechtsfolgenverweisung*).

By the way, in a footnote Wolff remarks that in the sources outside of Egypt the clause πρᾶξις ... καθάπερ ἐκ δίκης has the same impact, not replacing a judgement.[9] With some reason Meyer-Laurin countered: this cannot be correct; where *dikasteria* still existed, the clause did replace a court sentence.[10] However, just the existence of a *dikasterion* cannot be the criterion for the executive effect of a deed. One must take a closer look at the circumstances under which the clauses were used. — I hope that Peter Rhodes, the classicist of ancient Greek *dikasteria*, will benevolently accept this small, unorthodox contribution.

The Topic

The topic of the present paper is individually studying the sources outside of Egypt. Compared to the huge number of the quite uniform papyrus texts these sources are only few but manifold in character and different explanations may result. In the following, *praxis* dispositions will be divided into three groups by their appearance: 1) in contracts, 2) in penal sanctions of statutes, 3) in private penal sanctions (funeral charters).

1. καθάπερ ἐκ δίκης in contracts (bilateral transactions)
   a. Two-sided agreements are the closest parallel to the papyrus deeds. The earliest example and the only one preserved in a private contract is the sea loan *sungraphe* inserted into Demosthenes' speech *Against Lacritus* (Dem. 35.10–13, dated before 340 BC). The clause reads (§12): ... παρὰ Ἀρτέμωνος καὶ Ἀπολλοδώρου ἔστω ἡ πρᾶξις τοῖς δανείσασι καὶ ἐκ τῶν τούτων ἁπάντων καὶ ἐγγείων καὶ ναυτικῶν, πανταχοῦ ὅπου ἂν ὦσι, καθάπερ δίκην ὠφληκότων καὶ ὑπερημέρων ὄντων ('... against Artemon and Apollodorus [personally] shall be the enforcement by the creditors as well as out of their whole property ashore and at sea, wherever they [the debtors] may stand, just

---

[4] Wolff (1970: 533).

[5] Wolff (1970: 534) followed by Meyer-Laurin (1975: 197). Based on new findings Kramer and Sánchez-Moreno Ellart (2017: 41) hold that the *dikasteria* were abolished in 172 BC by royal ordinance. Rodrígez Martín (2017: 156–63) detected hints of the *diagramma* even after 170 BC.

[6] See the overview in Rupprecht (1994: 149–51).

[7] Wolff (1970: 531).

[8] Wolff (1970: 534), similarly Alonso (2016: 62); doubtfully Kränzlein (1976), Rodriguez Martin (2013: 260–264).

[9] Wolff (1970: 534 n. 36). In his view *dike* means "proceeding ... something going on rather than its conclusion."

[10] Meyer-Laurin (1975: 202).

as being sentenced in a lawsuit and being in default.'). Wolff is asking whether the plaintiff, one of the creditors, did not enforce directly due to the *praxis* clause, but rather is suing Lacritus, the deceased debtor Artemon's brother and heir.[11] Under normal circumstances, against the debtors themselves, the clause would have been effective in every polis where the debtors, being travelling maritime traders, would have been seizable by the creditors, notwithstanding the complex network of interstate treaties on seizure (*symbola*). The interstate dimension of this sea loan business alludes clearly to immediate enforcement.

b. Only a few years later is the date of the two loan deeds from Arcesine on the island of Amorgos (325–275, init. 3rd cent. BC, respectively), interstate loan businesses, too.[12] Private foreigners credited the polis considerable sums. Several times, the extensive documents grant the creditors the *praxis* against the polis 'just as being sentenced in a lawsuit that is conducted by a polis established as arbitration tribunal according to the treaty (*symbolon*) between the Naxiens and the Arcesinians.'[13] The clauses relieved the creditors of troublesome interstate arbitrations, of both the contentious pleading the merits of the case and the enforcement of a favorably rendered award through *dike exoules* (*Erkenntnisverfahren* and *Vollstreckungsverfahren*). Foremost, the latter clearly shows the executive character of the deed.

c. Although not an inscription but rather a papyrus document, chronologically and factually fitting is here the marriage contract from the garrison of Elephantine, P.Eleph. 1 of the year 311 BC. At that time, the Ptolemies had not yet enacted the jurisdiction *diagramma* and the military settlers drafted their documents according to the pattern they used at home. In case of severe misconduct the husband would have to pay his wife a penalty of 2000 drachmae, enforceable as follows (l. 12): ... ἡ δὲ πρᾶξις ἔστω καθάπερ ἐκ δίκης κατὰ νόμον τέλος ἐχούσης ... ('enforcement shall be just as following from a lawsuit that is conducted all the way through according to statute'). Since in Egypt a *dikasterion* was inaccessible the deed had to be enforceable immediately. In fact, a private arbitration court first had to declare the misconduct; in any case, the title of execution, probably under military control, was the private marriage agreement.

d. An inscription from later time preserves another interstate loan. It requires mentioning here although it does not use the phrase καθάπερ ἐκ δίκης. Nicereta from Thespiae granted a huge credit to the polis Orchomenos. In an extensive document of 223 BC an arduously negotiated compromise is preserved.[14] Some citizens, personally responsible as debtors, were subject to: πραχθήσονται κατὰ τὸν νό|μον[15] ('against them will be enforcement according to the law'). It is unimaginable that Nicereta after that troublesome compromise must sue the

---

[11] Wolff (1970: 534 n. 36). Not conclusive is his argument that the Athenian law may not have permitted immediate *praxis*; in fact, the problem could have been that the *praxis* clause was not valid against the debtor's heir (however, Lacritus' liability as heir is discussed already in Wolff, 1966: 76).

[12] *IG* XII 67B and 69 (Migeotte, 1984) no. 49 and 50.

[13] Migeotte (1984) no. 49.24, 28–29: καὶ ἐξέστω πράξασθαι Πασικλεῖ ταῦτα τὰ χρήματ[α] ... καθάπερ δίκην ὠφληκότων ἐν τῆι ἐκκλήτωι κατὰ τὸ σύμβολον τὸ Ναξ[ί|ω]ν καὶ Ἀρκεσινέων τέλος ἐχούσαν ... (similarly ll. 12–13 and 36–38). More precisely no. 50.15, 31 and 41, respectively: ... καθάπερ δίκην ὠφληκότων ἐξούλης ('just as being sentenced in an action based on withholding ownership'), hinting to seizure of encumbered land.

[14] *IG* VII 3172 (Migeotte, 1984) no. 13. For the original order of the eight parts of the document see Migeotte (1984: p. 53–54).

[15] Migeotte (1984) no. 13 VI 105–106 (*IG* A 28–29).

polis again. The clause *praxis kata ton nomon* made the loan deed negotiated anew, immediately enforceable.

e. Chronologically fitting, though highly hypothetically in nature, one may add here a phrase from a summons (*proklesis*[16]) to undergo arbitration that the polis Megalopolis (ἐγώ) directed to the polis Messene (σύ) in 182 BC (ll. 157–8, my restoration): ... ὅπως κριθεῖς πὸς ἐμὲ καθὼς | αὐ[τοῖς] ἐδικάσατε ('so that you against me get the award just as you had had a trial between yourselves'). In case both reading and restoration are correct the phrase allows the Megalopolitans, being victorious, to enforce the award against the Messenians like an intrastate Messenian verdict.

The five instances treated so far prove bilateral agreements about immediate enforcement. However, they are valid not because of the real existence of *dikasteria* (Meyer-Laurin) but rather due to the parties' private autonomy foremost in cases beyond the narrow jurisdiction of the *dikasteria* existing in the *poleis*. Likewise, the phrase καθάπερ ἐκ δίκης does not at all refer to an ongoing trial (Wolff), rather the parties feigned a condemnation in an orderly conducted lawsuit. It is important to note that in the classical and Hellenistic polis private creditors had to enforce (*eis-prattein*) their claims by personally seizing the debtors' assets. A *praktor* was in charge only of public claims.[17]

2. καθάπερ ἐκ δίκης in penal sanctions of general statutes

Chronologically quite close to the earliest loan documents a further field of applying the phrase καθάπερ ἐκ δίκης (and similar ones) can be found in orders to execute fines in penal clauses of statutes. On the one hand private persons can sue incorrectly acting officers (a), on the other officers must pursue disobedient private persons (b) and, finally, private persons vested with public competences penalize fellow citizens (c).

a. Enforcement against officials

It seems to be sufficient to deal here with three significant examples.

(1) An amnesty decree from Telos[18] (about 300 BC) orders: ἁ δὲ πρᾶξις ἔστω ‹τῶι› ἰδιώται καθάπερ ἐκ δί[κ]ας ('enforcement for the private person shall be just as following from a court procedure'). After readmitting oligarchic exiles, the *tamiai* and the *hierapoloi* of the polis had to restore to them their previously confiscated estates. If the officials disobeyed each of them had to pay a penalty of 5000 drachmae to the gods and double the value of the estate to the private owner. How to enforce the sacred penalty was no problem and is not even mentioned; normally a volunteer citizen, a *boulomenos*, interfered after the official was sentenced in an action of accountability or a similar one. However, this sentence did not help the private claimant. Instead of suing the officials for

---

[16] Preserved in the yet unpublished part of *SEG* 58.370, see my contribution quoted above, n. 1 and Thür (2013). I am grateful to Prof. Petros Themelis for the permission to discuss a few words here.

[17] Rubinstein (2010: 193–4 and 204 n. 37); differently, in Egypt the *praktor* is intervening in private cases too, Rupprecht (1994: 149).

[18] *IG* XII 4/1.132 lines 117–8; for the phrase see Rodriguez Martín (2013: 261–2) and Thür (2011: 349). The inscription is extensively discussed by Scafuro (2021) and Thür (2011).

private damage (*dike blabes*), here, the claimant could enforce immediately his loss against the officials because they had already been convicted in a public lawsuit for their misconduct. The value of the estate had already been estimated during the retrial procedure. The καθάπερ clause did not refer to a fictitious court procedure but rather was a legal-technical reference to the consequences of a privately conducted *dike* trial.

(2) In an honorary decree from Kyaneae[19] (ll. 14–15,) the clause prohibiting amendments is formulated similarly to the Telos text: ... ἢ αὐτὸς πρακτὸ] ς ἔστω εἰς τοὺς προγεγραμμένους θεοὺς καὶ τ[ὰ ὑπάρ|χοντα αὐτῶι· εἶναι δὲ τ] οἷς ἀγχιστεῦσιν [α]ὐτοῦ ἐπίτιμον καθάπερ ἐγ δί[κης.] ('...otherwise, against the [proposer] himself[20] shall be enforcement in favor of the aforementioned gods and against his fortune; the additional penalty shall be [accorded] to his relatives just as following from a court procedure'). The honored person had established a foundation the rules of which also were published in the present, fragmentarily preserved inscription. Whoever will move an amendment (which means acting in an official function) shall be fined twofold and subject to enforcement: first, in favor of the gods in the usual public way not further mentioned, and thereafter in favor of the founder's relatives according to the rules of the private *dike* (the amounts of the penalties are not preserved). Based on the public conviction, the polis bestowed immediate enforcing of the additional penalty (*epi-timon* in its original sense) to the private creditors through a legal-technical reference. Thus, the relatives didn't need to file an extra private suit.

(3) Legal-technical reference is to be supposed in another foundation document, also fragmentary.[21] If the managers (*dioiketai*) don't observe the statutes the following is ordered (ll. 6–12): ... ἀποτεισάτω ἕκαστος τῶν αἰ|τίων τῶι ἀνατιθέντι τὸ διάφορον δραχμὰς τρισχιλί|ας·[22] παθόντος δέ τι αὐτοῦ, ἐὰμ μὴ ἐπιτελέσωσιν | οἱ διοικηταὶ τὰ ἐπιτεταγμένα, ἀποτεισάτωσαν | τὸ αὐτὸ πρόσ[τι]μον τοῖς κληρονόμοις τοῖς Φαινίπ|που, τῆς πρά[ξεω]ς [οὔσ]ης κατ' αὐτῶν καθάπερ ἐγ δί|κης. ('... each culprit shall pay 3000 drachmae to the donator of the funds; if something had happened to him and the *dioiketai* don't perform the orders, they have to pay the same (additional) penalty to Phaenippus' heirs, whereupon against them [the *dioiketai*] enforcement shall be just as following from a court procedure'). In the inscription the passage ordering what persons are to be installed as managers is lost. If they were private persons, it is uncertain who is determining their disobedience and a *praxis* clause καθάπερ ἐκ δίκης makes no sense. Most probably an existing board of polis officials was appointed and first, before enforcing privately, the actual culprits out of them (ll. 6–7) were to be specified by demanding a public account. Apparently, private enforcement was permitted only in connection with a public verdict.

---

[19] Heberdey and Kalinka (1897) no. 28 (2nd cent. BC); friendly communicated by Prof. Kaja Harter-Uibopuu, Hamburg. Cf. also *I.Milet* I 3.134.22–28 and (in non punitive sense) I 3.145.63–64 (1st cent., 200–199 AD, respectively).

[20] Cf. the clause in Dem. 35.12 (above, section 1a) and in many papyrus contracts (e.g. *P.Eleph.* 1.13, mentioned above, section 1c). The (outdated) enforcement against the person (*Personalexekution*) is not the problem of this paper.

[21] *I.Iasos* 245 (1st cent. BC or Imperial time), foundation of Phaenippus; see Harter-Uibopuu (2013: 88–90).

[22] In line 8 the editors set a full stop. By the semicolon I would suggest that the *praxis* clause is concerning both alternatives.

b.   Enforcement by officials

To punish private persons or minor counterparts disobeying the law was one of the polis officials' essential duties. Examples of statutes empowering officers to do so run from the early fifth century to Hellenistic times are comprehensively collected by Lene Rubinstein (2010). However, within the penalty clauses rules how to enforce the fines are rare. The few ones, normally, refer to other statutes, whose content is mostly unknown, though never to the consequences of a private *dike* in general.[23]

c.   Enforcement by private persons invested with public competences

Poleis farm out some public duties or benefits by auction to private entrepreneurs, for example collecting taxes or customs, cultivating public land, or constructing public buildings. From the island of Kos a series of *diagraphai* is preserved, farming out priesthoods to the best offer.[24] The *diagraphai* determine the rights and duties of the respective priest, a private man or woman, and with the acceptance of the bid the documents become contract deeds. Some deeds contain the phrase καθάπερ ἐκ δίκης and others don't. Penalty clauses without the phrase concern fines in favor of gods.[25] Gods have no need of it; there are special means to secure their revenues, public ones because sacred debtors are state debtors. The phrase occurs in cases where the priests' revenues are concerned, mostly from sacrifices for private persons. One may suppose that the polis grants the priests, who had paid a lot for their offices, immediate enforcement against their defaulting clients.[26]

For enforcement by priests, the opposite is probable: the priest or the priestess, being private persons, have a weaker position than the gods. The system is disclosed in one text (no. 319.29–35): αἰ | δέ τίς κα μὴ ἐπιτελέσηι τι … | ἢ μὴ θύσει κατὰ τὰ ποτιτεταγμένα, ἀποτεισάτω τᾶι ἱεραίαι τὰ ἐφ᾽ ἑκάσ|τοις γεγραμμένα ἐπιτίμια, ἁ δὲ πρᾶξις ἔστω αὐτᾶι καθάπερ ἐγ δίκας | κατὰ ταὐτὰ δὲ καὶ αἴ τινά κα ἁ ἱέρεια μὴ ποιῇ τῶν ποτιτεταγμένων αὐ|τᾶι κατὰ τὰν διαγραφάν, ἀποτεισάτω δραχμὰς χειλίας ἱερὰς Ἀφροδί|τας, φαινέτω δὲ ὁ χρῄζων κατὰ τὸν νόμον. ('if someone doesn't … perform something or doesn't sacrifice according to the instructions he shall pay the priestess the fines stipulated in each case, she shall have enforcement just as following from a court procedure; on the same terms, also when the priestess doesn't perform something ordered to her by the diagraphe, she shall pay one thousand drachmae holy to Aphrodite; the phasis shall file whoever intends according to the law.')

---

[23] See Rubinstein (2010: 203–208). Texts similar to the καθάπερ ἐκ δίκης phrase are: ἐόντος πρ[άξεος …]…|… κὰτ τὸν νόμον τὸν ὑβριστ[ή]ριον (*SEG* 50.1195.37–8, Cyme, 3th cent.; cf. ὡς δίκην ὕβρεως in *IK Lampsakos* 9.34, 2nd cent.); τὰς δὲ πράξεις …|… ἐπιτελείτωσαν οἱ εὔθυναι καθάπερ καὶ τῶν ἄλλων τῶν δημοσίων δικῶν (*Syll.*³ 578.58–9, Teos, 2nd cent.); τὰς δὲ πράξεις εἶναι …|… κατὰ τὸν νόμον τῶν τοῦ ἐμπορίου ἐπιμελητῶν (*I.Milet* I 3.140C, lines 62–3, *StV* III 482, after 260 – all BC; for the last inscription = *IC* I 23.1.63–64 see the contribution of Gagarin in this volume).

[24] Published now in *IG* XII 4.1 (in the following quoted only by number and line). They date from the 3rd to the 1st cent. BC; see the extensive commentary by Parker and Obbink (2000); generally for sale of priesthoods Wiemer (2003), and Scafuro 2021 for contracting out in Kos.

[25] In favor of gods nos. 298.146–51, 315.21–2, 319.22–24, 325.15–16; in favor of humans nos. 302.26; 315.18–23; 319.1-2, 13–16, 29–32; 324.11–14; 325.22–23.

[26] Parker and Obbink (2000: 432–3), Wiemer (2003: 300).

Again, enforcement in favor of a god is contrasted with that in favor of a human. If the priestess transgresses the statute every citizen can file a *phasis* (denouncement action[27]) in favor of Aphrodite. After conviction in this 'contentious proceeding' in a second step the fine will be publicly enforced in support of the goddess; how this occurs was not worthwhile of mentioning. Outside persons are also authorized to exact fines in favor of priests (no. 315.20–21). In contrast, in that provision, just as here in no. 319, enforcement is mentioned (καθάπερ ἐκ δίκης) and the contentious proceeding is not. One may suppose that in these instances a *phasis* was effective too. However, because the fines were to pay private persons, the priests, not to support a god, a special provision was necessary: despite the public lawsuit, the *phasis*, enforcement follows private rules, καθάπερ ἐκ δίκης. This seems to have been the rule also when the priests themselves charge the penalty. First, they must file a suit, a *phasis*, and only afterwards, when the transgressor has been convicted, they are authorized privately to enforce the payment they are personally entitled to. In no way did the clause allow immediate enforcement to the priests. The clause was necessary because a public contentious proceeding, *phasis*, was combined with an enforcement in favor of a private person. He or she was worthy of protection through exercising public duties, the priesthood. Again, the clause is a legal-technical reference to applying private procedure.

In none of the instances dealt with in this section, where the phrase καθάπερ ἐκ δίκης is inserted in penal clauses of general statutes, is the beneficiary empowered to immediate enforcement. The phrase is used in cases where the culprit has previously been sentenced in a public lawsuit and on that basis a private person also could enforce a penalty on his or her own. Here, the phrase refers to the rules of jurisdiction in private cases. Similar phrases in favor of officials exacting fines simply refer to other statutes ruling public enforcement more precisely.

3.   καθάπερ ἐκ δίκης in private penal sanctions unilaterally ordained

Returning to private documents funeral inscriptions from Asia Minor also relate to our subject. The founder of a tomb was highly interested in ordaining who should have the right to be buried there afterwards. To ensure his or her disposition there were two options both published as their 'charters' at the gravesite: on the one hand to curse every transgressor and on the other to fix fines for illicitly burying. Treading the secular way, the founder ordered that every fellow citizen who wanted to do so (ὁ βουλόμενος) should intervene against any future violator (*Popularklage*). Primarily, the penalty has been in favor of the polis or a sanctuary and later, additionally, to the imperial *fiscus*; the intervening actor was to get a share of the fine. Here, the problem is not to be discussed on what legal base the private founder could authorize a random citizen to claim the money after his, the founder's, death. Anyway, it seemed to have worked. There are some hints that the actor had to file a public lawsuit first, and there is one example that, afterwards, a *praktor* was competent to enforce the fine.[28] Astonishingly under these circumstances, from the several thousand funeral inscriptions of Asia Minor just seven texts contain a clause πρᾶξις … καθάπερ ἐκ δίκης or a similar one. Did

---

[27] For the *phasis* procedure in Athens see Macdowell (1991), beyond Athens Rubinstein (2016: tab. 1) within the *boulomenos* cases.

[28] In the regions and *poleis* of Asia Minor the rules were different; see the survey of competent magistrates by Schweyer (2002: 86–7). For the *praktor* see Schuler and Zimmermann (2012: 575–82; no. 3, Patara in Lycia, 1st cent BC).

they permit the *boulomenos* immediate enforcement? The texts will be discussed according to their provenance from different regions, from Lycia and Caria.

a. Lycia

Four texts are relevant, three with the phrase καθάπερ ἐκ δίκης and one differently worded.

(1) The main source apparently to prove the doctrine of immediate enforcement has been *CIG* III 4300v 10–12 (*LBW* 1301, Simena, Central Lycia, Hellenistic; sarcophagus): ... καὶ ἀποτισάτωι ἐπιτίμιον[29] | τῶι δήμωι (δραχμὰς) ,ς τῆς προσανγελίας οὔσης παντὶ | τῶι βουλομένωι ἐπὶ τῶι ἡμίσει καθάπερ ἐγ δίκης ('... and he shall pay as fine to the demos 6000 drachmae whereupon the denouncement[30] shall be [possible] for everyone who wishes, [obtaining] the half [of the fine], just as following from a court procedure'). One has concluded that, because of the eminent public interest in funeral matters, immediate enforcement of the sum was allowed.[31] However, two inscriptions up to now not yet considered[32] point in another direction.

(2) *TAM* II 526.7–12 (Aloanda, West Lycia, 1st cent. BC; sarcophagus): ... ἢ ἀπ̣ο|τισάτω ὁ θάψας τῶι τε υἱ|ωνῶι μου Ἑρμολάωι δρα|χμὰς τρὶς χιλίας καθάπερ | ἐγ δίκης καὶ τῶι δήμωι τὸ ἴσον | πλῆθος ('... or the person who buries shall pay three thousand drachmae to my uncle Hermolaus just as following from a court procedure and to the *demos* the same amount.')

(3) *Petersen and Luschan, Reisen* II 56, no. 108.4–5 (Timiussa, Central Lycia, 1st cent. BC; sarcophagus): ... ἢ ὀφειλήσει ὁ παρὰ ταῦτα θάψας ἐπιτίμιον | καθάπερ ἐ[γ] δίκης Θρασυμάχῳ ἢ τοῖς ἐγγόνοις αὐτοῦ δραχμὰς χιλίας ... ('... or the person, who buries against these [orders], shall owe as a fine, just as following from a court procedure, to Thrasymachus or his progeny one thousand drachmae.')[33]

Exceptionally, only in the last two texts private persons who would get the penalty are specified by name, Hermolaus, the uncle of the deceased, and Thrasymachus, apparently being close to him, respectively. Normally founders left open who shall persecute violations of their charters on entitling to be buried. Overwhelmingly, they used the system that a *boulomenos* is encouraged to sue and get — as award — a share of the fine. In fact, painful disputes over gravesites occur between relatives, in the circle of the extended family, and a member feeling discriminated usually prosecuted as *boulomenos*; but also, it made sense if a powerful outsider was ready to take the duty upon himself. Funeral inscriptions need not explain how both contentious and enforcement proceedings in the *boulomenos* cases are to perform. This worked differently in the individual *poleis* of Asia Minor and we have very little knowledge of the legal proceedings there.

[29] *CIG* ἐπίτιμον : corr. Kalinka in his notebook, communicated by Dr. Christoph B. Samitz, Vienna.

[30] For the *prosangelia* see below, section c).

[31] See Rodriguez Martin (2013: 246–7 and n. 15) with further references.

[32] Friendly communicated by Dr. Karin Wiedergut, Vienna.

[33] It is unclear why in this inscription the *demos* is not involved; furthermore, one thousand drachmae is a low amount of a fine.

Authorizing an associated person instead of a *boulomenos* seems to be the answer to an ongoing or threatening family dispute. By nominating a person of confidence as beneficiary of the fine the founder of the grave primarily entrusts him to prosecute violations of the funeral charter. In Aloanda a certain Hermoas, son of Menneus, furnished the sarcophagus exclusively for himself, his wife, and their children. In case of violating this order Hermoas' uncle Hermolaus is addressed as recipient of the fine that is to be paid to the *demos*, too, together 6000 drachmae.[34] The text ends with a curse against the violator. The uncle, Hermolaos, had no proper right on the tomb. His only task was to uphold Hermoas' charter on burying. In this situation one can assume that a dispute with another competing relative was at stake.

A little bit different was the situation in Timiussa. Hegias, son of Sedeplemis, furnished the sarcophagus exclusively for himself and his wife. A violator shall owe Thrasymachus or his offspring 1000 drachmae. The text continues that also Thrasymachus, son of Archius, 'furnished' for himself, his wife, their children, and their offspring. Apparently Hegias was childless (in l. 3 of the inscription is a blank space exactly where one should expect the words καὶ τέκνοις). Probably Hegias had adopted Thrasymachus or had planned to do so (at least he had granted his family the right to be buried). This right should be protected by the charter. Disputes with Hegias' relatives were to be expected. When someone of them would violently open the sarcophagus to bury one of their members the beneficiary or one of his offspring and not a random *boulomenos* were the most competent persons to defend their rights.

It is not believable that a person specifically nominated would proceed in a different way than the *boulomenos*, generally not armed with the πρᾶξις ... καθάπερ ἐκ δίκης. First, differently to contracts where immediate enforcement is stipulated bilaterally, the present opponent or future violator did not agree to the unilaterally imposed fine. Thus, a court decision seems unavoidable. And because the violator would not bear any contractual or tortious liability, the nominated prosecutor, like the *boulomenos*, had to file a public lawsuit. Second, it is implausible that the system of enforcement by privately seizing the debtor's assets as practiced in the Classical polis survived in late Hellenistic Lycia. As in Ptolemaic Egypt, enforcement by self-help probably has vanished. Therefore, also in Lycia the clause seems to have been of no more legal relevance. The question remains: what was the reason for inserting it in those few funeral charters?

In the Classical polis enforcing a private claim against the convicted debtor was a task exclusively burdened upon the creditor. He relied on legitimate private self-help, and sometimes the issue ended in abuses and atrocities.[35] In contrast, a reluctant public debtor lost his civil rights and was threatened by public auction of his property. Thereby he was indirectly forced to pay. We have no sources that private self-help was the legal way of enforcement in Hellenistic *poleis*. Thus, the πρᾶξις ... καθάπερ ἐκ δίκης clause had lost its original scope of application. However, even if self-reliant private enforcement was no more practiced people may have known how it formerly had worked and remembered the dishonor involved. It seems possible that the founder of the grave wanted to furnish his confidant with an additional moral weapon: morally discrediting his relatives when they would disregard

[34] Cf. the case mentioned below, in n. 46.

[35] Enforcing monetary verdicts was performed through *enchyrasia* (taking in pledge), see Dem. 47.37 and Harrison (1971: 187–90), for violence Dem. 47.58-9; for seizing *enechyra* (enforcing penalties) beyond Athens see Rubinstein (2010: 195 and 208 n. 48). For private formal (ritualistic) violence in litigation in Greek *poleis* see Thür (2003).

his burying charter. Beside paying the fine, people violating his last will shall be socially humiliated too. Otherwise, because the *boulomenos* was not addressed personally this weapon normally was not put in the hands of the random citizen who would interfere as *boulomenos* against future violators, also uncertain persons. In these cases, the dispute remained at an impersonal level.

To sum up, the clause πρᾶξις ... καθάπερ ἐκ δίκης inserted in the inscriptions from Aloanda and Timiussa, above (2) and (3), was just moral reinforcement and had no legal importance.[36] Until now only in the Simena text (1) is the clause combined with appointing a *boulomenos*. In view of hundreds of *boulomenos* texts without the clause this instance is of no weight.[37] If there was, in fact, a background of familiar dispute we have no clue to it.

> (4) Finally, a misunderstanding of ancient forms seems to have occurred in the inscription Schweyer (2002: p. 269) no. 89.5–8 (*SEG* 43.980; Turant Assari, Myra, 1st cent. BC – init. 1st cent. AD): ... ἢ ὀφειλήσει ὁ θάψας τῇ Ἐλευθέρᾳ κιθαρη|φόρους ἑξακισχιλίας ὡς ἀπὸ καταδίκης τέλος ἐχού|σης, τῆς πράξεως οὔσης παντὶ τῷ βουλομέ|νῳ ἐπὶ τῷ τρίτῳ μέρει. ('... or the person burying shall owe [the goddess] Eleuthera six thousand citharephor [coins] as from a 'conviction' that is conducted all the way through whereupon the enforcement shall be [possible] for everybody who intends at [obtaining] the third.') In enforcement clauses the phrases ὡς ἀπὸ καταδίκης[38] and κατὰ δίκην ... τέλος ἔχουσαν[39] occur separately. Though, in combination they make no sense. The first designates the terminus of the lawsuit, the condemnation (*kata-dike*; to say "to bring it to an end" is odd); and the second means — inconsistent with the first — the whole length of the lawsuit. As it stands, the clause has just ornamental character.[40]

b.   Caria

Only marginally to be mentioned is a well-known inscription from Aphrodisias, *I.Aph.* 2007 12.1205.10–11 (*LBW* 1639, 2nd–3rd cent.): ... καὶ εἰσοίσει ἕκαστος αὐτῶν εἰς τὸν κυριακὸν φίσκον ἀ|νὰ (δηνάρια) μύρια ὡς ἐκ καταδίκης, ὧν τὸ τρίτον ἔσται τοῦ ἐκδικήσαντος. ('... and each of them shall bring ten thousand denars to the Imperial *fiscus* as from a conviction, a third of which shall belong to the intervening party.') Like the foundation inscription from Oinoanda[41] the text dates to Roman times. It stands completely isolated within the Carian funeral inscriptions and is of no value in informing us about the law of enforcement neither for the Hellenistic nor for the Roman time.[42]

---

[36] Already Mitteis (1891: 410) doubted the *"rechtliche Bedeutung"* of the clause in funeral inscriptions, followed by Wörrle (1988: 207 n. 141). See also below, n. 42.

[37] Two similar inscriptions yet unpublished (from Timioussa, again, and Corba, both Central Lycia) friendly communicated by Dr. Christoph B. Samitz, Vienna, cannot blur the statistical evidence.

[38] In a foundation text from Oinoander (*SEG* 38.1462.83; 124 AD); See Wörrle (1988: 204–7). Cf. also ὡς ἐκ καταδίκης in Aphrodisias, quoted below, at n. 41.

[39] S. above II 1b (n. 13) and 1c.

[40] Rodríguez Martín (2019: 488 n. 18) designates the phrase as "a lexical variation of καθάπερ ἐκ δίκης."

[41] See above, n. 38.

[42] See Mitteis quoted above, n. 36.

To sum up the section on funeral inscriptions one has to face the problem that there are only very few hints how penalty clauses even without the phrase καθάπερ ἐκ δίκης were enforced. Grave founders don't need to explain this item generally known to every citizen. Fragmentarily we know from Lycia that a *prosangelia* (denouncement, probably to an official[43]), an *apographe*[44] (registration, probably of the charge), and a *praktor*[45] (executory officer) were involved in such cases. Evidently, interfering in funeral matters the *boulomenos* had to follow strict rules we have no explicit knowledge about. Lawsuit and enforcement seem to have been public matters even when private persons were acting.[46] In this legal situation it seems unthinkable that a person, even a confidant of the grave founder, would be authorized to immediate enforcement against a future perpetrator who didn't submit to this kind of execution. Therefore, the *praxis* clause καθάπερ ... ἐκ δίκης in Hellenistic funerary inscriptions couldn't have had any legal relevance. Most likely it was a means of additionally humiliating the transgressor. Public enforcement, then up to date, should disgrace the culprit in the same way as personal seizure of his assets used formerly just as following from a *dike* procedure.

Ptolemaic contract deeds reconsidered

Against Wolff, Meyer-Laurin has come back to early orthodoxy whereupon in contract deeds of the Classical and Hellenistic *poleis*, beyond Egypt, by accepting the praxis clause καθάπερ ἐκ δίκης the debtor had agreed on immediate enforcement. However, the same clause used in penalty sanctions of statutes has been proven as a reference to enforcement orders stated in provisions elsewhere, just as Wolff has assumed for the papyrus contracts. In Egypt, in his opinion — not yet refuted, the phrase καθάπερ ἐκ δίκης was a special reminiscence to the *dikasteria* established by the *diagramma* no more in force. There, the phrase was of no further legal impact. Surprisingly a similar use of the phrase appears in some funerary inscriptions from Lycia. There, as sheer reminiscences to privately seizing the debtor's assets, the phrase probably had no legal effect, either.

Is this possible parallel occurring just by chance? One must not overlook the psychological components in Greek legal thinking. Especially in legal disputes honor and shame mattered. On that base I propose a — hypothetical — answer. As long as the *dikasteria* established by Ptolemy II Philadelphos administered justice the clause κατὰ τὸ διάγραμμα included the reference to the authority of the lawcourts of the ancient *poleis*. Even no more executed by private seizure but rather by public measures, enforcement of a *dikasterion* sentence could still have been feigned conducted like in Classical times. When substituted by the *chrematistai* courts the *dikasteria* had vanished, the phrase καθάπερ ἐκ δίκης referred to the authority of the earlier Egypt *dikasterion* system. And in the same way it referred to the dishonoring effects of the much older system of privately seizing the debtor's assets. In the Lycian funeral inscriptions the clause was used only rarely. In his lifetime the founder of the grave normally

---

[43] See above no. 3a(1) and at n. 30.

[44] *SEG* 56.1735, 1739, 1741.

[45] See above n. 28.

[46] Even when a private person is intervening, he enforces the penalty in favor of the polis (the *boule*: 3000 denars) whereas he may deduct 1500 for himself, *TAM* III 1.295.5–8 (Termessos, imperial time): ... ἐπεὶ ἐκτείσει τῇ | βουλῇ (δην.) ‚γ ἅπερ ἐξέσται παντὶ εἰσ|πράσσειν εἰς ἑαυτὸν καὶ τῇ βουλῇ | εἰσφέρειν τὰ ‚αφ‘ (δην.) ('... or [the perpetrator] shall pay 3000 denars to the *boule* to be enforced by anybody for himself and bring in to the *boule* 1500 denars'). In that times *eisprassein* has no more the meaning of self-reliant private seizure.

did not know which person would eventually violate his burial charter; a random *boulomenos* should intervene against a random violator. Only in a threatening or ongoing dispute the founder sometimes made use of this dishonoring weapon backing an entrusted prosecutor against an already existing opponent. In addition to the fine, the opponent should be struck by the same shameful effect of the enforcement as formerly in the Classical polis. Similarly, in a contract between two parties the creditor knows exactly the person of the debtor who eventually would default. Here a dishonoring clause makes perfect sense. In Egypt after 172 BC the phrase καθάπερ ἐκ δίκης — in my opinion — referred not only to the abolished *dikasteria* but also, and perhaps mainly, to the old way of shamefully enforcing. In both regions, in Lycia as well as in Egypt, the clause was of no legal relevance.[47] Nevertheless, Egyptian notaries automatically inserted it in the *praxis* clause of contract deeds. There, in daily use it might have lost a great deal of its dishonoring impact.

Bibliography

Alonso, J.L. 2016. Juristic Papyrology and Roman Law, in P.J. Du Plessis, C. Ando and K. Tuoriu, (eds) *Oxford Handbook of Roman Law and Society*: 59–69. Oxford: Oxford University Press.

Bagnall, R.S. 1976. *The Administration of the Ptolemaic Possessions Outside Egypt.* Leiden: Brill.

Harrison, A.R.W. 1971. *The Law of Athens.* Oxford: Clarendon Press.

Harter-Uibopuu, K. 2013. Bestandsklauseln und Abänderungsverbote. *Tyche* 28: 51–96.

Heberdey R. and Kalinka E. 1897. *Bericht über zwei Reisen im südwestlichen Kleinasien, Denkschriften der Kaiserlichen [Österreichischen] Akademie der Wissenschaften*, ph.-hist. Cl., 45.1. Wien: Gerold.

Kramer, B. and Sánchez-Moreno Ellart, C.M. 2017. *Neue Quellen zum Prozessrecht der Ptolemäerzeit. Gerichtsakten aus der Trierer Papyrussammlung (P.Trier I)*, Berlin: De Gruyter.

Kränzlein, A. 1976. Bemerkungen zur Praxisklausel καθάπερ ἐκ δίκης, in D. Medicus and H.H. Seiler (eds) *Festschrift für Max Kaser zum 70. Geburtstag*: 629–634. München: Beck.

MacDowell, D.M. 1991. The Athenian Procedure of Phasis, in M. Gagarin (ed.) *Symposion 1990*: 187–198. Köln: Böhlau.

Meyer-Laurin, H. 1975. Zur Entstehung und Bedeutung der καθάπερ ἐκ δίκης-Klausel in den griechischen Papyri Ägyptens, in H.J. Wolff (ed.) *Symposion 1971*: 189–204. Köln: Böhlau.

Migeotte, L. 1984. *L'emprunt public dans les cites grecques.* Québec: du Sphinx.

Mitteis, L. 1891. *Reichsrecht und Volksrecht in den östlichen Provinzen des römischen Kaiserreichs.* Leipzig: Teubner.

Parker, R. and Obbink, D. 2000. Sales of Priesthoods on Cos. *Chiron* 30: 415–49.

Rodríguez Martín, J.-D. 2013. Sobre la supervivencia de la cláusula καθάπερ ἐκ δίκης en los papiros romanos y bizantinos. *Revue Internationale des Droits de l'Antiquité* 60: 243–277.

Rodríguez Martín, J.-D. 2017. La relación entre las fórmulas καθάπερ ἐκ δίκης y κατὰ τὸ διάγραμμα en los papiros ptolemaicos y romanos, in M.J. Albarrán Martínez, R. (eds) *Estudios Papirológicos*: 143–170. Madrid: Fundación Pastor de Estudios Clásicos.

Rodríguez Martín J.-D. 2019. Avoiding the Judge: the Exclusion of the δίκη in Contractual Clauses, in A. Nodar and S. Torallas Tovar (eds), *Proceedings of the 28th Congress of Papyrology*: 484–493. Barcelona: Abadia de Montserrat.

---

[47] Notwithstanding the Ptolemaic rule over Lycia (295/94–197 BC, Bagnell 1976: 105–9, Wörrle 2012: 359. 367) direct influence seems hardly believable; in Egyptian contracts the phrase was used not before 172 BC and the relevant Lycian funerary inscriptions are dated in late Hellenistic time.

Rubinstein, L. 2010. Praxis: the Enforcement of Penalties in the Late Classical and Early Hellenistic Periods, in G. Thür (ed.) *Symposion 2009*: 193–215. Wien: Österreichische Akademie der Wissenschaften.

Rubinstein, L. 2016. *Reward and Deterrence in Classical and Hellenistic Enactments*, in D.F. Leão and G. Thür (eds) *Symposion 2015*: 419–49. Wien: Österreichische Akademie der Wissenschaften.

Rupprecht, H.-A. 1994. *Kleine Einführung in die Papyruskunde*. Darmstadt: Wissenschaftliche Buchgemeinschaft.

Scafuro, A. 2021. Koan Good Judgemanship: Working for the Gods in IG XII 4, 1 132, in E. Mackil, N. Papazarkadas (eds), *Greek Epigraphy and Religion: Papers in Memory of Sara B. Aleshire from the Second North American Congress of Greek and Latin Epigraphy* (Brill Studies in Greek and Roman Epigraphy 16): 248–282. Leyden and Boston: Brill.

Schuler, Ch. and Zimmermann, K. 2012. Neue Inschriften aus Patara I: Zur Elite der Stadt in Hellenismus und früher Kaiserzeit. *Chiron* 43: 567–626.

Schweyer, A.-V. 2002. *Les Lyciens et la mort*. Paris: Phoibos.

Thür, G. 2003. Sachverfolgung und Diebstahl in den griechischen Poleis (Dem. 32, Lys. 23, *IC* IV 72 I, *IPArk* 32 und 17), in G. Thür and F.J. Fernández Nieto (eds), *Symposion 1999*: 57–96. Wien: Österreichische Akademie der Wissenschaften.

Thür, G. 2011. Amnestie in Telos (IG XII 4/1,132). *Zeitschrift der Savigny Stiftung für Rechtsgeschichte, Romanistische Abteilung* 128: 339–51.

Thür, G. 2013. Gebietsstreit in einer neuen Inschrift aus Messene. *Zeitschrift für altorientalische und biblische Rechtsgeschichte* 19: 127–135.

Wachsmuth, C., 1885. Öffentlicher Credit in der hellenischen Welt während der Diadochenzeit. *Rheinisches Museum für Philologie* 40: 283–303.

Wiemer, H.-U. 2003. Käufliche Priestertümer im hellenistischen Kos. *Chiron* 33: 263–310.

Wolff, H.J. 1962. *Das Justizwesen der Ptolemäer*. München: Beck (2nd ed. 1970, with addendum).

Wolff, H.J. 1966. *Die attische Paragraphe*. Weimar: Böhlau.

Wolff, H.J. 1970. Some Observations on praxis, in D.H. Samuel (ed.) *Proceedings of the Twelfth International Congress of Papyrology*: 527–535.Toronto: Hackert.

Wörrle, M. 1988. *Stadt und Fest im kaiserzeitlichen Kleinasien*. München: Beck.

Wörrle, M. 2012. Anfang und Ende von Limyras ptolemäischer Zeit, in M. Seyer (ed.), *40 Jahre Grabung Limyra*: 359–369. Wien: Österreichische Akademie der Wissenschaften.

Part III - Politics

The Literary Sources for Athenian Prosopography[1]

John Davies

University of Liverpool
jkdavies@liv.ac.uk

Abstract

As a prolegomenon to a much revised re-edition of *Athenian Propertied Families*, and leaving fully reconstructed biographies (as in Nepos and Plutarch) aside for separate treatment, this paper attempts to survey and to evaluate as an entity the entire mass of disarticulated scraps of information about Athenian individuals that are preserved in later literary sources, whether as items on a list or as 'examples' selected for inclusion in a handbook or other systematic text. Such texts range from the C4 BCE to late Byzantine lexika, and vary widely by genre. However, the paper argues that they are best evaluated not individually but as a 'family' that shows common strands of knowledge and purpose. Three main strands – military, oratorical, and philosophical – that were of interest and value to an elite Greco-Roman readership are discussed in some detail, scholarly and belletristic strands being noted briefly. To view the ensemble in this way allows the biographer to separate what an individual did (his Leben) from how he was later regarded (his Nachleben).

Keywords

Athenians; biography; 'exemplum'; individuals; Nachleben; readership.

The long-drawn-out work of replacing *Athenian Propertied Families 600-300 BC* has required a total recast of content, citation systems, and format. The logic which drove that transformation has been set out elsewhere (Davies 2010), but it may now be of value to report the further consequences of the collective decision, taken in 1996, to cite not merely evidence about lineage and economic status (as in the 1971 edition), but rather all known data pertaining to each individual. That decision has prompted a far more wide-ranging review of the nature and the quality of the evidence that is provided by the various written modes of recording names and also some exploration of the characteristics and motors of the processes that created that evidence. Naturally, this brief paper cannot address every facet of such a review, but it can offer a framework for the evaluation of a major sector of one of those modes. It will not address the epigraphical or ceramic modes (which are being, or will be, reviewed elsewhere) but only the third, literary mode. For present purposes the term 'literary' principally denotes texts that have been preserved via the mediaeval manuscript tradition, but in the absence from Attika of any surviving documentary papyri it can also properly include the growing but still comparatively small mass of literary texts that are preserved on papyri.

---

[1] Throughout his long and distinguished academic career, Peter Rhodes has devoted much of his talents and energies to Athenian matters, and more recently to two notable Athenian individuals, Alkibiades and Perikles. A formal appreciation of his work appears elsewhere in this volume: here I report on my own work in progress on Athenian individuals and on the challenges which it has presented. I take great pleasure in being able to offer a contribution that reflects both personal affection and a strong collegiate sense of parallel enterprise and exploration. My thanks are due to an anonymous evaluator for constructive comments and helpful suggestions.

The corpus of such texts is, patently, a hundred-headed monster, comprising works that were written in a wide variety of genres for a huge range of audiences or readerships over a period of a thousand years and more. Again 'for present purposes' only, to permit coherent discussion, it is convenient to divide this corpus very roughly into three parts, distinguished by the kind and degree of contextualisation which is provided in this or that work for references to individuals. They can be (1) embedded in an extant primary continuous narrative or discursive text, or (2) decontextualised as an item in a list or as an example selected for inclusion in a discourse, or (3) recontextualised in a later construct, typically a biography. This paper is primarily concerned with category (2). That is because the texts in category (1) are comparatively straightforward to use, whereas those in categories (2) and (3) are not, while the texts in category (3) present specific complexities that will require separate discussion elsewhere.

Category (1) comprises most of the extant texts that were composed in or for an Athenian context between ca. 550 and ca. 320 BCE. They include lyric poetry, historical narratives, extant plays of the major tragic and comic dramatists, speeches of the Attic orators, technical treatises such as that of Aineias, works (genuine or attributed) of Plato, Xenophon, Hippokrates, and Aristoteles, and a number of unattributed texts such as the *Dissoi Logoi* and the *Old Oligarch*. For the purpose of identifying, reporting, and evaluating information about individuals, such texts are manageable. Being composed as entities and being for the most part substantial utterances, they are 'unproblematic' in the sense that contexts are usually clear and the nature of the light which the author has chosen to shine on the individual can be directly assessed.

This is not to say, of course, that such texts are always helpful or trustworthy. As the literature on *komodoumenoi* has shown, even full access to context does not always allow us to decode an abusive allusion in an Old or Middle Comedy. Michel Nouhaud's meticulous study of the use and misuse of history by the Attic orators (Nouhaud 1982) has painted a dismal picture of exaggeration, displacement and telescoping of events, vague chronology, false symmetry, false generalisation, and a general whitewashing of action by Athens and Athenians. Likewise, though Plato's detailed information about various lineages is most valuable, his various *mises-en-scène* can strain chronology to breaking-point and include much that is imaginative if not (like the eponym of the *Timaios*) imaginary.

The more general issue of the reliability of personal and social memory, much discussed in recent years (Castagnoli and Ceccarelli 2019; Fentress and Wickham 1992; Thomas 1989 and 2019), adds yet another layer of uncertainty. However, a first saving grace is that for so many of the texts in this first group scholarly work of the calibre of our honorand's *Commentary on the Aristotelian Athenaion Politeia* is accessible and allows the reader to make an informed judgement. A second saving grace is that one can be confident that references to individuals made in the texts of category (1) have been recorded in *PAA*. Since it was only the knowledge of the growing availability of its successive volumes that made a re-edition of *APF* a practicable ambition at all, it is only proper here to record my gratitude and admiration for that monument of scholarship.

However, the main business of this paper is with the disarticulated scraps of information about individual residents of Attika that the second category of literary texts presents. They are deeply problematic. Such scraps are widely scattered through the extant non-narrative literature of the Graeco-Roman world from Cicero to Macrobius and beyond, congregating indigestibly in Valerius Maximus, Aulus Gellius, and Polyainos, rubbing shoulders with legal and constitutional antiquities in Harpokration or the scholia to the orators, and populating every other page of Athenaios. As a mass they are repetitious, often misattributed or muddled, and focussed for the most part on a mere handful of high-status individuals. Nor, to tell the truth, are they hugely informative (it is therefore understandable that the reportage of these items in *PAA* is patchy at best): it is not so much that they add knowledge which the mainstream sources lack (though they do to some degree) as that frequently those mainstream sources alone provide the necessary context, rationale, and (often) correction. Hagiography rules, especially with the many anecdotes featuring Sokrates, and – understandably but unrealistically – success is far more often commemorated than failure. But, as always with florilegia, both the individual scraps, and the intellectual efforts that created the compilations in which such scraps appear, need respectful consideration.

Each aspect needs illustration. First, the individual scraps of information. Three examples will give the flavour and illustrate the range of value that could be added. Polyainos provides the first, a sketch of Alkibiades approaching an enemy city by sea, landing his troops, failing to entice the inhabitants into a landward engagement, and therefore ostensibly withdrawing while leaving troops in concealment who fell on the inhabitants when they dropped their guard (*Strategemata* I. 40, 2). Our honorand has renewed the identification of the probable historical context, the capture of Byzantion in 408, as well as Polyainos' attribution of the same stratagem to Thrasyllos a few sections later (*Strat*. I. 47.2; Rhodes 2011: 81-82 and 126 nn. 56-57). Here the survival of the fuller and earlier texts of Xenophon and Diodoros has allowed the citation to be re-attached to a mainstream narrative, but the same is not true for a second example, taken from one of the *Controversiae* of Seneca *père*. Its theme runs: 'When Philip was selling the captives from Olynthos, Parrhasios the Athenian painter bought an old man, brought him to Athens, tortured him and painted a Prometheus using him as a model. The Olynthian died in agony. Parrhasios set the picture up in the temple of Athene. He is accused of damaging the state.' (*Con*. X. 5 *praef*.) This poses a severe problem of method. Does one report and assess this and similar *progymnasmata* within a historical dimension of truth-values, within a pedagogic dimension of forensic values, or (as by Morales 1996) within a cultural dimension of conflict between artistic and ethical values? And if the latter, of which culture?

However, a third example is of a different calibre. While setting out provisions for his ideal law-code in his treatise *De Legibus*, Cicero notes, à propos of sacrilege and of 'the theft not merely of what is sacred but also of anything entrusted to what is sacred', that 'the custom of making such deposits still exists at many temples, and it is said that Alexander deposited a sum of money in a temple at Soloi in Kilikia, and that Kleisthenes, an eminent citizen of Athens, entrusted the dowry of his daughters to Hera of Samos when he was fearful for his own affairs' (*De leg*. II. 41, tr. Keyes LCL, modified, with Cromey 1979: 134). So far as I know, this information appears nowhere else. Cicero presumably picked up that for Soloi during his governorship of Kilikia in 51, though it stands in such disturbingly sharp contrast to the reports of Alexandros' harsh treatment of the city (Arrian, *Anab*. II.5.5; Curt. III. 7.2) as to create scepticism. That for Kleisthenes on the other hand has the ring of plausibility, especially when one recalls Xenophon's similar deposit with Artemis at Ephesos (Xen. *Anab*. V.3.6-7), and since no children of Kleisthenes are otherwise known it offers a potentially valuable accretion to Alkmaionid family history.

As these examples show, one can go some way, but only so far, at the level of the individual excerpt. One can attempt to evaluate the information, to identify (if possible) its ancestry in an earlier author, and to re-integrate it with the general corpus of knowledge: a task that is simple to formulate but frequently difficult to achieve, as the two previous paragraphs demonstrate. Beyond that point, one has to recognise that these are examples of 'examples', i.e. of entities with a peculiar ontological status: they are both in, and removed from, space and time. That is because they have lost their roots. Once such units of information are detached from their original contexts, they can function only as examples. They may figure as singletons, used (as by Cicero, above) to illustrate and strengthen a political or rhetorical or philosophical argument, or they can be used in multiple to form a repertoire, but there must always be a reason for citing them. Since it was citers such as Cicero, and especially compilers such as Seneca *père*, who made the decisions which have provided us with the particular array of examples that we have rather than others, it is essential both to disinter the logic that underlies each compilation and to address the second aspect identified above by viewing the 'family' of all such compilations synoptically and generically.

In doing so, it will be helpful to pay particular attention to two such compilations. Valerius Maximus' *Factorum et dictorum memorabilium libri novem* is one of the earliest of them to survive, though it sits chronologically near the centre of the seven-century-long sequence of the literature of citation of persons. Its title, language, date (ca. 30 BCE), innovative framework, and inferred social intention have combined to give it wide recognition as the prime exemplar of the 'Exemplum' art-form (Bloomer 1992; Maslakov 1984, with earlier references; Skidmore 1996). It comprises a congeries of hundreds of examples drawn from historical and oratorical texts: many concern Athenians and episodes that are not otherwise attested. It is carefully ordered, not by name or nation but by the human qualities and frailties that characterise such major areas of life as religion (book I), institutions and public life (book II), and virtues (books III-VI), as well as general behaviour (books VII-IX). Implicitly, it met a social need for *exempla* – not just as material for declamation and forensic pleading, but also as examples of behaviour that was appropriate for a Roman gentleman.

It therefore contrasts sharply with a second title, the twenty books of Aulus Gellius' *Noctes Atticae* (Holford-Strevens 2003). Written some 180 years later, its themes are many: antiquarianism in Roman customs and in language; citations of jurists; etymologies and correct use of language; moral and philosophical problems of behaviour and natural phenomena; the master-pupil relationship; *exempla* from the past; emendations and interpretations of texts; and anecdotes about philosophers. It reads as belletristic inconsequentiality, and the author admits as much: 'I used to jot down whatever took my fancy, of any and every kind, without any definite plan or order' (Praef. 2). Yet here too, amid the dross, there is information about Athenians to be winnowed out: the twenty books cannot be left on the shelf.

How then can one structure a general understanding of the contents and *raisons d'être* of a 'family' of titles that contains such unlike members? After much consideration of the problem, it has seemed best not to attempt a characterisation of individual compilers and compilations but rather, very briefly and schematically, to identify the various common strands of preoccupation and knowledge that ran across the range and through the centuries. At least six such common strands can be identified. Three of them have especial weight, since they consist of material that had been drawn from the spheres of skilled activity – military, oratorical, and philosophical – that were likely to be of most interest and concern to an educated elite as a readership.

(1) Hardly surprisingly, the military strand was early to emerge, itself taking two forms. One form, first extant in Xenophon's two treatises on horsemanship, eschewed *personalia* altogether in favour of impersonal advice, a mode which was followed two centuries later by Asklepiodotos and Onasandros, and semi-respected by Arrian's *Tekhne taktike* (he cites five names only, the one Athenian being Xenophon himself). Later still, probably in the 380s or 390s, Vegetius allowed himself some names of Romans and others, but no Athenian, and the anonymous Byzantine *Taktika* named no-one at all. In contrast, the second form, first represented by Aineias' *Poliorketika*, used illustrative examples extensively, both of collectives and of individuals. As noted above, Valerius Maximus followed suit, as did the two major extant compilers of *Strategemata*, Frontinus and Polyainos. Frontinus, indeed, followed it closely by classifying his *exempla* precisely under headings that identify the particular contingencies that commanders might encounter. In his text, again like Valerius's, though most of his *exempla* cite Roman commanders, Athenians figure not infrequently, many in ways that are not attested elsewhere and therefore add considerable value.

Polyainos's compilation of two generations later deserves even closer attention (Brodersen 2010, with references). It is much longer, organised by polity rather than by theme, and much wider in its range. Of its eight books, I is a hotchpotch of episodes from the Archaic period and the Graeco-Persian Wars, II to IV present Spartans, Athenians, and Macedonians respectively, V men of the Greek overseas foundations, VI various nations, VII non-Mediterranean powers, and VIII Romans and women. Athenians figure in Books I and III, and occasionally elsewhere, heavily enough to reveal Polyainos's choices and emphases very clearly, and here for once the details are worth setting out. Perikles and Kimon score a mere two entries each, eight commanders (Diotimos, Konon, Lakhares, Nikias, Xenophon, Peisistratos, Phormion and Khares) score from three to five entries each, Themistokles eight, Alkibiades nine, Khabrias 15, and Timotheos 17, but Iphikrates 63 -- a remarkable number, which regrettably cannot be dwelt on here. What is more, this was not a matter of collecting postage-stamps for display on the pages of an album. Just as Onasandros had claimed that his treatise 'will be a school for good generals, and an object of delight for retired commanders in these times of holy peace......' (*Strategikos*, Praef. 4), so too Polyainos' work was clearly seen as practically helpful, and it became canonical in consequence. At some uncertain later date, presumably so as to be of more practical utility, it was shortened and rearranged under 58 headings to form the so-called *Excerpta Polyaeni*. Later still it was again shortened and regrouped, this time under 29 moral-advisory headings as the Emperor Leo's *Strategikai paraineseis*.

(2) A second strand, that of the display and transmission of oratorical expertise, had an equally long life-span but is disappointingly uninformative about individuals. True, its leading text, Aristoteles' *Rhetorike Tekhne*, is a gold-mine of information, most of those cited being Athenians active in the 360s or the 350s, when Aristoteles was residing in Athens as a member of Plato's Academy, but the yield from the genre dwindles into near-insignificance thereafter. Typically, though Cicero's oratorical treatises such as *Brutus*, *De Oratore* I-III, and *Orator* are

long on the styles of the Athenian orators, they are either wholly silent or at best very short on biographical details. For example, his youthful *De Inventione* (I.51-53) and the surviving torso of *De Fato* (10, echoed in *Tusc.* IV.37) each offer precisely one relevant item, both of which reflect the Socratic tradition rather than being a practical *exemplum*.

Nor does the voluminous later stream of rhetorical texts and textbooks in Greek or Latin offer much. For example, Theon's *progymnasmata* allude spasmodically to now-lost speeches and at two points imply that there was more to know about the conspiracy of Kylon than is reported by Thucydides, but are otherwise unhelpful. Likewise, the two treatises attributed to Menander Rhetor provide illuminating blueprints of speeches for various occasions but yield precious little biographical information: instead, Phokion and Aristeides have become icons of righteousness devoid of personality. In the Latin tradition, too, the pickings are again sadly thin. Tacitus's *Dialogus* makes passing references to Athenian orators, but as stylists rather than as persons, and though Quintilian's *Institutio Oratoria* continually refers to Demosthenes and other Athenian orators and makes crisp and penetrating judgments both on them and on eminent practitioners in other creative fields, he gives very little biographical information outside the texts that have survived independently. Even worse, as seen above, the conventions of declamation as a genre seem to have precluded much respect for accuracy. Phokion and Aristeides are cardboard figures here too (Seneca *père C.* II. 1, 18), Iphikrates, Parrhasios, and Pheidias have become characters in violently telescoped scenarios, and Miltiades, Kimon, and Kallias feature in a pantomime-style caricature of historical reality (*ib.* IX. 9).

(3) A third strand, that of the philosophers and their Schools, is slightly more productive, especially in the texts of Cicero's would-be 'encyclopedia of philosophy'. True, some of his themes offered scant scope for *exempla*, but in three other treatises – *De Officiis*, *De Finibus*, and *Tusculan Disputations* – examples taken from earlier, and especially Athenian, history are frequent and pertinent, though they largely reflect or summarise information from surviving sources and offer little that is unique. However, Cicero's reminiscences of his student years in Athens are more valuable, because they show that his texts were superstructures, built on much older foundations. Those foundations had been laid by the collective but competitive efforts made by successive heads of Athenian philosophical schools and their assistants to illustrate their respective 'schemes for living' by citing as signifiers the acts and behaviours, for good or ill, of identifiable individuals of the past. But they also show that that primary process had all but ossified in the 80s and 70s BCE and that the examples which are quoted from it showed a strong bias towards the distant past (barely any Greek is named who was active later than 200 BCE, and even persons who were active after 300 BCE are rare). Nor did the Epicureans play the game at all. Cicero makes Triarius exclaim at one point that 'In the school of Epicurus I never heard one mention of Lycurgus, Solon, Miltiades, Themistocles, Epaminondas, who are always on the lips of the other philosophers' (*De Finibus* II.67; also II.116). It is hard to escape the conclusion that the 'examples' whom Cicero cites had lost their biographical individuality. Yet, even a century after Cicero, there was a residue. Among the mostly over-familiar Athenian names in the younger Seneca's *De beneficiis* two newcomers stand out, Kallistratos (VI.37.1) and Demades (VI.38.1), both attached to information that does not survive elsewhere.

Three other strands of information about Athenians must be noted more briefly. All three reflected other preoccupations, and offered correspondingly different sets of names. (4)

One such was small and clearly defined. The texts of Pausanias, Pliny the Elder, Quintilian, Vitruvius and others preserve much useful data about painters, sculptors and architects, as does Athenaios' Book XIII about Athenian *hetairai*, though the risks of such an approach are grimly exposed by the 'biographies' of the Greek poets (Graziosi 2002; Lefkowitz 2013). (5) Much larger was the scholarly or semi-scholarly strand, comprising commentaries, scholia, and descriptive or prescriptive works on language and vocabulary; Didymos, Harpokration, even Fronto all contribute names and details. (6) Last, overlapping untidily with (5), and most dispiriting (for the prosopographer, but not for the cultural historian) are the texts that comprise the so-called 'Second Sophistic', ranging from Gellius himself via the declamatory *rhetores* and Lucian's essays to Clement's *Stromateis* and Ailianos' *Pantodape historia*. All offer something *ad rem*, but all require a health warning: 'it is only in recent years that scholars have come to realise just how sceptical they ought to be in their attitude to all biographical material relating to figures from the classical period' (Wilson 1997: 9).

How then, in view of that warning, can one make the best use of the under-explored and decontextualised information about Athenian individuals that is offered by the texts of my second category? A simple provisional answer is to employ the concept of 'agency' and to distinguish as surgically as possible between an individual's Leben ('What X as actor made of his/her life') and his/her Nachleben ('How others then chose to use X's life'). That will allow most of the information that emanates from category (1) texts, and some of that from those of category (2), to be properly biographical, and will therefore allow it to be assessed historically, while most of what is attested in category (2), and some of the material in category (1), will count instead as a cultural artefact, to be assessed generically. To employ that distinction will have the further advantage of allowing such evidence as survives of the lively tradition of visual portrayal of historical individuals (Richter 1965; Richter and Smith 1984) to be integrated as a component of the collage of stories, characterisations, and representations that made up an individual's Nachleben, instead of being left in limbo as 'art history'. To proceed thus may also make it easier to follow the processes that extant biographers from Nepos onwards (Tuplin 2000) used to recontextualise the individuals whom they selected for portraiture. Those processes will need separate discussion.

Bibliography

Bloomer, W.M. 1992. *Valerius Maximus and the rhetoric of the new nobility*. London: Duckworth.

Brodersen, K. (ed.) 2010. *Polyainos: Neue Studien = Polyaenus: new studies*. Berlin: Verlag Antike.

Castagnoli, L., and P. Ceccarelli, P. (eds) 2019. *Greek memories: theories and practices*. Cambridge: University Press.

Cromey, R.D. 1979. Kleisthenes' fate. *Historia* 28: 129-147.

Davies, J.K. 2010. *Revising Athenian Propertied Families: progress and problems*, in R.W.V. Catling and F. Marchand (eds) with M. Sasanow, *Onomatologos. Studies in Greek Personal Names presented to Elaine Matthews*: 132-142. Oxford: Oxbow.

Fentress, J., and C. Wickham. 1992. *Social memory*. Oxford: Blackwell.

Holford-Strevens, L. 2003. *Aulus Gellius. An Antonine scholar and his achievement*, 2nd ed. (1st ed. 1988). Oxford: University Press.

Graziosi, B. 2002. *Inventing Homer. The early reception of epic*. Cambridge; University Press.

Lefkowitz, M.A. 2013. *The lives of the Greek poets*, 2nd edition. London: Bloomsbury.

Maslakov, G. 1984. Valerius Maximus and Roman historiography: A study of the Exempla tradition. *ANRW* II, 32 1: 437-496.

Morales, H. 1996. *The Torturer's Apprentice: Parrhasius and the limits of art*, in J. Elsner (ed.), *Art and Text in Roman Culture*: 182-209. Cambridge: University Press.

Nouhaud, M. 1982. *L'utilisation de l'histoire par les orateurs attiques*. Paris: Les Belles Lettres.

Rhodes, P.J. 1981. *A Commentary on the Aristotelian Athenaion Politeia*. Oxford: Clarendon Press.

Rhodes, P.J. 2011. *Alcibiades. Athenian playboy, general and traitor.* Barnsley: Pen and Sword.

Richter, G.M.A. 1965. *The portraits of the Greeks* I-III. London: Phaidon. Abridged and revised ed. by R.R.R. Smith, 1984. London: Phaidon.

Skidmore, C.J. 1996. *Practical ethics for Roman gentlemen: the work of Valerius Maximus.* Exeter: University Press.

Thomas, R. 1989. *Oral tradition and written record in Classical Athens*. Cambridge: University Press.

Thomas, R. 2019. *Polis histories, collective memories and the Greek world.* Cambridge: University Press.

Tuplin, C.J. 2000. *Nepos and the origins of political biography*, in C. Deroux (ed.), *Studies in Latin literature and Roman history*, X (Collection *Latomus* 254): 125-161. Bruxelles: Revue d'Études Latines.

Wilson, N.G. (ed. and transl.) 1997. *Aelian: Historical Miscellany*. Cambridge MA; London: Harvard University Press.

The Oligarchic Ideal in Ancient Greece

Roger Brock

University of Leeds
r.w.brock@leeds.ac.uk

Abstract

Social relations between the *kaloi k'agathoi* of archaic and classical Greece were governed by an unspoken code of behaviour, and acceptance required the ability to fit in and display the requisite style (*charis*), education and intelligence, above all in the symposium, where wine would reveal a man's essential character. However, sympotic poetry, especially the Theognid corpus, expresses apparently contradictory instructions as to how to behave, commending openness in one place while warning elsewhere of the dangers of trust, for example, and calling for moderation at one moment and 'madness' at another. There were no simple rules to follow: the appropriate choice was a matter of *kairos* and called for the ability to assess the circumstances and, like an octopus, adapt oneself to one's environment. That could only be learnt by experience, through associating with the minority of 'good' men (*agathoi, esthloi*) who were already 'wise' (*sophoi*): hence gaining admission to the elite was a matter of socialisation by apprenticeship to the virtuous few.

Keywords

ancient Greek oligarchy, social codes, symposium, Theognis

Although we probably tend to associate him above all with Athenian democracy and democratic institutions (and increasingly latterly with Greek historiography), our honorand has in his vast scholarly output also done characteristically authoritative work on oligarchic politics.[1] My subject in this modest tribute is something less solid than constitutional forms or political activity: the more nebulous world of ideology, and indeed the more nebulous end of that field. My concern is not (or only incidentally) with the high ideals that characterise the *aristoi*, the *kaloi k'agathoi*, but rather with the social code that marks out the elite as a select minority – and that, as we shall see, is a more slippery and elusive quarry.

I begin, somewhat at odds with my own political affiliations, with Margaret Thatcher. As leader of a Conservative party fragmented by ideological divisions, Thatcher famously used to ask of individual Members of Parliament 'is he one of us?' An answer in the affirmative could be cashed out in terms of adherence to her policy ideals – hard-line on economic policy (and specifically a believer in monetarism), conservative on social policy, Eurosceptic, a firm believer in the private sector, and so on – but the essential point is that membership of the inner circle was denoted by a coded expression which for insiders did not require such explication. The same point is made by one of my favourite footnotes in Kenneth Dover's *Greek Popular Morality*: 'I once heard the information, "He is a member of the Communist Party of Great Britain" conveyed by the words "He's a *very* nice man", spoken slowly and deliberately

---

[1] I have in mind particularly Rhodes (2000) and (2005), though Marr and Rhodes (2008) is germane, too, as are PJR's articles in *OCD*[3/4] *s.v.* aristocracy, *hetaireiai*, oligarchy, and Theramenes. My title is of course also a nod to Donlan (1980), a classic work on elite values, and the initial stimulus to investigate the topic came from the much-missed Anton Powell.

by one party member to another.'[2] This sort of coded labelling, then, is not confined to right-wing politics, but it *is* a typical feature of restricted in-groups concerned to police their membership and ward off undesirables.

A related policing of boundaries which is largely limited to elite circles is characterised by the monitoring of an unspoken code of social behaviour, any breach of which, commonly labelled a 'faux pas', unmasks the offender as not belonging. The classic illustrations of this practice are the cartoons by H.M. Bateman captioned 'The man who...' which depict the shock, horror or outrage of the assembled company at 'the man who lit his cigar before the royal toast' or 'threw a snowball at St. Moritz' or 'missed the ball on the first tee at St. Andrews'. What I want to argue here is that both these practices are also typical of the Greek elite of the archaic and classical periods, and that the oligarchic ideal is characterised by a control of membership through the use of coded language and the monitoring of standards of correct behaviour. The evidence comes mainly from archaic poetry, supplemented occasionally from later sources: while the aristocratic ideal develops and evolves, as Donlan demonstrated, the oligarchic ideal appears to remain largely consistent through archaic and classical times, as (for example) is implied by the persistent popularity of the Theognid corpus as a 'song-book' for classical Athenian symposia demonstrated by Robin Lane Fox. Hence, because the picture I am painting is essentially synchronic, I use 'Theognis' as a convenient shorthand for contributors to the corpus, without any implications as to authorship or date. Indeed, it was above all the symposium that served as the crucible in which social behaviour would be assayed, with wine serving as the efficacious solvent of men's true natures: as Theognis says, 'knowledgeable men recognise gold and silver in the flame, but it's wine that reveals the mind of man'. Yet whereas the measure of excellence in warfare or athletics was simple and clear-cut, a mark to aim at for a Pindaric javelin, the right way to behave turns out to be a much more elusive target.[3]

The appropriation and manipulation of language by the elite of ancient Greece to promote their ideology is now familiar: besides the contributions of Donlan, we should note also the appendix in R.A. Neil's brilliant edition of *Knights*, in this as in so much else decades ahead of his time.[4] Hence there is no need to rehearse in detail here the use of morally evaluative language such as *agathos*, *chrestos* and *aristos* to denote aristocratic excellence, though we should note in passing that, like Thatcher's 'one of us', this is coded language and, in itself, states nothing about what a man will say or do. That is less the case with certain other buzz-words which aristocrats attempted to monopolise in ways that circumscribed their definition. One thinks particularly of *eunomia* and *sophrosyne*, concepts sufficiently powerful to invite regular personification, but we might also note the case of *isonomia*, a term which, as we can see from the drinking songs that celebrate Harmodius and Aristogeiton, was originally claimed by aristocrats, to label the 'freedom' of a regime shared among themselves, as an antithesis to 'slavery' under the selfish rule of a tyrant; however, it slipped from their control and came to apply to conditions a good deal more equal than they would have liked, even if the claim of

[2] Dover (1974: 43 n. 21).

[3] Lane Fox (2000); cf. Nagy (1985: 33-36, 46-51). Wine as solvent: Thgn. 499-500; Pindaric javelin: *O*. 13.93-95, *P*. 1.44-45, *N*. 7.70-72, 9.55.

[4] Donlan (1980: esp. 127-129; 1978); Neil (1901: 202-209); Grossmann (1950) is also an early and under-appreciated study in the field.

the Thebans in the debate at Plataia in 427 that there could be an *oligarchia isonomos* indicates some continuing contestation.[5]

Perhaps more significant in terms of actual behaviour are terms denoting power or a capacity for action, *hoi dunatoi* or *dunatotatoi* or *hoi dunamenoi*, which relate to the role of members of the elite in the community at large. That in turn brings us on to language which is, or may be, concerned with the behaviour of individuals within the more circumscribed community of the elite itself. One key term is *pistos*, a word which, with its cognates, occurs more than twenty times in the Theognid corpus and in contexts which make it clear that loyalty and trustworthiness are normative aristocratic values. At the same time, these passages make very clear how problematic the operation of this code could be in reality, as Donlan showed. The analogy that Hans van Wees draws with the flexibility of the language and code of loyalty among Mafiosi is a salutary one.[6] The language of 'safety', *asphales* and *asphaleia*, may also be relevant here: Neil highlighted the use of *asphaleia* as 'a watchword of conservatism', and more recently Lowell Edmunds noted that it features in the language of faction in Thuc. 3.82; it also appears suggestively in the context of the oligarchic coup of 411 (8.66.5). It is noteworthy that this language is associated significantly with Sparta, just as Paula Debnar has pointed to a particular Spartan affinity for the terminology of *pistis*.[7] Another term markedly linked with Sparta is *epitedeios*: Thucydides refers programmatically in 1.19 to Sparta's establishment of oligarchies to rule 'σφίσιν ... ἐπιτηδείως' and the word recurs both with reference to Spartan policy in general and to her dispositions in the Peloponnese after the battle of Mantineia. Andrew Lintott also noted acutely the frequency of *epitedeios*, together with its antonym *anepitedeios*, in Thucydides' account of the oligarchy of the Four Hundred, in a way that suggests that it was a current slogan.[8] There may be something similar in the defence speech which Xenophon attributes to Theramenes in the *Hellenica*, where he uses without qualification the adjective *hikanos* to refer to Leon of Salamis, a man he has just labelled *kalos k'agathos*; I suggest that this curious usage denotes someone who should have been 'acceptable' to the Thirty. Another odd usage which might deserve more attention than it has received is Peisthetairos' explanation that he and Euelpides are not looking for a bigger city than Athens, but one which is 'προσφορωτέραν νῦν', to which the Hoopoe replies 'ἀριστοκρατεῖσθαι δῆλος εἶ ζητῶν': although this is a set-up for a reference to Aristocrates the son of Scellias, a favourite Aristophanic butt, the joke is less weak if the audience had a sense that those who favoured minority regimes had a penchant for the language of accommodation and fitting in. I suspect that a mind-set of this kind helps to explain the aristocratic fondness for invocations of Hesychia: what they had in mind, I think, was not only an untroubled political order, but also a social tranquillity analogous to Cicero's *cum dignitate otium*. Epicharmus declares that Hesychia is a gracious lady (χαρίεσσα γυνά) and lives next door to Sophrosyne, and Anacreon commends a friend who is 'one of the quiet ones' (τῶν ἀβακιζομένων), while Pindar observes in *Nemean* 9 that '*hesychia* loves a symposium'.[9]

---

[5] *Sophrosyne*: North (1966) and n.b. Neil (1901: 204); *oligarchia isonomos*: Thuc. 3.62.3; for the aristocratic origins of *isonomia* see Raaflaub (2004: 94-95, 99-100).

[6] Donlan (1985); van Wees (2000).

[7] *Asphaleia*: Neil (1909: 203-204, quotation from 203); Edmunds (1975: 81); Debnar (2001: esp. 42-3).

[8] *Epitedeios*: Thuc. 1.19, 144.2; 5.81.2, 82.1; 8.63.4, 65.2, 66.2, 70.2 with Lintott (1982: 181 n. 19); cf. Neil (1901: 205); Whibley (1896: 56 n. 8). *epieikes* is a borderline case: Neil (1901: 209); Dover (1974: 61-63, 191).

[9] Theramenes: Xen. *HG* 2.3.39; Peisthetairos: Ar. *Av.* 124-125; *hesychia*: Epicharmus fr. 100 KA; cf. Anacreon 416 *PMG*, Pi. *N*. 9.48 (with Braswell 1998: 137-138), P. 4.294-296; Neil (1901: 208-209), and n.b. Dover (1974: 189) for its assimilation

With the language of *charis* – in the sense of 'grace' – we are squarely in the world of the symposium; but while we might take this as primarily a matter of aesthetics, the charm that Anacreon aspired to in his poems (402c *PMG*), or the charms of the desirable youths often celebrated in poetry (Archil. fr. 9.10; Sim. el. 22.11, 15),[10] it clearly had a social aspect as well. That emerges clearly from another under-appreciated passage, in Herodotus' account of the career of Gelon: having reduced by siege the city of Megara Hyblaea, whose wealthy inhabitants had picked a fight with him, Gelon, contrary to expectations, absorbed them into the citizen body of Syracuse while deporting and selling into slavery the rest of the population. The same treatment was meted out to the Euboeans of Sicily: the explanation given for both cases was that the *demos* was a συνοίκημα ἀχαριτώτατον – 'really unpleasant to live with' (7.156.3).

The problem with the demos, as our sources make clear, was that they simply had no style. Pseudo-Xenophon laments that 'the demos has spoiled the athletic and musical activities at Athens' which they do not value because of their own incapacity (1.13: the text may be corrupt). We can see a democratic perception of oligarchic criticism of this kind reflected in the scenes at the end of Aristophanes' *Wasps* in which Bdelycleon tries to turn his father into the kind of cultured individual who will fit in at symposia: he fails, of course, but the failure is so wholesale as to be almost heroic, and in any case the audience's sympathy is with Philocleon, and the laugh on those whose pretensions are trampled underfoot in the process. More subtle is Anacreon's invective (388 *PMG*) against the nouveau-riche Artemon, whose lack of taste is shown by his effeminate love of luxury. Such breaches of decorum arise from a combination of a lack of restraint, *akolasia*, and a lack of intelligence, let alone education, that makes Megabyzus, the advocate of aristocracy in Herodotus' 'Constitutional debate', prefer to suffer abuse at the hands of a tyrant, because at least *he* knows what he is doing; pseudo-Xenophon likewise sneers that among the demos there is 'a maximum of *amathia*, *ataxia* and *poneria*'. Small wonder that such people do not know how to behave: only the *agathoi* have understanding, and the *agathoi* have always been few, as Theognis says: ἀνδράσι τοῖς ἀγαθοῖς ἔπεται γνώμη τε καὶ αἰδώς· οἳ νῦν ἐν πολλοῖς ἀτρεκέως ὀλίγοι. Pindar likewise identifies democracy with ὁ λάβρος στρατός and minority rule with οἱ σοφοὶ in *Pythian 2*, and Heracleitus explains in the same terms the lack of philosophic capacity among the masses, who follow the crowd, not knowing that the *polloi* are *kakoi* and the *agathoi* are *oligoi*.[11]

Such ignorance is fatal: wisdom is essential for correct social behaviour, because there is no simple rule to follow; what is appropriate is a matter of *kairos* and of judgement. This is perhaps most explicit in one of the Attic *skolia* (902 *PMG*): σύν μοι πῖνε, συνήβα, συνέρα, συστεφανηφόρει, σύν μοι μαινομένωι μαίνεο, σὺν σώφρονι σωφρόνει. Anacreon says something similar: ἐρέω τε δηῦτε κοὐκ ἐρέω καὶ μαίνομαι κοὐ μαίνομαι (428 *PMG*); so does a couplet in the Theognid corpus (313-314): ἐν μὲν μαινομένοις μάλα μαίνομαι, ἐν δὲ δικαίοις πάντων ἀνθρώπων εἰμὶ δικαιότατος. Different behaviour fits different occasions, and even

---

to *apragmosune* in democratic contexts.

[10] Homosexuality is of course often seen as performing a socialising function for *eromenoi*, but is rather different from the phenomenon I am examining inasmuch as it operates directly through the relationship between the particular partners (as it might be Theognis and Cyrnus) and the instruction would vary depending on the character of the individual *erastes*.

[11] *Akolasia*: e.g. Hdt. 3.81.2, Thuc. 6.89.5, Ps-Xen. *Ath.Pol.* 1.5. Good and wise are few: Thgn. 635-636; cf. 149-150, 1185-1186; Pi. *P.* 2.86-88; Heracleitus B104.

though *sophrosyne* is one of the key aristocratic virtues, sometimes it is appropriate for it to be replaced by madness.

What might release that madness, of course, was wine. In the wrong context, that could be disastrous: a fragment of Pindar describes the Centaurs 'coming to know the man-taming force of honey-sweet wine' (fr. 166 Maehler), with consequences depicted as a dreadful warning on many a work of art – *LIMC* under 'Kentauroi et Kentaurides' lists some 80 illustrations of the fight with the Lapiths, three-quarters of them from vase-painting. To be sure, the Centaurs were part-beast, but elsewhere Pindar speaks of *men* 'laid low by the arrows of the vine' (fr. 124b M). Theognis more than once observes that even a man who is *pinutos* or *sophron* will show himself up if he drinks *huper metron*;[12] what is needed is good judgement: 'To drink much wine is bad; but if one drinks it intelligently (ἐπισταμένως), it is not bad, but good' (509-510). Lines 467-498, one of the passages which West ascribes to Euenus (= 8a), presents an ideal symposiast advising his companion to serve those who still want to drink, and not to wake anyone who falls asleep; he for his own part is going home, having reached the most graceful state of inebriation (ὡς οἶνος χαριέστατος ἀνδρὶ πεπόσθαι), neither sober nor excessively drunk, and so not at risk of doing anything embarrassing. Before leaving, he chides his companion for being unable to resist 'just one more drink', but offers pointers for a symposium which will nonetheless be οὐκ ἄχαρι – the repeated language of *charis* is worth noting. Elsewhere, the poet reassures a friend that he won't get drunk enough to insult him (413-414), but drunkenness is by no means out of the question: in another passage (503-508) the speaker reports that wine has him on the run and that the room is going round and round; he is about to test whether wine also has control of his legs and wits (*nous*), fearful that in his well-fortified state he will do something stupid and embarrassing. 'Well-fortified (θωρηχθείς)' occurs five times in the Theognid corpus (413, 470, 508, 842, 884) alongside the neutral *methuo*: the existence of a slang term shows that this is a culture in which drunkenness is a familiar state; Archilochus provides another, 'οἴνωι συγκεραυνωθεὶς φρένας' (fr. 120.2).[13] Yet despite the potential hazards of drink, abstinence is not an option, for 'it is *aischron* to be drunk among sober men, and *aischron* to remain sober among drunkards' (Thgn. 627-628); the trick is to steer a course between the δισσαί ... πόσιος κῆρες, thirst and drunkenness (837-840). As a mock-oracular passage puts it, in another allusion to the characteristic post-party sense of disorientation, 'but when he who was above becomes below, then get thee home, ceasing from drink' (843-844).

That is good advice, since one further problem of drink is that it can lead you into bad company: οἶνος ἐμοὶ τὰ μὲν ἄλλα χαρίζεται, ἓν δ᾽ ἀχάριστος, εὖτ᾽ ἂν θωρήξας μ᾽ ἄνδρα πρὸς ἐχθρὸν ἄγηι (841-842). Even leaving aside that worst-case scenario, there is still the problem of how to engage with the company in which you find yourself, since 'many companions become friends by the mixing-bowl' (643 > 115). The problem of trust and disloyalty is a recurrent theme of sympotic poetry: I have already alluded to the persistent concern of Theognis as to

12 Wine and measure: Thgn. 497-498, 501-502; cf. 479-483; 509-510 > 211-212.

13 Garcia Soler (2010) surveys the use and abuse of wine; it is noteworthy that while sympotic poetry acknowledges drunkenness, with an implicit claim to be able to regulate this too, it draws a veil over the consequences in terms of bodily functions like vomiting and of misbehaviour, unlike vase-painting or comedy: elite symposiasts might well have seen the license to behave in such ways as among the privileges of their status (Pittacus was perhaps influenced by the misdeeds of the Penthelidai [Arist. *Pol.* 1311 b26-8] in remarking that it was 'hard to be *esthlos*' and legislating against drunken criminality: D.L. 1.76), but it does not form part of the idealising code.

219

who is *pistos*, and this is also a principal theme of the Attic skolia. 'If only it were possible to see what everyone is like by opening his breast, and, having looked at his mind, to close it up again and regard the man as one's friend for his guileless heart', laments one, but the truth is that 'under every stone lurks a scorpion'. Hence other songs attempt to direct drinkers into the path of virtue in the manner of animal fables, warning that it is not possible to 'play the fox' or befriend both sides, and offering the crab's advice to the snake that 'a comrade should be straight and not think crooked thoughts', or singing the praises of the man who does *not* betray his friends.[14] Yet this kind of protreptic just makes it plain that the problem was real and persistent: so what to do?

Plainly, caution is required, since 'wine is a peephole into a man', as Alcaeus put it (333 L-P), and can make one reveal one's real thoughts, as the proverb 'wine and truth' suggests (Alc. 366 L-P). Furthermore, even if it is bad form to remember afterwards what happened at a symposium, the lyric fragment which complains of it (1002 *PMG*) confirms that some men did so. The answer of Theognis is, as Bertie Wooster would put it, 'to wear the mask' (309-312):

> ἐν μὲν συσσίτοισιν ἀνὴρ πεπνυμένος εἶναι.
>   πάντα δέ μιν λήθειν ὡς ἀπεόντα δοκοῖ.
> εἰς δὲ φέροι τὰ γελοῖα – θύρηφι δὲ καρτερὸς εἴη –
>   γινώσκων ὀργὴν ἥντιν' ἕκαστος ἔχει.

Whatever one's own mood, one should conceal it – πῖν' ὁπόταν πίνωσιν· ὅταν δέ τι θυμὸν ἀσηθῆις, μηδεὶς ἀνθρώπων γνῶι σε βαρυνόμενον (989-990)[15] – and certainly not try to relieve one's feelings in bad times by big talk which can't be backed up, and will only embarrass one's friends (1029-1033). Alternatively, one can engage with others, but camouflage oneself, shifting the 'colour' of one's character with each companion in a kind of protective mimicry that imitates that of the octopus:

> θυμέ, φίλους κατὰ πάντας ἐπίστρεφε ποικίλον ἦθος,
>   ὀργὴν συμμίσγων ἥντιν' ἕκαστος ἔχει·
> πουλύπου ὀργὴν ἴσχε πολυπλόκου, ὃς ποτὶ πέτρηι,
>   τῆι προσομιλήσηι, τοῖος ἰδεῖν ἐφάνη.
> νῦν μὲν τῆιδ' ἐφέπου, τοτὲ δ' ἀλλοῖος χρόα γίνου.
>   κρέσσων τοι σοφίη γίνεται ἀτροπίης.

A fragment from Pindar's *Hymns* offers very similar advice: 'my child, make the way you think, whatever city you visit, most closely resemble the skin of the creature that lives in the sea's rock: do not hesitate to praise the men you are with, and think different things at different times'.[16] However, there are obvious problems with this policy, especially for Theognis. It is not unreasonable to commend caution, or even deceit, in dealing with *kakoi*, given that it is to be expected that they will do the same:

> μηδένα τῶνδε φίλον ποιεῦ, Πολυπαΐδη, ἀστῶν

---

[14] Opening the breast: 889 *PMG* (tr. Campbell); scorpion: 903; fox: 912a; crab: 892; loyalty praised: 908.

[15] Hence his criticism of a man who doesn't know how to do what he doesn't feel like doing (1085-6).

[16] Thgn. 213-218 (217-218 > 1073-1074); cf. Pi. fr. 43 M (tr. Olson at Athen. 513C).

ἐκ θυμοῦ χρείης οὕνεκα μηδεμιῆς·
 ἀλλὰ δόκει μὲν πᾶσιν ἀπὸ γλώσσης φίλος εἶναι,
χρῆμα δὲ συμμείξηις μηδενὶ μηδ' ὁτιοῦν
 σπουδαῖον· γνώσηι γὰρ ὀιζυρῶν φρένας ἀνδρῶν,
ὥς σφιν ἐπ' ἔργοισιν πίστις ἔπ' οὐδεμία,
 ἀλλὰ δόλους ἀπάτας τε πολυπλοκίας τ' ἐφίλησαν
οὕτως ὡς ἄνδρες μηκέτι σωιζόμενοι.[17]

Equally it is defensible, if slightly odd, to recommend inconsistency in one's treatment of outsiders: πικρὸς καὶ γλυκὺς ἴσθι καὶ ἁρπαλέος καὶ ἀπηνὴς λάτρισι καὶ δμωσὶν γείτοσί τ' ἀγχιθύροις (301-302), and even in the symposium, one sometimes has to associate with people one would sooner avoid (297-298). However, if honesty and consistency are required between *philoi*, as Theognis repeatedly states in a series of excerpts at lines 87-100 (cf. 851-852), and a friend should be a friend in deed, and not just at the mixing bowl (979-982), then concealing one's intentions from them (73-74) and masking one's feelings must surely be wrong; Theognis is ready enough to criticise others for putting on a front which can lead their associates to misread the 'false and knavish character' which it conceals (963-970). *Poikilia*, too, can be problematic, if it manifests itself as the kind of cunning deceit which leads to immoral behaviour (221-226); on one view, after all, virtue is simple and it is vice which is multifarious (Adesp. el. 3). Once again, what is required is the exercise of good judgement.

However, the model of the *polypus* doesn't only apply to self-presentation: it exemplifies the wider principle which we have observed, that there is no simple and consistent code of behaviour for the would-be *aristos* to adopt. Instead, he needs to adapt himself to his circumstances and to the nature, temperament and mood of those he is with: as Pindar puts it, 'I shall be small among the small, great among the great'. The key terms here are *metron* and *kairos*. The *agathoi* know how to keep to the *metron* in all things; that includes knowing their limits when it comes to wine, something alluded to by Euenus and Critias as well as Theognis.[18] Knowing the limit also means knowing when to keep quiet (611-614), even if 'it is difficult for a wise man among fools to say much, or keep entirely silent' (625-626). Here we are moving into the domain of *kairos*, what is fitting for the occasion, an issue we have already encountered with reference to drinking and 'madness', but which applies equally to poetry.[19] Pindar and Bacchylides express concern for 'singing in season' and particularly with the question whether it is appropriate to sing of war: both on occasion exclude it from epinician, Bacchylides observing that the lyre and choruses are equally out of place on the battlefield, while Anacreon does not love 'the man who while drinking his wine beside the full mixing-bowl talks of strife and tearful war', and prefers 'him who by mingling the splendid gifts of the Muses and Aphrodite remembers the loveliness of the feast'.[20]

---

[17] 61-68; cf. 283-286, 363-364.

[18] Pi. *P.* 3.107; keeping to the *metron*: Thgn. 614; knowing your limits: 475, 479, 498, 501, 694; Critias fr. 6.16, 22, Euenus fr. 2.1.

[19] And in a slightly different way to *ponos*, which is appropriate in pursuit of athletic excellence for Pindar and later in education or philosophy for Isocrates and Plato, but not as a means of earning a living; this kind of distinction by context is thus rather different from the clear definition of two types of equality analysed by Harvey (1965).

[20] 'Singing in season': Pi. *O.* 13.47-48, *P.* 1.81-82, 10.4; adesp. fr.1020 *PMG*; and warfare: Pi. *O.* 9.38-41, Ba. 14.12-18, Anacreon el. 2 (tr. Campbell). Pfeijffer (1999: 647-653) discusses *kairos* in Pindar (but with wider implications), emphasising that it 'is a relative notion' (647).

Indeed, although military valour was a central aspect of the aristocratic ideal, it could come into question at the symposium: Archilochus is notoriously insouciant about the loss of his shield, since he can get another just as good, and Alcaeus and Anacreon happily confess to having done the same thing.[21] Theognis offers a subtler spectrum of options, deprecating martial zeal when one is not fighting for one's own country, but conceding that once mounted up and on the scene it would be shameful 'not to look on tearful war' (887-890), while Pindar frankly confesses that war scares the hell out of the man who has any experience of it (fr. 110 M). Elsewhere, though, Theognis can praise a brave spearman (867-868), and chunks of Tyrtaeus were included in the Theognid song-book, just as the self-praise of the mercenary Hybrias found a place in the collection of *skolia* (909 *PMG*), so war is not entirely alien to sympotic poetry. Archilochus too could take a much more complex and subtle approach to flight, as Laura Swift's discussion (2012) of 'the new Archilochus' convincingly demonstrates. Yet again, what is needed is the wisdom to divine what is right for the occasion.

Indeed, the symposium is *par excellence* the venue for the exercise of intelligence, discernment and insight. Nothing there is obvious or as it appears on the surface, hence the frequent imagery of the touchstone as a test of worth which lies concealed.[22] Quite apart from the challenges of judging one's companions and the right way to behave, the entertainments of the symposium all call for intelligent discernment, too. Poetry is wisdom (Thgn. 769-72; Sol. 13.51-52; Xenoph. 2.12), but it is also subtle and indirect, and calls for wisdom in the hearers too, so that Bacchylides can represent himself as 'speaking for the wise' (Ba. 3.85; cf. fr. 5), while Theognis (or Euenus) goes a step further and labels his extended image of the ship of state 'a hidden riddle for the *agathoi*' (681). That is entirely appropriate, for riddles were also part of the entertainment at the symposium. In fact, there is one in the Theognid corpus: 'For I'm called home now by a carcass of the sea, that e'en in death speaks through a living mouth' (1229-1230, tr. West) – the answer is 'a conch', used as a trumpet. Further examples can be found in Athenaeus, who devotes almost a dozen pages to the phenomenon (448B-459B). Closely related are fables and proverbial expressions, both of which call for a pithy and oblique encapsulation of some truth. We have already encountered some instances of animal fables, to which should be added the numerous examples in Archilochus. One poet who was particularly fond of proverbs was Alcaeus, a phenomenon well studied by Lelli: two which he uses with political significance are his allusion to someone who 'is master, having moved the stone from the holy line', and his warning: 'this I know for certain, that if a man moves gravel, stone not safely workable, he will probably get a sore head'.[23] Another pastime of a similar character is the game of *eikones* ('comparisons'), which we know best from Old Comedy and from the literary symposia of Xenophon and Plato: this game again points to the appeal of the pithy, well-turned phrase in such circles, but also presented, yet again, the challenge of knowing how far to go in humorous mockery.[24] Even the equipment for the symposium could provide its own riddles and puzzles: some were visual, like the ships painted inside cups 'floating' on the wine, or the way an eye-cup formed a mask over the drinker who tipped it up; others were

---

[21] Archilochus fr. 5, Alcaeus 428a L-P, Anacreon 381b *PMG*.

[22] Thgn. 415-418, 447-452, 1105-1106; Adesp. el. 22; Ba. frs. 14, 33.

[23] Alcaeus frs. 351 (tr. Campbell) and 344 L-P; cf. Sapph. fr. 145 L-P; Lelli (2006: 23-70); Pütz (2007: 192-212) has a very useful collection of material mainly from comedy.

[24] *Eikones*: e.g. Ar. *Vesp.* 1308-1313 with MacDowell (1971); *Av.* 804-806 with Dunbar (1995); Pl. *Smp.* 215a; Xen. *Smp.* 6.8-10, where the scope for causing offence is evident.

practical, like the trick cups which emptied and filled themselves, or soaked the drinker, or rattled mysteriously.[25]

The symposium thus encapsulated the challenge facing would-be members of the elite. That this was so is underlined by the existence of passages of sympotic poetry which explicitly prescribe the appropriate behaviour for this all-important social gathering. We have already encountered the slightly smug ideal symposiast of Euenus; to him we can add the celebrated first fragment of Xenophanes, which begins by describing the ideal setting and ambience, and then prescribes the appropriate limit of drinking and content of conversation and poetry, banning strife and conflict whether mythical or historical. An anonymous elegiac fragment similarly lays out correct principles: 'Hail, fellow drinkers, age-mates: from this happy start I'll bring my discourse to a happy end. When friends forgather for occasions such as this, we ought to laugh and joke in high-class style, enjoy each other's company, make silly chat and banter such as fosters merriment. The serious talk should follow, with each speaker heard in turn: that's what symposiums are for. But let's be guided by the MC (in the Greek, τοῦ ... ποταρχοῦντος): that's what fine fellows must do, and show their eloquence' (Adesp. el. 27, tr. West). Fragment 6 of Critias is more narrowly concerned with the proper size of cups and the right amount to drink, and with propagandising for the virtues of Spartan society, but there is still a concern with the implications for appropriate behaviour and the aims of the symposium.

The role of the symposium and sympotic behaviour is beautifully brought out in one of the classic texts for the oligarchic ideal, Herodotus' account of the wooing of Agariste. Once their pedigrees had been vetted, Cleisthenes of Sicyon made trial of the suitors for his daughter's hand by testing their *andragathia*, character, education and manners through interaction with each, both individually and all together. The younger men had the chance to strut their stuff in the gymnasium, specially constructed for the occasion, but the key test lay in commensality: καὶ τό γε μέγιστον, ἐν τῇ συνεστοῖ διεπειρᾶτο.[26] After the lavish feast on the day of decision, the suitors competed in music and speaking in company: ἔριν εἶχον ἀμφί τε μουσικῇ καὶ τῷ λεγομένῳ ἐς τὸ μέσον. And it was here that the favourite, Hippocleides, famously blew his lead and his chances by inappropriate dancing. Herodotus nicely traces the stages of Cleisthenes' disillusionment: after the first round of dancing he has misgivings, after the Spartan and Attic table-dances he has written him out of the running, but it is only under the extreme provocation of Hippocleides' dancing on his head that his dismay gets the better of his self-restraint and he bursts out with 'Son of Teisander, you have danced away your marriage!' It is a nice coda to the story that the response, 'Hippocleides doesn't care' was so celebrated that it became proverbial in itself.[27]

There is a revealing contrast in the behaviour of the über-aristocrat Alcibiades. Plutarch describes how in his first exile from Athens he astonished the Spartans by assimilating himself completely to the Laconian way of life; he goes on to describe how Alcibiades' capacity to

---

[25] Lissarrague (1990: 47-67, esp. 47-52) for trick cups, on which n.b. also Kilinski (1986). Neer (2002: chs.1-2) elaborates a wider argument based on parallels between *poikilia* and riddles in the symposium and forms of visual ambiguity and paradox on sympotic vases, while Levine (1985) sees the symposium as 'a microcosm of the state' (194) in Theognis.

[26] So evidently the code continued to apply and to be policed beyond adolescence, at least on occasions when the assessment of men's character was important.

[27] Hdt. 6.126-129; Hermipp. fr. 16 KA, cited by late lexicographers as proverbial.

adapt to the lifestyle of whoever he was with outdid even the capabilities of the chameleon: chameleons cannot turn themselves to the pure white of paper, but for Alcibiades there were no limits. 'In Sparta he took exercise, lived frugally, and wore a frown on his face; in Ionia he was fastidious, companionable and easy-living; in Thrace he went in for hard drinking and hard riding; when he was with the satrap Tissaphernes he outdid the Persians, for all their magnificence, with his pomp and extravagance' (*Alc.* 23.3-6, tr. Waterfield). In all these elite environments with their differing requirements, he was able to fit in, not, as Plutarch goes on to say, by changing his fundamental nature, but by a deliberate alteration of the external impression he projected. If Alcibiades did have problems fitting in – and Plutarch follows up by narrating his alleged adultery with Timaea, wife of King Agis – they were not caused by an inability to present himself as whatever kind of gentleman was required at the time.

Our sources thus make it clear what the code was, and how it functioned; but how could aspiring members of this group learn to negotiate all its complexity and fluidity? How ought one to respond, for example, when one is told 'we're not barring you from partying (κωμάζειν), and we're not inviting you: you're welcome if you're here and a friend when you're absent' (Thgn. 1207-1208)? The answer Theognis gives us is, by association with those who already know: the *agathoi*, who are *sophoi* – and who, as we have seen, are also few in number. A passage early in the corpus (31-38) is programmatic:

> ταῦτα μὲν οὕτως ἴσθι· κακοῖσι δὲ μὴ προσομίλει
>   ἀνδράσιν, ἀλλ' αἰεὶ τῶν ἀγαθῶν ἔχεο·
> καὶ μετὰ τοῖσιν πῖνε καὶ ἔσθιε, καὶ μετὰ τοῖσιν
>   ἵζε, καὶ ἄνδανε τοῖς, ὧν μεγάλη δύναμις.
> ἐσθλῶν μὲν γὰρ ἄπ' ἐσθλὰ μαθήσεαι· ἢν δὲ κακοῖσι
>   συμμίσγηις, ἀπολεῖς καὶ τὸν ἐόντα νόον.
> ταῦτα μαθὼν ἀγαθοῖσιν ὁμίλει, καί ποτε φήσεις
>   εὖ συμβουλεύειν τοῖσι φίλοισιν ἐμέ.

Good men will teach you how to be good, and only from them can you learn this. Theognis returns to the point with variations later on: sit by an *esthlos* and take home his wise sayings as profit (563-566), the bad are not bad at birth, they develop that way from bad company (305-308), bad company has bad consequences (1169-1170). Always what matters is the immediate company you keep: Theognis and his ilk would simply have laughed at the proposition of the rather less elitist Simonides (fr. 15 W) that 'the *polis* teaches a man'.

What we have observed, then, was an unstated, subtle and elusive code of behaviour, though one both coherent and consistent with the broader aristocratic ideal, which required conformity to the shifting expectations of the established elite, and which could only be mastered by an apprenticeship in which the aspirant could be trained to fit in through socialisation: the oligarchic ideal was a beautifully constructed exclusionary code, both defined and policed by the virtuous few.

Bibliography

Braswell, B.K. 1998. *A commentary on Pindar Nemean Nine*. Berlin-New York: de Gruyter.

Debnar, P. 2001. *Speaking the same language: speech and audience in Thucydides' Spartan debates*. Ann Arbor: University of Michigan Press.

Donlan, W. 1978. Social vocabulary and its relationship to political propaganda in fifth-century Athens. *Quaderni Urbinati Di Cultura Classica* 27: 95-111.

Donlan, W. 1980. *The aristocratic ideal in ancient Greece*. Lawrence, KS: Coronado.

Donlan, W. 1985. *Pistos philos hetairos*, in T.J. Figueira and G. Nagy (eds) *Theognis of Megara: poetry and the polis*: 223-244. Baltimore: Johns Hopkins UP.

Dover, K.J. 1974. *Greek popular morality*. Oxford: Blackwell.

Dunbar, N. 1995. *Aristophanes Birds*. Oxford: OUP.

Edmunds, L. 1975. Thucydides' ethics as reflected in the description of stasis (3.82-83). *Harvard Studies in Classical Philology* 79: 73-92.

Garcia Soler, M.J. 2010. La consommation du vin en Grèce ancienne: idealisation et réalité. *Ktèma* 35: 39-49.

Grossmann, G. 1950. *Politische Schlagwörter aus der Zeit des Peloponnesischen Krieges*. Zurich: Leemann.

Harvey, F.D. 1965. Two types of equality. *Classica et Mediaevalia* 26: 101-46

Kilinski, K. 1986. Boeotian trick vases. *American Journal of Archaeology* 90: 153-158.

Lane Fox, R. 2000. Theognis: an alternative to democracy, in R. Brock and S. Hodkinson (eds) *Alternatives to Athens*: 35-51. Oxford: OUP.

Lelli, E. 2006. *Volpe e leone: il proverbio nella poesia greca: Alceo, Cratino, Callimaco*. Rome: Edizioni dell'Ateneo.

Levine, D.B. 1985. Symposium and the *polis*, in T.J. Figueira and G. Nagy (eds) *Theognis of Megara: poetry and the polis*: 176-196. Baltimore: Johns Hopkins UP.

Lintott, A. 1982. *Violence, civil strife and revolution in the classical city*. London: Croom Helm.

Lissarrague, F. 1990. *The aesthetics of the Greek banquet*. Princeton: Princeton UP.

MacDowell, D.M. 1971. *Aristophanes Wasps*. Oxford: OUP.

Marr, J.L. and Rhodes, P.J. 2008. *The Old Oligarch: the constitution of the Athenians attributed to Xenophon*. Oxford: Oxbow.

Nagy, G. 1985. Theognis and Megara: a poet's vision of his city. in T.J. Figueira and G. Nagy (eds) *Theognis of Megara: poetry and the polis*: 22-81. Baltimore: Johns Hopkins UP.

Neer, R.T. 2002. *Style and politics in Athenian vase-painting*. Cambridge: CUP.

Neil, R.A. 1901. *The Knights of Aristophanes*. Cambridge: CUP.

North, H. 1966. *Sophrosyne*. Ithaca NY: Cornell UP.

Pfeijffer, I.L. 1999. *Three Aeginetan Odes of Pindar*. Leiden: Brill.

Pütz, B. 2007. *The symposium and komos in Aristophanes*. Oxford: Oxbow.

Raaflaub, K. 2004. *The discovery of freedom in ancient Greece*. Chicago: University of Chicago Press.

Rhodes, P.J. 2000. Oligarchs in Athens, in R. Brock and S. Hodkinson (eds) *Alternatives to Athens*: 119-136. Oxford: OUP.

Rhodes, P.J. 2005. Democracy and its opponents in fourth-century Athens, in U. Bultrighini (ed.) *Democrazia e antidemocrazia nel mondo Greco*: 275-289. Alessandria: Edizioni dell'Orso.

Swift, L.A. 2012. Archilochus the 'anti-hero'? Heroism, flight and values in Homer and the new Archilochus fragment (*P.Oxy.LXIX* 4708). *Journal of Hellenic Studies* 132: 139-155.

van Wees, H. 2000. Megara's mafiosi: timocracy and violence in Theognis, in R. Brock and S. Hodkinson (eds) *Alternatives to Athens*: 52-67. Oxford: OUP.

Whibley, L. 1896. *Greek oligarchies: their character and organisation*. London: Methuen.

The Greek Polis and the Tyrant in the Archaic Age: Some Trends in the Relationship Between the Emergence of Tyranny and the Evolution of Political Community[1]

Aitor Luz Villafranca

Universidad Autónoma de Madrid
aitor.luz@uam.es

Abstract

Scholarly attention has recently returned to the consideration of ancient Greek tyranny, nuancing the traditional image provided by authors such as Mossé. The image of the tyrant as a political anomaly has been modified with the aim of integrating it into the development of Greek politics. In this sense, the main purpose of this article is to substantiate the occurrence of archaic tyranny in the consolidation of civil consciousness and citizenship of the Greek *poleis*, for which we are going to follow the line of revision initiated by Anderson (2005) and Stein-Hölkeskamp (2009). This chapter considers the role of tyranny in the transformations of archaic aristocratic polis systems, as well as the emergence of the motif of the monstrous tyrant as a tool used by the closed oligarchies.

Keywords
Archaic tyranny, *basileus*, *polis*, citizenship, demagogue, civic consciousness

Introduction

The traditional impression of archaic tyranny is that it was a destructive force that swept away the *polis* system.[2] Ancient sources concerning archaic tyranny are a good deal more varied than this traditional picture would suggest, in particular, sources from Herodotus onwards tended to be extremely hostile, generating a series of clichés that include the manipulation of the *demos*, the persecution of aristocrats, the application of excessive violence, and, in short, of a *hybris* that threatened to destroy the city.[3] To a large extent, the written sources emphasize

---

[1] I thank the editors for the invitation to participate in this volume honouring Peter Rhodes and to attend the conference in Portugal to celebrate Peter's eightieth birthday in 2020. Sadly, that meeting had to be cancelled because of covid. The editors asked for essays that reflect Peter's work and influence. Since he has managed to have an impact on practically all aspects of Greek history and politics, finding a topic on which to present fresh insights and appeal to him is not that easy. Hence the topic of this essay, which, like his work and life, were anchored in doing the right thing.

[2] On the Asian origin as the most widespread explanation of the origins of the lexical family tyrann-, see Koîv 2016: 17-18; Oliva 1982: 363. However, some authors such as Parker (2005: 147-149) have argued that the derivation from the luwian *tarwanis* is excessively complicated, as opposed to the possible Philistine root of the term. Therefore, this author considers that it is a term of Balkan origin that arrives in Greece during the Dark Age, when the Philistines settled in the historical region of the same name.

[3] The negative clichés of the paradigm of tyranny can be seen in Luraghi 2013; 2018. In this regard, Parker (1998: 145-172) has pointed out that in some of the passages of Greek literature, the term 'tyranny' is given a non-pejorative connotation. Dewald's (2003: 25-59) and Levy's (1993: 7-19) studies of the uses of 'tyranny' and *basileia* in Herodotus are extremely interesting. On the uses of tyranny in 4th century BC theorists, see Azoulay 2012: 337-370; Forsdyke 2009: 241-245; Luraghi 2018: 13-17.

the illegitimacy of tyranny. This illegitimacy is derived from two fundamental points: violent access to power through a military coup and questionable continuation in power through violence. Through these testimonies from Greek sources, a large part of the scholarship was satisfied with explaining tyranny as an autocratic phenomenon alien to the polis and largely destructive of it, that is, a violent regime opposed to the idea of a political community (Catenacci 2009: 22-24; Luraghi 2018).

For this reason, scholarship has looked for socioeconomic explanations that deepen the understanding of the emergence of tyranny in the culture of the polis. For example, the recent categorizations of the archaic tyrant as a 'demagogue tyrant',[4] a 'merchant prince',[5] or a 'warlord'[6] well reflect this socioeconomic trend. All these paradigms, however, were based on Aristotle's theorizations, and represent tyranny as a regime alien to the politics of the archaic polis and employing pre-political or apolitical methods. That said, some scholars, like Anderson (2005) or Stein-Holkeskamp (2009), have promoted an understanding of tyranny according to the canons of competition of archaic aristocracies. In this light, the current chapter analyzes the implications of tyrants' policies in the building of civic consciousness in the polis.

The tyrant and the citizenship system

Archaic tyrants have traditionally been seen to have disrupted the constitutional system of the polis by establishing a one-man government. The greatest example of this attitude is exemplified by the advice of Thrasybulus to Periander to 'cut off the heads of all the aristocrats' (Hdt. 5.92). Most of the sources testify that the tyrants ('allegedly') initiated a persecution against the *aristoi* and established a system staffed by their supporters. Related to the destruction of the polis framework, there is a proliferation of scenes in which the tyrant, after winning the favor of the assembly of citizens, allegedly dissolved and left it without any capacity of representation.[7] In short, the testimonies of classical literature reflect a regime which employs systematic violence through a professional corps of mercenaries, as well as the nullification of the citizen will and its methods of expression.[8]

However, the topic of tyrannical violence against citizens should be taken with a grain of salt as sometimes a discursive tool. Despite the widespread stereotype, it seems that not all the tyrants extensively modified the political framework that underpinned the functioning of the city-state. The Athenian sources, which are not suspected of arguing for tyranny, nonetheless

---

[4] The figure of the demagogue tyrant focused on the figure of Peisistratos. Accordingly, it has been considered that this tyrant builds his *arche* through the attainment of popular favor (Mossé 1969: 3-87).

[5] This theory arises from Thucydides' differentiation (1.13) between *basileia*, based on time, and tyranny, based on money. The paradigm of the 'merchant prince' was proposed by Ure (1922). This theory relates the rise of tyranny to the economic development and market opening of some cities (Fleck and Hansen 2013: 397).

[6] This paradigm considers that tyranny is only sustained through the use of private military force. In particular, certain authors adduced the use of mercenary forces in order to maintain their power in the polis, as in the case of Theagenes of Megara (Arist. *Rh.* 1.2.19) or of Peisistratos himself. In this regard, some have linked the origin of the minting of coins by tyrants with the hiring of mercenaries (cf. Trundle 2004: 5).

[7] In these passages, the tyrant is credited with using *metis* to rally the people, seize their arms and suspend the civic system (Trundle 2004: 5). Some examples of the disarmament of the *demos* are found in the passage of Aristodemos of Cumae (D.H. 7.7-8) or in the case of Peisistratos (Arist. *Ath.* 14.1; Hdt. 1.59).

[8] The stereotypes of violence in the tyrant's discourse are analyzed in Luraghi 2018: 19-21.

even generate the image of a judicious and law-abiding Peisistratos[9]. This impression from written sources has been corroborated from study of the list of archons of the 20s of the 6th century, where individuals belonging to both the Philaids and the Alcmaeonids achieved the highest magistracy of the state during the government of Peisistratids.[10] In turn, some tyrants cultivated a policy of intra- and inter-community alliances both with members of the elites and the *demos*, so that it does not seem that there was excessive reluctance in dealing with these 'autocrats'.[11] Consequently, it cannot be concluded that the methods, both coercive and alliance-based, employed by the tyrant differed greatly from the existing aristocratic system of the *polis*, as Anderson (2005: 185-190) or Lavelle (2005: 87-89) have pointed out in the case of the Alcmaeonids. It is not conceivable that tyranny is sustained only through the use of armed force since the sources describe contingents of soldiers employed by the tyrants as small in size. Tyrants, like aristocrats, use coercion, but also *philia* (friendship) and *megaloprepeia* (munificence) to sustain their power.

Therefore, some scholars have assumed that some tyrants carried out reforms in the *politeia* intending to consolidate their power. The passages concerning the modification of the tribes by Cleisthenes of Sicyon (Hdt. 5.67-68), as well as the naturalization of citizens by Peisistratos,[12] have been taken as evidence of a generalized manipulation of the citizenship system exercised by the tyrants to favor their permanence in power through the modification of the *politeia*. However, it is necessary to reconsider this image about tyrannical reforms of the civic system. First of all, the tyrants' political restructuration in terms of citizenship is greatly obscured in the sources. The reform of the *politeia* must be understood as a political tool available not only to the tyrants but also to the aristocratic *polis* to address its internal problems, generally sanctioned in a sacral manner.[13] The government of the polis in the Greek archaic age itself undertook reforms of the civic system to address the crisis of the city, as Solon's case demonstrates.[14] It must be admitted that the lack of stable peer rivalry in the

---

[9] Herodotus tells us that Peisistratos maintained the *thesmia* (1.59), while Thucydides speaks of laws established by him (Thuc. 6.54). In turn, Peisistratos seems to have created the image of a close link between himself and the legislator Solon, despite the latter's campaign to prevent the imposition of tyranny in Athens (Leão 2008: 162). On the relationship between Solon and Peisistratos, see Leão 2008.

[10] Numerous authors admit the presence of Cleisthenes and Miltiades in the list of archons (*IG*3.1031a) corresponding to the years 525/524 (Anderson 2005: 200-201; Plommer 1969; Valdés 2012: 336). However, Dillon (2006: 93-99) takes a position in favor of not identifying this Cleisthenes with the rival of Isagoras in 508/507.

[11] One of the most obvious cases is found in the marriage of Agariste, daughter of Cleisthenes of Sicyon (Hdt. 6.126-130). Herodotus reveals that young men of the Greek aristocratic classes concur to ask for the hand of the tyrant's daughter. In addition, there is evidence of a presumed matrimonial alliance between the Alcmeonid Megacles II and Peisistratos. On the extra- and intra-community relations with the elite (*xenia*, marriage...) of the tyrants, see Sierra 2014: 62-71; Taylor 2017: 190-194. In any case, tyranny, like any type of elite, tends to its self-perpetuation in which it employs methods of diverse character, from the alliance with the previous elite to its expulsion from the city.

[12] Aristotle (Arist. *Ath*.13.4–5) tells us of a *diapsephimos* carried out just after the expulsion of the tyrants with the aim of determining the citizens of 'impure origin' (*hoi to genei me katharoi*).

[13] Forsdyke (2011: 150-151) has suggestively proposed that the tribes established by Cleisthenes of Sicyon are actually the original *phylai* of the city, which have a local component. The original tribes would be modified by the three Dorians in the late 6th century by the aristocracy of Sicyon in an attempt to associate themselves more obviously with the Peloponnesian states.

[14] One of the mechanisms to solve the political crisis in the archaic age is the change of citizen ascription systems. In these processes, the action of the first legislators should be included. There is a very close association between the figure of the legislator and that of the tyrant in the archaic sources (Parker 2007: 36-37), and even Pythagoras and Periander are included among the Seven Sages of Greece. The best documented case of restructuring of the citizenship system to face a crisis in the city is shown in the case of Solon. Solon's legislation (Arist. *Ath.* 7) shows us the restitution of citizenship to numerous Athenians who had lost their status (Domínguez Monedero 2001: 60-62;

tyrants favors the change of the civic ascription system that is oriented in two directions, one vertical and the other horizontal. Solon's (Arist. *Ath.* 7) poems show us that a large part of the *demos* lacked legal rights and economic protections (Anderson 2005: 177-180; Dmitriev 2018: 131-132; Foxhall 1997: Gomes 2007: 23-32). The reform of the *politeia* by the tyrants does not venture so much into the exclusion of the already existing citizens, but into their redistribution to include elements not inserted in the civic corpus through processes of citizen naturalization[15]. Through this restructuring of the *politeia*, the tyrant gains the support of a *demos* with heterogeneous sectors but especially manages to break some of the client structures and local loyalties typical of peer competition of archaic aristocracies. Despite the scarce evidence in our sources, it can be understood that tyranny implies a centralization, but also a policy of resignification of the concept of citizenship (especially lower class or sub-hoplitic citizenship) to limit the aristocratic networks of power, although the degree of its action varies in each *polis* (Sierra 2014: 72).

In conclusion, the redistribution of systems of civic ascription constitutes a political tool used by the elites of the archaic Greek world in their attempts to build socio-economic control over the *polis*. As has been emphasized, the tyrants did not prefigure or seek to endow the *demos* with political participation of which it was devoid but simply employed administrative redistribution as a means of restructuring the spheres of influence in the *polis* environment (Gomes 2007). Throughout this section, it has become clear that tyranny, like previous aristocracies, developed a policy of self-preservation based on coercion, alliances, and administrative reforms. However, one of the most useful mechanisms for tyrants was the rationalizing centralization of civic elements around a central pivot, restricting the personal ties of the *gene* concerning the civic body.

The tyrant demagogue: *demos* and tyrannical politics

One of the elements traditionally assigned to the establishment of the tyrant in power is the decisive intervention of the *demos* (Cawkwell 1995: 85-86). However, it is not easy to document large-scale constitutional changes in the politics of tyrants, nor to determine the rights of the citizens below the elites. It has been widely recognized that archaic citizenship was not only a juridical notion (formalist position) but also a series of informal elements of belonging (Blok 2018; Duplouy 2018). In this sense, the tyrants developed a policy of 'public' spending from which the community as a whole benefited. Aristotle (*Pol.*1313b.29-35) explains the constructive policy on the part of the Greek tyrants as a manipulation of the popular masses, as well as a desire to employ a good part of the impoverished classes. Thus, the strategy of investment in infrastructures was attributed in ancient sources to the sole objective of manipulating the conscience of the *demos* for their benefit. Some authors have proposed that the tyrant acts like a 'big man' whose source of power lies in the constant public squandering of his wealth (Hall 2014: 144-152). However, the 'big man' is not a figure that bears such enormous similarities to the figure of the tyrant.[16] It is more accurate to envisage the tyrant

---

Valdés 2012: 332). On the uses of *politeia* and the naturalization of citizens in Solonian and post-Solonian Athens, see Dmitriev 2018: 181-190.

[15] Aristotle (Arist. *Pol.* 3.3.5, 1278a.30–35) recognizes that any regime makes concessions of *politeia* by decree in the case of necessity.

[16] Gygax (2016: 103-106) analyzes the similarities and differences between the figure of the 'big man' and the tyrant regarding generosity practices. The 'big man' is forced to squander his wealth to obtain status as the only way that

as developing policies of generosity and sumptuousness implicit in the relations between an elite charged with all the political power and a *demos* devoid of it (Anderson 2005: 192-193; Gygax 2016: 96-99). Moreover, it should not be underestimated that, behind the *topos* of the tyrant's enormous economic fortune, there is a centralization of the economic resources of the *polis* (Gomes 2007: 104-107).

One *leitmotif* of tyranny is the development of civil infrastructures, especially those related to the building of ports and water pipes. Among the infrastructures that favored maritime trade stands out the construction of the port of Samos by Polycrates (Hdt. 3.60) and the *diolkos* (D.L. 1.99), attributed to Periander. Also, the sources refer to the intensification of the tyrants in terms of the construction of water supply structures for the citizens.[17] Given the difficulty of massive distribution of land (*ges anadasmos*) in the city itself, as Solon's case demonstrates (Sagstetter 2013: 155), several tyrants developed a policy of economic intensification of sectors not covered by the aristocracy. Thus, craftwork or trade were promoted as ways to increase the economic possibilities of the *demos*. Through economic diversification, not only were the conditions of the non-landed people improved, but so too were the ties of the landed aristocracy weakened.

Numerous sources inform us of the construction of lavish temples dedicated to the divinities of the *polis*. Some outstanding examples are the Heraion of Samos (Hdt. 3.60) or the temple of the twelve Olympian gods (Thuc. 6.54) and the Olympieion (Arist. *Pol.* 1313b 23) by Peisistratos. In turn, the excavations in Corinth have shown us the importance of the sanctuaries erected by the Cypselids, among which it is necessary to underline the development of the central area of the agora (Dubbini 2016: 57-61).[18] Ultimately, the religious shrines are part of the importance of cults as elements of belonging, construction, expression, and manipulation of civic ideology. Tyrants obtained an excess of time over their opponents by embellishing the symbol of the communion of the civic community with the sacred sphere (Domínguez Monedero 1997: 85-86; Gygax 2016: 96 ss.).

In this process of attracting the *demos* and attaching civic consciousness, religious festivities also played a fundamental role, in which the tyrants seem to have excelled. In this regard, the case of Cleisthenes of Sicyon has been especially highlighted regarding the modification of the cults by the tyranny. Herodotus informs us of the change of the civic hero Adrastus for Melanippus while revealing the prohibition of recitation of Homeric poems (5.67-68). In the case of Peisistratos, the sources underline his use of a girl to disguise her as the goddess Athena (Hdt. 1.60) as well as the special interest in the reconfiguration of the *Panathenaia* (Thuc. 6.56-8) or the development of the Dionysian choruses (Valdés Guía 2012: 336).[19] Consequently, the

---

justifies his position. In the case of the tyrant, he possesses a military force that allows his establishment in power. Moreover, the tyrant can reinforce the hereditary character of his power. In the case of the Peisistratids, the tyrant not only squanders wealth, but can subject the *polis* to taxation (Gomes 2007: 106-107).

[17] The role of tyrants in the erection of water supply infrastructure is analyzed in Angelakis et al. 2012: 262-265. Among the most outstanding works, the tunnel of Eupalinus, erected by Polycrates of Samos (Hdt. 3.60), the fountain of Enneakrounoi by Peisistratos (Thuc. 2.15.5), the aqueduct of Naxos by Lygdamis, or the fountain of Peirene, in Corinth, should be mentioned.

[18] A compilation of the main temples built by the tyrants can be found at Domínguez Monedero 1997: 81- 127.

[19] There is a detailed discussion of the writing down of the Homeric poems by Peisistratos and his sons (Andersen 2011; Davison 1955; Finkelberg; 2017). Davison (1955: 15-21) and other authors have considered the establishment of a standard Homeric text carried out in the time of Peisistratos to be no more than a reinvention by the Pergamon school. However, along with Andersen (2011: 669) and Filkenberg (2017: 36-38) we concur that, although there are

Plommer, W.H. 1969. The Tyranny of the Archon List. *The Classical Review* 19/2: 126-129.

Raaflaub, K., Wallace, R. 2007. "People's Power" and Egalitarian Trends in Archaic Greece, in K. Raaflaub, J. Ober and R. Wallace (eds*) Origins of democracy in Ancient Greece*: 22-49. Berkeley, Los Angeles, London: University of California Press.

Raaflaub, K. 2013. Archaic and Classical Greek Reflections on Politics and Government, in H. Beck (ed.) *A Companion to Greek Government*: 73-93. London: Wiley Blackwell.

Salmon, J.B. 1997. Lopping off the Heads? Tyrants, Politics and the polis, in L. Mitchell, P.J. Rhodes (eds) *The Development of the Polis in Archaic Greece*: 60–73. London – New York: Routledge.

Sierra, C. 2014. La 'edad de los tiranos': una aproximación a las ambigüedades de la tiranía arcaica. *Gerión* 32: 57-77.

Sagstetter, K.S. 2013. Solon of Athens: The man, the Mith, the Tyrant? Unpublished PhD dissertation, University of Pennsylvania.

Stein-Hölkeskamp, E. 2009. The Tyrants, in K. Raaflaub, and H. van Wees (eds) *A Companion to Archaic Greece*: 100–116. Malden, Oxford, Chichester: Blackwell.

Taylor, J. R. F. 2017. Ancient Greek Tyranny: A New Phenomenon or a New Name for an Old Phenomenon? Unpublished PhD dissertation, Durham University.

Trundle, M. 2004. *Greek Mercenaries: From the Late Archaic Period to Alexander*. London-New York: Routledge.

Valdés Guía, M. 2012. *La formación de Atenas. Gestación, nacimiento y desarrollo de una polis (1200/1100 - 600 a.C.)*. Zaragoza: Pórtico.

Van Wees, H. 2000. Megara's mafiosi: timocracy and violence in Theognis, in R. Brock y S. Hodkinson, (eds) *Alternatives to Athens. Varieties of Political Organization and Community in Ancient Greece*: 52-67. Oxford: Oxford University Press.

A Tale of Two Cities: Studies in Greek Border Politics[1]

Lynette Mitchell

University of Exeter
l.g.mitchell@exeter.ac.uk

Abstract
In the fifth century both the Athenians and the Thebans struggled to take control of the mountainous border zone between the geographical regions of Attica and Boeotia. The cities there responded differently to the pressures of living in a war zone. Plataea and Tanagra, in particular, adopted different strategies for living in this border region. Plataea decided to ally themselves to Athens, while Tanagra remained Theban-facing, both to their cost. This chapter will consider how these two cities managed living in these borderlands as a way of understanding border identities and border politics in a Greek context more generally.

Keywords
Attica, Boeotia, Plataea, Tanagra, border politics

The mountain chain of Cithaeron and Parnes, stretching from the Corinthian Gulf to the Euboean Gulf, marked the boundary between Attica and Boeotia, at least in a geographical sense. For most of the fifth century this was a region of heightened tensions, as Thebes and Athens battled for control: Athens because dominance in Boeotia was something they desired as a route to fixing their influence in central Greece and Euboea, and Thebes because it allowed them to puncture Athenian interests and enhance their own political aspirations in what was to become, in the middle of the fifth century, the Boeotian *koinon*.

In this conflict between the competing interests of Athens and Thebes, the region between the gulfs, and between Attica and Boeotia, became a war zone. Most of the cities in the border zone were very small and were easily controlled by these larger cities at different times (whether forcibly or not), but two stand out for their very different responses: Plataea and Tanagra. While there has been extensive discussion of both cities individually, and their relations with their more powerful neighbours, they have never been considered together as part of the same border region. The way they managed the politics of the border zones was very different from each other, but also instructive for seeing what life in borderlands in a Greek context could be about.

We will begin this chapter by looking in more general terms at the border between Boeotia and Attica, and the language of border politics. We will then turn attention more specifically

---

[1] I would like to thank the editors for the invitation to contribute to this volume in honour of PJR. Peter has taught me much about Greek history and politics, and has continued to do so, over the many years of our friendship, not only about the practicalities of Greek politics, but also its psychology. He has often pushed me to explore further the limits of my thinking! It is with this in mind that I wish to take him to the border zone between Attica and Boeotia in the fifth century BC, and I offer him this chapter as my gift on the occasion of his 80-ish birthday. I also wish to give many thanks to kind friends who have read this chapter and made many important improvements: Neville Morley, Robin Osborne, Samuel Gartland, Greg Stanton and Peter Rhodes himself.

to consideration of the border politics of two cities (Plataea and Tanagra), and the way that they needed to play with their 'in-betweenness' in Boeotia and Attica, and finally look at what this tells us about border politics in the Greek world.

The border between Boeotia and Attica

Defining the limits of territorial control was important in Greek international relations.[2] Particularly at times of heightened political tensions, to transgress a border without permission could be seen as an act of aggression, and it was generally necessary at least to request permission before crossing another city's territory with an army.[3] Thucydides says, in the context of the Archidamian War, that all Greeks had come to regard crossing a neighbours' territory without permission as suspicious, so that, when the Spartan Brasidas wanted to travel north through Thessaly in 425 BC, he needed to summon his *xenoi* from Pharsalus to escort him, and even then their support was grudging and the crossing difficult (Th. 4.78).

However, this trenchancy about borders assumed that they were clear. Borders were often defined by natural features, such as rivers and mountains, although other physical markers, such as *horoi* ('boundary stones'), could also be used to mark territorial limits of various kinds. Pausanias, for example, says that Mount Parnon formed the border between Laconia, Tegea and Argos, and that in his time there were stone statues of Hermes on the borders to mark it (2.38.7). Likewise, Herodotus says that there was an inscribed stele set up by Croesus to define the border between Lydia and Phrygia on the River Halys (7.30.2; cf. 1.6.1, 28.1. 72.1, 103.2, 130.1), which remained an important fortified border-crossing (*ta oura*) under the Persians (Hdt. 5.52.1-2).

Nevertheless, the border between Attica and Boeotia, defined only in general terms by the mountain chain of Cithaeron and Parnes, was not always clearly articulated so that the whole region of the mountains and the corridor to the north of them running from one gulf to the other became a region of considerable contestation. To the north of the mountains, Ephorus says that the cities were of mixed descent (*summiktoi esan pallachothen: BNJ* 70 F 21) and were called the *Thebageneis*,[4] who seem to have been united not only by their proximity but also by a ritual whereby they dedicated a golden tripod at the Ismenion in Thebes (*Schol. Pind. Pyth.* 11.5).[5] They do seem to have been a diverse group of peoples, and Buck even suggests some of them (especially Hysiae and Eleutherae) may, like the people of Oropus, have spoken a non-Attic dialect of Ionian.[6] It is almost certain that this was the small group of cities along

---

[2] Cf. Raaflaub (1997: 52-53); cf. Ober (1995: 999). The main treatment of borders in the Greek world is that of Daverio Rocchi (1988).

[3] See Mosley (2007).

[4] On the etymology of the name, Mackil (2013: 186 n. 157) accepts that given by Ephorus (they were called *Thebageneis* because they were 'added to' the Thebans), although Hansen (2011) is sceptical.

[5] Mackil (2013: 185-188) argues that this was an early attempt by the Thebans to enforce political control of the cities in the borderland through the ritual giving of tripods by the *Thebageneis* at the sanctuary of Apollo Ismenios at Thebes.

[6] Buck (1968: 269-270). Buck suggests that there is evidence for the same non-Attic Ionic at Hysiae and Eleutherae, and that 'a good case can be made for believing that at least the whole Asopus valley spoke Ionic to a late date, and at Oropus it survived latest'.

either side of the Asopus (perhaps including Plataea) that formed a *sympoliteia* as part of the Boeotian *koinon* in 446 (*Hell. Oxyrh.* 19.3).[7] We will have more to say on that below.

The limits of Attica extended to the south of these mountains, from Oenoe, which Herodotus says was at the furthest edge of Attica (Hdt. 5.74), and Thucydides (2.18.2) says was in the *methoria ge* of Attica and Boeotia, in the 'borderland'.[8] Thucydides also says Oenoe was fortified, suggesting their aggression (or fear of an aggressive response) in occupying land that should have either been 'empty' or shared. In 422 the Athenian fort of Panactum, which was *en methoriois*, was seized by the Boeotians (Th. 5.3.5). Under the terms of the Peace of Nicias it was agreed that it should be returned to the Athenians (5.18.7; cf. 35), and it became a bargaining tool for the return of Pylos (5.36.2, 39.3, 44.3). However, the Boeotians demolished the fort the Athenians had built there on the grounds that there was an ancient agreement that this land would not be occupied but would be cultivated in common by the Athenians and Boeotians (5.42.1).[9] On this basis the building of the fort was itself an act of aggression in attempting to control this 'common land'.[10] On the other hand, these border cities were vulnerable to attack by invading Boeotians. In 506, as part of the joint effort with the Spartan Cleomenes, the Boeotians took Oenoe and Phyle (cf. Hdt. 5.74).[11] In this context it is useful to note that while on the southern side of the Cithaeron/Parnes chain Oenoe, Phyle and Deceleia were demes, a number of the border settlements, such as Panactum, were not.[12]

Further, the borders of Attica were sometimes defined in other, more fluid, terms. The Athenian ephebic oath defined the 'boundaries (*horoi*) of the fatherland' not in territorial terms, but as agricultural produce: wheat, barley, vines, olives, figs (RO 88.19-21). Ober thinks this list probably refers metaphorically to actual stone *horoi*, marking the limits of Attica.[13] However, a more literal reading is also possible, especially as the ephebes also swear to extend the fatherland (RO 88.8-11). Such a reading perhaps gives context to these fortifications within the *methoria ge*: the building of these fortifications was deliberate and aggressive colonialist activity to extend the control of the state over the resources in the borderland. The politics of the borderlands between Attica and Boeotia were not just – or only – about political control of territory for its own sake, but also about access to resources. The point has been well made that fortifications are not always (or only) about controlling access to routes and roads, but

---

[7] This *sympoliteia* included Scolus whose location was probably north of the Asopus River within Theban territory; on the location of Scolus to the north of the river, see Fossey (1988: 119-26); Hansen (*IACP* 452).

[8] Borders were also not always contiguous – there was often a 'borderland', a strip of land 'between the borders' (*methorios*) which did not clearly belong to anyone, and seems to have worked as a kind of 'common land', but could become the focus of conflict. Thucydides says that the Thyreatis/Cynouria was the *methoria* of Argos and Laconia (Th. 2.27.1, 4.56.2), but in 431 the Spartans gave land there to Aeginetans displaced by the Athenians, although they later made terms regarding it in 420 as part of their treaty with Argos (Th. 5.20). This land could be 'empty'/'unhabited' (*eremos*): Thucydides says that Mount Cercines in the *methorion* between the Sintians and Paeonians was *eremon* (Th. 2.98.1). Much of the confusion at the battle of Delium in 424 rested on doubts about the limits of Athenian controlled Oropia.

[9] Demosthenes in the fourth century mentions a campaign to secure Drymus and Panactum (19.326); Aristotle says that Drymus was 'sometimes Attic and other times Boeotian' (Arist. F 612 Rose). Ober (1985: 225) identifies the Skourta plain as the region of Drymus; cf. Daverio Rochhi (1988: 182-183).

[10] Munn (2010: 189-200).

[11] Herodotus says that the 'demes' taken were Oenoe and Hysiae, although a Theban dedication of a kioniskos indicates that it was actually Oenoe and Phyle: Mackil (2013: 188-189, 412-414).

[12] Whitehead (1986: 402).

[13] Ober (1995: 104-111).

also about controlling access to land for grazing or agriculture, a point made particularly about Eleutherae.[14]

In fact, Eleutherae was a border settlement which seems to have moved in and out of Athenian and Boeotian political control, and in antiquity there was some uncertainty about whether it should be considered Boeotian or Attic (Strabo 9.2.31). Pausanias says that Eleutherae was connected to Plataea by a main road (9.2.3), and that the people of Eleutherae changed their allegiance from the Boeotians to Athens because they wanted Athenian citizenship and felt threatened by the Thebans (Paus. 1.38.8; cf. 9.1.1), but the date of the change is unclear, and it seems that in the fifth century at least it was Boeotian;[15] certainly at the time of the writing of the *Hellenica Oxyrhynchia* it seems to have been under Theban control as part of the Boeotian federation (19.3 Chambers). What is interesting about Eleutherae, however, is its double liminality: Fachard, whose focus is mainly on the fourth-century fortress, has called it the 'Gates to Boeotia', but also points to its dual identity. Overlooking the Mazi plain (on the southern side of the Kaza Pass on Cithaeron), Eleutherae was at least as much 'the gates from' as 'the gates to' the hybrid space between it and Oenoe.

However, the Athenians were not the only aggressors on this border. The population of Hysiae was located within the territory of Plataea (Hdt. 5.76.2, 6.108.6) and so close to Plataea as to share a border with Thebes (Hdt. 6.108.6).[16] From Plataea, heading east, Pausanias describes how one turned off the main road to Eleutherae (and Attica through the Kaza Pass) for a road to Hysiae and Erythrae (Paus. 9.2.1, 3; cf. 3.24.1),[17] which were near the main routes that connected Boeotia to the Peloponnese (on 'Hammond's Road').[18] Both Hysiae and Erythrae at some point probably became part of the *sympoliteia* with Plataea and other cities of the Parasopia and later were brought under Theban control (along with Aulis and other wall-less cities in southern Boeotia), probably in about 431 (19.3, 20.3 Chambers).[19] This relocation of Hysiae was almost certainly as a consequence of the Theban attack on Plataea, or at least as part of the same aggressive plan by the Thebans to take control of the Plataïs; the people of Hysiae probably were given little real choice.

There were also other cities in this border zone who had a preference for the protection of Athens over that of their Boeotian neighbour, Thebes, and suffered for it – Thespiae, in particular. Although the Thespians fought with the Boeotians at Delium and sustained heavy losses at the hands of the Athenians (Th. 4.93.4, 96.3), Thucydides says that in 423 the Thebans took the opportunity caused by the decimation of the Thespians at Delium to take down their walls, accusing them of 'atticising' (Th. 4.133.1); it was certainly the case that there was a long

---

[14] Fachard (2013).

[15] McKesson Camp (1991: 199-202).

[16] Herodotus also says Hysiae was a 'deme' of Attica, but see n. 11 above.

[17] On the locations of ancient Hysiae and Erythrae, see Fossey (1988); Funke (2006).

[18] Routes into Attica (although noting the identification of Hysiae by Fossey 1988, and accepted by Funke 2006 and Hansen, *IACP* 440-441, 443): Ober (1985: 118-121). 'Hammond's Road': Hammond (1954: 103-122); cf. Ober (1985: 120-121); Pritchett (1980: 99-100, 190-191).

[19] The 'Hysiaeans' of *Hell. Oxyrh.* 19.3 must be the inhabitants of Hyettus: see McKechnie and Kern (1993: 157); Hansen (*IACP* 442). On the *synoikism* of these small Boeotian towns with Thebes, see Demand (1990: 83-84). The *Hellenica Oxyrhnchia* (20.3) also says that a number of small cities were relocated to Thebes at the beginning of the Peloponnesian War because they were unwalled.

history of Thespians who were sympathetic to Athens.[20] While Athens may have been keen to encroach on Boeotian territories from the south, Thebes was not a benign Boeotian neighbour on the southern Boeotian plain.[21]

What this survey of the border zone of Attica and Boeotia has shown is the complexity of these borderlands, especially north of the mountains. While there was a general sense of what it meant to be Athenian (although it is admittedly difficult to understand how Oropus and Plataea might fit into this sense of Athenianness – more on this below), 'Boeotianness' was a very variable set of ideas which were not defined simply by territory, language, cult or political organisation. It is true that, from the eighth century, regional and cultural identities north and south of this mountain chain were expressed through pottery styles, literary production and cult,[22] but 'to be Boeotian' could mean different things. An apparently early expression of 'Boeotianness' can be seen in the Homeric 'Catalogue of ships', which begins by detailing the 'Boeotians' who took part in the siege of Troy (*Iliad* 2.494-510); the names of cities later known as important 'Boeotian' cities in a territorial sense are included in the list, not just Thebes, Coroneia and Haliartus, but also Plataea, and Graea;[23] interestingly, and probably importantly, Orchomenus is listed separately as a city of the Minyans (*Iliad* 2.511-16). Tanagra is not included at all. The cult place of Athena Itonia, near Coroneia, celebrated the settlement of the *Boiotoi* together with the sanctuaries of Poseidon at Onchestus and Apollo Ptoeus near Acraephnium, which by the end of the sixth century had come under Theban control, formed a triad of sanctuaries which provided a focus for Boeotian ethnogenesis.[24] Shared coinage from the late sixth century also suggests shared economic interests which preceded the formalisation of the political *koinon* in the mid fifth century.[25] On the other hand, Kowalzig has highlighted the importance of joint story-telling and cultic ritual in the formation of 'Boeotianness' in the fifth century, from which Athens-facing Plataea and Thespiae seem to have been excluded.[26] In fact, in the late sixth and fifth centuries, it was generally Thebes who wanted to define what it meant to be Boeotian, although not everyone agreed with their understanding. On the other hand, there were some cities in the borderland who found strength in their resistance to their Athenian neighbour south of the border, even though that also made them vulnerable to their depredations. It is to the different reactions of the border cities, and especially of Plataea and Tanagra, that we turn next.

---

[20] An inscription dating to about 447 lists Thespian *proxenoi* being honoured by the Athenians (*IG* i³ 23), one of whom is called Athenaeus, which Lewis notes indicates the long-standing connection his family must have had with Athens (1992: 116 n. 74); in 424, one of the conspirators involved in the Delium campaign was probably from Thespiae: Th. 4.76.2 with Gomme et al. (1945-1981: 3.537) and Hornblower (1991-2008: 2.249-250); in 414 the *demos* of the Thespians made an unsuccessful attempt to overthrow the magistrates in power and were forced to flee to Athens: Th. 6.95.2 (cf. *IG* i³ 72).

[21] Note Gartland (2020).

[22] Cf. Coldstream (1983). Note also the sanctuary of Zeus on Mt Parnes, which van den Eijnde (2010-2011) argues was an important frontier cult centre until the sixth century, and location of significant competitive display because of its border position.

[23] Pausanias thinks Graea is in the territory of Tanagra (Paus. 9.20.1-2), and according to Strabo some say Graea is the same as Tanagra (9.2.11), although in the fifth century Thucydides says that the land which was called 'Graecan' was consonant with Oropus (Th. 2.23.3; cf. Aristotle fr. 613 Rose which also associates Graea with Oropia), which was at the time subject to the Athenians; Schachter (2016: 82-84) concludes that Graea is to be located within Oropia.

[24] Beck and Ganter (2015: 135-136).

[25] Mackil (2013: 247-249).

[26] Kowalzig (2007: 328-391).

A tale of two cities

This border zone could be a place of conflict and violence, but the violence could be directed as much towards Attica as Boeotia. In *Acharnians*, produced in 425 BC, at the height of the Archidamian War, Aristophanes refers to border raids through the mountain passes by Boeotians (1073-1077), and Andocides says that in 415 when the Boeotians heard of the mutilation of the Herms and its aftermath, they marched under arms to the borders (*epi tois horiois*) (Andoc. 1.45). However, as we have seen, there were also Boeotians who saw Athens as a better guardian of their interests than Thebes. In most of the rest of this chapter, I want to explore how two important cities in this border zone, Plataea and Tanagra, responded to the pressures of living in Boeotia, and being Boeotian, but with two more powerful neighbours, Athens and Thebes, who, for most of the fifth century, were trying to exert control in different ways over this border zone, and so secure their own place in central Greece.

Plataea was a city on the north slopes of Cithaeron in western Boeotia. According to Thucydides the Plataeans regarded themselves as 'inlanders' (*epeirotai*) (Th. 3.54.4), and, although Herodotus says they did send ships to the battle of Artemisium against the Persians in 480, they were not experienced in seamanship (Hdt. 8.1.1).[27] The Asopus marked the border between Plataea and Thebes, which was set by the Athenians at the end of the sixth century when Plataea first made overtures to the Athenians for a close diplomatic relationship because they were being pressured by the Thebans (Hdt. 6.108).[28] Certainly, from the late sixth century until their city's surrender to the Thebans, the Plataeans had been closely connected with the Athenians. This came about because of the heavy-handed pressure applied to them by Thebes to join the Boeotian project as defined by the Thebans. Herodotus says that when the Thebans required that they be reckoned as Boeotians (Hdt. 6.108.5: *es Boiotous teleein*),[29] they surrendered themselves to the Athenians (6.108.4). They perhaps even had Athenian citizenship from this early date (cf. Th. 3.55.3, 63.2, 68.5), although that is less clear.[30] In 427 Thucydides has the Thebans say that the Plataeans had never properly wanted to take part in 'Boeotianness': although the Thebans claimed to be the founders of Plataea, the Plataeans did not accept their leadership, and, separate from the other Boeotians, transgressed 'the *patria*', before turning to Athens (3.61.2).[31]

However, it is also unclear how Plataea fits into the picture of Athenian territorial, political and ideological control. Plataea was a *polis* in its own right. It was also clearly within Boeotia geographically-speaking, although the story was told in antiquity that the Plataeans took

[27] Pausanias says that nearby Creusis on the coast was the port of Thespiae (9.32.1).

[28] The Corinthians intervened in the dispute which arose with Thebes to fix the borders between Plataea and Thebes. Nevertheless, despite the Corinthian arbitration, the Boeotians attacked the Athenians as they were withdrawing, but lost the battle. The Athenians, as victors, then re-set the border (*ouron*) between Thebes and Plataea at the Asopus, so defining the area where they could enforce their control. Herodotus says the Plataeans submitted themselves to the Athenians, but it is unlikely that the relationship was one of *isopoliteia*: Hornblower (1991-2008, 1: 449-450 [on Th. 3.55.3], 464-466).

[29] Mackil (2013: 185-8) associates this early attempt by the Thebans to enforce political control of the cities with the ritual enforcement of the *tripodophoria*: see n. 5 above.

[30] The survivors of 427 were certainly given Athenian citizenship, and were fully incorporated into the Athenian *polis*: Isocrates 12. 94 and Demosthenes 59.103-4; cf. Lysias 23.2-3. See esp. Hornblower (1991-2008, 1:449-450, 458, 464-466).

[31] Kowalzig (2007: 356) comments on how important it was for the Thebans in particular that there *was* something that constituted 'Boeotianness'.

up the *horia* on the side of Attica before the battle of Plataea so that the Athenians could fight on their own land (Plut. *Arist.* 11.8). In fact, the Plataeans fought beside the Athenians at Marathon (Hdt. 6.108.1, 6.111), and together with the Thespians joined the Greek resistance to Xerxes' army, although the other Boeotians, led by the Thebans, gave 'earth and water' to the Great King (Hdt. 7.132.1; cf. 8.50.2).[32] On the other hand, we have already seen how Plataea had deep roots in Boeotian cult and story-telling, and, despite their connections with Athens, in the mid fifth century, Plataea seems to have been part of the *sympoliteia* with other small neighbouring cities and also a member of the Boeotian federation, possibly formalised in 446 (*Hell. Oxyrh.* 19.3 Chambers),[33] which suggests that their relationship to Athens was quite ambiguous by this time, or perhaps points to the fact that the *koinon* was as much a social and cultural organisation as a political one.[34]

In the spring of 431, the first act of outright aggression of the Peloponnesian War was the Spartan invasion of Attica, but it was preceded by the Theban assault on Plataea. The Thebans in their attack had been helped by pro-Theban sympathisers within the city who opened the gates to them (Th. 2.2.2). The majority of Plataeans, however, wanted to stay with the Athenian alliance (Th. 2.3.2), and the Thebans inside the city were put to death (Th. 2.5.7). This action on the part of the Plataeans in turn led to the Spartan siege (Th. 2.70, 75-78), which lasted from 429 until 427. It was the initial action at Plataea which Thucydides says broke the Thirty Years Peace (2.7.1); although the Spartans and their allies had voted in 432 that the Athenians had implicitly broken the treaty (Th. 1.87; cf. 125), they later changed their minds and conceded that it was the initial Theban attack on Plataea that was the cause for war (Th. 7.18.2), which may mean they knew about it in advance or that they at least tacitly condoned it.

In 429, the Spartans did not invade Attica, but, together with the Thebans, moved against Plataea (Th. 2.71). According to Thucydides, Archidamus the Spartan king, offered the Plataeans the possibility of joining them against the Athenians or to at least remain neutral (Th. 2.72-3). After consultation with the Athenians, and having been given assurances by the Athenians that they would not desert them (most of the wives and children of the Plataeans were already in Athens: Th. 2.72.2, 78.3), the Plataeans again decided to stay true to their alliance with the Athenians (Th. 2.73.2-74.1). The Plataeans, placed under siege in 429, surrendered to the Spartans in 427 (Th. 3.52). Judged by the Spartans and Thebans, the Plataeans' crime against 'the law of the Greeks' (cf. Th. 3.58.3) was that they did not agree to be neutral, and so took the side of 'the enslavers' of Greece (Th. 3.67.6, 68.1, cf. 2.72.1). Thucydides says that two hundred Plataean men were killed, twenty-five Athenians, and the women who had stayed to look after them were enslaved (Th. 3.68.2; cf. 2.78.3).[35] The city was razed in 426 and the land rented out by the Thebans on ten-year leases (Th. 3.68.3).[36] The Plataeans only returned when the

---

[32] Herodotus, however, also has Thespians and Thebans among the Greek resistance at Thermopylae (7.202), although only the Thespians stayed willingly, according to Herodotus (7.222, 226); see also Gartland (2020).

[33] Beck and Ganter (2015: 136-140); Mackil (2013: 22-46); but see Kowalzig (2007: 354).

[34] Mackil (2013: 336 n. 39; 2014: 45).

[35] On the apparent discrepancy in the numbers of those in Plataea, see Hornblower (1991-2008, 1: 463).

[36] Beck and Ganter (2015: 145).

Boeotian *koinon* was dissolved in 386 as a result of the King's Peace (Paus. 9.1.4),[37] which broke Thebes' hold on the Boeotian cities.[38]

It was a brave choice on the part of the Plataeans to hold firm to the Athenian alliance, since the Athenians were unable to honour their promises. With the outbreak of war in 431, the Spartan army seems to have had control of the routes from the Peloponnese into Attica and Boeotia and so of the border zone both south and north of Cithaeron and Parnes such that Archidamus was able to enter Attica at Oenoe and depart through Deceleia, and take the road from Tanagra, presumably returning to the Peloponnese on 'Hammond's Road' (near Hysiae). With such an obvious show of strength by the Spartans in the border zone, the cities of Plataea must have felt cut-off from their Athenian friends, and, other than garrisoning Plataea in 431 (Th. 2.6.4; cf. 2.78.3, 3.68.2), the Athenians seemed to be either unable or unwilling to offer much support once Plataea was placed under siege.

Tanagra, on the other hand, was an important Boeotian city, which was resolutely Boeotian ethnically and politically,[39] although the boundaries of the territory it controlled changed over time.[40] In the first phase of the Boeotian federation it contributed one of the eleven Boeotarchs and 60 of the 660 *bouleutae* (*Hell. Oxyrh.* 19.3-4 Chambers). It also controlled the sanctuary of Apollo at Delium on the coast facing Euboea (Th. 4.76.4).[41] It has sometimes been claimed on the basis of a coinage issue of the first part of the fifth century that Tanagra competed with Thebes for dominance in the southern Boeotian plain, but as Roisman argues this position is difficult to sustain, especially when there is positive evidence of co-operation between them at the end of the sixth century (Hdt. 5.79),[42] which is also perhaps evidenced in a shared interest in cult.[43]

To the east, Tanagra bordered on the territory of Oropus, which provided an important link for the Athenians between the mainland and Euboea through Deceleia (Th. 7.28.1).[44] Oropus was territorially Boeotian, but for most of the fifth century was a dependency of the Athenians (cf. Hdt. 6.101.1; Th. 2.23.3), although they lost control of it in 411 when it was betrayed to the Boeotians (Th. 8.60).[45] Interestingly, some Eretrians from across the Euripus were involved in the revolt of Oropus as they were also trying to bring about the revolt of Euboea (Th. 8.60).[46] It was largely because the Peloponnesian fleet was able to use Oropus as its base that it launched a successful attack on the Athenian ships and garrison at Eretria in the summer of 411 (Th.

---

[37] After the Athenian siege of Scione, and subsequent slaughter of the young men and enslavement of the rest, the Athenians gave Scione to the Plataeans (Th. 5.32.1).

[38] Beck and Ganter (2015: 146-147); cf. Hansen (*IACP*: 450-451, s.v. 'Plataiai').

[39] The poetess Corinna probably came from Tanagra (although possibly Thebes). Although it is now generally thought she dates to the fourth century, her poetry is very Boeotian in character: see Berman (2010).

[40] See especially, Schachter (2016: 80-112); cf. Faranetti (2011: 207-209).

[41] Schachter (2016: 80-98) has suggested that Mycalessus and Aulis were not part of the Tanagrais during the Classical period (accepted by Faranetti 2011: 207-9), although Fossey and Hansen do include them: Fossey (1988: 83-84, 222-223); Hansen (1995: 36-37; *IACP* s.v. 'Mykalessos' [no. 212], and 'Tanagra' [no. 220]).

[42] Roisman (1993: 81-83).

[43] Mackil (2013: 189-90).

[44] See Plant (1994: 272-273).

[45] Hansen (*IACP* s.v. 'Oropos' [no. 214]).

[46] The Boeotian historian Nicocrates (third century BC) thought that Oropus was originally settled by Eretrians (*BNJ* 376 F 1). The dialect of Oropus was also connected with Ionic from Euboea: Buck (1968: 269-270); see also n. 6 above.

8.95; Thucydides says that the loss of Euboea gave rise to greater panic in Athens even than the disaster in Sicily: 8.96.1). In 410 Diodorus says that the Boeotians and people of Chalcis built a bridge from Chalcis to Aulis in order to connect Euboea to Boeotia and prevent the Athenians re-taking Euboea (13.47.3-6; cf. Strabo 9.2.2 who says – citing Ephorus – that Euboea was made part of Boeotia by means of this bridge). We will return to the interest of some Eretrians in Tanagra.

Tanagra was also on a road to Plataea:[47] when the Persian Mardonius moved his army from Attica into Boeotia to encamp at Plataea he crossed Mount Parnes at Deceleia and from there moved down to Tanagra before following a route along the Asopus River to Scolus near Plataea (Hdt. 9.15). Likewise, after the first invasion of Attica in 431, Archidamus returned to the Peloponnese through Boeotia (his progress into Attica was by way of Eleusis), ravaging the territory of Oropus on the way (Th. 2.23, so presumably also following the Asopus past Tanagra, to pick up the main road near Hysiae to the Isthmus, the so-called 'Hammond's Road').[48] Tanagra, unlike Plataea, or other cities in the border zones, was always Boeotian/Theban-facing rather than Athens-facing.

In fact, Tanagra became an important location for conflict between the Athenians and Boeotians. For example, in 458 or 457 BC there was a major conflict at Tanagra between an army comprising the Spartans and their allies, and the Athenians and theirs,[49] the first confrontation between the super-powers in what has come to be called the First Peloponnesian War. This series of conflicts in the first instance was largely centred on Corinthian hostilities against Athens on the one hand (over control of the Saronic Gulf), and Argos on the other (over control of the sanctuary of Nemea).[50] Nevertheless, in 458 or 457, a series of incidents brought Athens and Sparta, together with their allies, into a battle that neither seemed to want to avoid. We have two narrative accounts of the battle, one in Thucydides and one in Diodorus (probably based on the fourth-century Ephorus), which diverge significantly and are probably not possible to reconcile, although the general thrust is that the Spartans positioned their army at Tanagra, the Athenians and their allies met them in battle (which was either a Spartan victory or inconclusive), the Athenians returned after the Spartans had departed to fight another battle at Oenophyta, which they won, and, as a result, gained control of all of Boeotia and Phocis.[51]

In considering this battle, most attention has been given to its purpose. Thucydides' and Diodorus' explanation that the preliminaries to the battle were Spartan interventions against the Phocians on behalf of the Spartan 'metropolis' Doris (Th. 1.107.2; Diod. 11.79.4-6) is generally doubted, and some ingenious alternative causes have been suggested. Simon Hornblower argues that the preliminaries to the battle arose out of the Spartans' desire, not

---

[47] In the third century BC, Heracleides Criticus described the road between Tanagra and Plataea (*BNJ* 369 F1): ὁδὸς ἡσυχῇ μὲν ἔρημος καὶ λιθώδης, ἀνατείνουσα δὲ πρὸς τὸν Κιθαιρῶνα, οὐ λίαν δὲ ἐπισφαλής; cf. Snodgrass (1992: 90). Mardonius' route took him from Tanagra to Scolus (in Theban territory) where he built a stockade which he used as his base for the attack on Plataea (Hdt. 9.15.1-3); cf. Pritchett (1980: 192-193).

[48] See n. 18 above.

[49] The date of the battle: Diodorus gives a date of 458 for the battle of Tanagra and 457 for the battle of Oenophyta (which Thucydides says happened two months later). Rhodes (2014: 254) notes that these archon dates could be right even if only two months apart.

[50] Hornblower (2011: 25-32).

[51] See Appendix.

how, in order for the campaign to work, it must only have been known to those in command (there was more than one occasion when decision-making even in democratic Athens could be made in secret without the involvement of the assembly).[64] However, these comments probably underestimate the importance of this campaign at this point in the Archidamian War, particularly as it took place in the year of the Spartan destruction of the city of Plataea (Th. 3.68.3).

The route from Tanagra to Plataea ran through southern Boeotia. We have already seen how Mardonius used a route from Tanagra to Plataea, when he crossed from Attica into Boeotia through the pass at Deceleia and then went to Plataea through Scolus (Hdt. 9.15.2). There were also links to Attica at a number of points over the ranges of Cithaeron (cf. Hdt. 9.38) and Parnes between Plataea and Tanagra, as well as a connection to the main road to the Peloponnese, 'Hammond's Road' (cf. Hdt. 9.19). The Athenian attack on Tanagra seems to have constituted not only a show of strength by the Athenians, but also a display of their ability to assert themselves in southern Boeotia, as well as a reminder of earlier defeats of the Boeotians: in 506 (at Euripus: Hdt. 5.77) and, more importantly, at Tanagra in the early 450s, as discussed above. It increased the scope of the border zone through a demonstration of the Athenian ability to transgress the legal boundary between Athenian controlled territory and Boeotia, to move in and out of this borderland, so acting as a destabilising force on the Boeotian cities, and possibly encouraging the Boeotian cities that were leaning towards Athens, especially Thespiae. As we have already seen, Aristophanes *Acharnians* makes plain that the Boeotians were making attacks on Attica in this period, probably by Boeotians based at Tanagra crossing Parnes. These raids seem to have caused considerable anxieties in Athens, so the attack on Tanagra, then, would have had a positive effect in Athens as revenge not just for Plataea, but also for the Boeotian incursions in Attica.

Indeed, this attack on Tanagra together with the attempt to bring Melos into the Athenian alliance, carried through so dramatically ten years later, was a demonstration of Athenian aggressive imperialism during the Archidamian War probably closer than we might suppose to the level usually associated with the mid 410s.[65] The fact that the Tanagran campaign was carefully planned and used a substantial body of troops seems to indicate that it was important on its own terms, even if not for material territorial gain. The campaign at Tanagra, while not adding to Athenian territories, was asserting their ability to transgress border districts, not just of the *polis* of Tanagra, but of the political entity that was now the Boeotian *koinon*.

This campaign against Tanagra in 426 should also probably be seen as the first stage of the campaign to establish an *epiteichismos* at Delium (in the Tanagrais) in 424, which could be used to make raids on Boeotian territories and to provide a focus for Boeotian dissidents, and, in a sense, to make more permanent a state of uncertainty in the border zone.[66] Thucydides says that some Boeotians had been in contact with two of the Athenian generals, Demosthenes and

---

[64] Hornblower (1991-2008, 1: 500).

[65] The attack on Melos in 416 is usually attributed to Alcibiades ([Andoc.] 4.22; Plut. *Alc.* 16.6), who was certainly one of the main agitators for the Sicilian campaign in the next year. Notably in the 420s it is Nicias (who, in Thucydides, later argued against the disastrous attack on Sicily) heading-up this campaign, perhaps suggesting that the gap between the activities of Nicias and those of Alcibiades might not always have been as polarised as Thucydides suggests, although there is of course some difference in the degree of violence perpetrated in both sequences of campaigning.

[66] See Westlake (1983: 17).

Hippocrates, with a view to inciting a democratic revolution among the Boeotian cities (Th. 4.76.2). To that end, Demosthenes and Hippocrates and the Boeotian rebels concocted a plan whereby Demosthenes and some of the Boeotians were going to bring over Siphae (on the Corinthian Gulf), exiles from Orchomenus were going to hand over Chaeroneia (bordering on Phocis), and Hippocrates and a contingent from Athens were to take the sanctuary of Delium in Tanagran territory (Th. 4.76.3-4), so a position on the Euboean Gulf.

In the event, everything went wrong, and by the time Hippocrates arrived at Delium, the plan had been uncovered and Siphae and Chareroneia were secure (Th. 4.89-90). The Athenians fortified and garrisoned the sanctuary, a battle was fought, and the Athenians were defeated (Th. 4.93-6). Thucydides says that the battle took place *en methoriois* (4.99; cf. 4.128.2), which, as Hornblower points out, made the question of legalities rather complicated.[67] There was considerable and elongated discussion over the Athenians' occupation of the sanctuary, and their rights to take up their dead. However, the objectives of the Athenian occupation of Delium help us to understand the psychology of border politics more generally.

Thucydides says the object was, by fortifying Delium, that, over time, it would be able to destabilise the Boeotian cities (Th. 4.76.5). As a strategy, *epiteichisis* was expected to cause internal instability of various kinds. Westlake talks about what he calls 'internal *epiteichismos*' where dissidents would set up a fort within the boundaries of their own state 'with the intention of harrying and, if possible, over-throwing the regime of their political opponents'.[68] In this sense, an *epiteichisis* was very like a siege (although much cheaper) as it limited access to polis' territory, and so brought hardship to the inhabitants of the city. Interestingly, a theme running through the work on how to survive sieges by the fourth-century Aeneas Tacticus is the possibility of internal treachery.[69]

It was thought that the presence of a hostile army was enough to destabilise a city. In 411, Thucydides says that Agis at Deceleia thought, after the oligarchic coup in Athens, that the sight of a large army would further unsettle the Athenians and that they would either surrender (because they would want to return to democracy), or be easily taken, and so summoned reinforcements (Th. 8.71). However, even with the uncertainty caused by the change from democracy to rule by the Four Hundred, the Athenians retained a calm external front and would only discuss terms for peace rather than capitulation. Nevertheless, it is an important point about the psychology of ancient warfare that Thucydides could interpret Agis thinking in this way.

---

[67] Hornblower (1991-2008, 2: 314-315). For the location of the *methorion*, and Athenian confusion about whether or not they were fighting in Boeotian territory, see Schachter (2016: 85-87).

[68] Westlake (1983: 13-15).

[69] Pretzler (2017). Westlake suggests that the helot occupation of Ithome would have been seen on the model of internal *epiteichisis*. Understanding the fortification at Ithome in this way helps to clarify the purposes (whether thought-through by the Athenians or not) and consequences of the Athenian fort at Pylos, established in 425. This fort not only provided a focus for deserting helots, but it also had an effect on Spartan morale because of their fear of revolution, not among the Spartiates, but among the helots, as they had seen before at Ithome (Th. 4.41, 55.1, 80.2, 5.14.3). Nevertheless, it was obviously the helots who had the potential to be disaffected, and it seems that the Spartans were genuinely concerned that, if the helots were supported, it might allow, not just the destabilisation or loss of Messenia, but also the possibility of the overthrow of their whole system (cf. the Cinadon conspiracy in 395).

It is with this in mind that we should consider the importance of Tanagra and its environs to both the Boeotians and the Athenians. Tanagra stood on an important land route into and out of Attica, although of course not the only one. It was also on an important corridor along the Asopus River through southern Boeotia. While other cities along this corridor and on the mountain-passes moved in and out of Theban/Boeotian and Athenian control, Tanagra seems to have consistently identified itself with Boeotian/Theban political interests and not Athenian ones. It was also accessible by sea from the important Euboean Gulf (and connections to Euboea were enhanced, of course, after the building of the bridge). It is significant that an inscription listing Tanagran war dead (which Low thinks must date to the battle of Delium)[70] includes two Eretrians (*IG* vii 585). We have already noted that Eretrians were involved in the revolt of Oropus in 411 and Euboea itself revolted in the same year.

Tanagra, as John Ma has argued, was a city that felt and expressed its liminality, in part through its sanctuaries for Hermes (Paus. 9.22.1-2), and used this as a way of positioning itself politically.[71] It was an important location for Theban/Boeotian attempts at destabilising Athenian interests, but it was also a location that the Athenians had an interest in being unstable so that it was less able to provide a focus for Boeotian activities against Attica and Athens. In 458/457 the possibility of the destabilising and even overthrow of Athens' fairly recently reformed constitution could well explain why the Spartans moved from Phocis to Tanagra and not just Thebes, which would have provided a closer link to Hammond's Road and the Peloponnese, and why the Athenians were prepared to send such a large force against them. Rather than trying to avoid a military engagement as Holladay has argued,[72] the Spartans' decision to camp its army 'on the border' was deliberate and aggressive.

Border politics

It has been argued recently that it was in Athenian interests to have access to Boeotia, and that, while generally the Athenians may have tried to secure this access peacefully, they were also prepared to use force, as we see them do in the fifth century.[73] By the same token, historical tensions between Athens and Thebes had deep roots (cf. Hdt. 5.74-81), and the Thebans were also prepared to use significant force to secure their interests, so that the border zone between Boeotia and Attica was a place of great uncertainty, political tension and violence. The push and pull of being neighbours of Athens and Thebes meant that political affiliations did not necessarily map onto ethnic or geographical ones. The resources of these regions must have been great to make them attractive places to live and keep living. Or, at least, the people of these border zones must have become inured to the vulnerability of living in a constant state of insecurity and 'in-betweenness'. The destruction of Plataea and the battles of Tanagra, and the events surrounding them, make this point so clearly. The landing in Tanagran territory by the Athenian general Dieitrephes of the Thracian mercenaries he was escorting home in 413 (Th. 7.29-30) also belongs in this context.[74]

---

[70] Low (2003: 103).

[71] Ma (2008: 196-199).

[72] Holladay (1977: 54-63).

[73] van Wijk (2020: 107-137).

[74] See Schachter (2016: 89).

In fact, we have seen the fluidity of political affiliations of the cities within the territory of Boeotia, and the difficulty of maintaining any kind of political cohesiveness. Aristotle says that some cities do not allow people on the borders to be involved in decision-making in times of war because of their conflicting interests (*Politics* 1330a 16-23). Even Plataea's participation, first probably in the *sympoliteia* based on the cities of the Parasopia and then in the Boeotian *koinon*, was not enough to save it from destruction in 427, even though its *chora* had also become in some sense a sacred site because this was where in mainland Greece the final battle with the Persians had been fought and where Greek soldiers had died and were buried (cf. Th. 2.71.2-4, 74.2, 3.57, 58.4-59.2; note also Hdt. 9.86.1).[75] However, it is also an indication of the importance of territory to polis-identity that the Plataeans returned to their border home in 386 (only to be expelled again by the Thebans in the 370s [Xen. *Hell.* 6.3.1; Isoc. 14 *passim*], and repatriated again by Philip II of Macedon [Paus. 4.27.10, 9.1.8]).

These very same reasons also demonstrate the resilience of the Tanagrans, and their commitment to the Theban-sponsored Boeotian project. Although they lived in a border zone, throughout the fifth century they were willing to endure steadfastly life in a war zone, to live dangerously on the edges – which says something about what border politics was about.

Despite the importance of borders for defining the physical shape and extent of Greek cities,[76] political borders also did not align with other kinds of boundaries or markers of identity, creating complex loyalties in the border zones. This was particularly true of the border between Attica and Boeotia. Indeed, the very fact that there was a rich 'language' of the borders shows that boundaries and borders were something that Greeks thought about, and the contested nature of the border between Boeotia and Attica gives an indication of why and how borders could become significant.

Appendix: Sources on the battle of Tanagra 458 or 457

In Thucydides' account, the preliminaries to the battle were a Spartan campaign with 1500 of their own hoplites and 10,000 of their allies, in Doris, to relieve one of the Dorian villages which had been seized by the Phocians; the reason (or excuse) for Spartan intervention was the fact that the Spartans considered Doris to be their metropolis (1.107.2). The campaign itself was successful, but their return was hindered by the Athenians who had control of Megara, and so a sea-crossing of the Corinthian Gulf, and had also garrisoned the land route at Mt Geraneia (1.107.3). The Spartans were unsure what was the safest way to return to the Peloponnese, so remained in Boeotia. Further, Thucydides says, they had been approached by some Athenians in secret who wanted to bring down democracy and stop the building of the long walls (1.107.4). A full Athenian contingent came out against them, together with 1000 Argives (who were then their allies), as well as other contingents from their other allies, altogether numbering 14,000, aware both of the plot against the democracy, and the dithering of the Peloponnesians about their return route (1.107.5-6). The Athenians also had some Thessalian cavalry with them, although these in fact defected to the Spartan side (1.107.7).[77]

---

[75] See Zatta (2011: 325-31).

[76] See Daverio Rocchi (2016: 70-74).

[77] The Thessalians made an alliance with both the Athenians and the Argives at about the same time as the Argive/Athenian alliance (Th. 1.102.4); their betrayal is indicative of Thessalian politics which tended to swing between pro- and anti-Athenian feeling (rather than to polarise between Athens and Sparta): see Rechenauer (1993: 241-242). In the

The battle took place at Tanagra, and Thucydides says it was a victory for the Spartans and their allies, although there was a great deal of slaughter on both sides (1.108.1). The Spartans then took advantage of the victory and cut their way through to the Megarid, over Geraneia and to the Isthmus (1.108.1). Despite this major defeat, Thucydides says the Athenians returned to Boeotia sixty-two days later, defeated the Boeotians at Oenophyta (generally assumed to be near Tanagra), over-ran Boeotia and Phocis, demolished the walls of Tanagra, and took as hostages a hundred of the Opuntian Locrians (1.108.2-3).

Diodorus' account is rather different. Hostilities begin in a similar way with Phocian aggression against the Dorians, Spartan reprisals, and the dispatch of an Athenian army, including Argives and Thessalians (11.79.4-80.1). It was at this point that the Spartans moved to Tanagra, and the Athenians lined up against them. A battle took place, during which the Thessalians defected, and many died in both armies (11.80.2). In Diodorus' account, the Thessalians then attacked (in the evening of the first day of the battle) a market [for supplies] (*agora*) coming from Attica, were given support by the Spartans, although the ensuing battle was indecisive, and both sides made a truce for four months (11.80.3-6). The Spartan army then seems to remain in Boeotia into the next archon year in order to strengthen Thebes (11.81.2-3). The Athenians responded by leading an army into Boeotia, won a great victory, and took Tanagra by siege (11.81.4-82.5). These actions then led to the battle of Oenophyta (Boeotians against Athenians), and all of Boeotia except Thebes came under Athenian control (11.83.1). Myronides, the Athenian general, then took Opuntian Locris and Phocis, and laid siege to Thessalian Pharsalus, although he wasn't able to take it (11.83.2-4).

As well as the narrative accounts, we also have evidence from inscriptions, but these are not straightforward. At Athens, as well as commemorating their own dead (Plato, *Menex.* 242c; Paus. 1.29.7), the Athenians commemorated the Argive dead (although the stone-cutter was an Argive) in a style similar (but not completely so) to their own commemorations of war dead (Pausanias also saw this monument together with the monument of the war-dead from Cleonae, presumably also from this battle: 1.29.7).[78] This commemorative document at least seems to confirm that the Argive number of dead were about a third of the total force (whereas hoplite warfare usually resulted in losses of between 5% and 14% depending on who were the winners and who were the losers).[79] It speaks to the significance of the battle in Athens that the Athenians wanted to commemorate not only their own dead but also those of their allies, which is certainly unusual, and it may be that the Athenians wanted to honour their allies (the point is often made that the Athenians were very enthusiastic about their new alliance

450s (after Tanagra) the Athenians had tried to restore the son of the 'king' of Thessaly who was in exile (Th. 1.111.1). That this Orestes was in exile is an indication of the political turmoil that persisted in Thessalian internal politics as different elite families jockeyed with each other for power and control of all of Thessaly: see Andrewes (1971: 219). Although not listed among the allies at Th. 1.2.9, Thessalian cavalry came to the support of the Athenians in 431 when the Peloponnesians made their first invasion of Attica (Th. 2.22.2-3). When Brasidas and his army marched through Thessaly in 424, Thucydides comments that the *plethos* of the Thessalians had good-will for the Athenians, and it was only because Thessaly at the time was controlled by a *dynasteia* that Brasidas was allowed to proceed (4.78.2-3), although on this contrast, see Hornblower (1991-2008, 2: 259-60); Rechenauer (1993: 140-1). In 422/421 the Thessalians resisted the Spartans' attempt to use Thessaly as a corridor again to the north Aegean (Th. 5.13.1), which seems to be the context in which Athens honoured the Thessalian Callipus of Gyrton with an honorific *proxenia* (OR 162).
[78] OR 111 with Papazarkadas and Sourlas (2012).
[79] On casualties in hoplite warfare: see Krentz (1985).

with the Argives after Spartans had sent them away from Ithome under a cloud of suspicion in 462/461: Th. 1.102.4).

There is some uncertainty in our sources over the outcome of the battle. As we have seen. Thucydides says the Spartans won, whereas Diodorus/Ephorus is more ambivalent. Nevertheless, the Spartans made a grand statement of their victory, by appropriating the newly built temple of Zeus at Olympia and erecting a golden shield as a thanksgiving offering on the east pediment of the new temple of Zeus for them and their allies (OR 112; Paus. 5.10.2-5), the temple itself having been a victory dedication by the Eleans over the Pisatans. The Spartans were not just claiming victory, but doing so in very strong panhellenic terms which promoted their claims to leadership both in the Peloponnese and in the Greek world more widely.[80] Other memories of the battle varied significantly. Pausanias, for example, thinks that the battle lasted over two days, and that the Thessalians betrayed the Athenians on the second day, but says the Spartans won (1.29.9).

Bibliography

Andrewes, A. 1971. Two notes on Lysander. *Phoenix* 21: 206-226.

Beck, H. and A. Ganter 2015. Boeotia and the Boeotian Leagues, in H. Beck and P. Funke (eds) *Federalism in Greek Antiquity*: 132-157. Cambridge: Cambridge University Press.

Berman, D.W. 2010. The Language and Landscape of Korinna. *Greek, Roman, and Byzantine Studies* 50: 41-62.

Buck, R.J. 1968. The Aeolic Dialects in Boeotia. *Classical Philology* 63: 268-280.

Coldstream, J.N. 1983. The Meaning of Regional Styles in the Eighth Century BC, in R. Hägg (ed.) *The Greek Renaissance of the Eighth Century BC: Tradition and Innovation. Proceedings of the Second International Symposium at the Swedish Institute in Athens, 1-5 June, 1981*: 17-25. Stockholm: Åström.

Daverio Rocchi, G. 1988. *Frontiera e Confini nella Grecia Antica*. Rome: L'Erma di Bretschneider.

Daverio Rocchi, G. 2016. Systems of Borders in Ancient Greece, in S. Bianchetti, M. Cataudella and H.-J. Gehrke (eds), *Brill's Companion to Ancient Geography*: 58-77. Leiden: Brill.

Demand, N.H. 1990. *Urban Relocation in Archaic and Classical Greece: Flight and Consolidation*. Bristol: Bristol Classical Press.

Eijnde, F. van den 2010-11. The Forgotten Sanctuary of Zeus on Mount Parnes. *Talanta* 42-43: 113-128.

Fachard, S. 2013. Eleutherai as the Gates to Boeotia. *Réma* 6: 81-106.

Faranetti, E. 2011. *Boeotian Landscapes: A GIS-based Study for the Reconstruction and Interpretation of the Archaeological Datasets of Ancient Boeotia*. Oxford: Archaeopress.

Fossey, J.M. 1988. *Topography and Population of Ancient Boiotia*. Chicago: Ares.

Funke, P. 2006. 'Hysiae' and 'Erythrae' in *Brill's New Pauly*, viewed 19/6/2021, <http://dx.doi.org/10.1163/1574-9347_bnp_e520350>.

Gartland, S.D. 2020. Silk Purses and Sows' Ears: Thebans, Boeotians and the Second Persian Invasion 480-79 BCE, in S. Medenieks (ed.), *Elite Responses to the Rise of Achaemenid Persia* (*Hermathena* nos 204-205): 41-63. Dublin: University of Dublin.

Gomme, A.W., A. Andrewes, and K.J. Dover, 1945-1981. *A Historical Commentary on Thucydides*. 5 volumes. Oxford: Oxford University Press.

---

[80] See also Scott (2010: 192-193).

Hammond, N.G.L. 1954. The Main Road from Boeotia to the Peloponnese through the Northern Megarid, *Annual of the British School at Athens* 49: 103-122.

Hansen. M.H. 1995. Boeotian Poleis, a Test Case, in M.H. Hansen (ed.) *Sources for the Ancient Greek City* (Acta of the Copenhagen Polis Centre): 13-63. Copenhagen: Munksgaard.

Hansen, M. H. and T.H. Nielsen 2004. *An Inventory of Archaic and Classical Poleis.* Oxford: Oxford University Press [*IACP*].

Hansen, V. 2011, 'Ephoros', *Brill's New Jacoby* [BNJ], viewed 20/06/2021, <https://referenceworks-brillonline-com.uoelibrary.idm.oclc.org/entries/brill-s-new-jacoby/ephoros-70-a70?s.num=2>.

Holladay, A.J. 1977. Sparta's Role in the First Peloponnesian War, *Journal of Hellenic Studies* 97: 54-63.

Hornblower, S. 1991-2008. *A Commentary on Thucydides.* 3 volumes. Oxford: Oxford University Press.

Hornblower, S. 2011. *The Greek World, 479-323 BC.* 4th ed. Abingdon: Routledge.

Kowalzig, B. 2007. *Singing for the Gods: Performance of Myth and Ritual in Archaic and Classical Greece.* Oxford: Oxford University Press.

Krentz, P. 1985. Casualties in Hoplite Battles, *Greek, Roman, and Byzantine Studies* 16: 13-20.

Lewis, D.M. 1992. Mainland Greece, 479-451 BC, in *The Cambridge Ancient History* v²: 96-120. Cambridge: Cambridge University Press.

Loraux, N. 1986. *The Invention of Athens: The Funeral Oration in the Classical City.* Cambridge Mass. and London: Harvard University Press.

Low, P. 2003. Remembering War in Fifth-Century Greece: Ideologies, Societies and Commemoration Beyond Democratic Athens. *World Archaeology* 35: 98-111.

Ma, J. 2008. The Return of the Black Hunter. *The Cambridge Classical Journal* 54: 188-208.

Mackil, E. 2013. *Creating a Common Polity: Religion, Economy and Politics in the Making of the Greek Koinon.* Berkeley; Los Angeles: California University Press.

Mackil, E. 2014. Creating a Common Polity in Boeotia, in N. Papazarkadas (ed.) *The Epigraphy and History of Boeotia: New Finds, New Prospects*: 45-67. Leiden: Brill.

Macleod, C. 1983. *Collected Essays.* Oxford: Oxford University Press.

Marr, J.L. and P.J. Rhodes 2008. *The 'Old Oligarch': The* Constitution of the Athenians *attributed to Xenophon.* Oxford: Oxbow Books.

McKechnie, P.R. and S.J. Kern 1993. *Hellenica Oxyrhynchia.* Warminster: Aris and Philipps.

McKesson Camp, J. 1991. Notes on the Towers and Borders of Classical Boeotia. *American Journal of Archaeology* 95: 193-202.

Mosley, D.J. 2007. Crossing Greek Frontiers Under Arms, in E.L. Wheeler (ed.), *The Armies of Classical Greece*: 228-235. London; New York: Routledge.

Munn, M. 2010. Panakton and Drymos: A Disputed Frontier, in H. Loman and T. Lorsten (eds), *Attika: Archäologie einer "zentralen" Kulturlandschaft*: 189-200. Wiesbaden: Harrassowitz.

Ober, J. 1985. *Fortress Attica: Defense of the Athenian Land Frontier 404-322 BC.* Leiden: Brill.

Ober, J. 1995. Greek Horoi: Artifactual Texts and the Contingency of Meaning, in D. Small (ed.) *Methods in the Mediterranean: Historical and Archaeological Views of Texts and Archaeology* (Mnemosyne Supplement 135): 91-123. Leiden: Brill.

Osborne, R. and P.J. Rhodes, 2017. *Greek Historical Inscriptions 478-404 BC.* Oxford: Oxford University Press. [OR]

Papazarkadas, N. and D. Sourlas 2012. The Funerary Monument for the Argives Who Fell at Tanagra (*IG* 1³ 1149): A New Fragment. *Hesperia* 81: 586-617.

Plant, I.M. 1994. The Battle of Tanagra: A Spartan Initiative?. *Historia* 43: 259-274.

Pretzler, M. 2017. The Polis Falling Apart: Aeneas Tacticus and Stasis, in N. Barley and M. Pretzler (eds) *Brill's Companion to Aineias Tacticus*: 146-165. Leiden: Brill.

Pritchett, W.K. 1980. *Studies in Ancient Greek Topography*. Vol. 3 (Roads). Berkeley; Los Angeles: University of California Press.

Raaflaub, K.A. 1997. Soldiers, Citizens, and the Evolution of the Early Greek *Polis*, in L.G. Mitchell and P.J. Rhodes (eds) *The Development of the Polis in Archaic Greece*: 49-59. London; New York: Routledge.

Raaflaub, K.A. 2004. *The Discovery of Freedom in Ancient Greece*. Chicago: University of Chicago Press.

Rechenauer, G. 1993. Zu Thucydides II 22,3 ... ἀπὸ τῆς στάσεως ἑκάτερος ..., *Rheinisches Museum fur Philologie* 136: 238-244.

Rhodes, P.J. 1993. *A Commentary on the Aristotelian* Athenaion Politeia, rev. ed. Oxford: Oxford University Press.

Rhodes, P.J. 2014. *Thucydides: History I*. Oxford: Oxbow.

Roisman, J. 1993. The Background of the Battle of Tanagra and some Related Issues. *L'Antiquité Classique* 62: 69-85.

Roller, D.W. 1989. Who Murdered Ephialtes? *Historia* 38: 257-266.

Schachter, A. 2016. *Boeotia in Antiquity: Selected Papers*. Cambridge: Cambridge University Press.

Scott, M. 2010. *Delphi and Olympia: The Spatial Politics of Panhellenism in the Archaic and Classical Periods*. Cambridge: Cambridge University Press.

Snodgrass, A. 1992. *An Archaeology of Greece: The Present State and Future Scope of a Discipline*. Berkeley and Los Angeles: University of California Press.

Stockton, D. 1982. The Death of Ephialtes. *The Classical Quarterly* 32: 227-228.

Westlake, H.D. 1983. The Progress of *Epiteichismos*. *The Classical Quarterly* 33: 12-24.

Whitehead, D. 1986. *The Demes of Attica, 508/7- ca. 250 BC*. Princeton: Princeton University Press.

Wijk, R. van 2020. The Centrality of Boeotia to Athenian Defensive Strategy, in F. Marchand and H. Beck (eds), *The Dancing Floor of Ares: Local Conflict and Regional Violence in Central Greece, Ancient History Bulletin*. Supplemental Volume 1: 107-137.

Zatta, C. 2011. Conflict, People, and City-Space: Some Exempla from Thucydides' *History*. *Classical Antiquity* 30: 318-350.

Empedocles *Democraticus*?

Carlo Santaniello

Independent Scholar – Rome
carlo.santaniello@gmail.com

Abstract

A tradition going back to Timaeus introduces Empedocles as one τῶν τὰ δημοτικὰ φρονούντων. This fragment is the only source apparently providing any support to the thesis that he nurtured "popular" feelings. Why did Empedocles dissolve the Gathering of the Thousand at Acragas after the fall of the tyrant Thrasydaeus? As an aristocrat, he may simply have contrasted an attempt to establish a new tyranny, in the same way as he had formerly reacted to the humiliations inflicted on him by a host with tyrannic aspirations. And Empedocles' denying a special site for the tomb of Akron's father is another example of his fondness of ἰσότης, of equal civil rights — nothing to do with the redistribution of land claimed by democrats of later times.

Even more doubtful are the recent efforts to look in the *Physical Poem* for confirmations of the supposed democratic feelings. The four elements, fire, aither, earth, and water, are not to be put on the same level as the two powers, Love and Strife. The powers comply with an agreement entered only by the two of them, and govern the elements. Nor does the social structure revealed by B112 (proem of the *Purifications*) back up any equalitarian hypothesis.

Keywords

Timaeus, democracy, Gathering of the Thousand, ἰσότης, social and cultural difference

Introduction

What we know of Empedocles' life and political engagement is very little and uncertain. This is so, not only because we have very scarce information, but also because the structure of the Laertian biography, by far our main source, is very complicated: it mixes extracts from several authors together, and patently ignores any 'rational' and chronologically straight distribution of events; indeed, it sometimes duplicates facts, for example adding the comparatively sober revision by Neanthes of Cyzicus to the sometimes picturesque exposition by Timaeus of Tauromenium.[1] Even essential data like the approximate date of birth and death of Empedocles are not so clearly obtainable from Diogenes' βίος.[2] Again, every meaningful event in Empedocles' political activity can only by inference, if ever, be linked to

---

[1] See the tale about the illicit divulgation of the Pythagoric doctrine by Empedocles in Timae., *FGrH* 566, fr. 14 (= D.L. 8.54) and the one in Neanth., *FGrH* 84, fr. 26 (= D.L. 8.55), where the latter makes use of less dramatic tones and also implicitly denies Timaeus' witness that Empedocles had listened to Pythagoras's teaching. Neanthes is now thought to have been active in the 4th century BC (so Schorn 2007: 115), and not between the end of the 3rd and the 2nd, as it was held before. — Presocratics' fragments (B) or testimonies (A) are quoted according to DK, if not differently specified, and all translations are mine.

[2] Perplexity might be caused also by some *topoi* in the *Life* which recur elsewhere in connection with other characters — consider, for example, the supposed bent of philosophers for fighting against tyrants. But, at least, Acragantine history, however only fragmentarily known, offers a more persuasive context to Empedocles' political endeavours than, for instance, the domination of the obscure Nearchus to Zeno the Eleates' fight against tyranny (D.L. 9.26–28=29A1).

a specific time. And, lastly, the authors quoted by Diogenes Laertius agree almost on nothing — not even on a famous feature of this story, the supposed exile of Empedocles and his death far from Sicily. This contribution attempts at putting some order into the matter and fixing some approximate dates; it also reacts to two recent papers, which contend that Empedocles was an extreme democrat and even an anarchist: Horky (2016) starts from a questionable interpretation of Aristotle's witness and from Timaeus, although acknowledging the strongly ideological character of the Tauromenian's work; while Coates (2018) is based upon an unsatisfying analysis of Empedoclean physics. All in all, I think it would be easier to disprove this thesis starting from the weakness of its philosophical foundations. But in this chapter I intend to focus on political and institutional history first. Also in this latter field there are clues that can lead us to what I consider to be the most satisfying solution to the problem.

Acragantine politics in the 5th century BC

Since Phalarides' times (probably, around the second quarter of the 6th century)[3] the power in Acragas was alternatively held by tyrants or by some oligarchic families; sometimes these opposed tyranny, but some other times their scions made themselves tyrants on their own. According to very flimsy information, Telemachus, grandfather of Theron,[4] may have seized the power wringing it from Phalarides, and securing it for his γένος, and thereby perspectively for Theron. This very uncertain scheme is further complicated by two rather mysterious figures, Alcamenes and Alcandros, who held the power for a space of time impossible to define, but included between Phalarides' death (perhaps 555–554) and Theron's access to tyranny (488). Theron's domination was characterized by his great qualities as a nobleman (riches and generosity also before rising to the power: Diod. 10.28.3; and moderation while exercising his rule: 11.53.2); he enjoyed wide consensus from higher and lower social strata. On the other hand, some rebellions against Theron's rule, and mainly the one led by his cousins Hippocrates and Capys (schol. Pind. *Ol.* 2.173f), uncover rivalries inside aristocracy, and even inside the γένος itself. After Theron's death (472), the sad end met with, one year later, by his son Thrasydaeus, who appeared to be eminently endowed with the vices opposed to his father's virtues, is represented as the result of moral unfitness to the standard required from an aristocratic leader (Diod. 11.53.2–5); but this episode seems to be part of the long conflict between Acragas and Syracuse for the control of south-eastern Sicily. We are now approaching the years we are especially interested in. Diodorus (11.53.5) — a source to which we cannot help turning, although it so often leaves us with a sense of frustration — relates that, after driving away Thrasydaeus, the Acragantines 'recovered democracy, sent an embassy to Hieron and thereby obtained peace'.[5] This is a key passage to understand the political *régime* and the society in Acragas at this time. Κομισάμενοι τὴν δημοκρατίαν: an exact parallel to this use of the verb κομίζομαι is to be found in Aristoph., *Av.* 549, where the chorus of the birds declares that it will not be worthwhile to live any longer unless they recover their reign (... εἰ μὴ κομιούμεθα... τὴν ἡμετέραν βασιλείαν). But what should we really understand for 'recovering democracy'? Surely, nobody would think that the tyranny of Theron and Thrasydaeus was preceded by democracy between the end of the 6th and the beginning of the 5th century! Unfortunately, we know almost nothing of Acragantine institutional history after the fall of Thrasydaeus

---

[3] Luraghi 1994: 21 n. 1.
[4] Luraghi 1994: 235.
[5] οἱ δ'Ἀκραγαντῖνοι κομισάμενοι τὴν δημοκρατίαν, διαπρεσβευσάμενοι πρὸς Ἱέρωνα τῆς εἰρήνης ἔτυχον.

in 471; but we have some indications that the oligarchic families who had acquiesced in the Emmenidai' power (and presumably also willingly accepted the defeat of Thrasydaeus at the hand of Hieron in 471) had still the upper hand in Acragas after 471, at least as far as Hieron tolerated it. First of all, as far as we know, no popular rising unleashed itself against the Emmenidai causing their fall; so, those of the oligarchic families who had not left Acragas during the Emmenidai' domination were probably ready to seize control after the expulsion of Thrasydaeus. Secondly, five years later, in 466, Syracusans rose against Thrasybulus, brother and successor of Gelon and Hieron, apparently under the leadership of the oligarchy (cf. Diod. 11.67.6),[6] and turned for help to several cities including Acragas (11.68). Of course, this is no indisputable proof that oligarchy, and not democracy, took the place of tyranny in Acragas as in several other cities, but such interpretation is shared by many scholars, like D. Asheri and N. Luraghi, although sometimes Diodorus' words have been taken at their face value.[7] It is worthwhile to compare the shrewd remarks by Aristotle in *Pol.* 4, 1297b: here the Stagirite explains that 'the ancients called δημοκρατίαι what we (i.e. Aristotle himself) call πολιτεῖαι'. In other words, the scarcity of the middle class in those times prevented the emergence of any true democracy, and therefore the ancient constitutions (down to the 5th century) were really either oligarchies or monarchies.[8]

Empedocles' life and political career

Empedocles' date of birth is fixed with comparative precision by Arist., *Metaph.* 1, 984a 11 (= A6), who connects it to Anaxagoras' birth — the latter was born earlier than Empedocles, but surely not many years earlier, if he wrote later than Empedocles.[9] Now, Anaxagoras was about twenty at the time of Xerxes' invasion of Greece (480), or even exactly twenty, if he died in 428 at the age of seventy-two (D.L. 2.7 = Anax. A1); then Empedocles may hardly have been born later than 495–492 — on this approximate date most scholars agree.[10] As Empedocles is said to have lived sixty years by Arist., περὶ ποιητῶν fr. 71 Rose³ (= D.L. 8.52; 8.74), he should have died around 435–432.[11] It is useful to bear in mind the structure of the Laertian *Life* of Empedocles:

---

[6] ... οἱ Συρακόσιοι προστησάμενοι τοὺς ἡγησομένους ὥρμησαν ἐπὶ τὴν κατάλυσιν τῆς τυραννίδος πανδημεί. Here Diodorus insists on the common effort of all the citizenship against the tyrant, but he also seems to suggest the allegiance of the people to the oligarchy, to whom οἱ ἡγησόμενοι are likely to have belonged.

[7] Asheri 1990: 486–490; Luraghi 1994: 267–268 ('sostanziale continuità tra il periodo pre-emmenide e quello post-emmenide'); *contra* Finley 1968: 59–60; Braccesi 1998: 60–65.

[8] Arist., *Pol.* 4.1297b 24–28: ... ἃς νῦν καλοῦμεν πολιτείας, οἱ πρότερον ἐκάλουν δημοκρατίας· ἦσαν δὲ αἱ ἀρχαῖαι πολιτεῖαι εὐλόγως ὀλιγαρχικαὶ καὶ βασιλικαί. δι'ὀλιγανθρωπίαν γὰρ οὐκ εἶχον πολὺ τὸ μέσον, ὥστ'ὀλίγοι τε ὄντες τὸ πλῆθος καὶ κατὰ τὴν σύνταξιν φαῦλοι ὑπέμενον τὸ ἄρχεσθαι. Cf. Mele 2007: 187–188.

[9] Ἀναξαγόρας δὲ ὁ Κλαζομένιος τῇ μὲν ἡλικίᾳ πρότερος ὢν τούτου, τοῖς δ'ἔργοις ὕστερος κτλ. Cf. Simpl., *Phys.* 25.19(= Emp. A7).

[10] See Diels 1884: 344 n. 2; Zeller I, 2, 1892⁵: 750 n. 1; Guthrie II, 1965: 128; Wright 1981: 5. Another clue is that Zeno of Elea and Empedocles, being fellow disciples of Parmenides (Alcid. ap. D.L. 8.56), were likely to be about the same age, and Zeno was described as being approximately forty in the Platonic dialogue *Parmenides*, staged in the historical context around 450. No proof is provided in the *Life* of the supposed ἀκμή (c. forty years of age) around 444, which could justify placing his birth about 484.

[11] D.L. 8.52: Ἀριστοτέλης γὰρ αὐτόν, ἔτι τε Ἡράκλειτον, ἑξήκοντα ἐτῶν φησι τετελευτηκέναι. 'In fact, Aristotle says that he died at sixty (and that so did Heraclitus)'. The reference to Heraclitus is preserved by DK and by the most recent edition of Diogenes Laertius by T. Dorandi, followed in this paper (see the discussion by Laurenti 1987, I, 230 n. 16); many others correct Ἡράκλειτον into Ἡρακλείδην. — The passage is assigned to the περὶ ποιητῶν also by R. Laurenti (fr. 2a), O. Gigon (fr. 18), and R. Janko (fr. 72a); see also D.L. 8.74 = fr. 2b Laurenti = 19 Gigon = 72b Janko. Unreliable information from other authors is reported by D.L. 8.73 (Empedocles would have died at seventy-seven from the aftermath of an accident while on a journey) and 8.74 (he would have died at one hundred and nine: an evident confusion with Gorgias).

family, distinctions gained by his relatives, philosophical teaching received, political career exemplifying features of his character, journeys, exile or rather exclusion from a return to his homeland, final years, and, lastly, conflicting and more or less amazing versions concerning his death. This scheme helps to understand why the *Life* contains a certain number of repetitions, and why it looks to the modern reader like a rather disorderly collection of news. Given the very modest room assigned to Empedocles' physical and religious theories, the core of the *Life* concerns his participation in politics — for which Diogenes Laertius largely depends on Timaeus of Tauromenium, a well-known hater of tyranny.[12] I will evaluate some anecdotes reported in the Laertian *Life*, and try to clarify their implications, debating — when necessary — those interpretations which I believe to be erroneous; and, while doing this, trying to set this information into a plausible chronological framework. A well-known episode concerns a double humiliation suffered by Empedocles at a symposium (Timae., *FGrH* 566, fr. 134 = D.L. 8.64 = A1). First the host, one of the leading men (τῶν ἀρχόντων) of Acragas, compelled his guests to wait a long time for a late-comer, 'the attendant (?) of the βουλή (τὸν τῆς βουλῆς ὑπηρέτην)', before allowing the wine to be served, and Empedocles was the only one who protested about such rudeness. Then, when the late-comer was finally there, he was chosen by the host as symposiarch, and forced Empedocles to drink lest wine be spilt on his head. Being forbidden to drink at all or, on the contrary, drinking under compulsion: nothing or too much. The anecdote has been judged strange sometimes, and even thought to be derived from a lost comedy.[13] I rather believe it to be a pointed description of the arbitrary power of tyranny, the arrogant violation of measure — in fact, a will to foreshadow tyranny is ascribed to the host (ὃς ὑπεγράφετο τυραννίδος ἀρχήν). Notably Empedocles' reaction in requiring that wine be served is qualified by the adverb μισοπονήρως, as μισοπονηρία ('the hatred of evil') is the name sometimes given to the virtue that inspires aristocratic resistance against tyranny.[14] Of course, far from being a way of humiliating a democrat, such behaviour was meant to offend an aristocrat as conscious of his dignity as our philosopher, and downgrade him.[15] Anyhow, the story ended with cold revenge by Empedocles: first, he accepted the imposition of drinking, but on the following day he dragged his two enemies to court, and had them condemned and executed. Timaeus thought that Empedocles' behaviour proved that he was δημοτικός, 'a democratic man'[16] — at least, so did Diogenes understand the purport of Timaeus' words. Diogenes saw in Timaeus' words a confirmation of Aristotle's judgement of Empedocles (Σοφιστής, fr. 66 Rose³ = D.L. 8.63): 'Aristotle says that he was free and alien from every kind of office, if he refused kingship offered to him — as Xanthus refers where he writes on him — evidently because he liked simplicity better'.[17] What did Aristotle mean by ἐλεύθερος καὶ πάσης ἀρχῆς ἀλλότριος? Likely not what was recently maintained by Ph.S. Horky, i.e. that

---

[12] Cf. Momigliano 1982: 228; *contra* Baron 2013: 258.

[13] Brown 1958: 52.

[14] Cf. Plut., *Tim.* 3.4; 5.1.

[15] Bibliography concerning the meaning of ὑπηρέτης in this passage is collected and discussed by Andolfi 2020: 213 n. 28. On the word in general see Richardson 1943, who argued in favour of the sense of 'subordinate'. Laurenti (1987, I. 231 n. 19) is probably right in suggesting the γραμματεὺς τῆς βουλῆς ('the secretary of the council') in the wake of Bidez.

[16] ... δημοτικὸν εἶναι τὸν ἄνδρα. On the meaning of this adjective cf. Ferreira 2008.

[17] Φησὶ δ'αὐτὸν καὶ Ἀριστοτέλης ἐλεύθερον γεγονέναι καὶ πάσης ἀρχῆς ἀλλότριον, εἴ γε τὴν βασιλείαν αὐτῷ διδομένην παρῃτήσατο, καθάπερ Ξάνθος ἐν τοῖς περὶ αὐτοῦ λέγει, τὴν λιτότητα δηλονότι πλέον ἀγαπήσας. Laurenti assigns the passage to the περὶ ποιητῶν (fr. 2c), and so does Janko (fr. 71), whereas Gigon puts it among the 'Fragmente ohne Buchangabe' (fr. 865). Cf. the commentary on this passage (Xanthos, *FGrH* 1001, fr. 1) by Schepens and Theys 2020.

Empedocles was an anarchist, opposing every kind of political authority.[18] He was ἐλεύθερος, 'free', because he freely reacted to every abuse of authority, as exemplified in the story of the *symposion*. And he was 'alien to every kind of office', because he liked 'simplicity' — this is proved by the fact that according to Xanthus, a more or less contemporary source,[19] he even refused to become king. This surprising revelation might be substantially true, even though not formally correct, if we take into account the frequent ascription by Pindar and Diodorus of the title of king to Sicilian tyrants, both Syracusan and Acragantine.[20] So, Empedocles might have refused to become a tyrant, presumably for the sake of consistency with his own opposition to tyranny, or, more precisely, he might have waived the offer of an αἰσυμνητεία.[21] Timaeus did not preserve for us the names of the rude host, one of the ἄρχοντες in Acragas, and of the ὑπηρέτης of the council, who was really at the service of this powerful leader. Anyhow, the request for capital punishment to be meted out to them was not disproportionate with Empedocles' point of view, because what was really at stake was the outcome of the fight against tyranny. Much evidence bears out this interpretation. From another, distant passage of the Laertian *Life* we glean something more. Neanthes (*FGrH* 84, fr. 28 = D.L. 8.72) referred that prodromes of tyranny started to show themselves after the death of Meton, Empedocles' father.[22] This might imply that engagement against tyranny was traditional with our philosopher's family. Other evidence points in the same way: according to D.L. 8.65 (unfortunately, this time the biographer does not quote his source), Empedocles prevented the βουλή from granting a site (evidently on public ground) to build a tomb for the famous physician Acron's father. The reason for denying such privilege was expounded by the philosopher in a speech focused on equality.[23] For the moment, suffice it to remark that both the anecdote on the symposium and the one on Acron concern attempts of two aristocrats to violate equality of rights. One might doubt whether it was equality of rights among all citizens or simply among those of the same social group as Empedocles, the aristocrats. But another piece of this jigsaw helps to clear this point, the Gathering of the Thousand.

The Gathering of the Thousand

This institution is attested for Acragas just by the *Life* of Empedocles. It is mentioned in a passage usually ascribed to Timaeus (*FGrH* 566, fr. 2 = D.L. 8.66): 'Afterwards [i.e. after the Acron's episode] Empedocles also dissolved the Gathering of the Thousand, which had been in existence for three years; therefore not only was he one of the rich, but also one of those who nurtured democratic feelings'.[24] This is the most meaningful event in Empedocles' public life, but, as to its chronological collocation, unfortunately, we only know that it was some time after the clash with Acron. The existence of Gatherings of the Thousand is witnessed elsewhere too: Rhegion, Locri, Croton, Opountian Locris, Cyme in Aiolis, and Colophon (even though historians often forget about the two last ones) — the Gathering of Colophon is recalled by Xenophanes (21B3.4), among other sources.[25] These Gatherings have been interpreted as oligarchic civic *corpora* composed of one thousand men, not councils — in other words, they are 'fixed-number oligarchies', theoretically fossils of the original citizenship dating from the times of the foundation. It is not a recent thesis, as it dates back to the end of the nineteenth century, although it has recently been reasserted by M. Giangiulio.[26] According to this scholar, 'l'età arcaica in realtà non conobbe regimi aristocratici, oligarchici, timocratici, democratici e ovviamente nemmeno "costituzioni" di qualsiasi tipo'. This sharp remark is intended to avoid transposing Aristotelian classifications back to earlier times. However, the scanty sources available associate these Gatherings of the Thousand with oligarchic or timocratic regimes: this is, for instance, the case of Rhegion in the 5th century, as described by Heraclid. Lemb. 55, p. 32 Dilts: 'They founded an aristocratic constitution. One thousand, chosen with regard to their wealth, administrate everything'.[27] Giangiulio recently maintained that the Gathering in Locri could have existed in the seventh century, in the age of Zaleucus (and I am inclined to agree that generally the origin of this institution is likely to be ancient, also because it is attested by Xenophanes);[28] but Giangiulio has also rightly acknowledged that 'nonetheless, in the classical age the numbered political bodies became more and more elitist and restricted. Only at that time did they become oligarchies'.[29] The relationship between the Gatherings and other institutions and political councils was investigated by G. Camassa.[30] If the vast powers assigned to the Thousand in Croton — as summarized by a late witness like Iamblichus — can offer a valid comparison in order to understand the role played by their homologues in Acragas, they could ask that political advice be given to the leaders of the government (Iambl., *VP* 45); act as judges (126); refuse the distribution of the land to the people (255); face the antipythagoric rebellion (257 and 260). It is conceivable that even the comparatively moderate Theron would not have borne the permanence in Acragas of such an important vestige of the pre-tyrannical regime as this body (if, as I believe, it dated back to those days). Therefore, in Acragas the Gathering of the Thousand might well have been dissolved two times: once, at the beginning of Theron's leadership or even before, and later, for the second time, by Empedocles.[31] Let us try to outline an approximate chronology. The fall of Thrasydaeus in 471

---

[24] Ὕστερον δ'ὁ Ἐμπεδοκλῆς καὶ τὸ τῶν χιλίων ἄθροισμα κατέλυσε συνεστὼς ἐπὶ ἔτη τρία, ὥστε οὐ μόνον ἦν τῶν πλουσίων, ἀλλὰ καὶ τῶν τὰ δημοτικὰ φρονούντων. — An alternative translation for ἄθροισμα... συνεστὼς ἐπὶ ἔτη τρία has been proposed by some scholars, among whom Gigante (1962: 409), 'l'assemblea dei Mille, costituita per la durata di tre anni'. — In the locution τῶν τὰ δημοτικὰ φρονούντων the words τὰ δημοτικὰ cannot indicate anything else than a political position, and not just moral qualities like unaffectedness or generosity.

[25] Sources and bibliography for Rhegion, Locri and Croton in Giangiulio 2003: 16 n. 6 (to whom Talamo 2011 should be added for Croton); Allasia 2014–2015: 19 nn. 79, 77, 78 for Opountian Locris, Cyme Aeolis and Colophon (to whom Beck 1999 should be added for Opountian Locris).

[26] Giangiulio 2016: 203–205, who goes through the bibliography.

[27] Πολιτείαν δὲ κατεστήσαντο ἀριστοκρατικήν. χίλιοι γὰρ πάντα διοικοῦσιν αἱρετοὶ ἀπὸ τιμημάτων.

[28] The fact that it apparently existed in the sixth century in Colophon seems to make it likely that it was old also elsewhere.

[29] See Giangiulio 2018: 283–285 and 293. This scholar also deals with the Six Hundred in Massalia (287–288).

[30] Camassa 1987: 630–656.

[31] This double dissolution is even taken for established by Ghinatti 1996: 28–29.

offers a first, provisional *terminus post quem* for the reconstitution of the Thousand. But we must take into account other relevant data:

As already said, the start of Empedocles' public life was the symposium episode (D.L. 8.64: ἀρχὴ μὲν οὖν αὐτῷ τῆς πολιτείας ἥδε), to which followed the Acron episode — the two anecdotes are linked by the contrast to the tyrannic aspirations of the host, and, respectively, the discourse denying the privilege requested by Acron and extolling ἰσότης.

Not long before Empedocles' access to public life, his father Meton is said to have died. This is suggested by the following circumstances:

a. According to Neanth., *FGrH* 84, fr. 28, at the death of Meton there appeared premonitions of the return of tyranny, which recall the political climate described above;
b. Empedocles would hardly have come to the forefront of the public scene (as he did reacting against the rude host and against Acron) before reaching the thirtieth year of age.[32] If Empedocles was born when his father Meton was around thirty, the latter's death may well have intervened some years later than the expulsion of Thrasydaeus — about the same time as our philosopher is said to have dissolved the Thousand, an initiative which he would hardly, in my opinion, have taken in the first person if his father had been still alive and politically active. It is noteworthy that, of the two anecdotes just recalled under b., the former implies a close relationship between Empedocles and the βουλή, and the latter mentions the opposition to Acron's request expressed by Empedocles' discourse to the βουλή, in all likelihood delivered as a βουλευτής. So, his public life opened with two speeches, a λόγος δικανικός and a λόγος συμβουλευτικός, as befits the inventor of rhetoric (Arist., Σοφιστής, fr. 65 Rose³ = D.L. 8.57=A1)[33] and the author of 'political discourses' (Arist., περὶ ποιητῶν, fr. 70 Rose³ = D.L. 8.57–58 = A1).[34] This start was fully inspired by the engagement against inequality (maybe in the wake of a policy started by Meton against all tyrannical temptations), and we learn from Neanthes that it was followed by a campaign led by Empedocles in order to 'persuade the Acragantines to desist from quarrels and practise political equality' (*FGrH* 84, fr. 28 = D.L. 8.72).[35] I will come back to this later. But then, when did Empedocles join public life? If we accept the approximate date (495–492) proposed above for the birth and a minimum age of thirty or a little less, the outcome is the second half of the sixties — a date next to the one (461) indicated by A. Mele on quite different grounds: i.e., at about that time our philosopher should have taught his disciple Gorgias, and in those same years many trials were celebrated in Sicily, as part of the aristocracy attempted to recover the properties of which they had once been dispossessed by the Emmenidai in favour of the latters' followers (cf. Arist., τεχνῶν συναγωγή, fr. 137 Rose³ = Cic., *Brut.* 12).[36] Of course, Mele's suggestion is useful, because

---

[32] We are forced to rely on analogy: thirty was the minimum age fixed for βουλευταί to be chosen by lot in Athens (Arist., *Ath.* 4, 3; cf. Rhodes 1985²: 116).

[33] = *Soph.* fr. 1a Laurenti= 39,1 Gigon.

[34] πολιτικούς (sc. λόγους): this is the reading accepted by the two last editors of Diogenes Laertius, M. Marcovich and T. Dorandi; cf. Gorg. A29. The passage is ascribed to the περὶ ποιητῶν also by Gigon (fr. 17), by Laurenti (fr. 1) and by Janko (fr. 73).

[35] Πεῖσαι τοὺς Ἀκραγαντίνους παύσασθαι μὲν τῶν στάσεων, ἰσότητα δὲ τὴν πολιτικὴν ἀσκεῖν.

[36] = fr. 125 Gigon. See Mele 2007: 185–186.

it sets the beginning of the public life of Empedocles into the context of the tensions among aristocracy and the 'new citizens' installed by the tyrants.[37] Empedocles may have faced an oligarchy elated at having got free of the 'new citizens'— an oligarchy sometimes even nourishing tyrannical aspirations in its turn.

The supposed exile

The romantic story of Empedocles' exile is really one of the vaguest features of the Laertian *Life*.[38] Indeed, the only passage of the *Life* which might explicitly refer to the exile — drawn from the historian Apollodorus — really seems to deny that Empedocles was ever even exiled (*FGrH* 244, fr. 32a = D.L. 8.52):

> Apollodorus the grammarian says in his *Chronicle* that (Empedocles) was son of Meton, and Glaucus says that he went to Thurii when the city had just been founded. Then, a little below: But those who narrate that he, being exiled (?) from his homeland to Syracuse, fought at the Syracusans' side against the Athenians, seem to me to fail to understand at all; in fact, either he was dead by then, or he was extremely old, which is inconsistent with the story.[39]

Apollodorus went on inferring such inconsistency from the already mentioned Aristotelian witness, according to which Empedocles died at sixty (fr. 71 Rose³ = D.L., *loc. cit.*). As a matter of fact, the information concerning the exile (οἴκοθεν πεφευγὼς εἰς τὰς Συρακούσας) sounds unreliable given the subsequent statement of Apollodorus himself that Empedocles could not have fought in defence of Syracuse against the Athenians for reasons of chronology.[40] Besides, the locution πεφευγὼς εἰς τὰς Συρακούσας can mean 'exiled to Syracuse', but also 'after fleeing to Syracuse'.[41] So, owing to the confused report by Apollodorus, some scholars have taken to regarding the foundation of Thurii (444/443) as a *terminus post quem* of his supposed exile.[42] But this is not confirmed by an unprejudiced reading of the source, as the verb used by Glaucus/Apollodorus is simply ἐλθεῖν, 'came'. Lastly, at D.L. 8.66–67 (again, the author does not quote his source) we read:

> While he stayed in Olympia, he was the object of the greatest attention, so that nobody was mentioned so often as Empedocles. (67) But afterwards, as Acragas was founded

---

[37] Apparently, part of the aristocracy had stayed in Acragas under Theron's tyranny, but the rest of it had not acquiesced in the *régime* and had gone on exile, losing their property (cf. Asheri 1990: 487).

[38] The exile was taken for granted by Diels (1898: 414), and by Tucker (1931: 50).

[39] Ἀπολλόδωρος δ'ὁ γραμματικὸς ἐν τοῖς Χρονικοῖς φησιν ὡς ἦν Μέτωνος μὲν υἱός, ἐς δὲ Θουρίους αὐτὸν νεωστὶ παντελῶς ἐκτισμένους Γλαῦκος ἐλθεῖν φησιν. εἴθ'ὑποβάς· οἱ δ'ἱστοροῦντες, ὡς οἴκοθεν πεφευγὼς εἰς τὰς Συρακούσας μετ'ἐκείνων ἐπολέμει πρὸς τοὺς Ἀθηναίους τελέως ἀγνοεῖν μοὶ δοκοῦσιν· ἢ γὰρ οὐκέτ'ἦν ἢ παντελῶς ὑπεργεγηρακώς, ὅπερ οὐ φαίνεται. 'Which is inconsistent with the story': this point is perfectly understood by R.D. Hicks. On Glaucus of Rhegium (here occurs fr. 6 Lanata) see Janko 2011: 536.

[40] This goes both for the siege of 415–412 and for the foregoing conflict of 424 (cf. Zeller I, 2, 1892⁵: 750–751 n. 1).

[41] Cf. Gigante's (1962: 403) translation 'fuggito dalla patria in Siracusa'. Instead, Hicks (1925: 369) rendered 'being exiled from his home'.

[42] Mele 2007: 190 understands the passage in Apollodorus as a witness concerning the exile; but he also explains Empedocles' move to Thurii as a consequence of the defeat suffered by Acragas (under supposed Pythagoric leadership) at the battle near the river Himera in 446 (cf. Hermipp., *FGrH* 1026, fr. 61 = D.L. 8.56, and fr. 25 = D.L. 8.40). This reconstruction is very uncertain.

again (?), the descendants of his enemies opposed his return; therefore, after retiring to Peloponnese, he died.[43]

This passage is very important, because of the much-debated locution τοῦ Ἀκράγαντος οἰκιζομένου.[44] Leaving this apart, there remains the news that 'the descendants of his enemies opposed his return'. Also this passage is sometimes supposed to prove that Empedocles underwent a condemnation to exile.[45] We do not know of any official decision in this sense, and we do not even know the source from which Diogenes drew this information (Jacoby made Timae., fr. 2 end at the close of §66 of the *Life*). It is open to speculation whether the denial of the return to Acragas was the response (ten or even twenty years later, as Timaeus refers to the 'descendants') to the dissolution of the Gathering by Empedocles — a reconstruction which was proposed by G. De Sensi Sestito.[46]

Ἰσότης πολιτική

It is difficult to grasp Empedocles' political position, as I.W. Rath wrote already in 1992.[47] Scholars have often thought that Empedocles was more or less warmly democratic.[48] Of course, the dissolution of the Gathering of the Thousand enforced by Empedocles (a piece of information which we may owe to Timaeus),[49] and his request to stop quarrels and observe the ἰσότης πολιτική (Neanth., *FGrH* 84, fr. 28 = D.L. 8.72) at least make it appear unlikely that the philosopher took a conservative stand (even this was upheld).[50] An interesting comparison is offered by an anecdote about Croton. Also there, if we trust a late source like Iambl., *VP* 257, the Thousand split into a group hostile to granting equal political rights to the people and another in favour of this innovation. The latter included three Pythagoreans, Hippasus, Diodorus and Theages, whereas other Pythagoreans sided with the aristocrats averse to extending political rights.[51] In this half-legendary reconstruction of the political

---

[43] καθ'ὃν δὲ χρόνον ἐπεδέμει Ὀλυμπίασιν, ἐπιστροφῆς ἠξιοῦτο πλείονος, ὥστε μηδενὸς ἑτέρου μνείαν γίνεσθαι ἐν ταῖς ὁμιλίαις τοσαύτην ὅσην Ἐμπεδοκλέους. (67). ὕστερον μέντοι τοῦ Ἀκράγαντος οἰκιζομένου, ἀντέστησαν αὐτοῦ τῇ καθόδῳ οἱ τῶν ἐχθρῶν ἀπόγονοι· διόπερ εἰς Πελοπόννησον ἀποχωρήσας ἐτελεύτησεν. On the interesting and much debated locution τοῦ Ἀκράγαντος οἰκιζομένου I am preparing a paper. Dorandi puts οἰκιζομένου between two *cruces desperationis*.

[44] Textual contributions are listed by Dorandi (2013: 639) in the apparatus.

[45] Bignone (1916: 108–109), and Wright (1981: 16–17) were rightly very cautious on this point.

[46] De Sensi Sestito 2016: 273–274.

[47] Rath 1992: 79.

[48] Surprisingly enough, not only was Diels (1898: 406) persuaded that Empedocles had a great role in the passage from tyranny to democracy, but also that his prestige worried the partisans of democracy themselves in the end, a circumstance which would have caused the philosopher to be exiled. Empedocles is regarded as a democratic also by Zeller I, 2 (1892⁵: 825); Bignone 1916: 65; 77–79; Burnet 1930⁴: 198–199; Guthrie II, 1965: 131. Wright (1981: 6–8) is wary of defining his political position; cf. Andò 1982: 47–48.

[49] See Timae., *FGrH* 566, fr. 2 (= D.L. 8.66). Timaeus is really mentioned in a sentence subsequent to that concerning the Thousand.

[50] For this position see Asheri (1990: 497–499). Of course, rejecting it does not necessarily imply believing that the Gathering of the Thousand had taken the place of a pre-existing popular assembly, and that the Gathering was abolished by Empedocles in order to resurrect such popular assembly.

[51] Καὶ λεγόντων ἐξ αὐτῶν τῶν χιλίων Ἱππάσου καὶ Διοδώρου καὶ Θεάγους ὑπὲρ τοῦ πάντας κοινωνεῖν τῶν ἀρχῶν καὶ τῆς ἐκκλησίας καὶ διδόναι τὰς εὐθύνας τοὺς ἄρχοντας ἐν τοῖς ἐκ πάντων λαχοῦσι, ἐναντιουμένων δὲ τῶν Πυθαγορείων Ἀλκιμάχου καὶ Δεινάρχου καὶ Μέτωνος καὶ Δημοκήδους καὶ διακολυόντων τὴν πάτριον πολιτείαν μὴ καταλύειν, ἐκράτησαν οἱ τῷ πλήθει συνηγοροῦντες. 'And when Hippasus and Diodorus and Theages from the Thousand themselves spoke in favour of open access to the offices for everybody and of the duty to submit a report of one's doings to people elected by lot among all citizens, whereas Alcimachus, Dinarchus, Meton and Democedes opposed

involvement of the Pythagoreans we perceive characteristic features of democratic ideology, like open access to public offices for everybody and election by lot. Whether Empedocles pushed himself so far in fifth-century Acragas or not, must remain an open question. At least, political equality was granted in Croton and, apparently, Empedocles successfully pleaded for it in Acragas. Instead, that main feature of extreme democracy, economic equality pursued through redistribution of land — which is not ascribed to Hippasus and his 'revolutionary' companions — was not included in Empedocles' proposal either (and it was anyway denied to the people also in Croton).[52] Rather, economic equality was bound to play a role in 4th-century Sicily.[53] It is interesting that a small part of the Pythagorean movement (a movement to which Empedocles cannot be assigned without any qualifications, but to which he was connected in several ways) supported political equality — all the more so, because a tradition, although rejected by its witness himself, Neanthes (FGrH 84, fr. 26 = D.L. 8.55), asserted that Empedocles had been a pupil of Hippasus.[54] Only one occurrence of πολιτικὴ ἰσότης is reported by the TGL and by LS: Plb. 6.8.4; here it signifies the equal dignity of all citizens, which is completely independent of social and economic inequalities: W.R. Paton translated 'civil equality', and G. Colesanti 'uguaglianza tra i cittadini'.[55] It is important to remark at this point that the demand to stop quarrels hardly sounds like a message of the leader of a political faction, but rather like a call addressed to the fellow-citizens by the main moral authority of the polis. Also the verb ἀσκεῖν in the locution ἰσότητα δὲ τὴν πολιτικὴν ἀσκεῖν suggests less a political frame of mind than the clever action of a divine craftswoman (as in the Physical Poem) or the careful cult offered to the gods.[56] On the other hand, the link between ἰσότης and φιλότης was a commonplace, repeated by poets and philosophers: see, for instance, E., Phoen. 535–538: ('... that is better, son, to honour equality, which always links together friends with friends and cities with cities; in fact, equality is right for people');[57] and Pl., Lg. 6, 757A ('Equality begets friendship').[58] This relationship was certainly constantly present to the mind of the poet/philosopher of Φιλίη, and could well inspire those who wrote about his life.

Politics and Philosophy in Empedocles

In the introduction I already mentioned and criticized Horky's thesis, according to which Aristotle considered Empedocles to be an anarchist. Besides, how could any anarchist turn to criminal courts to have would-be tyrants condemned and executed, and how could any anarchist address his fellow-citizens and demand that they give up fighting and establish a

---

this attempt at destroying the traditional constitution, the victory was of those who spoke in favour of the people'.

[52] Iambl., VP 255: Καὶ τὴν δορίκτητον διῳκήσαντο μὴ κατακληρουχηθῆναι κατὰ τὴν ἐπιθυμίαν τῶν πολλῶν. — 'And they decided not to portion out the land conquered in war, according to the desire of the many'.

[53] See Consolo Langher 2005. The popular insurrection in Syracuse led by Tyndarides in 454 (Diod. 11.86), mentioned by the same scholar (2007, 34), was quickly crushed by the χαριέστατοι.

[54] τὴν γὰρ περιφερομένην ὡς Τηλαύγους ἐπιστολὴν ὅτι τε μετέσχεν Ἱππάσου καὶ Βροτίνου, μὴ εἶναι ἀξιόπιστον — '(Neanthes said) that the letter divulged as written by Telauges, according to which (Empedocles) was a disciple of Hippasus and Brotinus, was not trustworthy'.

[55] Paton 1923: 285; Colesanti in Nicolai (1998: 287). Cf. TGL s.v. ἰσότης: 'Saepissime de aequalitate iuris dicitur et aequitate'.

[56] A divine craftswoman is described by Emp. B87 (γόμφοις ἀσκήσασα καταστόργοις Ἀφροδίτη — 'Aphrodite, having built ... with loving dowels'). Cult: Pind., Pyth. 3.108–109; Ol. 8.22.

[57] Κεῖνο κάλλιον, τέκνον, ἰσότητα τιμᾶν, ἢ φίλους ἀεὶ φίλοις πόλεις τε πόλεσι...συνδεῖ· τὸ γὰρ ἴσον νόμιμον ἀνθρώποις ἔφυ.

[58] Ἰσότης φιλότητα ἀπεργάζεται.

regime of equal political rights or any political regime at all? Rather, I am inclined to regard Empedocles as an unflinching adversary of tyranny and a supporter of equality of rights for all citizens (although not necessarily of an open access to public offices for all, and certainly not of redistribution of land).[59] Very recently another researcher, C.F. Coates, tried to draw proof of Empedocles' adhesion to democracy from his *Physical Poem*. The existence of a close correspondence of physics to politics and *vice versa* in some pre-Socratic authors since Anaximander's times is widely accepted; this line of research is no novelty, and it counts important antecedents, like G. Vlastos, W. Jaeger, and more recently, I.W. Rath.[60] But, in my opinion, it meets with a few serious difficulties, outlined below, at least as far as Empedocles is concerned.

a. Firstly, according to Arist., *Pol.* 6, 1317a 40–1317b 2, people are wont to say that the basis of the democratic constitution is freedom, as though they could take part in freedom only under that constitution (Aristotle clearly disagrees with them). Such freedom is characterized by two main features: alternation in government, because everybody in turn holds power and in turn is subjected to somebody else's power; and domination of the majority over the minority, so that 'the will of the mass is the aim, and it is what is right'.[61] Now, if government by turns is reflected in the sworn agreement between Love and Strife (B30), how does Empedocles represent the domination of the majority in his *Physical Poem*?

b. Secondly, if the Sphairos is supposed to represent monarchy, which is in due time dissolved in order to be substituted by democracy, what are we supposed to think (if we accept the cyclical interpretation of Empedoclean physics) of the subsequent reaggregation into the Sphairos? Might any fervent democrat accept a taken-for-granted return to monarchy (or tyranny)?

c. Thirdly, while Aristotle regards alternation in power and domination of the majority over the minority as the main democratic principles, he also takes into account another important feature of that constitution, the election by lot to all or most offices.[62] Where can we find any allusion to this in Empedoclean physics?

d. Fourthly, and most important of all, if democratic equality is really to be seen in the agreement between Love and Strife, sworn and faithfully observed by the two powers, what are we to make of the four elements? These are material, and now immortal now mortal, and lose and acquire again their divine condition; whereas Love and Strife are immaterial and constantly immortal.[63] The elements are disaggregated and aggregated again by the two powers, Love and Strife; so they are completely subjected to those two. Meaningfully, only the four elements are called πάντων ῥιζώματα ('roots of all things': B6), and this denomination is never extended to the powers.

---

[59] Concerning Empedocles' opposition to tyranny I agree with Andolfi 2020; but, as will be presently clear, I disagree with the idea, shared by her and others, that Empedocles' physics is consistent with a representation of democracy.

[60] Vlastos 1947; Jaeger 1947: 136–140; Rath 1992.

[61] Ὑπόθεσις μὲν οὖν τῆς δημοκρατικῆς πολιτείας ἐλευθερία (τοῦτο γὰρ λέγειν εἰώθασιν, ὡς ἐν μόνῃ τῇ πολιτείᾳ ταύτῃ μετέχοντας ἐλευθερίας...)· ἐλευθερίας δὲ ἓν μὲν τὸ ἐν μέρει ἄρχεσθαι καὶ ἄρχειν...ὅ τι ἂν δόξῃ τοῖς πλείοσι, τοῦτ᾽εἶναι τέλος καὶ τοῦτ᾽εἶναι τὸ δίκαιον.

[62] ...τὸ κληρωτὰς εἶναι τὰς ἀρχὰς...

[63] Immateriality of Love and Strife and materiality of the roots (or elements): Curd 2013; Wright 1981: 170–171. Love and Strife are immortal because their action is eternal, whereas the elements are in turn mortal (when they combine into things) and immortal (when they are separate): B17.6–13, and Curd 2016: 69; on the elements see also B35.14.

Consequently, it is impossible to put the elements on the same level as the powers, as Jaeger and Coates do,[64] as though the six of them were citizens enjoying equal rights in a democratic city. On the contrary, if this transposition from physics to politics makes any sense for Empedocles, the four elements cannot indicate anything but a status inferior to that represented by the two powers.[65]

Final remarks

My arguments have sought to draw as much as possible from a text like the *Life*, comparatively rich in data and at the same time elusive, and to challenge a political reading of Empedoclean physics as a close representation of democracy, which is not in my opinion well-founded on the text of the fragments of the Περὶ φύσεως. Is it possible, however cautiously, then, to answer the question posed in the title of this paper? Was Empedocles ultimately a democrat?

I think we should rather ask first: 'Was he a politician?'. In fr. B146,

> In the end they become prophets, poets, and physicians,
> and chiefs (πρόμοι) among men on the earth,
> and from these they shoot up as gods, excellent in honour,[66]

according to most scholars, the various roles played by Empedocles seem to be reflected here.[67] I think that they are right. First of all, Empedocles was apparently recognized as a god (B112.4–8),[68] even when he was still alive on earth and had not rejoined the community of the Blessed yet (cf. B147); so he was likely to be also the epitome of all the figures exalted in B146. Secondly, it seems safe to assume that he was a seer, μάντις (consider the μαντοσύναι he dispensed: B112.10), a poet (see his works), a physician (Satyr. fr. 13, p. 116 Schorn = D.L. 8.58 = A1; B111.1 and B112.10–12). Accordingly, it would be very strange if he were not also a πρόμος. Consequently, πρόμος here should indicate not a military chief (as in its use in Homer and *grosso modo* the tragic poets), but simply one of the outstanding figures (or the most outstanding figure) in his city.[69] Empedocles seems to be using the word metaphorically:

---

[64] But not, apparently, Vlastos (1947: 159 and n. 29), as recognized by Coates (2018: 434 n. 47).
[65] As to powers and elements, one passage has been discussed for decades (B17.27–29):
ταῦτα γὰρ ἶσα τε πάντα καὶ ἥλικα γένναν ἔασι,
τιμῆς δ'ἄλλης ἄλλο μέδει, πάρα δ'ἦθος ἑκάστῳ,
ἐν δὲ μέρει κρατέουσι περιπλομένοιο χρόνοιο.
'These are all equal and of the same age,
but each holds a different honour, each has its character,
and they dominate in turn as time comes round'.
Are ταῦτα the powers and the elements or just the elements? I prefer the second solution, which matches Aristotle's interpretation (*de gen. et corr.* 2, 333a 16–20), and is supported by Bollack III.1 (1969: 72); Diels (1901: 114); Wright (1981: 170–171). *Contra* Bignone (1916: 406–407); DK I, 317.
[66] Εἰς δὲ τέλος μάντεις τε καὶ ὑμνοπόλοι καὶ ἰητροί
καὶ πρόμοι ἀνθρώποισιν ἐπιχθονίοισι πέλονται,
ἔνθεν ἀναβλαστοῦσι θεοὶ τιμῆσι φέριστοι.
[67] See, for instance, Wright 1981: 291: 'It is probable that E. supposed all four types of life to be united in himself'.
[68] B112 is reproduced below.
[69] Bollack 2003: 111. *Contra* Picot and Berg (2015: 394–399). On semantic shifts from Homer to Empedocles cf. Bordigoni 2004.

he says πρόμος, 'champion qui combat hors des lignes', to indicate 'chef en général'.[70] Now, seers, poets, physicians, all of them, are essential categories in society, but all of them are pre-political categories. The same should be supposed of πρόμος, applied by Empedocles to Empedocles himself, a man capable of providing for all the needs of his fellow-citizens and — overcoming the boundaries usually imposed on ancient Greek politics — even of mankind at large.[71] This, of course, did not hamper the involvement of our philosopher in Acragantine politics, as we have seen. However, already a long time ago, in 1894, J. Bidez acutely remarked that Empedocles was not known to have founded democracy or any democratic institution in Acragas.[72] His policy — I would add — should rather be seen in the context of his ethical-religious engagement. Here we find an important point in common with Pythagoras.[73] This is really best described in fr. 112, reproduced below according to the text of D4 Laks–Most,[74] where also the social and cultural difference between the higher and the lower classes is clearly outlined:

> Friends, you who inhabit the great city along the fair Acragas,
> On the acropolis, you mindful of good deeds,
> Respectful harbours for foreigners, untouched by baseness,
> I greet you; I, an immortal god for you, no longer mortal,
> go among you, honoured, as it seems,   5
> crowned with headbands and rich garlands.
> Whenever I come to the flourishing cities, by them,
> Men and women, I am venerated; and others follow me,
> Thousands of them, asking where is the path to advantage,
> Some in need of vaticinations, others require to listen   10
> A word of remedy for all sorts of illnesses,
> Having long been pierced <by> cruel <pains>.

---

[70] Cf. Chantraine *et al.* 1968–1980, s. v. πρόμος.

[71] Empedocles' versatile capacities for curing moral and physical illnesses and natural catastrophes are illustrated in the *Life* (8.60–61), and in B112 itself in connection with his visits far from Acragas.

[72] Bidez 1894: 132: 'Il ne paraît guère qu'Empédocle ait joué à Agrigent le rôle d'un fondateur de la démocratie, comme tous l'ont cru jusqu'au présent. Timée énumère les tentatives auxquelles Empédocle s'est opposé, il n'indique pas une institution qui ait été son oeuvre'.

[73] About Pythagoras see Rath (1992: 74): 'Seine politische Tätigkeit bestand eher in Beratungsfunktion', and De Sensi Sestito (2016: 272): '...in nessun testo viene attribuita al Maestro una specifica attività legislativa, ma solo paideutica e parenetica'.

[74] ὦ φίλοι, οἳ μέγα ἄστυ κατὰ ξανθοῦ Ἀκράγαντος
ναίετ'ἀν'ἄκρα πόλεος, ἀγαθῶν μελεδήμονες ἔργων,
ξείνων αἰδοῖοι λιμένες, κακότητος ἄπειροι,
χαίρετ'· ἐγὼ δ'ὑμῖν θεὸς ἄμβροτος, οὐκέτι θνητός
πωλεῦμαι μετὰ πᾶσι τετιμένος, ὥσπερ ἔοικα,   5
ταινίαις τε περίστεπτος στέφεσίν τε θαλείοις.
τοῖσιν ἅμ'εὖτ'ἂν ἵκωμαι ἐς ἄστεα τηλεθάοντα,
ἀνδράσιν ἠδὲ γυναιξί, σεβίζομαι· οἱ δ'ἅμ'ἕπονται
μυρίοι ἐξερέοντες, ὅπη πρὸς κέρδος ἀταρπός,
οἱ μὲν μαντοσυνέων κεχρημένοι, οἱ δέ τι νούσων   10
παντοίων ἐπύθοντο κλύειν εὐηκέα βάξιν,
δηρὸν δὴ χαλεπῇσι πεπαρμένοι <ἀμφ'ὀδύνῃσι>.

Bibliography

Allasia, M. 2014–2015. Storia politica di Locri Epizefiri tra V e IV secolo. Il passaggio da oligarchia a democrazia. Unpublished PhD dissertation. Università di Torino, viewed 31 December 2020, <https://unito.academia.edu/ MatteoAllasia>.

Andò, V. 1982–1983. Nestis o l'elemento acqua di Empedocle. *Kokalos* 28–29: 31–51.

Andolfi, I. 2020. Empedocles *Arbiter Symposii*: Luxury, Political Equality, and Bizarre Dinner Parties in Fifth-Century Acragas. *Histos* 14: 206–230.

Asheri, D. 1990. Agrigento libera: rivolgimenti interni e problemi costituzionali, *ca.* 471–446 a. C. *Athenaeum* 68: 483–501.

Baron, Chr.A. 2013. *Timaeus of Tauromenium and Hellenistic Historiography*. Cambridge–New York: Cambridge University Press.

Beck, H. 1999. Ostlokris und die Tausend Opuntier. Neue Überlegungen zum Siedlergesetz für Naupaktos. *Zeitschrift für Papyrologie und Epigraphik* 124: 53–62.

Bidez, J. 1894. *La biographie d'Empédocle*. Gand: Clemm.

Bignone, E. 1916. *Empedocle*. Torino: Bocca.

Bollack, J. 1965–1969. *Empédocle. Les Origines*, I–III. Paris: Minuit.

Bollack, J. 2003. *Les Purifications*. Paris: Seuil.

Bordigoni, C. 2004. Empedocle e la dizione omerica, in L. Rossetti and C. Santaniello (eds) *Studi sul pensiero e sulla lingua di Empedocle*: 199–289. Bari: Levante.

Braccesi, L. 1998. *I tiranni di Sicilia*. Roma and Bari: Laterza.

Brown, T.S. 1958. *Timaeus of Tauromenium*. Berkeley and Los Angeles: University of California Press.

Burnet, J. 1930[4]. *Early Greek Philosophy*. London: Black.

Camassa, G. 1987. La codificazione delle leggi e le istituzioni politiche delle città greche della Calabria in età arcaica e classica, in S. Settis (ed.) *Storia della Calabria antica*: 613–656. Roma and Reggio Calabria: Gangemi.

Chantraine, P. *et al.* 1968–1980. *Dictionnaire étymologique de la langue grecque*. Paris: Klincksieck, I–IV.

Coates, C.F. 2018. Cosmic Democracy or Cosmic Monarchy? Empedocles in Plato's *Statesman*. *Polis* 35: 418–446.

Consolo Langher, S.N. 2005. Democrazia e antidemocrazia a Siracusa: ἰσότης e γῆς ἀναδασμός nelle lotte sociali del IV secolo, in U. Bultrighini (ed.) *Democrazia e antidemocrazia nel mondo greco*: 235–250. Alessandria: Ed. dell'Orso.

Consolo Langher, S.N. 2007: Le forme del potere nella Sicilia greca: tra democrazia e tirannide, in S.N. Consolo Langher, C. Raccuia and G. Mafodda. *Forme del potere, problemi storiografici, percorsi istituzionali in Sicilia*: 9–119. Messina–Civitanova Marche: A. Siciliano Editore.

Curd, P. 2013. Where are Love and Strife? Incorporeality in Empedocles, in J. McCoy (ed.) *Early Greek Philosophy and the Emergence of Reason*: 113–118. Washington, D. C.: CUA Press.

Curd, P. 2016. Powers, Structure, and Thought in Empedocles. *Rhizomata* 4: 55–79.

DK 1951[6]: Diels, H.–Kranz, W. (eds) *Die Fragmente der Vorsokratiker*, Berlin: Weidmann, I–III.

De Sensi Sestito, G. 2016. Qualche osservazione sui legislatori d'Occidente nella prospettiva pitagorica e storiografica del quarto secolo a. C., in *Poleis e politeiai nella Magna Grecia arcaica e classica*: 269–287. Taranto: Istituto per la Storia e l'archeologia della Magna Grecia.

Diels, H. 1884. Gorgias und Empedokles. *Sitzungsberichte der Königlich Preußischen Akademie der Wissenschaften zu Berlin* 49: 343–368.

Diels, H. 1898. Über die Gedichte des Empedokles. *Sitzungsberichte der Königlich Preußischen Akademie der Wissenschaften zu Berlin* 63: 396–415.

Diels, H. (ed.) 1901: *Poetarum Philosophorum Fragmenta*, Berolini: Apud Weidmannos.

Dilts, M.R. (ed.) 1971. *Heraclidis Lembi. Excerpta Politiarum*. Durham, NC: Duke University.

Dorandi, T. (ed.) 2013. *Diogenes Laertius. Lives of Eminent Philosophers*. Cambridge: Cambridge University Press.

Drachmann, A.B. (ed.) 1903–1927. *Scholia vetera in Pindari carmina*. Lipsiae: Teubner, I–III.

Ferreira, J.R. 2008. *Demotikos e demokratikos* na *paideia* de Plutarco, in C. Soares, J.R. Ferreira and M. do Céu Fialho (eds) *Ética e paideia em Plutarco*: 71–84. Coimbra: Imprensa da Universidade de Coimbra.

Finley, M.I. 1968. *A History of Sicily. Ancient Sicily to The Arab Conquest*. London: Chatto and Windus.

Freeman, E.A. 1891. *The History of Sicily from the Earliest Times*, Oxford: At the Clarendon Press, II.

Ghinatti, F. 1996. *Assemblee greche d'Occidente*. Torino: SEI.

Giangiulio, M. 2003. Ordinamenti pubblici e comunità politica in Magna Grecia: ancora sui regimi a numero fisso, in A. D'Atena and E. Lanzillotta (eds) *Da Omero alla costituzione europea: costituzionalismo antico e* moderno: 13–31. Tivoli: TORED.

Giangiulio, M. 2016. Le *politeiai* delle città della Magna Grecia: peculiarità e dinamiche, in *Poleis e politeiai nella Magna Grecia arcaica e classica*: 203–214. Taranto: Istituto per la Storia e l'archeologia della Magna Grecia.

Giangiulio, M. 2018. Oligarchies of 'Fixed Number' or Citizen Bodies in the Making?, in A. Duploy and R. Brock (eds) *Defining Citizenship in Archaic Greece*: 275–293. Oxford: Oxford University Press.

Gigante, M. 1962. *Diogene Laerzio. Vite dei filosofi*. Bari: Laterza.

Gigon, O. (ed.) 1987. *Aristotelis opera. Librorum deperditorum fragmenta*. Berlin: W. de Gruyter.

Guthrie, W.K.C. 1962–1981. *A History of Greek Philosophy*. Cambridge: Cambridge University Press, I–VI.

Hicks, R.D. (ed.) 1925. *Diogenes Laertius. Lives of Eminent Philosophers*. London: Heinemann; New York: Putnam, I–II.

Horky, Ph.S. 2016. *Empedocles Democraticus*: Hellenistic Biography at the Intersection of Philosophy and Politics, in M. Bonazzi and S. Schorn (eds) *'Bios Philosophos': Philosophy in Ancient Greek Biography*: 37–71. Turnhout: Brepols.

Jacoby, F. (ed.). *Die Fragmente der griechischen Historiker*. Leiden: Brill, 1923–1958, I–III; G. Schepens and S. Schorn (general eds), Leiden: Brill, 1998–2010, IV. [*FGrH*]

Jaeger, W. 1947. *The Theology of Early Greek Philosophers*. Engl. transl. Oxford: At the Clarendon Press.

Janko, R. (ed.) 2011. *Philodemus. On poems. Books 3-4, with the fragments of Aristotle, On poets*. Oxford: Oxford University Press.

Kingsley, P. 1995. Meetings with Magi: Iranian Themes among the Greeks, from Xanthus of Lydia to Plato's Academy. *Journal of the Royal Asiatic Society of Great Britain and Ireland* 5: 173–209.

Lanata, G. (ed.) 1963. *Poetica pre-platonica. Testimonianze e frammenti*. Firenze: La Nuova Italia.

Laurenti, R. 1987. *Aristotele. I frammenti dei dialoghi*. Napoli: Loffredo, I–II.

Liddell, H. G., R. Scott, and H. Stuart Jones, *A Greek-English Lexicon*. Oxford: Oxford University Press. [LS 1983[22]]

Luraghi, N. 1994: *Tirannidi arcaiche in Sicilia e Magna Grecia. Da Panezio di Leontini alla caduta dei Dinomenidi.* Firenze: Olschki.

Marcovich, M. 1999. *Diogenis Laertii Vitae Philosophorum*, I. Stutgardiae et Lipsiae: Teubner.

Mele, A. 2007. Empedocle e Agrigento, in G. Casertano (ed.) *Empedocle tra poesia, medicina, filosofia e politica*: 179–197. Napoli: Loffredo.

Momigliano, A. 1982. *La storiografia greca.* Torino: Einaudi.

Musti, D. 2005. *Magna Grecia. Il quadro storico.* Roma–Bari: Laterza.

Nicolai, R. (ed.) 1998. *Polibio. Storie. Libri IV-IX*, transl. by F. Cannatà, G. Colesanti, C. Tartaglini. Roma: Newton Compton.

Paton, W.R. 1923. *Polybius. The Histories* III. London: Heinemann. New York: Putnam.

Pezzullo, A. (ed.) 2017. *Aristotele. Politeiai di Samo, Colofone e Cuma eolica. Frammenti di tradizione indiretta.* Tivoli: TORED.

Picot, J.-C. and W. Berg 2015. Lions and 'Promoi': Final Phase of Exile for Empedocles' 'Daimones'. *Phronesis* 60: 380–409.

Rath, I.W. 1992. Die griechische Polis als Bezugsrahmen des vorsokratischen Denkens. Ein Versuch der sozial-historischen Verankerung. *Quaderni urbinati di cultura classica* 42: 63–81.

Rhodes, P.J. 1985[2]. *A Commentary on the Aristotelian Athenaion Politeia.* Oxford: Clarendon Press.

Richardson, L.J.D. 1943. ΥΠΗΡΕΤΗΣ. *Classical Quarterly* 37: 55–61.

Rose[3], V. (ed.) 1886. *Aristotelis qui ferebantur librorum fragmenta.* Lipsiae: Teubner.

Schepens, G. and Theys, E. (eds) 2020. 'Xanthos of Lydia', in S. Schorn (ed.), *Die Fragmente der Griechischen Historiker*, Part IV, viewed 10 November 2020 <http://dx.doi.org/10.1163/1873-5363_jciv_a1001> .

Schorn, S. (ed.) 2004. *Satyros aus Kallatis. Sammlung der Fragmente mit Kommentar.* Basel: Schwabe.

Schorn, S. 2007. 'Periegetische Biographie', 'Historische Biographie': Neanthes von Kyzikos (*FGrHist* 84) als Biograph, in M. Erler and S. Schorn (eds) *Die griechische Biographie in hellenistischer Zeit*: 115–151. Berlin: De Gruyter.

TGL: *Thesaurus Graecae Linguae*, ab Henrico Stephano constructus...1831–1865, I-VIII.

Talamo, C. 2011. I Mille, famiglie preminenti e pitagorismo a Crotone. *La Parola del Passato* 66: 171–179.

Tucker, G.M. 1931. Empedocles in Exile. *Classical Review* 45: 49–51.

Vlastos, G. 1947: Equality and Justice in Early Greek Cosmologies. *Classical Philology* 42: 156–178.

Wright, M.R. (ed.) 1981. *Empedocles: The Extant Fragments.* New Haven and London: Yale University Press.

Zeller, E. 1892[5]. *Die Philosophie der Griechen in ihrer geschichtlichen Entwicklung.* Leipzig: Reisland, I, 2.

From Chremonides to Chaeronea: Demosthenes' Influence in Later Athens[1]

Ian Worthington

Macquarie University, Sydney
ian.worthington@mq.edu.au

Abstract

This paper offers a different perspective on Chremonides' opposition to Antigonid rule and Athenian resistance in the Chremonidean War by considering the symbolism of Demosthenes' statue in the city. Demosthenes' strong anti-Macedonian line had ended in defeat at the battle of Chaeronea in 338. This he spun into a patriotic victory in his *Crown* oration: the Athenians had done the right thing in opposing Philip and followed in the tradition of their ancestors who fought the Persians for Greek freedom. His statue in 280/79, forty years after his death, called on the Athenians to continue doing the right thing by resisting Macedonian rule. Against this background, and despite continuing odds against them, the Athenians would always grasp any opportunity to fight for freedom and do the right thing (hence also their support for Mithridates against Rome in the 80s).

Keywords

Demosthenes; Athens; Macedonia; Chremonides; Chremonidean War.

The history of Athens after the death of Alexander the Great in 323 and throughout the Hellenistic and Roman eras is often marginalized when compared to the city's heyday in the Classical era.[2] Its form of government in the Hellenistic period has been called 'a mere caricature of the regime which had constituted the greatness of Athens',[3] with a muzzled Assembly passing mostly sycophantic decrees and the Areopagus reasserting its influence in political life. Its citizenry had been depleted because of the imposition of wealth requirements for citizenship by Antipater (of 2,000 drachmas) in 322,[4] and by Demetrius of Phalerum (of 1000 drachmas) in 317.[5] The city became a virtual oligarchy, with even the priesthoods losing their popular nature and exploited by aristocrats for political and social advancement especially in Roman times.[6] In addition, the city's artistic and cultural life dwindled away; the civic institution of the *ephebeia* became a shadow of its former self,[7] religious festivals were scaled

---

[1] I thank the editors for the invitation to participate in this volume honouring P.J. Rhodes and to attend the conference in Portugal to celebrate Peter's eightieth birthday in 2020. Sadly, that meeting had to be cancelled because of covid. The editors asked for essays that reflect Peter's work and influence. Since he has managed to have an impact on practically all aspects of Greek history and politics, finding a topic on which to present fresh insights and appeal to him is not that easy. Hence the topic of this essay, which, like his work and life, were anchored in doing the right thing.
[2] On this long period most recently see Worthington (2021).
[3] Mossé (1973: 108).
[4] Diod. 18.18.4; Plut. *Phocion* 27.3. Inconsistencies in our sources make the number of disfranchised citizens unknown, but perhaps there were as any as three thousand: see Worthington (2021: 27), citing bibliography.
[5] Diod. 18.74.3.
[6] Grijalvo (2005).
[7] Burckhardt (2004); Friend (2019); Habicht (1997: 233-237); Perrin-Saminadayar (2004; 2007).

back or even postponed because of a shrinking economy,[8] and as the Roman era progressed the city itself was even seen as a provincial one thanks to Roman-funded construction.[9]

The Athenians under Antigonid and Roman rule seem far removed from the days of their predecessors who resolutely faced down threats from Persia, Sparta, and Macedonia. They were subjects of outside powers, forced to do their bidding and endure the callous disregard of beliefs they held dear. Thus, they had to endure the ten-year regime of Demetrius of Phalerum (Cassander's puppet ruler) from 317 to 307, not to mention Demetrius I Poliorcetes' impious lifestyle while living in the Parthenon,[10] or his disregard of the law when, on the urging of his lover Cleaenetus of Cydathenae, he overturned the conviction and fine of Cleaenetus' father Cleomedon (Plut. *Demetrius* 24.3-4). Over two centuries later nothing had changed. Mark Antony, for example, could demand the Athenians call him the 'New Dionysus', hold Dionysiac processions, and (if we believe the story) marry their patron deity Athena and expect a dowry of one million drachmas.[11] And in the Augustan era Athena had to share the Acropolis with Roma, where was built the temple of Roma and Augustus, the likely focal point of the imperial cult in the city.[12]

But later Athens was not this sad postscript to its classical self, for one unifying, and often neglected, theme of this long period was the resilience of the people. The Athenians were never cowed and seized opportunities to revolt, as in the Chremonidean War (268-261) against Antigonus II Gonatas or in supporting Mithridates VI of Pontus against Rome in the 80s. Can we believe that after living for so long under foreign rule the Athenians naively believed they could regain their freedom – and be left alone if they did? After all, they knew their history. When attempting to overthrow Macedonian hegemony on the assassination of Philip II in 336 and on Alexander's death in 323, in the so-called Lamian War, they had been quickly subdued. In the latter instance, they had suffered badly at Antipater's hands, who, among other things, had established a garrison on the Munychia, demanded a heavy war indemnity, and imposed a wealth requirement for citizenship (see above), turning the city into a virtual oligarchy dominated by an elite sympathetic to Macedonia.

Still, the people's resolve made them revolt when they could, and more importantly, even as defeat loomed, they refused to back down. It is this latter point – refusal to back down till the bitter end – I wish to address in this essay. I take as an example the Chremonidean War, arguing that the people's attitude in holding out for so long against Antigonus may be traced back to the Demosthenic era – and that Chremonides deserves a different and arguably better press than that commonly bestowed on him.

The Chremonidean War of 268-261 is an oddity in the history of Hellenistic Athens.[13] By the time it broke out in 268, Antigonus II (r. 276 to 239) was firmly in control of Greece and Macedonia

---

[8] Mikalson (2007). Civic finances: Oliver (2007: 193-227). Foreign rulers even contributed to festival costs, for example at Callias' request Ptolemy II gave money to meet the expenses of the Great Panathenaea: Shear, T.L. (1978: 35-44); cf. Habicht 1997: 136.
[9] Shear, T.L. (1981).
[10] See Worthington (2021: 79-80), citing sources.
[11] New Dionysus: *IG* II² 1043, lines 22-23; see also Plut. *Antony* 60.3; Dio 48.39.1-2.
[12] Shear, T.L. (1981: 363-365); Worthington (2021: 257-258).
[13] War: Ferguson (1911: 170-182); Gabbert (1997: 45-53); Hammond and Walbank (1988: 276-289); O'Neil (2008); Tarn (1913: 295-310); Waterfield (2021: 159-173); Worthington (2021: 117-124). Outbreak in 268: O'Neil (2008: 68-71); Osborne (2012: 49-50, 68-69). Dreyer (1999: 276, 287-288, and 301) and Gabbert (1987) argue for 265/4. On the war

and focused on increasing his kingdom's military power, security, and economy.[14] Athens was wanting in all these areas, although it had been enjoying an increase in prosperity and even territorial gains starting two decades earlier after Demochares, on the Assembly's orders, had recaptured Eleusis.[15] When the carrot of joining Sparta and Ptolemy II against Antigonus and restoring their ancestral democracy was dangled before the city, Chremonides, after whom the war was named, persuaded the people to seize the carrot. That they anticipated war is shown by their swearing an oath by a number of gods, including the military deities Ares and Athena Areia.[16]

We are not concerned here with the events of the Chremonidean War, of which in any case we know only the bare outline even with what Chremonides' decree of 269/8 tells us about the war's causes and events.[17] But certain key points about it need to be made to show the Athenians' refusal to give up when all seemed lost.

Areus and Spartan troops were to march to confront Antigonus frontally, while Ptolemy's commander Patroclus (who had set up a base on the island of Gardonisi, close to Sunium), would either attack Antigonus from the rear or fight at sea.[18] Antigonus' rapid response thwarted their plan. His control of Corinth meant that he could prevent Areus leaving the Peloponnese during the summers of 267, 266, and 265, and in that last year he defeated and killed Areus close to Corinth.[19] He then moved to besiege Athens and so block Patroclus from landing in the Piraeus.

Nevertheless, the Athenians held out against Antigonus. The city's fortifications must have been shored up for an expected siege,[20] and the ephebes were clearly expected to play a major defensive role as their bravery is shown by a decree of 266/5 honouring the previous year's ephebes for the way they 'all held their ground, keeping good order, and obeying the laws and the *kosmetes*, and continued throughout the year to perform guard duties and all the instructions given by the general and for guarding the Museum, as ordered by the people'.[21] But by the spring of 261, with their grain crops devastated (and even the grove and temple of Poseidon Hippius, the cavalry headquarters by the Academy destroyed), the Athenians had no choice but to surrender.[22] Antigonus as a young man had studied in Athens under Zeno and maintained intellectual contacts with the city.[23] But while he may have been careful in his life to reflect the Stoic ideal of the equality of mankind, now was not the time for philosophy.

---

being a misnomer see Luraghi (2018: 23-26).

[14] Gonatas: Gabbart (1997); Lane Fox (2011); Hammond and Walbank (1988: 259-316); Tarn (1913); Waterfield (2021).

[15] Between September 285 and May 284: Shear, T.L. (1978: 84-86).

[16] On which, see Mikalson (1998: 138-139).

[17] *IG* II³ 1, 912, *SIG* 434/5; see too Paus. 1.7.3, 3.6.4-6; Justin 26.2.

[18] Vanderpool, McCredie, and Steinberg (1962); O'Neil (2008: 74-75).

[19] Hammond and Walbank (1988: 280-282); O'Neil (2008: 78-83).

[20] Theocharaki (2011: 126).

[21] *IG* II³ 1, 917, lines 9-13, with -Saminadayar (2007a: 56-57).

[22] The Athenians had never been able to suffer food shortages for long, witness, for example, their situation in 405/4 that led to surrender in the Peloponnesian War. Over a century later the situation had not changed when a chronic food shortage led to the tyranny of Lachares, toppled in 294 when he could not alleviate the distress – Poliorcetes, who had resumed control of the city, immediately gave 100,000 bushels grain to the people (Plut. *Demetrius* 34.1, 3-5). Good comments on Athens' need of grain: Oliver (2007: 127-131).

[23] Gabbert (1997: 69-70); Tarn (1913: 21-36).

According to a fragment of Apollodorus, Antigonus punitive measures included installing a Macedonian garrison in the city, 'stopping' the archons, and having everything done by 'the will of one man'.[24] But the Apollodorus fragment is rife with problems, including the identity of the 'one man' (presumably a governor); most likely there was not an individual governor but Antigonus himself who had the final say in Athenian affairs.[25] It has been supposed that in a blow to nationalistic pride and the economy he banned Athens from minting its own silver coinage, replacing it with Macedonian tetradrachms or 'Antigonids'.[26] Yet, if he did so, his action may have been because of a silver shortage from decreased production at the Laurium mines.[27] In any case, the Athenians had no need to mint their own coins, given the number of Macedonian ones in circulation in the city over the next years.[28] Still, the city suffered a military and economic fall, though its democracy continued, for in 261 the Assembly passed a honorary decree for Zeno, who died that year, showing that body continued to meet (Diog. Laert. 7.10-12; [Plut.], *Mor.* 183d).

The Athenians would not have known how Antigonus would treat them if they lost the war of course, but their hopes of victory must have been dashed once he had neutralized the threats from Sparta and Egypt and so ended any potential support from them for Athens. Yet the people held for some years, despite facing constant worry over their harvest as shown by *IG* II³ 1, 920, lines 8-10, a decree of 262, in which the archon was to performs a normal sacrifice for the welfare of Boule and the people, as well as 'for the safety of the crops in the countryside'.

Why were the Athenians prepared to resist Antigonus, despite his superior forces and when all seemed lost, for so long? And by extension, why go to war in the first place? The answer to the latter is usually seen as Chremonides' naïve idealism, who believed that Athens could return to its ancestral constitution.[29] But Classical democracy was long dead; Athens of the third century was a far different place from that of the fifth and fourth centuries, as we noted generally above, hence the unrealistic Chremonides is assigned blame for convincing the Athenians to go to war against Antigonid rule.

Yet, one would think that the Athenians would have learned by now not to keep falling for the slogan of Greek freedom, first touted by Philip II in the League of Corinth of 337 and again by Ptolemy so recently. Chremonides' decree makes it clear that Ptolemy wanted to champion the cause of Greek freedom, but the ideal was hardly at the heart of Ptolemy's thinking. In tandem with his sister-wife Arsinoe, he wanted to install Arsinoe's son Ptolemy from her previous marriage to Lysimachus on the Macedonian throne, secure the strategically important 'fetters' of Greece, and put an end to Antigonid ascendancy over the Aegean.[30] With a Macedonian garrison in the Piraeus, Ptolemy knew the lure of recovering the port would

---

[24] Apollodorus, *BNJ* 244 F 44, with the commentary of Williams ad loc.; with Ferguson (1911: 182-185); Habicht (1997: 150-172); O'Neil (2008: 85-86); Pouilloux (1946; 1982: 15-19, 43-63); Tarn 1913: 306-308. He may also have suspended the *ephebeia* (restoring it in 256): see Tracy (2004: 208-209).
[25] Worthington (2021: 122-123), on possible identities of a 'governor'.
[26] Ferguson (1911: 184); Habicht (1982: 34-47); Hammond and Walbank (1988: 286-287); Lönnqvist (1997); Tarn (1913: 308).
[27] Day (1942: 4-6); Habicht (1982: 34-42; 1997: 155).
[28] Lönnqvist (1997). It has been argued that the Athenians' silver coinage came to an end not in 262 but at least three decades earlier, and that the only Hellenistic kings to interfere in local currencies were the Ptolemies and Seleucids after the second century: Kroll (2003); Oliver (2001).
[29] Bayliss (2011: 109-112); Ferguson (1911: 157); Habicht (1997: 140); see too Luraghi (2018: 23-26, 36-41).
[30] Gabbert (1997: 45-46); Marquaille (2008: 47-48) especially. Antigonus' naval policy: Walbank (1982: 216-223).

prove irresistible to the Athenians.[31] In any case, the Athenians had to support Ptolemy: they relied on him for grain in times of emergency, and they carefully maintained friendship with the Ptolemies throughout the Hellenistic period.[32]

But this does not account for the people's determination to hold out until the bitter end or even whether they were naïve to follow Chremonides in the first place. I suggest another factor is at work, which may have prompted Chremonides to act as he did, which takes us into the realm of honorary statues. Athens' economic decline among other things impacted the quality and quantity of its artworks. The bestowal of statues on prominent individuals was not as affected, though in the Roman period the Athenians rededicated existing statues, which might have been to help save money as well as endear themselves to Rome.[33]

Of all the statues set up, the posthumous one to Demosthenes, successfully proposed by his nephew Demochares in 280/79, is arguably the most interesting and revealing.[34] Demosthenes had been dead for almost half a century by then, having taken his own life in 322 to escape capture by Antipater's agents as an enemy of Macedonia, and so had hardly done anything to benefit the city in 280.[35] But by 280 no Macedonian ruler had been living in the city since Poliorcetes' departure from Greece in 287; Demochares had recaptured Eleusis in 285-284; the Athenians had attempted to retake the Piraeus in 281 (albeit unsuccessfully); Ptolemy Ceraunus was now in control (shakily) of Macedonia; and chaos was about to break out with the Galatian invasions in 279.

This was the sort of background that offered hope to the Athenians of reasserting their independence and expelling the garrison in the Piraeus, and further, helps us to appreciate Demochares' decree, in which he waxes lyrical about Demosthenes' civic career and his constant support of 'freedom and democracy'. Demosthenes' reputation as a patriot had suffered greatly in the intervening years.[36] But his statue shows both his rehabilitation and a new spirit among Athenians; it echoes the anti-Macedonian documentary reliefs of the second half of the fourth century.[37] Indeed, the symbolism of Demosthenes' statue echoes to a great extent that of the statue to Lycurgus proposed by Stratocles of Diomeia in 307.[38] The latter's decree contrast Lycurgus' laws and contributions to the state and his pro-democratic spirit to the 'tyrant' Demetrius of Phalerum, who in 307 Poliorcetes had toppled after a ten-year regime.[39] With Demosthenes in 280, Athens could showcase another patriot if the people felt they were in an era of renewed democracy.[40]

[31] Habicht (1979: 108-109).
[32] Habicht (1992: 68-90); Marquaille (2008); Mattingly (1997: 129-133). Callias, sent on the motion of Demochares, had secured fifty talents of silver and 20,000 bushels of grain from Ptolemy II: Shear, T.L. (1978: lines 44-55).
[33] Keesling (2007; 2010); Shear, J.L. (2007).
[34] Plut. *Demosthenes* 30.5-6; [Plut.], *Mor.* 850f-851c, with Roisman, Worthington, and Waterfield (2015: 269-271); see too Worthington (2013: 339-341).
[35] Death of Demosthenes: Worthington (2013: 335-337).
[36] Cooper (2000); cf. Canevaro (2018).
[37] Lawton (2003).
[38] [Plut.] *Mor.* 843c-e, 847d, 852e, with Bayliss (2011: 105-106); Luraghi (2014: 208-214); Roisman, Worthington, and Waterfield (2015: 275-277).
[39] Luraghi (2014: 213).
[40] Habicht (1997: 139), claims it 'was tantamount to a declaration of war against Macedonia'.

But herein lies a problem. Demosthenes' stance, his entire policy, against Macedonia had failed. Philip II had imposed Macedonian hegemony over Greece when in 338 he had defeated a Greek coalition army headed by Athens and Thebes at Chaeronea, a battle that grew out of Demosthenes' famous alliance with Thebes the previous year.[41] Demosthenes does not seem the most obvious candidate for a statue in contrast to say, Lycurgus, who did not steer his city down a path to war and defeat. But I would argue that what sets Demosthenes apart, what justified his statue, and what made him so inspiring to Athenians even decades after his death, was not his anti-Macedonian standpoint, but what he made of it. This suggestion takes us to the famous Crown trial in 330.

The legal grounds for Aeschines' case against Ctesiphon and the details of the trial and speeches are well known and need no rehearsal.[42] Aeschines in his prosecution speech against Ctesiphon (3) had consistently attacked Demosthenes' anti-Macedonian stance throughout his career (3.49-167), especially the alliance with Thebes in 339 (3.140-151) that led to the battle of Chaeronea and defeat at the hands of Philip. The Athenians' shock and dismay were shown by their swift condemnation of their general Lysicles to death, calling him 'a living monument of our country's shame and disgrace' (Diod. 16.88.1-2).

But after Ctesiphon's short defence speech Demosthenes delivered the main response (18), reacting directly to Aeschines' assertions, defending his jingoistic rhetoric, and making no attempt to wriggle out of the defeat at Chaeronea (18.160-226). In doing so, he turned defeat into victory by arguing that at the end of the day his anti-Macedonian policy may have been flawed but it was still the right and only one to advocate because the Greeks had fought at Chaeronea for the noblest of ideals, their *eleutheria*. They therefore matched the patriotic standard of their ancestors in the Persian Wars (a common topos in oratory), as Demosthenes proclaims:[43]

> But you were not wrong, no, you were not, Athenians, to take on danger for the sake of the freedom and safety of all – I swear by your forefathers who led the fight at Marathon, by those who stood in the ranks at Plataea, by those who fought aboard ship at Salamis and Artemisium, and by the many other brave men who lie in the public tombs, all of whom the city buried, deeming them all equally worthy of the same honour, Aeschines, not just those among them who were successful or victorious. Rightly so, for they all performed the task required of brave men, and they each met with the fortune conferred on them by god.

Demosthenes was arguing that thanks to him and his policy he had given the Athenians another glorious episode in their history and had made their ancestors proud. He moved neatly from the gloomy historical presentation of the battle and its aftermath, on which Aeschines had focused, crafting a 'rhetoric of defeat' that in a near-epideictic style extolled the excellence of the city and made the battle a moral and patriotic victory.[44] That the Athenians realized Demosthenes' stance had been the right one is shown not only by his overwhelming acquittal

[41] Worthington (2013: 241-245 [alliance], 248-251 [battle]).
[42] Worthington (2013: 294-306), citing bibliography.
[43] Dem. 18.208; see too 18.63, 66-68, 192-195, 199, 206, 245-246, 208, 270-275.
[44] Worthington (2013: 302-304, 306) and Worthington 2022 (forthcoming).

at trial but also by being selected shortly afterwards to deliver the *epitaphios* for those who fell at Chaeronea (60).[45]

Aeschines failed because he had gone about reminding the Athenians of the recent past in the wrong way when the jury still did not want to face the truth of the battle. In the same year (330) Lycurgus had failed in his prosecution of Leocrates for desertion after Chaeronea for much the same reason.[46] Leocrates was almost certainly guilty of contravening an emergency law forbidding anyone to leave the city; even though Lycurgus had contrasted Leocrates' cowardice with the Athenians' ancestors patriotically fighting for freedom at Chaeronea (1.46-51, 59-62), he had emphasized only how Leocrates had put the city at risk and spoken too gloomily of what had been lost. By contrast Demosthenes presented a different version of the truth, reversing the defeat at Chaeronea by claiming that the Athenians had bravely done the right thing and could hold their heads high.

Thus, Demosthenes' statue takes on a new meaning – not simply honouring a man who served his city but a man who showed the people what was the right thing to do when the opportunity to restore *eleutheria* presented itself, even when the odds seemed unsurmountable. Joining with Sparta and Egypt against Antigonus was not a surprise. Nor was the Athenians' attitude to Macedonia, which remained covert and overt – Stratocles' move to secure a bronze statue for Lycurgus, mentioned above, is one such example, for this was the same Stratocles who proposed exorbitant honours on Antigonus I Monophthalmus and Demetrius I Poliorcetes in the same year (307), even calling them saviour gods and naming two new tribes after them (Antigonis and Demetrias).[47] Lycurgus' statue symbolized Athens' prosperity and its direct democracy, even a hearkening back to the Periclean era and thus a new age in Athens.[48] Demosthenes' statue thirty-seven years later – also set up in the Agora hence visible to everyone – bookended that of Lycurgus; it symbolized what the people should always strive for, and importantly why. Perhaps also the visual impact of the golden statue of Monophthalmus and Poliorcetes, deliberately set up next to that of the 'tyrannicides', had changed meaning from a sycophantic liberation monument to what Harmodius' and Aristogeiton's actions symbolized: saving the city from tyranny.[49]

The Chremonidean War thus takes on a new light. For several years after Antigonus came to power relations between him and the Athenians were amicable, with them even sacrificing to his prosperity as well as their own (*IG* II³ 1, 1009). But theirs was a surface relationship. Antigonus was always the enemy, a ruler who maintained a tradition of curbing Greek freedom that went back to Philip II. In 272 the Athenians had sided with Pyrrhus against him After Pyrrhus' death, Antigonus treated the city courteously, but there was no mistaking the reality of his hegemony and the garrison in the Piraeus. When the opportunity of revolt came in 268 with the Chremonidean War, the Athenians embraced it: it was the right thing to do, no matter the odds.

---

[45] Worthington (2013: 259-262). Thucydides 2.34 tells us that only someone 'most endowed with wisdom and preeminent in public esteem' was selected to give this formal speech.
[46] On the case, see Roisman and Edwards (2019).
[47] Diod. 20.46.1-2; Plut. *Demetrius* 10.2-11.1, with Bayliss (2011: 120-124); Ferguson (1911: 108-110); Habicht (1997: 68-69); Mossé (1973: 108-114); Worthington (2021: 72-74).
[48] Engels (1988; 1992); Faraguna (1992); Habicht (1997: 22-35); Mitchel (1965; 1973); Mossé 1973: 80-96; Rhodes 2010; and the reappraisal essays in Azoulay and Ismard (2011).
[49] Liberation monuments: Brogan (2003).

Likewise, Chremonides may well have been wrongly thought of as the idealist so out of touch with reality that he still believed in a return to 'the good old days'. With Demosthenes' statue serving as an inspiration to how Athenians of the past had defied enemies in the cause of freedom, Chremonides may have seen the triple alliance of Sparta, Egypt, and Athens as the chance for his city to shake off Macedonian rule not for any naively idealistic reason but because it was right for Athenians to resist and remain resolute. He was following in the steps of Demosthenes.

Even after Antigonus overcame them in 261, the Athenians were far from cowed. On the death of Demetrius II in 229, they moved quickly to regain their independence and unite the city and the Piraeus after over half a century of separation – albeit by bribing Diogenes, commander of the Piraeus garrison (Plut. *Aratus* 34.4; Paus. 2.8.6). They also made sure that institutions with civic and religious roles that gave prominence to the city and its culture were maintained, especially the *ephebeia* in the Hellenistic and Roman periods.

But warfare against Philip V of Macedonia after 200 brought Athens into the Roman orbit, and in 146 Rome folded Greece into its growing empire. By the 80s Rome was clearly the major power in the Mediterranean, yet when the belligerent Mithridates VI of Pontus dangled the carrot of freedom before the Athenians as he sought allies in a war against Rome, the people jumped at it. A terrible fate fell on them in 86 when Sulla sacked the city, the people suffering their 'fill of horrors' (App. *Mith.* 39).[50] Even so, they had demonstrated their resilience and will to do the right thing. That defiant attitude was again on view in 21 ahead of a visit from Augustus, when the Athenians daubed Athena's statue with blood and turned it to face westwards as though the goddess was spitting on Rome.[51]

A century later the city was catapulted to prominence again in the Greek world when Hadrian made it the centre of his Panhellenion, inaugurating a large Roman-backed building policy, adding to the notion that Athens had been turned into a provincial city.[52] Yet in many ways Hadrian's Arch, which the Athenians set up in AD 132, made it clear their city was still their own. On the east side of the Arch facing the completed temple of Olympian Zeus (the focal point of the Panhellenion), was an inscription that read: 'This is the City of Hadrian and not of Theseus'. On the other (west) side, facing the Acropolis and 'old' Athens was another inscription, proudly proclaiming: 'This is Athens, the ancient city of Theseus'.[53]

The Athenians after Chaeronea remained a force with which to be reckoned. If anything, given the city's depleted military forces, its economic distress, its loss of several thousand citizens from the property requirements, its muzzling because of Macedonian garrisons in the Piraeus and the city itself, the people's courageous defiance was a defining feature of their history. They had Demosthenes' statue as a visual reminder of why they fought against enemies and oppressors, no matter the odds, just as their ancestors had done against the Persians and against Philip at Chaeronea.

---

[50] Worthington (2021: 208-213), citing sources and bibliography.
[51] Worthington (2021: 245-252).
[52] The extent of 'Romanization' has been exaggerated: Worthington (2021: 287-288, 311-312; cf. 331-333).
[53] *IG* II² 5185; see too Worthington (2021: 327-331), citing bibliography.

Bibliography

Azoulay, V. and P. Ismard (eds) 2011. *Clisthène et Lycurgue d'Athènes: autour du politique dans la cité classique*. Paris: Éditions de la Sorbonne.

Bayliss, A.J. 2011. *After Demosthenes: The Politics of Early Hellenistic Athens*. London: Continuum.

Burckhardt, L.A. 2004. Die attische Ephebie in hellenistischer Zeit, in D. Kah and P. Scholz (eds), *Das hellenistische Gymnasion*: 193-206. Berlin: Akademie Verlag.

Canevaro, M. 2018. Demosthenic Influences in Early Rhetorical Education, in M. Canevaro and B. Gray (eds), *The Hellenistic Reception of Classical Athenian Democracy and Political Thought*: 73-92. Oxford: Oxford University Press.

Cooper, C. 2000. Philosophers, Politics, Academics: Demosthenes' Rhetorical Reputation in Antiquity, in I. Worthington (ed.), *Demosthenes: Statesman and Orator*: 224-245. London: Routledge.

Dreyer, B. 1999. *Untersuchungen zur Geschichte des spätklassischen Athen (322-ca. 230 v. Chr.* Stuttgart: Stuttgart.

Day, J. 1942. *An Economic History of Athens under Roman Domination*. New York: Columbia University Press.

Engels, J. 1988. Anmerkungen zum 'Ökonomischen Denken' im 4. Jahrh. v. Chr. und zur wirtschaftlichen Entwicklung des Lykurgischen Athen, *Münstersche Beiträge zur Antiken Handelgeschichte* 7.1: 90-132.

Engels, J. 1992. Zur Stellung Lykurgs und zur Aussagekraft seines Militär- und Bauprogramms für die Demokratie vor 322 v.Chr. *Ancient Society* 23: 5-29.

Faraguna, M. 1992. *Atene nell' eta di Alessandro: problemi politici, economici, finanziari*. Rome: Accademia Naz. Dei Lincei.

Ferguson, W.S. 1911. *Hellenistic Athens: An Historical Essay*. New York: Macmillan.

Friend, J. 2019. *The Athenian Ephebeia in the Fourth Century BCE*. Leiden: Brill.

Gabbert, J. 1987. The Anarchic Dating of the Chremonidean War. *Classical Journal* 82: 230-235.

Gabbert, J. 1997. *Antigonus II Gonatas: A Political Biography*. London: Routledge.

Grijalvo, E.M. 2005. Elites and Religious Change in Roman Athens. *Numen* 52: 255-282.

Habicht, C. 1979. *Untersuchungen zur politischen Geschichte Athens im 3. Jahrhundert v. Chr*. Munich: Beck.

Habicht, C. 1982. *Studien zur Geschichte Athens in hellenistischer Zeit*. Göttingen: Vandenhoeck und Ruprecht.

Habicht, C. 1992. Athens and the Ptolemies. *Classical Antiquity* 1: 68-90.

Habicht, C. 1997. *Athens from Alexander to Antony*, trans. D.L. Schneider. Cambridge: Harvard University Press.

Hammond, N.G.L. and F.W. Walbank, 1988. *A History of Macedonia* 3. Oxford: Oxford University Press.

Keesling, C.M. 2007. Early Hellenistic Portrait Statues on the Athenian Acropolis: Survival, Reuse, Transformation, in P. Schultz and R. von den Hoff (eds), *Early Hellenistic Portraiture: Image, Style, Context*: 141-160. Cambridge: Cambridge University Press.

Keesling, C.M. 2010. The Hellenistic and Roman Afterlives of Dedications on the Athenian Akropolis, in R. Krumeich and C. Witschel (eds), *Die Akropolis von Athen im Hellenismus und in der römischen Kaiserzeit*: 303-327. Wiesbaden: Reichert Verlag.

Kroll, J.H. 2003. The Evidence of Athenian Coins, in O. Palagia and S.V. Tracy (eds), *The Macedonians in Athens, 322-229 BC*: 206-212. Oxford: Oxbow.

Krumeich, R. 2008. Formen der statuarischen Repräsentation römischer Honoranden auf der Akropolis von Athen im späten Hellenismus und in der frühen Kaiserzeit, in S. Vlizos (ed.), *Athens During the Roman Period. Recent Discoveries, New Evidence*: 353-370. Athens: Benaki Museum.

Lane Fox, R. 2011. 'Glorious Servitude…' The Reigns of Antigonos Gonatas and Demetrios II, in R. Lane Fox (ed.), *Brill's Companion to Ancient Macedon*: 495-519. Leiden: Brill.

Lawton, C.L. 2003. Athenian anti-Macedonian Sentiment and Democratic Ideology in Attic Document Reliefs in the Second Half of the Fourth Century B.C., in O. Palagia and S.V. Tracy (eds), *The Macedonians in Athens, 322-229 BC*. 117-127. Oxford: Oxbow.

Lönnqvist, M. 1997. Studies on the Hellenistic Coinage of Athens: The Impact of Macedonia on the Athenian Money Market in the 3rd Century BC, in J. Frösén (ed.), *Early Hellenistic Athens. Symptoms of a Change*: 119-145. Helsinki: Suomen Ateenan-instituutin saatio.

Luraghi, N. 2014. Stratokles of Diomeia and Party Politics in Early Hellenistic Athens, *Classica and Mediaevalia* 65. 191-226.

Luraghi, N. 2018. Stairway to Heaven. The Politics of Memory in Early Hellenistic Athens, in M. Canevaro and B. Gray (eds), *The Hellenistic Reception of Classical Athenian Democracy and Political Thought*: 21-44. Oxford: Oxford University Press.

Marquaille, C. 2008. The Foreign Policy of Ptolemy II, in P. McKechnie and P. Guillaume (eds), *Ptolemy II Philadelphus and his World*: 39-64. Leiden: Brill.

Mattingly, H.B. 1997. Athens between Rome and the Kings, 229/8 to 129 B.C., in P. Cartledge, P. Garnsey, and E. Gruen (eds), *Hellenistic Constructs. Essays in Culture, History, and Historiography*: 120-144. Berkeley; Los Angeles: University of California Pres].

Mikalson, J.D. 1998. *Religion in Hellenistic Athens*. Berkeley; Los Angeles: University of California Press.

Mitchel, F.W. 1965. Athens in the Age of Alexander. *Greece and Rome* 12: 189-204.

Mitchel, F.W. 1973. Lykourgan Athens: 338-322, in *Semple Lectures* 2. Norman: University of Cincinnati Press.

Mossé, C. 1973. *Athens in Decline, 404-86 B.C.* Trans. J. Stewart. London: Routledge.

Oliver, G.J. 2001. The Politics of Coinage: Athens and Antigonos Gonatas, in A. Meadows and K. Shipton (eds), *Money and its Uses in the Ancient Greek World*. 35-52. Oxford: Oxford University Press.

Oliver, G.J. 2007. *War, Food, and Politics in Early Hellenistic Athens.* Oxford: Oxford University Press.

O'Neil, J.L. 2008. A Re-Examination of the Chremonidean War, in P. McKechnie and P. Guillaume (eds), *Ptolemy II Philadelphus and his World*: 65-89. Leiden: Brill.

Osborne, M.J. 2012. *Athens in the Third Century B.C.* Athens: Hellênikê Epigraphikê Hetaireia.

Perrin-Saminadayar, É. 2004. L'éphébie attique de la crise mithridatique à Hadrien: Miroir de la Société Athénienne?, in S. Follet (ed.), *L'Hellénisme d'Époque Romaine: Nouveaux Documents, Nouvelles Approches*: 87-103. Paris: De Boccard.

Perrin-Saminadayar, É. 2007. *Éducation, culture et société à Athènes. Les acteurs de la vie culturelle athénienne (229-88). Un tout petit monde. De l'archéologie à l'histoire*. Paris: De Boccard.

Pouilloux, J. 1946. Antigonos Gonatas et Athènes après la guerre de Chrémonidès. *Bulletin de Correspondance Hellénique* 70: 488-496.

Rhodes, P.J. 2010. 'Lycurgan' Athens, in A. Tamis, C.J. Mackie, and S.G. Byrne (eds), *Philathenaios. Studies in Honour of M.J. Osborne*: 81-90. Athens: Hellênikê Epigraphikê Hetaireia.

Roisman, J., Ian Worthington, and R. Waterfield 2015. *Lives of the Attic Orators: Pseudo-Plutarch, Photius and the Suda.* Oxford: Oxford University Press.

Roisman, J. and M. Edwards 2019. *Lycurgus, Against Leocrates*. Oxford: Oxford University Press.

Shear, J.L. 2007a. Reusing Statues, Rewriting Inscriptions and Bestowing Honors in Roman Athens, in Z. Newby and R.E. Leader-Newby (eds), *Art and Inscriptions in the Ancient World*: 221-246. Cambridge: Cambridge University Press.

Shear, T.L. 1978. Kallias of Sphettos and the Revolt of Athens in 286 B.C. *Hesperia Supplement* 17. Princeton: American School of Classical Studies.

Shear, T.L. 1981. Athens: From City-state to Provincial Town. *Hesperia* 50: 356-377.

Tarn, W.W. 1913. *Antigonos Gonatas*. Oxford: Oxford University Press.

Theocharaki, A.M. 2011. The Ancient Circuit Wall of Athens: Its changing Course and Phases of Construction. *Hesperia* 80: 71-156.

Tracy, S.V. 2004. Reflections on the Athenian Ephebeia in the Hellenistic Age, in D. Kah and P. Scholz (eds), *Das hellenistische Gymnasion*: 207-210. Berlin: Akademie Verlag.

Vanderpool, E., J.R. McCredie, and A Steinberg 1962. Koroni, a Ptolemaic Camp on the East Coast of Attica. *Hesperia* 31: 26-61.

Walbank, F.W. 1982. Sea-power and the Antigonids, in W.L. Adams and E.N. Borza (eds), *Philip II, Alexander the Great, and the Macedonian Heritage*: 213-236. Washington: University Press of America.

Waterfield, R. 2021. *The Making of a King: Antigonus Gonatas of Macedon and the Greeks*. Chicago: University of Chicago Press.

Williams, M. [s/d]. Apollodorus, *BNJ* 244. Leiden: Brill.

Worthington, I. 2013. *Demosthenes of Athens and the Fall of Classical Greece*. New York: Oxford University Press.

Worthington, I. 2021. *Athens after Empire: A History from Alexander the Great to the Emperor Hadrian*. New York: Oxford University Press.

Worthington, I. 2022. Dinarchus, the 'Recent' and the 'Very Recent' Past: Lessons from Lycurgus, Aeschines, and Demosthenes?, in A. Kapellos (ed.), *The Orators and Their Treatment of the Recent Past*: forthcoming.

Part IV - Epigraphy

Epigraphy's Very Own History

Robin Osborne

University of Cambridge
ro225@cam.ac.uk

Abstract

When we read an inscription we read words written at a particular moment in time for display in a particular space, and we read words that have undergone no subsequent editing. This paper explores the implications of place and time for the understanding of epigraphic texts, noting in particular that the context enables these texts to be economical with the truth – both in the sense of not needing to say some things and in the sense of giving a partial picture. It draws attention to the evidence provided by both private and public inscriptions for the absence of standardised forms of expression and for the positive preference for variation and difference and it unpacks some of the consequences of this both for epigraphic practice and for how we tell institutional histories. The very high degree of individualism displayed in the epigraphic record is an important aspect of Greek life more generally.

Keywords

Epigraphy, dedications, decrees, repetition, variation

Peter Rhodes began his historical research with a study of the Athenian *boule* (1972) that was rooted in epigraphy and he repeatedly returned to epigraphic documents and what can be done with them, above all in the volume on *The Decrees of the Greek States* (1997) written with David Lewis – quite apart from the three-volume endeavour to revise *Greek Historical Inscriptions* (2003; 2017; forthcoming) which he and I have undertaken together. In the 1960s and 70s it was customary to treat inscriptions as documents which just happened to be written on stone, with interest in their materiality largely limited to the possibility of dating stone documents on the basis of their letter forms. It is indeed a measure of that approach that Meiggs and Lewis's *Greek Historical Inscriptions* had no photographs illustrating the inscriptions it discussed. During Peter's long scholarly career, the 'material turn' of scholarship became more and more interested in the physical form of inscriptions, something reflected in the photographic coverage of the material in the latest fascicles of *Inscriptiones Graecae*.

In this paper I try to think a bit harder about how their material form affects the historical use of inscribed texts. I focus on two particular aspects of epigraphic texts, their being written for display in a particular place and their freezing of a particular moment in time. I argue that, if these aspects are taken into account, epigraphic texts acquire additional dimensions that enables a rather richer history to be written.

Place

Epigraphic documents are peculiar. Indeed, they are in general made to be peculiar; that is, most epigraphic documents, certainly in the ancient Greek world, were made to be unique. True, there are epigraphic documents which were one of a pair, with duplicates produced so that the same message could be displayed simultaneously in two locations, but these are the tiny minority. Rarer still are documents like the Athenian Standards decree (OR 155), produced in multiple copies for consumption by all Athens' allies in the Athenian empire.[1]

The peculiarity of the epigraphic document is crucial to its historical importance. Texts written to become known from papyrus copies, like texts run off a printing press, are texts written to be consumed in situations to a greater or lesser extent unknown to and unforeseen by the writer, situations removed, and often far removed, in either space or time or both. Epigraphic documents, even if losing out to the poetic ἀθάνατον μνᾶμα (CEG 393) or 'monumentum aere perennius' (Horace Odes 3.30.1) in perdurance over time, can boast that they will be read at some point that is temporally distant, as a Euboian stele of the fifth century (CEG 108) boasts cτέλεν ἀκάματον, | hάτις ἐρεῖ παρισι διαμερὲς ἄματα πάντα ('an unwearying stele, which will speak to passers by through all days'). But even if read at a more or less distant time, epigraphic documents can nevertheless reckon to be read in a particular and known space, and hence in a situation that can be more or less anticipated by whoever is responsible for the inscription.

Inscribed words are therefore different from the words of a poem or words written on papyrus. Words of a poem or words written on papyrus can travel anywhere, Pindar boasts, contrasting his ode to the works of a sculptor: Οὐκ ἀνδριαντοποιός εἰμ᾽, ὥcτ᾽ ἐλινύcοντα ἐργά-|ζεcθαι ἀγάλματ᾽ ἐπ᾽ αὐτᾶc βαθμίδοc | ἑcταότ᾽· ἀλλ᾽ ἐπὶ πάcαc | ὁλκάδοc ἔν τ᾽ ἀκάτωι, γλυκεῖ᾽ ἀοιδά, | cτεῖχ᾽ ἀπ᾽ Αἰγίναc διαγγέλλοιc... ('I am no maker of statues, so as to fashion sculptures which stand idle on the same base. Go sweet song on every ship and boat, away from Aigina making the announcement that...' Nemean 5.1–3). As Henry Spelman puts it in Pindar and the Poetics of Permanence (2018: 117): 'This epinician has statuesque durability but surpasses monumental commemoration on the spatial axis'.

The question of who might read what is written, and when and where they read it, is not a question simply about what form of writing will achieve what sort of communication. It is a question that affects what is written in the first place. Pindar, again, notes this: because he has to prepare his odes for reception by any reader anywhere, he has to prepare them for critical scrutiny by those with a full range of knowledge (in his case, both knowledge of what the victor and victor's family were like at home as well as full knowledge of the actual circumstances and nature of the victory). The only way to do that, Pindar suggests in Nemean 7.61-69, is never to lie.

Pindar's claim is sublime, but in some respects also ridiculous. Vast numbers of people, in antiquity and since, have had no interest in what he wrote. And if someone knows that what he says is untrue, what effect does that have, when the winged word has already taken flight? The theoretical possibility of reaching anyone does not translate into the practical possibility of reaching everyone. Like the readers of every text transmitted on papyrus, through poetic performance or, now, digitally, Pindar's readers were self-selected. The only people he needed to worry about were people for whom the world of the victory ode was an appealing one. Individuals decide whether they ever put themselves into a position where they might risk hearing poetry, and what those who never listen to poetry thought of him was irrelevant to Pindar – they would never commission an ode from him.

---

[1] This paper employs the following abbreviations: CEG: Hansen (1983, 1989); IG i³: AAVV (1981–1998); ML: Meiggs and Lewis (1969); OR: Osborne and Rhodes (2017); RO: Rhodes and Osborne (2003).

Inscriptions are, or at least can be, different.[2] Certainly, inscriptions can be carved in spaces that only a select few will ever visit. But they may also be carved in places where all sorts of people will see them – like graffiti in public conveniences in the modern world, or paederastic inscriptions on the cliffs next to a beach in the Greek world.[3] Not everyone who sees an inscription will be able to read it – though the degree of literacy required to recognise what an inscription says may be limited. Not everyone who can read will decide to read, but with short inscriptions many will find that they have already read it before they can decide whether to do so or not. The writers of these ancient and modern graffiti know, and work with, the situation in which their readers find themselves – in these two cases variously exploiting their enhanced body consciousness.

More peculiarly Greek are the inscriptions that mark the presence of gods by inscribing the names of those gods onto stone.[4] These have recently been discussed in the context of aniconism – the invoking of the presence of a god by some object that does not itself reproduce the physical appearance ascribed to the god. Part of the power of the name that is inscribed certainly comes from its associations – the impossibility of thinking about Zeus without thinking about stories about Zeus (in Herodotos' terms [2.53.2–3], of not thinking about the Zeus of Homer and Hesiod). But part of the power surely comes from the enduring fixity of a name that is inscribed: it is a mark of the gods that, unlike men, whom rupestral inscriptions record to have done things at this spot, but who are there no longer, gods are always present. The timelessness of the inscription brings the reader up short against not simply the possibility that Zeus (or whoever) is present here now, but against the fact that Zeus is always present here. Once made present by having their names inscribed here, the gods will never not be in this place.

Words inscribed on stone are unlike everyday spoken words in as far as they are available to be perceived not just on one particular occasion but every day, but they are like everyday spoken words in as far as are only available to be perceived in one place – they reach only those near enough to perceive them. As soon as the reader of the inscription moves out of reading distance, the ongoing life of the inscribed text becomes subject to the reader's memory. Like spoken messages given to messengers, once separated from its source the inscribed message is liable to distortion. For those not in a position to read them themselves, the truth of inscribed words is subject to compromise as the one who conveys what they have read in the inscription allows their account of it to be influenced by their own preferences or by the expectations of their audience. So Nikias, who fears a messenger from Sicily will not tell the horrific truth, writes a letter that can be read (Thuc. 7.8.2).

The most obvious class of inscriptions that exploit their being local, but long-lived, are rupestral boundary inscriptions. As scholarly debate about exactly what boundary is being marked shows, these boundary markers continue to indicate the presence of a boundary long after the local knowledge required to interpret them has been lost. Here is a case where the extreme fixity consequent upon writing on the living rock means that the inscription endures even while the local context so changes as to render the inscription incomprehensible. The

---

[2] For the variety of inscriptions see Osborne (2017: 115–129).
[3] See Garlan and Masson (1982: 3–22) and Coulié (1998: 445-453).
[4] For discussion of the names of the gods inscribed onto rocks in Thera see Gaifman (2012: 136-157).

laconic nature of these texts, which often simply read ὅρος/ hόρος ('boundary'), and is itself a product of their fixed position (those who needed to know that this was the boundary were people who necessarily knew what the boundary was of), means that an inscription designed to give crucial information comes to give no information at all.

The point of inscribing 'hόρος' was presumably often, at least, because the place that was marked had not always been the boundary – the very fixity was a mark that something had changed, and that that change, and with it the way in which this particular tract of nature had been turned into landscape by human intervention and ownership claims, had to be advertised. We might note the boundary stones of the classical Athenian Agora, stones which seem to date to the creation of the Agora as such in that location [*IG* i³ 1087–9]. We might think in similar terms about gravestones.[5]

With regard to grave markers too, the core function of a μνῆμα is to prolong the memory of the deceased – and they prolong it long past the time when any reader of the inscription will remember the person in question. They both mark the absence of the living person from this space, and at the same time make present the person who, without this marker, would, as far as the reader is concerned, never have lived. Making present a person at the place where their mortal remains lie is fundamental to the pathetic effect. Space and time get conflated here: the local serves to mark the way in which a life stopped at a particular point, a story came to an end, the dead person no longer moved around the place and did things for him- or herself but was placed at this spot.

Archaic Athenian tombstones repeatedly stress the placing of the monument. A straightforward example from the last quarter of the sixth century and from Athens would be *CEG* 46/*IG* i³ 1215: σε̃μα φί[λ]ο παιδὸς τόδε ἰδε̃ν Δι[όδορος]|ἔθεκε [:]/ Στεσίο, hὸν ꞉ θάνατο[ς δακρυ]|-όες καθ[έ]χει ('Diodoros put in place to see this marker of his dear son Stesias, whom tearful death holds'). More involved is the punning on putting in place found in another Athens stele of c. 510, *CEG* 50/*IG* i³ 1218: [σ]ε̃μα τόδε, Χσενόφαντε, | πατέρ σο<ι> θε̃κε θανόντι/| Σόφιλος, hο̃ι πένθος| θε̃κας ἀποφθίμενος. Ἀριστοκλε̃ς ἐποίεσεν ('Xenophantos, your father Sophilos put in place this marker to you when you had died, for whom in dying you had put in place grief. Aristokles made this'). Here the repeated use of the verb 'to place' emphasises the parallelism not simply between the stele that marks the tomb and the fixed place of the dead young man, but also stresses the fixity of the grief. Another variant in a gravestone of the same period (*CEG* 51, *IG* i³ 1219) puts stress on gazing upon the spot: οἰκίρο προσορο̃[ν]|παιδὸς τόδε σε̃μα| θανόντος ꞉/Σμικύθ[ο]| hός τε φίλον ὄλεσε|-ν ἔλπ᾽ ἀγαθέν ('Weep as you look upon this marker of the dead child Smiythos, who put an end to the good hope of his loved ones'). The finality of death, destroying hope, is here symbolised by the marker of the spot at which Smikythos lies. Those who look upon it, look upon how hope vanished as the marker roots Smikythos to this place, the only ongoing moment being the moment of his dissolution of all hope.

What all these inscriptions – graffiti, rupestral inscriptions of various kinds, gravestones – have in common is that their location enables them to be economical with the truth. They do not need to establish a discursive context because they count on local knowledge, the place

---

[5] Compare the mortgage *horoi* discussed below. Here too they mark something new – not a new boundary, but a new obligation born by the property of which they mark the boundary. Like ordinary boundary stones, where these are matters precisely, not just generally.

where they are seen establishes their discursive context (even the isolated names of gods seem not to occur randomly but in locations already marked out in other ways as sanctuaries or public meeting places). But are there inscribed texts that are economical with the truth in the sense that Pindar refers to, texts that perpetrate a view that, were it widely shared, would be vociferously denied and decried by some?

The prime candidates for such texts are war monuments. Indeed, the prompt erasure by the Spartans of the inscription which Pausanias had inscribed at Delphi announcing that he put up this memorial when he, Pausanias, as leader of the Greeks, destroyed the army of the Medes (Ἑλλήνων ἀρχηγὸς ἐπεὶ στρατὸν ὤλεσε Μήδων | Παυσανίας Φοίβωι μνῆμ᾽ ἀνέθηκε τόδε, Thuc. 1.132.2) nicely demonstrates both the temptation to lie (or at least to exaggerate) and the limitations on the location in which one could do so.[6] Three-quarters of a century later, however, Lysander got away with making a not dissimilar claim about his part in the defeat of the Athenians in the Peloponnesian war. Although the inscription on the thank-offering at Delphi for victory at Aigospotamoi led off with ascription of responsibility to Pollux, this was followed by an inscription that reads: 'Lysander set up his statue on this monument when, victorious with swift ships he destroyed the power of the children of Cecrops, crowning never-ravaged Sparta, fatherland of fine dancing' (εἰκόνα ἑὰν ἀνέθηκεν [ἐπ] ἔργωι τῶιδε ὅτε νικῶν | ναυσὶ θοαῖς πέρσεν Κε[κ]ροπιδᾶν δύναμιν | Λύσανδρος, Λακεδαίμονα ἀπόρθητον στεφανώσα[ς], κ]αλλίχορομ πατρίδα OR 192c). Lysander presumably got away with this in part because the crowd of statues that constituted the monument included many other named figures and not just him.[7] Plutarch refers to the monument as 'the sea captains' (On the Pythian Oracles, 395 b), despite the fact that Lysander, his seer and his helmsman were the only mortals in the front row of figures, and Lysander was shown being crowned by Poseidon.[8]

But the assumption of the lion's share of the glory by the commander was not the only way in which war memorials might make tendentious claims that their particular location prevented being challenged or ridiculed. If we believe the Athenian tradition, which comes to us primarily through Aischines 3.183–5, the Athenians got away with putting up a memorial at what became known as the Stoa of the Herms, northwest of the Agora, of the victory at Eion on the Strymon in the immediate aftermath of the Persian wars which claimed that these Athenians were the first to find a way to defeat the Medes (ἦν ἄρα κἀκεῖνοι ταλακάρδιοι, οἵ ποτε Μήδων | παισὶν ἐπ᾽ Ἡιόνι, Στρυμόνος ἀμφὶ ῥοάς, | λιμόν τ᾽ αἴθωνα κρατερόν τ᾽ ἐπάγοντες Ἄρηα | πρῶτοι δυσμενέων εὗρον ἀμηχανίην ('These were indeed enduring of heart who first found the weak point of cruel men when they brought powerful war and burning hunger to the sons of the Medes at Eion around the streams of the Strymon'). Earlier still there must have been many non-Athenians who would have taken exception to the claim, made in the dedication that marked the Athenian victory over the Boiotians and Chalkidians, supposedly

---

[6] Barron (1988: 617) finds ambiguity over who exactly is the subject of ὤλεσε, but the word order removes any ambiguity. The Doric version preserved in *Palatine Anthology* 6.197 has Pausanias use the first person. See ML, p. 60.

[7] Note also the careful 'mythicisation' of the victory by referring to the Athenians as 'children of Kekops'.

[8] For comparable tendentious celebration of an individual as responsible for military success see the early fourth-century dedications by the Lycian dynast Arbinas, RO 13. Note also the comparable sensitivity about individuals claiming credit for major buildings, and in particular temples, which is revealed by the fact that architraval dedications of that sort appear only in the fourth century and then sometimes in less conspicuous locations. See Hornblower (1982: ch. 10).

on the same day, in c. 506 BC, that what had been subdued was their *hybris* (δεσμῶι ἐν ἀχνύεντι (?) σιδερέοι ἔσβεσαν ὕββριν, ML 15/IG i³ 501A).

There are some circumstances in which cities make tendentious claims in other public documents.[9] Such claims are relatively rare in the decrees of the classical Greek city, which are notable in general for their reticence.[10] But such claims are more prominent in the Hellenistic period and particularly when a person's actions are described posthumously, either for praise or blame. In Athens one example, variously discussed recently by Luraghi, is the honours which Demochares had granted to Demosthenes in 280/279, the text of which is given in [Plutarch] *Moralia* 850f–851c.[11] Much might be said about this decree and its internal and external politics, but Demosthenes would certainly not have been described by his political enemies as the 'man who of all his contemporaries proved to be the best political adviser as far as freedom and democracy were concerned' ([Plutarch] *Moralia* 851c).

Outside Athens the dossier of records related to the tyrants of Eresos (RO 83) provides another example of the belated tendentious description of past activities as a contribution to present politics on the spot. As Ellis-Evans has shown, we are dealing here with a single monument written up on a single occasion between 306 and 301, a generation after the events described. The decision to put up this monument must have been a political one, with the publication part of an on-going debate: this 'is a tool of coercion and domination in the internal politics of Eresos, by which one faction within the city sought to redefine Eresian civic identity to its own advantage'.[12] The behaviour for which the people of Eresos had been invited to condemn the tyrants was described in some detail. The surviving parts detail the behaviour ascribed to Agonippos: 'he exacted 20,000 staters from the citizens; he committed piracy against the Greeks; he dug up the altars of Zeus Philippios; he made war on Alexander and the Greeks, and from the citizens he seized their arms and shut them all out of the city, and he arrested their women and daughters and confined them in the acropolis; and he exacted 3,200 staters; and he looted the city and the sanctuaries with the pirates and set fire to them and burned the bodies of the citizens; and finally he arrived before Alexander and told lies against and slandered the citizens' (RO 83 γ front 2–15). That this description would have been disputed is suggested not simply by its sweeping terms, but by the way in which 'the descendants of former tyrants, Heroidas son of Thetikon son of Heraios and Agesimenes son of Hermesidas ... offered to Alexander that they were willing to submit to judgement before the people concerning the charges' (RO 83 γ front 35–40).

The politics in this case, as in the case of the posthumous honours for Demosthenes and their extensive justification, is a local politics. Publicising to the world the misdemeanours of a long-dead tyrant, or a long-dead champion of lost freedom, made little sense, but republicising to fellow-citizens the way in which past work to free Athens from Macedon had been undermined by internal political struggle ('was exiled by the oligarchy after the fall of democracy' ([Plutarch] *Moralia* 851c), or of the way in which tyranny brought the loss of all

---

[9] Note e.g. RO 19 honouring Phanokritos of Parion for giving advice, which, had it been taken, would have led to the capture of enemy triremes.

[10] Osborne (1999: 341-358), reprinted with endnote in Osborne (2010: 64–82).

[11] Luraghi (2010: 247–263; 2018a: 21–43, at 32–34; 2018b: 209–228. For the status of the decrees in [Plutarch] and the question of the degree to which they have been edited, see Faraguna (2003: 479–503).

[12] Ellis-Evans (2012: 183–212, at 198).

law and order, the promotion of piracy, and dangers to financial security and the security of women and children, had enormous political value. It offered an effective way to keep before the eyes of the current generation, and in the space in which political life continued to be played out, the lessons that could be drawn from past generations. It is not so much that those reading these tendentious claims in this space would not recognise that they were tendentious, but that making these claims in that space defied those who regarded them as tendentious to make themselves known and challenge them.

Time

While it is true of all texts that they were written at a particular moment in time, this is true in a very particular way of epigraphic texts. We have no autograph literary texts from the ancient world, and all our literary texts are the product of a whole range of moments of writing. This is true in the relatively trivial sense that there were many acts of copying undertaken at different times to preserve literary texts for us. But it is also true in the sense that many literary texts were themselves products of processes of revision which may be more or less clearly indicated by the author. We may suspect spontaneity in our texts, but outside papyri or wooden writing tablets or lead letters which preserve pieces of ephemeral correspondence, we can never know whether the appearance of spontaneity was in fact the product of long study. When it comes to inscriptions, however, although in very many cases, as is occasionally visible, what appears on stone had previously been written on papyrus, what we see is the consequence of a single act of writing. More than that, the factors that have preserved inscriptions have been in important ways arbitrary. By contrast to the factors that have preserved both literary texts and sculpture, where what we have today has been heavily shaped by successive processes of canon formation, the selective interest of past generations has had relatively little effect on surviving inscriptions. Allowing for the very uneven distribution of excavation, we can take what survives on stone to be a more or less random subset of what was once inscribed on stone.

There are two historical questions for which the capturing by inscriptions of a single moment of writing matters. One of these concerns issues of corporate and individual identities, the other concerns what I shall refer to as the strength of institutionalisation. The former is best illustrated from private inscriptions, the latter from public.

Dedicatory inscriptions on or accompanying votive objects are on the whole – with the exception of some elaborate epigrams – relatively simple.[13] For all that dedicated objects take a very wide range of forms, from inexpensive pottery and terracotta, through bronze vessels and statuettes to life-sized and over-life-sized statues and statue groups, the words with which they signal themselves to be gifts to the gods are essentially the same. Dedicatory inscriptions comprise four elements, all of them optional: the verb of dedication, the identity of the god to whom the object is dedicated, the identity of the dedicator, and the identity of the object dedicated: 'so and so dedicated this such and such to so and so god'. As such, dedicatory inscriptions seem to beg for standardisation – if every inscription records the same information it makes it very easy for anyone to pick up the data they want if all take the same form, and given that in any given sanctuary the dedications are going to be obviously

---

[13] Cf. Lazzarini (1976).

dedications and likely to be largely to one god, standardisation would, in particular, help readers locate immediately the information they want, which is who dedicated the object (and, if given, why). Indeed scholars of Greek and Roman sculpture – and indeed artists – have in recent years put a great deal of emphasis upon the power of replication.[14]

A search through the dedications on the Athenian Acropolis from the sixth and fifth centuries, excluding the more developed longer dedications and those where the text is largely restored, reveals that dedicatory inscriptions variously take the forms laid out in Table 1. As the list in Table 1 shows, it would be an understatement to say that there is no single formula of dedication. Indeed, there is so little that is standard that, even among the examples I have included above, there are a number of cases where one must doubt whether we can have confidence in the restoration. In the hundred or so examples where enough survives for us to be reasonable confident that we have the full inscription, there are certainly some patterns that are repeated, but none is repeated more than a dozen or so times and many are unique or almost unique formulations.[15]

But how remarkable is such variation in the epigraphic record for a single type of inscription? A comparison with another sort of private inscription is telling – albeit the comparison is with a genre with a later chronological distribution: the *horos* inscriptions that marked mortgaged property.[16] These markers also combine a small number of fixed elements – the identification of the stone as a boundary stone, the nature of the property whose boundary it is, the nature of the financial transaction secured by the property, the person(s) or group whose money is so secured, and the amount of money involved. These elements invariably appear in this order, and variations are few: some *horoi* are prefixed with an archon's name; those that record property that is hypothecated may indicate who holds the paperwork rather than naming the creditor; those that record property sold upon redemption may indicate the paperwork holder before recording the creditor; those marking orphan estates name no creditor; and even when there are creditors and amounts in question both these elements may not appear at all – a number of *horoi* record no amount, and some also record no creditor. It is also the case that although *horoi* vary in physical appearance, that variation too is limited. With the exception of a very late example of dotal *apotimema* from second-century BC Brauron, which has up to 28 letters in a line, *horoi* in Attica have first lines of between 4 and 18 letters (and regularly between 4 and 10), and in general lines with more than 15 letters are rare (*horoi* outside Attica, on Naxos or Amorgos regularly have longer lines). So a degree of regularity and peculiarity of form (no other class of Athenian inscription looks like this) accompanies the degree of regularity of wording.

---

[14] See Trimble (2011), Settis, Anguissola and Gasparotto (2015), and, for the application of this to Greek sanctuaries, Vout (forthcoming). Among artists note the works of Edward Allington, especially *Perfect Pericles* (1974), *Roman from the Greek, in America* (1987) and *Victory Boxed* (1987), with Allington (1997: 152–167).

[15] The question of determinants of Greek word order in general have been much debated. Dover (1960), who included some epigraphic texts in his analysis, argued that the main determinants were logical, not syntactical. Dik (1995), concentrating on Herodotos, argued that, in the terms employed by functional grammar, 'Topic' comes first, and then 'Focus'. Dik's approach has been further extended by Matić (2003). For a recent discussion of epigraphic texts, arguing for Lycian influence on word order of some clauses in Greek funerary inscriptions from Asia Minor, see Macedo (2021).

[16] Finley (1985).

Formulas using a verb of dedication
Name of dedicator, verb of dedication (so *IG* i³ 528 Νικύλος ⋮| ἀνέθεκεν [small bronze base], 656 [Φ]σακύθε ⋮ ἀνέθεκεν [marble base])
Name of dedicator, verb of dedication, name of goddess with article (so *IG* i³ 527 Θειμάδες ἀν<έ>θεκεν τἀθενᾶι [bronze base]; 637 Ἐγέσαν[δρος]| ἀνέθεκ[εν] τἀθεναίαι [marble base])
Name of dedicator, verb of dedication, name of goddess with article, description of object (so *IG* i³ 526 Αἰσχίνες ⋮ Χαρίας ⋮ ἀνεθέ|τεν τἀθεναία<ι> ⋮ ἀπαρχέν [bronze base])
Name of dedicator, verb of dedication, name of goddess with article, description of object, description of dedicator (so *IG* i³ 702 Ἀριστίον ⋮ καὶ Πασίας ⋮ ἀνεθέ|τεν ⋮ τἐι Ἀθεναίαι ⋮ ἀπαρχέν | Λαμπτρἐ [marble base])
Name of dedicator, verb of dedication, name of goddess without article, description of object (so *IG* i³ 644.1-2 Λυσίας ἀνέθεκεν Ἀθεναίαι | ἀπαρχέν [abacus of marble column])
Name of dedicator, verb of dedication, object of dedication, name of goddess with article, description of dedicator (so *IG* i³ 546 Φρυγία ⋮ ἀνέθεκέ με τἀθεναίαι | ηε ἀρτόπολ[ις] [bronze miniature shield with image of Medusa])
Name of dedicator, verb of dedication, description of object, name of goddess with article (so *IG* i³ 540 Μελεσὸ ἀνέθεκεν | δεκά|τεν τἀθεναίαι [upper surface of bronze base]; 688 Κιρίας ⋮ ἀνέθεκεν | [δεκά]τ[εν ⋮ τἀθ]ενάαι [marble column])
Name of dedicator, verb of dedication, description of object, name of goddess without article (so *IG* i³ 644.2-3 Εὔαρχις ἀνέθεκεν | δεκάτεν Ἀθεναίαι [abacus of marble column])
Name of dedicator, verb of dedication, description of object, description of dedicator (so *IG* i³ 657 Πολυ- - | ἀνεθ[εκεν] | [δ]εκάτεν | [h]ο Χειμέρπο [marble column])
Name of dedicator, verb of dedication, description of dedicator (so *IG* i³ 622 Χναιάδες ἀνέθεκεν | ηο Παλενεύς [marble base])
Name of dedicator, verb of dedication, description of dedicator, name of goddess with article (so *IG* i³ 554 Πολυκλἐς ⋮ ἀνέθεκεν | ηο κνα<φ>εὺς ⋮ τἀθεναίαι [handle of large bronze bowl]; 681 [Διοκ]λείδες ⋮ ἀν[έθεκε]ν | ηο Διοκλέος ⋮ τἀθεν[αίαι] [large marble base])
Name of dedicator, verb of dedication, description of dedicator, name of goddess with article, description of dedication (so *IG* i³ 926 [Ὀνέσιμος] ἀν[έθεκεν ⋮ ὁ Σμικύθο ⋮ τἀ]θεναία[ι ⋮ ἀ]πα[ρχέν] [marble fragments]; restorations secured by 927–32)
Name of dedicator, verb of dedication, description of dedicator, description of dedication, name of goddess with article (so *IG* i³ 628 Νέαρχος ἀνέθεκεν [ηο κεραμε]ὺς ἔργον ἀπαρχὲν τἀθ[εναίαι] [column-mounted marble base of *kore*])
Name of dedicator, verb of dedication, description of dedicator, description of dedication, name of goddess with article, further description of object (so *IG* i³ 698 ηιπποθερίδες ⋮ ἀνέθεκεν ⋮ Ἀχαρνεύς | δεκάτεν ⋮ τἀθεναίαι τἀρ{ν} γυρίου [marble column with abacus, serving as base for bronze statue])
Name of dedicator, object of dedication, verb of dedication (so *IG* i³ 816 Θελοχ[άρες] μ' ἀνέθεκεν [marble column capital])
Name of dedicator, object of dedication, verb of dedication, name of goddess with article (so *IG* i³ 572 Μυρτό μ' ἀνέθεκεν ⋮ τἀθενᾶι [bronze jug handle]; 719 [Ε]ὐάνγελός με ἀνέ[[θ]εκεν τἐι Ἀθεναίαι [marble base for seated statue])
Name of dedicator, object of dedication, verb of dedication, name of goddess without article, description of goddess (so *IG* i³ 683 Ἰ<φ>ικίδε μ' ἀνέθεκεν Ἀθεναίαι πολιόχοι [marble column])
Name of dedicator, object of dedication, verb of dedication, descriptive phrase for goddess, description of object (so *IG* i³ 544 [Κ?]λιτοφõν μ' ἀ[νέθ]ε[κ]εν [Δ]ιὸ[ς] γ[λα]υγόπιδι φόρει *vacat* πολ[ι]όχοι [δ]ε[κ]άτ[ε]ν [bronze pomegranate])
Name of dedicator, object of dedication, verb of dedication, description of dedicator, description of object (*IG* i³ 600 Χε[ρ]ικ[ράτες μ' ἀνέ]θεκεν ηο Δεχ]σιθέ|ο τό[δε ἄγαλμα] [marble base])
Name of dedicator, object of dedication, verb of dedication, object of dedication, description of object (*IG* i³ 567 Μελί[τει]α [μ' ἀνέθε]κ[ε]ν ἱματίον δεκάτεν [bronze bowl])
Name of dedicator, object of dedication, verb of dedication, description of object, name of goddess with article, description of dedicator (so *IG* i³ 699.2-3 Ὀνέσιμος ⋮ μ' ἀνέθεκεν ⋮ ἀπαρχὲν | τἀθεναίαι ⋮ ηο Σμικύθο ηυιός [marble column capital])
Name of dedicator, description of object (so *IG* i³ 543 Πέσιδος ηικ|εσία [bronze ram])

293

Name of dedicator, description of object, name of goddess with article (so *IG* i³ 536 Γλύκε δεκά|τεν τἀθεναία<ι> [bronze base])
Name of dedicator, description of object, name of goddess without article (so *IG* i³ 547 Λύσιλλα ἀπαρχὲν Ἀθεναίαι [small bronze disc])
Name of dedicator, description of object, verb of dedication (so *IG* i 548bis Γλύκε ፧ δεκάτεν | ἀνέθεκεν [bronze mirror handle])
Name of dedicator, description of object, verb of dedication, name of goddess with article (so *IG* i³ 565 Καπανὶς δεκά[τ]εν ἀνέθεκεν τἀθεναίαι [shallow bronze bowl]; 767 Ἐμπεδία δεκάτεν ἀνέθεκεν [τ]ε͂ι Ἀθ[ε]ναίαι [marble column])
Name of dedicator, description of object, verb of dedication, name of goddess without article (so *IG* i³ 660 Τεισικλέες δεκάτεν | [ἀ]νέθεκεν Ἀθεναίαι [marble column])
Name of dedicator, name of goddess with article (so *IG* i³ 558ter Πυθονε͂λος ፧ τἀθεναίαι [handle of large bronze bowl])
Name of dedicator(s), name of goddess with article, description of object, verb of dedication (so *IG* i³ 696 χοι παῖδ[ες] | Ἐπιχάρες | Ὀφολονίδες | [Χ]αρῖνος | [Χ]αρίσιος - - κλε͂ς | [τ]ἀ[θεναίαι?] | ἀπαρχὲν | [ἀνέ]θεσαν [marble column])
Name of dedicator, name of goddess without article, verb of dedication (so *IG* i³ 571 Ἱμέρα Ἀθαναίαι ἀνέθεκε [bronze jug handle])
Name of dedicator, name of goddess without article, description of dedicator, verb of dedication, object of dedication (so *IG* i³ 658 Κρίτον <ι> Ἀθεναίαι ፧ hο Σκύθο ፧ ἀνέθεκέ με [marble column])
Name of dedicator, description of dedicator, name of goddess without article, object of dedication, verb of dedication (so *IG* i³ 754 Ὄφσι[ος κιθ]αροιδὸς Ἀθ[εναίαι μ’ ἀ]νέθ[εκεν] [marble base])
Name of dedicator, description of dedicator, name of goddess with article, object of dedication, verb of dedication (so *IG* i³ 894 [..... Π]ρέπιδο[ς γυνὲ | [Χσυπετ]αιόνος [τε͂ι] | [Ἀθεναί]αι ἀνέθ[εκεν] [abacus of marble column])
Name of dedicator, description of dedicator, name of goddess with article, object of dedication, verb of dedication, description of object (so *IG* i³ 934 [Καλ]λιστὸ Ναυκύδος θυγ[άτερ τἀθεναίαι μ’ ἀνέθεκε]ν ἀπαρχέ[ν] [marble fragment])
Name of dedicator, description of dedicator, verb of dedication (so *IG* i³ 758 Εὐθύδικος hο Θαλιάρχο | ἀνέθεκεν [marble column capital supporting *kore*])
Name of dedicator, description of dedicator, verb of dedication, name of goddess with article (so *IG* i³ 639 [Θρ]ᾶιχς Κορτυνίο | [ἀν]έθεκεν | [τ]ἀθεναίαι [limestone base])
Name of dedicator, description of dedicator, verb of dedication, name of goddess with article, description of object (so *IG* i³ 682 Διοκλ[ε͂ς hο Διοκλείδ]ο [huιὸς] | ἀν[έθεκε τἀθεναίαι ἀπαρχ]έν [large marble base])
Name of dedicator, description of dedicator, description of object (so *IG* i³ 883 hερμόλυκος | Διειτρέφος | ἀπαρχέν [marble base])
Name of dedicator, description of dedicator, verb of dedication, description of object, name of goddess with article (so *IG* i³ 905 Πολύχσενος ፧ hο Μνέσονος | τὸ [κνα]φέος ፧ ἀνέθ[εκεν]፡ ἀπαρχὲν [τἀθεναίαι] [marble fragment])
Name of dedicator, description of dedicator, object of dedication, name of dedicator, verb of dedication (so *IG* i³ 620 [Μ]νεσιάδες κεραμεύς με καὶ Ἀνδοκίδες ἀνέθεκεν [marble column])
Name of dedicator, having made a vow, description of dedicator, description of object, verb of dedication, name of goddess with article (so *IG* i³ 633 Πείκον εὐχσά|μενος κερα|μεὺς δεκάτεν | ἀνέθεκεν | τἀθεναίαι [small marble capital])
Name of goddess without article, verb of dedication, name of dedicator (so *IG* i³ 538 Ἀθεναιαι ἀν|έθεκεν Κλεαρέτε [bronze base])
Name of goddess without article, verb of dedication, name of dedicator, description of dedication, description of dedicator (so *IG* i³ 731 Ἀθεναίει ἀνέ[θε]σαν [Δι]ον[ύσι]ος | [καὶ Ἀ]θενόδορ[ο]ς ἀπ[αρχ]ὲν | [?Εὐρυ]κλείδο [marble column])
Name of goddess with article, name of dedicator, verb of dedication (so *IG* i³ 576 [τἀθεν]αίαι Δορόθεος ፧ ἀνέθεκε [lip of bronze jug])
Name of goddess without article, description of object, verb of dedication, description of dedicator, name of dedicator (so *IG* i³ 779 Ἀθενάαι δε[κάτεν ἔργον] | καὶ χρεμάτον ἀ[νέθεκ]εν | Κολλυτίδες Ἀρχενείδες [marble column])

(Name of goddess with article, description of object, description of dedicator, name of dedicator [order in which lines should be read and identification of which names are in genitive disputed] *IG* i³ 800 τἀθηναίαι | δεκάτην | χορίοω | Ἀθμονόθεν | Χαιρεδέμο Φιλέα [marble column])
Name of goddess without article, description of goddess, name of dedicator, object of dedication, verb of dedication, description of dedication, name of dedicator, description of dedicator, [description of goddess] (so *IG* i³ 783 Παλλάδι τρι[τογενεῖ Μέ]γυλος μ' ἀνέθε[κεν ἀπαρχὲν]] καὶ Χρέμες hυὺς [παιδὶ Διὸς μεγάλο] [marble column])
Description of object, name of goddess with article (so *IG* i³ 561bis ἀπαρχὲ τἀθεν[αίαι] [bronze bowl])
Description of object, name of goddess without article, description of goddess, name of dedicator, object of dedication, verb of dedication, description of dedicator (so *IG* i³ 775 δεκάτεν : Ἀθεναίαι : πολιόχοι | hιεροκλείδες : μ' ἀνέθεκεν : Γλαυκίο [marble column])
Formulas using 'sacred thing'/not using a verb of dedication
'Sacred thing', possessive of goddess without article (so *IG* i³ 541 h[ιε]ρὸς Ἀθεν[αί]ας [base of small bronze *kouros*])
'Sacred thing', possessive of goddess with article (so *IG* i³ 579 [hι]ερὸν τ̃ες Ἀθηναίας [bronze handle])
'Sacred thing', possessive of goddess with article, name of dedicator, description of object (so *IG* i³ 542 hιερός : τ̃ες Ἀθεναιάς | Φιλαίου δεκάτε [body of bronze athlete statuette])
'Sacred thing', dative of goddess with article (so *IG* i³ 583s hιερὸν τ̃ει Ἀθεναίαι [lip of bronze vessel])
'Sacred thing', verb of identification (so *IG* i³ 558 hιερὸν εἰμι [handle of large bronze bowl])
'Sacred thing', verb of identification, possessive of goddess with article (so *IG* i³ 583r hιερά εἰμ<ι> [body of bronze vessel])
Name of dedicator, 'sacred thing', verb of dedication (so *IG* i³ 755 Σπο[ῦ]δις : Λαισ[ποδίας : hι]έρον ἀν[έθεσαν] [marble base])
Possessive of goddess without article (so *IG* i³ 535 Ἀθεναίας [bronze base])
Possessive of goddess without article, verb of identification (so *IG* i³ 580 Ἀθεναίας | εἰμι τ̃ες [Ἀθεναίας] [bronze handle])

Table 1. Order of elements in dedicatory inscriptions from the Athenian Acropolis down to 403 B.C.

We might think it unsurprising that *horoi* are highly formulaic. Their whole purpose was to convey a number of items of information that constituted a legal contract, and the best way to do that was to give readers the information in the order that they expected. But, legal contract aside, the same is true of dedications. Those who made dedications had a common interest – to make it known that they had made a significant gift to a god. Repeat action lies at the very heart of ritual. If it was obvious to a worshipper that one dedication on the Acropolis was to Athena (though in fact we find dedications also to Poseidon and to Hermes), then it should have been obvious that all were (at least unless there was indication to the contrary). And if it was obvious to one worshipper that an object deposited on the Acropolis was a dedication, then that too should have been obvious to all. Yet every element of the dedicatory inscription – even the name of the dedicator – turns out to be optional, and the goddess, the object and the dedicator are all given the prominence of first place in the sentence in some examples. One consequence of this is that there are a number of examples where the order in which the inscription should be construed is up for debate (see *IG* i³ 756, 775, 800, 808, 809).

What we see on the Acropolis was no doubt encouraged by the presence of significant numbers of inscriptions that were in metre, and for that reason played with customary conversational word order. But the decision to make a dedicatory inscription metrical was presumably itself partly at least a consequence of the sense that the terms in which the gift was given, as well as the gift itself, should be pleasing to the goddess. The desire was not, as with mortgage *horoi*, simply to get noticed so as to convey certain items of information, but to stand out among the things noticed, and to impress as well as to engage the reader (both human and divine).

Any process of regularisation is resisted in dedications: the individual decisions of a great number of different dedicators advertise individuality as they are made permanent in bronze and stone. For all that many inscriptions on both bronze and stone must have been written by masons and other craftsmen, and not by individual dedicators, those inscriptions seem nevertheless to preserve and insist on the dedicator's peculiarity. Dedicators impress their own identity upon their dedications by presenting the information that they want to present in the manner and order that they want to present it. Only if we allow for individual dedicators positively seeking not to conform can we explain why so much variation prevails and persists over so long a period. These individuals made their voices, captured at the moment at which the dedication is made, individually heard.

The contrast between the anarchy of the Acropolis dedications and the routine formulae of the credit notices that are *horoi* raises the question of where decrees sit. Stephen Lambert has noted that as far as the form of stelai is concerned, the striking feature of the decrees from the third quarter of the fourth century is their variety: 'sameness was avoided, individuality emphasised'.[17] But what about their language? One of the great values of inscriptions, as emphasised above all by Peter Rhodes' work in *The Athenian Boule* and *The Decrees of the Greek States*, is the access that they give to institutions. But just how institutionalised was classical Athens in its political practices? How far was there an institutional identity that Athenians acquired when they took up magistracies? Or just how far did the public slaves who looked after magistrates turn what they did into look-alike products?

At one level, there is no doubt that the decrees of classical Athens were heavily institutionalised. Take the imposition of *stoichedon*, for instance. Everything the Athenians decided was turned into 'house style', and in the later fourth century there was even something a bit like a house font for the most routine of inscribed business.[18] But a certain uniformity of appearance may be quite independent of any uniformity of text. Just where do fifth-century Athenian decrees sit between the apparently unending variation of the dedications and the formulaic conformism of the *horoi*?

Some aspects of Athenian decrees, as is well known, become quite regularised. The Salamis decree (*IG* i³ 1) refers to itself as a decree of the *demos* only, but the next surviving decree opening (*IG* i³ 5) must have referred to the *boule* and *demos* and almost certainly made reference to the secretary of the *boule*. By the time we have further decrees preserved in the 450s, there seems to be an established pattern of reference to prytany, secretary, and president (*epistates*) (cf. e.g. *IG* i³ 9). But archon names seem to appear only occasionally (for instance in the renewal of treaties with Rhegion and Leontini in 433/2, OR 149, and in a decree concerning Miletos now dated to 426/5, *IG* i³ 15) until they become more regular at the end of the 420s. The heading of decrees and other public inscriptions to begin 'Gods' appears only in the 430s.

---

[17] Lambert (2012: 101).

[18] Tracy (1995: 2): 'The inscriptions of the late fourth century offer some special problems. Though individual idiosyncrasies abound and many cutters are easy to identify, these cutters are, in general more difficult to distinguish than their counterparts in the third and second centuries. Moreover, the accounts, inventories, and leases which constitute a large percentage of the inscriptions extant from the second half of the fourth century are inscribed in the tiniest letters possible... Such lettering allows very little room for individual variation. Indeed, I do not think that it is possible to discern with accuracy individual hands on most of these texts.'

Such regular features can mislead us into thinking that Athenian decrees in general were standardised. How far that is from the truth can be seen from some of the cases where standardisation would seem to be most likely. Take those two treaties with Rhegion and Leontini, renewed on the same day and on the proposal of the same man. Scholars have restored the texts to say substantially the same thing, but even if they are right to do so, the precise terms in which they say it are different. In the case of Rhegion Kallias proposes: χσυμμαχίαν εἶν]αι Ἀθεναίοις καὶ | [Ῥεγίνοις. τὸν δὲ hόρκο]ν ὀμοσάντον Ἀθενα|[ῖοι hίνα εἶ hάπαντα πι]στὰ καὶ ἄδολα καὶ h[απλᾶ παρ' Ἀθεναίον ἐς ἀΐ]διον Ῥεγίνοις ('There shall be an alliance between the Athenians and the Rhegians. The oath shall be sworn by the Athenians, so that everything may be faithful and without deceit and straightforward on the part of the Athenians for all time towards the Rhegians', lines 9–12). In the case of Leontini Kallias proposes: τὲμ μὲν χσυμμαχία|ν εἶναι Ἀθεναίοις καὶ Λεοντίνοις καὶ τὸν ὅρ|κον δόναι καὶ δέχσασ|[θαι. ὀμόσ]αι δὲ Ἀθεναί|[ος τάδε· σύ]νμα[χ]οι ἐσόμ|[εθα Λεοντ]ίν[οις ἀΐ]διο|[ι ἀδόλος κ]αὶ [ἀβλα]βôς ('There shall be the alliance between the Athenians and the Leontinians, and they shall give and receive the oath. The Athenians shall swear as follows: "We shall be allies of the Leontinians for all time, without deceit and unharmfully"', lines16–23).

We might imagine that the differences here, despite the identity of proposer, arise from different phrases having been negotiated at some earlier stage with the two different cities, and those phrases having been stuck to. But the fourth-century case of the Athenian imposition on the cities of Kea of rules forbidding the export of ruddle (RO 40) is not open to that explanation, yet shows the same phenomenon. For all that the rules imposed on Ioulis, Karthaia and Koresia are the same, they are differently expressed: in the case of Koresia, the rule is expressed in terms of export being allowed only on vessels indicated by the Athenians; in the case of of Ioulis, the rule is that export is only to Athens and to nowhere else; whereas particular provision is made in the case of Koresia to reward a slave who brings the prosecution (ἐὰν δὲ δοῦλος ἦι ὁ ἐνδείξας, 19), in the case of Ioulis the provision is for the slave who brings information (ἐὰν δὲ δοῦλος ἦι ὁ μηνύσας, 29).

Irregularity of expression is found all over classical Athenian decrees. Take, for example, the frequent provision that someone should be recorded on a stone stele as a *proxenos* and benefactor of the Athenians. We find this clause repeatedly, but very variously, expressed (Table 2 includes all examples that do not depend on extensive restoration), indeed no two fully-preserved inscriptions are the same. Should we emphasise the differences, or the similarities? Epigraphers tend to emphasise similarity, and stress the way in which the process of passing a decree encouraged similarity. But it is precisely because the process encouraged similarity that the degree of difference is so notable.

While the variety of forms of dedication, of decree stele and of funerary stelai might be explained with reference to the way in which they were competing for the attention of visitors to Acropolis or cemetery, this is an implausible explanation for variations in wording. So why so many ways of saying the same thing? Although the different individuals honoured did indeed experience different circumstances/earn the honour in different ways, that accounts for only a very small part of the variation that we see here. It is clear that there was no standardisation applied at any stage to the formulation even of these more regular of grants. That is, proposers took no care always to do things in the same terms (as the two treaties championed by Kallias indicate), neither the prytaneis nor the council as a whole,

| names/ἀναγρ[ά]φσαι/*proxenos* and benefactors/of Athenians/and their sons/on acropolis/on stone stele *IG* i³ 23.5–11 |
| names/(ἀνα)γράψαι/*proxenos* and benefactors/on stone stele/on acropolis/and on board in bouleuterion/ secretary of council/at ?'s expense *IG* i³ 155.5–9 |
| name/ἀναγράψαι/secretary of council/*proxenos* and benefactor/[restored clause]/and place on acropolis/reason *IG* i³ 227.8–11 |
| name/praise/reason/ἀναγράψαι/him/on stone stele/*proxenos* and benefactor/of Athenians/and his sons/deposit on acropolis *IG* i³ 92.9–13 |
| names/reason/ἀναγράψαι/*proxenos* and benefactor/of Athenians/on stone stele/at own expense [breaks off] *IG* i³ 95.7–10 |
| name/reason/ἀναγραψάτω/*proxenos* and benefactor/of Athenians/on stone stele/on acropolis/secretary of the council/and deposit on acropolis *IG* i³ 174.7–11 |
| name/reason/ praise/ἀναγράψαι/him/*proxenos* and benefactor/of Athenians/and his offspring/protection clause/ this decree/ ἀναγράψαι/secretary of the council/on stone stele/and deposit on acropolis *IG* i³ 110.13–24 |
| praise/names/reason/ἀναγραφσάτο/*proxenos* and benefactors/of Athenians/ like X/on stone stele/secretary of the council/and deposit on acropolis *IG* i³ 80.8–18 |
| praise/names/ ἀναγράψαι/and offspring/*proxenos* and benefactors/and everything else like X *IG* i³ 228.20–25 |
| cf. *IG* i³ 98.9–15 since *proxenos*/of Athenians/and benefactor/good deeds/former decree/write up/on stone stele/ secretary of council/currently serving/deposit on acropolis |

Table 2. Ways of expressing the grant of status of *proxenos* and benefactor in substantially preserved Athenian decrees down to 403 B.C.

nor the secretaries involved, imposed any regularity, and the discussion in the assembly and process of inscription similarly led to no editorial tidying. Despite the fact that what gets inscribed represents a boiling down of what must have been a very much more extensive case presented to council and assembly, and despite this editing evidently following some consistent principles (most notably the description of services rendered being rendered in stock and bland terms [see above n.8]), nothing has been done to impose a standard order of clauses upon these standard provisions.

Two conclusions seem required. First, that very little that happened in the Athenian council and assembly was a 'stock' occurrence, and individuals simply expressed themselves in the words that came to them on a particular occasion.[19] Second, no one in Athens was at all concerned to make it seem as if Athens had a single house style. Politics develops no significant 'technical' vocabulary beyond the names for particular magistrates and procedures, and certainly no chancellery style. The degree of regularity that was mustered for mortgage *horoi* was not replicated in the work of council and assembly: only it seems, when practical purposes require it, are the Athenians at all inclined to present information in a consistent and systematic way.[20]

I have concentrated here on the detailed wording of Athenian inscriptions, but what has emerged from that analysis is strongly supported by the similar variety in which equivalent bodies approached 'the same' task. A fine example of this is provided by the calendars of

[19] For another aspect of this – the high frequency in the fifth century with which decrees are amended by Athenians who are otherwise unknown to us – see Osborne (2018: 41–52; 2022: 217–228).

[20] Although I do not further explore this aspect here, the high degree of variety reveals how extremely problematic the restoration of clauses to fragmentary inscriptions is. *IG* i³ contains much more restoration than can be justified (for extreme examples involving *proxenos* and benefactor see *IG* i³ 91 [for one Proxenos son of Proxenides], 159).

religious sacrifices produced by Athenian demes in the fifth and fourth centuries.[21] No two of these calendars are organised in the same way. The earliest calendar, from Thorikos (OR 146), is organised by month, and lists the festivals/sacrifices to take place during each month, but without identifying specific days. The appropriate sacrificial victims are listed, and any special feature of the sacrifice, but no prices are given. The Teithras calendar (*SEG* 21.542), also organised by month, specifies the day of the sacrificial activity, the price, the god, the sacrificial victim, and any perquisites. The Marathon section of the Tetrapolis calendar (*SEG* 50.168) organises itself in three-monthly blocks, within those blocks giving the month (and, rarely, the day of the month), then the name of the god, then the sacrificial victim and the price, and sometimes the cost of perquisites; sacrifices carried out by the demarch are listed separately and the costs are never totalled. The Erchia calendar is in a sense not one calendar but five, with five columns dividing up the sacrifices in each month between them, apparently to produce sets of sacrifices to be paid for by five different deme liturgists. Days of the month are regularly specified, followed by the deity, the place in which the sacrifice is made, and the price, with stipulations given with regard to the ritual to be followed and perquisites specified when, and only when, a priestess (rather than a priest) is involved. All these demes have decided that they need a public record of their sacrificial activities, but they have come up with different specifications for what needs to be publicised – precise date, price, and place of sacrifice is considered necessary by some demes, but not by others. All the calendars, even that from Erchia, leave some aspects of what the deme does unrecorded (who gets what perquisites when a priestess is not involved in the case of Erchia): local knowledge is required and expected, but different local knowledge is required in different demes. Rather than reflect the petrification of records that had been refined over time to answer all the questions about their religious activity that demesmen might want to ask, what we have are documents which, despite their non-ephemeral nature, reflect one particular need at one particular moment of time.

Conclusion

In short, the inscribed record, both private and public, not only offers us monuments which were fixed in space and operated in a particular space, but also monuments that were fixed in time, in the sense that they captured a real and particular moment when an individual Athenian expressed himself or herself in this particular way. We do not know how many times a literary work may have been rewritten by its author, but that there were extensive processes of revision involved is very clear from e.g. the complicated pattern of references to later events in Thucydides' *History*. But with the inscribed record, beyond issues of inscribers correcting themselves or later erasure and replacement of passages, there seems to have been no process of revision and refinement. If the predilections and fashions of a day are going to be visible anywhere in ancient writing it is here, in the epigraphic record. And given the great variety that we find, the predilections and fashions of the day surely are indeed visible.

From all this there emerges a certain irony: scholars who want to know how the institutions of the Greek city worked have – beyond studying the Aristotelian *Athenaion Politeia* – no choice but to turn to the inscribed record; but the inscribed record reveals a world in which the regularity and consistency that institutions encourage, and even require, is found deeply

---

[21] Lambert (2018: 149–180); Whitehead (1986: 185–208).

unattractive. The ferocious individualism underlying the Greek city is patently inscribed upon these stones.[22] This is not just something that is to be found in instances where we might expect a conscious effort to stress difference in order to stress distinction. One might think, for example, that those honoured (in proxeny decrees and more generally) would be described in unique terms because making their honour stand out was part of the reason for inscribing the honour in the first place, but not only are there reasons to think that the qualities for which men are honoured were carefully limited, rather than rendered as varied as possible, but variation is equally if not more striking in genres of inscription (like sacred calendars) in which no such hortatory intention is in question.[23]

Ferocious individualism is the norm, and it is when we find high degrees of standardisation that we should reach for an explanation. That individualism actually makes these inscriptions more useful, not less, at revealing how institutions work. For whereas, when phraseology becomes formulaic and terms of description standardised, much change may occur in how business is actually done without any sign of this in the formulaic description changing, we have good reason to be confident that the descriptions that occur in Athenian inscriptions do not mislead. The more confident we are that what is inscribed upon stones is inscribed 'as it happened', putting on display the agendas and the rhetoric of the moment, the more transparent the epigraphic record becomes as evidence for the very particular life of the Greek city. The epigraphic display, simultaneously, of shared ends and individual means transports us to the very heart of what was special about the archaic and classical Greek city.[24]

Bibliography

AAVV, 1981–1998. *Inscriptiones Graecae.* Vol. 1 3rd ed. Berlin: De Gruyter. [*IG* i³]

Allington, E. 1997. Venus a Go Go, To Go, in A. Hughes and E. Ranfft (eds), *Sculpture and its Reproductions*: 152–167. London: Reaktion Books.

Barron, J. 1988. The Liberation of Greece, in J. Boardman, N.G.L. Hammond, D.M. Lewis, and M. Ostwald (eds), *The Cambridge Ancient History IV: Persia, Greece and the Western Mediterranean c.525 to 479 B.C.*: 592–622. Cambridge: Cambridge University Press.

Coulié, A. 1998. Nouvelles inscriptions érotiques à Thasos. *Bulletin de Correspondance Hellénique* 122: 445–453.

Dik, H. 1995. *Word Order in Ancient Greek : a Pragmatic Account of Word Order Variation in Herodotus.* Amsterdam : J.C. Gieben.

Dover, K.J 1960. *Greek Word Order.* Cambridge : Cambridge University Press.

Ellis-Evans, A. 2012. The Tyrants Dossier for Eresos. *Chiron* 42: 183–212.

Faraguna, M. 2003. I documenti nelle "Vite dei X oratori" dei Moralia plutarchei, in A.M. Biraschi (ed.), *L'uso dei documenti nella storiografia antica*: 479–503. Naples: Edizioni scientifiche italiane.

---

[22] Just as we might see it pictured in the absence of repetition within the iconography of Athenian painted pottery; see Osborne (2018b: 36-37). Of that individualism Dover (1960: 68) remarks: 'If the Greeks had not possessed so intense a degree of artistic self-consciousness, it may be thought likely that syntatctical patterns would have established themselves much earlier and much more firmly'.

[23] For the editing out of distinguishing detail from honorific decrees see Osborne (1999) and cf. Whitehead (1993: 37–75).

[24] I am grateful to Franco Basso for bibliographical help and to Stephen Lambert and Caroline Vout for comments on an earlier draft of this paper.

Finley, M.I. 1985. *Studies in Land and Credit in Ancient Athens 500-200 B.C. The Horos Inscriptions with a New Introduction by Paul Millett*. New York: Transaction Books.

Gaifman, M. 2012. *Aniconism in Greek Antiquity*. Oxford: Oxford University Press.

Garlan, Y. and O. Masson 1982. Les acclamations pédérastiques de Kalami (Thasos). *Bulletin de Correspondance Hellénique* 106: 3–22.

Hansen, P.A. 1983, 1989. *Carmina Epigraphica Graeca*, 2 vols. Berlin: De Gruyter. [*CEG*]

Hornblower, S. (1982). *Mausolus*. Oxford: Clarendon Press.

Lambert, S.D. 2012. *Inscribed Athenian laws and decrees 352/1-322/1 BC: epigraphical essays*. Leiden: Brill.

Lambert, S.D. 2018. Individual and Collective in the Funding of Sacrifices in Classical Athens: the Sacrificial Calendar of the Marathonian Tetrapolis, in F. van den Eijnde, J. Blok, and R. Strootman (eds), *Feasting and Polis Institutions*: 149–180. Leiden: Brill.

Lazzarini, M.L. 1976. *Le formule delle dediche votive nella Grecia arcaica*. Atti della Accademia Nazionale dei Lincei, 373. Memorie. Classe di Scienze Morali, Storiche e Filologiche, ser. 8, vol. 19, fasc. 2. Rome: Accademia nazionale dei Lincei.

Luraghi, N. (2010). The Demos as Narrator: public honors and the construction of future and past, in L. Foxhall, H.-J. Gehrke, and N. Luraghi (eds), *Intentional History: Spinning Time*: 247–263. Stuttgart: F. Steiner.

Luraghi, N. 2018a. Stairway to Heaven: the Politics of Memory in Early Hellenistic Athens, in M. Canevaro and B. Gray (eds), *The Hellenistic Reception of Classical Athenian Democracy and Political Thought*: 21–43. Oxford: Oxford University Press.

Luraghi, N. 2018b. Documentary evidence and political ideology in early Hellenistic Athens, in H. Börm and N. Luraghi (eds), *The Polis in the Hellenistic World*: 209–228. Stuttgart: F. Steiner.

Macedo, J.M. 2021. "Nobody else": word order in Greek funerary inscriptions from Asia Minor and in Lycian. *Glotta* 97: 158–77.

Matić, D. 2003. Topic, focus, and discourse structure: Ancient Geek word order. *Studies in Language* 27: 573–633.

Meiggs, R. and D.M. Lewis (eds) 1969. *A Selection of Greek Historical Inscriptions to the End of the Fifth Century B.C.* Oxford: Clarendon Press. [ML]

Osborne, R. 1999. Inscribing performance, in S.D. Goldhill and R. Osborne (eds), *Performance culture and Athenian democracy*: 341-358. Cambridge: Cambridge University Press.

Osborne, R. 2010. *Athens and Athenian Democracy*. Cambridge: Cambridge University Press.

Osborne, R. 2017. Greek epigraphy and archaeology, in A. Lichtenberger and R. Raja (eds), *The Diversity of Classical Archaeology*: 115–129. Turnhout: Brepols.

Osborne, R. (2018a). The Theatre of the Amendment in Fifth-Century Athens, in N. Villacèque (ed.), *À l'Assemblée comme au théâtre: Pratiques délibératives des Anciens, perceptions et résonances modernes*: 41–52. Rennes: Presses universitaires de Rennes.

Osborne, R. 2018b. *The Transformation of Athens: Painted Pottery and the Creation of Classical Greece*. Princeton: Princeton University Press.

Osborne, R. 2022. The politics of the amendment and the transformation of Athenian democracy, in A. Makres and P.J. Rhodes (eds), *Demosia Grammata: Studies in Memory of David M. Lewis (1928-1994)*: 217–228. Athens: Hellēnikē Epigraphikē Hetaireia.

Osborne, R. and P.J. Rhodes (eds) 2017. *Greek Historical Inscriptions 478-404 B.C.* Oxford: Oxford University Press. [OR]

Rhodes, P.J. and R. Osborne (eds) 2003. *Greek Historical Inscriptions 404-323 B.C.* Oxford: Oxford University Press. [RO]

Settis, S., A. Anguissola and D. Gasparotto 2015. *Serial / Portable Classic*. Milan: Fondazione Prada.

Tracy, S.V. 1995. *Athenian Democracy in Transition: Attic Letter-Cutters of 340 to 290 B.C.* Berkeley: University of California Press.

Trimble, J. 2011. *Women and Visual Replication in Roman Imperial Art and Culture*. Cambridge: Cambridge University Press.

Vout, C. forthcoming. The Stuff of Crowds, in M. Haysom, M. Mili, and J. Wallenstein (eds), *The Stuff of the Gods*. Stockholm: Svenska institutet i Athen.

Whitehead, D. (1986). *The Demes of Attica 508/7 – ca. 250 B.C. A Political and Social Study*. Princeton: Princeton University Press.

Whitehead, D. 1993. Cardinal virtues: the language of public approbation in democratic Athens. *Classica et Mediaevalia* 44: 37–75.

The Lost Dedicatory Inscription of the Serpent Column at Delphi

András Patay-Horváth

ELTE Institute of Ancient History / ELKH Institute of Archaeology, Budapest
pathorv@gmail.com

Abstract

The victory monument erected by the allied Greeks at Delphi is partially preserved, but its dedicatory inscription is lost. Literary sources mention that the original one was commissioned by Pausanias, the Spartan regent and leader of the Greek forces at Plataea but was erased soon afterwards to be replaced by the preserved list of poleis fighting against the Persians. This story is unanimously taken at face value but a comparison with epigraphically preserved epigrams and an analysis of the relevant written sources can be combined to suggest that it is most probably a literary fiction and the lost dedicatory inscription has to be reconstructed otherwise.

Keywords

Graeco-Persian wars, victory monument, Thucydides, epigraphy, Pausanias (the Spartiate)

The Serpent Column is a rare historical document of the 5th century BC and it has received particular scholarly attention.[1] Its inscriptions are partly preserved on the monument itself and are often discussed from different perspectives.[2] This paper focuses, however, on the two inscriptions which are only mentioned by various literary sources and proposes a radical reassessment of them. A comparison with preserved dedicatory inscriptions on archaic and classical monuments shows that the two epigrams which were allegedly engraved on the Serpent Column and are therefore seemingly lost to us, were in fact literary constructs and there is no reason to accept their authenticity. This conclusion has already been reached for one of them (the 'Diodorus-epigram') but the present paper will deal primarily with the story of the other, more famous inscription (the 'Pausanias-epigram') which is unanimously taken at face value. It will be argued that, contrary to the *communis opinio,* this inscription is equally fictitious. This new hypothesis arguably takes into closer account the facts preserved by our sources and as well as the conspicuous gaps in the literary record. Moreover, it is even possible to reconstruct, at least tentatively, the source of inspiration and the historical circumstances of the fiction. The real dedicatory inscription of the monument is therefore irretrievably lost and can only be reconstructed in broad terms.

---

[1] Most recently an entire monograph was written about this monument (Stephenson 2016) which offers an up-to-date summary of the research history. The vexed question of the correct reconstruction (cf. e.g. Gauer 1968, Laroche 1989 and most recently Steinhart 1997) is left out of consideration here, because it will be treated in more detail elsewhere and is almost entirely irrelevant for the present subject. Most recent treatments of the monument (Yates 2019: 29-60, Proietti 2021: 192-204 and MacGregor Morris 2022: 113-119) were unavailable for me and will be discussed elsewhere.

[2] Jacquemin et al. (2012: 43-44 no. 17); Jeffery (1990: 104); Meiggs-Lewis (1969: 57-60 no. 27); and *SEG* XLI 523 (with a slightly different reading).

have seemed quite misplaced at this moment and had Pausanias committed something scandalous like the unauthorized inscription of the common victory monument in Delphi, he would hardly have been acquitted.

It was only at a later stage, when Pausanias was recalled to Sparta for the second time, that the story of the inscription was somehow reconsidered or scrutinized as Thucydides (or his Ionian source) maintains and it was used against the general as the only unmistakable proof, although it was strictly speaking irrelevant for the case under consideration and the inscription certainly did not exist any more. Everyone who has witnessed or learned about the show trials in mid-20th century Eastern Europe, is immediately reminded of such procedures:[30] Pausanias, similar to the victims of the communist courts, was confident of his innocence and apparently thought that he would be acquitted as he previously was. As Thucydides (or his source) clearly admits (1.132) 'the Spartans had no manifest proof against him, neither his enemies nor the whole city, whereupon to proceed to his punishment'. But the outcome was preconceived by his political opponents and in such cases it was always possible to produce some kind of proofs, even if they were apparently fictive. The letters allegedly sent by Pausanias to the Persian king and the responses of the king cited verbatim by Thucydides (1.128-129) were plainly fakes and were rightly never considered authentic by modern research,[31] but they were obviously used during the first prosecution against Pausanias. They could apparently not achieve a condemnation at that time and were likely to strain the credulity of most contemporaries so they were not used again later on. But an inscription allegedly engraved on a well-known public monument and deleted immediately afterwards could be considered as an even better 'proof', since it was impossible to check its content and could be thus freely used (i.e. manipulated) to support the case against Pausanias. The documentary value of this kind of evidence is approximately equal to that of the fictive letters but could achieve a similarly great emotional effect. And the fictional character of the 'deleted' inscription was not as apparent as that of the correspondance and did not provoke any scepticism from Thucydides nor from modern researchers.[32]

To sum up, one cannot escape the impression that the epigram and the entire story which was 'reconsidered' during the final prosecution against Pausanias was in fact invented.[33] Moreover, it is even possible to identify a plausible source for this invention. Herodotus, who does not mention the Delphic scandal, referred in passing (4.81) to another dedication made by Pausanias, son of Cleombrotus. This was a bronze crater, i.e. a metal vessel similar to the Delphic tripod, and its inscription was regarded hybristic precisely because in this case Pausanias celebrated a military success (presumably the capturing of Byzantium) as his own achievement. The inscription was quoted by Nymphis, a local historian of Herakleia Pontike

named Kleonike: Plut. *Cimon* 6, Paus. 3.17.8-9.

[30] Such an awareness is shown perhaps by Cawkwell (1970: 50-51) when he says that 'we know enough of governments which are concerned to foster τῆς πολιτείας τὸ κρυπτὸν to suspend belief when they bolster charges of deviation with confirmatory details.'

[31] 'Unusually suspect' as Hornblower (1991a: 214) succinctly puts it with brief references to earlier literature.

[32] Some doubts concerning the historical reliability of the entire passage were occasionally expressed: 'It looks as if Thucydides has been less than usually critical' (Cawkwell 1970: 50) and in the entire excursus on Pausanias, Herodotus seems to be 'more cautious' than Thucydides (Hornblower 1991a: 217).

[33] Petrovic (2007: 270-271) discusses how the epigram may have been preserved and can only conclude that it was transmitted somehow orally. He does not seem to be aware of Westlake (1977) and the Ionian source likely followed by Thucydides.

(Athen. 12.50) and consisted of two elegiac couplets, which show some marked similarities to the two supposed Delphic dedications.[34]

μνᾶμ' ἀρετᾶς ἀνέθηκε Ποσειδάωνι ἄνακτι
  Παυσανίας, ἄρχων Ἑλλάδος εὐρυχόρου,
πόντου ἐπ' Εὐξείνου, Λακεδαιμόνιος γένος, υἱὸς
  Κλεομβρότου, ἀρχαίας Ἡρακλέος γενεᾶς.'

This monument of his prowess is dedicated to lord Poseidon
  by Pausanias, ruler of Hellas with its wide spaces
  at the Euxine sea; a Lacedaemonian by birth, the son of
  Cleombrotus of the ancient race of Heracles.
(English translation by Ch. B. Gulick)

The text of this Pontic dedication is unlikely to have been a forgery: contrary to the fake inscription in Delphi, it was preserved for centuries (at least the apparently reliable Nymphis asserted that the monument was still standing there at his time, the 3rd century BC, and he is likely to have copied the text from the original epigram) and gives both the patronymic and the home of Pausanias and of course the deity to whom it was dedicated. I think it was this monument and its inscription which most probably inspired the story about the Delphic tripod. A charge because of this dedication may have been part of Pausanias' trial after his first recall to Greece, especially because Nymphis makes the highly unusual claim that the Spartan commander appropriated a votive dedicated previously by someone else.[35] Later on, the entire story was simply transferred to another location and another monument, which was by then known to most Greeks (as Herodotus 4.81 clearly implies, the one at the entrance of the straits was not necessarily known to everybody) and could have a great impact in justifying the prosecution against Pausanias. The text of the dedicatory epigram was adjusted accordingly and it was easy to assert that it was erased since it was certainly not visible on the monument itself. As the list of the participant poleis may have been added as an afterthought to the dedicatory inscription and was most probably even altered afterwards in some cases[36] (and because this fact may have been generally known), it was easy to make people believe in the existence of a former dedicatory inscription and to use the well-known list as a tangible

[34] The Pontic dedication is occasionally mentioned (most recently Petrovic 2007: 268-269), but it is only Nafissi (2004: 72-73) who assumes a direct link between the two, suggesting that Pausanias offended by the removal of his Delphic epigram, compensated himself by this dedication. Of course, such a sequence or link cannot be ruled out and it is also conceivable that the two inscriptions were engraved roughly at the same time, but there is nothing to prove necessarily that the Delphic inscription really existed at all, while the existence of the Pontic dedication is beyond reasonable doubt.

[35] Since Nymphis does not reveal who the original dedicator was, his statement may also imply that Pausanias erased the original dedicatory inscription in order to apply his own one to the monument. But such a procedure would be highly unusual and Herodotus 4.81 does not indicate any crime by Pausanias in this case either, so the statement by Nymphis is suspect and may simply derive from an unwarranted slander against the victorious general. In fact, the epigram only mentioned Pausanias and omitted his fellow citizens or soldiers and may have been considered as a sign of tyrannical hybris partly because of this omission (cf. the tripod dedicated by Gelon referred to above and by contrast the inscribed helmet dedicated at Olympia by 'Hieron and the Syracusans' in the British Museum 1823,0610.1 = Jeffery 1990: 275, no. 7). The unofficial title 'general (archon) of broad Greece' may have been considered equally arrogant of course.

[36] See Herodotus 8.82 (with commentaries, e.g. Bowie 2007: 171) and the corresponding entry on the 7th coil of the Serpent column. Usually there are three names on each coil, but here the name of the Tenians seems to be added as a fourth entry and it is also incised in a different way from the other three.

and seemingly incontrovertible proof of an otherwise fictive story, even if the 'previous' inscription was obviously invisible.

Therefore, the well-known story and the inscription mentioned by Thucydides but deriving from an earlier Ionian source seem to have been fabricated most probably at Sparta, and we have to conclude that there is no trace left of the original dedicatory inscription. But a dedicatory inscription was surely an indispensable part of the monument and it was most probably engraved on the lost base. It was likely to have been a simple prose inscription, naming only the Hellenic symmachy led by Sparta, Apollon, and most probably the fact that it was erected as a military victory monument (e.g. the generic formula ἀπὸ τῶν πολεμίων). In this case both the preamble and the additional list of the *symmachoi* would make perfect sense and the complete silence of ancient literary tradition about this real dedicatory inscription would be also understandable.

Bibliography

Adornato, G. 2005. Il tripode di Gelone a Delfi. *Atti della Accademia Nazionale dei Lincei. Rendiconti Lincei* 16: 395–420.

Bowie, A.M. 2007. *Herodotus. Book VIII.* Cambridge: Cambridge UP.

Cawkwell, G.L. 1970. The Fall of Themistocles, in: Harris, B.F. (ed.), *Auckland classical studies presented to E. M. Blaiklock*: 39-58. Auckland; Oxford: Oxford UP.

Dittenberger, W. and K. Purgold. 1896. *Olympia: die Ergebnisse der von dem Deutschen Reich veranstalteten Ausgrabung. Textband 5: Die Inschriften von Olympia*, Berlin: Asher.

Fabricius, E. 1886. Das Platäische Weihgeschenk in Delphi. *Jahrbuch des Deutschen Archäologischen Instituts* 1: 176-191.

Fornara, Ch.W. 1967. Two Notes on Thucydides. *Philologus* 111: 291-295.

Frazer, J.G. 1898. *Pausanias' Description of Greece.* Vol. V. London: Macmillan.

Gauer, W. 1968. *Weihgeschenke aus den Perserkriegen* (IstMitt Beih. 2). Tübingen: Wasmuth.

Gomme, A.W. 1945. *An Historical Commentary on Thucydides. Volume 1. Introduction, and Commentary on Book I.* Oxford: Oxford UP.

Hansen, P.A. 1983. *Carmina epigraphica Graeca saeculorum VIII-V a. Chr. n.* Berlin; New York: DeGruyter.

Hornblower, S. 1991a. *A Commentary on Thucydides. Vol. I. (Books I-III).* Oxford: Oxford UP.

Hornblower, S. 1991b. *The Greek World 479-323 BC.* London; New York: Routledge.

Hölscher, T. 1974. Die Nike der Messenier und Naupaktier in Olympia, *Jahrbuch des Deutschen Archäologischen Instituts* 89: 70–111.

Jacquemin, A. 1999. *Offrandes monumentales à Delphes.* Paris: École Fraínçaise d'Athènes

Jacquemin, A., D. Mulliez, and G. Rougemont 2012. *Choix d'inscriptions de Delphes, traduites et commentées.* Athènes: École Française d'Athènes.

Jeffery, L.H. 1990. *The Local Scripts of Archaic Greece.* Oxford.

Kapparis, K.A. 1999. *Against Neaira [D 59].* Berlin-New York: DeGruyter.

Kienast, D. 1995. Die Politisierung des griechischen Nationalbewußtseins und die Rolle Delphis im großen Perserkrieg, in Schubert Ch. and K. Brodersen (eds), *Rom und der griechische Osten: Festschrift für Hatto H. Schmitt*: 117-133. Stuttgart: Steiner.

Laroche, D. 1989. Nouvelles observations sur l'offrande de Platées. *Bulletin de Correspondance Hellénique* 113:183-198.

Lazenby, J.F. 1975. Pausanias Son of Kleombrotos. *Hermes* 103: 235-251.

MacGregor Morris, I. 2022. Pausanias, Best of Men: Politics, Propaganda, and Memory, in: A. Konecny – N. Sekunda (eds.): *The Battle of Plataiai 479 BC*: 79-132. Wien: Phoibos.

Meiggs, R. and D. Lewis 1969. *A Selection of Greek Historical Inscriptions*. Oxford.

Nafissi, M. 2004. Pausania, il vincitore di Platea, in: Bearzot, C. (ed), *Contro le 'leggi immutabili', Gli Spartani fra tradizione e innovazione*: 53-90. Milano: Vita e Pensiero.

Parker, V. 2005. Pausanias the Spartiate as depicted by Charon of Lampsacus and Herodotus. *Philologus* 149: 3-11.

Petrovic, A. 2007. *Kommentar zu den Simonideischen Versinschriften* (Mnemosyne Suppl. 282). Leiden; Boston: Brill.

Proietti, G. 2021. *Prima di Erodoto*, Stuttgart: Steiner.

Raubitschek, A.E. 1949. *Dedications from the Athenian Akropolis*. Cambridge, MA: Archaeological Institute of America.

Rhodes, P.J. 1970. Thucydides on Pausanias and Themistocles. *Historia* 19: 387-400.

Rhodes P.J. 2018. Erasures in Greek Public Documents, in Petrovic, A., I. Petrovic and E. Thomas (eds), *The Materiality of Text – Placement, Perception, and Presence of Inscribed Texts in Classical Antiquity*: 145-166. Leiden; Boston: Brill.

Schachter, A. 1998. Simonides' elegy on Plataia: The Occasion of Its Performance. *Zeitschrift für Papyrologie und Epigraphik* 123, 25-30.

Steinhart, M. 1997. Bemerkungen zu Rekonstruktion, Ikonographie und Inschrift des platäischen Weihgeschenkes, *Bulletin de Correspondance Hellénique* 121: 33–69.

Stephenson, P. 2016. *The Serpent Column. A cultural biography*. Oxford: Oxford UP.

Trevett J. 1990. History in [Demosthenes] 59. *Classical Quarterly* 40: 407-420.

Westlake, H. D. 1977. Thucydides on Pausanias and Themistocles – a Written Source? *Classical Quarterly* 71: 95-110.

White, M.E. 1964. Some Agiad Dates: Pausanias and His Sons. *Journal of Hellenic Studies* 84: 140-152.

Yates, D. C. 2019. States of Memory. *The Polis, Panhellenism and the Persian War*, Oxford

Something to Do with Epigraphy? The 'Aegeus Episode' in Euripides' *Medea* and the Honorific Dimension of Athenian Tragedy[1]

Andrea Giannotti

Istituto Italiano per gli Studi Storici 'Benedetto Croce' / Durham University
andrea.giannotti1990@gmail.com

Abstract

This paper focuses on the concept of reciprocity in ancient Greek society by using as a test-case an interesting passage, the so-called 'Aegeus episode', from Euripides' *Medea*, where the Athenian king meets Medea and establishes a relationship based on mutual exchange and benefit with her. The analysis of the tragic episode sheds light on the linguistic and conceptual similarities between tragic reciprocations (i.e. those staged in the theatre) and historical reciprocations (i.e. those which occurred in real life and were textually attested by and ratified by inscribed honorific decrees). By highlighting the importance of τιμή ('honour') within human reciprocations, it will be plausible to argue that Euripides was so interested in Greek contemporary honorific practice that he utilised its same language and dynamics to stage his characters seeking for honour through reciprocal relationships.

Keywords
Euripides, Medea, Tragedy, Epigraphy, Honour

Tragic and epigraphic reciprocity: an overview

In his *Nothing to Do with Democracy*, P.J. Rhodes claimed that 'if we associate the festival [*sc.* of the Great Dionysia], and the plays performed at the festival, too intimately with the democracy of Classical Athens, we risk not only misunderstanding the plays and the festival by seeing them in too narrow a context but also misunderstanding the significance of democracy in Athens and of Athens in the Greek world'.[2] I do not aim here to discuss the ideology of the Athenian Great Dionysia, its surrounding civic context, and its dramas in connection with fifth-century BC democracy. Rather, my purpose is to draw another type of 'association', i.e. to investigate to what extent the language of Athenian tragic plays is related to the language of epigraphy, in particular that of honorific decrees praising the deeds and virtues of foreign benefactors (usually labelled as ἄνδρες ἀγαθοί, 'good men') by conferring titles on them.[3] These decrees,

---

[1] My undergraduate and graduate career in Pisa (2009–2015) has shaped my profile as a young scholar of Athenian tragedy and its relationship with Classical history and politics. My doctoral career in Durham (2015–2019) led me to develop – through the invaluable help of Professor P.J. Rhodes – a passionate interest in Greek epigraphy and, specifically, honorific decrees. The epigraphic shade of this paper, intertwined with the other 'tragic half' of my research, aims to be a humble, but sincere, homage to Professor P.J. Rhodes. I am grateful to Dr S. Knipe for having read and revised earlier drafts of this paper, and to the anonymous reviewer who has provided me with many precious suggestions.

[2] Rhodes 2003: 105.

[3] While the practice of gift-exchange and of rewarding benefactors goes back to archaic and pre-Classical times (and is later widely discussed by fourth-century BC oratory), honorific epigraphy started spreading from the mid-fifth century BC onwards (cf. e.g. Domingo Gygax 2016). Meyer 2013: 467–68 n. 69 counts at least 68 honorific decrees in the

inscribed and then erected in the most important and visible places in Athens (usually the Acropolis and the Agora),[4] established official relationships/exchanges between the city and outside individuals, and represented the ratified decision of the people. Moreover, honorific decrees were socially defining, insofar as they displayed the social behaviours both of the city, which attracted and conferred titles on the benefactors, and of the benefactors, who aimed to achieve honours by being socially useful. But they were also morally defining, insofar as they used a lexicon related to popular moral values, beliefs,[5] and recognised cardinal virtues (i.e. 'human qualities which the Athenians wanted to single out for praise and reward above all others').[6] Here the rules of reciprocity were crucial: χάρις χάριν γὰρ ἐστιν ἡ τίκτουσ' ἀεί (S. Aj. 522). Only through reciprocation (which could be extended across time) could the parties involved achieve τιμή, i.e. 'honour', understood both as concrete rewards and as the collective recognition of one's worthiness.[7]

Greek drama provides many examples of reciprocal relationships between people, such as Pelasgos and the Danaids, Philoctetes and Neoptolemos, Hecuba and Agamemnon, Heracles and Theseus, and so on.[8] Episodes depicting an encounter between two or more characters often mention the exchange of favours and/or gifts: as the above-quoted line from Sophocles shows, 'charis, in the language of fifth-century Greek tragedy, refers to a favor that is done with the expectation that repayment will be made, at some later point in time'.[9] That this mirrors the logic of honorific practice should not be surprising, as the playwrights were part of a civic system which, through its norms and values, deeply exploited such a practice to build, preserve, and promote its international social relationships. A comparative analysis of specific tragic episodes and epigraphic testimonies can thus help us to measure to what extent the logic of honorific practice permeated Athenian society (and its cultural products), and also to understand the significance of the logic of benefactions and exchanges in the tragic world.

Specifically, Euripidean drama presents many occurrences (more than 150) of the word τιμή (and cognates), more than we find in his fellow tragedians Aeschylus and Sophocles, in addition to a huge number of honour-related issues, and a deep involvement with the dynamics of reciprocity.[10] The crowded stage of Euripidean drama provides a chance to examine several reciprocal relationships between characters in action and to compare them with the language and functioning of reciprocal exchanges attested by epigraphical sources. Euripides' interest in using technical terms is noteworthy, as it testifies to a growing awareness in the language of honorific inscriptions – confirming, thus, that the language of those decrees was a daily component of the civic discourse (which was not divorced from a citizen's language). *Medea* is the earliest extant tragedy by Euripides and it does not yet display an extensive 'vocabulary of

---

period 451–404 BC. For the honorific decrees of the Classical period, cf. generally Veligianni-Terzi 1997.

[4] For a survey of the places of publication of Athenian state decrees, cf. Liddel 2003.

[5] Cf. Miller 2016: 386.

[6] Whitehead 1993: 42–43.

[7] On reciprocity in ancient Greece, cf. Gill, Postlethwaite, and Seaford 1998.

[8] The reciprocal relationships staged in Athenian tragedy have been analysed according to the concepts of αἰδῶς ('honour-shame'), φιλία ('friendship'), and supplication, along with the socio-ethical frictions and obligations they entail (cf. Cairns 1993, Belfiore 2000, Tzanetou 2012). Also, several social and legal relations between characters have been examined in the light of the Athenian legal system and its procedures (cf. Harris, Leão and Rhodes 2010).

[9] Mueller 2001: 481.

[10] Cf. e.g. Barbato 2020: 126–33. Cf. also Giannotti 2021a.

honour' as, for instance, *Children of Heracles* and *Heracles* do.[11] In the latter plays, the concepts of εὐεργεσία and proleptic honours are fully developed and, significantly, keep the image of beneficent Athens alive through the characters of Demophon and Theseus. In his *Medea*, Euripides still depicts some aspects of ξενία and its private dimension, but he also lightly touches upon the civic institution of προξενία.[12] Contemporary honorific decrees, which were pairing προξενία and εὐεργεσία as honorary titles in the name of reciprocal benefaction, gave Euripides the chance to explore that social field. The acknowledgement of this does not imply any (hyper-)historical reading of tragic plays, any daydreaming about direct allusions to specific decrees/events. Rather, it can open a new spectrum of inquiries on the nuanced relationship between drama and the contemporary socio-political context through the use of epigraphy as a valuable source to assess the involvement of drama in (and, perhaps, its rhetorical contribution to) Athenian social life and its mechanisms.

Owing to limitations of space, this paper examines the notions of honour and reciprocation in Euripides' *Medea*, while focusing on a passage of Euripides' *Medea* where an Athenian character, Aegeus, and a non-Athenian character, Medea, meet and establish a reciprocal relationship based on mutual exchange and benefit, in order to achieve an honourable status. An analysis of the language used by the two Euripidean characters while discussing and negotiating will not only unveil Euripides' incipient interest in the language and dynamics of honorific practice (with which his audience was surely familiar), but will also offer the chance to read and interpret further tragic scenes portraying reciprocation in action through the lens of the contemporary mechanism of benefactions and exchanges between πόλεις and individuals.

Medea ἄτιμος and Aegeus πρόθυμος πρόξενος: the benefits of reciprocity

Euripides' *Medea* revolves around the end of the relationship between Jason and Medea,[13] and it displays a rhetoric strongly related to the concept of reciprocity. However, the play provides a parallel and subtle discussion of τιμή related to reciprocity itself. Indeed, Euripides' stress on Medea's lack of τιμή, due to Jason's betrayal of his family and interruption of reciprocity (E. *Med.* 17, 32, 488–89, 495, 578, 778), can be analysed in the light of the dynamics of the Athenian honorific system by which τιμή was achieved through reciprocation.

Both the relationship between Jason and Medea and the new one between Jason and the royal family of Corinth are described as 'bonds' (76: κηδεύματα), thereby including the dimension of φιλία, understood as both kinship and friendship. By breaking his bond with Medea, Jason is no longer φίλος (77) to her. In the ancient Greek world, φιλία relationships required reciprocal solidarity both domestically (between relatives or friends) and diplomatically (between allies).[14] However, Medea finds herself in an unviable situation, as Jason's individualistic attitude (85–86) does not agree with the habit of reciprocating and of rewarding friends and benefactors: Jason only reached σωτηρία thanks to Medea (476, 482), who – as she herself admits – had been too πρόθυμος (which I would translate here as 'keen to do/receive good') and not wise enough to foresee Jason's selfishness (485). Medea has to acknowledge that Jason

---

[11] Cf. Giannotti 2022c

[12] On ξενία and προξενία, cf. Herman 1987: 130–42.

[13] Cf. Schein 1990.

[14] Cf. *IG* I³ 76 (422 BC), in which the Athenians and the Bottiaeans establish their τὲν φιλία[ν καὶ τὲν χουμμαχίαν (l. 25). Cf. Hdt. 1.69.1–2, Th. 1.57.2, X. *Mem.* 2.9.8. On friendship in Classical Greece, cf. Konstan 1997: 53–92.

will not πράξειν καλῶς (500) towards herself. The concept of 'doing good towards someone' in return for a benefit received (ἀντὶ ὧν εὖ πεποίηκεν) is common in honorific decrees, such as *IG* I³ 102 (*OR* 182; 410/9 BC), *IG* I³ 125 (405/4 BC), and *IG* II² 1 (*OR* 191 + *RO* 2; 405/4 and 403/2 BC).[15] Unfortunately, even the king of Corinth, Creon, does not reward Medea for her previous help in ending Corinth's famine (11-13, 20–22; cf. Σ *ad P. Ol.* 13, 74). Without Jason and Corinth giving Medea what she is entitled to, Medea lacks τιμή. Hence, in such a dishonourable and passive condition, this woman, while demanding οἵας ἀμοιβῆς ἐξ Ἰάσονος κυρεῖ (23) in vain, will ultimately be banished both by her husband and by the king of Corinth.

This is the situation in which Medea finds herself from the very first lines, as she is said to be ἠτιμασμένη (20, 33, 236–37, 1354) and ἠδικημένη (26, 165, 265, 314). However, it is interesting to consider a further term which the Chorus uses to label Medea's status: τάλαινα, φυγὰς δὲ χώρας / ἄτιμος ἐλαύνῃ (437–38). Here, we have something more than Medea's dishonourable condition in a moral sense: for while the middle perfect participle ἠτιμασμένη gives the idea of her poor treatment and the personal feeling of her current condition, the term ἄτιμος in ancient Greece indicated a specific legal status. It is not by accident that the term occurs twice in two somewhat technical contexts (i.e. in the Chorus' definition of Medea's status as an exile and in the 'Aegeus episode'), to distinguish ἄτιμος from ἀτιμάζειν. Such a distinction corresponds to the double, moral and legal, sense of the word ἀτιμία in Classical Athens. As Maria S. Youni has demonstrated, the literary occurrences of the term (from Homer, Pindar, and Tyrtaeus onwards) 'expressed the lack or loss of honour, respect or esteem, due to a god or human; it was a synonym to disgrace, indignity, humiliation, contempt, or insult'.[16] Conversely, in fifth-century BC inscriptions the term was used to indicate dishonour as a penalty deriving from specific infractions and legally determining the loss of rights and privileges. While the authors of these inscriptions employed ἀτιμία only in a technical sense, literary authors could use it in both a legal and moral sense (knowing that the Athenians would be able to infer its meaning from the context).

The Chorus' reference to the soon-to-be-exiled Medea as ἄτιμος would possibly have made the audience think of a specific legal status, perhaps similar to that of Arthmius of Zelea – the decree against whom was apparently inscribed on a bronze stele still visible on the Acropolis in the fourth century BC. Demosthenes says that Arthmius, a former πρόξενος of Athens, was made ἄτιμος καὶ πολέμιος τοῦ δήμου τοῦ Ἀθηναίων καὶ τῶν συμμάχων αὐτὸς καὶ γένος (9.42) for having brought Persian gold to the Peloponnesus (probably in the 470s BC).[17] Demosthenes here recalls the original consequences of being declared ἄτιμος: Arthmius was not ἄτιμος to the extent that he was deprived of civic rights (why should a non-Athenian care about that anyway?); rather, his ἀτιμία meant 'outlawry' and, as a banned outlaw, he could be killed by anyone with impunity. Medea's status is close to Arthmius' insofar as she is officially banished from the land[18] and risks being killed during her wandering (a possibility

---

[15] Cf. also *IG* I³ 91, *IG* I³ 95.

[16] Youni 2019: 374.

[17] Cf. D. 19.271–72, Aeschin. 3.258, Din. 2.24–25. Cf. also Meiggs 1972: 508–12 and, concerning the historicity of the event (with scholars' opinions), Dmitriev 2015: 35–39 (with references).

[18] In E. *Med.* 272 I opt for Harrison's reading Μήδει', ἀνεῖπον instead of C's Μήδειαν εἶπον as, in this way, we would have the verb used for institutional announcements (in inscribed decrees too, such as those stipulating a public proclamation of honours: cf. e.g. Giannotti 2022b).

which is maybe implied in 462–63).[19] After having been declared an enemy of the Athenians, Arthmius became an enemy of Athens' allies too. Accordingly, Medea is declared 'hostile' (323: δυσμενής) by Creon, who in turn has already been called an 'enemy' (along with his family and Jason, 278: ἐχθροί) by Medea herself.[20] Once Medea has settled her intentions, she calls herself ἐχθρά of the Corinthian royal family and Jason (875; but cf. already 16). Moreover, Jason offers an ultimate deal by which Medea could be hosted by Jason's ξένοι (612–13), i.e. guest-friends obliged to treat him – and be treated by him – respectfully. By rejecting both Jason's and his ξένοι's friendship, Medea becomes an enemy of Jason's ξένοι as well. The ἄτιμος Medea is thus forced to wander as an exile and to flee Corinth, Jason and their allies as their common enemy.

Epigraphy and oratory also attest to the meaning of ἀτιμία as the deprivation of rights and properties, as in: IG I³ 40 (OR 131) attesting to Athenian relations with Chalcis (446/5 or 424/3 BC); IG I³ 46 (OR 142) concerning the foundation of the Athenian colony at Brea (c. 440–432 BC); Andocides on the supporters of the Peisistratids (1.106); Thucydides on the homecoming of the Spartan prisoners from Sphacteria (5.34.2). It is clear that Medea is also ἄτιμος insofar as she is being deprived of something, i.e. she is deprived of her status as a wife. But more importantly, Medea is deprived of τιμή and, specifically, of that τιμή which comes from the reciprocation of χάρις. The term χάρις appears in honorific decrees only from the late fourth century BC onwards (e.g. IG II² 487, IG II² 555, IG II³,1 1028, IG II³,1 1386), but it is often associated with specific types of the so-called 'hortatory intention clauses', by which Athens aimed to publicise its habit of reciprocating.[21] This is what Medea unsuccessfully lays claim to, namely the public recognition of her favours. Indeed, Medea has proved her χάρις towards Jason (508: σοὶ χάριν φέρουσα), but her (overrated, in Jason's view: cf. 526) beneficent deeds (510: ἀντὶ τῶνδε) have not been reciprocated. Therefore, Jason is an ἀχάριστος man who does not honour (τιμᾶν) his friends (659–60). Most of all, he is the opposite of the ἄνδρες ἀγαθοί praised in honorific decrees: he is the κάκιστος ἀνδρῶν (488).

Given her situation, Medea desperately needs προξενία (35), δόμος (360, 387), σωτηρία (360), and ἀσυλία (387). As soon as the Chorus describes Medea as honourless, unworthy, homeless, friendless, and disgraced (627–62), Euripides stages Aegeus' timely entrance to redeem the woman's wretched status. Indeed, Aegeus is the one who can satisfy her needs. While it is clear that his φιλία serves to counterbalance Jason's violation of it,[22] it is extremely interesting that the king of Athens describes himself as πρόθυμος (720) and δίκαιος πρόξενος (724). The latter term was, properly speaking, a legal title usually indicating 'a citizen of the state in which he lived, appointed to look after the interest of, and visitors from, the state which appointed him; though over time such appointments became increasingly honorific'.[23] Hence, Aegeus should be considered a 'quasi-πρόξενος' since he is in Corinth at the moment, not in Athens – nor had he been officially nominated πρόξενος by Medea's city.[24] Despite this, Euripides was (even if metaphorically) using an official, institutional term and applying it to a tragic

---

[19] Concerning the dangers of wandering, cf. Montiglio 2005: 24–41.
[20] It is interesting how the three terms, though conveying different shades of 'enemy' (πολέμιος is a war enemy, ἐχθρός is one who has been previously a φίλος, and δυσμενής is one who refuses to be reconciled), equally imply an end/impossibility of reciprocity.
[21] Cf. e.g. Miller 2016.
[22] Cf. Mueller 2001: 487–90.
[23] Osborne and Rhodes 2017: 344.
[24] Cf. Perris 2017: 327–28.

context which, while obviously different from contemporary social life, still had diplomatic overtones. Conversely, the former specification, πρόθυμος, reminds us, for instance, of *IG* I³ 101 (*OR* 187; 410/9-c. 407 BC) where the people of Neapolis are said to be πρόθυμοι for their loyalty, financial help and more general benefactions and good services towards Athens. The term πρόθυμοι was also applied to Heracleides the Clazomenian (*IG* I³ 227 [*OR* 157]) in 423 BC (or later) and Oeniades of (Palae)Sciathus (*IG* I³ 110 [*OR* 184]) in 408/7 BC, when both were made πρόξενοι and εὐεργέται by Athens.[25] The decrees just mentioned are later than Euripides' *Medea* and προθυμία *qua* cardinal virtue in honorific decrees appears from the late fourth century BC onwards.[26] However, Aegeus turns out to be as πρόθυμος as those benefactors whom honorific decrees regularly call πρόθυμοι while describing and explaining their beneficent deeds. The fact that Aegeus calls himself πρόθυμος precisely when he decides to grant his favour to Medea (719–20: πολλῶν ἔκατι τήνδε σοι δοῦναι χάριν, / γύναι, πρόθυμός εἰμι, [...]) is noteworthy. In this respect, Aegeus' profile might embody a prototype of those zealous benefactors and just[27] protectors of strangers who were soon to be praised in stone.

In just one hundred lines, we find an official reciprocal exchange in action between two characters who are in dishonourable circumstances and seek τιμή: on the one hand, Aegeus, a man and king, is ἄπαις (670); on the other, Medea and her children are ἄτιμοι (696). However, there is a difference between the two characters: Aegeus is honourless in a moral sense as a king's (or just man's) sterility was considered shameful;[28] Medea, as said above, is ἄτιμος in the legal sense of the term and purposely describes herself and her children as ἄτιμοι so that her status can be rehabilitated by receiving χάρις (719). Only through a reciprocal exchange will Medea get her τιμή back: by solving the problem of Aegeus' sterility, she will again be a married and honourable woman in magnificent Athens, as described by the Chorus (824–65). Most importantly, Medea will obtain the ἀσυλία she is looking for (387). Again, we here find a term which, though rare, is related to honorific practice. Indeed, ἀσυλία,[29] literally 'immunity from seizure', was usually granted to foreign benefactors and πρόξενοι: from the fifth century BC we have *IG* IX,2 257 (*OR* 118), in which the Thetonians in Thessaly honour Sotaerus the Corinthian; *c.* 450-425 BC) and *IG* I³ 98 (*OR* 173), in which the Athenian oligarchical government honours Pythophanes; 411/10 BC.[30] It is interesting to note that most decrees that concern safeguarding[31] guarantee security (ἀσφάλεια) from external harm (μὴ ἀδικῆν μηδένα), and that ἠδικημένη Medea is equally looking for a πύργος ἀσφαλής (390).

It is clear how the process described by Euripides resembles the mechanism of reciprocity within diplomatic relationships attested by honorific epigraphy. The end of the 'Aegeus

---

[25] For other occurrences, cf. *IG* I³ 117 (*OR* 188; 407/6 BC), *IG* II² 1 (*OR* 191 + *RO* 2; 405/4 BC), *IG* II² 28 (*RO* 18; 387/6 BC).

[26] Cf. Whitehead 1993: 48–52. Fifth-century BC literary occurrences of the term (cf. Hdt. 9.91, Th. 8.40.3, Lys. 12.86 and 16.14) have little to do with later honorific contexts. A proper reciprocal context can be found in Th. 3.67.6. But cf. D. 20.45 for two fifth-century BC πρόθυμοι.

[27] On δικαιοσύνη as cardinal virtue in honorific decrees, cf. Whitehead 1993: 65, 67–68. The few (and heavily damaged) fifth-century BC inscriptions apparently using δίκαιος to describe honorands are *IG* I³ 37 and *IG* I³ 164. In *IG* I³ 53 (*OR* 149A), the Athenians describe themselves as 'faithful, [just], strong and unharmful allies' (ll. 13–14).

[28] Sterility was considered a terrible δυστυχία (cf. e.g. E. *Ion* 771–72) whose origin was usually attributed to women: for a brief but useful overview, cf. Senkova 2015; for the theme of the danger of sterility in ancient Greek literature (especially in Aristophanes' *Lysistrata*), cf. Tsoumpra 2020.

[29] Cf. Chaniotis 1996.

[30] Cf. *IG* II³,1 393. Cf. also Henry 1983: 245–46 (with n. 40 at 255).

[31] Cf. e.g. *IG* II² 1132, *IG* II² 1134, *IG* V,2 10. Cf. also Henry 1983: 163–90.

episode', with the swearing of an oath which serves to reassure Medea (734–58),[32] goes in this direction as well: in ancient Greece, each agreement between two or more parties always began with an oath before the gods[33] – the texts of inscribed laws and decrees too used to start with the invocation of θεοί. Speaking of diplomacy, it should not be forgotten that the play was staged in 431 BC, i.e. right before the outbreak of the Peloponnesian War, one of the most aggressive and anti-Athenian protagonists of which was Corinth, the setting of Euripides' play. Therefore, 'the play's contrast between a Corinthian king who expels an innocent woman and an Athenian king who agrees to protect her is no doubt significant'.[34] In light of this, it was appropriate and, at the same time, innovative for Euripides to use the language of honorific epigraphy due to the socio-political inclusion which its decrees guaranteed.

Bibliography

Allan, A. 2007. Masters of Manipulation: Euripides' (and Medea's) Use of Oaths in *Medea*, in A.H. Sommerstein and J. Fletcher (eds) *Horkos: The Oath in Greek Society*: 113–124. Exeter: Bristol Phoenix Press.

Allan, W. 2002. *Euripides: Medea*. London: Duckworth.

Barbato, M. 2020. *The Ideology of Democratic Athens. Institutions, Orators and the Mythical Past.* Edinburgh: Edinburgh University Press.

Belfiore, E.S. 2000. *Murder among Friends. Violation of* Philia *in Greek Tragedy.* New York and Oxford: Oxford University Press.

Burnett, A. 1998. *Revenge in Attic and Later Tragedy*, Berkeley, Los Angeles and London: University of California Press.

Cairns, D.L. 1993. *AIDŌS. The Psychology and Ethics of Honour and Shame in Ancient Greek Literature.* Oxford: Clarendon Press.

Chaniotis, A. 1996. Conflicting Authorities. *Asylia* between Secular and Divine Law in the Classical and Hellenistic Poleis. *Kernos* 9: 65–86.

Dmitriev, S. 2015. Athenian *Atimia* and Legislation against Tyranny and Subversion. *Classical Quarterly* 65: 35–50.

Domingo Gygax, M. 2016. *Benefactions and Rewards in the Ancient Greek City. The Origins of Euergetism.* Cambridge: Cambridge University Press.

Giannotti, A. 2021a. Debating Honor in Fifth-Century BCE Athens: Towards a Comparative and Intradisciplinary Approach. *Primerjalna književnost* 44(2): 39–52.

Giannotti, A. 2022b (forthcoming). Spatial Memory and the Public-Announcement Clause: The Case of Early Athenian Inscribed Public Honours, in I. Berti, C. Lasagni and D. Marchiandi (eds) *Inscribing Space. Topography and Communication in Attic Epigraphy*. Alessandria: Edizioni dell'Orso.

Giannotti, A. 2022c (forthcoming). Heracles' Honours: The Dynamics of Greek Honorific Practice on Stage, in P. Brillet-Dubois, A.-S. Noel and B. Nikolsky (eds) *Poétique et politique. Nouvelles lectures d'Euripide*. Lyon: MOM Éditions.

Gill, C., N. Postlethwaite, and R. Seaford (eds) 1998. *Reciprocity in Ancient Greece*. Oxford: Oxford University Press.

---

[32] For an analysis of the oath and its values in Euripides' *Medea*, cf. Allan 2007.

[33] Cf. Burnett 1998: 196–205.

[34] Allan 2002: 17.

Harris, E.M., D.F. Leão and P.J. Rhodes (eds) 2010. *Law and Drama in Ancient Greece*. London and New York: Bloomsbury.

Henry, A.S. 1983. *Honours and Privileges in Athenian Decrees: The Principal Formulae of Athenian Honorary Decrees*. Hildesheim: G. Olms.

Herman, G. 1987. *Ritualised Friendship and the Greek City*. Cambridge: Cambridge University Press.

Konstan, D. 1997. *Friendship in the Classical World*. Cambridge: Cambridge University Press.

Liddel, P. 2003. *The Places of Publication of Athenian State Decrees from the 5th Century BC to the 3rd Century AD*, ZPE 143: 79-93.

Meiggs, R. 1972. *The Athenian Empire*. Oxford: Clarendon Press.

Meyer, E.A. 2013. Inscriptions as Honors and the Athenian Epigraphic Habit. *Historia* 62: 453–505.

Miller, J. 2016. Euergetism, Agonism, and Democracy: The Hortatory Intention in Late Classical and Early Hellenistic Athenian Honorific Decrees. *Hesperia* 85: 385–435.

Montiglio, S. 2005. *Wandering in Ancient Greek Culture*. Chicago and London: The University of Chicago Press.

Mueller, M. 2001. The Language of Reciprocity in Euripides' *Medea*. *The American Journal of Philology* 122: 471–504.

Osborne, R. and P.J. Rhodes 2017. *Greek Historical Inscriptions 478-404 BC*. Oxford: Oxford University Press.

Perris, S. 2017. Is There a *Polis* in Euripides' *Medea*?. *Polis* 34: 318–335.

Rhodes, P.J. 2003. Nothing to Do with Democracy: Athenian Drama and the *Polis*. *The Journal of Hellenic Studies* 123: 104–119.

Rhodes, P.J. and R. Osborne 2003. *Greek Historical Inscriptions 404-323 BC*. Oxford: Oxford University Press.

Schein, S.L. 1990. *Philia* in Euripides' *Medea*, in M. Griffith and D.J. Mastronarde (eds) *Cabinet of the Muses: Essays on Classical and Comparative Literature in Honor of Thomas G. Rosenmeyer*: 57–72. Atlanta: Scholars Press.

Senkova, M. 2015. Male Infertility in Classical Greece: Some Observations. *Graeco-Latina Brunensia* 20: 121–131.

Tsoumpra, N. 2020. More than a Sex-Strike: A Case of Medical Pathology in Aristophanes' *Lysistrata*. *The Classical Journal* 116: 1–20.

Tzanetou, A. 2012. *City of Suppliants. Tragedy and the Athenian Empire*. Austin (TX): University of Texas Press.

Veligianni-Terzi, C. 1997. *Wertbegriffe in den attischen Ehrendekreten der Klassischen Zeit*. Stuttgart: F. Steiner.

Whitehead, D. 1993. Cardinal Virtues: The Language of Public Approbation in Democratic Athens. *Classica et Mediaevalia* 44: 37–75.

Youni, M.S. 2019. *Atimia* in Classical Athens: What the Sources Say, in L. Gagliardi and L. Pepe (eds) *Dike. Essays on Greek Law in Honor of Alberto Maffi*: 361–378. Milan: Giuffrè Francis Lefebvre.

Εὐθυνῶ τὴν ἀρχὴν:
Euthynai in the Sacrificial Calendar of Thorikos[1]

Kazuhiro Takeuchi

Japan Society for the Promotion of Science/Nagoya University
kazuhiro.takeuchi@mac.com

Abstract

The sacrificial calendar of Thorikos was inscribed on a large rectangular *stele* in stoichedon style with lines including 30 letters. The distinctive feature of the Thorikos calendar is its inclusion of the oath of the deme's *euthynos* and his *paredroi* as well as the *euthynai* procedure of deme officials at the end of the text. Although readings and restorations of the *editio princeps* presented by George Daux in 1983 have many issues, those continue to be preserved in the most recent editions. This article presents a fresh text based on autopsy, discusses four key clauses (on oath, *exoleia*, publication, *hypeuthynos*) with offering epigraphical observations, and even proposes new restorations for the oath and the *euthynai*. While several letters are left unrestored in the text, a new restoration suggests that the Thorikos' officials, by election or by sortition, responsible for preparing and conducting sacrifice should be all subject to audits. Moreover, although the similarity of the hands between the Thorikos calendar and the Kallias decrees has received wide recognition, the shapes of some characteristic letters (*nu*, *omicron* and *theta*, *rho*, *sigma*, *upsilon*, *omega*) on the two monuments are patently different.

Keywords

Sacrificial calendar of Thorikos, *euthynos*, oath, *euthynai* of deme officials, dating and lettering

The sacrificial calendar of Thorikos was first published from autopsy in 1983 by George Daux.[2] In 2005 it was republished in *Greek Sacred Law: A Collection of New Documents (NGSL)* by Eran Lupu after autopsy of the stone. His edition provides the basis for the texts in the epigraphical collections published in recent years: *A Collection of Greek Ritual Norms (CGRN)* by Jan-Mathieu Carbon, Saskia Peels, and Vinciane Pirenne-Delforge; and *Greek Historical Inscriptions 478-404 BC* by Robin Osborne and Peter J. Rhodes (OR).

Although the issues of its chronology and sacrificial ritual are under debate,[3] I find that there is still room to present a fresh text based on autopsy, offer epigraphical commentaries, and

---

[1] I would like to thank Delfim Leão, Rui Morais, and Daniela Ferreira for inviting me to contribute a paper in honor of Peter J. Rhodes. I am deeply indebted to Nikolaos Papazarkadas and Adele Scafuro for their helpful comments and for correcting my English text. I am grateful to Yuzuru Hashiba and Akiko Moroo for critically reading a draft. I also thank the director and the staff of the Epigraphical Museum for granting me permission to examine the stone EM 13537 and for facilitating my study in December 2012. This work was supported by JSPS KAKENHI Grant Numbers 19K23112, 21J01729.

[2] Except where otherwise indicated, all dates are BC. Readings which have been confirmed on stone are designated by the symbol [T.] (=Takeuchi).

[3] For the discussions of its sacrifice and the deme Thorikos, cf. Ekroth (2002: 158-159, 218-219); Humphreys (2004: 155-165; 2018: 991-992); Ismard (2010: 219-221); Osborne (2011: 29-32); Rosivach (1994: 22-29); Whitehead (1986: 194-199).

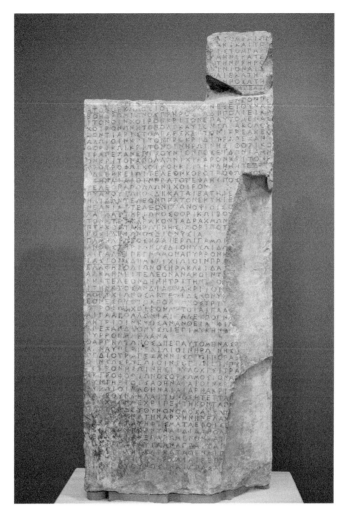

Figure 1. EM 13537 (front): Epigraphic Museum, Athens, Photo by K. Takeuchi © Hellenic Ministry of Culture and Sports / Hellenic Organization of Cultural Resources Development.

propose new restorations for the oath of the *euthynos* and the *euthynai* of officials appended to the end of the inscription (lines 57-65).[4]

Text and translation

A rectangular *stele* (EM 13537) of white marble, cut off square on the upper left and broken on the right below line 22 (Figure 1). The text is inscribed on the smooth front face in Ionic script and stoichedon style. The marginalia are added on the left (Figure 2) and right (Figure 3) sides by the different hands. The back is not original due to the secondary use of the stone as a

---

[4] For example, Parker (1987: 144-147) offered a translation and notes only for lines 1-57 that concern ritual. Kearns (2009: 225-230) also omitted a translation for lines 57-65.

Figure 2. EM 13537 (left side): Epigraphic Museum, Athens, Photo by K. Takeuchi © Hellenic Ministry of Culture and Sports / Hellenic Organization of Cultural Resources Development.

Figure 3. EM 13537 (right side): Epigraphic Museum, Athens, Photo by K. Takeuchi © Hellenic Ministry of Culture and Sports / Hellenic Organization of Cultural Resources Development.

Figure 4. EM 13537 (back): Epigraphic Museum, Athens, Photo
by K. Takeuchi © Hellenic Ministry of Culture and Sports /
Hellenic Organization of Cultural Resources Development.

threshold (Figure 4).[5] The dating remains uncertain, but most recently Osborne and Rhodes give a date of ca. 430. I shall return to the question of its chronology and lettering in the end.

Height 1.327 m; width 0.555 m; thickness 0.175-0.195 m; letter height 0.011-0.013 m (round letters 0.010-0.011 m); stoichedon grid, horiz. 0.0180-0.0184 m, vert. 0.019 m. Autopsy, Takeuchi 2012.[6]

---

[5] Unlike Lupu (2009: 125-126), I am not certain that the back of the stone had been inscribed. I confirm from autopsy that the marginalia on the left side started from the middle of words. I suspect that the lost beginnings of the words were in fact inscribed on the left side, not coming from the back. This may be illustrated by the restorations of the marginalia on the right side. I follow Jameson who first detected a reference to the Panathenaia on the right side. *IG* I³ 256 bis, right side, lines 4-6 [T.]: Μυκηνω[ι] τέ[λεον -?]]αν οἶν Π[α]ναθ[ηναί]]οις θύεν πρ[ατόν]; cf. Humphreys (2004: 157); Jameson (1999: 330, n. 32); Lupu (2009: 510); Osborne and Rhodes (2017: 271); Parker (2005: 75, n. 104); Shear (2021: 90, n. 32). If the restoration Π[α]ναθ[ηναί]]οις is right, at the least the thickness of four-letter spaces (letter height 0.010-0.015 m) has been lost from the back.

[6] The autopsy of the Thorikos calendar was carried out within the framework of my PhD dissertation on the cults of

Figure 5. EM 13537 (bottom lines): Epigraphic Museum, Athens, Photo by K. Takeuchi © Hellenic Ministry of Culture and Sports / Hellenic Organization of Cultural Resources Development.

Editions:[7] Daux (1983 = *Bull. ép.* 1984.190; *SEG* XXXIII 147); *IG* I[3] 256 bis (without text); Lupu, *NGSL*[2] 1; *CGRN* 32[8]; OR 146. Cf. Daux (1980; 1984); Parker (1984: 54); Whitehead (1986: 116-119, 194-199, 390-391, no. 127 = *SEG* XXXVI 203); Bingen (1991: 28-31, 35 = *SEG* XLI 251); Jameson (1999: 328-331 = *SEG* L 55); Humphreys (2004: 155-165 = *SEG* LIV 60); *Attic Inscriptions Online (AIO)* 847[9]; Takeuchi (2019: 266-271) (unpublished).

My text of lines 57-65 is as follows (Figure 5):

τὸν δ' εὔθυνον ὀμόσαι καὶ τ[ὸς παρέδ]-   stoich. 30
ρος, «εὐθυνῶ τὴν ἀρχὴν ἣν ἔλαχ[ον εὐθύν]-
εν κατὰ τὰ ψηφίσματα ἐφ' οἷς ε[.....7...]-
[.]εν ἡ ἀρχή». ὀμνύναι Δία, Ἀπόλλ[ω, Δήμητρ]-
α ἐξώλειαν ἐπαρώμενον, καὶ τ[ὸς παρέδ]-
ρος κατὰ ταὐτά. ἀναγρά{ι}ψαι [δὲ τὸν ὅρκ]-

60

Dionysos in the Attic demes. Takeuchi (2019).

[7] I omit the early editions which were not based on autopsy of the stone: Vanderpool (1975: 33-41 = *Bull. ép.* 1976.235); Dunst (1977 = *Bull. ép.* 1978.186; *SEG* XXVI 136); Labarbe (1977: 56-64, no. 50 = *Bull. ép.* 1979.187; *SEG* XXVIII 111). I do mention them, however, in *apparatus criticus* or commentaries, if applicable. Note that Michael H. Jameson was preparing a new edition of the Thorikos calendar from autopsy. Although it remained unpublished at the time of Jameson's death, this edition was available to Sally Humphreys, who engaged with it in her own analysis. On this see Humphreys (2004: 162, n. 81); Jameson (1988: 90, n. 7; 1999: 328, n. 27); Matthaiou (2009: 205-206).

[8] http://cgrn.ulg.ac.be/file/32, viewed 1 February 2021.

[9] https://www.atticinscriptions.com/inscription/AIO/847, viewed 1 February 2021.

[ο]ν ἐστήλῃ καὶ καταθε͂ναι π[αρὰ . . . ⁵ . .]-
[.]ιον, ὅσαι δ' ἂν ἀρχαὶ αἱρεθῶ[σι . . . ⁶ . . .]-
65   σιν ὑπευθύνος ε͂ναι ἁπάσα[ς.   *vacat*   ]
vacat ca. 0.078 m

Suppl. Daux, 59 63 Takeuchi 64 Whitehead || 57-58 τ[ὸς παρέδ]|ρος Graf apud Dunst || 59-60 ἐ[σελήλυʸ]|θεν Burkert apud Dunst in textu, ἐ[νέστηⁿ]|σεν Dunst in apparatu, ἐ[γκαθέστ]|ηκεν Daux post Labarbe || 61-62 [τὸς παρέδ]|ρος Daux, τ[ὸς παρέδ]|ρος Lupu || 62-63 ἀναγράψαι [τὸν ὅρκο]|ν vel [τὸν εὔθυνο]|ν Dunst in apparatu, ἀναγρά{ὶ}ψαι [τὸν ὅρκο]|ν Labarbe, [δὲ τὸν ὅρκ|ο]ν Daux, [δὲ τὸν νόμ|ο]ν Jameson apud Humphreys, [δὲ τὸν ταμί|α]ν Humphreys || 63-64 π[αρὰ τὸ Δελ<φί>|ν]ιον Daux, π[αρὰ τὸ . . . | .]ιον Bingen, π[αρὰ τὸ Κόρ|ε]ιον Humphreys || 64-65 αἱρεθῶ|σιν Daux, αἱρεθῶ[σιν ἢ ληχθῶ]|σιν Papazarkadas (per comm.), αἱρεθῶ[σιν ἢ λάχω]|σιν Takeuchi.

Translation

(57) The auditor (*euthynos*) and his assistants (*paredroi*) are to swear, 'I will audit the office which was allotted to me for auditing in accordance with the decrees on which the office [- - -]'. (60) To swear by Zeus, Apollo, Demeter, cursing utter destruction, and the assistants in the same way. (62) And to inscribe the oath on a *stele* and set it up [by - - -]ion. (64) All offices for which officials are elected [- - -] are to be subject to audits.

Oath clause (lines 57-60)

57-58: τὸν δ' εὔθυνον ὀμόσαι καὶ τ[ὸς παρέδ]|ρος. The auditor and his assistants were to swear an oath in Skirophorion, the last month of the year, when they were appointed by lot to examine the conduct of the officials of that year (see below). It is known from line 52 of the Thorikos calendar that their oath-taking could accompany a sacrifice of 'oath victim' (*horkomosion*).[10] *IG* I³ 256 bis.52 [T.]: Σκιροφοριῶνος, ὁρκωμόσιον <π>αρ[έχεν]. I follow Daux who restored the infinitive <π>αρ[έχεν] in connection with a similar formula inscribed in line 12, though with some doubt.[11] *IG* I³ 256 bis.12 [T.]: ὁρκωμόσιον πα[ρέ]χεν ἐς εὐθύνας. Here the oath victim was to be provided in Metageitnion, the second month of new year, when the auditor in fact carried out the audit (*euthynai*) of officials of the previous year.[12] At Halai Aixonides in 368/7 the demarch and treasurer rendered their accounts for the last year before [Metageitni]on (Wilhelm's restoration). *IG* II² 1174.10-13: τὰς δὲ εὐθ[ύνας διδόναι] | τῶι [ὑ]στέρωι ἔτει πρὸ [τῶ Μεταγειτνι]ῶνος μηνὸς ἐκ τῶν ἐκ [τῆς κιβωτοῦ λόγ]ων, ἐξ ἄλλων δὲ μή.

58-59: Daux's restoration εὐθυνῶ τὴν ἀρχὴν ἣν ἔλαχ[ον εὐθύν]|εν κατὰ τὰ ψηφίσματα was followed by all the later editors. To scrutinize the office in accordance with the decree(s)

---

[10] cf. Hsch. o 1236 s.v. ὁρκωμόσια· θύματα, ἐφ' ὧν ὅρκοι γίνονται. Cole (1996: 230-233) points out one more oath victim in the Thorikos calendar, that is, three animals (Labarbe's restoration) offered to Apollo Pythios in Mounychion. *IG* I³ 256 bis.41 [T.]: ἐς Πυθίο Ἀπόλλωνος τρίτ[τοαν]. On the oaths of office, see also Rhodes (2007).

[11] I confirm from autopsy that the initial *pi* of the infinitive is not inscribed and a left vertical with part of the upper loop is preserved on the right edge, likely of the *rho*. Throughout the extant text, however, that *pi* is the only supplied letter by Daux to be thought that the letter cutter omitted. Given the consistency in his lettering, it may be possible that the word actually begins in αρ-.

[12] On the audit of officials of the polis, see [Arist.] *Ath. Pol.* 48.4-5; Rhodes (1981: 561-564); cf. Piérart (1971); Scafuro (2014). On the audit culture of the Attic demes, see also Fröhlich (2004: 346-355).

Figure 6. EM 13537 (lower left edge): Epigraphic Museum,
Athens, Photo by K. Takeuchi © Hellenic Ministry of Culture
and Sports / Hellenic Organization of Cultural Resources
Development.

is well illustrated by the Halai inscription just cited above. *IG* II² 1174.15-18: ἐξορκούτω [δὲ ὁ δήμαρχος τὸν ε|ὔ]θυνον καὶ τὸς πα[ρέδρος εὐθύνεν κα|τ]ὰ τὸ ψήφισμα τὸ ἐ[ν τῆι ἀγορᾶι ἀναγε|γ]ραμμένον. As with the Thorikos calendar, the Halai's auditor and his assistants were both involved in the deme audit, but the decree was described as 'having been inscribed in the agora'.[13]

59-60: Daux's restoration κατὰ τὰ ψηφίσματα ἐφ' οἷς ἐ[γκαθέστ]|ηκεν ἡ ἀρχή was itself based on Labarbe's suggestion ἐ[γκαθέστ]|<ηκ>εν. It has been accepted in all the later editions uncritically, but I doubt it from autopsy. Labarbe first thought to restore two letters, *eta* and *kappa*, on stoichos 1 of line 60, whereas, Daux noted the *eta* inscribed between the *epsilon* on stoichos 1 of line 59 and the *kappa* on stoichos 1 of line 60.[14] When I examined the stone

---

[13] On the Halai decree *IG* II² 1174, see most recently Marchiandi (2019: 392-393).

[14] Daux (1983: 170-171); Labarbe (1977: 63).

at autopsy, however, I could see no traces of the two letters on the left edge due to damage (Figure 6). Lupu was also unable to verify Daux's reading 'beyond doubt', but he left the verb as it is in the text.[15]

On the other hand, it should be noted that there are several irregularities in letter-cutting throughout the Thorikos calendar:

1. The double *iota* of the dative singular Διί ('for Zeus') is always inscribed in a single stoichos (lines 10,[16] 13, 22, 25, 35, 47). The letters Δί in line 39 could be mistaken for Δι<ί>, since the *iota* is inscribed to left of center in the stoichos.[17]
2. The *iota* at the beginning or ending of a word is sometimes inscribed between two stoichoi, as in ΑΙΤ (line 5), ΙΙΕ (line 32), and ΑΙΤ (line 57). Daux's restorations Ποσ[ειδῶνι] 'for Poseidon' (line 23) and Φιλ[ωνίδι] 'for Philonis' (line 44) at line-ends are both followed by all the later editions, but each one letter too long for the stoichedon pattern. If the restorations are certain, as Daux assumed, one of the two *iotas* might have been inscribed between two stoichoi or in one stoichos with another letter.[18]
3. The small *lambda* of the phrase ἐφ' ἁλῆι 'at the salt-works' (line 23) is inscribed in the upper part of the space between two stoichoi (ΕΦΑᐩΗΙ *lapis*).
4. Erasures are made at several points at line end (lines 9, 21, 22) except for one (line 30), and the first three words in line 23 are characteristically crossed out by horizontal line. *IG* I³ 256 bis.23 [T.]: ⟦Ἀθηναίαι οἶν πρατὸν⟧ (⟦ΘΗΝΑΙΑΙΟΙΝΠΡΑΤΟΝ⟧ *lapis*).

Even after taking into consideration these irregularities, it should be stressed that Daux's reading and alignment of the two letters, *eta* and *kappa*, are quite uncertain.

The verb ἐγκαθίστημι means '*place* or *establish in*' (see LSJ⁹ s.v.). Daux thought the office (*arche*) has been instituted by the decrees.[19] If so, I suspect that the deme offices subject to audit for the performance of sacrifice, such as a demarch, priests, *hieropoioi*, etc. would have been all instituted or established by the decrees. Instead, it is, I think, more attractive to suppose that the office under the audit would have regulated or prescribed the official to carry out his task on the basis of the decrees. In 327/6, for example, the Kollytos decree ordered some official and the demarch to sacrifice round cakes and mixture(s) for all the gods and the heroes.[20] *SEG* LVIII 108.10-12: δεδόχθαι Κολλυ[τεῦσιν· θύειν . . . . . ¹⁰ . . . . . κα]|ὶ τὸν δήμαρχον τοῖ[ς θεοῖς πᾶσιν καὶ τοῖς ἥρωσιν] | πόπανα καὶ πελανὸ[- - -]. Nevertheless, the verb of the Thorikos calendar cannot be restored at all satisfactorily. I am currently inclined to leave the letters unrestored in the text.

---

[15] Lupu (2009: 120).

[16] Given the regularity of cutting Διί, its restoration in line 10 would leave 15 letter spaces on the missing beginning, not 14 of Μεταγειτνιῶνος. The month's name Metageitnion could be restored in the preceding lines, most likely in the beginning of line 7; cf. Lupu (2009: 130).

[17] Threatte (1996: 229-230, no. 56.021) has also pointed out the possibility of accidental omission of an *iota*.

[18] Daux (1983: 165).

[19] Daux (1983: 156) and Labarbe (1977: 59) translated the phrase in French, 'aux décrets sur la base desquels la magistrature a été instituée' and 'en fonction des décrets par lesquels cette magistrature a été instituée' respectively.

[20] On this restoration, see Matthaiou (2008).

Exoleia clause (lines 60-62)

60-61: ὀμνύναι Δία, Ἀπόλλ[ω, Δήμητρ]|α ἐξώλειαν ἐπαρώμενον. Daux's restoration [Δήμητρ]|α is supported by literary and epigraphical sources. cf. Ar. *Eq.* 941-942: Εὖ γε νὴ τὸν Δία καὶ τὸν Ἀπόλλω καὶ τὴν Δήμητρα; [Dem.] 52.9: (καὶ μὰ τὸν Δία καὶ τὸν Ἀπόλλω καὶ τὴν Δήμητρα, οὐ ψεύσομαι πρὸς ὑμᾶς, ὦ ἄνδρες δικασταί, ἀλλ' ἃ τοῦ πατρὸς ἤκουον, διηγήσομαι ὑμῖν); Schol. ad Aeschin. 1.114: τοὺς ὁρκίους (θεοὺς)] Ἀπόλλωνα πατρῷον καὶ Δήμητρα καὶ Δία, ὥς φησι Δείναρχος ὁ ῥήτωρ. The inscribed ordinances of Skambonidai dating to ca. 460 contain an oath to be sworn to 'the three gods', probably to Zeus, Apollo, and Demeter.[21] *IG* I³ 244.B.3-15 (OR 107) [T.]: «κα|ὶ τὰ κοιν|[ὰ] τὰ Σκαμ|βονιδõν | σõ : καὶ ἀ|ποδόσο : π|αρὰ τὸν ε|ὔθυνον : τ|ὸ καθε͂κο|ν» : ταῦτα ἐ|πομνύνα|ι : τὸς τρε͂ς θεός. In the late fourth century one may find a good parallel in the Myrrhinous decree,[22] which also attests the oath of the auditor himself. *IG* II² 1183.8-13 (RO 63) [T.]: «οὔτ' α[ὐ]τ[ὸς ἐγὼ] οὔτ[ε] ἄ[λ]λος ˅ ἐμοὶ οὐ|[δὲ ἄ]λλε(ι) εἰδότος <ἐ>μο[ῦ μηχανῆι ἢ τ]έ̣[χ]γ[η]ι οὐ̣δεμιᾶι· κ̣αὶ ἐάν μ[ο]ι δ̣οκεῖ ἀδικεῖν, κατ[ε]υ̣[θ]υνῶ α[ὐ]τοῦ [κα]ὶ [τιμήσ]ω οὗ [ἄ]ν μ[ο]ι δ̣ο̣κεῖ ἄξιον εἶ̣ναι τὸ ἀδί[κ]ημα· νὴ τὸν Δ[ία] νὴ τὸ[ν] Ἀπόλλω νὴ τὴν | [Δ]ήμ<η>τρα, εὐορ<κ>οῦντι μ[έ]ν <μ>οι πο̣λ̣[λ]ὰ̣ κ̣α̣[ὶ ἀγα]θά, εἰ δ' ἐπιορκο[ί]ην τἀναντία».

The phrase of cursing utter destruction (*exoleia*) is a distinctive feature of the Thorikos calendar. As Kyriaki Konstantinidou points out, '[n]ot limited to archaic times, the utter ruin (*exoleia*) of those swearing falsely – which denotes not only their own death, but can extend to the destruction of their offspring and, sometimes, even household – is the main manifestation of the explicit form of divine punishment, especially in formal oath-taking in all periods'.[23] It can be traced in Athenian treaties inscribed after the mid-fifth century, but was quite rare in Greek sacrificial calendars and ritual norms. A similar formula, along with an oath sworn by Apollo, Leto, and Artemis, can be found as early as ca. 457, in the Athenian decree dealing with the Delphic Amphiktyony. *IG* I³ 9.9-13 (OR 116): [ἐμμενε͂ν τε ὀ]μόσαντας ἐν [τε͂ι χσυνμαχίαι νὲ τ]ὸν Ἀπόλλο [καὶ τὲν Λετὸ καὶ τὲν] Ἄρτεμιν ἐ[χσ|ο͂λειάν τε καὶ ha]υτοῖς ἐπαρ[ομ|έ]νος ἐὰν παραβαί]νομεν. One could find an even closer parallel in the Athenian regulations for Erythrai, probably in late 435/4.[24] OR 121.16-17 (*IG* I³ 14): ὀμνύναι [δὲ? Δ]ία κα[ὶ] Ἀπόλλο καὶ Δέμε[τρα] ἐπαρομένο[ς ἐχσό]|λειαν ἐφ[ιορκõντι τε κ]αὶ παι[σ]ὶν; *IG* I³ 15.36-39: [τὸν δὲ hόρκο|ν ὀμνύναι κατὰ hιερõν καιομένον Δία καὶ Ἀπόλλο καὶ Δέμετ|ρα ἐναντί[ον τε͂ς βολε͂ς Ἐρυθρᾶσι καὶ τõ φρορáρχο, ἐφιορκõσι|ι] ἐπαρομέ[νος ἐχ]σόλε[ιαν καὶ παισί]; cf. *IG* I³ 75.25-27 (424/3?): ὀμνύντον δὲ | [καὶ] α[ὐ]τõ[ν πρέσβες καὶ ἐχσόλειαν ἐπ]αράσθον εἰ μὲ ἐμμ[[έ]νοιεν [ἐν τοῖς hόρκοις hὸς ὀμομόκα]σιν hαλιε͂ς. Moreover, Stephen Lambert restored the noun ἐξώλεια in an Athenian treaty dating to the mid-fourth century.[25] *IG* II³ 1, 488.11: [ἐξώ]λ[ε]ιαν εῖναι ἑαυτῶι κ[αὶ παισὶ].

---

[21] cf. Sommerstein and Bayliss (2013: 164 with n. 48).

[22] On its attribution to Myrrhinous, rather than Hagnous, see now Csapo and Wilson (2020: 195-201); Takeuchi (2019: 39-40).

[23] Konstantinidou (2014: 11). On related topics, especially in Homer and Hesiod, see now Gagné (2013: 159-205). I thank Nikolaos Papazarkadas for drawing my attention to this point.

[24] On this dating of the Erythrai decrees (*IG* I³ 14, 15, and probably 16), which I follow, see Moroo (2014 = *SEG* LXIV 30); cf. OR 121 (late 450s).

[25] Lambert (2007: 67, n. 3).

Publication clause (lines 62-64)

62-63: While the early editors already suggested the noun without the particle δέ, Daux's restoration ἀναγρά{ι}ψαι [δὲ τὸν ὅρκ|ο]ν ἐστήληι, with which I agree, was accepted in all the later editions. David Whitehead intriguingly commented that '[t]he stipulation that his oath be inscribed, followed by some provisions for the *euthynai* of deme officials, gives the document something of the character of a secular deme decree of its period'.[26] For inscribing the oath on a *stele*, cf. *IG* I³ 40.57-61 (OR 131) dating to 446/5 or 424/3: τὸ δὲ φσέφισμα τόδε καὶ τὸν | hόρκον ἀναγράφσαι Ἀθένεσι μὲν τὸν γρα|μμ[α]τέα τῆς βολῆς ἐστέλει λιθίνει καὶ κ|αταθεναι ἐς πόλιν τέλεσι τοῖς Χαλκιδέ|ον; *IG* I³ 11.11-12 (OR 166) dating to 418/7: [τὸ δὲ φσέ]φισμα τόδε καὶ τὸν [hόρκ]ο[ν] ἀνα[γρ]ά[φσα]ι ἐστέλει λιθίνει ἐμ π]όλει τὸν γραμματέα τῆς βολῆς; Thuc. 5.47.11: τὰς δὲ ξυνθήκας τὰς περὶ τῶν σπονδῶν καὶ τῶν ὅρκων καὶ τῆς ξυμμαχίας ἀναγράψαι ἐν στήλῃ λιθίνῃ Ἀθηναίους μὲν ἐν πόλει, Ἀργείους δὲ ἐν ἀγορᾷ ἐν τοῦ Ἀπόλλωνος τῷ ἱερῷ, Μαντινέας δὲ ἐν τοῦ Διὸς τῷ ἱερῷ ἐν τῇ ἀγορᾷ. On the other hand, Sally Humphreys preferred [τὸν ταμί[α]ν, 'the treasurer', as the official responsible for publication to Daux's [τὸν ὅρκ|ο]ν, 'the oath', or even to Jameson's unpublished restoration [τὸν νόμ|ο]ν, 'the law'.[27] Her restoration is one letter too long, however.

63-64: Daux's restoration καὶ καταθεναι π[αρὰ τὸ Δελ<φί>|ν]ιον has been followed by all subsequent editors. Daux first regarded the Delphinion as an important sanctuary due to its appearances twice in the Thorikos calendar (lines 6 and 11) with the definite article, then he thought two letters, *phi* and *iota*, inserted below the letters, *epsilon* and *lambda*, at the end of line 63.[28] His restoration, however, is not persuasive. As Jean Bingen pointed out, the suffix -ιον is commonplace for a sanctuary, thus he chose to print within the text simply π[αρὰ τὸ ...| .]ιον.[29] At the least, the Python is known from the Thorikos calendar. *IG* I³ 256 bis.41 [Τ.]: ἐς Πυθίο Ἀπόλλωνος τρίτ[τοαν]. The still unpublished Thorikos decree dating to ca. 460-440 could mention two sanctuaries, a Dionysion and a Herakleion.[30] More recently Lambert followed Bingen, refusing to restore the location of the *stele*, and instead offered the translation '[by the - - -]ion' (*AIO* 847, n. 1), with which I agree. Moreover, as Humphreys noted, even the restoration [Δελφίνι]ον in line 11 is 'unwarranted'.[31] In fact, there is no trace of letters visible at autopsy. *IG* I³ 256 bis.11 [Τ.]: π[αρ]ὰ τὸ [Δελφίνι]ο̲ν̲. Accordingly Humphreys suggested an alternative in lines 63-64 as π[αρὰ τὸ Κόρ|ε]ιον, the sanctuary of Demeter.[32] This seems to fit the stoichedon pattern but should remain conjectural. In the circumstances, the location of the *stele* should be left unrestored.

Nikolaos Papazarkadas has brought to my attention (personal communication) the letters of the Thorikos calendar, which were clearly painted red, and has pointed out that the good state

---

[26] Whitehead (1986: 194).

[27] Humphreys (2004: 162, n. 81). For inscribing the law of the polis, see for example the law against tyranny of 337/6. *IG* II³ 1, 320.22-24: ἀναγράψαι δὲ τόν|δε τὸν νόμον ἐν στήλαις λιθίναις δυοῖν τὸν γ|ραμματέα τῆς βουλῆς.

[28] Daux (1983: 170).

[29] Bingen (1991: 35, n. 31).

[30] On this see Matthaiou (2009: 206, no. 9, 208 = *SEG* LIX 58); Papazarkadas (2011: 113, 137).

[31] Humphreys (2004: 157, n. 69).

[32] Humphreys (2004: 162). The Koreion is rarely attested in literary sources but is known from the mid-fourth century deme decrees of Teithras, located at Pikermi. *SEG* XXIV 151.21-22: στήλην δὲ στῆσαι ἐν τῶι Κορε|[ίωι]; *SEG* XXIV 153.6-8: ἀναγρά|ψαι δὲ τόδε τὸ ψήφισμα ἐν στή[λ]ηι λιθίνηι καὶ στῆσα|ι ἐν τῶι Κορείωι.

of preservation of the color may suggest that the stone had been set up within a building. If, as is likely, the *stele* was located inside, we should be cautious about the meaning of the preposition π[αρὰ] with the accusative, 'beside, near, by' (LSJ⁹ s.v.). At any rate, the *pi* is fully visible on the stone and the preposition παρά is more likely than πρός (exclusively with the dative noun).

Hypeuthynos clause (lines 64-65)

64-65: ὅσαι δ' ἂν ἀρχαὶ αἱρεθῶ[σι . . . ⁶ . . .]|σιν ὑπευθύνος ἔναι ἁπάσα[ς]. Daux suggested here 'la liaison αἱρεθῶ|σιν', i.e., ending line 64 with αἱρεθῶ- and connecting it directly to -σιν at the opening of line 65, even though line 64 would then be 8 letters short.[33] If this is correct, the clause means that 'all offices for which officials are elected are to be subject to audits'. It has been accepted by others, but I follow Whitehead, who noted that 'Daux's αἱρεθῶ|σιν is unwarrantable'.[34] Lupu accepted Daux's αἱρεθῶ[vacat]|σιν, 'though with some doubt, since the stone is broken here'.[35] I also doubt that from autopsy, because the break to the lower right was seemingly cut off at one time. I confirm that the right half of the *omega* in stoichos 22 was broken away. If the whole letter of *omega* had been lost, would Daux have thought of directly connecting αἱρεθῶ- with -σιν in the next line? I am inclined to think that the ending -σιν at the beginning of line 65 is part of another verb, almost certainly in the third person plural.

Papazarkadas suggests to me (personal communication) the passive αἱρεθῶ[σιν ἢ ληχθῶ]|σιν, but that is one letter too long. As he points out, it is unlikely that the first verb does not have a euphonic *nu* before the vowel *eta*. In that case, the second *iota* of αἱρεθῶσιν might have been written between two stoichoi or within the same stoichos as the *nu*. On the other hand, I would rather suggest αἱρεθῶ[σιν ἢ λάχω]|σιν with the second verb in the active to denote the clause 'all offices for which officials are elected or allotted shall be subject to audits'. The verb λαγχάνω has the meaning '*obtain* an office *by lot*' (LSJ⁹ s.v. under I.2), and at least two methods of appointment are attested at the same time in a deme decree, though dating to the early third century. *IG* II² 1215.2-3 (Erikeia?) [T.]: [α]ἱρουμένων τῶν δημο[- - -]; 13-16 [T.]: ἐπὶ τεῖ ἐπαρχεῖ ἣν ἐπά|ρχονται οἱ δημόται ἀπὸ τῆς ἀρχῆς ἕ|καστος ἧς ἂν λάχει εἰς τὴν οἰκοδομ|ίαν.

It is well known that the Attic demes appointed their officials sometimes by election and sometimes by sortition. For the process of election,[36] see *IG* II² 1183.16-18 (Myrrhinous) [T.]: τ[ῶ]ι δὲ εὐθύ[ν]ωι μὴ ἐ<ξ>εῖναι ἐ<ξ>ελεῖ|ν τὴν εὔθυναν ἐὰν μὴ τοῖς [π]λέοσιν δ[ό]ξει τῶν δέκα τῶ<ν> αἱρ[ε]θέ<ν>των διαψηφιζομένοις [κ]ρύβ<δ>ην; *IG* II² 1205.3-8 (Epikephisia) [T.]: ἐπειδὴ οἱ αἱρεθέντες ὑπὸ τῶν δημοτῶν κατή|γοροι Νεοκλέους καλῶς καὶ | δικαίως ἐπεμελήθησαν τοῦ | ἀγῶνος καὶ εἷλον αὐτὸν ἐν τ[ῶ]ι δικαστηρίωι; *IG* II³ 4, 223.1-4 (Halai Aixonides): [οἱ αἱ]ρεθέντ[ες ὑπ]ὸ Ἀλα[ιῶν | τὸ ἄγ]αλμα πο[ι]ήσασθαι τεῖ Ἀφρ[οδίτει | στεφ]ανωθέντες ὑπὸ τῶν δη[μοτῶν | ἀνέ]θεσαν τεῖ Ἀφροδ[ίτει]; *SEG* XXI 519.12-14 (Acharnai): ἐπειδὴ οἱ αἱρεθέντες ἀποφαί[νο]|υσιν τὸ ἀ[ν]άλωμα τῆς οἰκοδομίας κα[ὶ οἱ] | ἀρχιτέκτονες; *SEG* XLII 112.4-6 (Halai

---

[33] Daux (1983: 171). He explained, 'Le graveur, n'ayant plus que 48 lettres à graver, n'a pas voulu le faire sur deux lignes dont la seconde n'aurait eu que 18 lettres et aurait été comme perdue, en bas du document, à la plus mauvaise place pour la visibilité et pour la lecture'.

[34] Whitehead (1986: 194, n. 99). Note that Whitehead himself saw and examined the stone on 13 April 1982 at the J. Paul Getty Museum, Malibu. See Whitehead (1986: 186, n. 53).

[35] Lupu (2009: 120).

[36] cf. Whitehead (1986: 144-148).

Aixonides): καὶ τὰ ἀγάλματα κεκόσμηκεν μετὰ τῶν αἱρεθέντων | ἐκ τῶν δημοτῶν, ἐπεμελήθη δὲ καὶ τῆς θυσίας τῶν Ζωστηρίων κατὰ τὰ | πάτρια, καὶ λόγους τῆς ἐπιμελείας ἔδωκεν τοῖς δημόταις. These elected officials seem responsible for unofficial and extraordinary tasks.

On the other hand, literary and epigraphical sources often attest to sortition.[37] cf. [Arist.] *Ath. Pol.* 54.8 (Peiraieus): κληροῦσι δὲ καὶ εἰς Σαλαμῖνα ἄρχοντα, καὶ εἰς Πειραιέα δήμαρχον; Dem. 57.25 (Halimous): ἔτι τοίνυν ἀρχὰς ἔλαχεν καὶ ἦρξεν δοκιμασθείς; *I.Eleusis* 101.6-8 (Eleusis): καὶ | [λ]αχὼν δήμαρχος κ[αλ]ῶς καὶ δικαίως | δεδημάρχηκεν; *IG* II² 1199.1-7[38] (Aixone): ἐπειδὴ οἱ | [λαχ]όντες ἱεροποιοὶ εἰς τὸ τῆς Ἥβη|[ς ἱ]ερὸν δικαίως καὶ φιλοτίμως ἐπ|[εμ]ελήθησαν τῆς θυσίας τῆ[ι] Ἥβηι κ|[αὶ] τοῖς ἄλλοις θεοῖς οἷς ἔδει αὐτοὺς θ|[ῦ]σαι καὶ λόγον καὶ εὐθύνας δεδώκα|[σ]ιν; *SEG* LVII 125.1-3 (Euonymon): ἐπ[ειδὴ Κτησικλ]είδης λαχὼν τῆς] ἀρχῆς [καλῶς καὶ φιλο]τίμως ἐπεμε]λήθη τῶν κ[οινῶν]. It should be noted that the officials responsible for sacrifice, that is, the demarch, the priest, and the *hieropoioi*, have been appointed by lot.

Jameson has pointed out that '[t]he principal aim of the Thoricus and the other deme calendars was the conscientious performance of a complex schedule of sacrifices. Unfailing attendance at the rites by members of the organization was not expected, and participation and spectacle, while desirable, were not of the first importance. Knowledge that these rites were being performed at the right time, in the right place with the right victims, was. The inscriptions themselves take on the task of declaring and making visible the community's recognition of its obligations. The inscriptions are spectacular, and the large, handsome, *stoichedon* lettering of the fifth century texts, in particular, confirms this function'.[39] At Thorikos the deme's officials, by election or by sortition, responsible for preparing and conducting sacrifice should be all subject to audits.[40] The *stele* of the Thorikos calendar was apparently standing in a sanctuary as a witness, not only of the oath-taking, but also of their sacrificial communication with the gods and the heroes.

Chronology and lettering

In the end, I return to the date and the lettering. Daux first dated the Thorikos calendar to 385-370 based on letter forms and orthography. Later, however, David M. Lewis suggested a date of 440-430 on the basis of letter forms and found the 'closest parallel' in the hand of the Kallias decrees *IG* I³ 52 (OR 144).[41] Harold B. Mattingly regarded both hands as 'certainly very close', and given the five old feminine dative plurals Ἡρωΐνησι in the Thorikos calendar (lines 18, 30, 48, 51 with line 58 of the left side), he could put it as late as ca. 420.[42] Jameson has dated the inscription 'from autopsy' to the 430s or 420s, and Lewis' higher chronology has been most recently favoured by Angelos P. Matthaiou and the subsequent editors.[43]

---

[37] cf. Whitehead (1986: 114-116).

[38] Based on Ackermann (2018: 294).

[39] Jameson (1999: 331).

[40] cf. Osborne and Rhodes (2017: 270).

[41] Daux (1983: 152); Lewis (1985: 108, n. 3; 1987: 57).

[42] Mattingly (1990: 111, 118-119). Instead, Leslie Threatte regarded the dative plural Ἡρωΐνησι as an archaistic use in the sacrificial calendar and suggested the date of ca. 380-375. See Threatte (1996: 99, no. 51.0331; 269, no. 56.043).

[43] Jameson (1988: 90, n. 7; 2000-2003: 26); Matthaiou (2009: 205-206); cf. *CGRN* 32 (ca. 440-430 [or ca. 380-375]); OR 146 (ca. 430); *AIO* 847 (ca. 440-420?).

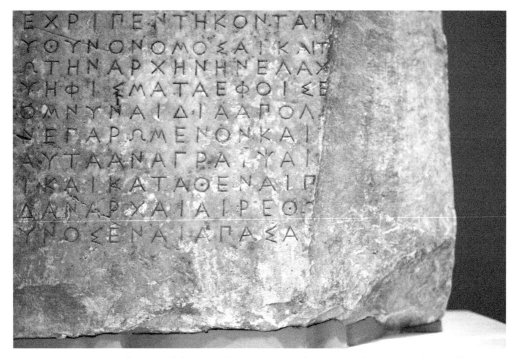

Figure 7. EM 13537 (lower right): Epigraphic Museum, Athens, Photo by K. Takeuchi © Hellenic Ministry of Culture and Sports / Hellenic Organization of Cultural Resources Development.

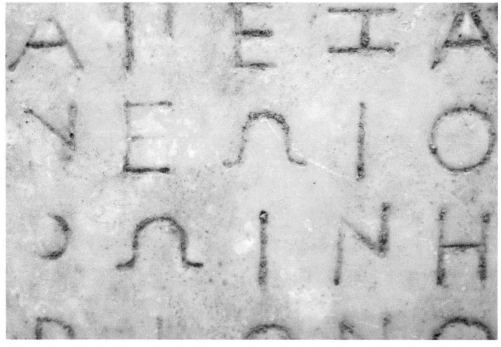

Figure 8. EM 13537 (detail): Epigraphic Museum, Athens, Photo by K. Takeuchi © Hellenic Ministry of Culture and Sports / Hellenic Organization of Cultural Resources Development.

On the other hand, Lupu has returned to the late date of 380-375, largely because the parallel calendars from the Attic demes all come from the fourth century, and he thought it may have been triggered by the republication of the Athenian polis calendar conducted between 410 and 399.[44] But Lupu's assumption is not convincing, unless any practical effect of the republished polis calendar can be detected on the fourth-century deme calendars.

Yet, I would like to bring up two points concerning the lettering. First, the similarity of the hands between the Thorikos calendar and the Kallias decrees has received wide recognition since Lewis first put it forward. However, the connection has not been substantiated. I myself have noticed the significant differences between some characteristic letters of the two inscriptions.[45] Autopsy has shown that the Thorikos calendar has a form of *nu* whose second vertical does not extend up and which is decidedly shorter than the first; *omicron* and *theta* that are not really small and, in fact, they are quite large; *rho* with rounded loop that covers half or more than half the height of the letter; backward leaning *sigma* whose central part does not reach the front of the letter; and *upsilon* made from curving strokes that meet a vertical that is half the height of the letter (Figure 7). In contrast, study of squeezes and photographs[46] shows that the Kallias decrees have *nu* whose second vertical extends up above the top, *omicron* and *theta* that are not as tall as the others, *rho* with rounded loop that covers less than half the height of the letter, upright or just slightly backward leaning *sigma* whose central part reaches the front of the letter, and *upsilon* formed by three strokes whose lower vertical covers half to two thirds the height of the letter. In fact, the shapes of the letters on the two monuments are patently different; in my view, the two inscriptions were cut by two different masons.

Second, less attention is paid to the fact that *omega* in the Thorikos calendar is very distinctive. The letter is round or slightly flat and almost open, with finials curving outward (Figure 8). At the moment, I have failed to find a parallel in Attic inscriptions.[47] Therefore, I am inclined to leave the matter open.

Bibliography

Ackermann, D. 2018. *Une microhistoire d'Athènes: Le dème d'Aixônè dans l'Antiquité*. Athens: École française d'Athènes.

Bingen, J. 1991. Thorikos ou l'épigraphie d'un dème (inédit), in J. Bingen (ed.) *Pages d'épigraphie grecque, I. Attique-Égypte (1952-1982)*: 27-39. Bruxelles: Epigraphica Bruxellensia.

Carbon, J.-M., S. Peels, and V. Pirenne-Delforge, 2017-. A Collection of Greek Ritual Norms (CGRN), viewed 1 February 2021 <http://cgrn.ulg.ac.be>.

Cole, S.G. 1996. Oath Ritual and the Male Community at Athens, in J. Ober and C. Hedrick (eds) *Dēmokratia: A Conversation on Democracies, Ancient and Modern*: 227-248. Princeton: Princeton University Press.

---

[44] Lupu (2009: 124-125); cf. *I.Eleusis* 175 (Eleusis, ca. 330); *SEG* XXI 541 (Erchia, ca. 375-350); *SEG* XXI 542 (Teithras, ca. 400-350); *SEG* L 168 (the Marathonian Tetrapolis, ca. 375-350?).

[45] For the methodology of approaching the lettering of inscriptions as a form of handwriting, see most recently Tracy (2016: 1-6).

[46] For excellent photographs, see the website of the Sara B. Aleshire Center for the Study of Greek Epigraphy at the University of California, Berkeley. http://aleshire.berkeley.edu/inscriptions/2155, viewed 1 February 2021.

[47] Akiko Moroo pointed out to me with photographs (personal communication) that *omega* in the religious decree of Miletus (*Milet* VI 3.1218; OR 143), dating to 434/3, closely resembles the one in the Thorikos calendar. But the shapes of other letters on both inscriptions are explicitly different.

Csapo, E. and P. Wilson, 2020. *A Social and Economic History of the Theatre to 300 BC, II: Theatre beyond Athens: Documents with Translation and Commentary*. Cambridge: Cambridge University Press.

Daux, G. 1980. Recherches préliminaires sur le calendrier sacrificiel de Thorikos. *Comptes rendus des séances de l'Académie des Inscriptions et Belles-Lettres* 124.2: 463-470.

Daux, G. 1983. Le calendrier de Thorikos au Musée J. Paul Getty. *L'antiquité classique* 52: 150-174.

Daux, G. 1984. Sacrifices à Thorikos. *The J. Paul Getty Museum Journal* 12: 145-152.

Dunst, G. 1977. Der Opferkalender des attischen Demos Thorikos. *Zeitschrift für Papyrologie und Epigraphik* 25: 243-264.

Ekroth, G. 2002. *The Sacrificial Rituals of Greek Hero-Cults in the Archaic to the Early Hellenistic Periods*. Liège: Presses Universitaires de Liège.

Fröhlich, P. 2004. *Les cités grecques et le contrôle des magistrats (IVe-Ier siècle avant J.-C.)*. Genève: Librairie Droz.

Gagné, R. 2013. *Ancestral Fault in Ancient Greece*. Cambridge: Cambridge University Press.

Humphreys, S.C. 2004. *The Strangeness of Gods: Historical Perspectives on the Interpretation of Athenian Religion*. Oxford: Oxford University Press.

Humphreys, S.C. 2018. *Kinship in Ancient Athens: An Anthropological Analysis*. Oxford: Oxford University Press.

Ismard, P. 2010. *La cité des réseaux: Athènes et ses associations VIe-Ier siècle av. J.-C.* Paris: Publications de la Sorbonne.

Jameson, M.H. 1988. Sacrifice and Animal Husbandry in Classical Greece, in C.R. Whittaker (ed.) *Pastoral Economies in Classical Antiquity*: 87-119. Cambridge: Cambridge Philological Society.

Jameson, M.H. 1999. The Spectacular and the Obscure in Athenian Religion, in S. Goldhill and R. Osborne (eds) *Performance Culture and Athenian Democracy*: 321-340. Cambridge: Cambridge University Press.

Jameson, M.H. 2000-2003. Athens and Phaselis, *IG* I³ 10 (EM 6918). *Horos* 14-16: 23-29.

Kearns, E. 2009. *Ancient Greek Religion: A Sourcebook*. Chichester: Wiley-Blackwell.

Konstantinidou, K. 2014. Oath and Curse, in A.H. Sommerstein and I.C. Torrance. *Oaths and Swearing in Ancient Greece*: 6-47. Berlin: De Gruyter.

Labarbe, J. 1977. *Thorikos: Les testimonia*. Leuven: Peeters Publishers.

Lambert, S.D. 2007. Athenian State Laws and Decrees, 352/1-322/1: IV Treaties and Other Texts. *Zeitschrift für Papyrologie und Epigraphik* 161: 67-100.

Lewis, D.M. 1985. A New Athenian Decree. *Zeitschrift für Papyrologie und Epigraphik* 60: 108.

Lewis, D.M. 1987. The Athenian Coinage Decree, in I. Carradice (ed.) *Coinage and Administration in the Athenian and Persian Empires*: 57. Oxford: BAR Publishing.

Lupu, E. 2009 (1st ed. 2005). *Greek Sacred Law: A Collection of New Documents (NGSL)²*. Leiden: Brill.

Marchiandi, D. 2019. Ancora sul peribolo di Menyllos ovvero la microstoria di una famiglia di Halai Aixonides. *Annuario della Scuola Archeologica di Atene e delle Missioni Italiane in Oriente* 97: 387-409.

Matthaiou, A.P. 2008. Νέο θραῦσμα τῆς ἐπιγραφῆς *IG* II² 1195, in A.P. Matthaiou and I. Polinskaya (eds) *Μικρὸς Ἱερομνήμων: Μελέτες εἰς μνήμην Michael H. Jameson*: 87-102. Athens: Greek Epigraphic Society.

Matthaiou, A.P. 2009. Attic Public Inscription of the Fifth Century BC in Ionic Script, in L. Mitchell and L. Rubinstein (eds) *Greek History and Epigraphy: Essays in Honour of P.J. Rhodes*: 201-212. Swansea: Classical Press of Wales.

Mattingly, H. 1990. Some Fifth-Century Attic Epigraphic Hands. *Zeitschrift für Papyrologie und Epigraphik* 83: 110-122.

Moroo, A. 2014. The Erythrai Decrees Reconsidered: *IG* I³ 14, 15 and 16, in A.P. Matthaiou and R.K. Pitt (eds) Ἀθηναίων Ἐπίσκοπος: *Studies in Honour of Harold B. Mattingly*: 97-119. Athens: Greek Epigraphic Society.

Osborne, R. 2011. Local Environment, Memory, and the Formation of the Citizen in Classical Attica, in S.D. Lambert (ed.) *Sociable Man: Essays on Ancient Greek Social Behaviour in Honour of Nick Fisher*: 25-43. Swansea: Classical Press of Wales.

Osborne, R. and P.J. Rhodes (eds) 2017. *Greek Historical Inscriptions 478-404 BC*. Oxford: Oxford University Press.

Papazarkadas, N. 2011. *Sacred and Public Land in Ancient Athens*. Oxford: Oxford University Press.

Parker, R. 1984. The Herakleidai at Thorikos. *Zeitschrift für Papyrologie und Epigraphik* 57: 59.

Parker, R. 1987. Festivals of the Attic Demes, in T. Linders and G. Nordquist (eds) *Gifts to the Gods: Proceedings of the Uppsala Symposium 1985*: 137-147. Uppsala: Academiae Upsaliensis.

Parker, R. 2005. *Polytheism and Society at Athens*. Oxford: Oxford University Press.

Piérart, M. 1971. Les εὔθυνοι athéniens. *L'antiquité classique* 40: 526-573.

Rhodes, P.J. 1981. *A Commentary on the Aristotelian* Athenaion Politeia. Oxford: Clarendon Press.

Rhodes, P.J. 2007. Oaths in Political Life, in A.H. Sommerstein and J. Fletcher (eds) *Horkos: The Oath in Greek Society*: 11-25. Exeter: Bristol Phoenix Press.

Rosivach, V.J. 1994. *The System of Public Sacrifice in Fourth-Century Athens*. Atlanta: Scholars Press.

Scafuro, A.C. 2014. Patterns of Penalty in Fifth Century Attic Decrees, in A.P. Matthaiou and R.K. Pitt (eds) Ἀθηναίων Ἐπίσκοπος: *Studies in Honour of Harold B. Mattingly*: 299-326. Athens: Greek Epigraphic Society.

Shear, J.L. 2021. *Serving Athena: The Festival of the Panathenaia and the Construction of Athenian Identities*. Cambridge: Cambridge University Press.

Sommerstein, A.H. and A.J. Bayliss, 2013. *Oath and State in Ancient Greece*. Berlin: De Gruyter.

Takeuchi, K. 2019. Land, Meat, and Gold: The Cults of Dionysos in the Attic Demes. Unpublished PhD dissertation, National and Kapodistrian University of Athens.

Threatte, L. 1996. *The Grammar of Attic Inscriptions, II. Morphology*. Berlin: De Gruyter.

Tracy, S.V. 2016. *Athenian Lettering of the Fifth Century B.C.: The Rise of the Professional Letter Cutter*. Berlin: De Gruyter.

Vanderpool, E. 1975. A South Attic Miscellany, in H. Mussche, P. Spitaels and F. Goemaere-De Poerck (eds) *Thorikos and the Laurion in Archaic and Classical Times*: 21-42. Ghent: Belgian Archaeological Mission in Greece.

Whitehead, D. 1986. *The Demes of Attica, 508/7-ca. 250 B.C.: A Political and Social Study*. Princeton: Princeton University Press.

Philip's (Serious) Joke: [ΦΙΛΙΠΠΟΥ] ΕΠΙΣΤΟΛΗ 12.14[1]

Adele C. Scafuro

Brown University
Adele_Scafuro@brown.edu

Abstract

In 'Philip's Letter to the Athenians', the twelfth text in Demosthenes' corpus, the Macedonian king mentions attempts to end his dispute with the Athenians over Halonessos by arbitration 'so that if the island was adjudged mine, it might be given to you by me; if yours, then I might give it back to you' (12.14). Whereas the verbal play of 'giving' and 'giving back' appears elsewhere in the same context and has been given much attention, hardly any at all has been bestowed upon Philip's *proklesis* to the arbitration (προὐκαλούμην κριθῆναι). I focus upon this 'new detail' here, explaining why a *proklesis* may be appropriate for a land dispute and also why, in a diplomatic letter, it might not be. The 'new detail' (the *proklesis*) is set within the context of the history of the letter's reception and an assessment of earlier arguments over its authenticity.

Keywords

Philip's letter; *proklesis* for arbitration

In a well-known passage in 'Philip's Letter to the Athenians', the Macedonian king mentions repeated attempts to end his dispute with the Athenians over the island of Halonessos by arbitration 'so that if the island was judged mine, it might be given to you by me (παρ' ἐμοῦ δοθῇ τὸ χωρίον ὑμῖν); if yours, then I might give it back to your people' (τότ' ἀποδῶ τῷ δήμῳ). The verbal play of 'giving' and 'giving back' appears elsewhere and belongs to the same geopolitical context (of course at [Dem.] 7.5 and Aeschin. 3.83; and in comedy as well: Plut. *Dem.* 9.5-6 and Athen. 6.223d-224b). Not surprisingly, it has received extensive (often repetitive) commentary, both philological and historical; what has been passed over in silence, however, is that Philip gives a *proklesis* to the Athenians to settle their dispute by arbitration (γνοὺς ἐγὼ ταῦτα προὐκαλούμην κριθῆναι περὶ τούτων πρὸς ὑμᾶς, ἵν' ἐὰν μὲν ἐμὴ γνωσθῇ, παρ' ἐμοῦ δοθῇ τὸ χωρίον ὑμῖν, ἐὰν δ᾽ ὑμετέρα κριθῇ, τότ' ἀποδῶ τῷ δήμῳ 12.14 and cf. 12.16 *apud fin.*). This is the point I eventually focus upon here; I explain why a *proklesis* may be appropriate for a land dispute (with comparanda from inscribed territorial disputes) and also why it might

[1] Peter J. Rhodes has been a guiding light to my research through his many books and essays that have been my companions for decades now; and also through his friendship over the last decade; most recently, I am grateful for an initial discussion last Thanksgiving about the essay presented here.

I am also grateful to Delfim Leão for his patience and encouragement—the essay would not have been finished without that. I am also grateful to three readers and their constructive suggestions: Gerhard Thür, Michael Gagarin, and Judson Herrman.

I have many others to thank—for, excepting the short section concerning early translations and histories of Philip II, deriving from research conducted mainly at Weston Library at Oxford for short periods over the summers 2016-2019, this essay was written mostly during the Covid lockdown in Athens. For their generosity in answering bibliographic queries or scanning essays, I thank the library staff of Brown University, Weston Library at Oxford, and Blegen Library, Gennadius, and the BSA here in Athens; indeed, the staff of Gennadius allowed me into the library one happy afternoon during lockdown to view, *inter alia*, Figliucci's *Undici Filippiche di Demosthene con una lettera di Filippo*.

I extend special thanks to Angelos Chaniotis for sending materials and answering queries while he was excavating in Crete, and also to Angelos Matthaiou who sent me materials and answered queries early on.

be considered wildly inappropriate in this particular diplomatic text. It may turn out that even such a mixed judgment as this might move the needle on the compass of the letter's authenticity in one direction or the other. To provide a critical context for the placement of this 'new' detail, the *proklesis*, in the history of the letter's reception, I first review some stand-out points in the long-running argument over its authenticity and also in that of its alleged response (Oration 11)—for better or worse, the two are intimately entwined in the scholarly record; in doing this, I am particularly interested in assessing the criteria and quality of argumentation. I then turn to the *proklesis* and verbal play.

The Letter's Reception

Philip's Letter to the Athenians, the twelfth text in the last two editions of OCTs of Demosthenes, is the only text in that series that is ascribed in its title to a specific individual other than Demosthenes.[2] Though some few orations were manifestly not penned by him—e.g., *On the Halonnesos*, is usually ascribed, on good grounds, to the fourth century politician Hegisippos, and a number of forensic speeches are often ascribed, again on good grounds, to Apollodoros, no one can possibly ascribe the 'letter of Philip' to Demosthenes; rather, the question is, can we in fact ascribe it to the Macedonian king?

The Ancient Commentators

The question has not always been raised. Ancient commentators, while aware of the existence of letters (for of course there was more than one letter sent by Philip), are not usually suspicious of their origins.[3] Their different descriptions, however, become the basis of many later arguments regarding the authenticity of 'Text 12'—a designation I shall use at times to distinguish it from other letters ascribed to Philip. Indeed, while for some later critics, the question becomes, 'which letter, amongst those mentioned in ancient sources, is to be attached to Oration 11 (the alleged response)', for others, especially those who do not believe in the authenticity of that Oration, the question becomes, what is 'Text 12'? It will be best to turn to the ancient commentators first.

1. Dionysios of Halicarnassos, *ad Amm.* 1.10 *apud fin.*, reports that in the archonship of Theophrastus (340/39), Demosthenes urged the Athenians to endure the war in a courageous spirit, 'since Philip had already declared it'; he calls the speech 'the last of the assembly speeches against Philip (τελευταία τῶν κατὰ Φιλίππου δημηγοριῶν), and cites its opening clauses (τῷ μὲν ἔργῳ πάλαι πολεμεῖ πρὸς τὴν πόλιν, τῷ δὲ λόγῳ νῦν ὁμολογεῖ διὰ τῆς ἐπιστολῆς). It is clear he is speaking about our Oration 11. In the next chapter (*ad Amm.* 1.11), he reports that Philochoros, in book 6 of his *Atthis* (FGrH 328 F 53-55) recounts that Philip, in that same archonship (Theophrastos, 340/39), first sailed against Perinthos, failed to take it, and then besieged Byzantion; Philochoros also recounts that Philip enumerated 'in the letter' (διὰ τῆς ἐπιστολῆς) all the complaints he had against the Athenians (ὅσα τοῖς Ἀθηναίοις ὁ Φίλιππος ἐνεκάλει) and added

---

[2] Not all series are so 'pure'; some ascribe Oration 7 to Hegesippos in the title to the speech, e.g. C. Rehdantz' *Neun Philippische Reden*, curated by Fr. Blass in 1886, 'VII: Hegesippos Rede über Halonnes'.

[3] See Schaefer (1858. 3.2: 104f.) on the absence of suspicion of Oration 11 and Text 12 in DH, Libanios, and Scholia and the absence of glosses on these texts in Harpokration and later lexica except for the *Lex. Seg.* Didymos' commentary on Demosthenes (which ushered in a new era of suspicion) was not published until 1904.

'when the people heard the letter and Demosthenes called on them to declare war and proposed a decree, they voted to take down the *stēlē* which had been set up about the peace and alliance with Philip, and to man ships and make other preparations for war'. DH has dated both Oration 11 and the letter to Theophrastos' archonship; it is clear he has attached the one to the other. Later scholars and critics sometimes agree; few, however, think Oration 11 is authentic, and while some identify 'Philochoros' letter' as the one that appears in the modern corpus as Text 12, yet many, possibly most, identify it as whatever letter DH (via Philochorus) thought was read to the people,[4] sometimes suggesting it may have been the letter that Demosthenes asks the court secretary to read aloud at Dem. 18.76,[5] but certainly not the letter that follows in 18.77-79—a letter that is generally agreed to be a later fabrication.[6]

2. Didymos in his treatise on Demosthenes also mentions a letter sent by Philip to the Athenians in three passages (cols. 1.70-74; 9.46-47; and 10.24-30 [Harding] from the end of the letter).

2a. In the lacunose end of col. 1, he refers to Book 6 of Philochoros' *Atthis* and quotes what appears to be the same sentence from our Oration 11 that appears in DH *ad Amm.* 1.11 ('when the people heard the letter . . .').[7] Didymos provides no separate commentary on the letter and moves from (what in modern editions is) Oration 11 straight on to Oration 13 (col. 13.14-25).[8] It is not clear whether Didymos knows Text 12; at least, he never mentions it.[9]

2b. In 9.46-47 and 10.24-30, he cites wording from the letter that differs from that preserved in modern editions of Text 12.[10]

---

[4] Böhnecke (1843: 520, n. 3), followed by Schaefer (1858.2:104), and Weil (1881: 402 n. 2) calls attention to Philochoros' description of the allegations διὰ τῆς ἐπιστολῆς in DH *ad Amm.* 1.11; the use of the article suggests that the letter was already known. Weil (1881: 402-404) maintains that 'the letter' is Text 12 but does not think Oration 11 is authentic (419-421), except for its opening sections; Böhnecke (1843: 520.4) has a convoluted hypothesis according to which there may have been no letter in Philochoros, but DH has falsely assigned one there (easily refuted by Schaefer 1858.3.2: 108). Schaefer's views are discussed in the text *supra*. Harding (2006: 114) thinks that Philochoros' letter fits the chronological indications of Oration 11 (regarding the sieges of Perinthos and Byzantium) and assesses the current *opinio communis* as agreeing that Text 12 does not. It might be added that when DH cites Philochoros' phrase διὰ τῆς ἐπιστολῆς in *ad Amm.* 1.11, he does that *after* he has used the same phrase in the preceding section when quoting the opening of Oration 11 (τῷ μὲν ἔργῳ πάλαι πολεμεῖ πρὸς τὴν πόλιν, τῷ δὲ λόγῳ νῦν ὁμολογεῖ διὰ τῆς ἐπιστολῆς); the article in 1.11 need only associate 'the letter' (in Philochoros) with the missive to which 'the last Philippic' (our Oration 11) refers—i.e., it need not refer to our Text 12 at all.

[5] E.g., Droysen (1839: 810 = 1893: 182); Wankel (1976.I: 447).

[6] Droysen (1839: 810 =1893: 182-183) argued that the letter inserted in Dem. 18 regarding Philip's siege of Selymbria is a fiction. Canevaro 2013 does not treat the letter, as being beyond the scope of his work, which focuses on decrees and laws; nevertheless, he makes useful general comments about Droysen, Oration 18, and the inserted letter on pp. 8-9 and 250 with n. 34.

[7] Didymos uses the same language as cited in DH; the text, however, is lacunose and restored on the basis of DH.

[8] Gibson (2002: 121 and 131). On the latter page, he points out that the numbering of the orations cannot confidently be ascribed to Didymos; rather, '[T]he more usual practice in antiquity was to refer to a speech by title (e.g., *Against Neaera*), by its number within a series (e.g., "the seventh of the Philippics"), and/or by the opening words of the speech (as in the closing title of Berol. 9780).

[9] For hypotheses on the absence of Text 12 from early editions of Demosthenes: Pohlenz (1928: 59); Wendland (1904: 436). It has often been pointed out that only two of the important manuscripts of Demosthenes carry the epistle (**F** and **Y** but not **S** and **A**). Canfora (2018: 433) thinks that the absence of Text 12 from **S** and **A** shows that 'its entry into the corpus evidently met with some resistance'; for Canfora's extended view, see n. 46 *infra*.

[10] There is no space for discussion of the differences here (the Greek text of Didymos' ending of the letter is given in n. 39 and that of Text 12 in n. 24). Some consider the endings are so different that they must belong to different letters: the passage in Didymos would in that case belong to the 'final ultimatum' and the conclusion to Text 12 would belong to an earlier one, a 'penultimate ultimatum'; see Pohlenz (1928: 57-60) and Wüst (1938: 134-5).

2c. About Oration 11 (col. 11.5-14), Didymos reports suspicions:[11]

> Well now, (these are) the circumstances of his speech of advice and this would be the culmination of the Philippics. One would not be off target to suspect (that) this little speech (λογίδιον) has been cobbled together, a cumulative accretion from some of Demosthenes' treatments (10) of the issues. And there are those who say (that) the speech of advice belongs to Anaximenes of Lampsakos [...] in the seventh (book) of his [Philipp]ika [...] has been inserted in almost the very words. (Trans. Harding 2006: 81 and 83)

These particular suspicions (arising from the 'Anaximenes hypothesis') will eventually be carried over to Text 12—but not until we are well into the modern era.

2d. Didymos col. 10.35-62-col. 11.2-5 mentions another important event, indeed, the spark for the war and Philips's 'greatest transgression', viz, the seizure of merchants' ships at Hieron. This happened, he explicitly says, in Theophrastos' archonship (340/39) according to Philochoros, the year to which he had assigned (again via Philochoros) Philip's letter and Demosthenes' exhortation to declare war. Didymos gives different numbers for the ships from Philochoros and Theopompos. The column ends with a quotation from the former (*FGrH* 328 F 162), detailing Philip's failure to take Chares' boats at Hieron and his seizure of the cargo. While the passage does not comment on the authenticity of letter or speech, the 'greatest transgression' will inform some later arguments on those topics.

3. Libanios for his part left no hypothesis for the letter, though he did so for the seventh oration and agreed with οἱ πρεσβύτεροι that it was not written by Demosthenes but by Hegesippos.[12]

4. The scholiast, sometimes designated as Ulpian, at the opening of Oration 11 (Schol. Dem. 11 Dilts 1; Dindorf, Vol. VIII, 209), sometimes designated as the *hypothesis* to Oration 11 (but not Libanios'), informs readers that Philip, when besieging Selymbria, suspected that the grain ships sent there by the Athenians were really sent to give assistance to the Selymbrians; Philip seized the fleet and sent a letter to the Athenians, charged them with aiding a city that was not included in their treaty and with unravelling the peace, and threatened them with requital with all his might; upon the letter being read [to the people], Demosthenes urged them to go to war. It would seem that the Scholiast of the *hypothesis* believes that the letter to which Oration 11 is a reply is the one that Demosthenes asks to be read to the court at Oration 18.76, though not necessarily the letter that is inserted there (18.77-79).[13] It is not clear that the scholiast has a copy of Text 12.

5. The scholiast of Oration 18 (Dilts Schol. Dem. 140; Dindorf, Vol. VIII, 289f.) gives a similar but lengthier report (about Philip's siege of Selymbria and his seizure of the fleet—with additions, e.g., his return of the fleet) at the point in the speech where Demosthenes asks that Philip's letter be read; at the end of the entry, he quotes clauses

---

[11] It is not likely that Didymos endorses this view of the origin of the speech from passages recycled from Demosthenes and its attribution to Anaximenes; Didymos is not known for original scholarship; see Harding (2006: 217-218); Wendland (1904: 420-421).

[12] Judson Herrman points out (pers. communication) that, as we lack Libanios' *hypotheseis* for Ds' letters and other 'different' material at the end of the corpus (speeches 60 and 61), it's not surprising that we lack a *hypothesis* for Text 12.

[13] Pohlenz (1924; 1929) and Wüst (1938), arguing that the *hypothesis* (Ulpian) to Oration 11 is distinct from the scholiast to Oration 18, give credence to the former and identify the letter mentioned there (Ulpian) with the one Didymos cites in *Dem.* cols. 9.46-47 and 10.24-30.

from the opening of Oration 11 (τῷ μὲν ἔργῳ πάλαι πολεμεῖ πρὸς τὴν πόλιν, τῷ δὲ λόγῳ νῦν ὁμολογεῖ διὰ τῆς ἐπιστολῆς).[14] Once again, the scholiast might believe the letter to which Oration 11 replies is the one requested by Demosthenes at 18.76.

Early Translators and Historians

If we turn to early translators of the letter (Text 12) and its use by historians more than a millennium later, there is little skepticism at the outset. M. Felice Figliucci, the first Italian (Tuscan) translator of the *Philippics* and the first to add the Letter (*Le undici Filippiche di Demosthene con una lettera di Filippo a gl' Atheniesi*, 1550), also includes Libanios' hypotheses and is therefore aware of discussions of authenticity elsewhere in the corpus (*Hyp. 7*); Figliucci, however, evinces no skepticism in his preface.[15] A century and a half later, the renowned French translator Jacques de Tourreil (1656-1714) entertained the question at the end of an encomium on the letter's style only to dismiss it immediately:[16]

> Cette Lettre me paroist un chef-d'oevre dans l'original. Il y regne une vivacité majesteuse & persuasive; une force & une justesse de raisonement soustenuës jusqu'au bout; une exposition de faits simples, & chacun suivi de sa consequence naturelle; une ironie delicate; enfin ce stile noble et concis, fait pour les Rois qui parlent bien, ou du moins qui sont d'assez bon goust, pour choisir qui les fasse bien parler. Que si Philippe lui-mesme est véritablement auteur de cette Lettre, comme La justice veut qu'un le croye, faute de preuves du contraire; on peut dire de lui ce qu'on a dit de Cesar*: Qu'il se servoit aussi-bien de la parole & de la plume, que de l'épée' (1701, original spelling retained).[17]

Among translators and historians over the next fifty years, concerns about the letter's authenticity glimmer infrequently. George Psalmanazar, who composed, inter alia, the section on Macedonian history in a multi-authored universal history (1736-1744), was fulsome in its praise and copied the entire letter into his text; in a footnote, he gave a nascent philological,

---

[14] The report here is somewhat consonant with the *hypothesis* to Oration 11 and the (fabricated) letter inserted at Dem. 18.77-79 but differs in details (see esp. Pohlenz 1924:38-39; the 'hypothesis' does not mention the nauarch (nor the release of the fleet); the scholion to 18 names the nauarch as Laomedon and mentions his capture and release as well as that of the fleet; the letter inserted at 18.77-79 names the nauarch as Leodamas and mentions the capture and release of the fleet but not that of the nauarch. Droysen (1839/1893) treats the inserted letter fully.

[15] Figliucci (1550: 133) offers as context that the letter impelled Demosthenes to incite the Athenians to go to war; the detail probably derives from DH *ad Amm.* 1.11. Figliucci, however, adds that Philip castigated the 'Senato' for listening to speakers who made accusations against him, and explicitly named Demosthenes. This is a point against which the latter argued in *On the Crown* (18.77 and 79), viz., that he is not mentioned in Philip's letter.

[16] The quotation (with original spelling) is from the *Philippiques* (re)published posthumously in his collected works (1721: 427); the *Philippiques* there duplicate the texts translated in the second edition (1701) which added several more Philippic speeches as well as the letter; the first edition was published in 1691. (For an annotated bibliography of Tourreil's works, see Douhain (1910: 259-263). The asterisk in the text above indicates Tourreil's footnote, *Quint. Instit. Orat. 10.1. *Eodem animo dixit, quo bellavit.*

[17] Leland's (1756; see n. 18 *infra*) English translation: 'This letter is a master-piece in the original. It has a majestic and persuasive vivacity: a force and justness of reasoning, sustained thro' the whole: a clear exposition of facts, and each followed by its natural consequence: a delicate irony; in short, a noble and concise stile made for kings who speak well; or have taste and discernment at least, to make choice of those who can make them speak well. If Philip was himself the author of this letter; as it is but just to believe, since we have no proof to the contrary, we may reasonably pronounce of him, as was said of Caesar, *that he wrote with that spirit with which he fought.* Eodem animo dixit, quo bellavit. Quinct. Inst. I.10 c.1 Tour.' (with Leland's original spelling, punctuation, and italics).

but mainly sentimental argument for the letter's genuineness: 'Happy would it have been for posterity, if more such letters as these had been preserved; but time has swallowed them up, and we have only a few short epistles, which serve barely to demonstrate, that this is truly *Philip*'s, from the conformity of its stile; as it must be allowed worthy of him from the consideration of its matter' (1747.8: 470).[18] Thomas Leland, in his 'translation/history' published in 1756, gave, as his first footnote to the letter, an English translation of Tourreil's encomium ('This letter is a master-piece in the original. . .'), duly ascribing it to the Frenchman and repeating the flickering possibility of fraudulence.[19]

Historians of the same era extinguished the flicker but magnified enthusiasm: Charles Rollin, the prolix French author of an earlier multi-volume universal history (1730-1739 first edition), quoted an excerpt from the Letter, prefaced it with a near verbatim quotation of Tourreil's 1701 encomium (without attribution), but omitted his slight suggestion that Philip might not be the author.[20] The anonymous English translator(s?) of Rollin's history followed suit (1736-1741) and automatically made the same omission.[21] Excerpts of the letter appear in histories of the period over and over again. L'Abbé Guyon, like Rollin, quotes the entire letter verbatim (1741.12: 88-92). Temple Stanyan gives some citation and proclaims it drawn 'with such a Spirit of Majesty throughout the Whole, that it may be look'd upon as one of the finest Pieces of Antiquity' (1739.2: 304-05).

The First Period of Modern Criticism: from John Taylor to Friedrich Blass

So far, post-Antique scholars offer no critiques of content but rather strong sentiments about what a letter from Philip should be and expressions of great pleasure in its style. Attacks on the letter's authenticity, however, soon followed, both on matters of style and historical content. I will designate as the long first period as beginning with John Taylor's mid-eighteenth century vilification that the *epistola* was *ea tempestate atque antiquitate... indigna* and ending with Friedrich Blass' second edition of *Die attische Beredsamkeit* (1887-1898) vindicating its genuineness.[22] During this period, two critical strategies evolved that endure to this day: the sentimental/rhetorical which includes an analytic strand (with 'unitarians' believing Oration 11 and Text 12 'stand or fall together' and 'separatists' believing they need not), and the historical; critics not infrequently use both. As we go forward now and consider the reception

---

[18] See Griggs (2007: 230-234) for Psalmanazar. Many later critics will throw out 'style' as a criterion for determining Philip's authorship, on the grounds that the letter may still be essentially Philip's even if written by a literary secretary.

[19] Leland (1756: 157). The full title of Leland's work suggests its dual genre: *All the Orations of Demosthenes, pronounced to excite the Athenians against Philip King of Macedon.* Translated into English; digested and connected, so as to form a regular History of the progress of the MACEDONIAN POWER: with notes historical and critical.

[20] I have not seen the first edition; I found the excerpt cited here in Weston Library, in vol. V, Book 8 *Histoire des Perses et des Grecs* 508f., in the second edition published in 1740.

[21] The English translation followed almost immediately on the heels of the first French edition. There are many editions—universal histories at this period were popular. (I note here an edition in modern Greek in the Gennadius Library in Athens published in 1750.) For this essay, I reviewed vol. VI, book 14 published in London in 1734, available online from Eighteenth Century Collections. Online at [https://www.gale.com/primary-sources/eighteenth-century-collections-online], accessed in October 2016 and Sept. 2021.

[22] *Not. ad Dem. Olynth.* II, p. 23. No date; *non vidi*; noted by Böhnecke (1843: 461 n. 5) who cites the phrase disapprovingly; it is cited in German by Jacobs (1833); in Latin by Westermann (1853-54: 17), with approbation; Schaefer (1858.3.2: 111) calls Taylor's judgment ungrounded. Taylor's editions of Demosthenes and Aeschines appeared between 1743 and 1757.

of the two texts, we do well to keep in mind an important date: P. Berol. 9780 was purchased in Cairo in 1901 and brought from there to Berlin; in 1904, it was published by Herman Diels and Wilhelm Schubart in two editions.[23] The papyrus contains Didymos' treatment of Dem. 9-11 and 13.

The decade of 1839-49 provides excellent exemplars of contemporary scholarship that provide a looking glass both into preceding decades and those to come. Karl Böhnecke, in his hefty study of the Attic orators and collection of decrees (1843) argued mostly in the sentimental/rhetorical mode and took on a slew of earlier critics beginning with Taylor. While 'Valckenaer und alle anderen gelehrten' judged Oration 11 a fabrication, only Böhnecke came to its defense (the connection between that and Text 12 becomes a peg in his overall argument):[24] critics were wrong to denounce the Oration for not specifically addressing the complaints of the letter: was Demosthenes expected to go 'point for point' immediately after the letter was read? Extemporaneous speaking was not his forte and besides, other speakers no doubt raised those issues before him. Critics were likewise wrong to complain that it used vulgar diction and had recycled passages from earlier speeches; Demosthenes does both elsewhere. More positively, Oration 11 and Text 12 are intimately connected: Philip's final clauses, ὑμᾶς ἀμυνοῦμαι μετὰ τοῦ δικαίου, καὶ μάρτυρας τοὺς θεοὺς ποιησάμενος διαλήψομαι περὶ τῶν καθ᾿ ὑμᾶς (later to be called 'the ultimatum to war' by some and 'the 'so-called ultimatum' by others), is a match for the Oration's opening statement that [Φίλιππος] τῷ μὲν ἔργῳ πάλαι πολεμεῖ πρὸς τὴν πόλιν, τῷ δὲ λόγῳ νῦν ὁμολογεῖ διὰ τῆς ἐπιστολῆς.[25] As for the letter itself, Böhnecke was one of very few who defended its authenticity;[26] while ignoring arguments about the author's mistaken designation of Sitalkes for Kotys (12.9) and his assertion of an early fifth century occupation of Amphipolis (12. 21) before the city existed,[27] he turned his attention elsewhere: earlier critics were wrong to identify Text 12 with the letter mentioned by Philochoros who had dated both letter and reply to Theophrastos' archonship in 341/340 (DH ad Amm. 1.11); there must have been an interval between the letter and the response to allow time for the raising of the siege of Perinthos and the commencement of that of Byzantion, both mentioned in the Oration but neither mentioned in Text 12; hence Philip's letter will have been sent in 341/340 and the response will have been delivered at the start of the following year; Philochoros' letter is not to be trusted.[28] Earlier critics were also misguided when they had objected, e.g., to the length of Text 12 as more appropriate for a sophist than a king; the royal letter to which Oration 7

---

[23] Harding (2006: 4).

[24] The description of 'the learned scholars' is Schaefer's (1858.3.2: 105); Böhnecke (1843: 463) also lists the non-believers.

[25] The full sentence ending Text 12 runs: Ἃ μὲν οὖν ἐγκαλῶ, ταῦτ᾿ ἐστίν· ὡς δὲ προϋπαρχόντων καὶ διὰ τὴν ἐμὴν εὐλάβειαν μᾶλλον ἤδη τοῖς πράγμασιν ἐπιτιθεμένων καὶ καθ᾿ ὅσον ἂν δύνησθε κακοποιούντων, ὑμᾶς ἀμυνοῦμαι μετὰ τοῦ δικαίου, καὶ μάρτυρας τοὺς θεοὺς ποιησάμενος διαλήψομαι περὶ τῶν καθ᾿ ὑμᾶς. While that sentence becomes the bone of contention in decades to come, Böhnecke is arguing against the scholiast of the hypothesis to Oration 11 who thinks the letter that incited war is the one that Demosthenes asks the secretary to read in Oration 18.76.

[26] Böhnecke (1843) was joined by one other (Winiewski 1829: 190-192) in defending the letter; Jacobs (1833) was uncertain.

[27] Jacobs (1833: 419-420 n. 9) on Sitalkes (pointing out the mistake) and 422 n. 16, quoting Auger (1788, non vidi) on Amphipolis, concluding: 'Es scheint, dass Philipp die Entfernung der Zeiten benutze, um ein hochst zweifelhaftes, wo nicht falsches Faktum aufzustellen.'

[28] Böhnecke (1843: 464, 468, and 520 n. 4) with a new hypothesis about 'Philochoros' letter' (see n. 3 supra). Böhnecke's reasoning is tortuous here: earlier scholars had been apt to throw out the letter because it makes no mention of the two sieges that are explicitly alluded to in Oration 11 and this omission remains problematic for some today; perhaps because Böhnecke wants to save both pieces, he moves the date of Text 12.

responded must have been of equal length. Moreover, the letter's authenticity was proven by the testimony of Diodorus Siculus (18.10.1-2) who ascribes a phrase to Philip (*procul dubio Diodorus ante oculos habuit epistolae locum*) that is used in Text 12.19.[29]

Later critics of this 'first period' would easily refute Böhnecke's arguments. As for Oration 11, Arnold Schaefer (1858 3.2: 105-110) met its lone champion head on: the speaker does not counter the accusations in Philip's letter; it can be no excuse that Demosthenes became tongue-tied upon compulsion to answer *ex tempore*—the letter would have been read to the Council first; everyone would know its contents before the Assembly met—and they would know Philip's complaints even without a letter! Moreover, the speaker does not offer any argument that could rouse the people to vote for war—which Philochoros reported was the direct result of Demosthenes' speech: could this patchwork of passages slightly reworked from earlier orations do the trick—passages that are out of tune with the wartime situation of Theophrastos' archonship! Rather, this is the compilation of a late rhetor, as diction and word choices demonstrate. As for Text 12, on the other hand, Schaefer all but capitulated to its genuineness; he would add to the argument on its 'sophistic tone'—and this would be iterated again and again—that there was no need to ascribe the letter to Philip's own hand; it could have been written for him—by the Byzantine envoy Python or by Eumenes, who had served as his secretary since 342.[30] Form and content were thus separate as criteria of judgment on the question of authenticity, apparently for good—except on one point: Benseler, in his 1841 treatise on hiatus, had shown that both Text 12 and the recycled passages that had been slightly re-worked for Oration 11 showed an avoidance of hiatus that was not characteristic of Demosthenes; *both* texts must derive from the same origin; the genuineness of Oration 11 and the Letter must stand and fall together.[31] While Schaefer here embraced a 'unitarian' theory for the authorship of the two texts, he was nevertheless loathe to maintain it. True, on historical grounds he thought Text 12 could not be Philip's work, whether his own or a secretary's—for neither the one nor the other could possibly have mistaken Sitalkes for Kotys (12.9); neither the one nor the other could have misrepresented the Peace of Philocrates as being separate from a treaty of alliance (12.22). Moreover, it was impossible to harmonize the date for the violation of the peace (according to Demosthenes at 18.73: καὶ μὴν τὴν εἰρήνην ἡ ἐκεῖνος ἔλυσε τὰ πλοῖα λαβών, οὐχ ἡ πόλις, Αἰσχίνη) with Philip's letter; Böhnecke's chronological corrections to Philochoros' explicit statements were purely arbitrary.[32] Still, there was much that was good in Text 12; after all, the essential contents of Philip's multiple complaints had been presented (DH *ad Amm.* 1.11); if the author did not have the work of Philochoros at hand, he must have had a good resumé.

At this point in the scholarly reception of Oration 11 and Text 12, almost every conceivable argument for and against authenticity had been articulated. Indeed, on that question (but not on the question of date), an *opinio communis* seems to have emerged even before Schaefer took pen to hand: George Grote in vol. 11 of his *History of Greece* (1853: 456) had written that,

---

[29] Böhnecke (1843: 658).

[30] MacDowell (2009: 365) suggests, whether tongue-in-cheek or seriously, that Isocrates himself was Philip's ghost writer; this would have the consequence of Isocrates paraphrasing or alluding to himself at Text 12.19 (cf. Isocr. 5.73).

[31] Schaefer (1856 3.2: 111-12 and n. 1) borrows the expression from Böckh (1845: 131), in the context of establishing Egyptian dates in the fourth century BC.

[32] Schaefer (1856.3.2: 508); on the violation of the peace that led to the Athenian declaration of war, see Schaefer (1886.2: 503-506): he has Justin 9.1, but not the date provided by Didymos col. 10.45-52.

after Philip had commenced his siege of Perinthos, he sent a 'manifesto and declaration of war to the Athenians,' enumerating many wrongs done to him for which he would take 'a just revenge by open hostilities.' Attached to Grote's account were two footnotes, one staunchly denying any veracity to the letter of Philip that was inserted in Dem. 18.77-79;[33] and the other, asserting the authenticity of Text 12, whether written by Philip 'or by some Greek employed in Philip's cabinet' and at the same time denying credibility to Oration 11 both for having 'no peculiar bearing on the points contained in the letter' and for being 'two or three months later in date...' Oration 11 thus seemed definitely out (as a fabrication) and Text 12 more or less in (as a genuine work). Friedrich Blass in both his first and second editions of *Die attische Beredsamkeit* (1868-77, 1887-98) more or less upheld the new status quo on Oration 11 and Text 12; spilling little ink on the former ('Demosthenes is only a source, not an author'),[34] he added little that was new on Text 12 except (1) to Schaefer's argument based on hiatus, he replied: if the same Sophist wrote both letter and response, then there would be more interplay of content and more specific similarity in form and style beyond hiatus; (2) to the complaint about the articulation of the Peace of Philokrates as separate from a treaty in 12.22, he maintained that the passage was corrupt;[35] additionally (3) he extrapolated from Philochoros' extract both that the letter (Text 12) must have been preserved in an archive and that it offered a fulness of facts, far more than that excerpt could have provided a fabricator (!). Beyond that, Blass offered a heightened rhetorical appreciation: 'die ganze Argumentation ist durchaus das, was wir von Philipp erwarten können: scharfsinnig und geschickt...'[36]

The wheel was being re-invented. Scholars had depleted the reservoir of arguments in a largely sentimental/rhetorical mode; there was very little that was historical: Sitalkes vs. Kotys and some concerns for chronology. A change, however, was about to take place. The publication of P. Berol. 9780 with Didymos' treatment of Dem. 9-11 and 13 in 1904 ushered in the second phase of the study of Text 12.

The second period of modern criticism: from Paul Wendland to Douglas MacDowell

The new detail that took scholars by surprise in Didymos' report (source 2c, *supra*) was not that readers could hold Oration 11 suspect for its cobbling together of passages from Demosthenic speeches—many critics had suggested that already; but rather that some said the Oration was Anaximenes' and that it was inserted into the seventh book of his *Philippika*. The gappiness of the papyrus, however, as well as Didymos' lack of endorsement left unclear whether Anaximenes had been the 'compiler' (and therefore 'author') of the speech in the first instance or had merely copied it from the original author. Paul Wendland came to the rescue almost immediately with an early study published in 1904; he first set out to show that the passages of Oration 11 that had been recycled from earlier speeches had indeed been re-worked by Anaximenes: stylistically, the alterations were of a piece with Anaximenes'

---

[33] No doubt that Droysen's treatise on the documents in that speech had become common knowledge to historians by this time; nonetheless, Grote named one ancient source after another who had made no mention of the city.

[34] Blass agreed with Schaefer that the avoidance of hiatus was an indication of authenticity; likewise the author's non-adherence to the rhythmic rules of Demosthenes' speeches. Since these features appear in Oration 11 from start to finish, he found it impossible to agree with Weil's assessment (1873) that the opening six paragraphs of of the speech were composed by Demosthenes; Weil heeded and (1881: 421) changed his mind.

[35] Wendland (1904: 444-445) ascribes the error to Anaximenes, an understandable error if he wrote twenty to thirty years after the Peace of Philokrates.

[36] Blass (1893.3.1: 395-96; 1st ed. 1877.3.1: 349-50).

writing; moreover, the arguments used to answer the letter did not evince the caliber and power of Demosthenes. Next, he set out to prove that Text 12 had also been re-worked by Anaximenes: once again, he used a stylistic argument, this time comparing the small bits and pieces of the letter that Didymos had quoted with the not quite parallel passages in Text 12 and once again he used comparanda from the fragments of Anaximenes: apparently, the bits and pieces quoted by Didymos belonged to the original letter; Text 12, on the other hand, was Anaximenes' elaboration.

By Wendland's 'Anaximenes hypothesis', Oration 11 and Text 12 were now inextricably bound together as genuine compositions—of Anaximenes. An early (pre-Alexandrian) edition of the Philippics had absorbed the historian's pieces, though the letter would drop out as interest in it ebbed—hence its absence in two of the major manuscripts, S and A.[37] Wendland's hypothesis became the new *opinio communis*: Beloch embraced the common origin of Oration 11 and Text 12 in Anaximenes' history in the second edition of his *Griechische Geschichte* in 1912 and designated Text 12 as 'Philipps Brief, d. h. Anaximenes'.[38] Felix Jacoby, persuaded by Wendland, hook, line, and sinker, incorporated the whole of Oration 11 and Text 12 into Vol. II of *FGrH* in 1926 as 72 Fragments 11b and 41 respectively.[39]

The wind soon shifted once again: in 1924 and in more detail in 1928, Max Pohlenz argued against the 'unitarian' view of Anaximenes' authorship of both pieces. While accepting Oration 11 as the work of the historian/rhetor, he gave a detailed commentary on Text 12 and argued for the authorship of the Macedonian king. Of special note, he saw differences between the ending of Text 12 and that provided by Didymos which indicated they belonged to different letters. Text 12 was an earlier letter, sent when Philip had brought his fleet to Perinthos; it outlined his complaints against Athens and its purpose was to delay a readily foreseeable outbreak of war. Didymos' version of the ending, on the other hand, belonged to a letter that was sent some months later, when Philip's attempts on Perinthos and Byzantion had failed, but after Philip was successful in taking an Athenian fleet of grain ships at Selymbria, as sketched in the *hypothesis* to Oration 11 (source 4 described at the outset of this essay); the taking of the fleet, after all, was the provocation that sparked the war and Demosthenes' proposal (Didymos. col. 10.35-62-col. 11.2-5; cf. D. 18.73: καὶ μὴν τὴν εἰρήνην γ᾽ ἐκεῖνος ἔλυσε τὰ πλοῖα λαβών, οὐχ ἡ πόλις, Αἰσχίνη). Both Didymos' letter (the final ultimatum) and Text 12 (an earlier letter of complaint), then, are genuine letters of Philip, written at different times and under different circumstances.[40]

[37] Wendland (1904: 435). Pohlenz (1928: 41) offers a wonderful description of this imagined edition.
[38] Beloch III² p. 24, cited by Pohlenz (1928: 41-42).
[39] Jacoby adopted Crönert's restoration of Didymos' text, which allows for the interpretation that Oration 11 was 'thought to be his [Anaximenes'] work, a speech put into the mouth of Demosthenes in the *Philippica*... and which later made its way into the canon of Demosthenes' (thus Pearson 1960: 245 and n. 11). Jacoby on Anaximenes F 11 (Oration 11): 'schriftstellerisch und historisch ist die einlage von brief und rede in diesem bedeutsamen moment gut. die von Demosthenes damals für den krieg gehaltene rede oder reden — Philochoros DH *ad Amm*. 11 p. 273, 1ff. vgl. Schäefer II 472, 7 — waren nicht publiziert. in der schule ist der moment öfters be handelt: P. Ox. 216 stammt aus solchem übungsstück, ist aber auch in einem geschichtswerk denkbar.' That Demosthenes had not published his speeches promoting the war is Jacoby's inference; he has bought into Wendland's interpretation of the Didymos papyrus.
[40] Didymos Comm. 10.24-30, quoting the end of the letter: Πρ[ο-]‖ ὑπαρχόντων ὁ(ὖν) ὑμῶν κ(αὶ) διὰ τὴν [ἐμὴ]ν εὐλά[βειαν μᾶλ[λον] ἔ[π]ικειμ(έν)ων κ(αὶ) διὰ τέλους ὡς |μάλιστα [δύν]ασθ[ε]‖ πρα[γ]ματευομ(έν)ων ὅπω[ς]‖ [ἔ]λ[οι] ς᾽ [ἂν] ἐμὲ πο[λέ]μ[ωι τὸ]ν πρότερον ὑ[μᾶς] ‖[εὐεργετήσαντα, ἐγὼ ὑμᾶς μ](ετὰ) τοῦ δικαίου ἀμ[υ-] | [νοῦμαι πάσηι μηχανῆι] ἀντιπ(αρα)ταττόμ(εν)ο[ς.]. Text of Pearson and Stephens from *TLG*. For the ending of Text 12, see n. 24 supra.

Pohlenz' argument soon won an important adherent in Fritz Wüst in his 1938 study of Philip II. Wüst mulled over the possibility that the Scholiasts' reports about Philips's siege of Selymbria and his capture of the cargo ships may not have been pure fiction. At the same time, however, he admitted the fragility of these sources[41] and so turned to a safer question, how could the tradition about Selymbria have originated: kann sie aus dem Nichts hervorgegangen sein? Wüst went on to create the attractive hypothesis that a siege of Selymbria, a city in alliance with Byzantion, and lying between that city and Perinthos, was a military necessity; after all, Philip would pass the city on his way to Byzantion and would need to secure it against aiding its ally.[42] In subsequent decades, the 'Selymbria hypothesis' would be rejected by Hermann Wankel (1976 I.447) but taken onboard by numerous others. For many of these latter scholars, Oration 11 was still 'out': it was inauthentic (whether composed by Anaximenes or some other compiler); but Text 12 was (more or less) 'in', an earlier letter of complaint sent by Philip to the Athenians—perhaps not unlike an even earlier letter of complaint (342) to which Hegesippos made a reply (Oration 7). Didymos' letter was also 'in' as Philip's final ultimatum that set the war in motion. Among those welcoming the new view were G.T. Griffith in 1979, though with some reservations, and Raphael Sealey in 1993.[43] Quite remarkably, N.G.L. Hammond wrote his own defense of Text 12 in 1993, broadly accepting the work of Pohlenz and Wüst and in particular arguing against Griffith's reservations; in so doing, he provided a credible explanation for the appearance of Sitalkes (that all precedents cited in the letter were from the fifth century), and in other ways elucidated the accuracy of the author, e.g., in designating the resolution of the cleruchs in the Chersonese as a *dogma* (12.16, cf. R&O no. 129, p. 149) and the decrees of the Athenians as *psephismata* (12.5, 6, 8, 9, 16).[44]

In the post-Didymos world, the criteria for declaring Oration 11 as now 'out' and Text 12 as now 'in' were quite different from those in the nineteenth century. Indeed, by the time that MacDowell undertook pronouncements on the authenticity of the two texts in 2009, the scholarly world seems to have been primarily occupied with the comments of the Berlin papyrus regarding the insertion of Oration 11 in Anaximenes' history and its vigorous scholarly wake. Nevertheless, except for a nicely logical and simple argument that Anaximenes himself could have copied Demosthenes' oration (rather than his own) into his history, MacDowell basically raised the same rhetorical defenses of Oration 11 as Böhnecke had in 1843.[45] He then raised similar rhetorical arguments for Text 12, with additions: Sitalkes was simply Philip's mistake; regarding the chronological misfit of the letter with Oration 11, there had been no need for Philip to speak of either the siege of Perinthos or that of Byzantion; moreover, while Selymbria may have been involved in Philip's attack on Perinthos, the Scholiasts who speak of a letter

---

[41] Wüst (1938: 138) agreed with Pohlenz that the so-called *hypothesis* to Oration 11 could be taken into account but not the Scholia to Dem. 18 which was tainted by its narrow connection to the false documents in that speech. See n. 13 for differences between the two.

[42] Wüst (1939: 138): 'Rein sachlich betrachtet, ist also die Belagerung von Selymbria, nicht nur wahrscheinlich, sondern müsste sie eigentlich auch ohne die Nachricht davon postuliern.'

[43] Sealey (1993: 187-88). Griffith (1979: 574 n. 2) accepts Wüst and Pohlenz and offers his own reasons for the unliklihood that 'the siege of Selymbria *in toto* is a scholiasts' fiction.' Griffith's argument in the lengthy footnote is compelling.

[44] Hammond (1993: 14) also got rid of Griffith's emendation (1979: 553, n. 3) to save the text from an 'unbelievable' piece of information, that 'Callias had taken all the cities of the Gulf of Pegasae': there was no need to change ἔλαβεν, as LSJ s.v. λαμβάνω offered an appropriate meaning at AIb, 'to take by violence', 'to carry off as prize or booty.'

[45] MacDowell (2009: 361-363) argues that the recycled passages are changed for their presentation in Oration 11; Harding's argument (2006: 217) that Demosthenes himself had 'cobbled together' the speech is unpersuasive.

of Philip mentioning its siege refer to the fabricated letter inserted in Oration 18; and finally, as for the ending of Text 12, it is perfectly suitable for interpretation as a declaration of war—MacDowell does not mention the different wording that appears in Didymos' commentary at col. 10.24-30.[46] MacDowell's views have been maintained more or less by recent scholars, but it is too early to determine whether a consensus has been reached; outliers remain.[47]

Assessment of reception and contextualization of the *Proklesis*

The purpose of this survey, as I said at the outset, was to contextualize the 'new' detail about the *proklesis* and to assess the quality of past arguments for (in-)authenticity. Assessment first: there is, overall, very little of anything that is historically solid. Dionysius of Halicarnassus has provided Philochoros' archon date for Philip sailing to Perinthos, his subsequent siege of Byzantion, and his sending of the letter with many complaints to Athens—a letter that impelled Demosthenes to propose war and the people to take down the *stele* about their alliance with Philip; we have Didymos' addition that the spark for the war and Philips's 'greatest transgression', viz, the seizure of merchants' ships at Hieron, also occurred in that same archon year (340/339), and the date is again provided by Philochoros. We have names that have caused problems, but some might argue, that at least Sitalkes' has found a resolution. We have a gappy notice from Didymos about the wholesale insertion of an oration into Anaximenes' history. We have hypotheses that both texts (11 and 12) must have that same origin (yet we might well embrace Rhodes' terse comment that they 'are better not ascribed to him' (i.e., Anaximenes).[48] We have attractive hypotheses based on an exciting narrative in two Scholia about Selymbria that have no reference elsewhere in any literary or epigraphical source; above all we have plenty of what I have called 'rhetorical arguments'—usually logical but without any dispositive anchor and certainly not decisive, the kind of argument that any smart person can make for one side of a question—and also, and at the same time, for the other. On the other hand, Pohlenz' close analysis of Text 12 revealed a shrewd and clear strategic thinker as the letter's author.[49] Indeed, the elements that I would point to as useful for authentication (that is, for claiming that Text 12 is an authentic document even if not composed by Philip himself) are harbingered by Pohlenz and suggested by Hammond; succinctly, these are specific indications of expertise in civic and international affairs of the fourth century.

---

[46] MacDowell (2009: 361-366); on the ending of the letter, cf. n. 9 and the Greek texts in nn. 24 and 39 *supra*.

[47] E.g., Jeremy Trevett in his translation of Demosthenes' speeches 1-17 (2011) and Ian Worthington, both in his study of Demosthenes (2013) and history of Philip (2014) follow MacDowell. On the other hand, Canfora (2018: 433) retains Wendland's view: he thinks that Anaximenes is responsible for Oration 11 (cobbled together from prior speeches: see source 2c, *supra*) and that he also re-worked Philip's letter; Philochoros' letter as cited by Didymos at col. 11.10-14 with col. 10.24-30 gives 'the real text of Philip's letter'; at the time when Didymos was writing, Anaximenes' re-elaboration of Philip's Letter (Text 12) had not yet entered the Demosthenic corpus (i.e., there was no letter at all in the corpus when he wrote).

[48] Rhodes (2010: 28).

[49] See e.g. Pohlenz (1928: 50-51). Indeed, Wüst (1938: 133) found the analysis so persuasive that he could not believe the text to be the sorry concoction or revision of a genuine letter—for in either of those cases the subtleties pointed out by Pohlenz would never have escaped the rhetorician's messy pen.

Indications of expertise

Some of these have been noticed, most recently by Angelos Chaniotis in his 2004a essay, 'Justifying Territorial Claims in Classical and Hellenistic Greece: The Beginnings of International Law', and decades before him in 1963 by Arnold Kränzlein in his justly famous *Eigentum und Besitz im griechischen Recht*. While there is certainly no universally recognized international law in the Classical and Hellenistic periods, still, as Chaniotis points out, there are doctrines and regulations quite consistently invoked and applied, especially in the settlement of territorial disputes; among these are 'a well-defined and differentiated legal vocabulary with regard to territorial claims' and also a consistency in the use of 'the same kinds of arguments to justify their claims to territory.'[50] As for the latter, Chaniotis goes to Text 12 time and again to demonstrate three fundamental arguments that Philip used in his claim to Amphipolis (12.21-23), 'original occupation, conquest in war, and recognition by treaty'—the same principles used by the Athenians in the same dispute (Aeschin. 2.31-33) and with parallels in Hellenistic inscriptions (e.g., *SEG* 47, 1745, 21ff).[51] As for the legal vocabulary that clearly distinguished ownership or 'lawful proprietary rights' (*Eigentum*) from possession (*Besitz*), Kränzlein had singled out [Dem.] 7.26 as the most important source for that distinction; there the topic is, once again, Philip's claim to Amphipolis and the speaker, Hegesippos, is lambasting it: 'He [sc. Philip] says that Amphipolis is his (ἑαυτοῦ εἶναι), for you [he said] decreed it belonged to him, when you decreed he should keep what he possesses' (ὑμᾶς γὰρ ψηφίσασθαι ἐκείνου εἶναι, ὅτ' ἐψηφίσασθε ἔχειν αὐτὸν ἃ εἶχεν). It is true that you passed that decree, but you never admitted his right to Amphipolis, for it is possible to "possess" what belongs to another, and not all "possessors" possess what is their own, but many are in possession of what is really another's (ἔστι γὰρ ἔχειν καὶ τἀλλότρια, καὶ οὐχ ἅπαντες οἱ ἔχοντες τὰ αὑτῶν ἔχουσιν, ἀλλὰ πολλοὶ καὶ ἀλλότρια κέκτηνται).'[52] The meaning of ἔχειν is clear, as Kränzlein points out: 'Philip should be seen as a possessor of foreign property, as the master of a city that does not belong to him. The speaker thus distinguishes between the possessor and the owner, between the actual use of force and lawful proprietary rights.'[53] These distinctions are found as well in Text 12.

The *proklesis*

Chaniotis' depiction of the consistency of territorial principles and Kränzlein's discussion of terminology provide a useful context for the new detail, the *proklesis*. To return to Oration 7 (spring 342) once again, Hegesippos, at the opening of the speech, had reported Philip's letter

---

[50] Chaniotis (2004a: 187).

[51] Chaniotis (2004a: 191-194 and 198f.); *SEG* 47, 1745 is a dossier of letters from Eumenes II to Tyriaion in the early second century. It makes no difference that the Macedonian claim on Amphipolis goes back to a period when the city did not exist—an historical and archaeological argument is made: Chaniotis (2004a: 201-202). Cf. Kränzlein (1963: 11-12) on [Dem.] 7.26 presenting Hegesippos' arguments against Philip's claim to Amphipolis; and p. 109, citing Philip's justification for his claim.

[52] Kränzlein (1963: 11). See the following note.

[53] Kränzlein (1963: 11); he continues: 'Die Athener hatten, wie der Sprecher nicht leugnen kann, im Friedensvertrag dem Fortbestand des makedonischen Besitzes zugestimmt, wenn auch unter dem Druck der militärischen und politischen Lage. Philipps Lage war daher mit der eines Räubers oder Diebes nicht vergleichbar. Sein Besitz war anerkannt, er besass in gewissem Sinne berechtigt. Das zeigt uns, dass die Griechen nicht jede berechtigte Sachherrschaft als Eigentum auffassten, sondern auch innerhalb des berechtigten Besitzes zwischen dem Haben fremder und eigener Sachen unterschieden.' For 'a *conditional* transfer of possession and not the unconditional change of ownership' see Chaniotis (2004a: 204) and n. 68 *infra*. In Dem. 5.25, Demosthenes says that Athens had conceded Amphipolis to Philip in the Peace of Philokrates.

regarding the island of Halonnesos: 'Philip begins by saying that he gives it as his own property (ἑαυτοῦ εἶναι) to you, but it is not right for you to demand it from him, for it was not yours (οὐ γὰρ ὑμετέραν οὖσαν) when he took it nor is it now when he has it (ἔχειν)' (7.2). Hegesippos then argues that Philip had taken the island from pirates and therefore his claim, that he is giving away his own property, is not legitimate.[54] Next he sums up the situation and poses a question: Philip does not fail to see that 'by whichever of the two terms you use, you will have (ἕξετε) the island, whether you receive (λάβητε) it or recover (ἀπολάβητε) it. Then what does he gain by using the wrong term and making a present (δωρειὰν) of it to you, instead of using the right term and giving it back (ἀποδοῦναι)?' (5-6). The answer, in a nutshell, is that Philip wants to humiliate the Athenians. Hegesippos now reports that Philip wants these matters to be decided (ἐθέλει διαδικάσασθαι) by arbitration[55]—another indication, according to the speaker, that Philip aims to insult the Athenians for being unable to protect their maritime possessions and thus accepting the verdict of any arbitral court (7.7: οἱ δὲ δικασταί, οἷς ἂν ἐπιτρέψητε, οἱ κύριοι τῆς ψήφου).[56]

In Text 12, the author (whom I shall designate 'Philip') returns to the contents of the earlier letter as reported by Hegesippos; this later discussion is part of an aggressive defense of Philip's treatment of the people of Peparethos who had driven the Macedonian garrison out of Halonnesos; Philip had punished them; the Athenians had instructed their general to retaliate. 'Philip' now makes a sophistic argument for his right to Halonnesos, namely, that he had neither robbed the Peparethians nor the Athenians of the island but only the pirate leader, Sostratos; accordingly, 'if you claim that you had handed it over to Sostratus, you are admitting that you dispatched pirates; but if he controlled it against your wishes, what terrible loss have you suffered as a result of my taking it and making the place safe for sailors?' (12.13, trans. Trevett). He continues (and one must keep in mind, as the last sentence shows, that he is speaking of the period before the Macedonian garrison had been removed by the Peparethians):

τοσαύτην δέ μου ποιουμένου πρόνοιαν τῆς ὑμετέρας πόλεως, καὶ διδόντος αὐτῇ τὴν νῆσον, οἱ ῥήτορες λαμβάνειν μὲν οὐκ εἴων, ἀπολαβεῖν δὲ συνεβούλευον, ὅπως ὑπομείνας μὲν τὸ προσταττόμενον τὴν ἀλλοτρίαν ἔχω ὁμολογῶ, μὴ προέμενος δὲ τὸ χωρίον ὕποπτος γένωμαι τῷ πλήθει. γνοὺς ἐγὼ ταῦτα προὐκαλούμην κριθῆναι περὶ τούτων πρὸς ὑμᾶς, ἵν᾿ ἐὰν μὲν ἐμὴ γνωσθῇ, παρ᾿ ἐμοῦ δοθῇ τὸ χωρίον ὑμῖν, ἐὰν

---

[54] Hegesippos' argument, that territory under the lawful authority (via conquest) of one sovereign state cannot become the property of another sovereign state by the conquest of temporary invaders such as 'pirates' is another of the ruling principles of the nascent 'international law' of the times; see Chaniotis (2004a: 198-199).

[55] That the author has 'arbitration' in mind is not determined by the verb διαδικάσασθαι (see the following note), but rather by a clause later in chap. 7: ὁπότε γὰρ ἡ μὲν δύναμις ἡ ὑμετέρα, ἡ ἐλευθερώσασα τοὺς Ἕλληνας, μὴ δύναται ὑμῖν τὰ ἐν τῇ θαλάττῃ χωρία σῴζειν, οἱ δὲ δικασταί, οἷς ἂν ἐπιτρέψητε, οἱ κύριοι τῆς ψήφου, οὗτοι ὑμῖν σώσουσιν... He uses διαδικάσασθαι once again in 7.41 in his paraphrase of (apparently) the same letter: ἀλλὰ καὶ πρὸς Καρδιανούς, οἳ οἰκοῦσιν εἴσω Ἀγορᾶς, ἐπιστέλλει ἐν τῇ νῦν ἐπιστολῇ ὡς δεῖ ὑμᾶς διαδικάζεσθαι, πρὸς Καρδιανοὺς τοὺς κατοικοῦντας ἐν τῇ ὑμετέρᾳ, εἴ τι πρὸς αὐτοὺς διαφέρεσθε. Little is known of this dispute; see Piccirilli (1973: no. 59).

[56] It is impossible to tell whether Hegesippos' emotionally charged paraphrase of Philip's letter accurately represents Philip's language; I rather think not. There is no other example of two equal opponents (here, Philip and Athens) using a *diadikasia* to settle a territorial dispute (Kränzlein 1963: 141). While Hegesippos might be inexpert in his application of the term (it is entirely uncertain whether one can settle property disputes in Athens via *diadikasiai*), yet he might also be misapplying the term purposefully, pretending it is a trivial matter of personal property which Philip has turned into a weapon for insulting Athens' maritime power. For the uncertainty regarding the existence of an 'ownership *diadikasia*', see Kränzlein (1963: 141); Thür (1982; 2012: 310-312; 2013).

δ ὑμετέρα κριθῇ, τότ' ἀποδῶ τῷ δήμῳ. ταῦτα δ ἐμοῦ πολλάκις ἀξιοῦντος, ὑμεῖς μὲν οὐ προσείχετε, Πεπαρήθιοι δὲ τὴν νῆσον κατέλαβον. (12.14)

Much could be said about the passage—not only about the use, once again, of the language of 'giving' and 'giving back' (phraseology to which we shall return in the end), or that of 'possessing the property that belongs to another' and 'property that is one's own' (as indicated here by the possessive adjectives ἐμέ and ὑμετέρα), the same language as used in Hegesippos' oration (7.2 and 41) and signaled by Kränzlein as belonging to the legal terminology of ownership and possession, but also about the speaker's concern for the opinion of the πλῆθος; nevertheless, it is the *proklesis* for arbitration that requires our attention here. A *proklesis* had not been reported in Hegesippos' report of Philip's quest for arbitration over Halonnesos (7.7 and cf. 7.41 for Kardia). Does it have a technical or juridical significance here in Text 12?

Prokleseis are well-known in Athenian private litigation where they serve manifold purposes before trial—e.g., one disputant might propose (προκαλεῖσθαι) that another disputant identify or produce a document, or that he end a dispute by arbitration, or by an oath, or by the examination of a slave under torture. While such 'proposals' might sometimes be useful for ending the dispute, more often they appear to be purely rhetorical[57] —they are designed to be refused and to inspire the judges' reprobation.[58] In addition to the kinds of proposals mentioned here already, Michael Gagarin recently argued that their range should be expanded to differentiate proposals between those aiming to end the entire dispute and those to resolve a specific issue; likewise they should be expanded to include those proposing that someone testify in court, and those proposing that someone undergo an *antidosis* (an exchange of property).[59] In a response to Gagarin's essay, Gerhard Thür suggested a further distinction between 'formal proposals' that had a juristic aspect and had been 'issued and documented for forensic use' (even if, in most cases, as part of a courtroom strategy) and 'informal' ones just vaguely narrated in the sources. Here he made an interesting and important observation about 'formal proposals' for an *antidosis*. He began by asking why an Athenian citizen did not use a summons to bring an allegedly more qualified citizen to court to carry out a liturgy; the reason may have been, he suggested, that the opponent had not committed a public or private wrong; he then proposed that the Athenians had 'created a kind of summoning that even a non-involved opponent couldn't resist.'[60] As a parallel, Thür, with reference to the 'new Messene inscription',[61] suggested that the Achaian League may have used the *proklesis* to start an international arbitration in this way: 'by a formal *proklesis* document, a member state of the League could summon another member to engage in an "obligatory" arbitration; obligatory means that in case of disobedience the League could impose a fine.'[62]

---

[57] 'Proposal' is Michael Gagarin's recent suggestion (2018: 165) for translating *proklesis*, often designated 'challenge' in the past.

[58] For *proklesis* in private suits in Athens, Thür 1977: 28-40 remains preeminent; also Gagarin 1997 and 2007; Mirhady 1991 and 1996. See also the *proklesis* in IK I 221.33, Tit. Calymnii 79 (Kalymnos-Kos, Arbitration of Knidos) =Ager 1996, no. 21.33, 43 and Magnetto 1997, no. 14: this is private litigation for the recovery of a loan; however, the dispute is between litigants from different *poleis* and on an international level similar to the Messene case (*infra*, n. 60).

[59] Gagarin (2018: 166).

[60] Thür (2018: 181-82).

[61] *SEG* 58.370: P. Themelis' *ed. pr.* of ll. 1-101; *SEG* 62.226; *SEG* 65.21.5. Ll. 102-190 remain unpublished; a text with the title ΠΡΟΚΛΗΣΙΣ ΜΕΓΑΛΟΠΟΛΙΤΩΝ occupies all of column III (55 lines). Thür, with Themelis' permission, uses the unpublished parts in his 2012 and 2013 essays (without the Greek text).

[62] Thür (2018: 181-82). For an example of penalties, see Luraghi and Magnetto (2012: 538 n. 88).

Thür's identification of this kind of formal *proklesis* allows us to distinguish it from its 'bastard brother', a *proklesis* that members of a league may have used without that league's bidding or superintendence; or a *proklesis* used by cities for whom an obligatory arbitration clause had been attached to an alliance or peace treaty—but vaguely and without specific provisions; in both cases, there would presumably be no penalty for one city to ignore the other city's proposal and participation would be voluntary. An example of the former is the successful arbitration of a boundary dispute between Hermione and Epidauros (Harter-Uibo-puu 1998 no. 10; Ager 1997 no. 63); while both cities were members of the Achaian League in the first half of the second century, it seems that the cities were acting independently of the League.[63] In such cases as this, one of the disputing parties would propose an arbitration to the other; if the latter agreed, then a preliminary document (a *compromissum* in modern literature) might be drawn up, setting the guidelines for the judges and their decision. On the other hand, Thuc. 7.18.2-3 offers parallels for proposals (*prokleseis*) emanating from a presumably vague arbitration clause of a treaty (the Thirty Years' Peace of 446/5)—but here the proposals came to naught.[64]

To return now to Text 12 and its author's proposal that Athens submit its dispute over Halonnesos to arbitration (12.14): at the time of the proposal in 343/2, when the two parties were living (uneasily, on the Athenian side) under the Peace of Philocrates, probably there was no clause in that agreement that had mandated the arbitration of disputes. We may assume, then, that the author's proposal is not 'juristic' in Thür's terms. Nonetheless, it surely was a serious proposal—after all, non-acceptance might precede if not precipitate the outbreak of war—though in this instance, it was hardly to be a leading cause.[65] The 'Philip' of Text 12 shows command both of the procedure and language of arbitration; e.g., he does not use the verb διαδικάσασθαι—he is not a later rhetorician copying his wording from Hegesippos' Oration. The author of Text 12 has expertise in fourth century international affairs and knows how to open an arbitration over a territorial dispute—*that* is the significance of the 'new detail.'

'Giving' and 'giving back'

Before drawing to a conclusion, a further point might be observed in the phrasing of 'giving' and 'giving back' both in Hegesippos' Oration and Text 12. Although coverage of the 'verbal play' has been extensive (as I said at the outset), much of it is repetitive and concerns two different matters. First, and less significantly, commentators and historians who have discussed 'giving' and 'giving back' in Oration 7 and Text 12, usually cite all the related passages where the terms are used, both in Aeschines and in the comic poets. The list is usually the same, and likewise its purpose: to show, via Aeschines 3.83, that Demosthenes had used the wordplay in the same context, and to suggest that the wordplay had early on become a focal point of mockery within Athens.[66] More significantly, they have discussed the precedents that might

---

[63] See the comments of Ager (1996: 7-8, and 172-73 on no. 63); Harter-Uibo-puu (1998: no. 10). The latter (p. 75 with n. 7) offers the parallel case of the (failed) *prokleseis* in Thuc. 7.18.2-3.

[64] See the insightful comments of Gomme, Andrewes, and Dover (1970: 394) on this passage along with further Thucydidean references on 7.18.2-3; also 1.34.2 with Thür (1977: 28, n. 9); and Piccirilli (1973 no. 21), on the arbitration clause in the thirty years' peace between Athens and Sparta.

[65] For a sympathetic and nuanced interpretation of Philip's motives here, see Harris (1995: 112-114).

[66] Weil is remarkable for seeing a broader comedy being played out: 'No doubt, if Philip had offered to give Amphipolis, it would have been absurd to refuse and to quibble over words, but one must not forget that Halonnesos was a mere islet, un rocher sans importance sérieuse. This explains both Philip's generosity and the patriots' obstinacy

be set by using one term or the other; thus, e.g., Trevett remarks, in the case of the disputed island, 'The issue was less petty than it might appear, since although Halonnesus itself was unimportant, the principle that Philip should give places back to the Athenians, implying that they belonged to Athens, could be applied to more important cities under his control such as Amphipolis.'[67]

True enough, but even more explicit attention can be given to the legal resonance of the verbs that convey the principle; indeed, as Thür has recently pointed out, ἀποδιδόναι denotes 'giving back, paying, and performing' due to a legal obligation;[68] διδόναι, on the other hand, can denote 'gift-giving' in the legal context of 'donations and inheritance'.[69] Putting both terms together, then: a city X (or its ruling regime) might 'give as a gift' some portion of a territory it occupies or owns to city Y, but if city X gives what legitimately belonged in the first place to city Y (because, e.g., city X had illegitimately taken possession of that territory), then it is 'giving back' or 'returning' what in fact belongs to city Y—it is giving back 'what is due' by law. As for ''gift-giving'', Chaniotis discusses cases of the 'donations' of territories in the 2004a essay mentioned earlier; e.g., when Arsinoe 'gave (δίδωμι) a disputed territory (in fact held by Nagidos) to Nagidos, following a request by the *strategos* of Kilikia; the grant of the land meant a full and permanent transfer of lawful ownership...'[70] Chaniotis' discussion and examples are extremely helpful, as are the examples provided by Dareste, Haussouillier, and Reinach more than a century ago (n. 68).

On the other hand, while examples are plentiful, I know of no discussion of ἀποδιδόναι in the context of 'giving back territory' as due by legal obligation.[71] A couple of quick searches in the online epigraphical corpora (PHI) and in my own studies show that quite often cities return

---

in refusing him the role, at so cheap a price, of bienfaiteur d'Athènes' (Weil 1881: 210-11). Both parties, then, were playing a game of masquerade, a pretense of seriousness over Halonnesos; it could not have been easy—and Aeschines had no patience for it. What is, I think, unique in Weil's treatment of the scenario, is his understanding of the real comedy of the situation (rather than the comedy of the comic poets), that Philip could make a pretense of proposing to amend the treaty, that the Athenians could pretend that Philip might conceivably give them back Amphipolos, and that both sides could continue the antiphonal ping-pong of 'give' and 'give back'. For Weil's serious formulation of 'giving back', see note 67 *apud fin.*

[67] Trevett (2011: 114-15 n. 6).

[68] I am grateful to Prof. Thür (pers. communication) for emphasizing the legal obligation inherent in ἀποδιδόναι—a meaning amply attested in LSJ s.v. ἀποδίδωμι A1. The closest approximation that I have found to Thür's neat formulation (in the context of the passages under discussion here) is Weil's depiction of the amendment to the Peace of Philocrates sought by Hegesippos and others: ils firent voter une nouvelle rédaction *attribuant à chacun ce qui lui revenait de droit.* C'était là demander implicitement la reddition des anciennes possessions d'Athènes, et particulièrement d'Amphipolis' (1881: 239, with n. 4 ; ital. mine).

[69] See Dareste, Haussoullier, and Reinach (1894-1904: II 116-45) for 'Donations entre Vifs' and also the following note.

[70] Chaniotis (2004a: 204). Chaniotis tracks other examples of δίδωμι in documentary evidence designating the transfer of property as a gift or testamentary donation; in n. 97, he refers to examples in Dareste, Haussoullier, and Reinach (1894-1904: II 132-45); in the first text (XXV A = Hatzopoulos, *Mac. Inst.* II 20, 305?-297 BC), Kassandros, king of Macedon gives (δίδωσι) to Perdikkas territory in Sinos, and near Trapezos, and Spartolos. Chaniotis also points out that the verb sometimes designates 'a *conditional* transfer of possession and not the unconditional change of ownership,' citing the treaty between the Kretan city of Praisos and its dependent community Stalai (*I.Cret.* III vi 7).

[71] I am grateful to Angelos Chaniotis for referring me to his 2004b essay on 'divine justice' with numerous instances of ἀποδίδωμι used of 'returning' on the basis of a legal obligation in *BIWK* (= Petzl 1994); thus the verb is used for repaying a debt to a sanctuary in *BIWK* 8, 17, 18, 28, 36, 46, 63, 71, and also for fulfillment of an expiation in *BIWK* 73 and 740 (see p. 26 n. 79); the term is related to 'the law of property and to inheritance law' as in ἀποδίδωμι συναχθεν κεφάλαιον 'repay the collected capital' (p. 32, n. 110); see also p. 37 n. 129. Chaniotis also points out that the verb is used with the same legal sense in *I.Metropolis* 1 = *SEG* 53.1312, an honorary decree in which Metropolis designates the freedom that it received from the Romans after the death of Attalos III as ἀποδεδομένη ἐλευθερία (thrice).

or pay (ἀποδιδόναι) 'thanks' to benefactors (and if not legally due, certainly they are due by the *nomos* of custom); perhaps most often, however, officials and individuals give back or pay money, whether obligated by a fine or agreement (as payment of rent or other contract) or they give back ships or ships' gear, as legally due in the *paradoseis* of the Athenian naval records, and likewise other items (including sums of money) belonging to temple treasuries. Nonetheless, there are also numerous examples of land being 'returned' by legal obligation. A well-known (but failed) proposal for an obligatory return of a mountain to Amphiaraos, on the grounds that the 50 *horistai* had set it apart for the god, appears in Hyp. *Euxenippos* 16-17 (ταύτας τὰς φυλὰς ἔγραψας ἀποδοῦναι τὸ ὄρος τῷ Ἀμφιαράῳ). By the decisions of the Koan judges regarding the numerous disputes of the Telians (*IG* XII 4.1.132, 306-301), the latter city is ordered to give back (ἀπο]-δόμεν) the confiscated property to the men who lost sacred cases (79-81); the city is also ordered to give back (ἀπο]-δόμεν) the price to the citizens who had bought those properties (85-87); and in general, the city is ordered to give back (ἀποδόμεν) the property as it is written up—and if they do not (αἰ δέ κα μὴ ἀποδῶντι), they will incur a penalty (112-15). In a letter of Lysimachos to Samos (*IG* 12.6.1.155, 283/2) about an ancient territorial dispute between Priene and Samos, the king mentions that Lygdamis had occupied the land for three years but later 'gave it back' (ἀποδιδόναι)—but only the Prienians received it (14-20). In *Labraunda* 33 (=*ILabraunda* 7, 220 BC), Philip V responds to a request of the Mylasians, that they be given back a temple and territory in Labraunda; Seleukos had returned (ἀποδοῦναι) the temple and land to them when he freed the city inasmuch as they had held it from the very beginning (ὥσπερ ἐξ ἀρχῆς εἴχετε, 33-36). These scattered examples are sufficient to show that in official documents, ἀποδιδόναι conveys the return of land under a legal obligation; the Labraunda and Koan texts are especially clear.

Once again, we see that the 'Philip' of Text 12 uses appropriate terminology in his proposal to the Athenians to settle their dispute over Halonnesos by arbitration: γνοὺς ἐγὼ ταῦτα προύκαλούμην κριθῆναι περὶ τούτων πρὸς ὑμᾶς, ἵν' ἐὰν μὲν ἐμὴ γνωσθῇ, παρ' ἐμοῦ δοθῇ τὸ χωρίον ὑμῖν, ἐὰν δ' ὑμετέρα κριθῇ, τότ' ἀποδῶ τῷ δήμῳ. In fact, the proposal is perfectly worded: 'if the island is judged mine, it will be given as a gift to you'—a legitimate action for a city or ruler to take, even if not motivated by generosity; 'if it is judged yours, I will give it back to you'—the very phraseology the anti-Macedonians insisted be used. Paradoxically, however, and for all its technical perfection, the magnanimous alteration of a judicial win or loss for Philip into a territorial gain for Athens cannot be a serious offer at all—at least in the eyes of some (perhaps many) Athenians. Philip had made an earlier offer—and if Hegesippos is to be trusted, even that offer had been technically correct: 'he has quite forgotten the letter that he sent to you while besieging Amphipolis, in which he admitted that Amphipolis was yours; for he said that when he had taken it, he would "give it back" (ἀποδώσειν) to you, on the grounds that the city belonged to you and not to those who were in possession of it. And apparently those who dwelled in Amphipolis before Philip took it were in possession of territory belonging to the Athenians, whereas after Philip took it, he possesses not the territory of the Athenians but his own' (7. 27-28).[72] While the circumstances surrounding the offer of Amphipolis are too

---

[72] 7.27-28: καὶ τοῦ μὲν Φιλοκράτους ψηφίσματος μέμνηται, τῆς δ' ἐπιστολῆς, ἣν πρὸς ὑμᾶς ἔπεμψεν ὅτ' Ἀμφίπολιν ἐπολιόρκει, ἐπιλέλησται, ἐν ᾗ ὡμολόγει τὴν Ἀμφίπολιν ὑμετέραν εἶναι· ἔφη γὰρ ἐκπολιορκήσας ὑμῖν ἀποδώσειν, ὡς οὖσαν ὑμετέραν καὶ οὐ τῶν ἐχόντων. κἀκεῖνοι μέν, ὡς ἔοικεν, οἱ πρότερον ἐν Ἀμφιπόλει οἰκοῦντες πρὶν Φίλιππον λαβεῖν, τὴν Ἀθηναίων χώραν εἶχον, ἐπειδὴ δὲ Φίλιππος αὐτὴν εἴληφεν, οὐ τὴν Ἀθηναίων χώραν ἀλλὰ τὴν ἑαυτοῦ ἔχει.

complicated to take up here,[73] the echoing rhetoric of ownership, possession, and giving back in Oration 7 and Text 12, held suspect in the former and jauntily bandied about in the latter, suggest that the formally correct proposal about Halonnesos would hardly serve as a serious invitation to a peace-making table—and has, instead, all the markings of a forensic advocate's bargain (consider, e.g. the *proklesis* to open the will in Dem. 45).[74] It is a precise and correct, serious insult and non-serious proposal for an arbitration, that offers, in Weil's words (see n. 65) 'un rocher sans importance sérieuse'. For its perfect construction and expertise, I reckon the text on the side of authenticity.

To conclude: this analysis of 12.14 has focused on the legal mechanism of a *proklesis* in a territorial dispute and its formulation with legal terms correctly deployed; the *proklesis* thus joins other details in the letter that display its author's skill in contemporary international arrangements and lawful maneuvers. These details reinforce the case (in my view, the case made by Pohlenz, Wüst, Griffith, and Hammond, and not the case argued by MacDowell) that the letter is an authentic document of the fourth century. We cannot know whether Philip himself wrote it, but we may be a bit more certain that someone in his political circle did.

Bibliography

AAVV. 1736-1768. *An universal history, from the earliest account of time.* Vol. 6, 1745 (Greece); Vol. 8, 1747 (Macedonia). London. T. Osborne. [Articles by George Sale, George Psalmanazar, Archibald Bower, George Shelvocke, John Campbell, John Swinton, and others. Consult Griggs *MIH* 2007: 228-237 for publication.]

Ager, S.L. 1996. *Interstate Arbitrations in the Greek World, 337-90.* Berkeley; Los Angeles; London: University of California Press.

Beloch, J. 1922-23. *Griechische Geschichte* III.2, Sec. ed. Berlin and Leipzig: W. de Gruyter and co.

Benseler, G.E. 1841. *De hiatu in oratoribus Atticis et historicis Graecis libri duo.* Fribergae: sumtus fecit F.F. Engelhardt.

Blass, Fr. 1877; 2nd ed. 1893. *Demosthenes* vol. 3.1, 1st ed. *Die attische Beredsamkeit.* Leipzig: B.G. Teubner.

Boeckh, A. 1845. *Manetho und die Hundssternperiode.* Berlin: Veit und Comp.

Böhnecke, K.G. 1843. *Forschungen auf dem Gebiete der attischen Redner und der Geschichte ihrer Zeit.* Berlin: G. Reimer.

Canevaro, M. 2013. *The documents in the Attic orators: laws and decrees in the public speeches of the Demosthenic corpus.* New York: Oxford University Press.

Canfora, L. 2019. Afterlife (Antiquity and Byzantine Era in G. Martin (ed.) *The Oxford Handbook of Demosthenes*: 431-451. Oxford: Oxford University Press.

Chaniotis, A. 2004a. Justifying Territorial Claims in Classical and Hellenistic Greece: The Beginnings of International Law, in E.M. Harris and L. Rubinstein (eds) *The Law and the Courts in Ancient Greece*: 185-213. London: Duckworth.

Chaniotis, A. 2004b. Under the watchful eyes of the gods: divine justice in Hellenistic and Roman Asia Minor, in S. Colvin (ed.) *The Greco-Roman East. Politics, Culture, Society* (Yale Classical Studies 31): 1-43. Cambridge: Cambridge University Press.

---

[73] Cf. Dem. 2.6, where D. claims that Philip offered to hand over (παραδώσειν) Amphipolis by a secretive diplomacy (mentioned by Theopompos *FGrH* 115 F 30). For discussion of these complicated events with reference to earlier bibliography, see Griffith (1979: 236-244); in regard to the matters discussed here, p. 238 n. 2 is insightful.

[74] See Scafuro (2011: 224-227) and Thür (2018:180).

Dareste, R., B. Haussoullier, and Th. Reinach 1891. *Recueil des inscriptions juridiques grecques : texte, traduction, commentaire.* II.1 Paris: Ernest Leroux.

Diels, H. and W. Schubart (eds) 1904. *Didymos Kommentar zu Demosthenes.* Berliner Klassikertexte I. Berlin: Weidmannsche Buchhandlung.

Diels, H. and W. Schubart (eds) 1904. *Volumina Aegyptiaca Ordinis IV, Grammaticorum Pars I, Didymi de Demosthene Commenta cum Anonymi in Aristocratem Lexico.* Leipzig: B.G. Teubner.

Dilts, M.R. (ed.) 1983-1986. *Scholia Demosthenica.* 2 vols. Leipzig: B.G. Teubner.

Dindorf, W. (ed.) 1851. *Demosthenes.* Vol. VIII. *Scholia Graeca ex Codicibus aucta et emendata.* Oxford: University Press.

Douhain, G. 1910. *Jacques de Tourreil, Traductuer de Démosthène (1656-1714).* Paris: Librarie Ancienne Honoré Champion.

Droysen, J. G. 1839. Über die Ectheit des Urkunden in Demosthenes Rede von Kranze. L. Chr. Zimmermanns *Zeitschrift für die Altertumwissenschaft* VIII.68. Sp. 537ff. (=1893. *Kleine Schriften zur alten Geschichte* vol. I: 95-256. Leipzig: Veit and Comp., with some corrections.)

Figliucci, M. F.1550 *Undici Filippiche di Demosthene con una lettera di Filippo a gl' Atheniesi.* Rome: Vincenzo Valgrisi.

Gagarin, M. 1997. Oaths and Oath-Challenges in Greek Law, in G. Thür and J. Vélissaropoulos-Karakostas (eds) *Symposion 1995, Akten der Gesellschaft für Griechische und Hellenistische Rechtsgeschichte* 27: 125-34. Köln-Weimar-Wien: Böhlau Verlag.

Gagarin, M. 2007. Litigants' Oaths in Athenian Law, in A.H. Sommerstein and J. Fletcher (eds) *Horkos: The Oath in Greek Society*: 39-47. Exeter: Bristol Phoenix Press.

Gagarin, M. 2018. Challenges in Athenian Law: Going Beyond Oaths and *Basanos* to Proposals in G. Thür, U. Yiftach, R. Zelnick-Abramovitz (eds) *Symposion 2017, Akten der Gesellschaft für Griechische und Hellenistische Rechtsgeschichte* 27: 165-78. Wien: Verlag der Österreichischen Akademie der Wissenschaften.

Gibson, C.A. 2002. *Interpreting a Classic. Demosthenes and His Ancient Commentators.* Berkeley Los Angeles London: University of California Press.

Gomme, A.W., A. Andrewes, and K.J. Dover. 1970. Vol. IV. *A Historical Commentary on Thucydides.* Oxford: Oxford Clarendon Press.

Griffith, G.T. 1979. See Hammond, N.G.L and G.T. Griffith 1979.

Griggs, T. 2007. Universal History from Counter-Reformation to Enlightenment. *Modern Intellectual History* 4.2: 219-247.

Grote, G. 1853. *A History of Greece*, vol. 11. New York: Harper and Brothers. (Repr. of the London Edition 1853: J. Murray).

Guyon, C.M., L'Abbé 1736. *Histoire des Empires et des Républiques, depuis le Déluge jusqu' à Jesus-Christ.* Vol. IV. Paris: Chez Hippolyte-Louis Guerin.

Hammond, N.G.L and G.T. Griffith 1979. *A History of Macedonia.* Oxford: Clarendon Press.[75]

Hammond, N.G.L. 1993. Philip's Letter to Athens in 340 BC. *Antichthon.* 27: 13-20.

Harding, P. 2006. *Didymos: On Demosthenes.* Oxford: Oxford Clarendon Press.

Harris, E.M. 1995. *Aeschines and Athenian Politics.* New York: Oxford University Press.

Harter-Uibopuu, K. 1998. *Das zwischenstaatliche Schiedsverfahren im Achäischen Koinon. Zur friedlichen Streitbeilegung nach den epigraphischen Quellen,* Akten der Gesellschaft für griechische und hellenistische Rechtsgeschichte, Volume 12, Köln-Weimar-Wien.

Jacobs, Fr. 1833. *Staatsreden: nebst der Rede für die Krone. Demosthenes; Übersetzt und mit Einleitungen und Erläuternden Anmerkungen.* Leipzig: Dyk'schen Buchhandlung.

---

[75] References in this essay are throughout to the portions written by Griffith (Part Two, except for chapter 20).

Jacoby, F. 1923-1958. *Die Fragmente der Griechischen Historiker*. Berlin: Weidmannsche Buchhandlung.

Kränzlein, A. 1863. *Eigentum und Besitz im griechischen Recht des fünften und vierten Jahrhunderts v. Chr.* Berlin: Duncker und Humblot.

Leland, T. 1756. *All the Orations of Demosthenes, pronounced to excite the Athenians against Philip King of Macedon. Translated into English; digested and connected, so as to form a regular History of the progress of the MACEDONIAN POWER: with notes historical and critical.* Dublin: University Press (William Slater).

Luraghi, N. and A. Magnetto. 2012. The Controversy between Megalopolis and Messene (With an Appendix by Christian Habicht). *Chiron* 42: 509-550.

MacDowell, D.M. 2009. *Demosthenes the Orator.* Oxford: Oxford University Press.

Magnetto, A. 1997. *Gli arbitrati interstatali greci: introduzione, testo critico, traduzione, commento e indici, II: dal 337 al 196 a.C.* Pisa: Marlin.

Mirhady, D.C. 1991. The Oath-Challenge in Athens. *Classical Quarterly* 41: 78-83.

Mirhady, D.C. 1996. Torture and Rhetoric in Athens. *Journal of Hellenic Studies* 116: 119-31.

Piccirilli, L. 1973. *Gli arbitrati interstatali greci: introduzione, edizione critica, traduzione, commento e indici, I: dalle origini al 338 a.C.* Pisa: Marlin.

Pearson, L. 1960. *The Lost Histories of Alexander the Great.* New York, NY: American Philological Association.

Petzl, G. 1994. (ed.) *Die Beichtinschriften Westkleinasiens* (*Epigraphica Anatolica* 22), Bonn: R. Habelt. (= *BIWK*).

Pohlenz, M. 1924. Der Ausbruch des zweiten Kriegs zwischen Philipp und Athen. *Nachrichten von der Gesellschaft der Wissenschaften zu Göttingen aus dem Jahre 1924. Philologische-Historische Klasse.* 1925: 38-42.

Pohlenz, M. 1928. Philipps Schreiben an Athen. *Hermes* 64.1: 41-62.

Rehdantz, C. 1886. *Neun Philippische Reden.* 5th ed. curated by Fr. Blass. Leipzig: B.G. Teubner.

Rhodes, P.J. 2010. The Literary and Epigraphic Evidence to the Roman Conquest, in J. Roisman and I. Worthington (eds): *A Companion to Ancient Macedonia*: 23-40. Chichester (UK), Malden (MA): Wiley-Blackwell.

Rhodes, P.J. and R. Osborne 2003 (eds). *Greek Historical Inscriptions 404-323 BC.* Oxford: Oxford University Press.

Rollin, C. 1740. *Histoire Ancienne des Égyptiens, des Carthaginois, des Assyriens, des Babyloniens, des Mèdes et des Perses, des Macédoniens, des Grecs.* Vol. 8. 2nd ed. Paris: Chez la Veuve Estienne, rue Saint Jacques, à la Vertu.

Rollin, C., Anon. English translation. 1734. *The Ancient History of the Egyptians, Carthaginians, Assyrians, Babylonians, Medes and Persians, Macedonians and Grecians.* Translated from the French. Vol. VI, Eighteenth Century Collections. Online https://www.gale.com/primary-sources/eighteenth-century-collections-online, accessed October 2016, September 2021. London.

Scafuro, A.C. 2011. *Demosthenes speeches 39-49, translated with introduction and notes.* Austin: University of Texas Press.

Schaefer, A. 1858. *Demosthenes und seine Zeit*, vol. 3. 1st ed. Leipzig: B.G. Teubner.

Schaefer, A. 1886. *Demosthenes und seine Zeit*, vol. 2. 2nd ed. Leipzig: B.G. Teubner.[76]

Sealey, R. 1993. *Demosthenes and his time: a study in defeat.* New York: Oxford University Press.

---

[76] For important differences between the first and second editions, see J.E. Sandys, *Classical Review* 2.1-2 1888: 31-33.

Stanyan, T. 1739. *Grecian History. From the End of the Peloponnesian War to the Death of Philip. Containing the Space of Sixty-eight Years.* London: J. and R. Tonson in the Strand.

Taylor, J. s.d. *Not. ad Dem. Olynth.* II (*non vidi*).

Thür, Gerhard. 1977. *Beweisführung vor den Schwurgerichtshöfen Athens: die Proklesis zur Basanos.* Akad. der Wiss., Sitzungsberichte 310. Wien: Verlag der Österreichischen Akademie der Wissenschaften.

Thür, Gerhard. 1982. Kannte das altgriechische Recht die Eigentumsdiadikasie? in J. Modrzejewski und D. Liebs (eds) Symposion 1977 *Akten der Gesellschaft für Griechische und Hellenistische Rechtsgeschichte* 3:55-69. Köln - Wien: Böhlau Verlag.

Thür, Gerhard. 2012. Dispute over Ownership in Greek Law: Preliminary Thoughts about a New Inscription from Messene, in B. Legras and G. Thür (eds) *Symposion 2011, Akten der Gesellschaft für Griechische und Hellenistische Rechtsgeschichte* 23:293-316. Wien: Verlag der Österreichischen Akademie der Wissenschaften.

Thür, Gerhard. 2013. Gebietsstreit in einer neuen Inschrift aus Messene. *Zeitschrift für altorientalische und biblische Rechtsgeschichte* (ZAR) 19: 127–35.

Thür, Gerhard. 2018. Formal Proposals in Athenian Law in G. Thür, U. Yiftach, R. Zelnick-Abramovitz (eds) *Symposion 2017, Akten der Gesellschaft für Griechische und Hellenistische Rechtsgeschichte* 27: 179-84. Wien: Verlag der Österreichischen Akademie der Wissenschaften.

de Tourreil, J. 1721. *Oeuvres de M. de Tourreil*; Vol. 1 *inter alia*, Philippiques de Démosthène, ou Harangues de Démosthène contra Philippe, traduites en francois. Third edition (posthumous). Paris: Chez Brunet grand'-Salle du Palais, au Mercure Galant.

Trevett, J. 2011. *Demosthenes speeches 1-17, translated with introduction and notes.* Austin: University of Texas Press.

Wankel, H. 1976. *Demosthenes, Rede für Ktesiphon über den Kranz.* 2 vols. Heidelberg: Carl Winter.

Weil, H. 1873 ; 2nd ed., 1881. *Les harangues de Démosthène: texte grec avec un commentaire critique et explicatif.* Paris: Libraire Hachett et Cie.

Wendland, P. 1904. Die Schriftstellerei des Anaximenes von Lampsakos. *Hermes* 39.3: 419-43.

Westermann, A. 1853-54. *De epistolarum scriptoribus Graecis Commentationis Pars Sexta.* Leipzig: Literis Staritzii (Edelmann).

Winiewski, F. W. 1829. *Commentarii historici et chronologici in Demosthenis Orationem de corona.* Münster: Coppenrath.

Worthington, I. 2013. *Demosthenes of Athens and the fall of classical Greece.* New York: Oxford University Press.

Worthington, I. 2014. *By the spear: Philip II, Alexander the Great, and the rise and fall of the Macedonian empire,* Oxford: Oxford University Press.

Wüst, F.R. 1938. *Philipp II von Makedonien und Griechenland in den Jahren von 346 bis 338.* München: C.H. Beck'sche Verlagsbuchhandlung.

Index

Wickham, C. 208
Wilamowitz-Moellendorff, U. von 143
Wilhelm, A. 176
Will, E. 104
Wilson, N.G. 213
Wolff, H.J. 191, 192, 201
Wooster, B. 220
Wüst, F. 348

X
Xanthus (of Lydia) 259, 260
Xenophanes 223, 261
Xenophon, Pseudo-Xenophon 41, 42, 208,
    217, 218, 222
    Anabasis 5.3.6-7: 209; 7.4.7-10: 58
    Cyropaedia 47
    Hellenica 1.2.6-11: 31-38; 1.2.6: 33; 1.13:
        218; 4.8.39: 56; 5.4.25: 56; 6.3.1: 251;
        7.4: 55; 7.4.31: 177
    Lakedaimonion Politeia 39-40, 152
    Symposion 2.12: 221; 8.34: 55; 8.35: 55
Xerxes 9, 243, 258

Y
Youni, M.S. 317

Z
Zaleucus 46, 261
Zeno (of Athens) 275
Zeno (of Elea) 274
Zeus 4, 45, 287